A Companion to Shakespeare's Works

This four-volume *Companion to Shakespeare's Works*, compiled as a single entity, offers a uniquely comprehensive snapshot of current Shakespeare criticism.

Complementing David Scott Kastan's *A Companion to Shakespeare* (1999), which focused on Shakespeare as an author in his historical context, these volumes examine each of his plays and major poems using all the resources of contemporary criticism from performance studies to feminist, historicist, and textual analyses.

Scholars from all over the world – Australi ew Zealand, the United Kingdom, and the Uni writing of new essays addressing virtually the rom a rich variety of critical perspectives. A r stablished scholars, their work reflects some o n currently being conducted in Shakespeare studi

Arguing for the persistence and utility of genre as a rubric for teaching and writing about Shakespeare's works, the editors have organized the four volumes in relation to generic categories: namely, the tragedies, the histories, the comedies, and the poems, problem comedies, and late plays. Each volume thus contains individual essays on all texts in the relevant category, as well as more general essays looking at critical issues and approaches more widely relevant to the genre.

This ambitious project offers a provocative roadmap to Shakespeare studies at the dawning of the twenty-first century.

Companion to Shakespeare's Works
Edited by Richard Dutton and Jean E. Howard

A Companion to Shakespeare's Works, Volume I: The Tragedies

A Companion to Shakespeare's Works, Volume II: The Histories

A Companion to Shakespeare's Works, Volume III: The Comedies

A Companion to Shakespeare's Works, Volume IV: The Poems,
Problem Comedies, Late Plays

Blackwell Companions to Literature and Culture

This series offers comprehensive, newly written surveys of key periods and movements and certain major authors, in English literary culture and history. Extensive volumes provide new perspectives and positions on contexts and on canonical and post-canonical texts, orientating the beginning student in new fields of study and providing the experienced undergraduate and new graduate with current and new directions, as pioneered and developed by leading scholars in the field.

A COMPANION TO

SHAKESPEARE'S WORKS

VOLUME III

THE COMEDIES

EDITED BY **RICHARD DUTTON**
AND JEAN E. HOWARD

Blackwell
Publishing

BLACKWELL PUBLISHING
350 Main Street, Malden, MA 02148-5020, USA
9600 Garsington Road, Oxford OX4 2DQ, UK
550 Swanston Street, Carlton, Victoria 3053, Australia

The right of Richard Dutton and Jean E. Howard to be identified as the Authors of the Editorial Material in this Work has been asserted in accordance with the UK Copyright, Designs, and Patents Act 1988.

First published 2003
First published in paperback 2006 by Blackwell Publishing Ltd

1   2006

Library of Congress Cataloging-in-Publication Data

A companion to Shakespeare's works / edited by Richard Dutton and Jean E. Howard.
p. cm. – (Blackwell companions to literature and culture ; 17–20)
Includes bibliographical references and index.
Contents: v. 1. The tragedies – v. 2. The histories – v. 3. The comedies – v. 4. Poems, problem comedies, late plays.
ISBN 0-631-22634-6 (v. 3 : alk. paper) — ISBN 1-4051-3607-3 (pbk. : alk. paper)
1. Shakespeare, William, 1564–1616 — Criticism and interpretation — Handbooks, manuals, etc. I. Dutton, Richard, 1948– II. Howard, Jean E. (Jean Elizabeth), 1948– III. Series.

PR2976 .C572   2003
822.3'3 – dc21   2002074602

ISBN-13: 978-0-631-22634-5 (v. 3 : alk. paper)
ISBN-13: 978-1-4051-3607-5 (pbk. : alk. paper)
ISBN-13: 978-1-4051-0730-3 (four-volume set)
ISBN-10: 1-4051-0730-8 (four-volume set)

A catalogue record for this title is available from the British Library.

Set in 11 on 13pt Garamond 3
by SNP Best-set Typesetter Ltd, Hong Kong
Printed and bound in the United Kingdom
by TJ International, Padstow, Cornwall

The publisher's policy is to use permanent paper from mills that operate a sustainable forestry policy, and which has been manufactured from pulp processed using acid-free and elementary chlorine-free practices. Furthermore, the publisher ensures that the text paper and cover board used have met acceptable environmental accreditation standards.

For further information on
Blackwell Publishing, visit our website:
www.blackwellpublishing.com

Contents

Notes on Contributors

John Michael Archer is Associate Professor of English at the University of New Hampshire, Durham. He has written *Sovereignty and Intelligence: Spying and Court Culture in the English Renaissance* (1993) and *Old Worlds: Egypt, Southwest Asia, India and Russia in Early Modern English Writing* (2002). He also co-edited *Enclosure Acts: Sexuality, Property, and Culture in Early Modern England* (1994).

Pamela Allen Brown is an Assistant Professor at the University of Connecticut, Stamford. Her book on women and popular culture, *Better a Shrew than a Sheep: Jesting Women in the Dramas of Early Modern Culture*, was published in 2002. Her articles on rogue literature, Jonson, and Shakespeare have appeared in various journals, and she is now co-editing a volume of essays (with Peter Parolin) on women players in England before the Restoration.

Julie Crawford is Assistant Professor of English and Comparative Literature at Columbia University. She has published on John Fletcher, Sir Philip Sidney, and Margaret Cavendish, and she is completing a book on post-Reformation popular literature.

Lloyd Davis is Reader in English at the University of Queensland, Australia. He has published on cultural studies, Victorian and early modern literature, as well as *Guise and Disguise: Rhetoric and Characterization in the English Renaissance*. He is the editor of *Sexuality and Gender in the English Renaissance: An Annotated Edition of Contemporary Documents* and *Shakespeare Matters: History, Teaching, Performance*, and he currently edits *AUMLA*, the journal of the Australasian Universities' Languages and Literature Association.

Mario DiGangi (Lehman College and the Graduate Center, CUNY) is the author of *The Homoerotics of Early Modern Drama*. His essays on Renaissance drama and lesbian/gay studies have appeared in *English Literary Renaissance, ELH, Shakespeare Quarterly, Textual Practice, GLQ,* and *Shakespearean International Yearbook.* He has contributed to the following volumes: *Marlow, History, and Sexuality; Shakespeare: The Critical Complex; Approaches to Teaching Shorter Elizabethan Poetry; Lesbian and Gay Studies and the Teaching of English; The Affectionate Sheperd: Celebrating Richard Barnfield;* and *Ovid and the Renaissance Body.*

Janette Dillon is Professor of Drama at the University of Nottingham. She has published widely on Renaissance drama, including Shakespeare, and her publications include *Language and the Stage in Medieval and Renaissance England* (1998), *Theatre, Court and City 1595–1610: Drama and Social Space in London* (2000), and *Performance and Spectacle in Hall's Chronicle* (2002).

Juliet Dusinberre is the author of *Shakespeare and the Nature of Women* (1975, second edition 1996), of many essays on Shakespeare, and of *Alice to the Lighthouse* (1987, second edition 1999) and *Virginia Woolf's Renaissance* (1997). She is a Fellow of Girton College, Cambridge, and is currently editing *As You Like It* for Arden 3.

Richard Dutton is Professor of English at Lancaster University, where he has taught since 1974. He has published widely on early modern drama, particularly on questions of censorship and authorship. He is general editor of the Palgrave Literary Lives series, and a general editor of the Revels Plays, for whom he has edited *Epicene* (forthcoming); he is currently editing *Volpone* for the new Cambridge Ben Jonson. From 2003 he will be Professor of English at Ohio State University.

Alison Findlay teaches at Lancaster University. Her publications include *Illegitimate Power: Bastards in Renaissance Drama* (1994) and *A Feminist Perspective on Renaissance Drama* (Blackwell, 1998). She is co-director of an interdisciplinary research project on early modern women's drama, and co-author of *Women and Dramatic Production 1550–1700* (2000). She is currently working on *Women in Shakespeare,* for the Athlone Shakespeare Dictionaries series, and *Macbeth* for the Arden *Shakespeare at Stratford* series.

Penny Gay is an Associate Professor in the English Department at the University of Sydney. Her publications include *As She Likes It: Shakespeare's Unruly Women* (1994), an edition of *The Merchant of Venice* (1995), and numerous articles on Shakespeare's female roles in performance. Her *Jane Austen and the Theatre* was published in 2002.

Helen Hackett is a Senior Lecturer in English Literature at University College London. She has written a study of *A Midsummer Night's Dream* for the *Writers and their Works* series (1997). Her other publications include *Virgin Mother, Maiden Queen: Elizabeth I and the Cult of the Virgin Mary* (1995) and *Women and Romance Fiction in the English Renaissance* (2000).

Barbara Hodgdon is Ellis and Nelle Levitt Distinguished Professor Emerita of English at Drake University. She is the author of *The Shakespeare Trade: Performances and Appropriations* (1998), *The End Crowns All: Closure and Contradiction in Shakespeare's History* (1991), *Henry IV, Part 2*, in the *Shakespeare and Performance* series (1996), and *The First Part of King Henry the Fourth: Texts and Contexts* (1997). A general editor of the Arden Performance Edition, she is presently editing the Arden 3 *Taming of the Shrew*.

Peter Holbrook is Senior Lecturer in English at the University of Queensland. He is the author of *Literature and Degree in Renaissance England: Nashe, Bourgeois Tragedy, Shakespeare* (1994) and co-editor (with David Bevington) of *The Politics of the Stuart Court Masque* (1998).

François Laroque is Professor of English Drama and Literature at the University of Sorbonne Nouvelle-Paris III. He is the author of *Shakespeare's Festive World* (1991, reprinted 1993) and *Shakespeare: Court, Crowd and Playhouse* (1993). He has edited and translated Marlowe's *Doctor Faustus* and is currently co-editing two volumes of non-Shakespearean drama.

Jeffrey Masten is Associate Professor of English and Gender Studies at Northwestern University, where he is also an Associate in the Interdisciplinary Ph.D. in Theatre and Drama. He is the author of *Textual Intercourse: Collaboration, Authorship, and Sexualities in Renaissance Drama* (1997), and, with Wendy Wall, editor of *Renaissance Drama*.

Ian Frederick Moulton is Associate Professor of English at Arizona State University West. He is the author of *Before Pornography: Erotic Writing in Early Modern England* (2000) as well as several articles on early modern literature and culture.

Lena Cowen Orlin is Professor of English at the University of Maryland, Baltimore County and Executive Director of the Shakespeare Association of America. She is author of *Private Matters and Public Culture in Post-Reformation England* (1994) and *Elizabethan Households* (1995), editor of *Material London ca. 1600* (2000), and co-editor (with Stanley Wells) of *Shakespeare: An Oxford Guide* (2002).

Gail Kern Paster is Director of the Folger Shakespeare Library and editor of *Shakespeare Quarterly*. She is the author of *The Idea of the City in the Age of Shakespeare* (1986) and *The Body Embarrassed: Drama and the Disciplines of Shame in Early Modern England* (1993), as well as many articles on Elizabethan and Jacobean dramatic culture. She has edited Middleton's *Michaelmas Term* for the Revels Plays (2000) and co-edited the Bedford *Midsummer Night's Dream: Texts and Contexts* (1998). She is currently working on a book entitled *Humoring the Body: Affects, Materialism, and the Early Modern Stage*.

Phyllis Rackin, a former president of the Shakespeare Association of America, is the author of numerous articles and books on Shakespeare and related subjects. These include *Shakespeare's Tragedies, Stages of History: Shakespeare's English Chronicles*, and, in collaboration with Jean E. Howard, *Engendering a Nation: A Feminist Account of Shakespeare's English Histories*. Her current project is a revisionist study of Shakespeare and women.

Garrett A. Sullivan, Jr. is Associate Professor of English at Pennsylvania State University. He is the author of *The Drama of Landscape: Land, Property, and Social Relations on the Early Modern Stage* (1998) and of articles in venues such as *ELH, Renaissance Drama*, and *Shakespeare Quarterly*. He is currently working on a book manuscript provisionally entitled *Planting Oblivion: Forgetting and Identity in Shakespeare, Marlowe, and Webster*.

Wendy Wall, Professor of English at Northwestern University, is author of *The Imprint of Gender: Authorship and Publication in the English Renaissance* (1993) and *Staging Domesticity: Household Work and English Identity in Early Modern Drama* (2002). She is also co-editor of *Renaissance Drama*.

Marion Wynne-Davies is Reader in English at the University of Dundee. Her publications include *Women and Arthurian Literature* (1996) and *Renaissance Women Poets* (1998), and with S. P. Cerasano she has co-edited *Renaissance Drama by Women: Texts and Documents* (1996 and 2002). She is presently working on familial writing in the early modern period.

Introduction

The four *Companions to Shakespeare's Works* (*Tragedies*; *Histories*; *Comedies*; *Poems, Problem Comedies, and Late Plays*) were compiled as a single entity designed to offer a uniquely comprehensive snapshot of current Shakespeare criticism. Complementing David Scott Kastan's *Companion to Shakespeare* (1999), which focused on Shakespeare as an author in his historical context, these volumes by contrast focus on Shakespeare's works, both the plays and major poems, and aim to showcase some of the most interesting critical research currently being conducted in Shakespeare studies.

To that end the editors commissioned scholars from many quarters of the world – Australia, Canada, France, New Zealand, the United Kingdom, and the United States – to write new essays that, collectively, address virtually the whole of Shakespeare's dramatic and poetic canon. The decision to organize the volumes along generic lines (rather than, say, thematically or chronologically) was made for a mixture of intellectual and pragmatic reasons. It is still quite common, for example, to teach or to write about Shakespeare's works as tragedies, histories, comedies, late plays, sonnets, or narrative poems. And there is much evidence to suggest that a similar language of poetic and dramatic "kinds" or genres was widely current in Elizabethan and Jacobean England. George Puttenham and Philip Sidney – to mention just two sixteenth-century English writers interested in poetics – both assume the importance of genre as a way of understanding differences among texts; and the division of Shakespeare's plays in the First Folio of 1623 into comedies, histories, and tragedies offers some warrant for thinking that these generic rubrics would have had meaning for Shakespeare's readers and certainly for those members of his acting company who helped to assemble the volume. Of course, exactly *what* those rubrics meant in Shakespeare's day is partly what requires critical investigation. For example, we do not currently think of *Cymbeline* as a tragedy, though it is listed as such in the First Folio, nor do we find the First Folio employing terms such as "problem plays," "romances," and "tragicomedies" which subsequent critics have used to designate groups of plays. Consequently, a number of essays in these volumes self-consciously examine the meanings and lineages of the terms used to separate one genre from another and to compare the way Shakespeare and his contemporaries reworked the generic templates that were their common heritage and mutually constituted creation.

Pragmatically, we as editors also needed a way to divide the material we saw as necessary for a Companion to Shakespeare's Works that aimed to provide an overview of the exciting scholarly work being done in Shakespeare studies at the beginning of the twenty-first century. Conveniently, certain categories of his works are equally substantial in terms of volume. Shakespeare wrote about as many tragedies as histories, and again about as many "festive" or "romantic" comedies, so it was possible to assign each of these groupings a volume of its own. This left a decidedly less unified fourth volume to handle not only the non-dramatic verse, but also those much-contested categories of "problem comedies" and "late plays." In the First Folio, a number of plays included in this volume were listed among the comedies: namely, *The Tempest*, *Measure for Measure*, *All's Well That Ends Well*, and *The Winter's Tale*. Others, such as *Pericles* and *Troilus and Cressida*, were not listed in the prefatory catalog, though *Troilus and Cressida* appears between the histories and tragedies in the actual volume and is listed as a tragedy, as is *Cymbeline*. *Henry VIII* appears as the last of the history plays; *Two Noble Kinsmen* does not appear at all. This volume obviously offers less generic unity than the other three, but it provides special opportunities to think again about the utility and theoretical coherence of the terms by which both Shakespeare's contemporaries and generations of subsequent critics have attempted to understand the conventionalized means through which his texts can meaningfully be distinguished and grouped.

When it came to the design of each volume, the editors assigned an essay on each play (or on the narrative poems and sonnets) and about the same number of somewhat longer essays designed to take up larger critical problems relevant to the genre or to a particular grouping of plays. For example, we commissioned essays on the plays in performance (both on stage and in films), on the imagined geography of different kinds of plays, on Shakespeare's relationship to his contemporaries working in a particular genre, and on categorizations such as tragedy, history, or tragicomedy. We also invited essays on specific topics of current interest such as the influence of Ovid on Shakespeare's early narrative poems, Shakespeare's practice as a collaborative writer, his representations of popular rebellion, the homoerotic dimensions of his comedies, or the effects of censorship on his work. As a result, while there will be a freestanding essay on *Macbeth* in the tragedy volume, one will also find in the same volume a discussion of some aspects of the play in Richard McCoy's essay on "Shakespearean Tragedy and Religious Identity," in Katherine Rowe's "Minds in Company: Shakespearean Tragic Emotions," in Graham Holderness's "Text and Tragedy," and in other pieces as well. For those who engage fully with the richness and variety of the essays available within each volume, we hope that the whole will consequently amount to much more than the sum of its parts.

Within this structure we invited our contributors – specifically chosen to reflect a generational mix of established and younger critics – to write as scholars addressing fellow scholars. That is, we sought interventions in current critical debates and examples of people's ongoing research rather than overviews of or introductions to a topic. We invited contributors to write for their peers and graduate students, rather than tailoring essays primarily to undergraduates. Beyond that, we invited a diversity of approaches; our aim was to showcase the best of current work rather than to advocate for any particular critical or theoretical perspective. If these volumes are in any sense a representative trawl of contemporary critical practice, they suggest that it would be premature to assume we have reached a post-theoretical era. Many lines of theoretical practice converge in these essays: historicist, certainly, but also Derridean, Marxist, performance-oriented, feminist, queer, and textual/editorial. Race, class, gender, bodies, and emotions, now carefully historicized, have not lost their power as organizing rubrics for original critical investigations; attention to religion, especially the Catholic contexts for Shakespeare's inventions, has perhaps never been more pronounced; political theory, including investigations of republicanism, continues to yield impressive insights into the plays. At the same time, there is a marked turn to new forms of empiricist inquiry, including, in particular, attention to early readers' responses to Shakespeare's texts and a newly vigorous interest in how Shakespeare's plays relate to the work of his fellow dramatists. Each essay opens to a larger world of scholarship on the questions addressed, and through the lists of references and further reading included at the end of each chapter, the contributors invite readers to pursue their own inquiries on these topics. We believe that the quite remarkable range of essays included in these volumes will be valuable to anyone involved in teaching, writing, and thinking about Shakespeare at the beginning of the new century.

1

Shakespeare and the Traditions of English Stage Comedy

Janette Dillon

> Our wooing doth not end like an old play:
> Jack hath not Gill. These ladies' courtesy
> Might well have made our sport a comedy.
> (*Love's Labour's Lost*, 5.2.874–6)[1]

Here Shakespeare signals his awareness, in a relatively early play, written in 1594–5, of a conscious departure from existing stage tradition. Indeed *Love's Labour's Lost*, as I have argued elsewhere, is a highly fashion-conscious play, deliberately playing with modishness and parodying very contemporary trends in both theatre and London life (Dillon 2000). Yet the force of this rejection, with its bid to create new fashion, can only be visible to an audience familiar with older tradition, an audience that recognizes the difference between old and new in what it sees. It is the aim of this essay not only to show how far Shakespeare is indebted to the old in his comic writing, but also to illustrate the degree to which the stance of *Love's Labour's Lost* is characteristic of his work. While his plays so evidently grow out of English stage traditions (which are very varied in themselves, and include several different strands of classical and European influence), their characteristic attitude towards tradition is dialogic, playful, and exploratory. That conscious dialogism works by constructing an audience alert to allusions, quotations, and in-jokes. Thus, if we wish to recover the full comic experience of Shakespeare's comedies we must by definition seek to reconstitute an awareness of tradition.

Yet "tradition" does not merely mean the long familiar and well established. It can mean everything that is already in place, even if only for a short while. This point is worth emphasizing because, in England, comedy itself, as we now understand it, as a dramatic genre defined by structure, was only a generation or so older than Shakespeare. "Is not a comonty a Christmas gambold, or a tumbling-trick?" asks Christopher Sly in *The Taming of the Shrew* (1593–4; 1.1.137–8), thereby demonstrating his unfamiliarity with the term. The classical derivation of the word points to its origins in the humanist revival of interest in classical drama, and terms such as *commedia* and *comédien* first emerged in common use for plays and players in European languages in the mid-sixteenth century, around the same time as the emergence of professional playing companies (Salingar 1974: 257).[2] Several strands of English tradition to which Shakespeare was indebted can be traced back to classical origins. Translations and adaptations of Plautus and Terence had been performed in elite circles since the beginning of the sixteenth century, and English humanists had been importing the plots and character types of classical comedy since about the 1530s in plays such as *Thersites* (1537) and *Ralph Roister Doister* (ca. 1547–8). Such adaptations could anglicize their material in different ways and for different ends, so that while *Gammer Gurton's Needle* (ca. 1551–4), for example, located these recognizably classical types and shapes in the vernacular setting and mores of an English village, thus exploiting the possibilities for rustic humour, *Jack Juggler* (1553–8) used them to incorporate witty play on the very fraught topical question of Reformed church doctrine. Another highly fashionable strand of elite English drama looked back to classical forebears through the writers of Italian *commedia erudita*, so that George Gascoigne's debt to the classics in his *Supposes*, performed at Gray's Inn in 1566, comes through Ariosto's *I Suppositi* (1509), which he is translating. And in addition to plays themselves, a considerable body of theoretical writing, formulated in response to Aristotle's *Poetics*, had been building first in Italy and later in England, most famously in Sir Philip Sidney's *Apology for Poetry*, which Shakespeare almost certainly knew.

More obviously and insistently, of course, Shakespeare was immersed in popular English stage tradition through his professional involvement with the theatre as an actor and sharer as well as a dramatist. The distinction between classical and popular (English vernacular) theatre is not wholly satisfactory, though it was one that contemporaries recognized, as in the opposing terms for different modes of Italian theatre, *commedia erudita* (learned theatre) and *commedia dell'arte* (professional theatre).[3] Popular theatre at this time is characterized by a magpie ability to pick up pieces from different sources; and any source, including classical or classically influenced sources, was fair game. Stephen Gosson noted in 1582 that "baudie Comedies in Latine, French, Italian, and Spanish, haue beene thoroughly ransackt to furnish the Playe houses in London"; and more recently, Kent Cartwright has persuasively argued that the debt cuts both ways, with learned dramatists also absorbing the dramaturgical techniques of popular tradition (*Plays Confuted in Five Actions*, Chambers 1923: IV, 216; Cartwright 1999). Shakespeare's own use of foreign models was noted more approvingly by another contemporary, John Manningham, who recognized his *Twelfth Night* as "most like and neere to that in Italian called Inganni" (*Riverside Shakespeare*, p. 1840).[4]

The professionalization of the stage was a process concurrent with Shakespeare's own lifetime. Until about half-way through his life, the English stage was a collection of *ad hoc* practices. Drama proliferated according to occasion, most performance was amateur, and venues ranged from inns, churches, village greens, marketplaces, guildhalls, quarries, fields, and private gardens to the halls of great houses or the court. Performers were sometimes offering different fare for different occasions and different clienteles, but they were also adapting the same material for those different audiences. The notion that different kinds of engagement belonged in different kinds of plays was alien. Hence the anachronism, outside an academic context, of terms like "comedy", used to categorize drama as one kind of genre or another. Dramatists sought variety instead. They looked to make audiences laugh and weep from moment to moment, so that the experience of the play was one of plenitude rather than unity. Tragedy and comedy were ingredients, not definitions. It was a virtue in plays to be flexible, open to improvisation and adaptation, cutting and extending, and it was not uncommon for the prefatory material to advise on how it might be played with different sized companies or cut for audiences who wanted fun without teaching. "Yf ye lyst ye may leve out muche of the sad [serious] mater", advises John Rastell with regard to *The Four Elements* (ca. 1517–ca. 1518).

When the terms "tragedy" and "comedy" were used (outside an academic context), the difference from our present usage is evident. The same play can be described on its title page as "A Lamentable Tragedie, mixed full of plesant mirth", while the running heads call it "A Comedie of King Cambises" (1561). Even Richard Edwardes, Master of the Chapel Children, a highly educated court dramatist writing on a classical subject in his *Damon and Pythias* (1565), performed before Queen Elizabeth and at Merton College, Oxford, presents his play as a "tragical comedy" presenting "matter mixed with mirth and care" (Prologue, ll.37–8). And as late as 1612, Heywood, though he began Book III of his *Apology for Actors* with Greek and Roman definitions of genre, went on to define a comedy, in English playhouse practice, as a kind of play "pleasantly contrived with merry accidents, and intermixt with apt and witty jests, to present before the prince at certain times of solemnity, or else merily fitted to the stage" (Heywood 1841: 54).

From about the late 1570s, when drama begins to become more theory-conscious, more aware of the notions of unity associated with the name of Aristotle,[5] some English writers, both theorists and dramatists, begin to regard the miscellaneous character of English drama as something in need of reform. Hence Sidney's complaints about plays that are "neither right tragedies, nor right comedies" (Sidney 1973: 135).[6] Yet the revived classical precept of bringing together the *utile et dulce*, the useful and the pleasing, is not sufficiently distinct from the popular "mingling [of] kings and clowns" (ibid.) it seeks to dismiss for the distance between the two to remain fixed. John Lyly, writing for elite audiences at court and the Blackfriars in the 1580s, is evidently influenced by both Sidney and classical drama, and echoes Sidney's wording in his prologues, yet his statements of intent could stand as unwitting defenses of less learned drama. "We have mixed mirth with counsel and discipline with delight, thinking it not amiss in the same garden to sow pot-herbs that we set flowers," he writes in the Blackfriars prologue to *Campaspe*; while in his Blackfriars prologue to *Sappho and Phao* (probably first performed, with *Campaspe*, in 1583) he writes of "knowing it to the wise to be as great pleasure to hear counsel mixed with wit as to the foolish to have sport mingled with rudeness." The attempt to differentiate himself from popular tradition is evident, but the conceptual framework of mixing mirth with matter remains the same.

> *Amiens.* What's that 'ducdame'?
> *Jaques.* 'Tis a Greek invocation, to call fools into a circle.
> (*As You Like It* 2.5.58–60)

As the lines from *Love's Labour's Lost* are cited at the start of this essay in order to focus Shakespeare's comic dialogue with tradition, so these lines epitomize a starting point for examining some of the shapes of that deviation, shapes I propose to look at through concentration on one comedy, *As You Like it*, written ca. 1599. The lines are almost the last lines in a short scene that begins with Amiens' song in praise of the green-wood life, an idealistic piece in the pastoral tradition. Jaques responds with a song of his own, mocking both the song and thus the pastoral tradition by conceiving of retirement as stubborn willfulness and gross folly:

> If it do come to pass
> That any man turn ass,
> Leaving his wealth and ease
> A stubborn will to please,
> Ducdame, ducdame, ducdame!
> Here shall he see
> Gross fools as he,
> And if he will come to me. (2.5.50–7)

When Amiens asks about the meaning of its refrain: "What's that 'ducdame'?," Jaques promptly turns the whole notion of concord and harmony underpinning comic form in on itself: " 'Tis a Greek invocation, to call fools into a circle." When Jaques and the others are gathered round Amiens as he sings, the tableau is idealistic, seeming to present the "golden world" of art that Sidney recommends as superior to the "brazen world" of nature in a consciously literary idiom (see further below). What Jaques does is to puncture the moral idealism of that tableau and expose it momentarily as foolish and sentimental gullibility. In performance the fools gathered round him in a circle either fall back awkwardly or continue to hold the pose; but, even if the pose is held unaltered, its look is changed. The audience can no longer see it as an image of con-tentment because they have been invited to see it as false and ridiculous. The easy and traditional pleasure of pastoral idealism is denied.

The pleasure of comedy, however, is not denied, but it is changed. The dialogue with tradition opens up a space for a more skeptical engagement that offers compet-ing kinds of comic pleasure. Besides the straightforward joke of turning pastoral nostalgia temporarily upside down, there is the further witty play with classicism in Jaques' affirmation that "ducdame" is "a Greek invocation." The term has become a textual crux for modern editors, who gloss it as anything from Latin to Italian, Welsh, Romany or pure nonsense (the note on it in the Variorum edition of the play covers almost three pages). But if there is one thing the context makes clear, it is that Jaques is playing with his onstage auditors and Shakespeare is playing with his audience. And what the line does at this distance in time is highlight for us simultaneously that playfulness, its importance in relation to the play's stance towards its classical forebears and the fact that we may have to reconcile ourselves to the irrecoverability of its exact nuances.

Yet we can go a little further than this. Even without being certain of the precise implications of one word, we can see that Shakespeare is playing with his source and with theoreticians like Sidney as well as with classical and newly fashionable pastoral.[7] He is consciously changing the tone of Lodge's *Rosalynde*, the prose novella that is his primary source, by adding an extra character whose function is precisely to play with the other characters and with the literary frame within which they are set. He is quite consciously defying Sidney's contempt for English plays that proceed by "thrusting in clowns by head and shoulders" (Sidney 1973: 135). In fact, he thrusts in not one clown but two, since Touchstone is also an addition to Lodge; and both characters are named in such a way as to indicate their capacity to stand outside the fiction as commentators: Jaques with lavatorial innuendo and Touchstone with possible sexual innuendo ("stones" are testicles) and extradiegetic reference to the actor playing the part (if indeed the part was taken by Robert Armin, who was a goldsmith by trade), besides the more obvious literal suggestion that here is a character who functions as a testing ground for the pretensions of other characters, and perhaps of the play itself.

One the most famous pieces of commentary in the canon is Jaques' speech on the seven ages of man, yet all too often scant attention is paid to its speaker. As commentary, the speech is of course highly detachable in one sense; yet that should not lead us to undervalue its contextual importance. "All the world's a stage" is scarcely any more novel or exciting an observation in Shakespeare's time than it is in our own. But, in theatrical terms, the speech is not merely a skillful variation on a well-worn metaphor; it is also part of the play's ongoing dialogue with theatre tradition and with familiar modes of representation. The roll-call of figures is not just, perhaps not even primarily, an encapsulation of the ages of a man's life; it is also a sequence of recognizable theatrical characters (lover, soldier, old man, and so on), which the term "pantaloon," with its explicit allusion to the *commedia dell'arte*, underlines. And Orlando's entry with Adam on his back as Jaques finishes with the "last Scene of all," the portrait of helpless old age, provides a further link between the speech and the play itself, with its own character-parts, and the varying levels of role-consciousness they inhabit. Jaques, the speaker, repeatedly calls attention to his melancholy as a role, and his self-staging invites the audience to think about other plays they have seen, other stage representations of the melancholic, at least as much as about the fashion for melancholy in late sixteenth-century London. What his speech on the seven ages does in context is force the audience to pause and think about *As You Like It* within the wider framework of theatrical history, to reflect on its pantaloons, melancholics, and lovers in relation to stage traditions, whether English, Italian, or classical.

The sheer excess of commentators in the play is one measure of its interest in evaluating its own position in relation to both stage tradition and literary tradition, in particular pastoral, which Italian dramatists like Tasso and Guarini were making fashionable, and which Shakespeare himself had already introduced more fleetingly into *Two Gentlemen of Verona* (1594). One point at which stage tradition meets fashion in this period is in the way that, season by season, the different companies seek to "answer" plays staged by their rival. This is especially true of the 1590s, when, for much of the decade, there were only two licensed companies, the Chamberlain's and the Admiral's Men. In 1598 the Admiral's Men had staged two plays about Robin Hood, *The Downfall of Robert Earl of Huntingdon* and *The Death of Robert Earl of Huntingdon*. Ballads and plays of Robin Hood had been popular since the Middle Ages, but there was also a particular vogue for them in the 1590s, a vogue of which *The Downfall* registers awareness in a dialogue between Little John and the Friar itemizing the kind of content such plays normally contained: "ieasts of Robin Hoode, . . . merry Morices of Frier Tuck, . . . pleasant skippings vp and down the wodde, . . . hunting songs, . . . coursing of the Bucke" (ll.2210–13). Lodge's *Rosalynde* has Rosalynde's father, Gerismond, living "as an outlaw in the Forrest of Arden" (Bullough 1957–75: II, 169), but Shakespeare develops this passing remark into four scenes representing the life of banishment, and in so doing specifically alludes to and builds on the two earlier Robin Hood plays.[8] Early in the play he also goes out of his way to make the Robin Hood reference explicit, when he has Oliver ask Charles where the banished Duke will live, and Charles reply:

> They say he is already in the forest of Arden, and a many merry men with him; and there they live like the old Robin Hood of England. They say many young gentlemen flock to him every day, and fleet the time carelessly, as they did in the golden world. (1.1.114–19)

The reference to the golden world is equally carefully placed as a signpost. Just as the Robin Hood reference points to two particular plays of the previous season and more widely to an English tradition of ballad and romance, the golden world reference points specifically to Sidney's *Apology for Poetry* and more widely to a classical and Italian tradition of pastoral. The Robin Hood plays represented a very English manifestation of pastoral, which had already been introduced into the English theatre in more learned and continental style in George Peele's *The Arraignment of Paris* (1583) and in John Lyly's *Gallathea* (1585), a play to which Shakespeare's debt in *As You Like It* is very substantial. Pastoral was a particularly compelling predecessor to engage with at this point in time, because, besides being currently very fashionable in London, its avowed depiction of a golden world, a time and place of uncorrupted innocence and simple pleasures, linked it to current theoretical discourse on art itself as depicting a golden world. As Sidney writes in defence of poets:

> Nature never set forth the earth in so rich tapestry as divers poets have done; neither with pleasant rivers, fruitful trees, sweet-smelling flowers, nor whatsoever else may make the too much loved earth more lovely. Her world is brazen, the poets only deliver a golden. (Sidney 1973: 100)[9]

Imitation, as Sidney and many Renaissance theorists understand it from their reading of Aristotle and Italian commentators, is not a realistic mirroring of the real world, but an idealized representation of the state to which the real world might aspire, and it is this that gives art its moral grounding. To the accusation that poets are liars, Sidney replies that poets feign with moral purpose, in order to show truth as distinct from reality. The business of art is to "imitate," or represent, the highest ideals, and thereby inspire humans to imitate (in the sense of copy) those representations of ideal truth. For Sidney, "the question is, whether the feigned image of poesy or the regular instruction of philosophy hath the more force in teaching," and the answer is that poetry, because "the feigned may be tuned to the highest key of passion," has the greater power to teach: "For [the poet] doth not only show the way, but giveth so sweet a prospect into the way, as will entice any man to enter into it." Art, like "a medicine of cherries," inspires readers and spectators to love "the form of goodness" (ibid: 108–14). Shakespeare is consciously targeting the Sidneian view when he thrusts in yet more clowns to play mischievously with Sidney's notions of truth and feigning:

> *Touchstone.* Truly, I would the gods had made thee poetical.
> *Audrey.* I do not know what 'poetical' is. Is it honest in deed and word? Is it a true thing?
> *Touchstone.* No, truly; for the truest poetry is the most feigning, and lovers are given to poetry; and what they swear in poetry may be said as lovers they do feign.
> *Audrey.* Do you wish then that the gods had made me poetical?
> *Touchstone.* I do, truly; for thou swear'st to me thou art honest. Now, if thou wert a poet, I might have some hope thou didst feign.
> *Audrey.* Would you not have me honest?
> *Touchstone.* No, truly, unless thou wert hard-favor'd; for honesty coupled to beauty is to have honey a sauce to sugar. (3.3.15–31)

Both Touchstone and Audrey are additions to Lodge, and Shakespeare knows exactly what he is doing with them. As with Jaques, their comic function consists partly in making us laugh by detaching us from the comic structure of plot in order to make us look consciously at the comic and theoretical traditions it both embraces and refuses.

Pastoral tradition is explored precisely by bringing together a range of miscellaneous and, generically speaking, incompatible stage traditions. But, in a much looser and more pragmatic way, the play remains true to the traditions of English popular form by refusing classical or generic unity. It evidently delights in weaving together seemingly incompatible modes in a way that invites an audience to become self-conscious about the identifying features of each. Thus Silvius and Phoebe, the verse-speaking shepherd and shepherdess taken from Lodge, and by Lodge in turn from a variety of pastoral sources, including vernacular adaptations such as Lyly's *Gallathea* and Montemayor's *Diana* (a Spanish prose romance), represent the classically derived vein; Duke Senior and his men represent the nostalgic, equally idealized, English popular vein; Jaques and Touchstone stand apart as well-read, courtly commentators, witty fools, who have read their Lodge and Lyly; while Audrey and the mischievously named William (perhaps, as T. W. Baldwin (1960) long ago suggested, played by Shakespeare) are clowns whose very appearance may provoke laughter, as the famous Tarlton was said to do just by peeping his head round the curtain.

Yet the urge to classify and categorize separate strands of influence as one thing and not another can also falsify, as noted above. It would be misleading to suggest that the pastoral mode on the English stage descended wholly from a line traced back from Lyly to Virgil and Theocritus through Guarini, Tasso, and Sannazaro. As the vernacular tradition of Robin Hood demonstrates, forms of pastoral were already deeply rooted in medieval English tradition, both on and off stage, wherever romantic plots created opportunities for flight or retreat. Religious and secular tradition alike had long been enamored of knights errant, forest hermits, persecuted saints, long-suffering heroines, abandoned children, and wild men of the woods. *Sir Clyomon and Sir Clamydes* (ca. 1570–83), one of three surviving stage romances predating Peele's and Lyly's learned adaptation of classical pastoral[10] "and sundry times Acted by her Maiesties Players," shows how the popular English stage brought together some of the features recognizably present in Shakespeare's comedy. Most striking, since Shakespeare's comic heroines are sometimes said to initiate roles for assertive women on the Elizabethan stage, is the role of Neronis. Like Rosalind, Neronis falls in love at first sight with a man who may be her social inferior and finds herself torn between her desire to express her love openly and the social decorum of "shamefastnesse and womanhood" that "bids vs not seeke to men" (l.1020). She becomes a servant to a shepherd named Corin, who rightly predicts that the village wenches "will loue thee bonnomablely in euery place" (l.1329). The play's depiction of him as a working countryman rather than an idealized literary shepherd-type may well also have contributed to Shakespeare's depiction of the rural group of Corin, Audrey, and William in *As You Like It*, two of whom are additions to Lodge, and all of whom contest the literary artificiality of Lodge's shepherds.

Neronis, however, though her resemblance to Rosalind is striking, is not the only model of an assertive woman on the pre-Shakespearean English stage. English plays had been developing representations of women more complex than the saints and temptresses of miracle, mystery, and morality plays since *Fulgens and Lucres* (ca. 1496–7), and Greene and Lyly, two of Shakespeare's most prominent immediate predecessors, had made strong women central to their plays. Greene had depicted a woman's decision to venture into an unfamiliar world disguised as a man in his *James IV* (ca. 1590), while Lyly had explored the tensions between love and duty for a woman of power who falls in love with a social inferior in his *Sappho and Phao*. Shakespeare's greatest debt to Lyly in *As You Like It*, however, is to his *Gallathea*, from which Lodge too may have borrowed in writing *Rosalynde*.[11] Shakespeare shares with, and perhaps learns from, Lyly the interest in moving away from narrative drive to circle around the tonal and textural exploration of ideas. Thus, where Neronis and other pre-Shakespearean heroines such as Greene's Dorothea disguise themselves in male attire in order to achieve their ends (or, critically speaking, further the plot), Lyly and Shakespeare are more interested in pausing to experiment with what crossdressing feels like, what its implications are, and how the audience might position themselves psychically and emotionally to view it. Both are also fascinated by the dramaturgy of symmetry, and Shakespeare learns from Lyly how to parallel characters, scenes, and speeches with satisfying and sometimes comic precision. In *Gallathea* there are two girls in male disguise, and from this a set of parallel ironies proceeds. When they first meet, each hopes to learn from the other how to behave as a boy, and both express blushing discomfort with their disguise, but each immediately falls in love with the other. From their first meeting to the end of the play their scenes are constructed as parallel. When one speaks, the other echoes her, whether in an aside or a reply; when one enters alone and expresses inward thoughts, the other enters alone and expresses the same thoughts in the next scene. Same-sex attraction, played with in the enactment but finally denied in the resolution of As *You Like It*, is much more openly and curiously explored in *Gallathea*, where Phyllida asks herself, "Art thou no sooner in the habit of a boy but thou must be enamored of a boy?" (2.4.3–4), and each girl in male attire openly laments the accident of sex:

> *Phyllida.* It is a pity that Nature framed you not a woman, having a face so fair, so lovely a countenance, so modest a behavior.
> *Gallathea.* There is a tree in Tylos whose nuts have shells like fire, and being cracked, the kernel is but water.
> *Phyllida.* What a toy is it to tell me of that tree, being nothing to the purpose! I say it is pity you are not a woman.
> *Gallathea.* I would not wish to be a woman, unless it were because thou art a man.
> (3.2.1–8)

The conundrum of the tree in Tylos is indeed crucial to the play in a way that is not the case in As *You Like It*. The gods in *Gallathea* have to do more than merely descend to bless the marriage, as Hymen does in Shakespeare's play. Nothing, says *Gallathea's* Venus, is "unpossible" to "love or the mistress of love": one of the girls must simply be transformed into a boy at the church door when they come to marry, and neither must know which of them it will be until that point. Gallathea, played by a boy in a play performed entirely by boys, speaks an epilogue of a quite different tone from Rosalind's, urging all ladies to yield themselves to love, which can work "things impossible in your sex" (Epilogue 3). The tone of the two plays throughout is very different, but the focus of interest, the scenic construction, and the patterned speeches have much in common. Both "tickle our senses with a pleasanter vaine, that they make vs louers of laughter, and pleasure, without any meane, both foes to temperance," as Gosson despised comedy for doing (*Plays Confuted in Five Actions*, Chambers 1923: IV, 215).

The tone of As *You Like It*, in which its chief difference from Lodge, Lyly, and anything else on the English stage before Shakespeare's own plays resides, may be examined further through analysis of three passages where the tone can be specified more closely by looking at them in relation to the English stage before Shakespeare: Silvius' wooing of Phebe in 3.5; Rosalind's feigned swoon in 4.3; and the descent of Hymen in the closing scene. While isolating individual passages, however, it is also necessary to recognize the extent to which their tone is determined by how they are placed within the play. By the time Silvius' wooing of Phebe is set before us in 3.5, we have seen a sequence of wooing rituals displayed in comic conjunction. First we see Orlando hanging verses to Rosalind on trees, speaking parodically inflated verse:

"Run, run, Orlando, carve on every tree / The fair, the chaste, and unexpressive she" (3.2.9–10). We do not hear the verses until they are read aloud, later in the same scene, by Rosalind and Celia in front of Touchstone, so that we are distanced from their content by the critical ear that each of them applies to Orlando's poor rhymes and metre. A meeting between Rosalind and Orlando follows in which Rosalind, already flirting indirectly with Orlando, proposes the love-cure;[12] and that in turn is followed by Touchstone's marriage proposal to Audrey, in the first scene that has shown them together, a scene that ends with the wonderful rhyme for which Shakespeare must surely have named Audrey: "Come sweet Audrey, / We must be married or we must live in bawdry" (3.3.96–7). The next scene shows Rosalind playing the distracted lover to visible extremes, with Celia's mocking responses calling attention to the absurdity of Rosalind's performance; and only then, after all these competing modes of courtship, love, and playing at love have been displayed, does Corin invite Rosalind and Celia to come and see "a pageant truly play'd / Between the pale complexion of true love / And the red glow of scorn and proud disdain" (3.4.52–4).

"Pageant" is the key word that positions the audience for viewing this scene. Just as the absurdity of Orlando's versifying is underlined by the foregrounding of its formal inadequacies by Rosalind, Celia, and Touchstone, so the foregrounding of this scene as a well-worn tableau highlights its absurdity and distances us from any emotional engagement with the characters as feeling beings, as does the fact that Corin refers to the players, not by name, but as the "shepherd" and "shepherdess" (48, 50). Lodge's Silvius and Phebe are a source for innumerable and prolonged songs, presented as an embellishment of the narrative; and Lodge in turn is drawing on the rarefied shepherds and shepherdesses of Italian stage pastoral.[13] Shakespeare's pair speak in verse, and his Silvius adopts the literary conceits of the Petrarchan lover wholesale, but Phebe mocks the literary stereotype with brutal realism:

> I would not be thy executioner;
> . . .
> And if mine eyes can wound, now let them kill thee.
> Now counterfeit to swound; why, now fall down,
> Or if thou canst not, O, for shame, for shame. (3.5.8–18)

Rosalind punctures the self-dramatizing moment of adoring shepherd and cruel shepherdess with a much franker realism, advising Phebe directly that, since she is no beauty, she should

> thank heaven, fasting, for a good man's love;
> For I must tell you friendly in your ear,
> Sell when you can, you are not for all markets. (58–60)

The scene takes a further step into the literary and theatrical stereotype of love at first sight (already noted in the brief account of *Gallathea* above) as Phebe gazes at

Rosalind, but again signals that step with another overt distancing mechanism that invites us to see the play as in conscious dialogue with tradition, this time the quotation of the dead Marlowe's *Hero and Leander:*

> Dead shepherd, now I find thy saw of might,
> 'Who ever lov'd that lov'd not at first sight?' (81–2)

The address to Marlowe as shepherd, playing as it does on the traditional shepherd/poet topos, marks the mechanism of the quotation even more emphatically. And Phebe's languishing for Rosalind after her departure, in particular for "his complexion [and] a pretty redness in his lip, / A little riper and more lusty red / Than that mix'd in his cheek; . . . just the difference / Betwixt the constant red and mingled damask" (116–23) not only mocks tradition in itself, by recalling traditional literary praise of women and Rosalind's scorn for Phebe's own "cheek of cream" (47), but by recalling realist Rosalind's earlier languishing for Orlando in 4.4. The traditions of loving at first sight and dying for love, on which so much earlier theatre, including Shakespeare's own *Romeo and Juliet* (1595–6), is based, are made ridiculous in Silvius and Phebe; they in their turn unwittingly parody Rosalind and Orlando, with their love at first sight and their stagy languishing; while Rosalind and Orlando themselves pull back mischievously from the stereotypes they play through Orlando's failure to display the "lean cheek" and other features of the stage-lover (3.2.373–84) and Rosalind's later denial, with a further direct reference to Marlowe's *Hero and Leander*, that any lover ever died for love (4.1.94–108). Added to this, Corin's reminder in the middle of the wooing sequence of act 3 that shepherds are men whose hands are greasy with handling their ewes (3.2.53–4) and Touchstone's accusation that they make a living "by the copulation of cattle" (3.2.80) function to mock the easy romanticizing of both pastoral and love. The fact that one of the truly idealistic pastoral speeches of the play is inserted between these two moments and uttered by Corin is characteristic of Shakespeare's method, where no perspective is allowed to dominate and all are in perpetual dialogue with each other.

The tone or, more truly, tones of Rosalind's swoon similarly arise out of the very careful preparation and juxtaposition of earlier material, particularly in relation to feigning. First, the simple life of the banished Duke and his fellows celebrates a rejection of the false posturing and artifice of the court. As Amiens sings, "Most friendship is feigning, most loving mere folly" (2.7.181). Touchstone, as noted above, takes up the theme of feigning with sophisticated irony, linking it to lovers and teasing Audrey with her lack of artifice or understanding (3.3.15–41). Phebe, as we have seen, specifically chooses swooning as an example of the falseness of lovers' large claims when she challenges Silvius to "counterfeit to swoon" if he really wants to play the lover. Rosalind herself has been involved in deceit since first disguising as a boy, and has worked herself deeper into deception through the game of the love-cure, earning Celia's rage for her dishonesty: "You have simply misus'd our sex in your love-prate. We must have your doublet and hose pluck'd over your head, and show the world what the bird hath done to her own nest" (4.1.201–4).

By the time we reach Rosalind's swoon in 4.3 we have seen love played out in a number of different kinds of performances and routinely signaled as precisely that: a performance. Yet before Rosalind swoons, there is one more love-performance, this time clearly signaled as spontaneous, uncontrollable, and not consciously performed: Orlando's swoon. As Oliver narrates the event, it is continuing loss of blood from a lion's bite that causes Orlando to faint and to "[cry] in fainting upon Rosalind" (149); and it is precisely as a token of the reality of his wound, and its prevention of his promised visit to Rosalind, that he sends her the "napkin / Dy'd in [his] blood" (154–5), which in turn provokes her swoon. Swooning is the last thing any man would feign, since it seems to call his manhood into question ("Be of good cheer, youth", Oliver responds to Rosalind-Ganymede's swoon, "You a man? / You lack a man's heart" (163–4)), but then Orlando does not swoon, or even claim to swoon, for love. Rosalind's swoon is equally clearly not feigned, since she is dressed as a man; but it equally clearly *is* for love, since she swoons not at the point when she sees the bloody napkin, which she inquires about quite calmly (138), but at the point when she realizes that the blood is Orlando's. The joke, but also the emotional intensity, of the moment is encapsulated in the fact that she needs to become doubly deceptive in claiming that the real swoon was counterfeit. Again, the Shakespearean tone lies in the sure combination of humour, wit, and poignancy in a single stage action, which is then pushed even closer to the edge, following Oliver's chiding of Ganymede as lacking in a man's heart:

> *Rosalind.* I do so, I confess it. Ah, sirrah, a body would think this was well counter-feited! I pray you tell your brother how well I counterfeited. Heigh-ho!
> *Oliver.* This was not counterfeit, there is too great testimony in your complexion that it was a passion of earnest.
> *Rosalind.* Counterfeit, I assure you.
> *Oliver.* Well then, take a good heart and counterfeit to be a man.
> *Rosalind.* So I do; but, i' faith, I should have been a woman by right.
> *Celia.* Come, you look paler and paler. Pray you, draw homewards. (165–78)

The playing becomes sharper, the wordplay more risky, the intrusion of the imagined physical body more insistent and dangerous.

The two crucial ingredients of this scene are found together in an earlier scene from another of Lyly's plays, *The Woman in the Moon* (1590–5), which has both a swoon and a bloody napkin. Another pastoral play, it centres around the creation of a woman, Pandora, for the shepherds of Utopia, and the working of her downfall by the planet-ary gods, who make her faithless and changeable. When the faithful Stesias rightly accuses her of wantonness, Pandora feigns a swoon in order to express false outrage ("Then dye, Pandora! art thou in thy wits / And calst me wanton?"), thus prompting Stesias to instant repentance: "Divine Pandora! rise and pardon me!" (4.1.84–7). Pandora's feigning knows no limits. She concocts an absurd story, which Stesias will-ingly believes, and the pastoral imagery brutally contrasts his simpleness with her guile:

Stesias. I cannot stay, my sheepe must to the fould. *Exit.*
Pandora. Go Stesias as simple as a sheepe;
And now Pandora summon all thy wits,
To be reuenged vpon these long-toungd swaynes. (107–10)

Her revenge on the other three shepherds who love her includes sending a bloody
napkin (dipped in lamb's blood) to one of them with the message that she has stabbed
herself for his sake and is now calling on him as her only love. The parallels with *As
You Like It* are striking, but the elements have been reworked in a wholly different
style, so that what was primarily a piece of simple plotting in the earlier play becomes
a complex exploration of the boundaries between genders and between counterfeit and
truth. Ironically, despite the unsophistication of this scene in *The Woman in the Moon*,
it may have been Lyly, as *Gallathea* illustrates, who partly inspired Shakespeare's interest in exploring this kind of territory.

The ending of *As You Like It*, even more than those scenes examined already,
reworks a series of debts to the earlier English stage. The paralleling of characters and
language becomes even more pronounced as the play moves towards its climax, and
again Lyly is the most obvious precedent here. The memorable repetitions of 5.2,
matching the lovers up in sequence:

Phebe. Good shepherd, tell this youth what 'tis to love.
Silvius. It is to be all made of sighs and tears,
And so am I for Phebe.
Phebe. And I for Ganymed.
Orlando. And I for Rosalind.
Rosalind. And I for no woman. (83–8)

can be regularly paralleled in Lyly's plays,[14] though Shakespeare emphasizes and partly
parodies the patterning by breaking it off with an abrupt move into realism:

Phebe. If this be so, why blame you me to love you?
Silvius. If this be so, why blame you me to love you?
Orlando. If this be so, why blame you me to love you?
Rosalind. Why do you speak too, "Why blame you me to love you?" (103–7)

As I have argued elsewhere, this strategy works to give Rosalind greater depth and
seriousness (Dillon 2001: 52). Shakespeare characteristically brings different tones and
modes into marked conflict, making it seem as though the characters are speaking in
two different plays, and thereby bringing genre and tradition openly into the frame
of the audience's viewpoint.

Yet it is not the case that the only effect is parody, for the patterning also works
to underline our sense that the play is approaching a resolution. Latham speaks for a
widely shared dislike of this kind of dramaturgy in recent times when she dismisses
it as "characteristic enough of Lyly's dramatic style, but . . . less to be expected in a
mature play by Shakespeare" (Latham 1975: lxii); but she also points out earlier in

the same essay, quite rightly, that Shakespeare's plays, from first to last, "show a tendency to some kind of formalism at the conclusion" (ibid: xxi). She is thinking about stagecraft rather than language when she writes this, and in particular about the masque of Hymen, but the dialogue echoes the pageant-like quality of the stage-picture in its privileging of the aesthetic. The language of spectacle, typically combined with very formal speech, if speech figured at all, was entrenched in stage tradition at all levels from the popular to the elite. The entry of Hymen stands in a long line of spectacular descents and tableaux, stretching back through public playhouses, court masks, royal entries, and civic shows, to the mystery cycles, with their assumptions of the Virgin and descents of God. Though Glynne Wickham (1979) has shown that even playwrights writing as late as the end of the 1580s could not take it for granted that public playhouses would have a machine for ascents and descents,[15] such machinery had long been known and used in a variety of theatrical venues, including even moveable street pageants, and evidently playwrights often sought to present such effects where possible. This is perhaps unsurprising in plays written for court performance, like Lyly's *Woman in the Moon*, with its uncompromising orders for ascents and descents of the planetary gods. But even the rougher, more popular *Clyomon and Clamydes*, in a scene that Shakespeare echoes more directly in *Cymbeline* than in *As You Like It*, instructs that Providence descend to stay Neronis' hand from killing herself in despair and then reascend; and the wording of the stage direction, "Descend Providence" (l.1549), is as uncompromising as Lyly's.

Descent, however, is only one possible aspect of what critics usually refer to as the "masque" of Hymen. Both the word and its spelling are instructive. A tradition of court revels going back to at least the start of the sixteenth century in England included entertainments commonly known as masks (a term not clearly distinct in early use from "disguisings" and "mummings"). These shows often had to claim space and attention in the middle of an evening's banqueting and festivity, and a spectacular irruption was one sure way of doing this. Typically, a large wheeled pageant car, constructed to resemble a castle, a rock, or a garden, bearing one central figure or a group of figures, richly and often allegorically costumed, together with singers and musicians, would enter the hall and play out its allegory. The event always came to an end with dancing, usually between the masked or costumed participants and the guests for whom they had played their pageant. Speech was optional and subordinate in this kind of performance. The primary stage language was visual and kinetic.

The playwright most noted for drama in this vein in Shakespeare's lifetime was George Peele. Peele wrote for very different kinds of performance: the Chapel Children at court; Paul's Children at their private indoor playhouse; the adult companies at the public playhouses; and the civic street performance of the Lord Mayor's Show. The tendency to construct scenes as tableaux, part of civic pageantry by definition, is visible across all these different forms of writing. *The Arraignment of Paris*, written for court performance before Queen Elizabeth in 1583, in the same season as *Campaspe* and *Sappho and Phao*, has not only its spectacular mode but its mythical subject matter in common with those of mask and pageant. The coronation pageants for Anne Boleyn in 1533, for example, were underpinned by the conceit that Anne's entry would bring about a return to the Golden Age and included "a ryche pageaunt full of melodye and song, in whiche pageaunt was Pallas, Juno and Venus, and before them stode Mercury, whiche in the name of the .iii. goddesses gave to her a balle of gold devided in thre, signifiyng thre giftes the which thre Goddesses gave to her, that is to saye, wysdome, ryches and felicitie."[16] The shows of the goddesses in *The Arraignment*, 2.2, are especially close in style to the Tudor court mask, with their music, song, bejeweled props, and richly costumed attendants. Juno's show specifies a mechanically ascending and descending tree: "*Heereuppon did rise a Tree of gold laden with Diadems and Crownes of golde*" (456); "*The Tree sinketh*" (462). Other entries are in more processional mode, and though pageant cars are nowhere specified, they are not improbable, as in the following entry for Helen of Troy: "*Here Helen entreth in her braverie, with 4. Cupides attending on her, each having his fan in his hande to fan fresh ayre in her face*" (497). Spectacle is enhanced by music, Italian song, and formal verse. Perhaps Shakespeare had this scene in mind, alongside North's prose, when he wrote Enobarbus' description of Cleopatra in the barge. Certainly, in the early 1590s, when Peele himself was writing, Shakespeare wrote a spectacular pageant-car entry for Tamora and her sons in *Titus Andronicus* (5.2). Echoes of mask and pageant are widespread in Elizabethan dramatic writing, not confined to any particular style of dramaturgy.

The stage direction for the entry of Hymen does not mark it as a descent or a visual spectacle, but the provision of "still music" signals the entry as an important visual tableau. So too does the formal verse that follows, both in the set speech of Hymen, which echoes Peele in its deliberate highlighting of metrical variation, and in the combining of patterned speech with patterned movement. The repetition of the lines that follow Hymen's first speech:

> *Rosalind.* [*To Duke Senior*] To you I give myself, for I am yours.
>   [*To Orlando*] To you I give myself, for I am yours.
> *Duke Senior.* If there be truth in sight, you are my daughter.
> *Orlando.* If there be truth in sight, you are my Rosalind. (5.4.116–19)

is the repetition of dance; it includes repeated gesture and movement in different directions, shaping the revelations and reconciliations into the elegance of measured time and space. The move into song creates an extended pause in which the spectators can appreciate and savor the tableau. The parallel with Tudor mask is evident. Even the closing dance and epilogue, so familiar an aspect of early Shakespearean and Elizabethan comedy generally, echo the *rapprochement* between performers and spectators in the dancing that always follows on from the spectacular entry in mask. Yet the word "mask," with its early Tudor spelling, is almost never used in Shakespeare studies. Critics throughout most of the twentieth century typically acknowledge only the influence of "masque," the term given to the revived version of these revels at the Jacobean court, which always included speech, and usually employed noted literary men like Samuel Daniel or Ben Jonson to write it; and even then they would typically be more comfortable if Shakespeare could only have grown out of such childish things. As Dover Wilson expresses it, "There is no dramatic necessity for this masque-business" (quoted in Latham 1975: xxi). The need to substitute the awkward and dismissive phrase "masque-business" for straightforward "mask" or "masque" is revealing. Wilson, like many others, is uncomfortable with the privileging of the visual over the verbal, indeed with the various modes of Elizabethan dramatic writing that seek to give pleasure to eye or ear in a manner that flaunts the distance from realism, feeling such writing to be somehow naive, embarrassing, or "immature."[17] Work on the Stuart masque since Dover Wilson's time has made it more acceptable to study the link between Shakespeare's dramaturgy and masque, but the Tudor mask awaits full rehabilitation and incorporation into Shakespeare studies.[18]

Shakespeare and his contemporaries would have been puzzled by this resistance to a style of dramaturgy which was both traditional and fashionable, as the discussion of descent machinery in the public playhouse implies. It is likely that the first playhouse to incorporate descent machinery was the Rose, and likely furthermore that the incorporation of that machinery at the Rose was part of the alterations to the building made by Henslowe in 1592–5. Expensive refurbishment of the Theatre in 1592 might conceivably also have been to incorporate this kind of machinery (Wickham 1979: 2–5). Neither Philip Henslowe nor James Burbage would have dreamed of going to the expense and inconvenience of closing the theatres and carrying out costly building works had they not been virtually certain of attracting bigger audiences following refurbishment. And if visual spectacle was fashionable at the public playhouses, this was partly because it was already a defining feature of both private, elite performance, and large-scale, prestige outdoor performance.

Characteristically, however, the perspective of mask is not given sole dominance in this closing scene, any more than any single perspective is ever given dominance throughout the play. Between the song and the dance of mask-form a new character enters, Jaques de Boys, announcing the sudden conversion of Duke Frederick after "meeting with an old religious man." The suddenness of this, together with its unnecessariness (as Dover Wilson might put it) and its introduction of a new character, seem to represent another playful and affectionate gesture towards the implausible plot resolutions of older romance tradition. *As You Like It* could easily end without this implausibility. The conversion is there precisely to call attention to itself and to remind the audience again of what the theatrical traditions and options are at this stage of a play. It also, by interrupting the mask, distances the audience from that mode of engagement too, allowing them to see the two traditions of mask and romance side by side, vying as it were for dominance over the form. As Duke Senior seeks to restore the resolution of mask, by summoning music and dance ("Play, music; and you brides and bridegrooms all, / With measure heap'd in joy, to th' measures fall" (178–9)), so Jaques interrupts again with a further distancing mechanism, rejecting straightforward dance or mask, marriage or conversion, and opting instead to be a spectator on the edge: "To him will I. Out of these convertites / There is much matter to be heard and learn'd" (184–5). At one level this is the position Shakespeare, through all these distancing mechanisms, is inviting his spectators to adopt: they are to be outside, on the edge, viewing . . . and learning? Or perhaps not. Given Shakespeare's ongoing dialogue with the theorists as well as the stage in this play, there seems to be one more joke in Jaques' sober decision to pursue learning while those around him pursue their "pleasures" (Jaques' term, 1.192). Sidney justified art above all for its capacity to teach; Gosson attacked contemporary English romantic comedies for being too foolish to teach: "When the soule of your playes is eyther meere trifles, or Italian baudery, or wooing of gentlewomen, what are we taught?" (*Plays Confuted in Five Actions*, Chambers 1923: IV, 216). For Shakespeare, the best joke is to laugh, with his audience, at those who think that comedy needs to be justified on moral grounds. Though he incorporates much that is new in his remaking of English stage tradition in this play, he is not new-fangled enough to dispense with the implicit and traditional assumption of theatre practitioners, as opposed to theorists: that plays are for pleasure.

NOTES

1   Quotations from Shakespeare are taken from *The Riverside Shakespeare*, ed. G. Blakemore Evans; 2nd edn. (Boston: Houghton Mifflin, 1997).

2   "Comedy" is in earlier use in English, but without specifically dramatic application.

3   Despite the distinct terms, however, the Italian genres are indebted to each other, and part of the problem of distinguishing popular from literary sources in English drama stems from the interdependence of the sources.

4   Though Manningham writes of *Gl'Inganni*, he almost certainly meant *Gl'Ingannati*.

5   Aristotle, it should be noted, only advocated unity of action. He did not prescribe unity of time or place.

6   Sidney's *Apology* circulated in manuscript before his death in 1586. It was printed by two different printers in 1595, under two different titles, *An Apologie for Poetry* and *The Defence of Poesie*.

7   Italian pastoral was already fashionable in England. The two best-known Italian pastoral plays were Tasso's *Aminta* and Guarini's *Il Pastor Fido*, probably written in 1572–3 and 1580–5 respectively, and published together in England in one volume by John Wolfe, working with Giacopo Castelvetro (nephew of the famous critic), in 1591. *Il Pastor Fido* had been published in Italy only a year before, but already, according to Castelvetro's dedication, there was a real demand for an English edition (Henke 1997: 46–7). As Louise George Clubb (1989) has shown, however, these two have come to be falsely regarded as typical of the genre. Italian pastoral was much more diverse than these two plays (also very different from one another) suggest.

8   The case has been argued more fully by A. H. Thorndike (1902), who also demonstrates the extent to which *As You Like It* takes on the ethos of repentance and forgiveness from the Robin Hood plays in place of the warlike resolution of Lodge's *Rosalynde*. Thorndike also lists the known Robin Hood plays between 1589 and 1599.

9   The Robin Hood plays also seem to demonstrate familiarity with this more literary vein of writing. Robin has a set-piece speech very like Duke Senior's in *As You Like It* on the "tongues in trees, books in the running brooks, / Sermons in stones" (2.1.16–17), in which his praise of an outdoor life, where "For Arras hangings, and rich Tapestrie, / We haue sweete Natures best imbrothery [embroidery]" (*The Downfall*, lines 1374–5) sounds like a dispute with Sidney.

10 The other two are *Common Conditions* (1576) and *The Rare Triumphs of Love and Fortune* (1582).

11 This point is made by Agnes Latham in her introduction to the Arden edition of the play. I am indebted throughout this essay to her thorough analysis of the play's sources.

12 The love-cure is not in Lodge, and may represent a possible further debt to Lyly, who portrays three shepherds cured of their love for Pandora in an earlier pastoral play, *The Woman in the Moon* (1593).

13 Not all Italian pastoral is so artificial, and some script low-born clowns alongside idealized shepherds, but Tasso and Guarini, as noted above, were the familiar models.

14 Lyly is not the only source, of course, nor is drama alone in producing this kind of speech. Agnes Latham demonstrates the parallel with Bartholomew Young's translation of Montemayor's *Diana*, completed in 1583 and published in 1598: "And it was the strangest thing in the world to heare how Alanius sighing saide, Ah my Ismenia; and how Ismenia saide, Ah my Montanus; and how Montanus saide, Ah my Selvagia; and how Selvagia saide, Ah my Alanius" (Latham 1975: viii).

15 Wickham cites the stage direction from *Alphonsus, King of Aragon* (ca. 1587–8) that reads *"Exit Venus. Or if you can conueniently, let a chaire come downe from the top of the stage, and draw her vp"* (ll.2109–10), to argue that Greene is catering for all possibilities. Wickham himself notes, however, that this provisionality is in conflict with the opening stage direction, which instructs unequivocally that *"Venus be let downe from the top of the Stage"* (ll.1–2).

16 The quotation is from Hall's Chronicle, and the text is quoted from my edition for the Society of Theatre Research, *Performance and Spectacle in Hall's Chronicle* (London, 2002). The same coronation entry included another pageant figuring prominent descent machinery, in which a falcon (Anne) first descended, followed by an angel who crowned it. The theme of the judgment of Paris had already been used for the Edinburgh reception of Margaret Tudor, sister of Henry VIII, in 1503 (Anglo 1997: 225).

17 The phrasing here is of course anachronistic, since no Elizabethan writer would have thought of realism as any kind of norm or criterion. The dramatists are simply writing to their own standards. The "criterion" of realism needs to be introduced as a way of explaining later critics' embarrassment or awkwardness in dealing with drama that does not start from that premise.

18 See further my forthcoming paper in the collection of papers from the SCAENA conference, 2001, ed. Aebischer, Esche, and Wheale.

REFERENCES AND FURTHER READING

Anglo, S. (1997). *Spectacle, Pageantry and Early Tudor Policy*, 2nd edn. Oxford: Clarendon Press.

Baldwin, T. W. (1960). William Shakespeare as William in *As You Like It. Shakespeare Quarterly*, 11, 228–31.

Bevington, D. M. (1962). *From 'Mankind' to Marlowe: Growth of Structure in the Popular Drama of Tudor England*. Cambridge, MA: Harvard University Press.

Bullough, G. (1957–75). *Narrative and Dramatic Sources of Shakespeare*, 8 vols. London: Routledge and Kegan Paul.

Cartwright, K. (1999). *Theatre and Humanism: English Drama in the Sixteenth Century*. Cambridge: Cambridge University Press.

Chambers, E. K. (1923). *The Elizabethan Stage*, 4 vols. Oxford: Clarendon Press.

Clubb, L. G. (1989). *Italian Drama in Shakespeare's Time*. New Haven, CT: Yale University Press.

Clyomon and Clamydes (1913). Malone Society Reprints. Oxford: Oxford University Press.

Cordner, M., Holland, P., and Kerrigan, J. (eds.) (1994). *English Comedy*. Cambridge: Cambridge University Press.

Death of Robert Earl of Huntingdon, The (1965). Malone Society Reprints. Oxford: Oxford University Press.

Dillon, J. (2000). Fashion, City and Theatre in Late Sixteenth-Century London. In E. J. Esche (ed.) *Shakespeare and His Contemporaries in Performance*. Aldershot: Ashgate, 161–76.

——(2001). Elizabethan Comedy. In A. Leggatt (ed.) *The Cambridge Companion to Shakespearean Comedy*. Cambridge: Cambridge University Press, 47–63.

——(2002). *Performance and Spectacle in Hall's Chronicle*. London: Society for Theatre Research.

Downfall of Robert Earl of Huntingdon, The (1964). Malone Society Reprints Oxford: Oxford University Press.

Edwards, Richard. The Works of (2001). Ed. Ros King. Manchester: Manchester University Press.

Gibbons, B. (1990). Romance and the Heroic Play. In A. R. Braunmuller and M. Hattaway (eds.) *The Cambridge Companion to English Renaissance Drama*. Cambridge: Cambridge University Press, 207–36.

Greene, R. (1905). *The Plays and Poems of Robert Greene*, 2 vols, ed. J. Churton Collins. Oxford: Clarendon Press.

——(1926). *Alphonsus King of Aragon*. Malone Society Reprints. London: Oxford University Press.

Hattaway, M. (1982). *Elizabethan Popular Theatre*. London: Routledge and Kegan Paul.

Henke, R. (1997). *Pastoral Transformations: Italian Tragicomedy and Shakespeare's Late Plays*. Newark: University of Delaware Press, Associated University Presses.

Heywood, T. (1841). *An Apology for Actors* [1612]. Rpt. for Shakespeare Society.

Latham, A. (ed.) (1975). *As You Like It*. London: Methuen.

Leggatt, A. (1992). *Jacobean Public Theatre*. London: Routledge.

Levenson, J. Comedy. In A. R. Braunmuller and M. Hattaway (eds.) *The Cambridge Companion to English Renaissance Drama*. Cambridge: Cambridge University Press, 263–300.

Lyly, J. (1969). *Gallathea* and *Midas*, ed. Anne Begor Lancashire. London: Arnold.

——(1902). *The Complete Works of John Lyly*, 3 vols, ed. R. Warwick Bond. Oxford: Clarendon Press.

——(1991). *Campaspe* and *Sappho and Phao*, ed. G. K. Hunter and David Bevington. Manchester and New York: Manchester University Press.

Mincoff, M. (1961). Shakespeare and Lyly. *Shakespeare Survey*, 14, 15–24.

Peele, G. (1952–71). *The Life and Works of George Peele*, 3 vols, ed. C. T. Prouty. New Haven, CT: Yale University Press.

Salingar, L. (1974). *Shakespeare and the Traditions of Comedy*. Cambridge: Cambridge University Press.

Shakespeare, W. (1997). *The Riverside Shakespeare*, 2nd edn, ed. G. Blakemore Evans. Boston: Houghton Mifflin.

Sidney, P. (1973). *An Apology for Poetry*, ed. Geoffrey Shepherd. Manchester: Manchester University Press.

Thorndike, A. H. (1902). The Relation of "As You Like It" to Robin Hood Plays. *Journal of English and German Philology*, 4, 59–69.

Weimann, R. (1978). *Shakespeare and the Popular Tradition: Studies in the Social Dimension of Dramatic Form and Function*. Baltimore, MD: Johns Hopkins University Press.

Wickham, G. (1979). "Heavens," Machinery, and Pillars in the Theatre and Other Early Playhouses. In H. Berry (ed.) *The First Public Playhouse: The Theatre in Shoreditch 1576–1598*. Montreal: McGill-Queen's University Press, 1–15.

Wiles, D. (1987). *Shakespeare's Clown: Actor and Text in the Elizabethan Playhouse*. Cambridge: Cambridge University Press.

2

Shakespeare's Festive Comedies

François Laroque

Contrary to Ben Jonson who wrote lengthy and pedantic prologues or long theoretical exchanges (as in the dialogue between Mitis and Cordatus in *Every Man Out of His Humour*, 3.6.191–211) to define and justify his brand or style of comedy, Shakespeare "slyly" effaces himself behind the drunken tinker, Christopher Sly. Indeed, in the second scene of his Induction to *The Taming of the Shrew*, after he has accepted the sweet dream that he is indeed the Lord of the house, Sly exclaims:

> *Sly.* Am I a lord, and have I such a lady?
> Or do I dream? Or have I dreamed till now?
> I do not sleep: I see, I hear, I speak,
> I smell sweet savours and I feel soft things.
> Upon my life, I am a lord indeed,
> And not a tinker, nor Christopher Sly . . .
>
> *Enter a Messenger*
>
> *Messenger.* Your honour's players, hearing your amendment,
> Are come to play a pleasant comedy;
> For so your doctors hold it very meet,
> Seeing too much sadness hath congealed your blood
> And melancholy is the nurse of frenzy –
> Therefore they thought it good you hear a play
> And frame your mind to mirth and merriment,
> Which bars a thousand harms and lengthens life.
>
> *Sly.* Marry, I will. Let them play it. Is not a comonty a Christmas gambold or a tumbling trick?
>
> *Bartholomew.* No, my good lord, it is more pleasing stuff.
>
> *Sly.* What, household stuff?

Bartholomew. It is a kind of history.

Sly. Well, we'll see't. (Induction, 2.64–136)

Sly's dream that he has become a lord and may be treated to a private performance of a "comonty" in his own house certainly anticipates Bottom's dream that he was loved by the fairy queen before waking up and walking away from the woods to play Pyramus at the marriage revels at Duke Theseus' court. Sly remains passive and a simple spectator of the play within, while Bottom is an actor in a "brief scene" of "tragical mirth" (5.1.56–7).[1] But both fictions are used by Shakespeare to illustrate his style of popular, romantic comedy as opposed to the more learned, elitist form of play which Ben Jonson was to advocate a few years later. Sly's malapropism brings out the common nature of comedy, associated with the life of the community and the "common" people, and its links with popular entertainment and festivity ("Christmas gambold," "tumbling trick"). This spontaneous and quasi "natural" association between the world of the stage (the entertainment industry of Elizabethan London) and the cyclical holidays of the calendar – May Day, Midsummer, Whitsun, Christmas, Twelfth Night – is not a chance or fortuitous association but a form of discreet manifesto inscribed in the margins of one of Shakespeare's early playtexts. The titles of his festive comedies refer to some well-known seasonal celebrations and thus become associated with mirth, sexual excitement and freedom and, in the case of *A Midsummer Night's Dream*, Peter Holland reminds us that

> this rustic celebration of fertility combines neatly with the pleasures of sex in the woods that Hermia resists when Lysander proposes it (2.2.45–71). But its presence in the play is set against the notion of Midsummer itself, strongly associated with bonfires, watches, magic, and carnival parades. (Holland, in Shakespeare 1995a: 105)

So, at this early stage, without anticipating the various criteria used to define the sub-genre known as Shakespeare's "festive comedies," it may be useful to give the short list of the titles considered as definitely belonging to it. In my view, even though it remains a fairly awkward attempt at it, *Two Gentlemen of Verona* is Shakespeare's first sketch of his future festive "forest" comedies, *A Midsummer Night's Dream* and *As You Like it.* Shakespeare's "English" comedy, *The Merry Wives of Windsor*, is also certainly to be included in the list in spite of its bourgeois backgrounds and moralistic features, were it only because of the huge carnivalesque presence of Sir John Falstaff. Finally, *The Merchant of Venice* and *Twelfth Night*, two plays that have no real "green world" of their own, should nevertheless also be added because their subplots (the enchanted world of Belmont and the carnivalesque, below-stairs atmosphere of Olivia's household) are far more than simple counterpoints to the main plots. In a way, Portia on the one hand and Feste and Sir Toby on the other do contribute a lot to the final triumph of the spirits of carnival and reveling over the sour, anti-festive stance of Shylock and Malvolio. In a way these two plays offer both negative versions (since they use carnival and festivity as a punishment of the puritanical figures) and complements to the ebullient, topsy-turvy energies of *A Midsummer Night's Dream* and

As You Like It. So I would certainly consider this group of four plays as the core of the festive group with its complex, subtle arrangement of echoes, variations, and correspondences.

The Backgrounds of Shakespeare's Festive Comedies

Indeed, in Shakespeare's days, long after the Reformation, the calendar as it had been established by the church with its series of days consecrated to saints and its fixed and movable feasts, still played a role of major importance. It constituted a matrix of time, the effect of which was to subordinate events of secular life to those of the sacred cycle of the year (the movable feasts of the Christian liturgy governed by the Eastern cycle and ranging from Shrove Tuesday to Corpus Christi) and to commemorate a host of popular beliefs and folkloric traditions that had developed over centuries. The year was by and large divided into two halves: the winter or sacred half ranging from Christmas to June 24, which corresponded to Midsummer but also to the latest possible date for the feast of Corpus Christi, and the summer half with its mainly agrarian feasts and host of local and occasional celebrations which went from June 25 to Christmas.

Shakespeare, as a playwright, is unique in the place and importance he ascribes to popular festivity and holidays in his work, thus giving "a local habitation and a name" to what might otherwise have been regarded as "airy nothing" (*A Midsummer Night's Dream*, 5.1.16–17). He indeed includes all and sundry, court and country, in his festive kaleidoscope firmly set on the fertile ground of the variegated traditions and customs of "Merry England," and this without nostalgia or satire. He imbues the spirit of holiday with mirth, making it akin to the freedom necessary to comedy, as when Rosalind in male attire joyfully says to Orlando: "Come woo me, woo me, for now I am in a holiday humour, and like enough to consent" (*As You Like It*, 4.1.62–5). His festive comedies stage repressed or forbidden desires which are ultimately liberated and lawfully expressed in marriage through disguises, tricks, or apparently miraculous events that find a rational explanation at the end. According to Lawrence Danson,

> the happiness resides in the overcoming of potential conflict between the public business of familial alliance and the private business of emotional and sexual compatibility. The marriage of Kate and Petruchio becomes the socially acceptable equivalent of a fertility ritual; their indulgence in licensed sexuality brings renewed life to the community. Shakespeare did not need anthropology to tell him about the ancient connections between comedy and the rituals and myths which ensure and explain the cycle of the seasons . . . Christianity revised the ancient myth of seasonal return in its own celebration of a god's death and resurrection, and in the process did its best to de-sexualize the miracle; Shakespeare's comic marriage plots restore the sexual connection. In Shakespearean comedy the reward of virtue . . . is the life-giving energy of sex contained within the licensed arena of marriage. (Danson 2000: 64–5)

Thus the festive occasion, loosely associated with the play and the sexual freedom and love games which it encouraged, can also be regarded as a rite of passage for the young, leading to their integration or incorporation through marriage into the group or community. Writing about this phenomenon in *As You Like It*, Marjorie Garber describes it in terms of "communitas" and of "transforming Shakespearean confraternities" (Garber 1981: 8).

Even though local traditions were pretty strong and accounted for important holidays and celebrations in the various parts of the realm, the main source of recreation came from a number of court activities which gave the impression that royal festivals provided the general impulse and rhythm for all sorts of different rites and rejoicings taking place in the provinces and at all social levels. In other words, the queen was regarded as the center, the *primum mobile* of all forms of merry-making and festivity. The queen's year was also divided into two halves. The season of the Revels in winter used to begin on November 17 when, in a jolly atmosphere of bell-ringing, bonfires, and jousts, Queen Elizabeth returned to Whitehall to celebrate the anniversary of her accession to the throne in 1558. During the twelve days of Christmas, the court was alive with all sorts of entertainments, including plays, organized by the Master of the Revels. On Candlemas or Shrove Tuesday the court set off for Greenwich or Richmond, when the ceremony of the washing of the feet of twelve poor people took place on Maundy Thursday. The Garter ceremony was traditionally held at Windsor castle on St. George's Day, April 23. The summer was devoted to royal progresses through the provinces. The entertainments (Kenilworth, Elvetham, etc.) organized for the queen were highly extravagant affairs laid on by the great aristocratic families of the realm. The whole court followed and the high favor which was then granted to one of them to lavish princely hospitality to the sovereign and her train for several weeks certainly called a great deal of national attention to the house and county on whom the expensive honor befell. Shakespeare alludes to these events in Oberon's description of the magic flower called "love-in-idleness" in *A Midsummer Night's Dream*, which is generally thought to have been inspired by the extraordinary festivities organized for Elizabeth at Elvetham in 1591:

Oberon. My gentle puck, come hither. Thou rememb'rest
Since once I sat upon a promontory
And heard a mermaid on a dolphin's back
Uttering such dulcet and harmonious breath
That the rude sea grew civil at her song
And certain stars shot madly from their spheres,
To hear the sea-maid's music.

Puck.   I remember.

Oberon. That very time I saw, but thou couldst not,
Flying between the cold moon and the earth
Cupid all armed. A certain aim he took
At a fair vestal thronèd by the west,
And loosed his love-shaft smartly from his bow,

As it could pierce a hundred thousand hearts.
But I might see young Cupid's fiery shaft
Quenched in the chaste beams of the wat'ry moon,
And the imperial vot'ress passed on,
In maiden meditation, fancy-free. (2.1.148–64)

This passage probably conflates memories of this particular entertainment, which had apparently been one of the most spectacular and lavish in the entire reign of Queen Elizabeth, with its gorgeous water pageantry and its mythological apparatus, with the cult of the chaste vestal identified with the "cold moon" Cynthia and the celebration of the "Virgin Queen" (Strong 1977: 16). For Louis Montrose, "the pervasive cultural presence of the Queen was a condition of the play's imaginative possibility" (Montrose 1996: 160). Interestingly, this subtle and oblique poetic evocation of the queenly presence by Shakespeare offers a striking contrast with Jonson's masque-like epiphany of Queen Elizabeth at the end of *Every Man Out of His Humour*. This rather obtrusive impersonation of the queen at the closure of comedy was used by Shakespeare's rival to replace the traditional reconciliation concluding festive comedy. Stephen Orgel argues that, by openly miming the person of the queen on stage, "the theater was considered to have overstepped its bounds . . . Only Jonson would have presumed so far, using the power of royalty to establish the authority of his fiction" (Orgel 1985: 23).

Even in the heart of the woods, the real source of power was rarely forgotten or ignored. But if Jonson's characters in *Every Man Out* begin in the country and end in the city, Shakespeare's festive comedies are structurally built on a contrary movement that takes its protagonists away from court into the green world. As Anne Barton puts it, "Shakespeare's comedies deliberately bypass the teeming life, not only of contemporary London, but of cities generally. They are filled with evasions of the urban" (Barton 1994: 305). The contrast between London and the provinces was then to become an increasingly important one with the spectacular urban and commercial boom that took place in the last decades of the sixteenth century. To Jonson and the upholders of city comedy, London was the center of throbbing life, a kaleidoscope of manners, of intrigue, vices and folly, and a great source of comic inspiration. Not so Shakespeare. In fact, the opposition between the city and the country lay at the heart of the whole phenomenon of festivity, for even if it was through the towns that festivals were developed, embellished and enriched, the festival itself was still the product of a rural, popular culture whose seasonal rhythms and pre-Christian beliefs were linked with the mysteries and the magic of natural fertility. For Shakespeare and his contemporaries, the countryside lying outside the city walls was still the object of superstition and deep-rooted fears. The forest associated with royal privileges was the domain of hunting, of wildness and the sacred (Marienstras 1981: 58–9). There was also the world of folklore and the ballads of the "old Robin Hood" as well as the iconography of the *homo sylvarum* or Wild Man echoed in texts as different as Spenser's *The Fairie Queene* or the anonymous play *Mucedorus* (1590), which was performed by Shakespeare's troupe, the Chamberlain's Men.

As Elizabethan England was gradually shifting from a ritualistic and relatively static system to a more secular one, the themes and images of popular festivals were disseminated at the very moment when their existence was being questioned by Puritan pamphleteers like Philip Stubbes in his *Anatomy of Abuses* (1583). It is quite possible that these attacks made local games and traditions better known, as attention was drawn to them when University Wits like Thomas Nashe stood up in the defense of popular pastimes, a tradition later continued by Ben Jonson, Robert Dover with his Cotswold Games (Laroque 1991: 163-4), and by such remote disciples of the Tribe of Ben as Robert Herrick, the genial, nostalgic poet of *Hesperides* (1648). The defense of the traditions of "Merry England" led to what Leah Marcus (1986) has called "the politics of mirth," thus arousing a pre-ethnological interest as it were for the forgotten games, customs, and festivals in the most remote corners of the land. A famous letter by Robert Laneham, giving an account of the royal progress at Kenilworth, tells of a local craftsman and colorful figure called "Captain Cox" and of his efforts to ask Queen Elizabeth to stand in defense of the "Hocktide" games which had been banned by the local Puritans (Laroque 1991: 337; Montrose 1996: 183).

Shakespeare, whose childhood in rural Warwickshire and possible Catholic background (Honigmann 1985; Wilson 1997: 11–13) made him particularly alive to the importance of ritual and festivity, was then to find out what astounding dramatic use he could make in his comedies of all the local games and traditions and of the vestiges of folklore. He had the flair and vision to see what profit he could make in his festive comedies with these generally despised bits and pieces of local popular culture. He quickly assimilated the fairly primitive dramatic structures emerging from seasonal mimes and dramas like the folk plays and the morris dance, and then incorporated them in his plots or subplots or in his poetic imagery. Ass-headed Bottom in *A Midsummer Night's Dream* has thus been compared to a mummer wearing an animal mask for some local performance (Holland, in Shakespeare 1995a: 78–9), while the foresters' song in *As You Like It* ("What shall he have that killed the deer?" 4.2.10–19) seems reminiscent of the Abbots Bromley Horn dance in Staffordshire (Laroque 1991: 167).

The May Day and Midsummer morris dance was also a significant festive occasion, even though, as Hamlet complains, the hobby horse was often "forgot."[2] Indeed, as David Wiles puts it, this "centre-piece of Elizabethan folk culture . . . symbolized the sense of community that everyone supposed to have existed in some past golden age. It was . . . associated with anti-authoritarian summer festivals in which the boundary between game and rebellion was ill-defined" (Wiles 1987: 44). Michael Mangan explains how it progressively left the green of the local village to become incorporated on the London stage:

> Morris dancing itself forms a significant strand in the development of comedy: part entertainment and part ritual, it acts as a bridge between the general festivities of the country community and the performance in the London theatres . . . As the dominant culture of England became more urban . . . the spirit of misrule grew away from its seasonal roots. (Mangan 1996: 40)

In fact, Shakespeare's comedies take us back to the roots of romance away from the urban centers. The park in *Love's Labour's Lost*, the woods near Athens in *A Midsummer Night's Dream*, Windsor forest with its local legends and folklore in *The Merry Wives of Windsor*, or the forest of Arden in *As You Like It*, are all Shakespearean versions of the pagan, ritualized vision of a traditional green world with its hunting rites and grounds, chance or sporting games and its utopian, topsy-turvy scenarios. The green world was regarded as a place of escape from the constraints of the law and of every-day life, a place of change (of gender or of identity or both) and deep interior trans-formation. According to Edward Berry, the confrontation with these "enchanted landscapes" is an experience which is "akin to the sacred places of initiation":

> Often located in nature, these landscapes can be anywhere . . . for they represent a geography of the mind. Sometimes hostile, sometimes benign, these realms always disorient; their contours are the meandering lines of identities in transition. (Berry 1984: 144)

This sense of disorientation is expressed through images related to the labyrinth, while the world suddenly becomes a maze for the lovers ("the mazed world . . . / Knows not which is which": *A Midsummer Night's Dream*, 2.1.113–14). Sometimes, on the con-trary, the adoption of the pastoral convention made the contact with nature and "old custom" the source of content and fulfillment, as Duke Senior's in *As You Like It*:

> Now, my co-mates and brothers in exile,
> Hath not old custom made this life more sweet
> Than that of painted pomp? Are not these woods
> More free from peril than the envious court? . . .
> And this our life, exempt from public haunt,
> Finds tongues in trees, books in the running brooks,
> Sermons in stones, and good in everything. (2.1.1–17)

But the green world is not just limited to forest and green pastures. It also corre-sponds to Portia's home in Belmont where Lorenzo and Jessica listen to the harmonies of celestial music at night (5.1.1–88) and, in this particular case, it becomes a byword for perfection and enchantment. But not all festive comedies insist so much about harmony.

Indeed, in *The Taming of the Shrew* Shakespeare explores the theme of comic sexual warfare between men and women, a theme to which he will return in a more sophis-ticated way in *Much Ado About Nothing*. The taming of Katherina by Petruchio may indeed be taken as a dramatic variation on the traditional Hocktide games that play-fully opposed the sexes in Warwickshire at Easter-tide (Laroque 1991: 108–9). In *Much Ado* the theme of sexual warfare leading to marriage is verbalized in the witty sparring between Beatrice and her cousin Benedick:

> *Leonato.* You must not, sir, mistake my niece. There is a kind of merry war betwixt Signor Benedick and her. They never meet but there's a skirmish of wit between them. (1.1.57–60)

The merry interlude at Messina represents the equivalent of a carnival period when the local court indulges in a hectic bout of laughter, alcohol, and dancing after the trials and dangers of the war that has just come to an end. In this "weak piping time of peace" (*Richard III*, 1.1.24), love games also form "dangerous liaisons" beset with all sorts of risks even when they are pursued amid the rowdiness of the ball and the carefree festive intrigues that take place at the governor's palace. But in spite of the jolly atmosphere that seems to prevail at the surface of things, the happy ending and final marriages are difficult to achieve. Benedick tries his best to be a festive, romantic lover, but he confesses that he "cannot woo in festival terms" (5.2.31). It is true that the frictions or "flyting" games remain somewhat marginal in Shakespeare's plays, since his festive comedies teem with examples assessing the preeminence of women, which probably simply reflects the fact that in many popular celebrations they often happened to be more numerous or more active than the men. According to Susan Snyder, this phenomenon "harks back to the festival roots of comedy, those rites of spring in which women played a prominent part. May queens were more common in English village festivals than May kings" (Snyder 1979: 27). This is also why feminist criticism in the wake of Juliet Dusinberre, Linda Bamber, Jeanne Addison Roberts, Irene Dash, Marianne Novy, and many others has expressed preeminent interest in the gender games and subversion of patriarchy found in Shakespeare's festive comedies.[3]

Late spring festivals prompt confusion and disorientation as well as a questioning of identity and sexual desires. Shakespeare indeed associates the popular May Day festival with the disorder of the senses. In A *Midsummer Night's Dream* he plays on the similarities between the festive customs of May Day and Midsummer in order to add to the overall confusion. The sequence of comic chaotic situations symbolizes the unpredictability of the festive time in the green world ("there's no clock in the forest" says Orlando in *As You Like It*, 3.2.291–2), marked by fortune, chance, or luck. Enchanted time, now suspended, now accelerated, working in mysterious lunar cycles, is the true counterpart of these enchanted places.

In popular memories, Midsummer was still linked to the London parades. The famous Midsummer Watch, suppressed in 1539, was replaced by the Lord Mayor's Show on St. Simon and St. Jude on October 28. It was usually staged at nightfall with torches, with the presence of St. George and the dragon (popularly referred to as "Old Snap"), of giants and of Wild Men ("woodwoses") all equipped with candles, lanterns, or "cressets" (Laroque 1991: 344–6). This created among its audiences a tinge of delight and fear, analogous to the ambivalent reactions prompted on contemporary English stages by fairies' magic as well as by demonic or ghostly apparitions. "Why, this is very midsummer madness" (*Twelfth Night*, 3.4.53) Olivia exclaims when she sees her besotted steward sporting yellow stockings cross-gartered with a large conniving smile, suggesting that Malvolio has been "moon-struck" and now behaves like a lunatic or like one of these fantastic Midsummer dreams or apparitions. The whole moment is steeped in a sort of crazy topsy-turvydom, like much of what happens in this fairly somber comedy of eros and errors. This is not just an innocent or chance proverbial saying on the part of Olivia in a comedy that takes its title from an allusion to the winter solstice, or rather from the twelfth night that follows, and it looks ahead to its summer counterpart or calendrical antipodes, six months later.

After the summer, essentially marked by open-air pastoral rejoicings (harvest home, Lammas or sheep-shearing) in the country, and fairs and wakes in the towns and parishes, came the autumn festivals. Besides these great holiday cycles, echoed and sometimes mirrored in the situations or imagery of his comedies, Shakespeare was also attentive to occasions and commemoration. But the calendrical allusions are far from being systematic or even accurate, since not all of these customs were consistently observed. In *A Midsummer Night's Dream* there is as much confusion in festival dates (the night of the comedy could be situated any time between St. Valentine's Day and Midsummer) as in the phases of the moon; this, in spite of a number of sophisticated scholarly explanations (Wiles 1993), is certainly deliberate on the part of a playwright who generally refuses to follow any strict, rigid series of rules. This muddle over the calendar is analogous to Shakespeare's usual disruption of the unities of space, time, and action in Aristotelian, classical dramaturgy, except for a few, highly visible exceptions like *The Comedy of Errors* or *The Tempest*. Such desire to break free from constraints of all sorts was one of his main disagreements with Jonson who, quite unlike him, was a poet and playwright constantly obsessed with the introduction and discussion of rules and theory in his plays. Shakespeare's point is to use festivity in a romantic way, as a means of abolishing continuous time altogether and to make it the equivalent of sleep or a form of "re-creation," so that a sense of wonder or enchantment may be produced.

The feast of Hallowmas is only mentioned in a rather puzzling passage in *The Merry Wives of Windsor* when Simple asks a rather astounding and apparently nonsensical question about a book of riddles: "*Book of riddles?* Why, did you not lend it to Alice Shortcake upon Allhallowmas last, a fortnight afore Michaelmas?" (1.1.184–6). By putting the order of festivals upside down (Michaelmas corresponds to September 29 and Hallowmas to November 1), Simple provokes hilarity among the audience. Time seems to be running backward in this saturnalian, festive comedy with an English background. But there may be another meaning in this passage, as Jeanne Addison Roberts suggests, confirming that Shakespeare's one English, citizen comedy is in fact steeped in an autumnal background as well as a number of connections with carnival and charivari customs (Roberts 1972: 107–12).

At the end of year, Christmas and its train of twelve happy days represented a long parenthesis that had been originally devised to bridge the gap between the solar and the lunar calendars. In *Love's Labour's Lost* (5.2.460–8) and *The Taming of the Shrew* (Induction 2.131–2) Shakespeare associates Christmas with the performances of the minstrels or mummers who were all vaguely associated with the spirit of comedy and mirth.

Though rare and rather paradoxical in comedy, a song of winter may be used to end a festive comedy. This is indeed the case at the end of *Love's Labour's Lost*, which closes on a "Song of the cuckoo and the owl" where the two birds respectively stand for Spring and Winter and compete with rival themes. This final song echoes and encapsulates the main topic of the comedy, which could be interpreted as a long struggle between the forces of Lenten meditation and study, on the one hand, and those of Carnival, love-making, and marriage, on the other. Contrary to all the other comedies, marriage is finally postponed when the death of the French king is announced and the play that had begun with a vow of asceticism and penance ends in frustration, atypically and ironically confronting the young men with their anti-festive pledge:

> *Princess.*   . . . go with speed
> To some forlorn and naked hermitage,
> Remote from all the pleasures of the world:
> There stay until twelve celestial signs
> Have brought about the annual reckoning.
> If this austere insociable life
> Change not your offer made in heat of blood;
> If frosts and fasts, hard lodging and thin weeds
> Nip not the blossom of your love . . .
> Come challenge me, challenge me by these deserts,
> And, by this virgin palm now kissing thine,
> I will be thine . . .
>
> *Berowne.* Our wooing doth not end like an old play;
> Jack hath not Jill. These ladies' courtesy
> Might well have made our sport a comedy. (5.2.782–858)

This ending is totally unconventional for a festive comedy since it turns its back on "old play(s)," but it may be explained in part by the desire to prepare the audience for a sequel which may well have been the mysterious *Love's Labour's Won*, a comedy that was probably lost and for which many different hypotheses are regularly being proposed (Mangan 1996: 149).

Definitions of Festive Comedy

Comedy is in itself hard to define — most critics agree on this point. Shakespearean comedy is even more elusive as there is no theoretical definition of it and even less a sort of master code or master key to explain it. "It is impossible to provide a magic formula," says Kenneth Muir (1979: 2). Some critics are happy to define it in a chrono-logical manner (early comedies, mature or romantic comedies, problem comedies, and late comedies or romances), while others have tried to make them fit a number of pre-defined molds or categories. In *Shakespeare and the Traditions of Comedy* Leo Salingar (1974) by and large distinguishes between three main groups: the woodland com-edies, *Two Gentlemen of Verona*, *Love's Labour's Lost*, *A Midsummer Night's Dream*, and *As You Like It*, whose plots are situated in a park or forest and marked by the influence of pastoral romances like Sidney's *Arcadia* or Lodge's *Rosalynde*; then comedies based on classical sources or Italian plays belonging to *commedia erudita*, like *The Comedy of Errors*, *The Taming of the Shrew*, and *The Merry Wives of Windsor*; finally, the problem plays, *The Merchant of Venice*, *Much Ado About Nothing*, *All's Well That Ends Well*, and *Measure for Measure*, which are derived from Italian *novelle*. This way of classifying the comedies by looking at their sources or at the specific "comic tradition" they belong to rather than by analyzing their specific plots and forms is certainly interesting and intellectually stimulating, but it also offers the risk of downplaying Shakespeare's own invention, additions, or variations in his playtexts. And in the case of his festive comedies the importance taken on by the sources (as in *Love's Labour's Lost* or *A Midsummer Night's Dream* for instance) seems precisely less than in his other works. This is why Northrop Frye, who was marked by anthropology and myth-oriented studies, remains one of the most influential critics of Shakespearean comedy. It is he who first associated Shakespeare's comedy with what he calls "the drama of the green world," thus presenting the reader with a fascinating account of Shakespeare's use of symbolic geography in a way that turns its back on the traditional fear and refusal of "la selva oscura":[4]

> The earlier tradition established by Peele and developed by Lyly, Greene and the masque writers, which uses romance and folklore and avoids the comedy of manners, is the one followed by Shakespeare. Those themes are largely medieval in origin, and derive, not from the mysteries or the moralities or the interludes, but from a fourth dramatic tradition. This is the drama of folk ritual, of the St George's play and the mummers' play, of the feast of the ass and the Boy Bishop, and of all the dramatic activity that punctuated the Christian calendar with the rituals of an immemorial paganism. We may call this the drama of the green world and its theme is once again the triumph of life over the waste land, the death and revival of the year impersonated by figures still human and once divine as well. (Frye 1948: 85)

This is indeed a green world in the sense of an enchanted, golden world where summer triumphs over winter and fertility prevails over sterility and death. The winners of comedy are then the characters who place themselves in tune with the natural forces of life renewal and who corroborate the idea that nature is the great ally of love. In a later study, *A Natural Perspective*, Frye (1965) develops parallels between Shakespeare's comic structure and three phases of seasonal ritual: a dark and rather tense moment of preparation, a time of license when the world is put upside down, which is then followed by a period of fertility and celebration (marriage revels with music, songs, and dancing).[5]

This was the line taken up by C. L. Barber in his pioneering and seminal book, *Shakespeare's Festive Comedy* (1959). According to him, the main function of festive elements in Shakespearean drama is to trigger an emotional release and help create an atmosphere of joyful liberation in the face of an archaic moral order or tyranny. This, according to his optimistic view, is bound to produce a movement of clarification in the characters themselves, but also in the various complications or entanglements of the play:

> The *clarification* achieved by the festive comedies is concomitant to the release they dramatize: a heightened awareness of the relation between man and "nature" – the nature

celebrated on holiday. The process of translating festive experience into drama involved extending the sort of awareness traditionally associated with holiday, and also becoming conscious of holiday itself in a new way. (Barber 1959: 8)

Barber's analysis sounds on the whole more Freudian than historical or political and it argues that the presence of a popular festival energizes the younger characters in the comedy and presents them with a possibility of reaching freedom and emancipation from patriarchy so as to express their own desires against the mutilating or castrating nature of the law of the father. In this connection, carnival, with its saturnalian inversion of rank or gender roles, seems to offer the occasion or the welcome detour that allows the young to get away with transgression and abuse. When Jessica elopes from old Shylock's house and "gilds" herself with her father's ducats (*The Merchant of Venice*, 2.6.49–50), she evolves in a jolly atmosphere of revelry and almost innocent revolt.

Strangely enough, Barber includes only five of Shakespeare's comedies in his study, namely *Love's Labour's Lost*, *A Midsummer Night's Dream*, *The Merchant of Venice*, *As You Like It*, and *Twelfth Night*, thus leaving out comedies like *Much Ado About Nothing* and *The Merry Wives of Windsor*. He preferred to deal with the carnivalesques Falstaff of *1* and *2 Henry IV* rather than with the slightly farcical, ludicrous knight who is simultaneously courting two perfectly respectable wives of a provincial and bourgeois community. In an article called "The Two Worlds of Shakespearean Comedy" Shearman Hawkins (1967) has proposed a second type presenting a number of significant variations on the original model. According to this critic, comedies like *The Comedy of Errors*, *Love's Labour's Lost*, *Much Ado About Nothing*, and *Twelfth Night*, are built on an "alternate pattern" according to which, instead of leaving the court to move into the green world, the characters stay put and are visited by outsiders who upset the daily life of the community (like Cesario arriving in Illyria, for instance) (ibid: 67–8). The obstacles to love do not come from the opposition of a tyrannical old father but from inside the lovers themselves, so that the conflict of generations is replaced by the battle of the sexes. Shearman Hawkins calls these the "comedies of the closed world" and their two principles are "acting out" (releasing latent desires or impulses) and "fixing the blame," thus locating the madness or evil in one particular character (Falstaff, Don John, or Malvolio) who may be overpowered or driven out of the community (ibid: 71). Two remaining comedies, *The Taming of the Shrew* and *The Merry Wives of Windsor*, are "mixed comedies," in that they combine both patterns in their double plots (ibid: 65).

Besides these proposed variations on the "green world" model, other reproaches have been leveled against Barber's anthropological method, namely that he depends for his approach on a now obsolete anthropological model, which is no other than the one worked out by Sir James Frazer and the Cambridge ritualists, Francis Cornford and Margaret Murray. Moreover, his analysis of Elizabethan festivity remains general and tentative and often lacks historical detail. After the books of Keith Thomas, David Underdown, David Cressy, or Ronald Hutton, to name only a few of the historians of popular holiday, the political dimension of festivity has become increasingly important to modern critics. As Richard Wilson puts it:

If modernist Shakespeareans obeyed Henry James's dictum to 'Dramatize! Dramatize!' a timeless contemporaneity, postmodernist critics take as their watchword Frederic Jameson's imperative to 'Always historicize.' From James to Jameson, the historical turn in Shakespeare studies is a shift, then, of global to local, order to process, speech to writing, and *langue* (language as a system) to *parole* (specific utterance). (Wilson 1993: 20)[6]

For Marxist critics like Mikhaïl Bakhtin, Robert Weimann, or Michael Bristol, on the other hand, festive license is deeply indebted and fundamentally allied to popular culture. Bakhtin's concept of carnival as a form of popular culture showing subversive irreverence for authority and a way of indulging verbal exuberance and vulgarity, even obscenity, that revels in ambivalence (confusing high and low, birth and death . . .) and celebrates the pleasures of the body, especially in its orifices, protuberances, and appetites, has been the most widely used and discussed over the past thirty years. To the eyes of the Russian critic, carnival makes mutability and topsy-turvydom the main energizing poles of the popular culture of the late Middle Ages and the Renaissance:

> During the century-long development of the medieval carnival, prepared by thousands of years of ancient comic ritual, including the primitive Saturnalias, a special idiom of forms and symbols was evolved – an extremely rich idiom that expressed the unique yet complex carnival experience of the people. This experience, opposed to all that was ready-made and completed, to all pretense of immutability, sought a dynamic expression; it demanded ever changing, playful, undefined forms. All the symbols of the carnival idiom are filled with this pathos of change and renewal, with sense of the gay relativity of prevailing truths and authorities. We find here a characteristic logic, the peculiar logic of the 'inside out' (*à l'envers*), of the 'turnabout,' of a continual shifting from top to bottom, from front to rear, of numerous parodies and travesties, humiliations, profanations, comic crownings and uncrownings. A second life, a second world of folk culture is thus constructed; it is to a certain extent a parody of the extracarnival life, a 'world inside out.' (Bakhtin 1984: 11)

This taste for putting the world upside down, for travesties and "uncrownings," is certainly echoed in the atmosphere of *A Midsummer Night's Dream*, where Bottom's hairy head literally "translates" him into an "ass," a visual and grotesque pun that also amounts to a form of bodily reversal emphasizing the "lower bodily stratum" so important in carnival and popular culture according to Bakhtin.[7]

For Bakhtin and his followers, carnival grotesqueries in Shakespeare are indeed endowed with a truly subversive power and with a desire to destabilize authority and its serious, official, one-sided, vertical vision of the world. Popular festivals and charivaris, local forms of popular justice against sexual offenders also known as "skimmingtons" or "rough music" (Underdown 1985: 100–3), thus contributed to the expression of dissent, to the simultaneous presence of multiple voices, including those of children and women (through the rites of inversion of the Boy Bishop or cross-dressing). Contrary to the historian David Underdown, who argues that "on the stage, as in carnival, gender inversion temporarily turns the world upside down – but to reinforce, not subvert, the traditional order," Louis Montrose claims that "in specific instances, such marginal symbolic actions [i.e., "game, play, or drama"] may have constituted intervals of a creative or contestatory counter-order that generated critical perspectives upon, or rowdy parodies of, ideologically dominant forms and practices" (Montrose 1996: 121).

It would seem that popular festivity, even when staged in a play, cannot be reduced to the function of a simple interval or "safety valve." The context of a network of communal obligations might suggest that it was not indispensable for each individual to take responsibility for his own destiny, while Shakespeare's entire work lays stress on the promotion of self-knowledge rather than on any particular action or mode of behavior recommended within some ritualized system. For all that, Shakespeare's festive comedy is certainly to be contrasted with Ben Jonson's gallery of eccentrics in a comedy like *Every Man in His Humour*, which Gabrielle Bernhard Jackson has called a "comedy of non-interaction," opposing it to Shakespeare's "comedy of interaction" (Jonson 1969: 2) where the minds of the lovers have been "transfigured so *together*" and "grow to something of great constancy" (*A Midsummer Night's Dream*, 5.1.24–6).

Clowns and Jigs

In the London playhouses that attracted increasing numbers in the 1590s due to the establishment of fixed and professional stages, but also to fierce competition between them, the stage clown was to become a most significant figure for the whole atmosphere, life, and structure of Shakespearean comedy, from Launce and his dog in *Two Gentlemen of Verona*, to Feste in *Twelfth Night*. The clown was indeed one of the last upholders and defenders of the old popular tradition of the carnivalesque. One of his functions was to cut down intellectual pretension and to draw attention to what Bakhtin has subsequently called "the material bodily lower stratum" (Bakhtin 1984: 368–436), i.e., the vulgar world of anality and sex associated with basic human appetite. This is a way of giving the spectator a chance to distance himself/herself from high-minded activity and discourse, as in *Love's Labour's Lost*, where Costard and Jaquenetta unabashedly express their bodily needs against the high-flown, far-reaching and pretentious aspirations of the courtiers: "Such is the simplicity of men," says Costard, "to hearken after the flesh" (*Love's Labour's Lost*, 1.1.214–15). In *A Midsummer Night's Dream* it is the sphere of romantic love itself which is refracted in a burlesque, farcical manner in the mechanicals' bungled performance of "Pyramus and Thisbe," while the bergamask at the end (5.1.354) is clearly a reminiscence of the pantomime wooing dances or jigs performed at seasonal festivals and weddings (Berry 1984: 117). In *Much Ado About Nothing* the "shallow wits," Dogberry and his hilariously inefficient watch, "bring to light" the simple truth that the wiser characters could not discover (*Much Ado About Nothing*, 5.1.205–6); in *The Merchant of Venice* the clown Gobbo gives a farcical version of the main plot and of the tense family relations inside the Christian and Jewish communities. Strangely enough, Shakespeare's most extraordinary clown and expert in all tricks and saturnalian disguises and reversals – carnivalesque jokes, theatrical ad-libbing, bibulous word games or superb comic monologues to obfuscate his lies or cover his bad faith – Sir John Falstaff – is mostly present in *1* and *2 Henry IV* and appears in one comedy only, *The Merry Wives of Windsor*. In his one and only English comedy with a semi-urban, semi-rural background, the fat knight of the Henriad is purged of his lust as well as of his sexual and financial pretensions to make him cut a sorry figure at the end. The festive side is far from ignored, but it is the corrective dimension that clearly prevails in the main plot, which presents a rather un-Shakespearean form of sexual, urban comedy with tentative seduction of married middle-class women by a down-and-out, aged aristocrat, with resulting male jealousy and the fear of cuckoldry as some of its main comic ingredients, while the romantic strain is only present and pre-served in the subplot. Indeed, the secret love between Anne Page and Master Fenton allows them in the end to get rid of rivals and of parental opposition and to turn the confusion of the final comedy of tricks and errors to their own advantage and marriage.

It is interesting that, in Elizabethan England, neoclassical writers regularly criti-cized the presence of clowns on the stage. Sir Philip Sidney delivers strictures to plays "mingling kings and clowns" (Sidney 1965: 135), while Ben Jonson made the deci-sion to eliminate this character from the genre of comedy and indeed managed to do without one in his last two comedies (Bednarz 2001: 113). Against them, Shakespeare made sure that the clown – and here no strict distinction should be made between country rustic and court jester, since the line between the two is blurred in plays where the entertainer is alternately called "fool" and "clown" – kept an important place and function in his festive comedies. In *As You Like It* Touchstone is pitted against the satirist Jaques, and he embodies festive comedy in all its facets and con-tradictions. The difficulty seems to have remained at the level of the critical inter-pretation of the plays where, as David Wiles explains, the clown has remained "an embarrassment":

> So long as the accepted task of the critic was to seek out the moral purpose of the text, the unity of the play's construction, truth and consistency of character, the inspirational kernel which generated the play's themes, then the clown remained an embarrassment. The theory of 'comic relief,' with its mysterious cathartic overtones, was evolved to conceal a conceptual vacuum. The clown escaped from marginalization only when such critics as C. L. Barber, Northrop Frye, and Robert Weimann began to show how Shake-spearean comedy was patterned by the popular festive tradition, and not by classical notions of form. (Wiles 1987: 165)

So the understanding of the real importance of the clown in the festive comedy of the Elizabethan stage was definitely achieved by a number of anthropology-oriented studies that demonstrated the structural links that existed between Shakespeare's comedies and seasonal mirth and misrule.

Mirth vs. Laughter

There are two main types of comic strategies. One uses laughter to ridicule some deficiency or error in a character that can be shown as foolish. This tradition belongs to corrective comedy, a genre best depicted by the famous Latin motto *castigat ridendo mores*.

The second type relates comedy to festive rejoicing and it presents us with convivial laughter in which simple mirth is opposed to the more aggressive aspect of ridicule. The latter, which is meant to expose, cleanse, or correct vices and follies, encourages one to laugh *at* someone else, while in mirth and foolery, people laugh *with* the fool or rejoice with the happy crowd that is making merry. Mirth provokes release and it licenses the potentially anarchic and subversive spirit of carnival with the celebration of the life-force that triumphs over its enemies.

These two comic attitudes may be called derisive laughter and festive mirth. In *An Apology for Poetry* or *The Defence of Poesy* Sir Philip Sidney clearly opposes the two notions, which he defines at some length:

> But our comedians think there is no delight without laughter; which is very wrong, for though laughter may come with delight, yet cometh it not of delight, as though delight should be the cause of laughter; but well may one thing breed both together. Nay, rather in themselves they have, as it were, a kind of contrariety . . . Delight hath a joy in it . . . Laughter hath only a scornful tickling. For example, we are ravished with delight to see a fair woman. We laugh at deformed creatures, wherein certainly we cannot delight . . . But I speak to this purpose, that all the end of the comical part be not upon such scornful matters as stirreth laughter only, but, mixed with it, that delightful teaching which is the end of poesie . . . For what is it to make folkes gape at a wretched beggar, and a beggarly Clowne: or against lawe of hospitalitie, to ieast at a straunger, because they speake not English so well as we do? (Sidney 1965: 136–7)

In general, the scurrilous and satirical humor represented by the Old Comedy of Aristophanes is condemned at that time. On the other hand, mirth is well regarded, and Nicholas Udall, the author of the first English comedy, *Ralph Roister Doister*, starts with an apology of mirth in the Prologue to his play:

> For mirth prolongeth life, and causeth health,
> Mirth recreates our spirits and voideth pensiveness,
> Mirth increaseth amity, not hindering our wealth. (ll.8–10)

This quasi-therapeutic function of comedy that dispels the darker humors and is the source of good health is taken up by Shakespeare at the end of the Induction of *The Taming of the Shrew* (see above, p. 23). Heywood, in his *Apology for Actors*, seems to support this view when he explains that the lessons of comedy

> are mingled with sportful accidents, to recreate such as of themselves are wholly devoted to melancholy, which corrupts the blood: or to refresh such weary spirits as are tired

with labour or study, to moderate the cares and heaviness of the mind, that they may return to their trades and faculties with more zeal and earnestness, after some small soft and pleasant retirement. (Heywood 1612: sig. F4)

Such a view is fairly close to the safety-valve theory of misrule and festive irreverence as a temporary transgression of established order, whose function is not to upset authority permanently but, on the contrary, to reinforce it. We find a similar attitude in an observer of the time, the Dijon physician Pierre Gringoire, for whom

the feast of fools and celebrations of misrule served the same function for a rigidly hierarchical society as the bung-holes did for a wine-cask: these indeed needed to be opened occasionally to release the pressure of the fermenting wine and to prevent the barrels from breaking altogether. (Mangan 1996: 37)[8]

These two poles of the comic are naturally, not mutually, exclusive or incompatible, since they are often combined in Shakespeare's comedies. In *A Midsummer Night's Dream* things are perhaps a little more complex as – if the mutual scoffs and taunts of Helena and Hermia (3.2) may be placed in the first category of scornful jests – the main stress in the play remains the one often put on the incongruous, as in the nightly encounter and embrace of Bottom and Titania, and on the display of delightful absurdity, as in the performance of "Pyramus and Thisbe" which Hippolyta describes as "the silliest stuff that ever I heard" (5.1.209). Sometimes the plays take on the dimension of a charivari used to punish whores or unruly women reputed to cuckold or beat their husbands. In *The Taming of the Shrew*, for example, the courting of "wild Kate," the shrewish Katherina, seems so problematic that old Grumio cantankerously suggests replacing the ritual of seduction by shaming practices:

Baptista. If either of you both love Katherina
Because I know you well and love you well
Leave shall you have to court her at your pleasure.

Gremio. To cart her rather! She's too rough for me. (1.1.52–5)

The court/cart pun here obliquely refers to the Shrove Tuesday practice of dragging prostitutes from houses of ill-fame and parading them through the town in carts for the crowds to jeer at them (Laroque 1991: 100). But in other cases it was the husband or his nearest neighbor who were publicly humiliated for allowing his wife to have deceived or humiliated him:

I have sometimes met in the streets of London a woman carrying a figure of straw representing a man, crown'd with very ample horns, preceded by a drum, and followed by a mob, making a most grating noise with tongs, gridirons, frying-pans and saucepans. I asked what was the meaning of all this; they told me that a woman had given her husband a sound beating for accusing her of making him a cuckold, and that upon such occasions some kind neighbour of the poor innocent injured creature generally performed this ceremony. (Misson 1698: 70)

This form of popular justice corresponds to the situation of Falstaff when he is seen wearing the ample horns of Herne the hunter at the end of *The Merry Wives of Windsor* (5.5.1–120). When, after being pinched by the Windsor fairies, he finds out that he has been gulled (made an "ass" or an "ox") and made the victim of the two wives' hoax, he realizes that the horns are more the badge of humiliation than of sexual potency, contrary to what he had thought (Salingar 1974: 236–7; Laroque 1984: 27). As in a local charivari, he is now wearing the horns of the cuckolded husband. He has become a substitute or *doppelgänger* of Ford disguised as Master Brook, a character whom his pathologically comic jealousy leads to the door of cuckoldry with the help of Falstaff, whose lust and financial appetite he is unwittingly encouraging. If the furious husband is finally purged of his jealousy, Falstaff has become a comical sexual outlaw who must be banished from the community for offending its codes.[9] It is ironical that the motto of the Order of the Garter (*Honi soit qui mal y pense*) is here turned into a moral condemnation to scoff at the "corrupt and tainted in desire" (*The Merry Wives of Windsor*, 5.5.68, 89).

So, on a general level, the two comic attitudes of laughing *at* and laughing *with* define the two main trends or strains of comedy: the satiric and the jocular. If one subtext of comedy is indeed carnival, festivity, rejoicing, and liberation, another is containment, exclusion, and regulation. One is Dionysiac and celebratory, the other normative and corrective.

Festive Comedy vs. Comical Satire

Festivity, celebration, carnival – these are words that have positive, genial, exciting connotations attached to them, while laughter, satire, ridicule, and folly sound cruel, punitive, expository. The first group implies freedom or liberation, the belief in the power of imagination and of the dream, and a surrender to nature and to the irrationality of desire in the hope that all will end well and that Jack shall have Jill. The second group is linked to scrutiny and suspicion, to a form of intolerance towards difference, deviance, or eccentricity, as well as towards all forms of vices and follies that must be exposed and laughed away at the expense of the vain, the selfish, or the gullible. It is in this sense that the city comedy developed by Ben Jonson is poles apart from Shakespeare's sensibility and personal preferences, even if in his comedies of the "closed world" he does not refuse the idea of scapegoating Don John, Shylock, or Malvolio. In a festive comedy like *A Midsummer Night's Dream*, the unmarried young lovers find in the natural environment of the green world a locus where they freely indulge in the irrationalities of desire, where the complications of the double plot add tricks and errors only to disentangle their misalliances towards the end in a dream-like, miraculous way that allows the comedy to end happily. Even though the comic follies of the lovers are fully displayed in a sometimes rather harsh and bitter manner, the magic of the green world soon takes over to produce its beneficent effects and exorcize the potential violence. So the "story of the night" does produce a sense of estrangement, loss, and amazement, as in the lots that were traditionally drawn on

Valentine's Day (Laroque 1991: 106–7) or in the excesses often noted on the night of May Day or Midsummer eve. But in the end a "great constancy" (*A Midsummer Night's Dream*, 5.1.26) is discovered which restores not only harmony and peace but sexual satisfaction and happiness. Indeed, the two companionate marriages which Egeus, as *senex iratus*, was stubbornly opposing at the beginning are now possible and are about to be celebrated and consummated. In a nutshell, the freedom from constraints and subversion of authority, observable both in the erotic alliances and erratic wanderings in the forest, on the one hand, and in the text's noted absence of sources, on the other, produce a truly carnivalesque euphoria and energy.

Far from this, the marriage feast in Jonson's comedy of humors often proves impossible. Indeed, at the end of *Every Man in His Humour*, the wedding feast turns into a violent tavern scene in *Every Man Out*, a play that focuses on the collapse of Delirio's marriage to Fallace. Contrary to the happy ending of *A Midsummer Night's Dream*, the satirical play reveals how marriage may be destroyed by a husband's discovery of his wife's unfaithfulness. In his treatment of sexual attraction, Jonson puts the stress on exposure and he challenges Shakespeare's faith in the intrinsic value of desire at the expense of reason and judgment. Shakespeare sanctions desire in the spectacle of numerous weddings at closure, while Jonson subjects his characters to the chastening or humiliating vision of satire that exposes their folly or gullibility. This corresponds to what Ian Donaldson has called "leveling comedy," namely "comedy of unmasking, comedy which reveals unexpected and embarrassing brotherhood in error, comedy which . . . stuns, disables and humbles its protagonists" (Donaldson 1984: 108). Jonson's public humiliation runs against Shakespeare's encouragement or condoning of a spirit of rebellion against the constraints of law. It is true that in *Romeo and Juliet* he wrote a play which may be regarded as a companion piece to *A Midsummer Night's Dream* and which illustrates the dangers of blindly following the dictates of Cupid and ignoring the law in favor of passion and romantic love.

According to James Bednarz, Shakespeare wrote two of his festive comedies, *As You Like It* and *Twelfth Night*, in order to counter Jonson's move to try to displace romantic comedy, whose inner flaw was supposed to be its absence of rules and authority, with comical satire and the comedy of humors (Bednarz 2001: 13), an interpretation that partly accounts for the complexity and sophistication of these two highly metatheatrical comedies. Indeed, by returning to pastoral and to a plot based on a prose romance by Thomas Lodge, *Rosalynde*, after writing the urban comedy of *Much Ado About Nothing*, Shakespeare tried to test the standards of art and judgment against the more spontaneous impulses of nature and "folly." His festive comedy deliberately included "cross-wooing" and a "clown," two elements which Jonson had censured in *Every Man Out of His Humour* when Mitis derides weak comic plots with "cross-wooing [and] a clown to their servingman" (3.6.198). So the Stratford man was returning to authorities which Jonson would have disapproved of as "artless." Furthermore, in *As You Like It* the clown Touchstone is allowed to baffle and silence the bitter satirist Jaques (to be pronounced "Jakes" in order to bring out the pun on a "privy" or closestool), who is generally thought to represent Ben Jonson himself, later to be purged under the character of Ajax (with always the same pun on "jakes") in *Troilus and Cressida* (Bednarz 2001: 107). According to James Bednarz,

> Touchstone, like Rosalind, exemplifies C. L. Barber's notion of 'a mocking reveler,' a character who yields to festivity by accepting the natural as irrational . . . In contrast to Jonson's attempt to distinguish the judicious from the humoured, Shakespeare emphasizes their common fallibility. Whereas Jonson's satirist makes absolute moral judgments and resists desire, Shakespeare's fool derides a natural condition he embraces. (ibid: 112)

The holiday, carefree atmosphere of the forest of Arden imbues the comedy with a sense of natural teleology, since the green world, in this romantic perspective, can only bring about maturation and reconciliation. As Susan Snyder puts it, "chaos is held in check by comedy's arbitrary natural law" (Snyder 1979: 55).

In his last festive comedy, *Twelfth Night*, Shakespeare returns to cross-wooing with a fool with a backward glance at his first Plautine comedy, *The Comedy of Errors*. He contrasts the selfless love of Viola for Orsino with Malvolio's ridiculous self-infatuation and, according to the other festive comedies that insist on the restoration of a broken or impossible union, this play "presents mutability as a laudable component of desire" (Bednarz 2001: 188). The comic resolution is not achieved through fidelity, but through fluidity or flexibility, as Olivia is quite happy to take Sebastian for Viola and Orsino Cesario–Viola for Olivia. At the same time, unrequitable desire is exposed and stigmatized in Aguecheek and Malvolio, who embody the antitypes of hypocritical restraint on the one hand, and ridiculous excess on the other. The below-stairs carnivalesque subplot may provide some boisterous or obscene moments in performance, as in Adrian Noble's production for the RSC in 1998:

> Later as the fool, Andrew, and Toby sang 'Hold thy peace,' Feste mimed the erection of an enormous 'piece' (or phallus) from the front of his trousers, up which the knights apparently climbed as though it were an invisible beanstalk. This totemic penis was then carried above their heads as they processed drunkenly around the kitchen and only following the entry of the incandescent Malvolio was the wilting erection fed back into the flies of the jester.[10]

Maybe modern audiences need to be presented with linguistic puns in this visual, insistent manner so that they can understand what "cakes and ale" really mean! This also looked ahead to the sexual frustration of Malvolio. By allowing Olivia's steward to isolate himself in the subplot and commit himself to an angry promise of revenge ("I'll be revenged on the whole pack of you," 5.11.368), Shakespeare powerfully illustrated "the wisdom of folly" in a farewell to the genre which may certainly also be read as a manifesto in favor of the superiority of festive comedy over comical satire (Bednarz 2001: 190). According to Leo Salingar, *Twelfth Night*, whose title "proclaims an affinity with the season of Christmas and carnival," "deals with the psychological value of revelry and its limits as well" and should be read as "a comedy about a comedy" (Salingar 1974: 239–42).

So, at a time when Puritan ministers and pamphleteers repeatedly attacked the abuses and excesses of "papist" rejoicings and popular festivals that were taken to be pagan remnants and forms of superstitious or licentious idolatry, Shakespeare stood in the defense of "old holiday pastimes," as these seemed to him to anchor his plays deeply in local tradition while allowing him a measure of flexibility as well as a world of phrases, images, and symbols, all chiming together to create a tightly woven network of associations and resonances. In his festive, green-world comedies and later romances, he chose festivity and mirth rather than the city intrigue and comical satire advocated by his colleague and rival Ben Jonson.

Shakespeare's festive comedies revel in a carnival spirit of liberty and irreverence. They sanction sexual desire to be crowned and licensed by companionate marriage and they praise the wisdom of folly, as constancy and happiness are ultimately proved right once the young lovers are allowed to leave the labyrinth of errors, tricks, or illusions that have been wrought upon them.

Songs, music, and lyrics are particularly important in Shakespeare's festive comedies. They are there to entertain the audience, but also to contribute to the general mirth and to the dancing spirits that accompany the rites of love and restore harmony like some final, almost impossible miracle. Contrariwise, Jonson's comical satires or Shakespeare's subplots that take up the tricks of humours and the cruel games of deception and exposure – illustrated in the conflicts between Shylock and Antonio in *The Merchant of Venice* or between Sir Toby, Feste, and Malvolio in *Twelfth Night* – insist on dissonance and cacophony or on men who have no music in them. *As You Like It* presents the character–singer Amiens who, though he is shivering with cold, sings the "green holly," repeating that "this life is most jolly" (2.7.175–94). To C. L. Barber "the songs evoke the daily enjoyments and the daily community out of which special festive occasions were shaped up. And so they provide for the conclusion of the comedy what marriage usually provides: an expression of the going-on power of life" (Barber 1959: 118). This evocation of the "daily enjoyments of the daily community" does indeed seem to tie in with Christopher Sly's "comonty," i.e., with the special, subtle, unmistakable festive note which it is otherwise so difficult to isolate and define. Yet, for Philip Edwards, the festive comedies do not really end in clarification and in a resolution of the contrary forces of holiday and everyday: "A strong magic is created: and it is questioned" (Edwards 1968: 70). This shows that one cannot do away with the basic discrepancy between ritual and reality and it is also meant to remind the spectator–reader of Shakespeare's festive comedies that it is quite necessary to reestablish a critical perspective after enjoying the sweet impossibilities of romance.

Notes

1   See Peter Holland in Shakespeare (1995a: 18–19).
2   *Hamlet*, 3.2.125. On this see Liebler (1995: 173–95).
3   Dusinberre (1975); Bamber (1982); Roberts (1991); Dash (1981); Novy (1984).

4 Dante, *Inferno*, Canto 11.2.
5 Frye (1965: 73).
6 The first three chapters of the book, "'A mingled yarn': Shakespeare and the cloth workers", "'Is this a holiday?': Shakespeare's Roman carnival" and "'Like the old Robin Hood': *As You Like It* and the enclosure riots", offer an excellent illustration of this method of historicizing and politicizing festivity and using it as a background for reinterpreting Shakespeare's text as a distant echo of these ideological or social disputes.
7 On this see Laroque (1984: 25).
8 This refers to a text by a doctor of Auxerre, Pierre Gringoire, comparing the clergy to "nothing but old wine casks badly put together [that] would certainly burst if the wine of wisdom were allowed to boil by continued devotion to the Divine Service". Quoted in Welsford (1935: 202).
9 Louis Montrose (1996: 119) finds that the "fundamental contradiction of the Elizabethan gender system that was articulated in charivaris may also have found controlled expression in the anxious and aggressive aspects of Elizabethan courtship comedies such as Shakespeare's". He mentions in particular what he calls "the ubiquitous jokes and fears about cuckoldry" which are found in *The Taming of the Shrew*, *The Merry Wives of Windsor*, and *Much Ado About Nothing*.
10 Review by Peter J. Smith, *Cahiers Elisabéthains*, 54 (October 1998), p. 131.

References and Further Reading

Bakhtin, M. (1984). *Rabelais and His World*, trans. H. Iswolsky. Boston, MA: MIT Press; Indianapolis: Indiana University Press.

Bamber, L. (1982). *Comic Women, Tragic Men: A Study of Gender and Genre in Shakespeare*. Stanford, CA: Stanford University Press.

Barber, C. L. (1959). *Shakespeare's Festive Comedy: A Study of Dramatic Form and its Relation to Social Custom*. Princeton, NJ: Princeton University Press.

Barton, A. (1994). *Essays, Mainly Shakespearean*. Cambridge: Cambridge University Press.

Bednarz, J. P. (2001). *Shakespeare and the Poets' War*. New York: Columbia University Press.

Berry, E. (1984). *Shakespeare's Comic Rites*. Cambridge: Cambridge University Press.

Bristol, M. (1985). *Carnival and Theatre: Plebeian Culture and the Structure of Authority in Renaissance England*. London: Methuen.

Cressy, D. (1989). *Bonfires and Bells: National Memory and the Protestant Calendar in Elizabethan and Stuart England*. London: Weidenfeld and Nicolson.

——(1997). *Birth, Marriage and Death: Ritual, Religion, and the Life-Cycle in Tudor and Stuart England*. Oxford: Oxford University Press.

Danson, L. (2000). *Shakespeare's Dramatic Genres*. Oxford: Oxford University Press.

Dash, I. G. (1981). *Wooing, Wedding and Power: Women in Shakespeare's Plays*. New York: Columbia University Press.

Donaldson, I. (1984). Justice in the Stocks. In D. J. Palmer (ed.) *Comedy: Developments in Criticism*. Basingstoke: Macmillan, 103–14.

Dusinberre, J. (1975). *Shakespeare and the Nature of Women*. Basingstoke: Macmillan.

Edwards, P. (1968). *Shakespeare and the Confines of Art*. London: Methuen.

Frye, N. (1948). The Argument of Comedy. *English Institute Essays*, 58–73.

——(1965). *A Natural Perspective*. New York: Columbia University Press.

Garber, M. (1981). *Coming of Age in Shakespeare*. London: Methuen.

Hawkins, S. (1967). The Two Worlds of Shakespearean Comedy. *Shakespeare Studies*, 3, 62–80.

Heywood, T. (1612). *An Apology for Actors*. London.

Honigmann, E. A. J. (1985). *Shakespeare: The 'Lost Years'*. Manchester: Manchester University Press.

Hutton, R. (1994). *The Rise and Fall of Merry England: The Ritual Year 1400–1700*. Oxford: Oxford University Press.

Jonson, B. (1925–52). *Ben Jonson*, 11 vols, ed. C. H. Herford and P. Simpson. Oxford: Clarendon Press.

——(1969). *Every Man in His Humour*, ed. G. B. Jackson. New Haven, CT: Yale University Press.

Laroque, F. (1984). Ovidian Transformations and Folk Festivities in *A Midsummer Night's Dream*, *The Merry Wives of Windsor* and *As You Like It*. *Cahiers Elisabéthains*, 24, 23–36.

——(1991). *Shakespeare's Festive World: Elizabethan Seasonal Entertainment and the Professional Stage*. Cambridge: Cambridge University Press.

Liebler, N. (1995). Hamlet's Hobby Horse. In *Shakespeare's Festive Tragedy: The Ritual Foundations of Genre*. London: Routledge.

Mangan, M. (1996). *A Preface to Shakespeare's Comedies 1594–1603*. Harlow: Longman.

Marcus, L. (1986). *The Politics of Mirth: Jonson, Herrick, Milton, Marvel and the Defense of Old Holiday Pastimes*. Chicago, IL: University of Chicago Press.

Marienstras, R. (1981). *Le Proche et le lointain. Sur Shakespeare, le drame élisabéthain et l'idéologie anglaise aux XVIe et XVIIe siècles (New Perspectives on the Shakespearean World)*. Paris: Editions de Minuit.

Misson de Valbourg, H. (1698). *Mémoires et observations faites par un voyageur en Angleterre et sur ce qu'il y a trouvé de plus remarquable*. The Hague.

Montrose, L. (1996). *The Purpose of Playing: Shakespeare and the Cultural Politics of the Elizabethan Theatre*. Chicago, IL: University of Chicago Press.

Muir, K. (1979). *Shakespeare's Comic Sequence*. Liverpool: Liverpool University Press.

Novy, M. (1984). *Love's Argument: Gender Relations in Shakespeare*. Chapel Hill: University of North Carolina Press.

Orgel, S. (1985). Making Greatness Familiar. In D. Bergeron (ed.) *Pageantry in the Shakespearean Theater*. Athens, GA: University of Georgia Press, 19–25.

Roberts, J. A. (1972). *The Merry Wives of Windsor* as a Hallowe'en Play. *Shakespeare Survey*, 25.

——(1991). *The Shakespearean Wild: Geography, Genus, and Gender*. Lincoln: University of Nebraska Press.

Salingar, L. (1974). *Shakespeare and the Traditions of Comedy*. Cambridge: Cambridge University Press.

Shakespeare, W. (1969). *Two Gentlemen of Verona*, ed. C. Leech. London: Methuen.

——(1981). *Richard III*, ed. A. Hammon. London: Methuen.

——(1984). *The Taming of the Shrew*, ed. A. Thompson. Cambridge: Cambridge University Press.

——(1987). *Hamlet*, ed. G. R. Hibbard. Oxford: Oxford University Press.

——(1988). *Much Ado About Nothing*, ed. F. H. Mares. Cambridge: Cambridge University Press.

——(1993a). *As You Like It*, ed. A. Brissenden. Oxford: Oxford University Press.

——(1993b). *The Merchant of Venice*, ed. J. L. Halio. Oxford: Oxford University Press.

——(1994a). *Love's Labour's Lost*, ed. G. R. Hibbard. Oxford: Oxford University Press.

——(1994b). *The Merry Wives of Windsor*, ed. T. W. Craik. Oxford: Oxford University Press.

——(1995a). *A Midsummer Night's Dream*, ed. P. Holland. Oxford: Oxford University Press.

——(1995b). *Twelfth Night*, ed. R. Warren and S. Wells. Oxford: Oxford University Press.

Sidney, P. (1965) [1595]. *An Apology for Poetry* or *The Defense of Poesy*, ed. G. Shepherd. Manchester: Manchester University Press.

Snyder, S. (1979). *The Comic Matrix of Shakespeare's Tragedies: Romeo and Juliet, Hamlet, Othello and King Lear*. Princeton, NJ: Princeton University Press.

Strong, R. (1977). *The Cult of Elizabeth*. London: Thames and Hudson.

Stubbes, P. (1877–9). *Philip Stubbes' Anatomy of Abuses in England in Shakespeare's Youth, A.D. 1583*, 2 vols, ed. F. J. Furnivall. London: New Shakespere Society.

Thomas, K. (1971). *Religion and the Decline of Magic: Studies in Popular Beliefs in Sixteenth and Seventeenth Century England*. London: Weidenfeld and Nicolson.

Udall, N. (1984). In *Three Sixteenth-Century Comedies*, ed. C. W. Whitworth. Tonbridge: Ernest Benn.

Underdown, D. (1985). *Revel, Riot and Rebellion: Popular Politics and Culture in England 1603–1660*. Oxford: Oxford University Press.

Weimann, R. (1978). *Shakespeare and the Popular Tradition in the Theater*. Baltimore, MD: Johns Hopkins University Press.

Welsford, E. (1935). *The Fool: His Social and Literary History*. London: Faber and Faber.

Wiles, D. (1987). *Shakespeare's Clown: Actor and Text in the Elizabethan Playhouse.* Cambridge: Cambridge University Press.

——(1993). *Shakespeare's Almanac: A Midsummer Night's Dream and the Elizabethan Calendar.* Cambridge: D. S. Brewer.

Wilson, R. (1993). *Will Power: Essays on Shakespearean Authority.* Hemel Hempstead: Harvester Wheatsheaf.

——(1997). Shakespeare and the Jesuits. *Times Literary Supplement*, December 19.

3

The Humor of It: Bodies, Fluids, and Social Discipline in Shakespearean Comedy

Gail Kern Paster

The classical doctrine of the four humors gave early modern English playwrights – Shakespeare included – a theory of personality, behavior, status, gender, age, and ethnicity that had the distinct advantage of being rooted in what they believed to be indisputable facts about the human body and its relation to the natural world. The humors – blood, phlegm, choler or yellow bile, and melancholy or black bile – were "real bodily fluids to which largely hypothetical origins, sites and functions were ascribed" (Siraisi 1990: 105). The humoral body's internal organs produced the four fluids and sent them out into the bloodstream to deliver their qualities of cold, hot, moist, and dry to all the body's parts. From blood came the qualities of hot and moist; from phlegm, cold and moist; from choler, hot and dry; and from melancholy, cold and dry. At every moment in the course of a day, a month, a season, or a lifetime, these humors and the qualities residing in them were thought to calibrate a body's internal heat and moisture – what the Elizabethans called its temper or complexion. Certainly before publication of Harvey's discovery of the circulation of the blood in 1628 and even for some time thereafter, the body constructed by Galenic humoralism was distinguished by its openness to the world around and by the variability of its humors as they moved sluggishly around their "semi-permeable, irrigated container" (Paster 1993: 8–11). It is the full-to-bursting contents of such a humoral body that Prince Hal identifies disparagingly in (and as) Falstaff – "that trunk of humors, that bolting-hutch of beastliness, that swoll'n parcel of dropsies, that huge bombard of sack, the stuff'd cloak-bag of guts, that roasted Manningtree ox with the pudding in his belly" (*1 Henry IV*, 2.4.449–53). But everyone was, or had, a trunk composed of humors – if ordinarily a somewhat smaller and more decorous one than Falstaff's.

Given that, physiologically, bodies differ very little from one century to the next, we might wonder why humoral language matters to understanding the role of bodiliness in Shakespeare's plays. Judith Butler has mounted a response to that question by insisting that the "materiality of bodies" – that which appears not to change much over time – must be understood as historically variant because it is discursively variant. Bodily matter "matters" textually as an "effect of a dynamic of power, such that the matter of bodies will be indissociable from the regulatory norms that govern their materialization and the signification of those material effects" (Butler 1993: 2). In other words, the language descriptive of bodies is not an effect of their materiality but helps to produce it; bodily materiality is not an irreducible precursor to signification but part of what is to be signified. If she is right, readers of Shakespearean comedy – a genre where questions pertaining to bodily appetites are so often at the heart of the action – may as well begin by assuming that the early moderns' humoral construction of the body implies significant change in bodily self-experience between then and now – and then test out such a proposition by reading for difference in the language of bodily self-experience. They can look for particular sites of difference in the comedies, either where the language of the humors is explicitly invoked or where casual, subthematic locutions of bodily affect and experience seem to organize that which is being thought and said.

In my view, the biggest source of historical otherness to be found in the bodies represented in Shakespearean comedy lies in the fact that, in the humoral interaction of the four qualities, the early moderns accounted for a person's thoughts and deeds in a way that did not distinguish, as we tend to do, between the psychological and the physiological. This is because the physical model underlying ancient and early modern psychology was, as historian Katharine Park has noted, "a simple hydraulic one, based on a clear localisation of psychological function by organ or system of organs" (Park 1988: 469). The forces of cold, hot, wet, and dry comprised the material basis of any living creature's characteristic appraisals of and responses to its immediate environment; they altered the character of a body's substances and, by doing so, organized its ability to act or even to think. "The Minds inclination follows the Bodies Temperature," the jurist John Selden noted in *Titles of Honor* (Selden 1614: sig. b4), repeating a Galenic commonplace of his age. Heat stimulated action, cold depressed it. Sound judgment and prudent action required the free flow of clear fluids in the brain, but melancholy or choler altered and darkened them. The young warrior's choler gave him impulsiveness and the capacity for rage; phlegm helped to produce his cowardly opposite's lethargy and was responsible for the general inconstancy of women. Youth was hot and moist, age cold and dry; men as a sex were hotter and drier than women (Filipczak 1997: 14–23, 68–77; Paster 1998: 416). And over all these individual qualities arched the defining humoral attributes of geographical latitude – the cold that gave northern peoples their valor, hardiness, and slow-wittedness; the heat that gave southerners their sagacity and quickness of response (Floyd-Wilson 2002).

As these generalizations of humoral thought suggest, the qualities were physical, psychological, and even cultural in effect, explaining not only an individual's characteristic responses to circumstances but also those of whole peoples. In the dynamic reciprocities between self and environment imagined by the psycho-physiology of bodily fluids, circumstance engenders humors in the body and humors in the body help to determine circumstance by predisposing the individual subject to a characteristic kind of evaluation and response. Such evaluation and response were thought to occasion subtle but important changes in a person's substance – change in the humoral fluids coursing through the body, change in the color and flow of brain fluids, change in the temper of the flesh carrying out the heart's commands. Modern uses of the word "humor" suggest how far we have come from thinking about bodily self-experience in the terms understood by Shakespeare and his contemporaries. Except in ophthalmic instances, as when an eye doctor refers to the viscous humor of the eyeball, humor does not now refer to bodily fluids at all but to characteristics we tend to designate as non-bodily and abstract. In its modern sense as denoting the temporary mood, good or bad, of a person or group (*OED* 4), humor clearly refers to disembodied mental and emotional states. As the word (*OED* 7a) for what makes something funny – whether event, text, performance, or person – humor also denotes an abstract characteristic, an effect that may be caused by something physical but is not physical in and of itself. As for the proprietary possession of that faculty known as a "sense of humor" (*OED* 7b), it is usually held to be among an individual's defining characteristics, even a litmus test of a person's likeability, popularity, and affinity for social life in general. We often think of a distinctive sense of humor functioning as a perdurable point of view, a particular lens of irony, wit, playfulness, or even satire determining a person's characteristic appraisal of and response to the world – especially perhaps to an absurd or irrational world.

As such specific meanings suggest, the multiple definitions and documentary citations for "humor" in the *Oxford English Dictionary* write a history for the word that throws into sharp relief the epistemic differences between early modern theories of human psychology and behavior and the gradual movement towards abstraction and dematerialization that in the Enlightenment overtook early modern locutions of body and mind (Hadfield 1992: 343–50; Sutton 1998: 117–18). A sense of humor, for example, is not at all unlike the predisposition that a particular combination of the four humors produced in an individual, rendering him or her by nature inclined to be choleric, melancholic, phlegmatic, or sanguine. But in contemporary usage a sense of humor is a quality of mind and, as such, lacks the bodily basis that made humoral typologies of personality persuasive to the early moderns as an explanation for different forms of agency and response. Even at the end of the seventeenth century it was still possible for William Congreve to characterize female deficiencies of wit in humoral terms:

> Methinks something should be said of the Humour of the Fair Sex; since they are sometimes so kind as to furnish out a Character for Comedy. But I must confess I have never made any Observation of what I apprehend to be the true Humour in Women. Perhaps Passions are too powerful in that Sex, to let Humour have its Course; or may be by reason of their Natural Coldness, Humour cannot Exert it self to that extravagant Degree, which it often does in the Male Sex. (Congreve 1964: 183)

Some of the current meanings for "humor" were also available to early modern English speakers. In general, however, the word "humor" denoted the fluids in plants and animals (*OED* 2a), the four bodily humors, and the physiological disposition or temperament which those four fluids acting in combination produced in an individual (*OED* 2b).

Probably because the humors were volatile in action though not unpredictable in effect, they became associated early on with impulse and whim (*OED* 6), with an idiosyncratic tendency to fix upon a course of action that, to others, seems groundless or fanciful or even unanswerable. This, according to J. B. Bamborough, is the chief meaning the word came to have for London gallants at the time, who may have cited their humors profligately to excuse lapses in behavior, to garner notice, to promote their individual eccentricities of style and address, or to claim affective privilege (Bamborough 1952: 103). In *The Gull's Hornbook* (1609) Thomas Dekker satirically describes the "true humorous gallant" as one who "desires to pour himself into all fashions" and "to excel even compliment itself must as well practise to diminish his walks" – that is, walk only in the places that fashionable men walk and adopt their proud gait while doing so – "as to be various in his salads, curious in his tobacco, or ingenious in the trussing up of a new Scotch hose" (Dekker 1968: 88; see Correll 1996). The association of this kind of self-preoccupation with the humors serves Ben Jonson as the basis for his own brand of London humor comedies, especially *Every Man In His Humour* (1598) and *Every Man Out Of His Humour* (1599), which focus satirically on the socially disabling manifestations of personal eccentricity, ego, and overweening appetite in groups of (mostly) men living in contemporary London. We can see something of this meaning in *A Midsummer Night's Dream* when Bottom announces to his fellow theatrical aspirants: "My chief humour is for a tyrant" (1.2.27–8). He means both the strong desire he feels for such a role at that particular moment and the predilection for dominance that might lead him to choose it. In truth, as we soon discover, his chief humor is to play *all* the roles in *Pyramus and Thisbe*, including that of the lion: "I will roar, that I will do any man's heart good to hear me," he tells Peter Quince (1.2.61–2).

But among Shakespeare's characters, it is irascible Corporal Nym of the second tetralogy and *The Merry Wives of Windsor* who most relies on the term *humor* in the Jonsonian sense, defending his actions by citing his humor as that force within him which simply and unanswerably moves him to feel and do: "I have an humor to knock you indifferently well," he tells Pistol early in *Henry V*; "I would prick your guts a little in good terms, as I may, and that's the humor of it" (2.1.55–9). For Nym, the possibility of verbal recourse to "humor" – as a placeholding word that substitutes for his lack of ideas and vocabulary – makes his world full of self-evidence. Humor is both a force in him and a force in all other things as well. Humor is thus synonymous with, or metonymic for, things as they are; humor is the badge of Nym's self-acceptance and the source of his resistance to alteration. In *Merry Wives*, with Nym's reliance on the term perhaps even more pronounced than in the history plays, the word is deliberately evacuated of denotative meaning in order, I think, that we may ponder the nature of its usefulness not as a description of the world but as a mode of social practice. In act 2, for example, Nym greets Masters Page and Ford with the following odd and abrupt declaration: "my name is Nym, and Falstaff loves your wife. Adieu. I love not the humor of bread and cheese and there's the humor of it" (*Merry*

Wives of Windsor, 2.1.134–6). Page's bemused response cues us to marvel at Nym's inarticulateness and the odd discontinuity of his speech: "Here's a fellow frights English out of his wits" (138–9). The phrase is wonderful, encompassing both Nym's effect on language – frightening English out of its ability to mean – and the effect of his language on Nym himself. But in Nym's eyes as self-declared humoral subject, the socially recognized autonomy of the humors serves not only to excuse his boorishness but also to justify his unwillingness to regulate, articulate, or reflect upon his words and actions – or indeed upon the curious nature of his world. The running of his bad humors against others, in that sense, *are* his actions, the stream of impulsive behaviors and disconnected speech that through their repetition constitute psychologically continuous self (such as it is) in Nym. From being a physiological attribute, the humors expand to become the basis of a way of life, a way of being in the world – in Nym's case, a maladaptive and inarticulate way identified by a prominent impulsiveness and aggressiveness that he and others see in humoral terms. "I never heard such a drawling, affecting rogue," Page complains (2.1.141) on Nym's departure.

Shylock too uses the humors for purposes of self-justification in a world he correctly believes to be stacked against him, but he does so with far more brilliance and effect than Corporal Nym. The concept is conveniently available when he rejects the Duke's plea to accept repayment of Antonio's debt in ducats rather than flesh, or even to give reasons for his refusal to do so. The Duke has framed the plea in terms of sympathy as the response properly ordained by nature – the touch of "humane gentleness and love" (25) – to the spectacle of extreme suffering, a response so natural that it is to be found even among peoples Elizabethans tended to regard as cultivating ferocity. Even "stubborn Turks, and Tartars never train'd / To offices of tender courtesy" (4.1.32–3), the Duke remarks hyperbolically, would pity Antonio. But the Duke's rhetorical strategy of calling on natural passion not only to authorize Shylock's change of heart but to proclaim his city's confident expectation of it backfires when Shylock invokes the equally natural status of his bodily "humor" to explain his obduracy:

> You'll ask me why I rather choose to have
> A weight of carrion flesh than to receive
> Three thousand ducats. I'll not answer that;
> But say it is my humor, is it answer'd?
> . . .
> Some men there are that love not a gaping pig;
> Some are mad if they behold a cat;
> And others, when the bagpipe sings i' th' nose,
> Cannot contain their urine: for affection,
> [Mistress] of passion, sways it to the mood
> Of what it likes or loathes.
>   (*Merchant of Venice*, 4.1.40–52)

The brilliance of this reply lies precisely in Shylock's determination to broaden the scope of the natural to allow not only for the predictability of appetite's objects –

those things most men actively like, such as roasted pig and bagpipe music, or those things they tolerate with indifference, such as the "harmless necessary cat" – but for its evident unpredictability as well. He thus reduces his animosity to Antonio – animosity grounded complexly in personal history, wounded self-interest, and religious hatred – to an intense humoral incompatibility. His strategy is less to remind the Duke of culture's strong effect on behavior – a Jew's allusion to the dietary prohibitions against roasted pig would accomplish that – than to ground behavioral difference in the undeniable variety and obduracy of the physical body's appetites and their resistance to reason. He uses bodily humors as an agreed-upon instance of what comes before cultural inscription, before religious and ethnic difference, before the history of Christians and Jews. In this respect, the humors become a perfect instance of what Butler sees as body materiality's uncontested status in Western discourse as a sign of the irreducible (Butler 1993: 28). Shylock initially bases his refusal on the inviolability of his contract with Antonio – "if you deny it, let the danger light / Upon your charter and your city's freedom" (4.1.38–9) – but he goes on to turn the Duke's own discourse of the natural body and its capacity for pity strongly against him. The effect is subversive: to point out how dominant elites use the discourses of natural knowledge for their own ends. Shylock, in support of his defiance of his Christian enemies and the Venetian state, can then invoke the doctrine of bodily humors himself as a determinative part of innermost bodily being that evades state manipulation and the subject's own articulation:

> As there is no firm reason to be rend'red
> Why he cannot abide a gaping pig,
> Why he, a harmless necessary cat;
> Why he, a woollen bagpipe, but of force
> Must yield to such inevitable shame
> As to offend, himself being offended;
> So can I give no reason, nor I will not,
> More than a lodg'd hate and a certain loathing
> I bear Antonio . . . (4.1.53–61)

Perhaps Shylock's most telling irony here is located in the multiple analogies among the several sorts of bodies affected by humoral theory's doctrine of reciprocity between the early modern subject and its social and physical environment (Sutton 1998: 39–410). Shylock ironically constructs the Duke's request to explain himself as one involving a mutual shame – the shame of the humoral body offended by an environment containing things that it cannot help but find disgusting (pig, cat, bagpipe, Antonio) and the shame of an environment (here Venice) offended against its will by the social consequences of that disgust. Venice is shamed, Shylock insinuates, by being reminded that someone so highly valued as Antonio could be found "naturally" disgusting by an abjected low Other such as Shylock. What Shylock defines as the humoral body's inability to be other than it is – what we might call the Nym defense – becomes emblematized in the incontinent body of the man who is caught unaware by bagpipe music and also, by extension, in his own body, physically unable (he says) to cease hating Antonio and to identify with him through pity. But the logic of his argument extends further to encompass the political body of the state that suddenly finds itself legally unable either to regulate or to expel *him*. In their embarrassment, all these humorally determined bodies point proleptically to the body of Antonio, its outer envelope of clothing opened to reveal the chest vulnerable to Shylock's penetrating knife.

Perhaps equally important, at least for my purposes here, is the image that Bassanio employs in his outraged reaction to Shylock's refusal: "This is no answer, thou unfeeling man, / To excuse the current of thy cruelty" (63–4). Though Bassanio claims to be unpersuaded by Shylock's humoral logic, his reference to Shylock's cruelty as a current is itself humorally based, a localization of "psychological function by organ or system of organs." Cruelty acts as a current in the blood because it is the effect of choler – the sharp humor produced by the gall bladder. Though choler is what Hamlet famously accuses himself of lacking ("I am pigeon-liver'd, and lack gall / To make oppression bitter," 2.2.577–8), Shylock, for whom oppression is bitter indeed, does not lack for gall however we might wish to interpret it – as vengeful cruelty or as something more sympathetic, such as embattled courage, determination, or even self-defense.

It is key to recognize that all parties in this play's dispute, whatever else their disagreements, recognize the natural basis of the humors and status of the passions they release as environmental determinants. By acknowledging Shylock's cruelty as a current in his blood, Bassanio in effect agrees to Shylock's brilliant naturalization of his hatred for Antonio as a form of material irreducibility. Antonio concedes much the same when he tells his friend despairingly that he may as well dispute with tide or wind as "seek to soften that – than which what's harder? – / His Jewish heart!" (79–80). The anti-Semitism of such remarks distracts us from their contemporary logic: that the drying and hardening effects of choler, the bodily fluid produced by cruel or grasping behavior and reciprocally productive of it, would toughen the flesh of any heart and render it less receptive to entreaty. The same logic underlies Lear's anguished cry about his cruel daughters: "Is there any cause in nature that makes these hard hearts?" (3.6.77–8) (Erickson 1997: 15). Even Portia concedes the naturalness of Shylock's cruelty by figuring its opposite emotion, mercy or compassion, as a liquid belonging equally to the body and its environment – not as raging wind or mounting tide but as "gentle rain from heaven" dropping "upon the place beneath" (185–6). Whether or not the place beneath – in this case Shylock's heart – would soften as a result of such gentle (and here gentile) moistening would thus depend, literally, on how hard it was in the first place; the change of heart will have to be a literal one. In this early modern conception of passions as belonging fully to the natural order, human relations take on an ecological character. This is, at least in part, why Portia assumes the too-hardness of Shylock's heart and turns to his written word instead, discovering release in a strict interpretation of the bond. She allows Shylock's excision of Antonio's flesh only on the condition that "in the cutting it, if thou dost shed / One drop of Christian blood, thy lands and goods / Are by the laws of Venice confiscate" (4.1.309–11). In this stipulation, both nature and culture work on Portia's behalf

– nature because Shylock cannot hope to cut flesh without spilling blood, culture because the legal distinction which she invokes between Christian and Jewish blood is located in a discursive register conveniently independent of the old fluid physiology. (The classical antecedents of humoralism recognized geography as a form of innate difference in bodies, but not religion.)

Shylock and Portia manipulate different aspects of humoral discourse – Shylock its theoretically undeniable basis in nature, Portia its actual susceptibility to hegemonic redefinition or even displacement through the symbolic complexity of blood. It is in Shylock's interest – and perhaps a conventional element of Shylock's character as stage Jew – to portray the humors as fixed and irreducible. More often in humoral discourse, however, the humors are represented as a part of the natural body that can and must be manipulated through various dietary regimes for the achievement of physical health and emotional stability (Schoenfeldt 1999: 25). But though in one sense all bodies were equally humoral since they were equally material – being composed of the same four humors – they were, as we have seen, humorally different. For a traditional society like that of early modern England, humoral difference guaranteed that humoralism would reflect hierarchical social values and could be used powerfully to naturalize them. Thus in *The Comedy of Errors* one part of service in the Syracusan servant Dromio is to subordinate his humor to that of his moody master Antipholus. "A trusty villain, sir," the wandering Antipholus tells a friendly merchant, "that very oft, / When I am dull with care and melancholy, / Lightens my humor with his merry jests" (1.2.19–21). Antipholus here invokes the neo-feudal assumption that Dromio's service to him proceeds from the whole man, from body and mind, from interior and exterior, from his humorally saturated and socially subordinated flesh. The duty of the "villain" – the rascally low-born man – would thus include the subjection of his bodily substances to those of his master, here by directing his bodily humors into the production of jests in order to leaven his master's heaviness of mood. It doesn't matter whether we understand the jests to derive naturally and spontaneously from Dromio's humorality or to be produced by Dromio for purposes of entertainment. The jests' social significance in this context lies in their ability to temper the humors of his master and, not coincidentally, to express Dromio's own subordination. It is not surprising, then, that the Syracusan Antipholus reacts with outrage when the Ephesian Dromio fails to answer his question about the money entrusted to him: "I am not in a sportive humor now: / Tell me and dally not" (1.2.58–9). Dromio, expecting to receive what significantly he calls a "dry" or choleric "basting" (2.2.63), becomes the object of his master's anger because it seems that he has neglected a fundamental discipline of service in hierarchical society – what we might call the humoral right of way and who gets to have it. This discipline, in his master's words, is "to know my aspect, / And fashion your demeanor to my looks" (2.2.32–3). The play suggests that Dromio's inability to do so is in part a function of low-born men's unruly humoral propensities (to make ill-timed jokes or otherwise not know their place) and in part a function of the play's eerie duplication of masters, the confusing replication of Antipholuses to whom the bewildered servant-twins must respond. The play, that is, steers neatly between the poles of humoral determination and environmental construction, finding a middle course in which the Dromios – being far less distinguishable from one another than the Antipholuses – both are and are not representatives of the humoral common man and the natural basis of servitude.

But in satiric or courtly contexts the ability to reflect the mood of another with a counterbalancing humor was seen as the sign of unmanly sycophancy, a trait unworthy of the independent man. Thus in Jonson's *Sejanus* the rise of the flatterer is described as entailing a willed subjection of mood; they are men who "laugh when their patron laughs; sweat, when he sweats; / Be hot, and cold with him; change every mood, / Habit and garb, as often as he varies" (1.33–5). The melancholy Prince Ferdinand in Webster's *Duchess of Malfi* rebukes his courtiers for daring to laugh without his permission: "Methinks you that are courtiers should be my touchwood, take fire when I give fire; that is, laugh when I laugh" (1.1.122–4). Ferdinand is a prime example of those aristocrats whom the English moral philosopher Thomas Wright complains of:

> Gentlemen by blood and Noblemen by birth, yet so appassionate in affections that their company was to most men intolerable . . . and men had need of an Astrolabe always to see in what height or elevation his affections are, lest by casting forth a spark of fire his gunpowdered mind of a sudden be inflamed. (Wright 1986: 92)

As the thermal imagery in this model of human relations suggests, the subjection produced by the requirements of social deference has a humoral component. The emotions associated with servitude would ostensibly be the cooler ones of timidity or even fearfulness, just as the emotions associated with mastery are hotter. The properly deferential servant – the servant who *feels* the subjection required of his place – would in theory have a natural, bodily basis for matching his mood to that of his master, as the Syracusan Dromio used to do, balancing his master's heaviness with his own lightness. As a matter of bodily *habitus*, the servant should learn to incorporate his social inferiority into the quality of his substances and to limit the character of his moods. By the same token, the independent gentleman would claim possession of his own humor rather than seek subordination to those of others. The willingness of the sycophantic courtier to relinquish this emotional autonomy for the sake of social advancement prompts Jonson's contemptuous description of emotional vacuity in *Sejanus* and, significantly, the unfirm flesh that goes with it, "the soft and glutinous bodies, that can stick, / Like snails, on painted walls" (1.8–9). Such softness, contemptible in the body of an independent gentleman, is a signifier of humoral unworth and grotesque abjection.

If, as Linda Charnes has argued, identity can be understood as a relatively fixed and objective feature of social (and/or textual) being and subjectivity as the moment-to-moment experience of that identity, then appropriate humoral subjectivity involves a temperate correspondence between one's humoral interior and the immediate environment, so to speak, of one's exterior social identity (Charnes 1993: 75). Humoral inflection in the discourse of subjectivity is, as we have seen, a matter of qualities – of hot and cold, wet and dry. In *Twelfth Night*, for example, Fabian rebukes Sir Andrew

Aguecheek for lacking the warmth proper both to his elite station as a knight and to the role of ardent suitor of Olivia. The latter's show of favor to Cesario, Fabian tells Sir Andrew disingenuously when the knight threatens to quit the household and give up his suit, was intended "to put fire into your heart, and brimstone in your liver. You should then have accosted her, and with some excellent jests, fire-new from the mint, you should have bang'd the youth into dumbness" (3.2.20–3). By wasting the opportunity, "you are now sail'd into the north of my lady's opinion, where you will hang like an icicle on a Dutchman's beard" (27–8; Paster 1997: 122). From a humoral point of view it is easy to see that, by contrast with the thermally deficient Andrew, the steward Malvolio is almost literally too full of himself, too full of radical heat and moisture and the prepossessing behaviors associated with them. It outrages Sir Toby and other members of the household that Malvolio should be found "yonder i' the sun practicing behavior to his own shadow" (2.5.16–17), mirroring himself to himself in a parodic imitation of gentlemen's conduct manuals. At this moment we recognize in Malvolio a form of humoral vanity and self-satisfaction that leads him to imagine Olivia's attraction to him: "I have heard herself come thus near, that should she fancy, it should be one of my complexion" (24–6). Released here by his fantastic aspirations of marriage from the affective subjection required of social subordinates, Malvolio imagines himself as future determiner of affect in his little world, the weather-maker of his micro-climate. He sees himself, newly ennobled and having sexually pacified Olivia with daytime dalliance that has left her sleeping on a daybed, as a man dictating mood, time, and place to others: "And then to have the humor of state; and after a demure travel of regard – telling them I know my place as I would they should do theirs – to ask for my cousin Toby . . . I extend my hand to him thus, quenching my familiar smile with an austere regard of control" (2.5.52–5, 65–6). In that imaginary quenching of the smile – the disciplinary coolness which dampens what Malvolio insinuates either as his own (hypothetical) tendency to brotherly warmth or the inappropriate warmth of boisterous Sir Toby – lies the humoral triumphalism of the new man on top.

    What Malvolio finds in the forged letter – the letter that Fabian hopes will win Malvolio "liver and all" (95) – are not only the specific requests for clothing and behaviors, but an overall injunction to rise up humorally, to embolden his bodily substance: "Thy Fates open their hands, let thy blood and spirits embrace them, and to inure thyself to what thou art like to be, cast thy humble slough and appear fresh" (2.5.146–9). The exhortation is to a new mode of self-presentation in Malvolio that, while it eventuates in bold smiles and yellow stockings, begins as an elevation and expansion of bodily stuff. In its focus upon the expressive production of bodily liquids, the letter's advice strongly resembles the encouragement that Sir Toby delivers to Sir Andrew: "My very walk should be a jig. I would not so much as make water but in sink-a-pace" (1.3.129–31). Even more interesting, perhaps, it resembles that moment of erotic encounter in *A Midsummer Night's Dream* when Titania, newly enthralled with Bottom, promises to etherealize him by means of a program of delicate sensual allurements produced by fairy attendants and designed to "purge thy mortal grossness so / That thou shalt like an aery spirit go" (3.1.160–1). As I have argued elsewhere, the reformation through purge that Titania promises is both spiritual and physical in its aims and methods since, along with the refinements in his environment, it involves a distinctly laxative diet of "apricocks and dewberries, / . . . purple grapes, green figs, and mulberries" (3.1.166–7). We are asked to imagine (if not necessarily to believe) that such a diet would have the effect of lightening his bodily substance and thus of refining the words and behaviors coming from it (Paster 1993: 130–1). The encouragement in all these cases presupposes the metonymic significance of fluids in the humoral body – blood and spirits standing here for bold behaviors, urination (as a still possible mode of male public display) standing in for ejaculation. Like Sir Andrew, Malvolio is being invited not just to change his external demeanor – his "humble slough" of steward's clothing and deferential manner – but in effect to alter his internal substance, or at least to perform the prepossessing behaviors that would signal (or, in the reciprocity of humoral logic, even produce) such an alteration. The advice, Maria tells Toby later, is specifically designed to offend Olivia in terms of humoral antipathy not unlike those Shylock has offered the Duke of Venice – presenting her with a color she abhors, a fashion she detests, and with a feigned mirth unsuitable for her mood as Maria reads it: "he will smile upon her, which will now be so unsuitable to her disposition, being addicted to a melancholy as she is" (200–2). And indeed, Olivia does exclaim right away to Malvolio about the inappropriateness of his affective display: "Smil'st thou? I sent for thee upon a sad occasion" (3.4.18–19). Like Dromio, Malvolio has offended against the humoral proprieties proper to their relation as mistress and servant, even if the mistress herself is criticized as being "addicted to a melancholy" (2.5.202) – that is, to the by-products, both psychological and physiological, of her own complexion.

The evident social fluidity, especially the fluidity of gender, that has so preoccupied recent criticism of *Twelfth Night* is – again as I have argued elsewhere – everywhere contained in the play by a more conservative biological discourse which prescribes the blood and heat – hence the behavior – humorally proper to men and women, to the elite and their social inferiors (Paster 1998: 434–5). Humoral impropriety in the case of the class-jumping Malvolio turns less upon gender than upon status, especially since his attentions are fixed on a woman who herself threatens the "natural" boundaries of gender by presuming to control male access to her person and fortune, to choose the object of her affections for herself, and to act vigorously in pursuit of those affections (Howard 1988: 432–3). That both lady and steward threaten social norms in similar ways is clear in the exposure to which they are jointly subject in the famous dirty joke that emerges from Malvolio's attempts to decipher her handwriting: "By my life, this is my lady's hand. These be her very c's, her u's, and her t's, and thus makes she her great P's" (3.1.86–8). As critics have noted, Malvolio's spelling out of "c-u-t" – an Elizabethan slang word for vagina – enacts the misogynist reduction of all women to their genitalia, the metonymical displacement of the writing hand as the emblem of individuality by the vagina as emblem of female lowliness and unworth (Goldberg 1986). That reduction is itself aggravated in the satiric identification of Olivia, who wants to be walled off and self-enclosed in her household, with great "pees." It is an identification of the female body with incontinence and physical uncontrol. For Malvolio to know Olivia's great pees, more-over, is to associate him with the lowly household task of waste removal, a job proper only to servants far below him in rank (Paster 1993: 32–4). This image of excretion, coming so early in a scene where Malvolio thinks he is being enjoined to an elevation of bodily matter and social *habitus* thanks to the fates' recognition of his worthy blood and spirits, functions as a leveling reminder of the social limits of humoral transfor-mation. For the behaviors that Maria's forged letter asks Malvolio to perform on command – the expenditure of spirit in incessant smiling, the cross-gartering which numbs and swells his legs – represent an extreme of humoral manipulation. "Sad, lady?" Malvolio exclaims when he first appears to Olivia in costume, "I could be sad. This does make some obstruction in the blood, this cross-gartering . . . Not black in my mind, though yellow in my legs" (3.4.20–1, 26–7). In humoral terms, Malvolio is punished physically for the excessive warmth of his aspirant blood and spirits by the imposition of "obstruction in the blood" – a mechanical obstruction that would slow and cool his blood. In this play, the steward "sick of self-love" who "tastes with a distemper'd appetite" (1.5.90–1) is not allowed to aspire romantically to the lady he serves. And he is also not allowed to enjoy the warmth and increase of blood and spirits such aspirations evidently produce; indeed he is humiliated because of them. The madness of which he is accused – "midsummer madness" (3.4.56) or the mad-ness produced by the drying of the brain and spirits in hot weather – ironically acknowledges the great expenditure, again both physiological and psychological, that Malvolio's performance has required. In bodily terms, Malvolio has been trapped into committing a particularly egregious form of humoral insubordination – the failure to suit one's own humor and behaviors to those of one's social superiors – and is punished, spectacularly, with the symbolic social nullification and physical isolation reserved for those possessed by alien spirits. Even Sir Toby's allusion to Malvolio as being inhabited by scriptural devils – "if all the devils in hell be drawn in little, and Legion himself possess'd him" (3.4.85–6) – fosters the humoral context of Malvolio's entrapment: "Legion" was the name of an "unclean spirit" (Mark 5: 8–9); here it is the domestic equivalent of the socially "unclean" spirit that the household revelers accuse Malvolio of becoming.

But the bodies I would nominate as most conspicuously subject to humoral manip-ulation in all of Shakespearean comedy belong to Christopher Sly and Katherine Minola, protagonists respectively in the frame and main plots of *The Taming of the Shrew*. It is no accident, as this essay has already implied, that the bodies of the low-born man and the choleric but well-born woman should be targeted for humoral repro-gramming. The achievement of good temper involved a manipulation of diet and other environmental factors theoretically available to all. (Like the early moderns, I am defining environment broadly here to include all six of the Galenic non-naturals including diet, fullness and emptiness, sleep and waking, air, rest and exercise, and the passions.) But in practice (as we have seen) humoral thinking and humoral tex-tualization tend to reproduce – and thus to biologize – prevailing narratives of social difference.[1] In vernacular medical texts, all the bodily fluids of humoralism, but espe-cially blood, are routinely classified in ethically and socially weighted language –

a discourse of purity, clarity, and differential worth. In *The Taming of the Shrew* the sodden, lethargic tinker and the unruly choleric woman are represented humorally as opposites but socially as homologous in terms of their capacity for social disruption and unproductiveness. The play's actions present them both as subjects of behavioral experimentation through opposite means – pleasure therapy for Sly, aversion therapy for Kate. Together the two experiments in behavioral manipulation serve to question how far the mind's inclination really does follow the body's temperature, for they presume the possibility – though not the extent – of subjective transformation through environmental means.

The Induction makes Sly a test-case for human potentiality and productivity by constructing what I see as a set of humorally telling contrasts – with Sly in the middle between the lord's trained hunting dogs at one end of a localized scale of nature and the lord himself at the other. Such a contrast is implicitly a reminder that in this cosmology animals, too, were humoral creatures, their differences in flesh, blood, behavior, and temperament humorally determined, and hierarchically ranked.[2] Though the lord is not represented as a humoral subject himself (the question of his own temperament being mostly occluded), his trick upon Sly does seem to be the result of lordly whim or caprice – humor in that sense of the term. And Sly's treatment is cast throughout as humoral therapy, both fictional (since Sly is not in fact a distracted lord) and real (since the means resemble actual practice on the insane). The lord comes upon Sly just after he and his huntsman have been discussing the care of his hounds and debating their merits. The dogs' traits identified as socially useful, pleasurable, and significant to the lord – their breeding; their individuality of voice and temperament; their responsiveness to training, management, and care; their economic value – are precisely at issue in Sly. Indeed, his social progress in the two scenes is like an ascent of the scale of nature, since at first he seems barely to qualify as animate, to be more a feature of the landscape than of the human world: "What's here? One dead, or drunk? See, doth he breathe?" (Induction, 1.30–1). Once established as alive, he looks to the lord like the wrong kind of human animal: "O monstrous beast, how like a swine he lies" (34). Since, in early modern cosmology, to know a thing is to know what it resembles, the resemblance of man to pig is more disturbing to the conscious man at the top of the social order than to the barely conscious one at the bottom (Stallybrass and White 1986: 44–59). From this point of view, the lord's stated goal of seeing if he can make Sly "forget himself" (41) is paradoxical, since it asks Sly to forget the self-forgetting already epitomized in his swinish drunkenness. The higher form of self-forgetting that is supposed to occur by having him awaken suddenly as lord of an aristocratic household is a classic exercise in Galenic stimulation, designed to raise the slothful man's radical heat and moisture and clear the vapors of confusion from his sodden brain (here varied from the norm in that one form of confusion is being supplanted by another). The lord's tools are a significant elaboration of Titania's, ranging from the sensual enhancements of distilled waters, sweet smells, and music, to the social enhancements of costly apparel, servants, a "lady wife," and the comic entertainment provided by the visiting players. Together these features constitute an almost complete transformation of the six non-naturals and thus, within the terms of psychological materialism – of mind following the body's temperature – they signify analogously as the means of subjective overhaul. We can see, too, how the page Bartholomew's masquerade as Sly's wife is intended to function as a form of humoral subordination, to give to Sly what Malvolio imagined for himself as "the humor of state" in Olivia's household. "Such duty to the drunkard let him do," the lord instructs, "With soft low tongue and lowly courtesy, / And say, 'What is't your honor will command, / Wherein your lady, and your humble wife, / May show her duty and make known her love?'" (Induction, 114–17). In effect, the lord's trick mimics the terms of Malvolio's gulling, offering up a dream of social elevation against the "humor" of lowness, but in this case offering it to an unready object, one in whom the humoral ground is unprepared, one not already enamored of his own complexion. Returning to consciousness, Sly holds fast to the particularities of his identity – his name and social origins, his habits of drink and clothing, his series of lowly occupations. The lord pretends to find illness in this ordinary health, to find a disturbing continuity in Sly's residual lowness of nature: "Heaven cease this idle humor in your honor! / O that a mighty man of such descent, / Of such possession, and so high esteem, / Should be infused with so foul a spirit" (Induction, 2.13–16). The sensual inducements which Sly is then offered – the soft bed, the invitation to hunt, the visual and physiological stimulation of erotic scenes from Ovid – are intended literally to warm him into activity from the lethargy associated with lowness and drink. That metatheatrical reminder of the gender ideology of the Elizabethan playhouses – the page's deferral "for a night or two" (Induction, 2.119) of Sly's sexual demands on him – also has a plausible medical explanation, given that ejaculation was understood as a sometimes dangerous expenditure of spirit. As a well-known aphorism from Avicenna put it, the loss of seed "harmeth a man more, then if hee should bleed forty times as much" (quoted in Vaughan 1612: 70). Even the comedy which the visiting players provide for Sly's entertainment – the comedy which becomes the main plot of Shakespeare's play – is presented to him in humoral terms:

> your doctors hold it very meet,
> Seeing too much sadness hath congeal'd your blood,
> And melancholy is the nurse of frenzy.
> Therefore they thought it good you hear a play,
> And frame your mind to mirth and merriment,
> Which bars a thousand harms and lengthens life.
> (Induction, 2.131–6)

The underlying medical thought here is analogous both to Maria's exhortation of Malvolio's blood and spirits and to Titania's promise of Bottom's fleshly rarefication through purging. The evidence of transformation in Sly's case, however, is even more equivocal than in the others'. While the tinker comes to accept that he is a lord on the basis of his new surroundings – "I smell sweet savors, and I feel soft things" (Induction, 2.71) – he asks at the same time for a "pot o' th' smallest ale" (75), the original signifier of his swinish lowness and the means of his potential return to oblivion. Tellingly, the lord's arousal of Sly's blood and spirits is more clearly successful in phallic terms – the terms of nature, perhaps – than in social ones, since the tinker grants his lady wife's demur only with reluctance: "it stands so that I may hardly tarry so long. But I would be loath to fall into my dreams again. I will therefore tarry in despite of the flesh and the blood" (125–8). The comedy which he agrees to watch is thus a kind of erotic surrogate, a therapy of gratification through deferral whose ultimate impact on Sly's transformation is left unresolved. Whatever threat to the meaning of hierarchy might be embodied in Sly's transformation, it is fragmentary and imperfect – in part because we know that Sly is the unconscious victim of lordly caprice, more a threat to himself than to others in his immediate world, in part because the transformation is so equivocal and its final outcome left so unresolved by extant texts of the play. We do not find out in the extant Shakespearean text of this play what humoral effect seeing the inner play of Kate and Petruchio has had on Sly.

While the Induction leaves no doubt that any man would prefer to be a lord not a tinker, its antithetical presentations of lordliness in Sly and the lord himself only beg the question of what might constitute a true humoral reformation of this lowly subject once the unfolding of that reformation is displaced by the main play. Certainly, however, Shakespeare's strategic placement of Sly's gulling between the lord's discussion of his hunting dogs and Baptista Minola's introduction of Kate focuses attention on the play's underlying interest in social regulation of the natural and the appropriateness of the means for doing so. What complicates this question in the relation between Kate and Petruchio is that – unlike Sly and the lord – both protagonists of this plot are constructed as humoral subjects prone to the socially outrageous behaviors produced by chronic humoral imbalance. Both are given to violence throughout the play, both take delight in "crossing" others. The play does seem to offer an overall endorsement of Kate's taming and assigns Petruchio the task of undertaking it as the crux of his own masculinization. As Lyndal Roper has argued, "The real man was household head, a little patriarch ruling over wife, children, servants, journeymen, and apprentices . . . What gave access to the world of brothers was one's mastery of a woman which guaranteed one's sexual status" (Roper 1994: 46). The language of the play flirts with the possibility of defining Katherine as untamed nature – "intolerable curst / And shrowd and froward" (1.2.89–90) – and Petruchio as the self-motivated bearer of culture: "Tell me her father's name, and 'tis enough; / For I will board her, though she chide as loud / As thunder when the clouds in autumn crack" (1.2.94–6). Even the play's strong emphasis on Petruchio's economic motivation in the wooing serves to enhance the rationality of his motives and his control over appetite (however inappropriate such mercenary decisions seem in the context of romantic comedy). But his choleric nature is established independent of Kate's introduction onstage, his servant Grumio insisting not on his rational self-control but rather on his excessive combativeness and imperviousness to persuasion. When Hortensio counsels Petruchio to think twice about courting Katherine, Grumio declares,

> I pray you, sir, let him go while the humor lasts, A' my word, and she knew him as well as I do, she would think scolding would do little good upon him. She may perhaps call

him half a score knaves or so. Why, that's nothing; and he begin once, he'll rail in his rope-tricks. (1.2.107–12)

To see his courting Kate as a whim – while the humor lasts – is to make it equivalent to the lord's reforming Sly as a moment's caprice. But the play obscures the balance between humoral determinism and rational self-control in its representation of Petruchio by underscoring the strategic calculation and the deliberateness behind even his most outrageous behaviors, especially the sexual self-discipline signified by deferral of his marriage's consummation.

Typically, encouraging strategic calculation in the planning of long-range goals and discouraging impulsiveness are the goals of Renaissance conduct books, which represent self-management in elite men and women as the sign of clear thought and humors in balance. Elsewhere in Shakespeare, for example, we see the historical success of the strategic subject in the overdetermined contrast between the impulsive, choleric, and socially archaic Hotspur and that princely epitome of rational calculation, his rival Hal (Paster 1997: 121). Here, it is not that Petruchio's combination of calculation and choleric impulsiveness balances itself out into good temper but that, in the project of taming the choleric woman, Petruchio finds a way to make his own choler socially productive by directing it against an even less socialized, even more disruptive object than himself. In this respect *The Taming of the Shrew* is a clear demonstration of the asymmetries of humorality and gender ideology working in tandem, because only the choleric man could be tasked with taming the choleric woman, never the reverse. The play thus becomes a comic, perhaps even parodic instance of the social concern voiced in the period in pedagogic and conduct manuals about how best to correlate the individual's natural temperament with society's needs for diverse talents. In a treatise translated in English in 1594 as *The Examination of Mens Wits*, the Spanish physician Juan Huarte argued that "well ordered common wealths, ought to have men of great wisedome and knowledge, who might in their tender age, discouer ech ones wit and naturall sharpnesse, to the end they might be set to learne that art which was agreeable, and not leave it to their owne election" (Huarte 1959: 23).

Taming Kate offers Petruchio the opportunity to alter himself materially in two ways: the social alteration derived from marriage to a wealthy heiress and the physical alteration of expending choler against a socially sanctioned target. I make this argument not in order to excuse what I regard as Petruchio's physical and psychological abuse of Kate, but to note the ideological underpinnings of the play's humoral logic in which both protagonists undergo humoral reformation, but only the woman's reformation is called a taming. Most of the deprivations which Petruchio makes Kate undergo he also experiences himself, as when he explains the rationale of throwing out meat uneaten because, he says, it was overcooked:

> I tell, Kate, 'twas burnt and dried away.
> And I expressly am forbid to touch it;
> For it engendreth choler, planteth anger,
> And better 'twere that both of us should fast,

> Since of ourselves, ourselves are choleric,
> Than feed it with such overroasted flesh.
> And for this night we'll fast for company. (4.1.170–7)

His reference to the choleric humor they share is, of course, only a mock effort at consolation, since his emphatic, if ironic, pronouncement about what they are going to do – fast together companionably – underscores the obvious difference between voluntary and involuntary acceptance of a humoral regime. Similarly, Petruchio's attempts at rational persuasion of her are only mock ones, brute exercises in physical and psychological intimidation, as when he is reported to deliver a "sermon of continency" in her chamber in a manner far from contained: "And rails, and swears, and rates, that she, poor soul, / Knows not which way to stand, to look, to speak, / And sits as one new risen from a dream" (4.1.184–6). In the notorious analogy between taming a wife and a falcon, Petruchio presents his taming as unrelenting, patient labor in the manipulation of Kate's environment: he must fling the bedcovers around the room and create disorder, he must stay awake to keep her from sleeping, he must "rail and brawl" to unsettle her relation to her world and make her realize her powerlessness. Petruchio's question, only mock-rhetorical – "He that knows better how to tame a shrew, / Now let him speak; 'tis charity to shew" (4.1.210–11) – acknowledges the possible obnoxiousness of his methods and the sadistic thrust of the play's action to alter the inclinations of her soul by altering – here by lowering – the temperature of her body.

In its apparent ratification of Petruchio's boorishness and use of physical force, the play seems to enact a virulent misogynistic mandate that social historians and literary critics have seen as reflecting widespread gender disorder in late sixteenth-century England (Underdown 1985: 116–19). The play invites us to take much more pleasure in Petruchio's taming of Kate's humor than in the self-taming of his own and to accept that his dominion over her is socially more significant than any increase in his own self-dominion. But a more interesting way to take the play's pleasure in watching Petruchio is in terms of the anti-conduct manuals that, as Barbara Correll has explained, offered mock-praise for boorish behaviors as a way of re-instilling the self-regulatory demands of the civilizing process on masculine subject-formation (Correll 1996: 25–7). In these terms, the violent behaviors manifest in both husband and wife, but especially in Petruchio, become humoral manifestations of the unruly bodiliness they both must contain in order to earn their places at the communal feast. Even so, Petruchio's self-taming can only be partial – his boorishness incompletely refined – because he still needs a store of choler, what Bassanio called a "current of cruelty," in order to maintain dominion over his wife. Within their own household, Petruchio's taming of Kate thus becomes a distinctive example of the privilege of humoral autonomy that must be claimed, as we have seen, in order for princes to have sway over courtiers, masters over servants, and here – exaggerated and extended by the programmatic violence of its means – by husbands over wives. This is why, from Petruchio's point of view, Kate cannot be returned to the paternal household that had failed to contain her humorally until she subordinates her humor to his and thus ratifies gender norms. He complains: "Look what I speak, or do, or think to do" – here he covers the full range of his potential behaviors – "You are still crossing it" (4.3.192–3). Petruchio is willing to make the return journey only when she accepts his definitions of the phenomenal world as her own, when she agrees in effect to perceive the world through the spectacles of his humor even when that humor is willfully changeable. In the famous sun and moon scene, this involves not only relinquishing her independence of judgment but denying the evidence of her senses as well: "What you will have it nam'd" – she says of the sun standing metonymically here for all of reality – "even that is, / And so it shall be so for Katherine" (4.5.21–2).[3]

This moment is a famously dismaying one for feminist scholarship and, in terms of humoral subordination too, Kate's capitulation would seem to be complete. In order to underscore that dismay, but also by way of conclusion, I would like to emphasize the importance of this exchange to an understanding of humoralism's overall significance in Shakespearean comedy. For, in its broadest application, the classical doctrine of the four humors is not a theory of personality at all but a discourse of nature and the human body's place within it. It is evidence of early modern phenomenology if we understand phenomenology – bodily self-experience – as a form of lived cosmology. In a universe constructed through what John Sutton has nicely called "a nested system of spirits in the cosmos, the environment, the human body, and in inanimate objects" (Sutton 1998: 36), the humors bring the natural world almost directly into the body and extend the body out to the natural world. The humors and the passions they release operate upon the body very much as strong movements of wind or water operate upon the natural world: they are the body's internal climate of mood and temper, inward motions carried to the sentient flesh by the animal spirits.

As we have seen in other early modern characters seeking mastery over others, Petruchio requires Kate to symbolize her wifely submission through humoral subordination to his internal climate. His fantasy of control, built on fear and intimidation, resembles that of Webster's Prince Ferdinand but is, perhaps, even more grandiose. At this moment, requiring her to accept his definition of time, place, and mood as equivalent to accepting a wholesale mediation of reality, Petruchio puts himself in the place of nature for Kate. As the new principle of signification for a body that – even if female – is never simply the material unsignified, it is he who would be the means of bringing her body into the world, the world into her body. His apparently successful programmatic alteration of her humorality expands from being a crude caricature of customary socialization practices to being a fantasy of ownership of her bodily substance from the inside out. The goal is thus not to reform her humorality but to erase it, to take away her independent ability to appraise and interact in characteristic fashion with her environment. Kate becomes, at least for the moment, a woman neither in nor out of her humor, but a woman without right to a humor at all. It is as if Petruchio has solved the problem Othello describes as the "curse of marriage! / That we can call these delicate creatures ours, / And not their appetites" (3.3.268–70).

We may not believe Kate's private capitulation here – or later in her famous public pledge to place her hand beneath her husband's foot – to be anything other than strategic, external compliance only for the sake of self-preservation. But in a cosmology governed by psychological materialism, where the psychological is not yet divorced from the physiological, Kate's soul is thus proved to have followed her body's temperature whether the compliance is external or internal. In the reciprocities of humoralism, external compliance means internal alteration and internal alteration manifests itself in behavior. For Petruchio and Shakespeare's audience, watching the tamed Kate is humoral comedy, a ratification of male dominance – no matter how ironic we understand that ratification to be, given the emergence of Bianca as Padua's latest shrew. For Kate herself – having acquired a forbidding, new kind of mediation in bodily self-experience, having lost the humoral right of way – experience of the world has lost definition and savor, and the result is more than tragicomic.

NOTES

1 Here is where I disagree most emphatically with the central thesis of Michael Schoenfeldt's *Bodies and Selves*, which stresses "the empowerment that Galenic physiology and ethics bestowed on the individual" (Schoenfeldt 1999: 11). The implication of such phrasing – that all individuals are equal under the laws of Renaissance Galenism – simply ignores the realities of social and gender hierarchy everywhere in the period.

2 The naturalist Edward Topsell noted, for example, that "nature hath framed no simpathie or concord betwixte the noble and coragious spirite of a horsse, and the beastlie sluggish condition of a swine" (Topsell 1607: 303).

3 As Fran Dolan points out, the relations of sun and moon are conventionally emblematic of the relation of husband and wife (Dolan 1996: 30).

REFERENCES AND FURTHER READING

Bamborough, J. B. (1952). *The Little World of Man*. London: Longmans, Green.

Butler, J. (1993). *Bodies That Matter: On the Discursive Limits of Sex*. London: Routledge.

Charnes, L. (1993). *Notorious Identity: Materializing the Subject in Shakespeare*. Cambridge, MA: Harvard University Press.

Congreve, W. (1964). An Essay Concerning Comedy. In J. C. Hodges (ed.) *William Congreve: Letters and Documents*. New York: Harcourt, Brace, and World.

Correll, B. A. (1996). *The End of Conduct: Grobianus and the Renaissance Text of the Subject*. Ithaca, NY: Cornell University Press.

Dekker, T. (1968). The Gull's Hornbook. In E. D. Pendry (ed.) *Thomas Dekker*. Cambridge, MA: Harvard University Press, 69–109.

Dolan, F. E. (ed.) (1996). *The Taming of the Shrew: Texts and Contexts*. Boston, MA: Bedford Books.

Elam, K. (1991). The Fertile Eunuch: Early Modern Intercourse, and the Fruits of Castration. *Shakespeare Quarterly*, 47, 1–36.

Erickson, R. A. (1997). *The Language of the Heart, 1600–1750*. Philadelphia: University of Pennsylvania Press.

Filipczak, Z. Z. (1997). *Hot Dry Men, Cold Wet Women: The Theory of Humors In Western European Art 1575–1700*. New York: American Federation of Arts.

Floyd-Wilson, M. (2002). *English Ethnicity and Race in Early Modern Drama*. Cambridge: Cambridge University Press.

Goldberg, J. (1986). Textual Properties. *Shakespeare Quarterly*, 37, 213–17.

Hadfield, G. (1992). Descartes' Physiology and Its Relation to Its Psychology. In J. Cottingham (ed.) *The Cambridge Companion to Descartes*. Cambridge: Cambridge University Press, 333–70.

Howard, J. E. (1988). Crossdressing, the Theater, and Gender Struggle in Early Modern England. *Shakespeare Quarterly*, 39, 418–40.

Huarte, J. (1959) [1594]. *The Examination of Mens Wits*, trans. R. Carew, ed. C. Rogers. Gainesville, FL: Scholars' Facsimiles and Reprints.

Jonson, B. (1981). *Sejanus*. In G. A. Wilkes (ed.) *The Complete Works of Ben Jonson*. Oxford: Clarendon Press, 2.

Neely, C. T. (1991). Recent Work in Renaissance Studies: Did Madness Have a Renaissance? *Renaissance Quarterly*, 44, 776–91.

Park, K. (1988). The Organic Soul. In C. B. Schmitt et al. (eds.) *The Cambridge History of Renaissance Philosophy*. Cambridge: Cambridge University Press, 464–84.

Paster, G. K. (1993). *The Body Embarrassed: Drama and the Disciplines of Shame in Early Modern England*. Ithaca, NY: Cornell University Press.

——(1997). Nervous Tension: Networks of Blood and Spirit in the Early Modern Body. In D. Hillman and C. Mazzio (eds.) *The Body in Parts: Fantasies of Corporeality in Early Modern Europe*. New York: Routledge, 107–25.

——(1998). The Unbearable Coldness of Female Being: Women's Imperfection and the Humoral Economy. *English Literary Renaissance*, 28, 416–40.

Roper, L. (1994). *Oedipus and the Devil: Witchcraft, Sexuality, and Religion in Early Modern Europe*. London: Routledge.

Schoenfeldt, M. C. (1999). *Bodies and Selves in Early Modern England: Physiology and Inwardness in Spenser, Shakespeare, Herbert, and Milton*. Cambridge: Cambridge University Press.

Selden, J. (1614). *Titles of Honor*. London: William Stansby for John Helme.

Shakespeare, W. (1997). *The Riverside Shakespeare*, ed. G. B. Evans. Boston, MA: Houghton Mifflin.

Siraisi, N. G. (1990). *Medieval and Early Renaissance Medicine: An Introduction to Knowledge and Practice*. Chicago, IL: University of Chicago Press.

Stallybrass, P. and White, A. (1986). *The Politics and Poetics of Transgression*. Ithaca, NY: Cornell University Press.

Sutton, J. (1998). *Philosophy and Memory Traces: Descartes to Connectionism*. Cambridge: Cambridge University Press.

Taylor, C. (1989). *Sources of the Self: The Making of the Modern Identity*. Cambridge, MA: Harvard University Press.

Temkin, O. (1973). *Galenism: Rise and Decline of a Medical Philosophy*. Ithaca, NY: Cornell University Press.

Topsell, E. (1607). *The Historie of Foure-Footed Beastes*. London: William Jaggard.

Underdown, D. E. (1985). The Taming of the Scold: The Enforcement of Patriarchal Authority in Early Modern England. In A. Fletcher and J. Stevenson (eds.) *Order and Disorder in Early Modern England*. Cambridge: Cambridge University Press, 116–36.

Vaughan, W. (1612). *Approved Directions for Health, Both Natural and Artificiall*, 4th edn. London: T. S. for Robert Jackson.

Webster, J. (1997). *The Duchess of Malfi*, ed. J. R. Brown. Manchester: Manchester University Press.

Wright, T. (1986) [1601]. *The Passions of the Mind in General*, ed. W. W. Newbold. New York: Garland.

4

Class X: Shakespeare, Class, and the Comedies

Peter Holbrook

Scan critical bibliographies on English Renaissance drama and you will be awash with titles featuring gender, race, sexuality, and other relations of subordination. "Class" barely appears. To quote Celia in *As You Like It*: it is "most wonderful-wonderful . . . and after that out of all whooping" (3.2.176–7) that in a field as fixated, currently, on social questions as early modern drama studies there is no big book on *Class in Renaissance Drama*. Or perhaps it isn't so surprising. Sharon O'Dair's *Class, Critics, and Shakespeare* identifies a systematic silence about class in academic literary criticism. The silence reproduces the notorious unmentionability of class in America – which is, we know, "classless," and where most Shakespeare criticism finds a home. Might not race and gender dominate recent critical discourse because American capitalism in the Age of Diversity has less difficulty addressing inequities based on such categories than it does the reproduction of economic inequality? While gender–racial equality is celebrated in the democracies, proposing that class inequality be abolished is extremist, unrealistic, etc. The amount of academic talk about race–gender – "there are now more than a hundred books on women or gender in early modern England, and well over a thousand articles" (Wiesner-Hanks 2000: 4) – can look like a way of *not* mentioning economic inequality.

Perhaps another reason for criticism's lack of interest in class is its sheer pervasiveness in the plays – all those lords, ladies, dukes, kings, servants, waiting-women, and so on: is it worth commenting on something so obtrusively there? When in *Love's Labour's Lost* Holofernes observes that "the gentles are at their game" (4.2.151) we don't perhaps register the class marker, so bent are we on unearthing the play's "deep" thematic concerns. But if critics find class boringly obvious, this wasn't true of Shakespeare and his peers. It was a prime subject of their restlessly explorative drama – continually talked or joked about, always noticed. The fascination with class is as true of Shakespeare's apparently escapist comedies as of his other, more "serious" plays.

Take *A Midsummer Night's Dream*, one of Shakespeare's most fantastic comedies and one regularly addressing class. The first of the checks to "true love" Lysander catalogs involves class: lovers are often "different in blood" – "too high to be enthralled to low" (1.1.135–6). Property and status (as so often in these plays focused on marriage) is taken for granted: Lysander's first line of defense of his love for Hermia is to insist he is "as well derived" as his rival (1.1.99). Even the fairy world has its orders: Puck, "lurk[ing] . . . in a gossip's bowl" (2.1.47), is closer to the world of "rude mechanicals" (3.2.9) than Oberon or Titania. Yet he is a strange social amalgam – "gentle" at 4.1.61. The play assumes a weaver becoming the consort of a Fairy Queen is ridiculous, but at other times suggests this is too literal a perspective; after all, "Things base and vile, holding no quantity, / Love can transpose to form and dignity" (1.1.232–3). The love theme is closely bound up with the class interest: Bottom-in-love is a "gentle mortal," "gentleman," "my gentle joy" (3.1.121, 146; 4.1.4) – a fit companion for Titania, "a spirit of no common rate" (3.1.136) – and the humor of the Bottom–Titania scenes revolves around the disparity between high and low. Yet it isn't always clear what we are laughing at – the "Hard-handed men that work in Athens" (5.1.72)? If so the play sets us up for a fall, because it's clear – if only from Theseus' words about nothing being "amiss / When simpleness and duty tender it" (5.1.82–3) – that the prole-bashing the nobles engage in at its end is distasteful. (Weirdly, neither Theseus, nor Hippolyta – both sensitive to the plight of "wretchedness o'ercharged, / And duty in his service perishing" (5.1.85–7) – follow their courteous instincts, and are as rude as Demetrius, who calls the plebeians "asses" (5.1.153): Hippolyta says the play is "the silliest stuff" she's ever heard and Theseus calls Snug's Lion a "goose" (5.1.207, 225).) None of this snobbery, however, may matter. Bottom, after all, can "discourse wonders" (4.2.25) and the elite perspective on these simple men seems in some ways narrow – an effect of the play's juxtaposition of social spheres. The famous many-sidedness of Shakespeare's drama includes above all this class aspect: we can never see the action simply in noble terms, because Puck and others re-cast it for us – at the end of 3.3 we see the well-born lovers in a less illustrious, more proverbial light: "Jack shall have Jill, / Naught shall go ill, / the man shall have his mare again, and all shall be well." The class dynamics of *A Midsummer Night's Dream* are tortuously complicated. The Epilogue addresses the audience as "gentles." Does that mean the play appeals to snobbery? Possibly, but it also invokes, through the mechanicals and Bottom especially, different standards of evaluation from those of an aristocratic elite. If what I say here about *A Midsummer Night's Dream* seems tentative, that is because I believe (and hope to show in this essay) that Shakespeare's own "social vision" is undecided and contradictory. One thing, however, is certain: class was at the heart of his imagination.

That last point is meant literally. Shakespeare's *image-making* is frequently class-inflected (note, for example, the all-pervasive antithesis in his work between "high" and "low," "noble" and "base"). We can – should – trace the importance of class in Shakespeare at the level of word-pictures. When in *The Merchant of Venice* Salerio, endeavoring to allay Antonio's anxieties about his ships' fate, represents "argosies with portly sail" as being "Like signors and rich burghers on the flood" that "overpeer the petty traffickers / That . . . do them reverence" (1.1.9–13), it's notable that the images he draws on make play with social distinctions. Shakespeare's fellow Elizabethans were obsessed with rank; it's not surprising his means of representation invoke it. Modern critics may find class unexciting, but part of this essay's purpose is to suggest Renaissance poets and audiences did not.

There are non-ideological reasons for Shakespeare critics not talking about class. As social historians like Harold Perkin (1969) have pointed out, it's not clear "class" as such existed in the early modern period. We are all historicists now, and have learned to be wary of using certain words – "homosexuality," "racism" – that only make sense in the era after, say, 1900. "Class," it is said, is one such category – i.e., anachronistic when used to describe early modern societies. People in the close-knit, hierarchical communities of Elizabethan England, Perkin argues, did not think of themselves as belonging to "classes" – saw themselves instead in relation to those above and below them, "vertical" relations of deference and superiority being more important than "horizontal," solidaristic ones. We shouldn't read back into early modern social formations the mentality of modern workers gathered into large workplaces. And there is, perhaps, another problem with the concept "class": its irreligiousness. It was invented by the godless sociology of the nineteenth century. Recent criticism, it has been suggested, neglects the religious character of early modern life (see Shuger 1997). Was "social thought" possible in the period? Thinking about society in purely power-based or economic terms is probably not what Tudor people did. The secularism of the sociological imagination may mislead us.

These arguments suggest students of Renaissance literature shouldn't use the word "class" but alternative categories like "degree." "Degree" invokes a divinely ordered cosmology based on the principle of hierarchy; it may more accurately reflect the mentality of Tudor–Stuart people. That doesn't imply (as it once did) that people couldn't question or rebel against hierarchy, but it does put a brake on anachronism.

The present essay retains the word "class," using it interchangeably with others like "rank" and "degree." That is because I believe people were (at times) capable of the "horizontal" solidarity "class" implies. But I try to remember that early modern people certainly did not always think of their social identities in this way, and often conceived them in ways alien to us (for example, in terms of "service"). The chapter hopes to make a modest, yet I believe important and too little noticed, point: that Shakespeare, in his comedies as much as in other genres, was preoccupied with rank. That's not, notice, "consistently supported social hierarchy." As we shall see, such a conservative attitude does appear in the comedies, but so does a more egalitarian perspective. By way of preface, then, four propositions:

- Class is central to Shakespeare's drama.
- Tudor–Stuart playhouses were distinctive social spaces in which hierarchical social relations, especially those of class, were explored, reinforced, and challenged.
- The comedies display a range of attitudes to social subordination, not all of them compatible with each other.
- Shakespeare's own social position, and that of the players generally, is relevant to how his plays represent class: as someone both inside and outside the dominant culture, his attitudes to hierarchy were contradictory. Searching the plays for a

consistent opinion about hierarchy is hopeless because he felt and thought contradictory things about it. His own socially ambiguous position as a successful player–poet made this dividedness virtually inevitable.

To sum up: we need to register the complexity of what Shakespeare's plays do *vis-à-vis* class; criticism's lack of interest in the poet's treatment of this category is a major blindspot.

will Shakspere gent[1]

There is a bardolatrous criticism that finds it vulgar to ascribe to Shakespeare an opinion. In this perspective, Shakespeare always contains multitudes – his mind is so "comprehensive" (Dryden 1668: 79) that it is futile to try to pin him down to anything; this is Shakespeare as Proteus. This belief isn't always wrong and I will sail near it myself when arguing Shakespeare does not have a single "view" on class. Yet the attitude that Shakespeare did not have attitudes is misleading because it etherealizes him, divorcing him from material and social life and making it impossible for his art to intervene in issues of the day. It kills the author to make a god. Despite contemporary criticism's justified skepticism about biographical approaches, there is good reason for taking account of Shakespeare the man. Like everyone else who has ever lived, Shakespeare existed in a particular time and place; his art grew out of specific conditions. In an effort, then, to free ourselves of the bardolatry that finds that Shakespeare says everything because he was himself nothing, let us begin with the man – someone, it turns out, whose attitudes to class were bound to be complicated. There are three pertinent facts:

1   Shakespeare became very rich, but via a profession barely socially acceptable.
2   In 1592 Robert Greene, a graduate and rival playwright, called him "an upstart Crow, beautified with our feathers."
3   In 1596 Shakespeare's father, John, applied successfully for a grant of arms. As a result William joined the main and most numerous status group of early modern English society; he became a gentleman.

These facts tell us that William Shakespeare was both a member of the elite of Elizabethan–Jacobean England and an outsider to it. Nothing is more crucial for understanding Shakespeare's representation of social subordination than this insider–outsider position (not unique to him but shared by numerous of his fellow playwrights and actors – on the socially ambiguous status of many English Renaissance writers see Holbrook 1994). Shakespeare spent much of his life connected to the court. As a royal servant (Honan 1998: 303) he was granted cloth to make a gown for James I's procession into London. Yet despite such ties to greatness he was in other ways a stranger to its world, the son of a local worthy but not at all a part of the illustrious "Great House" or aristocratic milieu a Sir Philip Sidney belonged to (see Danby 1952).

This betwixt-and-between position bears upon Shakespeare's representation of social relations but, because it is ambiguous, it is difficult to describe. What is the view on social hierarchy of one who acquires, rather than inherits, wealth and position? Of one whose wealth has been made in a "profession" that is disreputable (see Hunter 1997: 30)? A herald objected to grants of arms being made to "base and ignoble persons," citing in this connection Shakespeare (Honan 1998: 229). The Elizabethan playhouse, as has long been known, was a socially ambiguous place, frequented by all classes. It was here Shakespeare made the wealth that enabled him to return to Stratford as a grandee, if a dubious one. To grasp the extent to which association with the public theatre might complicate pretensions to gentility (or poethood) consider that a play might be followed by an entertainment in which

> Dogs were made to fight singly with three bears . . . after this a horse was brought in and chased by the dogs, and at last a bull, who defended himself bravely. [Then] a number of men and women came forward from a separate compartment, dancing, conversing and fighting with each other; also a man who threw some white bread among the crowd, that scrambled for it. Right over the middle of the places a rose was fixed, this rose being set on fire by a rocket: suddenly lots of apples and pears fell out of it down upon the people standing below. Whilst the people were scrambling for the apples, some rockets were made to fall down upon them out of the rose, which caused a great fright but amused the spectators. After this, rockets and other fireworks came flying out of all corners, and that was the end of the play. (Report of Lupold von Wedel, visitor to Southwark in 1584; quoted in Hunter 1997: 131n.)

Is it possible Shakespeare felt ambivalent about his association with this institution, as sonnet 111 suggests? The fear that, like "the dyer's hand," his "nature" has become "subdued / To what it works in" – that "public means . . . public manners breeds" – is the fear of an aspirant to higher place. In short, Shakespeare, like many of his contemporaries, quite probably aspired to be a poet but found himself instead a player. "Gentle" (i.e., non-plebeian) Shakespeare – as Ben Jonson and other colleagues called him – was divided about his calling, on class grounds.

Shakespeare's biography suggests he was socially and materially ambitious. By 1597, when he purchased New Place, he presumably felt socially secure. But in other ways not. Getting wealth is always different from inheriting it; and what if you get status in a depressingly ambiguous sense? Shakespeare may have been a snob – someone who keenly desired to be thought a gentleman, as Katherine Duncan-Jones (2001: 83) suggests – but he was also the object of snobbery. Hunter (1997) reminds us of the envy and contempt with which impecunious, university-trained poets regarded the rich player. Discussing Greene's *Groats-worth of Wit* (1592) in which a poor graduate, Roberto, is employed by an actor as his writer, Hunter notices how taken aback Roberto is when he learns his new employer's profession: "A player, quoth Roberto, I took you rather for a gentleman of great living." As Hunter says, working for a player, no matter how financially rewarding, is humiliating: "money earned under these circumstances" cannot "secur[e] socio-economic status" (Hunter 1997: 29, 30).

Greene's attack on Shakespeare as an "upstart Crow" hurt – so the retraction by Henry Chettle, Greene's publisher, presumably obtained by influential friends of Shakespeare's, suggests (Honan 1998: 162). In-jokes in *The Merry Wives of Windsor* and *As You Like It* indicate Shakespeare dwelt on such slurs. In the former play the schoolboy William answers questions about Latin grammar. The scene sends up the pedantry, as Shakespeare would have it known, of his more academic rivals. Shakespeare pokes fun at the ignorance of Mistress Quickly, who thinks "horum" means "whore" (4.1.52–4) – humor appealing to educated spectators. Yet when Mistress Page complains that "my son profits nothing in the world at his book" (4.1.11–12) William Shakespeare's implication is clear: "my enemies evaluate my scholarship as no sounder than a schoolboy's!" The further joke, however, is that William doesn't do too badly: "That is a good William," says Sir Hugh Evans, and Mistress Page admits: "He is a better scholar than I thought he was" (4.1.32, 69); Evans confesses he has "a good sprag [lively] memory" (4.1.70). The scene responds beautifully to the estimation of Shakespeare by the University Wits. It confidently projects Shakespeare's ability to laugh off the contempt held for him by classically trained arbiters of taste.

A similar moment comes in *As You Like It*. The yokel William in the Forest of Ardenne (the details recall William Shakespeare's birthplace as well as his Christian and mother's name) confronts the court clown Touchstone as a rival for the hand of the very ordinary Audrey (Touchstone's "gentle Audrey" (5.1.1) is heavily ironic). "William" surely alludes to Shakespeare; yet the character, as Stanley Wells (1997: 171) notes, is "sublimely inarticulate" – the joke is delicious. Shakespeare plays up to – and thus de-fangs – snobbish contempt for him as a peasant. William admits he is not "learned" though has a "pretty wit" (5.1.27–36) – not an inaccurate picture of Shakespeare. (Cf. Rosaline in *Love's Labour's Lost*: "Well, better wits have worn plain statute-caps," i.e., apprentices have outwitted lords or scholars (5.2.281).) Yet while the scene satirically acknowledges that there are those who sneer at Shakespeare as a "clown," it also casts the poet's critics as absurd pedants (Shakespeare enjoys jokes against the teaching profession). Touchstone may lord it over William –

> Therefore, you clown, abandon – which is in the vulgar leave – the society – which in the boorish is company – of this female – which in the common is woman; which together is, abandon the society of this female, or, clown, thou perishest; or, to thy better understanding, diest; or (to wit) I kill thee, make thee away . . . (5.1.43–8)

– but the pretentiousness of his language is ridiculous. One must hope Shakespeare played William; the joke would have been exquisite.

We mustn't underestimate the importance of Greene's attack for Shakespeare's representation of class. As O'Dair (2000: 2) argues, one of the most important facts we know about Shakespeare – that snobs despised him – has received scant critical attention. The wound inflicted by the attack rankled for some time: Holofernes and

Armado in *Love's Labour's Lost* are partly Shakespeare's revenge against the academic writers – the sort of people who, like Holofernes, "prove . . . verses to be very unlearned, neither savouring of poetry, wit, nor invention" (4.2.145–6). When Armado says to Holofernes "Arts-man, *preambulate*. We will be singled from the barbarous" (5.1.68–9); when Armado (to Holofernes' toadying approval) specifies that "afternoon" is what "the rude multitude" call "the posteriors of this day" (5.1.75–6), we see Shakespeare using satire to construct an alternative social identity for himself, one not at the mercy of snobs like Greene.

Reading the plays in this way – as moves in a complex game of authorial self-presentation – may seem reductive. And so it would be if it was weirdly asserted that that was all or mainly what the plays were. That's not argued here. But recalling Shakespeare's biography in the way I've done helps situate his works as pieces of social symbolism, sometimes of a personal kind. Shakespeare's own sensitivity to status, and his desire for advancement, is not reasonably in question. He and his colleagues were the "Lord Chamberlain's," later the "King's," men: the company drew on the prestige that went with those significations. The plays – with their almost uniformly aristocratic, royal subjects (it is surely significant Shakespeare did not in the main devote himself to "citizen" subjects) – are partly bids for gentility on his part.

The period's discourses on style, language, and art are saturated with the vocabulary of class. *Troilus and Cressida*'s prefatory epistle, stressing it has never been "clapper-clawed with the palms of the vulgar," illustrates how "aesthetic" judgments in the period are shot through with class ones. "Art" is synonymous with "gentle" and the issue of Shakespeare's "art" (or lack of it) inseparable from the issue of his identity: poet or player? Jonson's Folio tribute – "the race / Of Shakespeare's mind, and manners brightly shines / In his well turned, and true filed lines" – conflates style and gentility. By insisting upon Shakespeare's art Jonson conveniently presents himself as gentle (i.e., capable of discerning art): "Thy art, / My gentle Shakespeare . . ." Chettle's apology is likewise imbued with the language of distinction: "my self have seen his demeanour no less civil than he excellent in the quality he professes; besides, divers of worship have reported his uprightness of dealing, which argues his honesty, and his facetious grace in writing, that approves his art." The Folio presents Shakespeare as a gentleman (in doing so his friends, Heminges and Condell, accrue to themselves his prestige). For Jonson, he is "gentle Shakespeare" (in both "To the Reader" and "To the Memory of my Beloved, the Author Mr. William Shakespeare . . ."); for Hugh Holland, "the Famous Scenic Poet, Master William Shakespeare" – no mere player but a "Poet first, then Poet's King"; for the editors – who dedicate the volume to nobles – "a most gentle expresser" of Nature. Like Chettle, Heminges and Condell emphasize Shakespeare's facility: "what he thought, he uttered with that easinesse, that we have scarce received from him a blot in his papers" – thus associating Shakespeare with the courtly ideal of the amateur rather than the reality of the hard-working professional (on this distinction see Saunders 1951). "To the Great Variety of Readers" and "To the most Noble and Incomparable Pair of Brethren" balance the poetic against theatrical character of the "writings" (twice), "works," and "papers" of this "Author" (twice); the dedication's threefold reference to "trifles" recalls Sidney's use of the word in the letter to his sister prefacing *Arcadia* ("a trifle, and that triflingly handled"). Shakespeare's poems are now "absolute in their numbers." The poetizing language is telling and, since Heminges and Condell made two of the three colleagues remembered in Shakespeare's will, this tilting Shakespeare's reputation in the direction of non-professional poet probably reflected his wishes. Jonson's Shakespeare is a "Star of Poets" whose plays "did take Eliza and our James": even as theatre his was a royal art. There is no pretending Shakespeare did not write for the theatre. But Jonson injects the language of the study into his portrait: "book" (thrice); "volume"; "lines" (four times) – not to mention "muses," "laurels," etc. Leonard Digges's "To the Memory of the Deceased Author" works similarly ("book" twice, "works" twice, "volume . . . ," "line," "verse," and so on). We can't know why *The Tempest* was placed first in the volume, but the editors may have felt it portrayed their friend as an "Author" aware of the classical rules of time and place – again giving the impression of a "gentle Shakespeare."

My point has been simple: Shakespeare was socially ambitious and sensitive to class. Working in a kind of no-man's land in the social hierarchy, yet rising in wealth and status, made this sensitivity inevitable. All of which suggests class was a subject of his writing.

Class and Classics

Academic criticism has largely given up on value judgments, but I make one here: in respect of social relations, mid-to-late Shakespeare is better than early. I want to argue that *The Comedy of Errors*, for instance, is more committed to traditional notions of social hierarchy than later plays. Nevertheless the social symbolism of *Errors* is not without ambiguity: it looks forward to the egalitarian potential of later plays.

Errors is the work of an ambitious young playwright eager to be seen as capable of handling, even sending up, academic models. Strongly marked by the schoolroom, it doubles the plot complications of its source; out-Plautusing Plautus, Shakespeare shows his mastery of the Roman or school tradition. A virtuoso piece, it displays Shakespeare's ability to handle complex plotting (Wells 1997: 54), the soul of drama for the classical tradition. Elements look ahead to the destabilizing social vision of the comedies that follow, such as *A Midsummer Night's Dream* or *As You Like It* – plays that transform the social order (see Ryan 1989: ch. 3). That radical vision is almost absent from *Errors* – Shakespeare has not yet found the imaginative trajectory that will take him to a skeptical attitude towards social hierarchies.

Errors is a bid for a desirable social identity on the part of a writer at a social disadvantage *vis-à-vis* some of his contemporaries. Unlike the University Wits who transform the London stage in the 1580s, Shakespeare can lay no claim to an academic background. Social insecurity must have weighed heavily on this poetically and socially ambitious writer. *Errors* is a grab for academic prestige in the competitive, status-conscious arena of the Elizabethan stage and provided the perfect answer to Greene.

In garnering the social capital associated with the academic tradition, Shakespeare took over some of that tradition's values. In this respect it was a false start. The attitudes encoded into this kind of comedy were not those that, ultimately and thankfully, shaped Shakespeare's art, which views hierarchy critically. Like all Shakespeare plays, *Errors* contains contradictory ideological impulses. Its social symbolism is mobile and ambiguous, capable of being interpreted in different ways by diversely positioned audience members, from groundling to grandee.

Discussing University drama at Cambridge, Alan H. Nelson writes that "one play that adheres in strictest possible measure to the rules for academic comedy is *The Comedy of Errors*" (Nelson 1997: 66). The 1594 Gray's Inn performance signals Shakespeare's closeness at this date to academic theatre culture. As Nelson writes: "Shakespeare in his early days adhered much more closely than any of his professional colleagues to the English academic staging tradition. Perhaps he learned of the academic performance tradition at the grammar school in Stratford" (ibid: 67 n.6). Nelson contrasts the "fixed locale" of this tradition – the city street – with the "dynamic" one common in the professional theatre, in which the stage may represent a council chamber, forest, battlefield, and so on. Such flexibility, Nelson argues, gave the professional theatre opportunity for striking effects of juxtaposition (for example, between country and city; ibid: 64); perhaps such contrasts also allowed more searching social investigation than the restricted *mise-en-scène* of the academic theatre permitted. In addition, we need to remind ourselves of the placement of this academic tradition in institutions firmly committed to rank, namely universities and colleges. Ann Jennalie Cook illustrates this theatre's preoccupation with hierarchy by citing the seating regulations devised for a 1629 Trinity College Cambridge performance. The chancellor stipulates that

> no scholar under a Master of Arts do presume to take any place above the lower rail, or bar, either upon the ground, or the side scaffolds. The space above the said bar unto the stage with the scaffolds on both sides, to be for the regents in their caps, hoods, and habits, and for the fellow commoners; the space upon the ground beyond the stage, and the scaffold above at the end of the hall, for non-regents and knights' eldest sons. Yet so, that they also leave the lowest seat of the said scaffold, at the end of the hall, with both the side scaffolds, which reach to the stage, for the doctors, and for such courtiers, as shall not sit with the chancellor and the ambassador. (Cook 1997: 309)

The regulations amply indicate the institution's jealous regard for degree. The academic dimension of Shakespeare's *Comedy of Errors* is signaled by a similarly obsessive focus on hierarchical relations, one less marked by the skeptical, even oppositional, perspective of later comedies. The play's wit combats between young masters and servants I take to be material especially appealing to an audience of upwardly mobile young men well-schooled in rhetoric – the audience the play encountered at Gray's. Instances of master–servant exchanges in *Errors* make the point (and are paralleled in another early comedy also marked by academic culture, *The Taming of the Shrew*). Here Antipholus of Syracuse wants to know what Ephesian Dromio has done with the money Antipholus thinks he left in his charge:

> I am not in a sportive humour now.
> Tell me, and dally not, where is the money?
> . . .
> Come, Dromio, come, these jests are out of season.
> . . .
> Come on, sir knave, have done your foolishness,
> And tell me how thou hast disposed thy charge.
> . . .
> . . . I shall break that merry sconce of yours
> That stands on tricks when I am undisposed.
> . . .
> What, wilt thou flout me thus unto my face,
> Being forbid? There, take you that, sir knave! (1.2.58–92)

Like many other such exchanges in the play between master and servant, this one concludes with a beating. Dromio receives another from Adriana, Ephesian Antipholus' wife, immediately afterwards –

> Back, slave, [to fetch Antipholus], or I will break thy pate across.
> . . .
> Hence, prating peasant. Fetch thy master home.

– and is given the servant's stock complaint:

> Am I so round with you as you with me,
> That like a football do you spurn me thus?
> You spurn me hence, and he will spurn me hither,
> If I last in this service you must case me in leather. (1.3.77–84)

Part of the pleasure *Errors* offers its audience lies in the complication and enforcement of relations of subordination – ends logically, but not dramatically, contradictory. As so often, Shakespeare – keen to maximize audience satisfaction – plays both sides of the street. The beatings have a slapstick, unreal quality, but do they not also offer elite audiences a certain sadistic amusement? It isn't easy to define the social symbolism of this everlasting necessity for beating incorrigible slaves:

Antipholus E. Thou whoreson, senseless villain.
Dromio E. I would I were senseless, sir, that I might not feel your blows.
Antipholus E. Thou art sensible in nothing but blows, and so is an ass.
Dromio E. I am an ass indeed. You may prove it by my long ears. I have served him from the hour of my nativity to this instant, and have nothing at his hands for my service but blows. When I am cold, he heats me with beating. When I am warm, he cools me with beating. I am waked with it when I sleep, raised with it when I sit, driven out of doors with it when I go from home, welcomed home with it when I return. Nay, I bear it on my shoulders, as a beggar wont her brat, and I think when he hath lamed me, I shall beg with it from door to door. (4.4.22–35)

Dromio's speech has its own power: servingmen or apprentices might have detected a hit at master brutality (if the speech's content is resigned to such treatment, its stylistic energy is not). Yet criticism hardly allows for the possibility that it is such brutality we are meant to find funny. *Errors*, I suggest, belongs to an academic vein of humor committed to the policing of social distinctions, an approach Shakespeare later swapped for more ironic treatments of hierarchy (think of *A Midsummer Night's Dream*, dating from not long afterwards). It's difficult to find a critical language that notices the comedy of snobbism in the play without sounding miserably parsonical about it; nonetheless, that is the comedy operating in the exchange between master and servant in the extended description of Nell, she of the "swart" and sweaty complexion and globular shape, "no longer from head to foot than from hip to hip." This fat "kitchen-wench" (3.2.101, 94, 112) is an instance of the humor the play prefers – that likely to confirm a group of young gentlemen in their good opinion of themselves. It would not be hard to find in later Shakespearean comedy examples of wit that similarly bolster feelings of social superiority (think of Autolycus' tormenting of the Shepherd and his son in *The Winter's Tale*, 4.4.695ff.). But I believe such material is generally complicated by the presence of perspectives correcting such self-congratulatory attitudes. For instance, I would invoke the Caliban-defense – giving a negative character lines makes it difficult to dismiss him or her – in the case of *As You Like It*'s Audrey who, while Nell-like in some ways – "I am not a slut, though I thank the gods I am foul" – also says "I do not know what 'poetical' is. Is it honest in deed and word? Is it a true thing?" (3.3.31; 13–14), a profound query suggestively bearing upon the poetry-maddened conception of life of Shakespeare's comic young men, Orlando included. Making such young men face reality, as in *Love's Labour's Lost*, where, it seems, "Jack hath not Jill" (5.2.852), is often part of the comedies' ethical work. Audrey asks an important Shakespearean question.

Errors, then, is an academic comedy heavily invested in social hierarchy. And "academic" in this context means in part "verbal wit." *Love's Labour's Lost* is perhaps a turning point, stigmatizing representatives of that academic tradition within which Shakespeare began writing comedy, i.e., the bright but shallow young things of Navarre's court. The play questions the very wit that is that tradition's *raison d'être*. Rosaline's words to Biron recognize wit's limitations:

> Oft have I heard of you, my Lord Biron,
> Before I saw you; and the world's large tongue
> Proclaims you for a man replete with mocks,
> Full of comparisons and wounding flouts,
> Which you on all estates will execute
> That lie within the mercy of your wit. (5.2.818–23)

Biron is a lord. I take "all estates . . . [lying] within the mercy of your wit" to mean "your inferiors" – precisely the humor of *Errors*, with its jokes about kitchen wenches. Rosaline wants to "choke" Biron's "gibing spirit" (835) – the rhetorical mode of the earlier play – with its "comparisons and wounding flouts" directed at the Nells and Dromios.

Errors's wittiness – a value *Love's Labour's Lost* indulges and ironizes – may be intrinsically socially orthodox. The play is concerned with mistake: its disruptions of identity are errors. That's not how Shakespeare imagines challenges to identity in subsequent plays, where it's not clear that the self born out of some catastrophe – Bottom "translated" (*Midsummer Night's Dream*, 3.1.105) into the Fairy Queen's consort, say, or Edgar as Poor Tom – is merely a mistaken version of the old self. In *The Comedy of Errors* only misapprehensions are at issue; clearing up illusions puts old realities back together. The play describes a perfect circle – it's *almost* possible to say nothing is changed at its close. Its wit resides in extreme entanglement of action and deft disentanglement. In later plays, however, confusion refuses to be labeled as simply that; something is left over from the "story of the night" (*Midsummer Night's Dream*, 5.1.23) and the reality at play's end is different from that at its beginning. In *Errors* wit consists in redescribing a reality taken as given (the kitchen wench *is* a certain type of person, comparable to X); in later plays, reality itself is seen as contradictory and unstable (Bottom is both foolish *and* a genius). As a consequence, a more critical, interrogative attitude is taken towards it. This is an ideological, as well as poetic, revolution in Shakespeare's writing.

It's sometimes said *Errors* anticipates Shakespeare's interest in effects of wonder, which would connect it with plays (like *A Midsummer Night's Dream*) that have this transformative or utopian sense of reality. This is true but easily exaggerated. Adriana may, when her husband appears outside the abbey's walls, exclaim that this appearance is "past thought of human reason" (5.1.190), but the truth is she is merely mistaken as to the identity of the man inside. Rather than wonder – the revelation of some order challenging that of the everyday – the play deals with tricks, distortions: "I think you are all mated, or stark mad" (5.1.282) exclaims the Duke. The confusions of the day do not point towards a truth the characters need to know; no larger perspectives emerge. Instead the degrading nature of the confusions is dwelt upon, especially the "deep shames and great indignities" (5.1.254) Ephesian Antipholus undergoes, locked out of his own house and bound in a cellar. Shakespeare imagines the loss of male power in the most lurid terms: "Beyond imagination is the wrong / That she this day hath shameless thrown on me" (202–3). The play's exploration of male–female relations is strikingly different from that in comedies such as *Love's Labour's Lost, Much Ado About Nothing, As You Like It*, or *All's Well That Ends Well*, which encourage a wry, skeptical, or critical look at masculine folly, injustice, or vanity and which unhysterically countenance a much greater degree of female initiative and independence. Perhaps it was only by exiting a rather masculinist academic tradition of play-writing that Shakespeare was able to arrive at this more emancipated outlook.

I've suggested that ideologically *The Comedy of Errors* was a dead-end for Shakespeare: it doesn't look forward to the radical social symbolism of later work. That's not, however, entirely true. As I suggested above, it's possible to find in the play wryly humorous expressions of servant discontent. And its final lines suggest, to qualify a point made earlier, that this "one day's error" (5.1.399) has not ended in a mere reprise of the social reality with which the play began. I mean the touching moment when the two Dromios agree that, since they are twins, they should forego the principle of seniority: "We came into the world like brother and brother, / And now let's go hand in hand, not one before another" (5.1.426–7). That exchange hints at the egalitarian fantasies imbuing subsequent comedies (and other plays) by Shakespeare. It's to such fantasies I now turn.

Masters and Men

In P. G. Wodehouse's *Joy in the Morning* the feather-brained Bertie asks his servant savant Jeeves whether he'd like a gift. Jeeves requests the "new and authoritatively annotated edition of the works of the philosopher Spinoza" (Wodehouse 1946: 11). The delight of the Wooster stories, whose atmosphere Alexander Cockburn (1976: xii) compares to that of Shakespeare's comedies, resides in their wonderful reversal of hierarchy. Even Bertie acknowledges that Jeeves is in every way – except socially – his superior. The Bertram Wooster Theory of Class illuminates Shakespeare's playing with relations of subordination in the comedies.

The Taming of the Shrew opens with Lucentio's resolve to undertake a "a course of learning and ingenious studies" in "fair Padua, nursery of arts" (1.1.9, 2). It's a Woosterish moment, since no sooner has Lucentio uttered these laudable words than his able and literate servant Tranio – later his master's adroit impersonator – injects some reason into these vaporings. Tranio begs Lucentio not to be "so devote to Aristotle's checks / As Ovid be an outcast quite abjured" (1.1.32–3). Tranio speaks wisely: Shakespeare enjoys taking to task such callow, unbalanced intellectualism as Lucentio's. (Intellectualism features in a number of comedies – *The Taming of the Shrew*, *Love's Labour's Lost*, *The Two Gentlemen of Verona* – in which "study" is part of male self-improvement plans.) The schoolroom atmosphere of *Shrew* is pronounced (for instance in arguments between the supposed tutors "Cambio" and "Licio" (3.1)). As I've indicated, Shakespeare must have been sorely conscious of how he fell outside that university-educated group of writers who revolutionized the Elizabethan stage. I've suggested he takes at times an ironical, amused view of the academic tradition: keen to show his ease in it he is also its wry critic. (Shakespeare often pokes fun at bookishness.) It's hardly irrelevant he probably experienced some discomfort about his own lack of a university education, one of the clearest marks of gentility being possession of a university degree (Palliser 1983: 70): the ironic treatment of learning in the plays is a piece of self-defense. (Sharon O'Dair (2000) notes an ambivalence about books in *The Tempest*: see pp. 23–41.) It's also significant that Shakespeare has servants ballast upper-class waffling. It's perhaps an obvious point, but not always given its due: Shakespeare's lower-class figures regularly act as guides and confidants to upper-class ones. This isn't to suggest lower-class figures are the center of the play, just that they often supply balance. Moreover, Shakespeare frequently presents his most attractive characters (Hamlet, or Rosalind and Orlando in *As You Like It*) as those who have struck a mean between courtly virtues of grace, wit, eloquence, and idealism and a plebeian grasp of reality. They are partly popular. "The people praise [Rosalind] for her virtues" (1.2.247) and "pity her" (1.3.73); the tyrannical Oliver confesses that

Orlando is "so much in the heart . . . of my own people, who best know him, that I am altogether misprizd" (1.1.143–4).

As You Like It is perhaps the comedy of Shakespeare's that most deliberately plays with egalitarian social fantasies (see Wilson 1993). It also exemplifies the contradictory character of Shakespeare's thinking about hierarchy. The opening conversation between Adam and Orlando reinforces hierarchical ideology, the latter complaining that Oliver keeps him "rustically at home . . . call you that keeping for a gentleman of my birth?" (1.1.6–8). "You have trained me," he accuses Oliver, "like a peasant, obscuring and hiding from me all gentleman-like qualities" (1.1.57–9). The play (as often in Shakespeare) encourages audience identification with this upper-class perspective. Like much art at all times, this was one function Renaissance drama performed: as the Captain in *Twelfth Night* says, "What great ones do the less will prattle of" (1.2.29). To some extent the medium made an aristocratic bias inevitable: a high, poetic drama like that of the Elizabethans would naturally be drawn towards "gentle" characters, topics, themes. Moreover, playwrights and actors had a class interest in accruing to themselves the cultural capital that went with a deft, rhetorically sophisticated representation of upper-class manners, styles, and preoccupations. The companies' names – Lord Chamberlain's, King's – suggest that. Yet contradictory social fantasies are at work in the plays which, after all, had to appeal to a cross-section of the nation. *As You Like It* is a good example. The play reinforces the ideology of aristocratic precedence yet also, as Wilson (1993) shows, attacks inequality. Oliver's brutality towards Adam ("Get you with him, you old dog") and the servant's dignified reply ("Is 'old dog' my reward? Most true, I have lost my teeth in your service" (1.1.69, 70–1)) frame the play's sylvan republicanism, which trades the "painted pomp" of the "envious court" for the fellowship of a band of "co-mates and brothers in exile" (2.1.3, 4, 1). The forest is bourgeois not feudal: the Duke sympathizes with the "poor dappled fools, / . . . native burghers of this desert city" (2.1.22–3). Yet Adam is a faithful servant, "not for the fashion of these times, / Where none will sweat but for promotion" (2.3.60–1). The idealization of service and of a loving, mutually beneficial hierarchy sits alongside egalitarianism. Orlando's bearing an exhausted Adam – "Come, I will bear thee to some shelter, and thou shalt not die for lack of a dinner if there live any thing in this desert. Cheerly, good Adam" (2.6.12–14) – is almost as daring a piece of social symbolism as the servants challenging Cornwall in *King Lear*. His not eating until "necessity be served" (2.7.89) likewise adopts a radical perspective on hierarchy: servants' needs are as important as nobles'. "There is an old poor man," says Orlando to Duke Senior's offer of food; "Who after me hath many a weary step . . . / Till he be first sufficed . . . / I will not touch a bit" (2.7.128–32). Mutuality and solidarity evaporate at the end of the play when "every of this happy number, / That have endured shrewd days and nights with us, / Shall share the good of our returned fortune, / According to the measure of their states" (5.4.161–4), though there is an interval before this reassertion of "states": "Meantime, forget this new-fallen dignity, / And fall into our rustic revelry" (5.4.165–6). Perhaps, however, a vestige of rustic republicanism will survive into the post-Ardenne order: Duke Frederick has "thrown into neglect the pompous court" (5.4.171) and Jacques, for one, is keen to find out more.

At times Shakespeare's comedies can seem positively anti-aristocratic. In *The Merry Wives of Windsor* a self-consciously bourgeois setting sees the comeuppance of a debauched knight, an out-and-out snob who calls Ford a "mechanical salt-butter rogue," "knave," and "peasant" (2.2.246, 239, 249). Ford ironically presents Falstaff as a "court-like" and "learned" knight of "admirable discourse" (2.2.200–4) and Falstaff quotes Sidney while attempting to seduce Mistress Ford: "Have I caught thee, my heavenly jewel?" (3.3.35). So the degradations he undergoes (hid under "stinking clothes that fretted in their own grease" (3.5.98) for instance) might be a dig at the Great House tradition of poetry (see Duncan-Jones 2001: 98). *The Merry Wives* is obsessed with class (Anne mustn't marry Fenton because he is "of too high a region" (3.2.62)) and the play revolves around court–bourgeois tension, which eventually dissipates in harmonious laughter "by a country fire" (5.5.218). But the play's concerns are not unique. *Much Ado About Nothing* also relies on a contrast between courtly and popular life. Conrad calls Dogberry an "ass" at 4.2.66, which is fair enough: the sentimental notion that Dogberry fingers the villains overlooks the role of the Sexton, a more educated figure who has to guide Dogberry's investigations ("Master Constable, you go not the way to examine, you must call forth the watch that are their accusers" (4.2.29–30)). Dogberry's proletarian *saeva indignatio*, with its playing on ass's "ears" – "Dost thou not suspect my place? Dost thou not suspect my years?" (4.2.67–8) – makes him a figure of fun. As with Bottom, lower-class stupidity is a main comic resource. Yet we are also invited to prefer good-hearted simplicity to the villainy or plain callousness ("What your wisdoms could not discover, these shallow fools have brought to light" (5.1.205)) of Don John, Claudio, or Don Pedro.

Shakespeare's comedies are preoccupied with master–servant relations, but these relations, I've argued, are not easily described. On the one hand there is much violence directed at subordinates: "Fie, fie on all . . . mad masters . . . Was ever man so beaten?" complains Grumio in *The Taming of the Shrew* after arriving at Petruccio's house (4.1.1–2). The first scene in which we encounter Petruccio concludes with him beating Grumio because of the latter's misconstrual of his command to "knock me here soundly" (1.2.8). Does the play then reinforce hierarchy? Yes, but the relation between masters and men is not a simple power one. Servant impudence is as prominent as beatings – "A slave," says Proteus of Launce in *Two Gentleman*, "that still on end turns me to shame" (4.4.54) – and masters and men are often intimate: Hortensio greets Grumio warmly as "My old friend" (1.2.20; on this scene, see Moisan 1991). In *Shrew*, as in other Shakespeare comedies, master–men relations are wonderfully freewheeling. Grumio's incorrigibility, Lucentio's dependence on Tranio: such material at the least complicates official notions of obedience. Petruccio's household is instructive. Although a hierarchy it is also a rough, masculine community. Petruccio's abuse of servants – "logger-headed and unpolished grooms! . . . heedless jolt-heads and unmannered slaves" (4.1.106, 147) – is male shrewishness in action; the servingman Nathaniel comments amazedly to one of his fellows: "Peter, didst ever see the like?" (4.1.160); this isn't Petruccio's normal self. Just as, it is arguable, the play treats the marriage relation with a humor and realism tempering its orthodox commitment to "aweful rule, and right supremacy" (5.2.113) – Kate's assured final speech doesn't *sound* like a slave's, despite its content – so the play modifies the idea that masters are the natural superiors of their men: otherwise how do we account for Tranio's eloquence while impersonating Lucentio in 2.1?

In *The Taming of the Shrew*, as elsewhere in Shakespeare, social roles are astonishingly liquid: Tranio, son of "a sailmaker in Bergamo" (5.1.65), effortlessly plays a well-born youth. The subversiveness of the idea that social positions are transferable *roles* rather than fixed orders of nature is immense: perhaps the single most radical thing about Shakespeare's theatre was this highlighting of the extent to which social roles were part of culture not nature. As David Scott Kastan puts it: "In the theaters of London, if not in the *theatrum mundi*, class positions are exposed as something other than essential facts of human existence, revealed, rather, as changeable and constructed" (Kastan 1993: 107). *The Taming of the Shrew* depicts the overturning of normal class distinctions. Watching a low-born servant abuse a master (5.1), or a tinker treated like a lord, is material a society as obsessed with degree as that of Tudor England must have found intoxicating, scandalous, hilarious. Such topsy-turvydom can show how artificial such distinctions are: we have already seen Tranio speak eloquent verse. At the same time the play appeals directly to the snobbery it elsewhere overturns – for example in Petruccio's uproarious abuse of the Tailor in 4.3. The social perspective of Shakespeare's comedies, like that of Renaissance drama generally, is contradictory, partly as a result of the players' own complicated social position, partly because they were written for diverse audiences. Their social vision is irreducibly various.

How Not to Be a Servant

In *The Two Gentleman of Verona* the servant Launce has been "two days loitering" (4.4.38). One of the blissful things about Shakespeare's comedies is the lower orders' frequent obliviousness to their inhabiting a hierarchy; they need reminding their purpose in life is serving their betters. *The Merry Wives*'s Slender hounds Peter Simple for his truancy: "How now, Simple, where have you been? I must wait on myself, must I?" (1.1.167–8). He's just another of the comedies' refractory menials. Elizabethan society enforced social distinctions as part of daily life (Palliser 1983: 81–2). By contrast, social relations in Shakespeare's comedies are remarkably undisciplined: the plays are like lessons in being a bad servant.

Servant impudence is a subject of *Two Gentlemen*. Speed, a servant wit, jokes about sheep in a way highly disrespectful to Proteus' Julia: "I, a lost mutton, gave your letter to her, a laced mutton" (1.1.93–4; laced mutton being slang for prostitute). As in other Shakespeare comedies the license of servant speech is breathtaking. The pertness of Julia's maid Lucetta in the letter scene – "That you may ruminate" she off-handedly remarks to Julia as she exits (1.2.49) – must have been piquant to Elizabethans of high as well as low rank. (Recall how servant impudence is given a tragic dimension elsewhere in Shakespeare, for instance in the greasy Oswald's blasé treatment of Lear.) In *Two Gentlemen*, as in other comedies, master–servant relations bear little resemblance to Tudor norms: "Is't near dinner-time?" asks Julia; "I would it were," replies Lucetta, "That you might kill your stomach on your meat / And not upon your maid" (1.2.67–9). At 2.1.71–2 Speed blithely confesses that yesterday he didn't "wipe [Valentine's] shoes" because he "was in love with [his] bed"); his repartee elicits Valentine's resigned recognition that his man will "still be too forward" (2.1.11). Perhaps the most extreme case of plebeian impertinence in the comedies is the prisoner Barnadine's blunt refusal in *Measure for Measure* to be executed (4.3). However, it's a feature of all of them. In *Love's Labour's Lost* Costard's insousiance provokes his monarch to scream "Peace!" (1.1.220). His address to the Princess is typical: "Are not you the chief woman? You are the thickest here"; exasperated, she demands "What's your will, sir? What's your will?" (4.1.51–2). In *Twelfth Night* Feste turns back on his mistress her request that the servants "Take the fool away": "Do you not hear, fellows? Take away the lady" (1.5.33–4). This is cute for a modern audience; in the fastidiously rank-conscious world of Elizabethan England it must have seemed not only funny but wondrous.

Similarly with the closeness frequently obtaining between masters and servants of the same sex. Lucetta and Julia, Lucentio and Tranio: these couplings aren't friendships, but neither are they unambiguous relations of subordination. Warmth, humor, irony, affection enter into them. The to-and-fro between superior and subordinate sometimes conveys the pleasure Shakespeare's lovers' banter does. "You, minion, are too saucy" Julia observes tartly to Lucetta in *Two Gentlemen* (1.2.93). But the minion has a shrewd comeback: "Ay, madam, you may say what sights you see. / I see things too, although you judge I wink" (1.2.93, 138–9). The back-and-forth suggests intimacy. Julia begs Lucetta – "the table wherein all my thoughts / Are visibly charactered and engraved" – for "[c]ounsel." And Lucetta is the voice of "reason" (2.7.1, 3–4, 23). Quick-witted, perceptive, and eloquent, Lucetta is in most respects Juliet's equal as well as friend; the difference is that she is not given her mistress's emotional range, a deficiency Shakespeare (or Shakespeare and Fletcher) repaired in the affecting portrait of the Jailer's Daughter in *The Two Noble Kinsmen*. Low-born, witty, and likable characters like Tranio and Lucetta open up the whole question of egalitarianism in the comedies.

The Jeeves Principle

The Dromios exiting "hand in hand, not one before another" is not a unique moment: it's easy to find in Shakespeare's comedies broadly egalitarian sentiments. In *The Merchant of Venice* Aragon deliberates before the caskets. The silver casket's motto ("Who chooseth me shall get as much as he deserves") prompts this outburst:

> O, that estates, degrees, and offices
> Were not deriv'd corruptly, and that clear honor
> Were purchased by the merit of the wearer!
> How many then should cover that stand bare

How many be commanded that command?
How much low peasantry would then be gleaned
From the true seed of honor . . . ? (2.9.35, 40–6)

It's fascinating that Shakespeare thought this meritocratic aria, which must have prompted some spectators to reflect on Elizabethan injustices, interesting enough to give to Aragon. And yet it's Aragon who gets the idiot's head and who says in this same speech that he "will not choose what many men desire [i.e., gold], / Because [he] will not jump with common spirits / And rank [himself] with the barbarous multitudes" (2.9.30–2). The speech switches between egalitarianism and haughty disdain of "the mob."

Aragon's speech underlines the point that we shouldn't look for a consistent social symbolism in the plays, for reasons already outlined. Nevertheless the Jeeves principle – the master is not smarter or in general braver or more deserving than the man – obtains in Shakespeare's comedies. And not only that: plebeians function as a brake on the excesses and absurdities of upper-class behavior. In *Love's Labour's Lost* the aristocrats ridicule the entertainment put on by their inferiors. "This is not generous, not gentle, not humble" says Holofernes (5.2.617). It's a powerful moment, revising class-based ideas of worth: gentility is a matter of conduct not birth. One shouldn't underestimate the subversive power of this ancient notion. *Love's Labour's Lost* ends with a song portraying rural, lower-class life; it's almost literally a breath of fresh air after the preciousness of the upper-class comedy. Here lower-class life functions as a moral corrective to what has gone before, the unpretentious song echoing the ladies' stern lessoning of the men. This sentimental use of the popular – bringing the lords down to earth – is not uncommon in the plays. It operates, for example, in *A Midsummer Night's Dream*. That play's snobbery is evident – the mechanicals are ridiculous, as their names, malapropisms, aesthetic naivety, etc., indicate – but Bottom is also its moral center. One needs ears to hear it, but it's possible to extract a message from the comedies that challenges the elite's claim to natural superiority.

Thus one of the noticeable things about the comedies is how wit – a self-consciously aristocratic attribute – is not confined to aristocrats. "[N]ow you are metamorphosed with a mistress" says Speed to Valentine (2.1.26–7); the whole speech illustrates how servants are wit's fount as well as object. Speed has to explain to Valentine that Silvia has wooed him "by a figure" (2.1.132). Not only is he cleverer than his noble master, he is more down-to-earth – "though the chameleon love can feed on the air" Speed is "nourished by . . . victuals" (2.1.154–5) – and a witty poet (2.1.121–8, 146–51).

The comedies explore what makes a master or a man. The amount of upstairs-downstairs interaction shows this is a principal subject. And there are distinctions to be drawn: not all plebeians are alike. Launce is the type of the simple servant, like Gobbo in *The Merchant of Venice*, Dogberry in *Much Ado*, or Bottom's friends in *A Midsummer Night's Dream*; they are distinguishable from the Tranios, Lucettas, Speeds. But Launce et al. aren't dismissable. They often embody a sentimentalism the play hails as wisdom. Launce's chiding of his dog as a "cruel-hearted cur" that doesn't "shed one tear" on leaving Verona (2.3.8) is both ridiculous and contrasted with his master Proteus' villainy.

In her introduction in *The Riverside Shakespeare* Anne Barton (1997: 179) gives a catalog of the moral failings of the gentle characters in *Two Gentlemen*. Launce's sentimentality shows up the rather heartless elite posturing in the play. It's a familiar strategy: here as in other plays elite and popular characters are measured against each other – with the latter comparing favorably. Proteus calls Launce a "whoreson peasant" (4.4.37). Was this insult neutral in effect? I think it's more likely an audience noticed it as yet another black mark against Proteus' name, just as it would have noted with discomfort Bertram's snobbery about Helena in *All's Well*. Proteus is the perfect gentleman – "With all good grace to grace a gentleman" (2.4.67) – yet his shameless facility at slander, a skill he tutors the Duke in at 3.2.31ff., not to mention his attempted rape of Silvia, aligns him with Bertram, whose play draws a pungent contrast between bourgeois rectitude (Helena's fidelity) and aristocratic rascality. *Two Gentlemen* has the riddling title of other Shakespeare plays. The Duke thinks Valentine "a gentleman, and well derived" (5.4.143). Yet his handing over of Silvia to her would-be rapist sits awkwardly with this courtly image.

Like all Shakespeare plays, *Two Gentlemen* invokes antitheses of "high" and "low," contrasts having a clear social dimension. But knowing which term is normative is not always easy. Launce's complaisant attitude to female inconstancy confirms his clownishness. Or does it? "Of her tongue," Launce reasons, "she cannot" be "liberal" because "that's writ down she is slow of. Of her purse she shall not, for that I'll keep shut. Now of another thing she may, and that cannot I help" (3.1.335–8). Recall Shakespeare's interest in the horrific consequences of sexual jealousy in *Othello* or *The Winter's Tale* and Launce's unillusioned view of marriage seems, like Emilia's in the former play, a necessary counter-perspective. *Two Gentlemen* is full of such ironies. Some of the outlaws Valentine falls in with are "gentlemen" who "detest such vile, base practices" as rape (71); yet First Outlaw casually refers to murder as a "petty" crime (4.1.42, 71, 50). So are, or are they not, "gentlemen"?

Launce is not an "ass," or not only, but a "madcap" (the word is used of one of Shakespeare's wittiest lords, Biron in *Love's Labour's Lost* (2.1.214)). Like the elite characters, Launce's fault is punning: "Well, your old vice still, mistake the word" (3.1.277) Valentine observes. In *Much Ado* Benedick says of Margaret, Beatrice's waiting-woman, that her "wit is as quick as the greyhound's mouth, it catches" (5.2.9–10). There is no fundamental difference between the wit of the upper-class characters and the Launces, Speeds, and so on.

Shakespeare's comedy invites us to laugh at servants. But it also takes their side. Much of the humor of the plays consists in offenses against hierarchy – Launce's dog "mak[ing] water against a gentlewoman's farthingale" for example (4.4.32–3). Proteus may think him a "foolish lout" (4.4.58), but the play measures Launce's simplicity against his master's falseness (4.2.1). Launce covers for his dog's misdemeanors: "How many masters would do this for his servant?" he asks: "When a man's servant shall play the cur with him, look you, it goes hard. One that I brought up of a puppy, one that I saved from drowning when three or four of his blind brothers and sisters went to it" (4.4.25, 1–4). Even Launce, it turns out, is a master – but a kindly one. Many a servingman or apprentice in the audience must have longed for such a master.

Language

Shakespeare's is a language-conscious drama. What isn't noticed enough is that its language is consistently socially marked. When Biron declares that "Henceforth my wooing mind shall be expressed! / In russet yeas and honest kersey noes" (*Love's Labour's Lost*, 5.2.412–13) he makes the point: thoughts come in proletarian or gentle dress. Language in the period is regularly conceived in such terms. It marked social distinctions and the drama exploited these. This doesn't mean words only operated in one social register. When Armado and Mote chant "But O, but O / The hobby-horse is forgot" (3.1.23–4) we are reminded that popular culture, then as now, crossed class barriers.

Nevertheless, in the Renaissance, facility with language – like musical facility – signified gentility. The Princess in *Love's Labour's Lost* knows this: "Good wits will be jangling, but, gentles, agree": verbal wit and gentility are part of the same code (2.1.224). First and foremost Renaissance stage language communicated class: even before an auditor knew *what* was being said he or she knew, via the distinction, for example, between prose and verse, *who* was saying it – that is, a gentle or plebeian. Language, like costume, identified rank. Class was the *primary* meaning of everything said on stage. What was represented *first of all*, visually and aurally, was *class*: as soon as characters opened their mouths they made known their rank (and few things in Elizabethan society were more significant than that). Shakespeare enjoyed complicating sociolinguistic distinctions – making his plebeians "wit-crackers" (*Much Ado*, 5.4.98) for instance – but that didn't make the distinctions any less real. They were his material.

There are few features of Shakespeare's language that can't be referred to social distinctions. Consider his predilection for socially hybrid verbal doublets ("incarnadine, / Making the green one red" (*Macbeth*, 2.2.60–1)): one part for the less, another for the better, educated. It needs to be noticed how often Shakespeare's comic language is the comedy of class. When Mote says Samson "was a man of good carriage, great carriage, for he carried the town-gates on his back like a porter" (*Love's Labour's Lost*, 1.2.65–6), the witticism lies in the yoking of high and low. The technique is so central to Shakespeare's writing it is observable at the level of the line. When Biron swears not to "woo in rhyme, like a blind harper's song" (5.2.405) the line's jest lies in the deflating effect of its second half. So much of Shakespeare's verbal singularity relies on such disconnects between social spheres. When in a passage of high lyricism Lysander describes love as being as "Brief as the lightning in the collied night" (*A Midsummer Night's Dream*, 1.1.145) *collied* has its primary meaning "coal-black," but also summons up the proverbially dirty trade of coal-carters and miners. That mingling of social levels preserves Shakespeare's verse from cliché and monotony. When Armado tells Mote to bring Costard "festinately hither" (3.1.4) the joke appeals to the latined and unlatined; in any case it revolves around this class distinction (similarly for the playing around with "Remuneration" or "guerdon" (*Love's Labour's Lost*, 3.1.125–6, 156–8)). On the other hand, if Dull misunderstands Holofernes' "*haud credo*" for "old gray doe" (4.2.10; see note in *The Riverside Shakespeare*) the play is serving up an in-joke for gentles.

Love's Labour's Lost sends up academic (i.e., gentle) language and manners. It contrasts "barbarism" (1.1.112) – for example that of Costard – with learning, but without preferring learning. It asserts its author's mastery of scholarship while repudiating scholarship's sense of superiority. Throughout it pokes fun at pomposity and "high-borne words," identifying eloquence with breeding (Armado is a "refined traveller of Spain" and says he is "a gentleman" (1.1.170, 161, 226)). But if Shakespeare skewers pompous speech – "Great deputy, the welkin's viceregent" (1.1.213) – he also lays claim to eloquence. He plays a double game, making fun of gentle eloquence but securing the very thing he exposes as ultimately unimportant or pretentious.

Throughout, characters comment on language in social terms. Mote, making fun of Armado's addiction to verbal decorum – the love of the "congruent epitheton" (1.2.12) – notes that "one more than two" is called by "the base vulgar . . . three" (1.2.44–5). Inkhornisms ("tender juvenal" (1.2.7)) abound. The Princess says Boyet's flattery is like the "base sale of chapmen's tongues" (1.2.16). Everywhere the play invokes sociolinguistic distinctions, in the process reminding us how capacious the Elizabethan vocabulary for stratification was. The play is obsessed with rank, yet sends up that obsession. Armado, who falls for "a base wench" (1.2.54), won't answer Mote's question "How many is one, thrice told," replying: "I am ill at reckoning; it fitteth the spirit of a tapster" (1.2.37–8).

Shakespeare's lexicon of class needs critical attention. Consider the word "fair." When Maria tells Olivia "there is . . . a young gentleman much desires to speak with you . . . a fair young man, and well attended," there is an association between fairness and gentility (1.5.85–9). Of course "fair" means "beautiful," but it is not class-neutral. In *Love's Labour's Lost* Biron's "fair tongue" tells jokes in "apt and gracious words" (2.1.72–3); the word signifies courtly grace. In this scene of high elegance, in which the Princess and her ladies first meet the King and his lords, "fair" is a motif, used sixteen times in the space of 258 lines; "grace" (or variants) appears eight times, and the words "gentle" and "virtue" feature. All these words express nobility. One may suppose mastery of "noble" scenes like this, full of such high language, lent a certain social prestige to Shakespeare and his colleagues. "Fair" might, of course, mean simply "beautiful" in 2.4 of *The Merchant of Venice*, where it is applied to Jessica four times, the first usage alluding to the whiteness of her hand (2.4.12–14). Yet Lorenzo describes her as "gentle" twice in this scene, which is, after all, part of Shakespeare's attempt to ennoble Jessica and separate her from her father's taint. (Even Jessica's white hand is, of course, a class marker – contrast the shepherdess Phoebe's "leathern hand . . . a housewife's hand" in *As You Like It* (4.3.24, 27).) "Fair" is an instance of the way Shakespeare's diction is saturated with class significance.

In his very funny book *Class*, Paul Fussell (1983) postulates a "class X" – a bohemian, intellectual class outside normal status hierarchies. Shakespeare's representation of class needs to be understood as, among other things, a mode of self-presentation, a way of positioning his own identity as both outside (or free of) and inside the usual status hierarchy. Shakespeare knew he was no Sidney. Yet he aspired to social distinction and claimed it when and how he could. As a result his plays, including the comedies, are deeply preoccupied with rank. They reveal a writer often treating high and low social spheres as it were from outside. The ironic treatment of social class is part of their many-sided, complex perspective on the social scene. *The Merry Wives of Windsor* sends up *both* the pretensions of a neo-feudal aristocracy (Pistol's "O base Hungarian wight, wilt thou the spigot wield?" (1.3.18)) as well as the simplicity of the populace (Mistress Quickly's "allicholy" for "melancholy" (1.4.134)). And because Shakespeare's plays had to please a socially diverse audience, they articulated as many perspectives on class as that audience contained. If class doesn't matter to Shakespeare's critics, it did matter to him.

Note

1 Burial entry in parish records of Holy Trinity Church, Stratford-upon-Avon; see *The Riverside Shakespeare*, p. 1952.

References and Further Reading

Note: Shakespeare quotations are from *The Norton Shakespeare*, ed. S. Greenblatt, W. Cohen, J. E. Howard, and K. E. Maus (New York: Norton, 1997); unless otherwise indicated, all quotations from contemporary documents concerning Shakespeare are also from this volume (spelling modernized).

Barton, A. (1997). Introduction to *The Two Gentlemen of Verona* in *The Riverside Shakespeare*, 2nd edn. Boston: Houghton Mifflin.
Berry, R. (1988). *Shakespeare and Social Class*. Atlantic Highlands, NJ: Humanities Press International.
Bristol, M. D. (1985). *Carnival and Theater: Plebeian Culture and the Structure of Authority in Renaissance England*. New York: Methuen/Routledge.
Cockburn, A. (1976). Introduction to P. G. Wodehouse, *The Code of the Woosters*. Mattituck, NY: Rivercity Press.
Cohen, W. (1985). *Drama of a Nation: Public Theater in Renaissance England and Spain*. Ithaca, NY: Cornell University Press.
Cook, A. J. (1997). Audiences: Investigation, Interpretation, Invention. In J. D. Cox and D. S. Kastan (eds.) *A New History of Early English Drama*. New York: Columbia University Press.
Cressy, D. (1976). Describing the Social Order of Elizabethan and Stuart England. *Literature and History*, 3, 29–45.
Danby, J. (1952). *Poets on Fortune's Hill: Studies in Sidney, Shakespeare, Beaumont and Fletcher*. London: Faber and Faber.
Dryden, J. (1900) [1668]. *An Essay of Dramatic Poesy* in vol. 1 of *Essays of John Dryden*, ed. W. P. Ker. Oxford: Oxford University Press.
Duncan-Jones, K. (2001). *Ungentle Shakespeare: Scenes From His Life*. London: Arden Shakespeare.
Empson, W. (1966). *Some Versions of Pastoral*. Harmondsworth: Penguin Books.
Erickson, P. (1987). The Order of the Garter, the Cult of Elizabeth, and Class–Gender Tension in *The Merry Wives of Windsor*. In J. E. Howard and M. F. O'Connor (eds.) *Shakespeare Reproduced: The Text in History and Ideology*. New York: Methuen.

French, H. R. (2000). The Search for the "Middle Sort of People" in England, 1600–1800. *Historical Journal*, 43, 1, 277–95.

Fussell, P. (1983). *Class: A Guide Through the American Status Systems*. New York: Summit.

Holbrook, P. (1994). *Literature and Degree in Renaissance England: Nashe, Bourgeois Tragedy, Shakespeare*. Newark: University of Delaware Press.

Honan, P. (1998). *Shakespeare: A Life*. Oxford: Oxford University Press.

Hunter, G. K. (1997). *English Drama, 1586–1642: The Age of Shakespeare*. Oxford: Oxford University Press.

Kastan, D. S. (1993). Is There a Class in this (Shakespearean) Text? *Renaissance Drama*, n.s. 24, 101–23.

Moisan, T. (1991) "Knock me here soundly": Comic Misprision and Class Consciousness in Shakespeare. *Shakespeare Quarterly*, 42, 276–91.

Montrose, L. (1983). Of Gentlemen and Shepherds: The Politics of Elizabethan Pastoral Form. *English Literary History*, 50, 415–59.

Nelson, A. H. (1997). The Universities: Early Staging in Cambridge. In J. D. Cox and D. S. Kastan (eds.) *A New History of Early English Drama*. New York: Columbia University Press.

O'Dair, S. (2000). *Class, Critics, and Shakespeare: Bottom Lines on the Culture Wars*. Ann Arbor: University of Michigan Press.

Palliser, D. M. (1983). *The Age of Elizabeth: England Under the Later Tudors, 1547–1603*. London: Longman.

Perkin, H. (1969). *The Origins of Modern English Society: 1770–1880*. London: Routledge and Kegan Paul.

Reay, B. (1997). The Cultures of the People in Early Modern England. *Journal of British Studies*, 36, 4, 467–73.

Ryan, K. (1989). *Shakespeare*, 2nd edn. New York: Harvester.

Saunders, J. W. (1951). The Stigma of Print: A Note on the Social Bases of Tudor Poetry. *Essays in Criticism*, 1, 139–64.

Shakespeare, W. (1997). *The Riverside Shakespeare*, 2nd edn., ed. G. B. Evans and J. J. M. Tobin. Boston, MA: Houghton Mifflin.

Shuger, D. K. (1997). *Habits of Thought in the English Renaissance: Religion, Politics, and the Dominant Culture*. Toronto: University of Toronto Press.

Tillyard, E. M. W. (1943). *The Elizabethan World Picture*. London: Chatto and Windus.

Wells, S. (1997). *Shakespeare: The Poet and His Plays*. Revised edition of *Shakespeare: A Dramatic Life*. London: Methuen.

Wiesner-Hanks, M. (2000). Gender in Early Modern Europe: Introduction to Recent Studies. *The Sixteenth Century Journal*, 31, 1, 3–7.

Wilson, R. (1993). Like the Old Robin Hood: *As You Like It* and the Enclosure Riots. In *Will Power: Essays on Shakespearean Authority*. Detroit, MI: Wayne State University Press.

Wodehouse, P. G. (1946). *Joy in the Morning*. London: Herbert Jenkins.

5

The Social Relations of Shakespeare's Comic Households

Mario DiGangi

Shortly into the opening scene of one of Shakespeare's earliest comedies, an inebriated tinker is made to believe that he is the master of a noble household. The duping of the disorderly Christopher Sly has long been recognized as an apt beginning to a play devoted to the taming of an "uncivil" wife. Yet in its representation of the operations of desire and discipline within and across the boundaries of the domestic, the Induction to *The Taming of the Shrew* also offers a useful point of departure for an analysis of the Shakespearean comic household.[1]

From the start, the Induction associates Sly's disorderliness with his absence from, and perhaps complete lack of, a proper home. Ejected from the tavern (itself probably contiguous with the Hostess's home), Sly makes a "bed" of the ground (Induction, 1.29). Consequently, he falls under the harsh gaze of his social opposite: an aristocratic householder who competently manages his servants and possessions – the hounds that he "esteem[s]" and charges his huntsmen to "tender well," "sup . . . well," and "look unto" (23, 12, 24).[2] In a stark emblem of social hierarchy, the commanding Lord stands above the prostrate beggar, moralizing about his inferior's beastly loss of self-mastery: "O monstrous beast! How like a swine he lies" (30). By "practis[ing]" on Sly, thereby amusing himself and punishing an idle drunk, the Lord actively expresses his social superiority (32). The opening scene of *The Taming of the Shrew* thus appears to unfold as an illustration of early modern theories of household government: the noble householder maintains his status through judicious management of servants and possessions; the "simple peasant," having lost control over his own person and identity, is physically removed to the Lord's household as if a servant or possession (131).

Nonetheless, the overt theatricality of the Lord's disciplinary methods produces results that run counter to prescriptive theories of household management. Through his practice against Sly, the Lord introduces the deceptive schemes – or "counterfeit supposes" – that tend to violate patriarchal order in the play proper (5.1.99). For example, by exchanging clothes with Tranio, Lucentio can infiltrate Baptista's household, woo Bianca, and ultimately arrange a clandestine marriage, hence usurping Baptista's authority. The Lord's scheme actually demystifies the "natural" foundation of his own social and moral authority. If the Induction represents gender not as a natural, innate quality but a performative effect – recruited to play Sly's wife, the page Bartholomew mimes the conventional "grace, / Voice, gait, and action of a gentlewoman" (Induction, 1.127–8) – it likewise reveals that social status depends on the theatrical deployment of material properties. Sly's social transformation requires that he be invested with the signs of the Lord's aristocratic privilege:

> What think you: if he were conveyed to bed,
> Wrapped in sweet clothes, rings put upon his fingers,
> A most delicious banquet by his bed,
> And brave attendants near him when he wakes –
> Would not the beggar then forget himself? (33–7)

Ironically, the Lord's use of such properties to make Sly "forget himself" would appear to exacerbate the alcohol-induced self-forgetfulness against which he has already inveighed. Of course, the humor of the trick comes from Sly's *inability* to forget himself; interpellated as a Lord, he still responds as a beggar. Nonetheless, the Induction's emphasis on the performance of high rank, especially through the consumption of luxury goods and cultural artifacts like Ovid, suggests that aristocratic power is sustained by a process of acculturation – learned civility – rather than by "blood" or innate honor.[3]

The transformative power of theatricality thus works not only to dupe Sly but also to distract the Lord from maintaining the ideologically naturalized household order that displays his elite status. Turning his attention from the good husbandry of domestic management to the management of a "pastime passing excellent, / If it be husbanded with modesty," the Lord paradoxically indulges immodest fantasies of seeing his page "husbanded" by Sly: "I long to hear him call the drunkard husband" (Induction, 1.63–4, 129). Perhaps most significantly, in addressing Sly the Lord appears to be addressing his mirror-image rather than his social opposite:

> Dost thou Love hawking? Thou hast hawks will soar
> Above the morning lark. Or wilt thou hunt,
> Thy hounds shall make the welkin answer them
> And fetch shrill echoes from the hollow earth.
> (Induction, 2.41–4)

Ultimately, the success of the Lord's practice requires not only that the beggar believe that he is a propertied lord, but also that the Lord project onto the beggar his own passions, habits, and signs of rank. Hence the Lord's homoerotic interest in his cross-dressed page's impersonation of femininity produces erotic desire in Sly, who urges his reluctant "wife" to come to bed. Turning his household into a theatre of desire, the Lord, not Sly, we might justly suspect, has come to "forget himself" (Induction, 1.42). The Induction intimates that theatricality not only bolsters the status of the propertied household through the performance and display of rank; it also threatens to disrupt or render unstable the hierarchical structure of the household through the mutation of supposedly fixed social identities and roles.

Sly's confused equation of the traveling players' "comonty" with "household stuff" (Induction, 2.132, 134) inadvertently articulates the link between comedy and domestic life that the Induction stages and that is a staple of Renaissance genre theory (Orlin 1994: 75; Comensoli 1996: 142). Nevertheless, some of the most significant scholarship on domesticity in early modern drama has focused not on comedy but on domestic tragedy. Frances Dolan, Lena Cowen Orlin, and Viviana Comensoli, among others, have examined the contradictions and tensions of domestic hierarchy in plays like *Arden of Faversham* and Heywood's *A Woman Killed with Kindness*. Analyzing the household's ideological function as a model for political order, they have fruitfully demonstrated the complex interarticulation of the public and private realms in early modern England. Domestic tragedies undoubtedly give us access to the stress points of everyday household functioning. Yet comedies also explore the frustrations, prohibitions, and rivalries – as well as the pleasures, liberties, and alliances – afforded by domestic experience. Renaissance domestic comedy differs from domestic tragedy not so much in kind as in degree; namely, in the degree to which the passions and conflicts that cause destruction in tragedy can be successfully dispelled or contained by the harmonious gestures attending the formation of new households in the comic denouement.

Apart from questions of genre, a further consideration in interpreting domestic comedy involves the theatrical transformation of everyday discourses and practices. On the one hand, Shakespeare draws upon the familiar structures, ideologies, and practices that inform the theoretical discourses as well as the lived experiences of early modern domesticity: patriarchal social organization; differentiated duties and responsibilities according to gender, age, rank, and occupation; surveillance and management of property; the importance of sexual and social credit; the expectation of hospitality and civility; the recognition of the social order's dependence upon private discipline. On the other hand, Shakespearean comedies refract the theoretical discourses and lived experiences of the household in multiple, overdetermined ways.

In what follows I aim to provide an historical analysis of Shakespeare's comic households that pays close attention to the dramatic and ideological shaping of cultural materials in specific plays. My argument will proceed in three distinct but interrelated parts, each concentrating primarily on a pair of plays and exploring key issues that have occupied the relevant scholarship – mainly feminist, materialist, and queer scholarship – in those areas. First, I will examine Shakespeare's representation of the social and economic exchanges of courtship that create new households. Assertions of patriarchal power in *A Midsummer Night's Dream* and *The Taming of the Shrew*, I will argue, expose the gaps and inconsistencies in gender ideologies that open space for resistance to that power. Next, I will consider the struggle for financial, sexual, and political control over the household in *The Comedy of Errors* and *The Merry Wives of Windsor*. These plays show how conflicts over the proper boundaries of spousal authority impact relationships between male householders as well as between husbands and wives. A look at the practices of hospitality and service in the early modern household, as depicted in *Much Ado About Nothing* and *Twelfth Night*, will conclude my discussion. In these later comedies the noble household remains open to public surveillance (in the form of guests) even as it fosters secret alliances through the intimacy of servants with their masters. The uneasy accommodation of guests and servants within the domestic space reveals at once the early modern householder's deepest aspirations – a reputation for civility, generosity, and effective domestic government – and deepest fears – the public exposure of private disorder, the proliferation of illicit sexual practices, the treachery of unruly subordinates.

Household Formation and the Exchanges of Courtship

As a social and economic rite of passage, marriage bestowed the responsibilities and privileges of adulthood. Shakespeare's comedies dramatize the obstacle-strewn process by which young women transfer allegiance from paternal households to conjugal households and by which young men advance from domestic subordinates to householders. For instance, at the beginning of *As You Like It* Orlando complains that Oliver, his older brother and household head, refuses to educate him like a gentleman; in a cultural fantasy of social advancement, Orlando overcomes the strictures of primogeniture, establishing his own household as son-in-law of the restored Duke.[4] Through this process, domestic patriarchalism is subjected to negotiation and contestation, as older and younger brothers contend with the "ideological contradiction between spiritual fraternity and political patriarchy," and as Rosalind and Orlando engage in a courtship that "revolves around the issue of mastery in the shifting social relationship between the sexes" (Montrose 1995: 53, 61). Focusing on the shifting relations of courtship, Carol Thomas Neely argues that in Shakespeare's comedies "the most important impediments to comic fulfillment lie within the couple themselves," and not, as is often asserted, with "blocking figures" like oppressive fathers (Neely 1985: 26). Other feminists likewise challenge the notion of patriarchal hegemony. Marianne Novy posits that Shakespeare's depictions of gender relations "keep elements of both patriarchy and mutuality in suspension" (Novy 1984: 6); Karen Newman asserts that in early modern England patriarchalism was not a "given" but "a dominant trope through which social relations were perceived, a strategy whereby power was embodied and institutionalized" (Newman 1991: 17–18). In Shakespearean comedy, women's agency in choosing a marriage partner is one area in which the "tropes" of patriarchal authority are most vigorously articulated and resisted.

A contest over patriarchal power initiates the action of *A Midsummer Night's Dream*. Conventional wisdom might dictate that "they which are called fathers are called by the name of God, to warn them that they are in stead of GOD to their children," but Theseus' admonition to Hermia – "To you your father should be as a god" (1.1.47) – exposes the analogy between father and god as an ideological gambit that sometimes fails to naturalize patriarchal power. Hermia's resistance of her father's right to choose her husband shows that, when ideological interpellation fails, the practical application of this axiom depends upon coercion.[5] In fact, Egeus' absolute, seemingly arbitrary, power to prefer Demetrius over Lysander violates the early modern ideal of "benevolent patriarchy, not authoritarian government" (Amussen 1988: 39; also Ezell 1987: 59–61).

Even as he complains of Hermia's disobedience, Egeus paradoxically implies that she does not act on her own will, having been "bewitched" by Lysander (1.1.27). In *Othello* Brabantio asserts that only literal bewitchment could incite his daughter to marry a black man. There is nothing overtly objectionable about the prosaic Lysander, who, in showering Hermia with "rings, gauds, conceits, / Knacks, trifles, nosegays, sweetmeats" (1.1.33–4), uses the most conventional witchcraft. Nonetheless, by inflating Lysander's powers of seduction, Egeus diminishes his shame at Hermia's refusal to function as a "gift" in the male–male social and economic exchanges of betrothal (Findlay 1999: 135). Lysander's generosity, Egeus alleges, deviously facilitates his theft of household property and propriety: "With cunning hast thou filched my daughter's heart, / Turned her obedience which is due to me / To stubborn harshness" (1.1.36–8). Describing Lysander's gifts as "messengers of strong prevailment" (1.1.35), Egeus protests that he has been bypassed, hence robbed, in the transfer of properties and promises between his daughter and her suitor.

Egeus has been denied the conventional right of parents to manage the reconfiguration of the patriarchal household that betrothal entails, a right fully dramatized in *The Taming of the Shrew*. Before courting Katherine, Petruccio requires a single piece of information from Hortensio: "Tell me her father's name and 'tis enough" (1.2.90). Baptista's name is "enough," that is, to situate Katherine within a male homosocial network – "I know her father, though I know not her, / And he knew my deceased father well" (1.2.97–8). Through this network Petruccio can offer himself to Baptista as the known heir, and improver, of a gentleman's land and reputation:

> You knew my father well, and in him me,
> Left solely heir to all his lands and goods,
> Which I have bettered rather than decreased.
> Then tell me, if I get your daughter's love,
> What dowry shall I have with her to wife? (2.1.114–18)

Whether or not Petruccio actually acquires Katherine's "love" remains a subject of debate. At the very least, Katherine accuses Baptista of abdicating his duty to find her a suitable mate: "You have showed a tender fatherly regard, / To wish me wed to one half-lunatic" (2.1.278–9). Tellingly, Baptista considers the party at risk in the marriage to be not Katherine but himself: "Faith, gentlemen, now I play a merchant's part, / And venture madly on a desperate mart" (2.1.318–19). Tranio responds: " 'Twas a commodity lay fretting by you. / 'Twill bring you gain, or perish on the seas" (2.1.320–1). Imagining Katherine as a drowned commodity, Tranio troubles Baptista's commercial metaphor of marriage. Baptista softens the implication that he has hazarded Katherine's welfare for his own profit by professing that the only "gain" he seeks is "quiet in the match" (2.1.322). Nevertheless, the possibility of the alternative outcome – that Katherine might "perish on the seas" of her tempestuous marriage – is neither addressed nor dispelled. Instead, Baptista immediately reaps the profit of Katherine's "venture" by offering his more marketable daughter, who now becomes available, to the suitor with the most wealth. Unlike Lysander, Bianca's suitors pledge their property and wealth for her dower; moreover, they send to Baptista's house not love tokens but tutors and books as "messengers" of their concern for her proper education.

Although Katherine bears the stigma of shrewishness, Hermia transgresses further than she by removing herself altogether from the circuit of exchange between father and suitor. To recover the theft of Hermia's heart, Egeus asserts his absolute pro-prietary right to "dispose of" her body either to the man of his choice or to death (1.1.42). Theseus' support of Egeus reveals how much is at stake in Hermia's counter-assertion of self-sovereignty. As is typical of Shakespeare's comic households, there is no mother here to intervene on Hermia's behalf against the severity of male authority.[6] More remarkable is Theseus' erasure of the maternal role in conception:

> What say you, Hermia? Be advised, fair maid.
> To you your father should be as a god,
> One that composed your beauties, yea, and one
> To whom you are but as a form in wax,
> By him imprinted, and within his power
> To leave the figure or disfigure it. (1.1.46–51)

The Aristotelian science behind this claim holds that in procreation the male acts as the active, imprinting spirit and the female as the passive, imprinted form; yet by displacing the image of the "form in wax" from mother to daughter, Theseus com-pletely elides the mother's role in "compos[ing]" the child. This elision of female agency in the birth of his female child bolsters Egeus' claim to have sole power to "figure or disfigure" Hermia's adult body as well.

Against the power of such masculinist ideology, Hermia's assertion of autonomy is all the more shocking. Instructed that she must marry Demetrius, be executed, or live cloistered like a rose "withering on the virgin thorn" (1.1.77), Hermia translates this enforced decision into an exertion of self-mastery:

> So will I grow, so live, so die, my lord,
> Ere I will yield my virgin patent up
> Unto his lordship whose unwishèd yoke
> My soul consents not to give sovereignty. (1.1.79–82)

Evoking the notion of consent, Shakespeare engages on Hermia's behalf the contem-porary debate over spousal choice. In an analysis of early modern discourses about marriage, Ann Jennalie Cook finds that the most widely accepted "ideological mandate" was the father's duty to find an appropriate mate for his child (Cook 1991: 69–70). Although they admit variations, the formal advice books and sermons Cook examines agree on the importance of parental approval. Some even support Egeus' equation of children with property: "For the childe (in respect of the body) is part of the parents goods."[7] On the other hand, commentators acknowledge the importance of affection between partners and describe the misery of forced marriages (ibid: 71–2). George Whetstone's *An Heptameron of Civil Discourses* (1582) attempts to balance the claims of parents and children, to temper the "satisfaction of fancy," which is "the source of joy in marriage," with the rational "foresight" of the parents in determining a socially appropriate partner. A couple joined without "free choice" and mutual desire will not be happy; neither will a marriage based solely on the couple's "fancy" thrive (quoted in McDonald 2001: 293). The marriage with the greatest chance of success combined the child's submission to the parents' judgment with the parents' acknowledgment of the child's emotional needs.

Hermia challenges the orthodox Protestant discourse on marriage not only by denying her father's "foresight" in approving a partner, but also by rejecting Theseus' punitive construction of life-long virginity as a state equivalent to death. His authority symbolized by his martial and marital power over his conquered Amazon queen, Theseus stigmatizes life in an all-female household as "barren": Hermia will be "mewed" in a dark cloister, fruitlessly "[c]hanting faint hymns to the cold fruitless moon" (1.1.72, 71, 73). That Hermia could prefer such an anemic existence to married life makes available the subversive knowledge that the institution of marriage, not simply enforced marriage, places an "unwishèd yoke" upon women (1.1.81). Of course, what Hermia demands is not the right to remain a virgin but the right to choose the husband to whom she will grant "sovereignty" over her body (1.1.82). Nonetheless, her resistance to the patriarchal control of her "virgin patent" evokes the threat of what Theodora Jankowski has called "queer virginity." Jankowski describes as queer virgins women like Hermia who "challenge the necessity of patriarchally mandated marriage" or like *Measure for Measure*'s Isabella who repudiate marriage altogether, thus "maintain[ing] their personal autonomy and resist[ing] control by men" (Jankowski 2000: 193).

As Jankowski's concept of the "queer virgin" implies, marriage represents a loss as well as an achievement for those women who have resisted the cultural mandates of femininity. Yet instead of diminishing the sense of that loss in an attempt to naturalize the teleology of marriage and reproductive sexuality, *A Midsummer Night's Dream* calls it to our attention. In a nuanced reading of domestic conflict in the play, Louis Montrose deconstructs patriarchy's pretenses to hegemonic control over gender and erotic relations. Showing the repressive mechanisms of patriarchy to be "tentative, partial, or flawed," Montrose argues that "patriarchal norms are compensatory for men's perceptions that they are vulnerable to the powers of women" (Montrose 1996: 129, 151). For instance, the play repeatedly "enacts a masculine disruption of an intimate bond between women" (ibid: 137): Theseus' abduction of Hippolyta from the Amazons; Oberon's theft of the votress's son from Titania; and the destructive rivalry between Hermia and Helena over Lysander and Demetrius. If the formation of new conjugal households sunders the friendship of Hermia and Helena and renders them silent throughout the last scene of the play, it solders the friendship of Demetrius and Lysander and reconciles them to Theseus. Whether such a state of affairs is regarded as a triumph of the natural order or of masculine political will largely depends on the degree of benevolence one attributes to the social function of the early modern household and the ideological function of comedy in representing its formation.

Household Economy and Domestic Authority

Feminist critics in particular have long debated the social and ideological implications of household discipline in *The Taming of the Shrew*. Recently, Frances Dolan has intervened in this debate by emphasizing the importance of status relations as well as gender relations in the early modern household. Dolan examines contemporary representations of wives not only as objects of physical discipline, but also as authorized disciplinarians of subordinates such as children and servants. That Katherine can be "simultaneously tamed and domineering" reflects the fundamental contradictions of Renaissance conjugal theory: the wife was the inferior member of a nonetheless "mutual" and spiritually egalitarian conjugal partnership; the household, while theoretically governed by the husband, was in actuality "the arena in which [women] could most readily and legitimately exercise authority" (Dolan 1999: 209–10).[8] As Louis Montrose has observed regarding William Gouge's popular tract *Of Domestical Duties* (1622), "It is the intermittent presence of such reciprocal, companionate, and egalitarian elements that produces recurrent moments of rhetorical and ideological strain within Gouge's predominantly hierarchical discourse" (Montrose 1996: 116–17). In *The Taming of the Shrew*, although Petruccio disciplines Katherine, she shares his prerogative of physically disciplining domestic subordinates: her younger sister, her music teacher (Litio/Hortensio), and her husband's servant Grumio.[9] As part of his taming program. Petruccio teaches Katherine not to be less violent, but "how to use violence to assert dominance in more socially acceptable ways" – that is, to demonstrate her privileges as a woman of gentle status (Dolan 1999: 218).

Petruccio's complementary goal of teaching his wife how properly to display her economic privileges has been productively analyzed by Natasha Korda. According to Korda, by refusing to indulge Katherine's desires for fashionable apparel, Petruccio harnesses her appetite for status objects (or "cates") at the same time that he teaches her how to deploy such objects publicly as symbolic capital reflecting his status and wealth (Korda 1996: 127). Petruccio aims to train Katherine for "the housewife's managerial role as a consumer and caretaker of household cates" (ibid: 129). Early modern marriage manuals typically granted wives authority over everyday household matters regarded as too "trivial" to distract husbands from greater public responsibilities. As Susan Amussen explains, this "theory of complementary abilities and duties helped many writers of household manuals gloss over the contradiction between a wife's responsibility for the household and her subordination to her husband, but it did not completely resolve it" (Amussen 1988: 44). In *The Taming of the Shrew* Katherine's authority in domestic affairs is likewise glossed over in her final speech, which evokes the political analogy of the husband's sovereignty over the wife to "devalu[e] her role in the household economy" (Korda 1996: 130). Nonetheless, the cultural logic of economic exchange subjects Petruccio as well as Katherine to the symbolic power of commodities – the obligation to acquire, manage, and display them as signs of gentle status.

Whereas Petruccio asserts firm control over Katherine's exercise of both disciplinary and economic agency in the household, much of the humor (and violence) of *The Comedy of Errors* involves a husband's humiliating subjection to his wife's domestic authority. Significantly, the conflict between Antipholus of Ephesus and his wife Adriana arises from the conventional gendering of space in early modern England: the wife occupies the "private" household, and the husband, whose "business still lies out o' door," the public market (2.1.11). When Antipholus fails to come home for dinner, Adriana complains of the masculine "liberty" that allows him to disregard her domestic management (2.1.10). Drawing upon the same ideological resources as Katherine's submissive oration in *The Taming of the Shrew*, Adriana's sister Luciana defends male sovereignty over women. Yet *The Comedy of Errors* shatters Katherine's unbroken, rhetorically coherent, discourse into a dialogue among competing perspectives on domestic authority. As Adriana wryly observes, her unmarried sister remains unaffected by the wifely subservience and sufferance that she advocates: "This servitude makes you to keep unwed" (2.1.26). Antipholus' complaint about his wife's "shrewish" behavior is no less self-serving than Luciana's unsympathetic assessment of her sister's fretting (3.1.2). Unlike Katherine, Adriana is not generally reputed to be a shrew; rather, Antipholus construes her anger as shrewish when he himself provokes it by his neglect and resort to a courtesan. Whereas Katherine fumes that Petruccio keeps her "starved for meat" (4.3.9), Adriana laments that she remains "at home starve[d] for a merry look" (2.1.86). Again, Luciana attributes marital discord not to Antipholus' disregard but to Adriana's "self-harming jealousy" (2.1.101), and again the audience is left to evaluate these competing accounts of household unrest.

The conflict heightens when Adriana, mistaking Antipholus of Syracuse for her husband, shuts the latter out of the house. Having invited the goldsmith Angelo and the merchant Balthasar home for dinner, Antipholus of Ephesus finds his entry refused and his identity denied: "Your wife, sir knave? Go, get you from the door" (3.1.64–5). Had Adriana deliberately locked her husband out to punish him for his "liberty," he might have justifiably blamed the ensuing chaos on her "shrewish" behavior. Instead, Adriana tries to reform the man she mistakes for her husband, gently appealing to their conjugal bond and admitting her dependence on him: "Thou art an elm, my husband; I a vine, / Whose weakness, married to thy stronger state, / Makes me with thy strength to communicate" (2.2.174–6). Whereas Antipholus of Syracuse is so welcomed by Adriana, Antipholus of Ephesus does not gain access to his own house until Adriana, having found him to be mad, arranges for his incarceration there. As he bitterly recounts, "They fell upon me, bound me, bore me thence, / And in a dark and dankish vault at home / There left me and my man, both bound together" (5.1.247–9). Antipholus' imprisonment is particularly mortifying not only because it denies him the liberty previously identified as the sign of male supremacy, but also because it reverses his earlier humiliation in being locked out of the house by his wife.

At stake in Antipholus' loss of domestic control is his credit as a male householder. Lorna Hutson has shown that the late sixteenth-century concept of "good husbandry" (*oikonomia*) implied the householder's ability to use persuasive narratives and textual negotiations to "manage people and situations" (Hutson 1994: 87). Thus in Terentian comedies like *The Comedy of Errors*, "the deliberate introduction of error or ambiguity or uncertainty into discursive exchange is read, not as irresponsible credit fraud with intention to deceive, but as the masculine exercise of prudence" (ibid: 201). But if effective husbandry depends on the opportunistic production of persuasive discourse, such persuasive techniques might also be used to seduce (other men's) women, who are "naturally" prone to err. Consequently, male husbandry gets identified with the policing of female sexuality.

When Adriana bars Antipholus from his house, the mere impression of her infidelity threatens to destroy his "very reverend reputation" as a citizen "of credit infinite, highly beloved, / Second to none that lives here in the city" (5.1.5–7). To avoid being labeled a cuckold, Antipholus must carefully avoid behaving as if adultery were a plausible explanation of his wife's strange actions. Balthasar warns Antipholus that to reassert his domestic mastery by breaking down the door would only encourage curious neighbors to "discover" the sexual disorder hidden inside:

> Herein you war against your reputation,
> And draw within the compass of suspect
> Th' unviolated honour of your wife.
> . . .
> If by strong hand you offer to break in
> Now in the stirring passage of the day,
> A vulgar comment will be made of it,
> And that supposèd by the common rout
> Against your yet ungallèd estimation,
> That may with foul intrusion enter in
> And dwell upon your grave when you are dead.
> For slander lives upon succession,
> For ever housed where once it gets possession. (3.1.87–9, 99–107)

As Angelo and Balthasar know, good estimation or "credit" – a reputation for honesty, solvency, and the maintenance of domestic order – was crucial to the householder's status in the community (Amussen 1988: 152–5). Describing slander as a "foul intrusion" that will "dwell" forever "housed where once it gets possession," Balthasar intimates that Antipholus' violent intrusion into his own house would essentially amount to self-slander. Whether or not he trusts his wife, Antipholus must publicly display his credit in her chastity in order to retain his own credit as an effective husband.

Yet Balthasar's reasonable counsel throws Antipholus into a dilemma, for by surrendering his household to his wife's control in order to avoid sexual slander, his only recourse against her increasingly apparent usurpation of domestic authority is to slander her himself. The domestic tragedy *Arden of Faversham* (1592), in which Alice

Arden and her lover plot to assassinate her husband, stages an extreme version of the kind of conspiracy Antipholus comes to fear from Adriana and "her confederates" (4.1.17; Dolan 1994: 59–60). Following his arrest, Antipholus sends Dromio of Syracuse home with a key, instructing him to alert Adriana that "in the desk / That's covered o'er with Turkish tapestry / There is a purse of ducats" (4.1.103–5). Apparently, this key opens either a locked desk or a private study: "essentially a strongbox writ large" to which the householder alone had access and which thereby "invested his own isolation with a derivative prestige" (Orlin 1994: 183, 186).[10] When the other Dromio returns sans purse, Antipholus concludes that his wife and her co-conspirators have indeed usurped his position:

> You minion, you, are these your customers?
> Did this companion with the saffron face
> Revel and feast it at my house today,
> Whilst upon me the guilty doors were shut,
> And I denied to enter in my house? (4.4.55–9)

If Adriana, unlike Alice Arden, does not intend to murder her husband, she nonetheless seems bent on destroying his reputation: "Dissembling harlot, thou art false in all, / And art confederate with a damnèd pack / To make a loathsome abject scorn of me" (4.4.96–8). Ironically, by publicly denouncing his wife as a harlot, Antipholus makes himself an abject scorn – and hence a victim of the "self-harming jealousy" about which Luciana had previously warned Adriana (2.1.101).

Near the end of the play, Adriana receives a lecture on domestic politics that recalls Katherine's closing speech in *The Taming of the Shrew*. Reprimanding Adriana for disturbing her husband "in food, in sport, and life-preserving rest," the Abbess concludes that "[her] jealous fits / Hath scared [her] husband from the use of wits" (5.1.84, 86–7). Petruccio tames his wife precisely by disrupting her comfort "in food, in sport, and life-preserving rest"; evidently, a wife's deployment of such strategies against her husband can yield only madness. Yet the Abbess's diagnosis of Adriana's responsibility for Antipholus' supposed madness is incorrect, and the play's concluding focus on Egeon's miraculous reunion with his lost wife (the Abbess) and his sons (the Antipholi) leaves the marital conflict unresolved. There is no attempt to mend the rift between husband and wife or to formulate relevant lessons about the jealousy and mistrust that have contributed to their mismanagement of household affairs. It may well be that, as the play turns from satiric urban comedy to the harmonies of romance, the tensions inherent in the gendered division of household authority can no longer be directly acknowledged.

The lack of conjugal reconciliation in *The Comedy of Errors* is all the more striking given the emphasis on reordering a similarly disrupted household in *The Merry Wives of Windsor*. In *The Merry Wives of Windsor* Mistress Ford does not close the door against her husband; rather, she freely opens the door to Falstaff, a would-be seducer. Yet Master Ford's fears of cuckoldry are no less based than Antipholus' in a paranoid interpretation of his wife's exercise of domestic authority as conspiratorial. More than any

other play by Shakespeare, *The Merry Wives of Windsor* displays the household's function as the "dominant space" for Renaissance women, "the place where they spent
most of their lives" and where they exerted the most control (Henderson 1995: 176).
Whereas Adriana unknowingly locks her husband out of the house, the Windsor wives
deliberately manipulate the household for their own ends. It is precisely Mistress
Ford's superior knowledge of and control over domestic matters that elicits Ford's
panic over his reputation as a husband.

As Richard Helgerson and Natasha Korda have recently demonstrated, *The Merry
Wives of Windsor* presents the household as a private, female space embedded within,
yet distinguished from, the public worlds of community and nation. Examining the
strategies by which the wives exert and justify their control over their bodies and
properties, Helgerson argues that Falstaff and Ford are punished for assuming, the
former wishfully and the latter anxiously, that "if a woman chose to open her house,
her buck basket, or her body to an outsider, there was little her husband could do to
prevent her" (Helgerson 1999: 170). Through their skillful management of domestic
space, the women defend their chastity and defeat those men who try to diminish or
appropriate their authority. Nonetheless, Korda emphasizes the price the wives pay
for such domestic autonomy. She reads the play in terms of "the birth of consumer
culture in early modern England," which "turned housewifery among the middling
sort into a task centered on the care, safekeeping, and display of 'household-stuff'"
(Korda 2001: 87). Although the Windsor wives protect their households "by demonstrating their competence as disciplined, yet discreet, domestic supervisors," they
must constantly monitor the vigilance and chastity of their own gazes, thus subjecting themselves to a "disciplinary regime of self-supervision" (ibid: 90, 98). Taken
together, Helgerson and Korda illuminate both the liberating and restricting aspects
of women's domestic control; however, the effect of the wives' authority on the rivalry
between their husbands remains to be explored.

In *The Merry Wives of Windsor* the social relations of the household are fully inscribed
within those of the neighborhood and even the nation.[11] Consequently, the conduct
of household members significantly impacts on the householder's reputation. Warned
of Falstaff's adulterous intentions, Page and Ford each asserts his right to intervene
on his wife's behalf, albeit in antithetical ways. Whereas Page would set his wife upon
Falstaff, Ford would leash in his:

> *Page.* If he should intend this voyage toward my wife, I would turn her loose to him;
> and what he gets more of her than sharp words, let it lie on my head.
> *Ford.* I do not misdoubt my wife, but I would be loath to turn them together. A man
> may be too confident. I would have nothing lie on my head. I cannot be thus satisfied.
> (2.1.160–5)

These divergent responses do not simply indicate the difference between a trusting
and a suspicious personality; rather, they reflect theories of household governance that
pull in contrary directions. On the one hand, early modern household manuals justify
Ford's impulse to curtail his wife's association with Falstaff: "a man may show his

wife and his sword to his friend, but not too far to trust them. For if thereby grow unto him any infamy, let him not blame his wife, but his own negligence," warns Edmund Tilney in 1568 (quoted in Orlin 1994: 166). As Ford admits, he would not have the infamy of cuckoldry "lie on [his] head." On the other hand, manuals like Richard Whitford's *A Work for Householders* (1530) justify Page's refusal to pry into his wife's personal affairs: "A noble heart and high gentle mind will never search of women's matters" (quoted in Orlin 1994: 105). The contest between Falstaff and the wives thus pits Ford against Page as representatives of different approaches to household management.

The desire to humiliate Page significantly motivates Ford's quest to discover the truth of his wife's conduct. Ford regards his neighbor not as less jealous but as less observant than himself – Page is a "secure fool" and "secure ass" who fails to recognize the signs of adultery that Ford has witnessed between his wife and Falstaff: "She was in his company at Page's house, and what they made there I know not" (2.1.202, 2.2.264, 2.1.203–4). Anticipating the ruin of his sexual, financial, and social credit – "My bed shall be abused, my coffers ransacked, my reputation gnawn at" (2.2.257–8) – Ford attempts to displace his imminent shame onto his rival: "I will prevent this, detect my wife, be revenged on Falstaff, and laugh at Page" (2.2.271–2). When he discovers Mistress Page with Falstaff's page, moreover, Ford blames Page's lax domestic government for his own wife's rebellion:

> Has Page any brains? Hath he any eyes? Hath he any thinking? Sure they sleep; he hath no use of them . . . He pieces out his wife's inclination; he gives her folly motion and advantage. And now she's going to my wife, and Falstaff's boy with her . . . Good plots – they are laid; and our revolted wives share damnation together. Well, I will take him; then torture my wife, pluck the borrowed veil of modesty from the so-seeming Mistress Page, divulge Page himself for a secure and willful Actaeon, and to these violent proceedings all my neighbors shall cry aim. (3.2.25–6, 28–30, 32–7)

By exposing the unruliness of the Page household, Ford aims not only to distinguish himself from his neighbors but also to earn general acclaim for uncovering a threat to the community: "I shall be rather praised for this than mocked" (3.2.39–40).

Ford imagines social reputation as a zero-sum game in which one man's acclaim requires another's disgrace. Hence he guarantees his neighbors the "sport" of ridicule if they will accompany him home as witnesses to his wife's infidelity (3.2.67). If Falstaff indeed lurks in his home, "I will show you a monster" he promises (3.2.67–8). Alternatively, "If I suspect without cause, why then, make sport at me; then let me be your jest – I deserve it" (3.3.125–7). The resourceful wives use their "merry" scheming to enjoy the sport of ridiculing Falstaff with the buck basket, but Ford's flawed scheming as Master Brooke only betrays himself to general ridicule:

> *Page.* Fie, fie, Master Ford, are you not ashamed? What spirit, what devil suggests this imagination? I would not ha' your distemper in this kind for the wealth of Windsor Castle.
> *Ford.* 'Tis my fault, Master Page. I suffer for it.

Evans. You suffer for a pad conscience. Your wife is as honest a 'omans as I will desires among five thousand, and five hundred too.
Caius. By gar, I see 'tis an honest woman. (3.3.181–8)

Finding evidence of his wife's honesty instead of a spectacle of illicit sexuality, Ford's neighbors bear witness to his poor domestic management. Because his mistaken account of household disorder actually produces that disorder, Ford himself becomes subject to communal discipline: "But trust me, we'll mock him," promises Page (3.3.194).

Unreformed by his humiliation, Ford concludes that he erred not in suspecting his wife, but in being outwitted by her. He determines not to make the same mistake twice:

> I will now take the lecher. He is at my house. He cannot scape me; 'tis impossible he should. He cannot creep into a halfpenny purse, nor into a pepperbox. But lest the devil that guides him should aid him, I will search impossible places. Though what I am I cannot avoid, yet to be what I would not shall not make me tame. If I have horns to make one mad, let the proverb go with me: I'll be horn-mad. (3.5.124–30)

Ford hales his neighbors home yet again and ransacks the buck basket, corroborating the collective opinion that he is indeed horn-mad, "the proverbial expression for a husband beside himself with jealousy or anger" (Kahn 1981: 130). As Evans implies, Ford in his "horn-mad" jealousy gives himself the cuckold's horns as well by displaying his wife's dirty laundry: " 'Tis unreasonable: will you take up your wife's clothes?" (4.2.122). Frustrated by his failure to discover Falstaff underneath women's clothes, Ford redirects his anger against the witch of Brainford – Falstaff underneath women's clothes. Ford's powers of observation have been so diminished through an irrational fear of female conspiracy that, in his furious determination to find Falstaff even were he concealed in a "halfpenny purse" or "pepperbox," he fails to penetrate the rather obvious ruse right before his eyes. In contrast, by judiciously deploying the resources of the household to restore social and moral propriety, the wives demonstrate that they are the most perceptive, and most effective, managers of their bodies and properties.

Nonetheless, to demonstrate their chastity truly, the wives' household management must ultimately serve their husbands' interests. The wives include their husbands in the final, public, humiliation of Falstaff, thereby acknowledging their function as custodians over the domestic order that maintains their husbands' social credit. The maintenance of citizen honor in *The Merry Wives of Windsor* requires that Falstaff's breach of domestic integrity be publicly healed. In recognition of her virtue and his fault, Ford ultimately relinquishes to his wife the domestic autonomy she has already enjoyed:

> Pardon me, wife. Henceforth do what thou wilt.
> I rather will suspect the sun with cold
> Than thee with wantonness. Now doth thy honour stand,

> In him that was of late an heretic,
> As firm as faith. (4.4.5–9)

Admonishing Ford not to be "as extreme in submission / As in offence" (4.4.10–11), Page recognizes the compromised position of the excessively jealous husband, who exposes himself to public ridicule as well as private humiliation. Page implies that a husband's trust in his wife's chastity should never become a matter of religious faith, for household order ultimately depends not upon an essentialized notion of honor, but rather on the husband's continual balancing of the community's demand for accountability with the householder's prerogative of domestic sovereignty.

The Open Household: Hospitality and Service

The citizen households in *The Merry Wives of Windsor* are remarkably open to various outsiders: guests from court; friends and neighbors; Welsh and French residents of Windsor; a country magistrate and his nephew; servants from other households. This openness reflects the "communal surveillance" of the early modern household, as well as the practices of hospitality through which the householder could "dramatize his generosity, and thereby reveal his hegemony" (Orlin 1994: 7; Heal 1990: 6). On the social advantage that could accrue to a generous host, Felicity Heal (ibid) cites Henry Wotton's *Elements of Architecture* (1624), which describes a man's home as the "*Theater* of his *Hospitality*" and "a kinde of private *Princedome*." Aside from immediate family members, Shakespeare's comic households are populated by guests who are welcomed into the "theater of hospitality" – as beneficiaries of and witnesses to the host's virtue – and by numerous servants who symbolically embody its status and pragmatically keep it running smoothly (Heal 1990: 45–8). However, the disruptive, sometimes dangerous, agency of guests and servants in plays like *Much Ado About Nothing* and *Twelfth Night* reveals faultlines in the civilized order of the early modern household.

In *Much Ado About Nothing* Don John takes advantage of the expectation of hospitality to undermine Hero's reputation and to betray his host. When Don Pedro initially greets his host with much ado – "Good Signor Leonato, are you come to meet your trouble? The fashion of the world is to avoid cost, and you encounter it" – Leonato gracefully makes nothing of his duty: "Never came trouble to my house in the likeness of your grace; for trouble being gone, comfort should remain, but when you depart from me, sorrow abides and happiness takes his leave" (1.1.77–83). Behind Leonato's courteous figuration of hospitality in the terms of "comfort" and "happiness" lies a concern with his obligation to a visiting prince, who is positioned with respect to Leonato as both "your trouble" and "your grace." We can detect a strain in the civil discourse between host and guest because the bonds of friendship and courtesy they construct are "not entirely guaranteed by affective feelings but by external influences such as wealth, social position, and family objectives" (Comensoli 1996: 141). For instance, Don Pedro obliquely raises the possibility of his host's insincerity when he informs Claudio and Benedick that Leonato "heartily prays some occasion may detain us longer. I dare swear he is no hypocrite, but prays from his heart" (1.1.121–3). Given Don John's later success at slandering Hero and thereby dishonoring both Leonato and Don Pedro, it is significant that in the very gesture of reaffirming his welcome to his honored guest, Leonato also welcomes his guest's treacherous brother into the household.[12]

Shame comes upon Leonato's household both from without and within, from a stranger (guest) and a familiar (servant). Courting Margaret at Hero's chamber window as if the maidservant were the mistress, Don John's follower Borachio arranges for Claudio and Don Pedro to witness Hero's apparent infidelity. Margaret's complicity in the plot remains ambiguous to the end, despite Leonato's efforts to determine the truth of disorder in his household: "But Margaret was in some fault for this, / Although against her will as it appears / In the true course of all the question" (5.4.4–6). Leonato's qualifications ("some," "as it appears"), reversals ("But . . . Although"), and contradictions ("in fault . . . against her will") belie the authoritative tone by which he reasserts his domestic control. Whatever her intentions, Margaret's susceptibility to Borachio's seduction is clear. The play's emphasis on Margaret's sexuality reflects contemporary anxiety about the potentially harmful influence of maidservants on their mistresses (Burnett 1997: 127–9). Margaret makes "illegitimate construction" of other women's words, as in her response to Beatrice's complaint of a stuffed nose: "A maid, and stuffed! There's goodly catching of cold" (3.4.41, 55). Even after Hero's denunciation as a whore, Margaret flirts with Benedick, goading him to praise her beauty and alluding to her unfulfilled sexual needs: "Give us the swords. We have bucklers of our own" (5.2.16).

Although bawdy exchanges also characterize the mistress–maidservant relationships in *Two Gentlemen of Verona* and *The Merchant of Venice*, the maidservant's discretion in these plays minimizes any threat to the mistress's chastity. Whereas Margaret imitates Hero without her knowledge, Julia and Portia ask their maidservants for assistance in romantic matters. Both Julia and Portia enter their respective plays discussing potential husbands with their women. In her first words – "But say, Lucetta, now we are alone" (1.2.1) – Julia establishes intimacy before soliciting her servant's opinion about various suitors. Julia later requires her advice on how to reunite with Proteus:

> Counsel, Lucetta. Gentle girl, assist me,
> And e'en in kind love I do conjure thee,
> Who art the table wherein all my thoughts
> Are visibly charactered and engraved,
> To lesson me, and tell me some good mean
> How with my honour I may undertake
> A journey to my loving Proteus. (2.7.1–7)

When Julia decides to disguise herself as a page, Lucetta rather immodestly recommends the use of a prominent codpiece; nonetheless, she also tries to protect her mistress's honor and to mitigate the "extreme rage" of her passion (2.7.22). Julia reveals confidence in the discretion and secrecy of Lucetta by entrusting her to manage her "goods," "lands," and "reputation" in her absence (2.7.87). As head of her own household, Portia exerts greater authority over her maidservant than does Julia.[13] In *The Merchant of Venice* it is the mistress, not the maidservant, who evaluates the mistress's suitors. Furthermore, when Portia announces her intention to crossdress, she, unlike Julia, seeks no advice from her servant; instead, she informs Nerissa: "I have work in hand / That you yet know not of" (3.4.57–8). Strategically controlling her sexual destiny through the somber disguise of a master of law, Portia relegates Nerissa to Julia's role as the submissive, homoerotically alluring page, the "little scrubbèd boy" about whom her husband fantasizes "couching with" (5.1.161, 304).[14]

Unlike Lucetta and Nerissa, Margaret jeopardizes instead of sustains her mistress's good reputation. She therefore epitomizes the figure of the unreliable servant that provoked such anxiety in early modern England. In comedies, servants are often entrusted to act as secret instruments in the plots of their social superiors. For instance, Tranio trades identities with Lucentio to fool Baptista; Mistress Quickly carries messages to help the wives trick Falstaff. Facilitating their masters' designs, these stage servants enact the anatomical metaphor of dependence found in Dod and Cleaver's *A Godly Form of Household Government*:

> For as the hand is said to be the instrument of instruments . . . so is the servant said to be an instrument of instruments, because he keepeth all the instruments of the household occupied . . . [But] he differeth from all other instruments. For where they are things without soul, he is divinely enriched with a soul: and herein he differeth from the hand, for that the hand is fastened and united to the body, but he is separate and disjoined from his master. (Quoted in Neill 2000: 422 n.18)

If the wife supervises the "instruments of household," the servant employs them for the sustenance, comfort, and convenience of the family. Yet far from a passive instrument under the householder's direct control, the servant is an agent who might not achieve the master's ends. As Neill (ibid) observes, the "image of a hand that is at once faithfully instrumental and yet disjoined nicely suggests the contradictions of the servant's role during the early modern transformation of household government." On the one hand, nostalgic accounts of the faithful household retainer – like old Adam in *As You Like It* or his counterparts in I. M.'s *A Health to the Gentlemanly Profession of Serving-men* (1598) – celebrated the servant as a self-sacrificing family member (Burnett 1997: 82–5). On the other hand, "the notion of what it meant to be a 'servant' was progressively narrowed and specialized until it came to refer almost exclusively to a form of domestic wage-labor, a potentially degrading occupation fundamentally distinct from other forms of 'service'" (Neill 2000: 46). As a result of the greater affective and social distance between master and servant created by a wage economy, servants were increasingly represented as potentially rebellious agents within the household, concerned only with profit and advancement (ibid: 39–41; Dolan 1994: 3–6).

In *Twelfth Night* Olivia's dependence on ambitious servants at once extends and destabilizes her domestic authority. Jessica Tvordi argues that Olivia and Maria unite "to secure their female authority, subdue male dissenters, and discourage male suitors" (Tvordi 1999: 124). Although it is reasonable to assert that "Olivia employs Maria to strengthen her authority" (ibid: 123), it is less clear that Olivia would endorse all of her maidservant's actions. Maria is not a menial servant like Dromio, who might well lament his subjection to his master's every command: "Thither I must, although against my will; / For servants must their masters' minds fulfil" (*Comedy of Errors*, 4.1.112–13). As a gentlewoman, Maria enjoys considerably more intellectual and physical freedom than Dromio's stale axiom allows. Mark Burnett rightly observes that in reprimanding Sir Toby and Feste, Maria "begins to dismantle a carefully gradated system of household allegiances by appropriating some of the mistress's traditional responsibilities" (Burnett 1997: 142). For Tvordi, Maria carries out Olivia's authority; for Burnett, she goes beyond it.

Yet neither critic acknowledges that Maria fails to use Olivia's authority effectively. Maria's inability to contain domestic disorder tends to support Burnett's view of a household weakened by the dispersal of power. The first time Olivia's household appears on stage, Maria is warning Sir Toby that Olivia "takes great exceptions to [his] ill hours," to which he dismissively responds: "Why let her except, before excepted" (1.3.4–5). When Maria then enjoins Sir Toby to "confine" himself "within the modest limits of order," he snaps: "Confine? I'll confine myself no finer than I am," translating a servant's attempt to restrict his liberty into a declaration of his superior ("finer") social status (1.3.6–8). At the next appearance of Olivia's household, Maria enters admonishing Feste – "My lady will hang thee for thy absence" (1.5.3) – but the mere invocation of Olivia, who is not there to support Maria's threats, fails to intimidate him. Echoing Sir Toby's dismissal of Olivia's authority, Feste impudently replies "Let her hang me" (1.5.4). Of course, Maria does succeed in disciplining Malvolio. However, she thereby not only augments her power at the expense of the household's highest-ranking officer, but also deprives Olivia of the comfort she had taken in his sobriety. Perturbed by her desire for Cesario, Olivia asks Maria: "Where's Malvolio? He is sad and civil, / And suits well for a servant with my fortunes. / Where is Malvolio?" (3.4.5–7). Malvolio enters at precisely this moment, "tainted in's wits" from reading Maria's forged letter, further to trouble Olivia with his "midsummer madness" (3.4.13, 52).[15]

Even worse, while Maria's impersonation of Olivia might justifiably punish Malvolio for his presumptuous desire to marry his mistress, it also promotes the objectification of Olivia's body that underlies that very desire. When Malvolio identifies Olivia's handwriting on the forged love-letter – "These be her very c's, her u's, and her t's, and thus makes she her great P's" (2.5.78–9) – he puts her private parts (her "cut") on public display for the amusement of other men (Callaghan 2000: 38). Referring to Maria's "ambivalent sexual identity as Amazon Queen, Penthesilea" and to her "(mis)representation of [Olivia's] body," Dympna Callaghan suggests her complicity in the humiliation of her mistress. Callaghan does not, however, consider the political implications of a maidservant's ability to place her mistress's genitalia on display (ibid: 37). In this regard, Maria's transgression clearly parallels that of Margaret in *Much Ado About Nothing*: each maidservant, urged on by an unruly suitor, theatrically performs her mistress's sexual availability for her own benefit. In Cristina Malcolmson's more positive formulation, Shakespeare links Maria and Viola as intelligent women who "use language and counterfeited appearances to manage" men of higher status (Malcolmson 1991: 38). Viola wins Orsino's trust by imitating a gentleman; Maria wins Sir Toby's admiration by imitating a countess. Malcolmson concludes that *Twelfth Night* represents social advancement "through women who, though servants, are as capable as their male masters, and who rise out of their role as servants" (ibid: 31). Nonetheless, Malcolmson does not acknowledge that the ingenuity through which Maria secures an aristocratic husband not only proves her worthy of her "male master," but also troublingly diminishes the power of her aristocratic mistress.

If Olivia's domestic authority becomes a casualty of Maria's cross-rank impersonation, Malvolio's domestic authority is its ground zero. The household conspiracy that had existed only in the paranoid imaginations of Antipholus and Ford actually materializes in *Twelfth Night* – albeit not against a master but a servant who desperately wants to be a master. Given the success of Maria and Viola in marrying above their social rank, why must Malvolio's similar ambition be so brutally crushed? As Malcolmson interprets the play's ideological bias, "the desire of an inferior to be matched with a superior is acceptable as long as it is motivated by love; to the extent that desire is self-interested, it is foolish and dangerous" (ibid: 39). Self-interested and self-loving, Malvolio is unworthy to master Olivia as a husband; moreover, he becomes unworthy even to serve her as a steward. Through his secret fantasies of domestic ascendancy, Malvolio approaches the contemporary stereotype of the household officer who abuses his authority and engages in secret sexual vices (Burnett 1997: 160–71). Although Malvolio attempts to fulfill the steward's conventional duty to set a moral example for other servants and "to reprimand actions inimical to wider domestic harmonies" (ibid: 159), his tyrannical authority also subverts aristocratic prerogatives. Leonard Tennenhouse maintains that, resenting his exclusion from aristocratic society, Malvolio "takes it upon himself to enforce the principle of exclusion when acting as the overseer of Olivia's household." Specifically, he "appropriates the voice of the community to which he wants to belong . . . and uses it to assault certain practices of courtly life" (Tennenhouse 1986: 67). Adopting the style of "Count Malvolio," the steward uses his "prerogative of speech" to condemn Sir Toby's festive indulgences as an "uncivil rule" (2.5.30, 63; 2.3.111).

Malvolio's hostility towards Sir Toby is particularly out of place considering that the central principle of early modern civility, as formulated by Erasmus' extremely influential *Manners for Children*, was the public display of "good will toward others" (Revel 1989: 184). In a more political vein, Viviana Comensoli describes the early modern understanding of civility as "a collective obligation which promises to ensure social cohesion and continuity" by investing both domestic and national power in a single governor (Comensoli 1996: 66). As a parodic emblem of his usurpation of domestic power, his self-elevation above other servants, and his fostering of social ill-will, Malvolio is gulled into wearing the clownish yellow stockings and cross-garters that he believes will transform him from a steward into a lover and finally a count.

William Gouge inveighs against the sartorial outrages of such ambitious servants: "One end of apparel is to show a difference betwixt superiors and inferiors, persons in authority and under subjection . . . Exceeding great is the fault of servants in their excess apparel" (quoted in Neill 2000: 425 n.39). Engaged in a status crossdressing even more socially transgressive than the gender crossdressing of Viola (Callaghan 2000: 34), Malvolio violates the very household civility he has been authorized as a steward to uphold.

Conclusion

> *Fabian.* Why, we shall make him mad indeed.
> *Maria.* The house will be the quieter.
>   *(Twelfth Night* 3.4.119–20)

In a chapter entitled "'A Twenty Years' Removed Thing': *Twelfth Night*'s Nostalgia," Eric Mallin argues that in marrying off Olivia Shakespeare symbolically "rewrites the unfulfilled history of [Queen] Elizabeth's frustrating Anjou courtship" (Mallin 1995: 202). Yet if Queen Elizabeth did attend a performance of *Twelfth Night* in 1601, the play might have reminded her not only of Anjou's "frustrated" courtship in the 1570s, but also of the eruption of conjugal frustration involving another Elizabeth during the same period. In 1579 Lady Elizabeth Willoughby, wife of the courtier Sir Francis Willoughby, suffered a domestic humiliation curiously reminiscent of Malvolio's. Provoked by his wife's continuous disobedience and disruption of household order, Sir Francis placed her under "a sort of house arrest." As Alice Friedman recounts this episode, Sir Francis compelled his wife "to submit to the authority of two of his officers" and "restricted her movements to specific rooms within his house." Additionally, he gave their children over to a nurse's care, barred his wife "from entering the room where household stuffs were laid," and took away all her "authority to command anything in the house." Outraged by this degrading treatment, Lady Willoughby "fell into a most violent passion, threatening to make away with herself, and being denied a knife would have struck her scissors into her belly if she had not been prevented." Ultimately, she threatened "to bring the case to the attention of the Queen" (Friedman 1989: 62–3). Malvolio's ordeal replicates the major incidents of Lady Willoughby's: the violently passionate behavior; suspension of domestic authority (which in a steward's case would specifically entail debarment from household stuffs); incarceration; subjection to (inferior) servants; demand for justice; and threat of revenge.

  Despite their significant differences, the punishments of Lady Willoughby and Malvolio fundamentally share a recognition of the profound loss of identity – a kind of social madness – that follows from the violation of one's place in the domestic hierarchy. Viviana Comensoli illuminates the "link between social alienation and madness" in early modern England through an analysis of *A Yorkshire Tragedy* (1605), a domestic tragedy about a gentleman (simply called Husband) who murders his children

(Comensoli 1996: 100). As the play opens, the Husband has already "consume[d] his credit and his house" through gambling and whoring (2.3). He abuses his wife, denounces his children as bastards, and scorns the advice of his neighbors, one of whom admonishes that "he's more than mad / That wounds himself; whose own words do proclaim / Scandals unjust to soil his better name" (2.106–8). Whether domestic authority is abdicated by the head of household, as in *A Yorkshire Tragedy*, or usurped from below, as with Malvolio and Lady Willoughby, the result of such "uncivil rule" is the same: an irrational self-wounding (recall Lady Willoughby's attempt to stab herself), a descent into social incoherence. Having refused the social identities conferred upon them by their proper places in the civilized household, the "mad" husband, wife, and servant who disrupt domestic order all lose their customary authority. Or, to return to the scene of household discipline with which this essay began, these untamed subjects have come to "forget themselves."

Yet Malvolio's "midsummer madness" should not simply be attributed to a moral flaw in his character, for it emerges as well from the political structure of the household and from the dramatic logic of comedy. In *Twelfth Night* the comic confusion of identities that blesses Sebastian with a socially advantageous marriage to Olivia (who thinks she is marrying the identically dressed Cesario) also constitutes a kind of madness. Having received Olivia's proposal, a baffled Sebastian twice denies that he is experiencing "madness" before conceding that perhaps he is indeed "mad, / Or else the lady's mad" (4.3.4, 10, 15–16). Significantly, Sebastian's perception of Olivia's domestic government, her ability to "sway her house, command her followers, / Take and give back affairs and their dispatch / With such a smooth, discreet, and stable bearing," convinces him that she cannot be mad (4.3.17–19). Sebastian certainly has an interest in assuming that some as yet undisclosed error can explain Olivia's odd behavior, for this is the discreet wife and the orderly household that he will now master, no matter how bizarre the circumstances of their obtainment.

Putting aside Sebastian's own appeal to good "fortune" (4.3.11), how can we explain his advantageous marriage to a countess in less mystified terms? If the play rewards Viola and Maria with socially advantageous marriages because they have loved and served their husbands, the same is obviously not true of Sebastian, who has never met Olivia before and who displays more affection for Antonio. Conversely, if the play punishes Malvolio for his "mad" desire to marry a powerful and wealthy woman whom he does not love, then why isn't the "mad" Sebastian similarly thwarted? The simplest, and most telling, answer lies in Orsino's attempt to comfort Olivia upon her discovery that she has married a stranger: "Be not amazed. Right noble is his blood" (5.1.257). According to the socially conservative bias of the comedy, "the Lady of the Strachey [who] married the yeoman of the wardrobe" is stigmatized because she violates status boundaries (2.5.34–5). However accidental or ironic – for Olivia, too, has been seduced by a wardrobe – the Countess's union with a fellow aristocrat nevertheless stays within status boundaries. As Maria anticipates, stigmatizing Malvolio as a madman might make the house quieter, but thereby silenced is the knowledge of the political interests served by the selective enforcement of the household's social hierarchy.

NOTES

1   The household was "a unit of residence and of authority: a group of people living under the same roof and under the authority of the household head – usually, though not always, an adult male"; most households were "nuclear," consisting of parent(s) and children (Wrightson 2000: 30–1). About 29 percent of all households contained servants, who were usually between 10 and 30 years of age and unmarried (Burnett 1997: 1). Moreover, "by law all those between the ages of fifteen and forty-five who were unmarried and without estates of their own were required to be in service" (Amussen 1988: 48).

2   I will be using *The Norton Shakespeare* for all citations. On the significance of dogs as members of the household in Shakespearean comedy, see Boehrer (1999).

3   On the conflict between "patriarchy" and "play" in the Induction, see Novy (1984: 45–7). Newman argues that "relationships of power and gender" that are naturalized in orthodox Elizabethan discourses are here "subverted by the metatheatrical foregrounding of such roles and relations as culturally constructed" (Newman 1991: 38).

4   On this process, see Montrose (1995). For men, marriage "conferred social status because it inaugurated the household in which any man and every householder had the opportunity to realize the theoretically absolute political power of domestic patriarchalism" (Orlin 1994: 138).

5   Henry Smith, *Preparative to Marriage* (1591), quoted in Orlin (1994: 99).

6   Although mothers "were active agents in marriage negotiations and the transmission of property, many Renaissance discourses on the family continue to conceptualize motherhood as a private, almost pre-social interaction between mother and baby or small child" (Rose 1991: 300).

7   Matthew Griffith, *Bethel, or A Form for Families* (1633), quoted in Cook (1991: 72).

8   According to John Dod and Robert Cleaver's *Godly Form of Household Government*, the household "should function as 'a little commonwealth' whose rulership, both civil and 'righteous,' must be exercised by the husband or 'cheefe' with the support of his wife or 'fellow-helper'" (quoted in Comensoli 1996: 18).

9   Moisan (1991: 276–82) discusses violence against servants in *Shrew*.

10   On the private closet or study, see Friedman (1989: 146–7); Ranum (1989: 225–7); and Stewart (1997: 161–87).

11   Like Helgerson (1999), Wall (1998: 32–5) links domesticity and nationalism.

12   Palmer (1992: 77) demonstrates how "guests make the household – and the authority of the male host – vulnerable." On Don John's appropriation of the aristocratic prerogative of theatricality, see Howard (1987: 172–83).

13   Portia represents women who "escaped direct patriarchal control because they were left fatherless"; perhaps one in three children lost their father before reaching maturity (Ezell 1987: 17–18).

14   The homoerotics of service are discussed in Jardine (1992) and DiGangi (1997: 64–99).

15   Burnett (1997: 156–9) describes the steward's pragmatic and symbolic importance as maintainer of order.

REFERENCES AND FURTHER READING

A Yorkshire Tragedy (1969). In K. Sturgess (ed.) *Three Elizabethan Domestic Tragedies*. Harmondsworth: Penguin Books.

Amussen, S. D. (1988). *An Ordered Society: Gender and Class in Early Modern England*. New York: Columbia University Press.

Belsey, C. (1999). *Shakespeare and the Loss of Eden: The Construction of Family Values in Early Modern Culture*. New Brunswick, NJ: Rutgers University Press.

Boehrer, B. (1999). Shylock and the Rise of the Household Pet: Thinking Social Exclusion in *The Merchant of Venice*. *Shakespeare Quarterly*, 50, 152–70.

Burnett, M. T. (1997). *Masters and Servants in English Renaissance Drama and Culture: Authority and Obedience*. New York: St. Martin's Press.

Callaghan, D. (2000). *Shakespeare Without Women: Representing Gender and Race on the Renaissance Stage*. London: Routledge.

Comensoli, V. (1996). *"Household Business": Domestic Plays of Early Modern England*. Toronto: University of Toronto Press.

Cook. A. J. (1991). *Making a Match: Courtship in Shakespeare and His Society*. Princeton, NJ: Princeton University Press.

Cressy, D. (1997). *Birth, Marriage, and Death: Ritual, Religion, and the Life-Cycle in Tudor and Stuart England*. Oxford: Oxford University Press.

DiGangi, M. (1997). *The Homoerotics of Early Modern Drama*. Cambridge: Cambridge University Press.

Dolan, F. E. (1994). *Dangerous Familiars: Representations of Domestic Crime in England, 1550–1700*. Ithaca, NY: Cornell University Press.

——(1999). Household Chastisements: Gender, Authority, and "Domestic Violence." In P. Fumerton and S. Hunt (eds.) *Renaissance Culture and the Everyday*. Philadelphia: University of Pennsylvania Press, 204–28.

Ezell, M. J. M. (1987). *The Patriarch's Wife: Literary Evidence and the History of the Family*. Chapel Hill: University of North Carolina Press.

Findlay, A. (1999). *A Feminist Perspective on Renaissance Drama*. Oxford: Blackwell.

Friedman, A. T. (1989). *House and Household in Elizabethan England: Wollaton Hall and the Willoughby Family*. Chicago, IL: University of Chicago Press.

Girouard, M. (1978). *Life in the English Country House: A Social and Architectural History*. New Haven, CT: Yale University Press.

Heal, F. (1990). *Hospitality in Early Modern England*. Oxford: Oxford University Press and Clarendon Press.

Helgerson, R. (1999). The Buck Basket, the Witch, and the Queen of Fairies: The Women's World of Shakespeare's Windsor. In P. Fumerton and S. Hunt (eds.) *Renaissance Culture and the Everyday*. Philadelphia: University of Pennsylvania Press, 162–82.

Henderson, D. E. (1995). The Theater and Domestic Culture. In J. D. Cox and D. S. Kastan (eds.) *A New History of Early English Drama*. New York: Columbia University Press, 173–94.

Howard, J. E. (1987). Renaissance Anti-Theatricality and the Politics of Gender and Rank in *Much Ado About Nothing*. In J. E. Howard and M. F. O'Connor (eds.) *Shakespeare Reproduced: The Text in History and Ideology*. New York: Methuen, 163–87.

Hutson, L. (1994). *The Usurer's Daughter: Male Friendship and Fictions of Women in Sixteenth-Century England*. London: Routledge.

Jankowski, T. A. (2000). *Pure Resistance: Queer Virginity in Early Modern English Drama*. Philadelphia: University of Pennsylvania Press.

Jardine, L. (1992). Twins and Travesties: Gender, Dependency, and Sexual Availability in *Twelfth Night*. In S. Zimmerman (ed.) *Erotic Politics: Desire on the Renaissance Stage*. New York: Routledge, 27–38.

Kahn, C. (1981). *Man's Estate: Masculine Identity in Shakespeare*. Berkeley: University of California Press.

Korda, N. (1996). Household Kates: Domesticating Commodities in *The Taming of the Shrew*. *Shakespeare Quarterly*, 47, 109–31.

——(2001). "Judicious Oeillades": Supervising Marital Property in *The Merry Wives of Windsor*. In J. E. Howard and S. C. Shershow (eds.) *Marxist Shakespeares*. London: Routledge, 82–103.

McDonald, R. (2001). *The Bedford Companion to Shakespeare: An Introduction with Documents*, 2nd edn. Boston, MA: Bedford–St. Martin's Press.

Malcolmson, C. (1991). "What You Will": Social Mobility and Gender in *Twelfth Night*. In V. Wayne (ed.) *The Matter of Difference: Materialist Feminist Criticism of Shakespeare*. Ithaca, NY: Cornell University Press, 29–58.

Mallin, E. S. (1995). *Inscribing the Time: Shakespeare and the End of Elizabethan England.* Berkeley: University of California Press.

Mertes, K. (1988). *The English Noble Household 1250–1600.* Oxford: Blackwell.

Moisan, T. (1991). "Knock Me Here Soundly": Comic Misprision and Class Consciousness in Shakespeare. *Shakespeare Quarterly,* 42, 276–90.

Montrose, L. (1995). "The Place of a Brother" in *As You Like It*: Social Process and Comic Form. In I. Kamps (ed.) *Materialist Shakespeare: A History.* London: Verso, 28–54.

——(1996). *The Purpose of Playing: Shakespeare and the Cultural Politics of the Elizabethan Theatre.* Chicago, IL: University of Chicago Press.

Neely, C. T. (1985). *Broken Nuptials in Shakespeare's Plays.* Urbana: University of Illinois Press.

Neill, M. (2000). *Putting History to the Question: Power, Politics, and Society in English Renaissance Drama.* New York: Columbia University Press.

Newman, K. (1991). *Fashioning Femininity and English Renaissance Drama.* Chicago, IL: University of Chicago Press.

Novy, M. L. (1984). *Love's Argument: Gender Relations in Shakespeare.* Chapel Hill: University of North Carolina Press.

Orlin, L. C. (1994). *Private Matters and Public Culture in Post-Reformation England.* Ithaca, NY: Cornell University Press.

——(1995). *Elizabethan Households: An Anthology.* Washington, DC: Folger Shakespeare Library.

Palmer, D. W. (1992). *Hospitable Performances: Dramatic Genre and Cultural Practices in Early Modern England.* West Lafayette, IN: Purdue University Press.

Ranum, O. (1989). The Refuges of Intimacy. In P. Ariès and G. Duby (eds.) *A History of Private Life, Vol. 3: Passions of the Renaissance,* ed. R. Chartier, trans. A. Goldhammer. Cambridge, MA: Harvard University Press and Belknap Press, 207–64.

Revel, J. (1989). The Uses of Civility. In P. Ariès and G. Duby (eds.) *A History of Private Life, Vol. 3: Passions of the Renaissance,* ed. R. Chartier, trans. A. Goldhammer. Cambridge, MA: Harvard University Press and Belknap Press, 167–205.

Rose, M. B. (1991). Where are the Mothers in Shakespeare? Options for Gender Representation in the English Renaissance. *Shakespeare Quarterly,* 42, 291–314.

Shakespeare, W. (1997). *The Norton Shakespeare,* ed. S. Greenblatt, W. Cohen, J. E. Howard, and K. E. Maus. New York: Norton.

Stewart, A. (1997). *Close Readers: Humanism and Sodomy in Early Modern England.* Princeton, NJ: Princeton University Press.

Tennenhouse, L. (1986). *Power on Display: The Politics of Shakespeare's Genres.* New York: Methuen.

Tvordi, J. (1999). Female Alliance and the Construction of Homoeroticism in *As You Like It* and *Twelfth Night.* In S. Frye and K. Robertson (eds.) *Maids and Mistresses, Cousins and Queens: Women's Alliances in Early Modern England.* New York: Oxford University Press, 114–30.

Wall, W. (1998). "Household Stuff": The Sexual Politics of Domesticity and the Advent of English Comedy. *English Literary History,* 65, 1–45.

Westfall, S. (1997). "A Commonty a Christmas Gambold or a Tumbling Trick": Household Theater. In J. D. Cox and D. S. Kastan (eds.) *A New History of Early English Drama.* New York: Columbia University Press.

Wrightson, K. (1982). *English Society 1580–1680.* New Brunswick, NJ: Rutgers University Press.

——(2000). *Earthly Necessities: Economic Lives in Early Modern Britain.* New Haven, CT: Yale University Press.

6

Shakespeare's Crossdressing Comedies

Phyllis Rackin

A surprising number of the plays written for the early English professional stage featured crossdressed characters. Michael Shapiro lists eighty in the appendix to his book *Gender in Play on the Shakespearean Stage* (1994) but his list does not claim to be exhaustive, and it is impossible to know exactly how many there were.[1] Of the thirty-eight surviving plays attributed to Shakespeare, about one fifth involve crossdressing. In seven of those plays female characters disguise themselves as young men. In three – *The Merchant of Venice*, *As You Like It*, and *Twelfth Night* – crossdressing is central to both the complication and the resolution of the plot. The heroines also disguise themselves as men in *The Two Gentlemen of Verona*, one of Shakespeare's earliest plays, and in *Cymbeline*, one of his latest. In *The Taming of the Shrew* and in *The Merry Wives of Windsor* male characters are disguised as women. In addition to all these crossdressed disguises, three of Shakespeare's earliest history plays feature female characters who probably appeared in masculine battle-dress (Joan in Part I of *Henry VI*, Margaret in Part III, and Eleanor in *King John*).

Crossdressing had a variety of functions in these plays, some deriving from the material conditions of performance, others from the conflicted status of gender roles in the culture at large. The uses of crossdressing varied over time and across class. The amphitheatres that catered to an audience composed largely of citizens had significantly different repertories from the indoor playhouses that catered to more privileged audiences, and both differed from the repertory of Shakespeare's company, which attracted a more heterogeneous audience, especially after it acquired the Blackfriars in addition to the Globe. However, the uses of crossdressing also varied from one play to another, even within the productions of a single playwright or theatrical company.

Crossdressing in Performance

In one sense, of course, all the female characters on the professional stage in Shakespeare's time were crossdressed, because all the actors who played their parts were male. Although the fact that the professional companies in Shakespeare's England did not employ female actors is well known, the reasons are still a subject of scholarly conjecture and debate. The practice is sometimes assumed to be traditional, but it was actually rather anomalous, since Shakespeare and his original audiences could and did see women performing in a variety of other physical and social settings. Women performed in the guild plays, May games, and civic entertainments that were regular features of village life, and there were also women among the itinerant musicians, acrobats, and other performers who toured the English countryside (Stokes 1993). Women also performed in private entertainments in aristocratic households and in court masques. Even on the London commercial stage there were occasional performances by foreign professional companies that included female actors. In 1574, for instance, Thomas Norton complained to the Lord Mayor about "assemblies to the unchaste, shamelesse and unnatural tomblinge of the Italian Woemen" (Chambers 1923: 273). Fifty-five years later, Thomas Brande was similarly contemptuous of "certaine vagrant French players": "*those women*," he wrote, "did attempt, thereby giving just offence to all vertuous and well-disposed persons in this town, to act a certain lacivious and unchaste comedye, in the French tonge at the Blackfryers." Despite Brande's condemnation, the women's performance was apparently popular with London playgoers: William Prynne claimed in his *Histriomastix* that "there was great resort" to see the "*French-women Actors*, in a Play not long since personated in *Blackefriers Play-house*," and the same company also performed at two other playhouses, the Red Bull and the Fortune (Orgel 1996: 7).

Although performances by French and Italian women were condemned by moralists throughout the period, there was no law prohibiting women from appearing on the English professional stage. Various explanations for the exclusion of women have been proposed. Taking the moralists at their word, some scholars have explained it in terms of cultural taboos against women's public speech or anxieties about the powerful erotic allure of female players. Others have suggested that the players desired to exploit the even more powerful erotic allure of boys dressed in female clothes; but the reason why the English professional companies excluded women has never been satisfactorily explained.[2]

The players clearly knew that their practice was anomalous, but that very anomaly seems to have been a point of pride for them. Thomas Nashe's 1592 defense of playgoing in *Pierce Penilesse his Supplication to the Divell* used the masculine purity of the English companies as a basis for both national and professional pride: "Our Players," he boasted, "are not as the players beyond Sea, a sort of squirting baudie Comedians, that have whores and common Curtizens to playe womens partes" (Chambers 1923: 239). Nashe's boast suggests that the exclusion of women from the English professional companies may have been an attempt on the part of the players to distinguish themselves from the foreigners who did include women in their companies and to insulate themselves from both the taint of effeminacy that was associated with acting and the low social status of traveling players. In excluding women from their stages the new London professional companies were following the practice of the male students who performed Latin plays at Oxford and Cambridge, rather than that of the amateurs who performed in village festivals and the wandering professionals who had traveled across the countryside from time immemorial, both of which included women as well as men.

The recent film *Shakespeare in Love* treated crossdressing from a distinctly – and anachronistically – modern perspective. In *Shakespeare in Love* the male actor who was cast as Juliet was "naturally" unable to play the part convincingly; and the players' production of Shakespeare's play did not really come to life until he was replaced by the Lady Viola, disguised as a boy actor, but actually a real woman (and a woman in love to boot), who was herself played by the beautiful Gwyneth Paltrow. In Shakespeare's time, however, the assumption seems to have been just the opposite. Visiting a Venetian playhouse where women performed the female parts, Thomas Coryate wrote:

> I saw women acte, a thing that I never saw before, though I have heard that it hath beene sometimes used in London, and they performed it with as good a grace, action, gesture, and whatsoever convenient for a Player, as ever I saw any masculine Actor. (1611, quoted in Bentley 1984: 114)

Coryate was surprised to see that the women performed the female parts as effectively as the male players he had seen in London. John Downes, as a book keeper and prompter in the Restoration theatre, had seen both male and female actors performing women's parts, but he doubted that any of the women could equal the achievement of Edward Kynaston. Kynaston, he wrote,

> made a Compleat Female Stage Beauty, performing his parts so well . . . that it has since been Disputable among the Judicious, whether any Woman that succeeded him so Sensibly touch'd the Audience as he. (quoted in Bentley 1984: 115)

One traditional explanation for the popularity of crossdressed heroines among Shakespeare's contemporaries seems to rest on the same anachronistically modern assumption we saw in *Shakespeare in Love*. Shakespeare put his heroines into male disguise, it was claimed, because it was easier for the boy actors to play as boys. This explanation never made much sense because most of Shakespeare's female characters, including such demanding roles as Lady Macbeth and Cleopatra, never take on male disguises. Moreover, a boy portraying a female character disguised as a boy would probably have performed in subtly different ways from a boy portraying a character who was actually a boy, so the double-cross may have been even more difficult to perform than the straightforward impersonation of a woman. A more likely explanation, which acknowledges the well-documented skill and effectiveness of the boy actors, is that the disguise gave them additional opportunities to put their virtuosity on display. The kind of seamless, unbroken dramatic illusion demanded by the post-Shakespearean classic realist theatre was clearly not a requirement in a theatre where actors frequently stepped forward to address the audience directly in asides and soliloquies that emphasized the present reality of dramatic presentation. When female characters took on male disguise the ambiguous gender identity of the actors who played their parts could be foregrounded in the performance, calling attention to their virtuosity and inviting the playgoers to admire their accomplishment. The cross-dressed boy, in fact, became the living embodiment of the mystery of theatrical impersonation, a craft that produces a body in which the represented character and the representing actor are simultaneously present to the audience.

In Shakespeare's England this craft of professional playing was still a novelty. The first purpose-built professional playhouse was not constructed until 1576, and although the London playing companies rapidly developed a remarkable degree of professionalism, they were still not numbered among the guilds that organized the more traditional crafts. The boys who played the women's parts were apprentices to the mature actors in their companies, but not – at least not officially – to the craft of playing. As Stephen Orgel points out,

> only members of guilds could have apprentices, and there was no actors' guild. The boys were apprenticed instead to those actors who happened to be guild members, of which there were a substantial number – in Shakespeare's company, for example, John Heminges was a grocer, Robert Armin and John Lowin were goldsmiths, and a number of other guilds were represented as well. (Orgel 1996: 65)

The novelty of the actors' trade provoked numerous attacks (Howard 1994). Antitheatrical invective typically featured the charge that dramatic impersonation was a form of deceit, the players misrepresenting their true identities. In these attacks the deceitfulness of playacting was repeatedly conflated with the deceitfulness of dressing in real life in clothing that rightly belongs to someone of a higher status or different sex. A typical example is Stephen Gosson's charge in *Playes Confuted in Five Actions* (1582): "In Stage Plays for a boy to put one the attyre, the gesture, the passions of a woman; for a meane person to take upon him the title of a Prince with counterfeit porte, and traine, is by outwarde signes to shewe them selves otherwise then they are, and so with in the compasse of a lye" (Chambers 1923: 217).

Many playscripts encode the players' awareness of these attacks, reproducing the antitheatrical charges and implicitly answering them as well. A good case in point is Shakespeare's *Two Gentlemen of Verona*, where the fickle, deceitful lover is named Proteus, and Julia, the faithful lady he abandons, is the first of Shakespeare's cross-dressed comic heroines. Proteus, the shape-shifting god of classical antiquity, was used by both admirers and detractors of the players as a prototype for their craft of impersonation (Barish 1975: 99–197). Shakespeare's portrait of Proteus as a treacherous deceiver seems to echo the detractions, but his representation of the crossdressed lady seems clearly designed to answer them. In an often-cited dialogue, Julia, disguised as the boy Sebastian, is asked whether (s)he knows Julia. Foregrounding the duplicity of both the character's and the player's identity, the supposed boy replies: "I know her almost as well as I do know myself" and "have wept a hundred several times" while "thinking upon her woes." Asked how tall Julia is, Sebastian replies that they are so close in height that he was able to wear her gown in a pageant where he played "the woman's part," a claim that might have reminded Shakespeare's original audience that the same boy actor who was now dressed as the boy Sebastian had earlier taken on "the woman's part" of Julia by wearing her gown. This reminder would have carried extra resonance for Elizabethan playgoers, who were subject to sumptuary laws that regulated dress to ensure that no man would misrepresent his social identity by wearing luxurious clothing that signaled a position higher than the one he actually occupied. To be sure, there were no laws against crossdressing, but in a theatre where parts were habitually doubled, any change of costume was inevitably read as a change of identity (Hooper 1915; Jones and Stallybrass 2000: 193–206).

The supposed boy's description of his crossdressed performance in the pageant, with Julia herself as one of the spectators, conjures up a *tour de force* of layered impersonation – the boy actor, impersonating Julia, who impersonates a boy, who claims to have impersonated a woman in a pageant in which he wore Julia's dress to play the part of Ariadne, abandoned by Theseus,

> Which I so lively acted with my tears
> That my poor mistress, movèd therewithal,
> Wept bitterly; and would I might be dead
> If I in thought felt not her very sorrow. (4.4.161–4)

The dizzying whirl of identification in the represented action – Julia is Sebastian is Ariadne – is resolved only when Julia's sympathetic response to the performance unites actor and spectator in imagined sorrow and real tears. The description invites the playgoers' admiration, both by calling attention to the player's art of impersonation and by modeling the response of a sympathetic spectator.

These same elements of layered, cross-gendered impersonation and solicitation of the playgoers' admiration reappear in the Epilogue to *As You Like It*, which insists that the speaker is both Rosalind and the male actor who played her part. Here, as in *The Two Gentlemen of Verona*, the crossdressed heroine uses her indeterminate gender identity to celebrate the players' craft. At the beginning of the speech the speaker seems to be the female character, when she says: "It is not the fashion to see the lady the epilogue." Later in the same speech, however, it is the male actor who played her part who offers: "If I were a woman I would kiss as many of you as had beards that pleased me, complexions that liked me, and breaths that I defied not." But this is not the end, for (s)he quickly adds: "And I am sure, as many as have good beards, or good faces, or sweet breaths will for my kind offer, when I make curtsy, bid me farewell." At this point – the last lines in the playtext, which were presumably followed by a curtsy – the gender of the speaker becomes completely indeterminate.

The Epilogue invites the audience to applaud the entire performance, embodied in the person of the doubly crossdressed actor who performed the part of a woman disguised as a boy. Here, as in *The Two Gentlemen of Verona*, the crossdressed heroine implicitly answers the charge that dramatic representation is a form of deception by echoing the distinction Sir Philip Sidney had made in his *Defense of Poesie* (1595), when he argued that because the poet "nothing affirms" he "never lies." Like Sidney's defense of poetic fictions, both plays insist upon the categorical distinction between deceit in real life and the make believe of dramatic representations. Like the antitheatricalists' attacks on the players' deceits, they focus the argument in the figure of the cross-dressed boy actor.

Early in *As You Like It*, in the very first scene where Rosalind and Celia appear, they engage in an elaborate repartee with the clown, Touchstone, involving a "certain knight that swore by his honour" that some pancakes were good while the mustard was not. To demonstrate that the knight was wrong but not forsworn, the clown asks Rosalind and Celia to step forward, stroke their chins, and take an oath by their beards; "if you swear by that that is not," he explains, "you are not forsworn" (1.2.62–3). The script of *As You Like It* uses the word "if" more than any other Shakespearean play, repeatedly insisting that the entire action takes place in the conditional tense that insulates it from the offstage dichotomy of truth and falsehood. In the resolution scene, for instance, when Rosalind appears in female dress to marry Orlando and enable the marriage of Phoebe and Silvius, the immediate result is a chorus of "ifs":

> *Duke Senior.* If there be truth in sight, you are my daughter.
> *Orlando.* If there be truth in sight, you are my Rosalind.
> *Phoebe.* If sight and shape be true,
> Why then my love adieu!
> *Rosalind.* [*to the* Duke] I'll have no father if you be not he.
> [*to* Orlando] I'll have no husband if you be not he,
> [*to* Phoebe] Nor ne'er wed woman if you be not she. (5.4.107–13)

In each case the crux of the matter is the regendered appearance that identifies the actor as Rosalind, but the "ifs" bracket the entire resolution as an exercise in make believe, a matter of appearance rather than reality.

Just before Rosalind's entrance, Touchstone entertains the assembled characters, and the audience, with an extended description of the way quarrels are resolved at court. The quarrel, like the plot complications that are about to be resolved by Rosalind's appearance as a woman, is resolved by the use of an "if," which is used to avoid "the Lie Direct." "I knew," says Touchstone,

> when seven justices could not take up a quarrel, but when the parties met themselves, one of them thought but of an "if," as "If you said so, then I said so," and they shook hands and swore brothers. Your "if" is the only peacemaker; much virtue in "if." (5.4.88–92)

Clearly, Touchstone's joke, like the Epilogue and the responses to Rosalind's entrance, insists on the virtue of "if." In ways that may not be so clear, it also raises the issue of gender because the occasion for the quarrel that Touchstone imagines is his statement that he disliked the cut of a certain courtier's beard. Here, as in his dialogue with Rosalind and Celia at the beginning of the play and in the Epilogue's flirtation with the audience, the joke involves what Will Fisher has demonstrated was the essential sign of manhood in the period – a beard, which was considered the evidence of the mature, procreative sexuality that distinguished adult males from boys and women alike (Fisher 2001). Fisher's theory requires that we enlarge our understanding of theatrical crossdressing to include not only the male actors who played the roles of women, but also the boys in the children's companies who put on false beards to perform the roles of adult men. The binary divisions between male and female persons and homo- and heterosexual desire derived from modern understandings of sex and gender may be too simple to account for the cultural matrix in which male actors played the parts of female characters on Shakespeare's stage.

Just as the implications of the jokes about the beard are likely to be lost on a modern audience, the implications of all those "ifs" are also less apparent in modern productions where a female actor plays the part of Rosalind and the crossdressing represented on stage no longer gestures towards the crossdressing involved in the theatrical performance itself. Perhaps the best modern analogue for the theatrical appeal of crossdressing in a play like *As You Like It* is the popularity of ballets that represent dolls who come to life, undoing what ballet does in order to celebrate and advertise its accomplishments. The strenuous disciplines of classical ballet transform the living bodies of the dancers into graceful machines that can accomplish spectacular *tours de force* for the pleasure of a viewing audience. In a sense, what ballet does is to make living bodies into dancing machines, but ballets like *Petrouchka*, *Coppelia*, and *The Nutcracker* bring mechanical bodies to life to foreground the marvel of their own performance. Similarly, in a theatre where boy actors played female characters, female characters playing boys foreground the virtuosity of the actor and the transformative power of the entire performance.

Cultural Questions: Testing the Water

This is not the whole story, however. It is worth noting that the fantasy of a mechanical creature that comes to life achieved its greatest popularity in an age of mechanical reproduction, not only reproducing in reverse the conditions of the dancers' performance but also undoing cultural anxieties about the mechanization of human life outside the theatre. Those same anxieties are dramatized in a more disturbing form in a variety of modern theatrical fictions, such as Charlie Chaplin's 1936 film *Modern Times*, where the tramp becomes mechanized by his work on a factory assembly-line, and Karel Čapek's 1921 play *R.U.R.*, where robots (a word derived from the Czech word meaning "forced labor" and first used in this play) rebel against their roles as mechanical slaves. Similarly, although crossdressing can be used – as it is used in *As You Like It* – as the basis for elaborate metadramatic games with the audience, that is not the only function served by the device: the popularity of crossdressed comedies had larger cultural roots that extended beyond the material practices of the English stage. Crossdressed heroines, in fact, were also popular in Italian comedy, even when the actors who played their parts were female. Moreover, the public stage was not the only place where fictional representations of crossdressing were popular in Shakespeare's England. They appeared in a variety of non-dramatic texts ranging from the *Arcadia* and *The Faerie Queene* to popular ballads and pamphlets concerning the exploits of Long Meg of Westminster. Long Meg was a real person, and there was also a vogue for masculine fashions among actual women in Jacobean London. However, it would be difficult to explain the widespread popularity of fictions of crossdressing as mere imitation of actual practice. The vast majority of women in Shakespeare's England did not adopt transvestite disguise, or even the masculine fashions that were favored for a time by fashionable ladies and their imitators. The reality the cross-gendered comedies did address was more pervasive but also much more complicated: a sex–gender system beginning to undergo the radical renegotiation that would finally produce an ideological regime based on the assumptions about the essential, biologically grounded differences between men and women that came, until very recently, to be taken for granted.

Traces of this renegotiation can be seen in virtually every area of life. Patrilineal inheritance was giving way to the personal acquisition of wealth as the ground of masculine status and identity. Propagandists for an emergent nation-state mystified the authority of husbands and fathers to rationalize monarchical power. Women's work was increasingly distinguished from men's as women were excluded from crafts and trades in which they had previously worked. The household was redefined as a private, feminized space, divided from the public sphere of masculine economic and political activity. The widespread practice of wet-nursing was increasingly discredited as mothering came to be seen as every woman's most important duty. In anatomical theory the traditional belief that female genitalia were simply an imperfect version of the male was challenged by theories that anticipated the modern conception of the two sexes as anatomically discrete. Gender difference was increasingly grounded in the body, and sexuality was increasingly linked to gender. In 1594, for instance, the medical term *hermaphrodite* was generalized to include gender in a usage that conflated social role with physical structure. During the same period the grammatical term *epicene* was similarly transformed, figuratively transferred in 1601 to a person of indeterminate gender and in 1633 to mean an "effeminate" man.

The trajectory I have suggested, leading finally to a recognizably modern ideology of sex and gender in which the differences between men and women were sexualized and grounded in the body and nature, can be traced in retrospect, but in Shakespeare's time the sex–gender system was not yet stabilized in modern terms, and its instability made it a subject of intense interest. Dramatic representations of crossdressed characters reproduce this instability, putting the gender of the characters in flux to complicate the dramatic action. The resulting stories work like successful dreams, dramatizing fantasies of gender confusion only to sort everything out at the end. In so doing they played their own part in the long cultural struggle to rationalize and ground a threatened gender hierarchy and ultimately to redefine what it meant to be "male" or "female"; but taken one by one these plays raise far more questions than they answer.

Put in their simplest terms, the central questions raised in these stories of crossdressing have to do with the differences between men and women. *Twelfth Night*, for instance, stages, in the persons of differently sexed but otherwise identical twins, what amounts to a fictional test of those differences. The fantasy works in some ways like recent scientific studies of identical twins separated at birth. In these studies the fact that the twins are genetically identical serves as a scientific control, enabling any differences between them to be attributed to their different life experiences. In the context of a culture which affords radically different privileges and opportunities to white and black, rich and poor, these twin studies provide ammunition for hotly contested political battles about the relative weight of environment and heredity in the construction of personal identity and success. Can and should anything be done about the inequalities of opportunity that our supposedly meritocratic and egalitarian culture affords? Or are success and failure genetically predetermined and impervious to well-meaning efforts to compensate for racial and economic inequalities? These issues also underlie the popular film *Trading Places* (1983), in which a wealthy white man from Philadelphia's Main Line temporarily switches places with a poor black man from the inner city; playing with the issues of racial and economic inequality, the film uses an improbable plot and comic action to dissipate the anxieties they provoke.

In *Twelfth Night* serious cultural questions about the differences between men and women are similarly defused. Viola and Sebastian are twins, and they are identical in almost everything that mattered in Shakespeare's time, since their identical birth and parentage serve as surrogates for identical nature, nurture, and social rank. Even their situations in the play are similar, both shipwrecked, both landing in Illyria, both assisted by seamen, so when Viola imitates the "fashion, colour, ornament" of Sebastian's dress to disguise herself as a boy, their identity is complete in everything except sex. To all the other characters the twins are indistinguishable. Antonio, who loves Sebastian, mistakes the disguised Viola for him (3.4). Olivia, who loves the disguised Viola, is so entirely convinced that Sebastian is Cesario that she marries him.

Neither appearance nor manners nor sexual attraction is sufficient to establish sexual difference. Here, as in the 1992 film *The Crying Game*, the crossdressed character is the object of desire from a character of the same sex, but in striking contrast to that film, *Twelfth Night* does not frame the issue of homoerotic desire as a shocking secret or a serious threat. Antonio's love for Sebastian is unconsummated, but it is not condemned. The only desire punished severely enough in the play to mark it as a focus of cultural anxiety is Malvolio's desire to marry Olivia: the problem is disparity of social rank. Cesario's sexual ambivalence is easily incorporated into the socially desirable resolution, which is enabled by the fact that Olivia desires the crossdressed female character. Both Olivia's and Viola's desires are gratified at the end of the play when the existence of the identical opposite-sex twins is revealed – in effect splitting the doubly gendered Cesario into two conveniently sexed bodies. Viola will get the man she served in the guise of his page, and Olivia will get the real man that the disguised Viola had imitated. Moreover, the fact that Cesario's femininity makes him desirable to women is presented as a given. Orsino knows that Cesario will make an ideal surrogate suitor for Olivia because, as he says,

> Diana's lip
> Is not more smooth and rubious; thy small pipe

> Is as the maiden's organ, shrill and sound,
> And all is semblative a woman's part.
> I know thy constellation is right apt
> For this affair. (1.4.30–5)

Orsino is right. Olivia is immediately attracted to the feminine boy, and her only concern has to do with his social status. The first question she asks when she begins to fall in love is "What is your parentage?" (1.5.248). Having received the desired answer – "I am a gentleman" – she begins to pursue him. At the end of the play, when it is revealed that Olivia has married Sebastian rather than the man she thought she knew in Cesario, Orsino reassures her: "Be not amazed. Right noble is his blood" (5.1.257).

Distressed when Olivia falls in love with her, Viola calls her crossdressed disguise "a wickedness" (2.2.25); but the plot of the play rewards her for crossdressing as a boy, while humiliating Malvolio for another kind of crossdressing – dressing across rank. When Malvolio dresses in yellow stockings and cross-garters, he too is cross-dressed, because he has cast off the sober garments that express his role as Olivia's steward; but his new clothing does not disguise him or enable him to assume the role of Olivia's suitor that he desires. In Viola's case, by contrast, the disguise appears impenetrable. So long as she imitates Sebastian's manner of dressing, the difference between them remains invisible to all of the other characters.

Speaking directly to the audience, Viola does gesture towards embodied sexuality as the crucial difference between the twins. When she first hears that Sir Andrew is determined to fight her, she says: "Pray God defend me. A little thing would make me tell them how much I lack of a man" (3.4.169); and when she discovers that Olivia has fallen in love with her she refers to her disguised self as a "monster," presumably a hermaphrodite (2.2.32). However, even in the recognition scene, after Orsino has heard all the evidence that establishes his servant's true identity, he still addresses him as "Boy" (5.1.260). This does not prevent Orsino from deciding to marry his former servant, but their courtship cannot begin until he sees Viola in her "women's weeds" (5.1.266). In *Twelfth Night* embodied sexuality appears to be less important than clothing in establishing gendered identity. The power of crossdress-ing, it seems, is so great that verified knowledge of Viola's true sex is insufficient to displace the masculine gender identity established by her costume. Disguised as Cesario, Viola easily succeeds in the sexual conquest of Olivia, who is unsuccessfully courted by Orsino, Sir Andrew, and Malvolio. She also prevails easily in her battles of wits with the clown.

The only arena in *Twelfth Night* where Viola's true sex seems to make a difference is that of armed combat. The only thing Cesario cannot do is fight, and this is the only visible manifestation of the sexual difference between the twins; but although it differentiates Viola from Sebastian, it makes no difference at all between her and Sir Andrew. Sir Toby mischievously encourages the cowardly knight to challenge the equally cowardly Cesario to fight. At first, the joke goes as expected, with each of the would-be combatants comically terrified of the other and exposed as deficient in masculine valor, but when Sir Andrew mistakenly confronts Sebastian, the male twin easily beats the cowardly knight and prepares to take on Toby as well. At the beginning of the recognition scene the two enter with bloody coxcombs, and a minute later Sebastian enters to reveal his responsibility and the existence of the real man that Cesario only imitated.

The ability to fight also appears as a test of manhood in Jonson's *Epicoene*, where the gallants play a practical joke on Daw and LaFoole almost identical to the one Toby attempts on Cesario and Sir Andrew, but with a more successful outcome, since there is no Sebastian to intervene, and both victims are easily exposed as cowards when they readily agree to give up their swords and undergo physical punishments and humiliations rather than attempting to fight. In other plays, however, this test is itself put to the test, and it comes up short. In some, such as *The Roaring Girl* and Part I of *The Fair Maid of the West*, although blustering men are exposed as cowards, they are beaten not by other men but by women in crossdressed disguise; and in Shakespeare's *Henry VI* plays, women in their own persons are shown beating the greatest warriors at their own manly game of swordsmanship. Joan easily defeats the Dauphin in single combat, and she fights Talbot, the greatest warrior on the English side, to a draw. Margaret leads victorious armies on the battlefield, and she captures and kills the Duke of York, the leader of the army that opposes her husband's regime.

In all these plays, swordsmanship is depicted as a quintessentially manly activity, but although the inability to fight makes a man defective, it does not establish the difference between men and women, which remains elusive. Viola's cowardice is no greater than Sir Andrew's. Here, as in his other comedies of crossdressing, Shakespeare plays with the issue of gender distinction, but never really resolves it. The identical twins remain indistinguishable even at the end of the play, because Viola's resumption of her female dress and identity is deferred until after the conclusion. In fact, in the last lines of the play, Viola is still Cesario because she is still wearing her disguise. "Cesario, come –" Orsino says,

> For so you shall be while you are a man;
> But when in other habits you are seen,
> Orsino's mistress and his fancy's queen.

Modern Responses: The Erotics of Crossdressing

It is probably no coincidence that fictions of crossdressing have become interesting again in our own time, a period when the long-entrenched assumptions about sex and gender associated with modernity have come into question. Crossgender casting has never penetrated the mass-market film industry, but films that feature crossdressed characters have done very well. In June 2000, when the American Film Institute polled 1,800 people in the movie industry to determine the hundred funniest American films, two films that centered on male characters disguised as women – *Some Like It Hot* (1959) and *Tootsie* (1982) – came out first and second. Now, as in

Shakespeare's England, gender ideology is a contested subject, interrogated in everything from sexual mores to employment legislation, and comic drama that features characters in crossdressed disguise has again become popular. This is not to say that our own anxieties about sex and gender can be mapped onto those that troubled Shakespeare's original audiences. The fact that the crossdressed characters in modern popular entertainments are typically male rather than female marks a profound difference, and so does the fact that aside from the notable exception of *The Crying Game*, their disguises are rarely convincing and are almost always an occasion for derisive jokes. However, the popularity of crossdressing as a dramatic device in both periods derives from its ability to address and defuse the anxieties arising from the cultural change and dislocation produced by an unstable gender ideology.

Within this context it is not surprising that the use of crossdressed characters in the plays of Shakespeare and his contemporaries has attracted widespread scholarly attention and that these studies have yielded very little consensus in regard to what they tell us about early modern understandings of sex and gender. In fact the debates about their implications have made this discourse an arena where our own battles about gender and sexuality are fought out. At a time when feminists defined their agenda as "women's liberation," major feminist scholars often emphasized the liberatory potential of Shakespeare's representations of crossdressed comic heroines. Juliet Dusinberre argued in her pioneering 1975 study *Shakespeare and the Nature of Women* that they "freed the dramatist to explore . . . the natures of women untrammelled by the customs of femininity" (Dusinberre 1996: 271). In another influential early feminist study, Catherine Belsey proposed that the crossdressed heroine released "for the audience the possibility of glimpsing a disruption of sexual difference" (Belsey 1985: 183). Other critics offered readings that were much less optimistic for women. To Stephen Greenblatt, the point of a comedy like *Twelfth Night* is that "men love women precisely as *representations*, a love the original performance of these plays literalized within the person of the boy actor . . . The open secret of identity – that within differentiated individuals is a single structure, identifiably male – is presented literally in the all-male cast" (Greenblatt 1988: 93). Greenblatt used Thomas Laqueur's theory that there was only "one sex" in Renaissance anatomical theory and the fact that all the actors on stage were male to theorize a masculinist fantasy of a world without women. Lisa Jardine argued that the spectacle of a boy "playing the woman's part" was "an act for a male audience's appreciation." "These figures are sexually enticing *qua* transvestied boys," she contended, and "the plays encourage the audience to view them as such" (Jardine 1983: 31, 29).

Although Greenblatt identified the appeal of the crossdressed boys as a version of heteroerotic desire and Jardine insisted that the desire they evoked was homoerotic, both grounded their interpretations on masculine erotic desire. What neither seemed to consider is that there were women in the audience as well as men – perhaps, in the view of some theatre historians, more women than men – and the prologues and epilogues to many plays explicitly mark the players' awareness that they needed to please female playgoers. The Epilogue to *As You Like It*, for instance, addresses both male and female playgoers, but the appeal to the women comes first, and its wording –

"I charge you, O women, for the love you bear to men, to like as much of this play as please you" – suggests that the "you" in the play's title refers primarily to them. As Jean E. Howard has observed, in a theatre "where men and women alike were both spectacles and spectators, desired and desiring," the women, no less than the men, "could become desiring subjects" (Howard 1994: 91, 79). Contesting Greenblatt's use of *Twelfth Night* to construct a paradigmatic example of the way erotic desire was directed in Shakespeare's crossdressed comedies, Valerie Traub argues that although *Twelfth Night* relies on a "predominantly phallic and visual" erotic economy, "the erotics of *As You Like It* . . . are diffuse, non-localized, and inclusive . . . [with] provocative affinities with the tactile, contiguous, plural erotics envisioned by Luce Irigaray as more descriptive of female experience" (Traub 1992: 142).

The tendency of recent scholarship to emphasize the ways the crossdressed boy might have served as a focus for male homoerotic desire is also difficult to square with the fact that within the represented action of these plays it is the women, at least as much as – perhaps more than – the men, who desire the crossdressed heroines. It is also significant that Olivia's infatuation with Cesario and Phoebe's for Rosalind both focus on the *femininity* of the figures they take for young boys. Olivia, who has vowed to remain in seclusion for seven years to mourn her brother's death, abruptly reverses herself and agrees to admit Cesario as soon as Malvolio describes him as an effeminate figure: "Not yet old enough for a man, nor young enough for a boy . . . he speaks very shrewishly. One would think his mother's milk were scarce out of him" (1.5.139–44). Phoebe describes the object of her desire as a "pretty youth," "not very tall," with "a pretty redness in his lip" (3.5.113–21). The premise underlying these infatuations is that what women naturally desire is not mature, virile men, but effeminate boys whose bodies are more like their own. In Jonson's *Epicoene* a young page is casually identified as his master's "ingle" (1.1.23), but he also reports that "The gentlewomen play with me and throw me o' the bed, and carry me in to my lady, and she kisses me with her oil'd face and puts a peruke o' my head and asks me an' I will wear her gown" (1.1.12–15). In that same play, there is no indication that the crossdressed boy who is the title character is desired by any of the men. Morose decides to marry Epicoene, not because he desires him but because "her" silence and youthful fertility will enable him to beget an heir to disinherit Dauphine without subjecting himself to the unbearable noise of a chattering wife. The two fools, Jack Daw and Sir Amorous LaFoole, claim to have had sex with Epicoene, but there is no indication that either of them actually desired her and they have no inkling that she is actually a boy in disguise.

This is not to deny that the crossdressed characters mobilize men's desire as well as women's. Antitheatrical warnings that the boys inflamed male spectators with sodomitical passion are well known, and Rosalind stages her entire courtship with Orlando in the person of a boy with the suggestive name of Ganymede. "Sebastian," the name adopted by the disguised Julia and the name of the brother the disguised Viola imitates, had similar implications. In real life, female prostitutes wore male attire to make themselves more alluring to male customers. In 1587 William Harrison wrote, "I have met some of these trulls in London so disguised that it hath passed my skill to discover whether they were men or women" (Harrison 1968: 147). In 1620 the misogynist pamphlet *Hic Mulier or The Man-Woman* described the woman in masculine attire as wearing a "loose, lascivious . . . French doublet, being all unbuttoned to entice . . . and extreme short waisted to give a most easy way to every luxurious action" (*Hic Mulier*: 267). In Middleton and Dekker's *The Roaring Girl*, the title character, Moll, who never impersonates a man but dresses in male attire and excels in masculine activities such as swordfighting, is repeatedly slandered as a whore, and she is also depicted as eminently desirable sexually. Laxton, for instance, fantasizes,

> Heart, I would give but too much money to be nibbling with that wench. Life sh' has the spirit of four great parishes, and a voice that will drown all the city! Methinks a brave captain might get all his soldiers upon her . . . Such a Moll were a marrowbone before an Italian: he would cry bona-roba till his ribs were nothing but bone. I'll lay hard siege to her – money is the *aquafortis* that eats into many a maidenhead: where the walls are flesh and blood, I'll ever pierce through with a golden auger. (2.1.187–97)

When Moll supplies the romantic heroine, Mary Fitzallard, with a male disguise for a secret meeting with her lover, he comments at length on the erotic appeal of the crossdressing. When Moll remarks that it looks "strange" to see "one man to kiss another," Sebastian responds: "I'd kiss such men to choose, Moll; / Methinks a woman's lip tastes well in a doublet" (4.1.46–7):

> As some have a conceit their drink tastes better
> In an outlandish cup than in our own,
> So methinks every kiss she gives me now
> In this strange form is worth a pair of two. (4.1.53–6)

Although recent criticism has been understandably fascinated by the erotic excitement activated by crossdressed heroines, it is difficult to read, at this distance, the nature and directions of the erotic feelings mobilized under a sexual regime that was strikingly different from our own. Conditioned by the assumption that the sexed body is the unshakable ground of gender identity, we are likely to classify the spectacle of two male actors, both dressed in male attire, kissing as they do here or courting as they do in *As You Like It*, as a performance specifically designed to elicit homoerotic desire in male spectators. However, Laxton, delighted at the suggestion that Moll may be "both man and woman," exclaims: "That were excellent: she might first cuckold the husband and then make him do as much for the wife" (2.1.211–12). In this play, unlike *As You Like It* and *Twelfth Night*, none of the female characters is depicted as desiring Moll (most of them, in fact, dislike her as a sexual rival); but Laxton's reaction is a comic version of the erotic excitement that crossdressed characters could elicit from characters and spectators of both sexes. This excitement, like the ambiguous gender identity of the characters themselves, resists analysis in terms of the modern division between homo- and heteroerotic (or even bisexual) desire. It derives from the very ambiguity that those classifications would dismantle.

The Sexual Politics of Crossdressing

The scholarly preoccupation with the erotics of crossdressing runs the risk, as Valerie Traub reminds us, of "ignoring gender differentials altogether, in an energetic pursuit of 'sexuality'" (Traub 1992: 144). Traces of gender differentials historically distant from our own, the representations of crossdressed characters on the early modern English stage offer an opportunity to historicize and thus to demystify oppressive assumptions that are often taken for granted in our own culture. A striking example of the way crossdressing can challenge an oppressive gender hierarchy can be found in *The Taming of the Shrew*. In many ways this play offers the closest Shakespearean analogue to contemporary crossdressing films, since it is one of the only two plays of Shakespeare's that feature male-to-female disguise, and it is also the play that addresses most directly the issue of the sex–gender hierarchy. The play is one of Shakespeare's earliest, and it has not usually been thought of as one of his best, but it has proved remarkably popular with recent audiences, as questions of male privilege and female autonomy have come to the forefront of our own cultural controversies. Undoubtedly, the same anxieties that made Laura Doyle's guidebook for women, *The Surrendered Wife: A Practical Guide to Finding Intimacy, Passion, and Peace with Your Man* a best-seller in the year 2001 have made Kate's taming a deeply satisfying fantasy to audiences ranging from Harold Bloom to the many filmgoers who paid to see the more than eighteen movies that have made *Shrew* one of the most popular of all Shakespeare's plays for production on the modern screen (Henderson 1997: 148). Women have also bought into the fantasy. They are, after all, the primary audience for *The Surrendered Wife*. Deirdre Donahue wrote in *USA Today* that the book's author, "a self-described 'former shrew,' offers a surprisingly honest recipe for getting along with the man you married." Bloom describes his admiration for *The Taming of the Shrew* in strikingly similar terms: "One would have to be tone deaf (or ideologically crazed) not to hear in this [the dialogue between Kate and Petruchio at 5.1.130–8] a subtly exquisite music of marriage at its happiest" (Bloom 1998: 33). Meryl Streep, who played the part of Katherine for Joseph Papp, seems to have heard the same music: "Really what matters," she has said, "is that they have an incredible passion and love; it's not something that Katherine admits to right away but it does provide the source of her change" (Henderson 1997: 161).

It is significant, I think, that most of these modern productions of the *Shrew* cut the Induction, the only part of the play that involves crossdressing. Despite Kate's vocal resistance to the role of submissive woman, she never crossdresses, and her final speech of submission relies heavily on the fiction of a woman's body beneath her costume, arguing, as it does, that women's submission to men is required by their embodied weakness:

> Why are our bodies soft, and weak, and smooth,
> Unapt to toil and trouble in the world,
> But that our soft conditions and our hearts
> Should well agree with our external parts. (5.2.169–72)

The speech, which naturalizes women's subordination, works even better in a modern production, where the actor who plays Kate really is a woman. The ideological work it accomplishes is less assured if it is performed (as it often is not) with the Induction framing the action. For there, in the page's crossdressed disguise as Christopher Sly's wife, feminine submission is staged as an act designed to trick a drunken tinker with delusions of grandeur. "Wrapped in sweet clothes," with rings on his fingers, "A most delicious banquet by his bed, / And brave attendants near him when he wakes" (Induction 1, 34–6), Sly is still not convinced that he really is a noble-man who has lost his memory until he is told that he has a beautiful lady who has been weeping about his affliction. The page Bartholomew, crossdressed in a lady's clothes and weeping with the help of an onion concealed in a napkin, is needed to complete the illusion. "My husband and my lord, my lord and husband," Bartholomew says: "I am your wife in all obedience" (Induction 2, 103–4), fore-shadowing in direct parody Kate's declarations of submission to Petruchio at the end of the play and destabilizing the performance of femininity by the boy actor who played her part. It is almost unbearable for many modern feminists, as it was for George Bernard Shaw, to hear "the lord-of-creation moral" of the speech when it is "put into the woman's own mouth." Presented by a crossdressed boy, however, Katherine's proclamation can be seen as a male performance of female compliance, espe-cially if the play is performed with the Induction, which proleptically parodies Kate's obsequious speech when the crossdressed page persuades a drunken tinker that he is truly a lord by performing the role of his obedient wife. Here, as in the Epilogue to *As You like It*, although the marriage plot reaffirms the authority of patriarchy, the hegemonic force of the represented action is undermined by the reminder to the audience that what they are watching is a performance of theatrical shape-shifting.

This capacity of crossdressed performance to destabilize the gender norms of the represented action was often cited in early feminist studies of Shakespearean crossdressing. However, crossdressing can also be used to reinforce those norms by emphasizing the stereotypically feminine qualities of the female character, unchanged by her male attire. In *Two Gentlemen of Verona*, for instance, Julia's disguise as a boy never interferes with what the editor of the 1969 Arden edition of the play called "her feminine appeal to our sympathy" (Leach 1969: xli). "Breeches parts" were enormously popular on the post-Restoration stage, where the actresses who played the parts of the disguised women could put their actual, sexed bodies on display for the pleasure of male spectators. Instead of disturbing the gender identity of the crossdressed heroines, these performances insisted on its stability. In the context of a sex/gender system increasingly grounded in biology, the spectacle of a woman's body in male attire reassuringly emphasized that the sexed body persisted beneath the otherwise gendered clothes. But even in Shakespeare's time, when the modern, biologically grounded sex–gender system was only beginning to take shape, similar implications appear in a number of playtexts. From this distance it is difficult to read those implications with total assurance, just as we cannot surely know what Jacobean women had in mind when they adopted masculine fashions. Since costume had long been regulated by law to ensure that it would express a man's social status and identity, we might assume that these women were attempting to challenge the constraints implicit in their identities as women. However, since social gender was increasingly rationalized as the product of a biologically sexed body, and clothing may have lost some of its significance after 1604 when the sumptuary laws were repealed, they may have been wearing male attire, as the *Hic Mulier* pamphlet claimed, to reveal their essentially and unchangingly female sexed bodies as a temptation for male erotic desire.

Shakespeare's only Jacobean crossdressed comic heroine – Imogen in *Cymbeline* – seems, when she assumes the disguise of a boy, to lose all the assertiveness that marked her initial characterization. In her own person she has defied her father in her choice of a husband and defied her stepmother by rejecting Cloten. In the Welsh wilderness, disguised as a youth, she takes on the role of "housewife" to Belarius and her disguised brothers (4.2.44), who are delighted with her "angel-like" singing and "neat cookery" (4.2.49–50). After her apparent death, the men, still believing she is the boy Fidele, mourn her as the "sweetest, fairest lily" (4.2.203). They declare that the boy's tomb, haunted by "female fairies," will be decked with the "flower that's like [his] face, pale primose," the "azured harebell, like [his] veins," and the "leaf of eglantine," which "outsweetened not [his] breath" (4.2.222–5). In the recognition scene, still disguised as a boy page, she faints when Posthumus strikes her. The revelation of her true identity immediately follows.

It is interesting to compare this scene with the fainting scene in *As You Like It*, which leads, not to a revelation of Rosalind's true identity, but to a reminder of the boy actor's virtuosity in acting the doubly gendered part. Disguised as the boy Ganymede, Rosalind faints at the sight of the napkin stained with Orlando's blood, prompting Oliver's response: "You a man? You lack a man's heart." Even at this moment of crisis, Rosalind takes control of the discourse, turning the subject to the issue of play-acting: "I do so [lack a man's heart]," she says, "I confess it. Ah, sirrah, a body would think this was well counterfeited. I pray you, tell your brother how well I counterfeited." The word "counterfeit," which was commonly used for acting, echoes throughout the exchange, tied always to the issue of Ganymede's ambivalent gender.

Oliver. This was not counterfeit. There is too great testimony in your complexion that it was a passion of earnest.
Rosalind. Counterfeit, I assure you.
Oliver. Well then, take a good heart, and counterfeit to be man.
Rosalind. So I do; but i' faith, I should have been a woman by right. (4.3.163–74)

Both fainting scenes were literally counterfeit, performed by actors on a stage, but only Rosalind's is explicitly marked as such. In this case, the fainting scene provides an occasion to reiterate the instability of the performer's layered identity as male and female, actor and character. The fainting scene in *Cymbeline*, by contrast, reinforces the dramatic illusion of the character's gendered identity as a woman, which is unaffected by her disguise in male attire and untroubled by any reminder that she was portrayed by a male actor.

As these examples indicate, crossdressing does not necessarily destabilize the gender identity of the crossdressed heroine. Neither does it necessarily empower her. In *Twelfth Night* Olivia never crossdresses, but as a wealthy heiress she is always more powerful than the shipwrecked Viola disguised as the boy Cesario, whose social status as Orsino's servant is vastly inferior to her own. Perhaps the most powerful of Shakespeare's crossdressed heroines is Portia in *The Merchant of Venice*, but it would be difficult to argue that she is more powerful in disguise than out of it. Her disguise as a young lawyer enables her to argue Antonio's case in the Venetian lawcourt, but the power she wields as a wealthy heiress in Belmont is even greater. Betrothing herself to Bassanio, she describes that power but states that it is now his:

> But now I was the lord
> Of this fair mansion, master of my servants,
> Queen o'er myself; and even now, but now,
> This house, these servants, and this same myself
> Are yours, my lord's. (3.2.166–9)

Nonetheless, when the letter arrives, describing Antonio's predicament, Bassanio waits for Portia's permission before leaving for Venice to be with his friend (3.2.320–2); and in act 5, when Portia herself returns from Venice, "this house, these servants and this same myself" are still identified as Portia's property. Nerissa recognizes the music playing as "your music, madam, of the house" (5.1.97); and Portia tells her to "give order to my servants" (5.1.118). In the ensuing action, when Portia promises that Bassanio will never come to her bed until she sees her ring and also threatens to sleep with the young doctor to whom Bassanio thinks he gave the ring, "this same myself," like the house and the servants, is also identified as her own to withhold or bestow as she pleases.

One play where crossdressing might seem to empower the heroine is Thomas Heywood's *Fair Maid of the West*. In Part I Bess, dressed in male disguise, trounces the swaggerer Roughman and later, again in disguise, captains her own ship on the high seas. Confronted by a Spanish warship, she vows to "face the fight, / And where the bullets sing loud'st 'bout mine ears, / There shall you find me cheering up my men" (4.4.91–3). In Part II Bess never crossdresses, she is constantly vulnerable to threats of rape and always dependent on the male characters, even Roughman, for protection and advice. Here, as in Part I, Bess is, as the subtitle proclaims, "A Girl Worth Gold," but while she earns most of the money she acquires in Part I, the money she receives in Part II comes to her in the form of gifts from wealthy men, such as the Duke of Florence and the King of Fez, who are overwhelmed by her beauty and desire to possess her sexually.

One explanation that has been advanced for the striking differences between the two parts of *Fair Maid* is that they may have been designed for historically distinct audiences. Part I may have been written at or before the beginning of the seventeenth century, Part II as much as thirty years later. But it would be difficult to explain Bess's disempowerment in Part II simply as the result of her confinement to female costume.

The Bess of Part I is powerful in female dress as well as male. Having intimidated Roughman with her sword while disguised as a "pretty, fair, young youth" (3.1.109), she then proceeds to do the same thing in her own person, threatening that "in this woman shape I'll cudgel thee / And beat thee through the streets. / As I am Bess, I'll do't" (3.1.124–6). She also wields remarkable economic power, managing her tavern so well that she accumulates a sizable fortune – so sizable, in fact, that the Mayor solicits her as a "fit match" for his son (4.2.14). Departing to sea to search for her beloved Spencer, she leaves a will that includes £1,000 to set up young beginners in trade, £500 to relieve those who have had loss at sea, another £10 to every maid married from the town whose name is Elizabeth, £10 a year to relieve maimed soldiers, £500 to Captain Goodlack, as well as other legacies which are not enumerated. Bess's crossdressing is merely one of many manifestations of the remarkable power she has in Part I of *The Fair Maid of the West*. Any anxieties that power might provoke surface only in the responses of misguided and unsympathetic characters, all of whom are easily shown the error of their ways. In Part II, by contrast, those anxieties seem to dictate the entire action of the play, as Bess is stripped not only of her masculine attire but of every other manifestation of self-reliance and ability. She retains nothing of her earlier character except for her name, her devotion to Spencer, and her remarkable beauty.

Many other examples could be adduced to show that while Shakespeare and his contemporaries were clearly fascinated by crossdressed characters, the uses to which they were put were consistent only in their variety, and their implications are often more difficult to read than modern critics have tended to assume. Falstaff's humiliation while dressed as a woman is clearly legible to modern audiences who have long been conditioned to see male-to-female crossdressing as an occasion for derisive laughter. But in the Induction to *The Taming of the Shrew* the focus for derisive laughter is identified as Sly's transformation into a lord, not that of the page into a lady. To an audience accustomed to seeing all female characters played by crossdressed boys, the mere sight of a male character in women's clothes is unlikely to have provoked the kind of automatic, uneasy laughter that made films like *Tootsie* and *Some Like It Hot* so hilariously funny to twentieth-century audiences and reviewers. Some of Shakespeare's comedies, such as *Cymbeline*, depict their crossdressed heroines in ways that seem relatively transparent today. Others, such as *As You Like It* and *Twelfth Night*, reveal traces of a gender ideology that is so different from our own that it is impossible to read with assurance from this distance in time. All these inconsistencies, like the popularity of the crossdressed figure on stage, are symptoms of a sex–gender system undergoing radical renegotiation.

The direction in which that renegotiation was headed can be seen not only in Bess Bridges' transformation but also – and even more clearly – in another seventeenth-century play, *Love's Cure, or The Martial Maid*,[3] where crossdressing is depicted as symptomatic of a kind of disease. That play, generally attributed to John Fletcher, Shakespeare's successor as the leading playwright for the King's Men, looks in some ways like a rewriting of Shakespeare's experiment in *Twelfth Night*. The main plot, which also features a crossdressed girl who has taken her brother's place, is directly and explicitly concerned with the production of gender difference. Condemned to death for murdering a domestic enemy, Alvarez has spent the past sixteen years in foreign wars, accompanied by his daughter Clara, whom he dressed as a boy called Lucio and reared as a soldier. His posthumous son, the real Lucio, at home with his mother, has been dressed and reared as a girl in order to protect him from the vengeful family of the murdered man. The play begins when Alvarez returns, and the two parents attempt to "cure" the "unnatural" behavior of both their progeny. Both the problem and the cure are defined in strikingly modern terms. Not surprisingly, the play privileges heterosexual desire, male dominance, and female submission. In a last desperate effort to reform his effeminate son, Alvarez declares: "ther's only one course left, that may redeem thee, / Which is, to strike the next man that you meet / And if we chance to light upon a woman, / Take her away, and use her like a man" (4.3.37–40). Lucio never becomes a rapist, but both his problem and Clara's are finally resolved when both siblings fall in love and heterosexual desire reorients their inappropriately gendered behavior. Lucio learns to fight and dominate, and Clara learns to suffer and submit, promising to "abjure all actions of a man . . . / To suffer like a woman," and to "show strength in nothing, but my duty and glad desire to please" the man she loves (4.2.185–92).

For both siblings, crossdressing is strenuously marked as unnatural, and sexed bodies are invoked to rationalize the gender roles the characters are expected to adopt. Clara, a joyous and accomplished swordfighter, is reminded that "nature hath given you a sheath onely, to signifie women are to put up mens weapons, not to draw them" (2.2.88). Lucio, who prefers needlework, is told "you have a better needle . . . if you had grace to use it" (1.2.17–18). The play takes considerable pains to establish that Lucio is ridiculous in his female clothing, and he is explicitly reminded that "the best of a man lies under this Petticoate" (1.2.8–9). Clara, who prefers masculine attire, is forced to acknowledge that "nature's privy Seale assures me" a woman (2.2.139). All these admonitions seem clearly legible in modern terms. They become much more complicated, however, if we remember that Clara's role was written to be performed by a crossdressed boy.

NOTES

1 Contemporary documents refer to the titles of numerous plays whose texts are now entirely lost: the papers of the theatre manager Philip Henslowe, for instance, give the names of 280 plays, only forty of which have survived. In addition, scholars have estimated that there were probably about 500 plays for which even the titles have been lost (Saeger and Fassler 1995: 63).

2 For exceptionally thoughtful – and productively different – discussions of this issue, see Orgel (1996) and Callaghan (2000).

3 Although *Love's Cure* defines both the problem and its solution in strikingly modern terms, the gender ideology that shapes the action cannot be associated with a specific author or theatrical milieu or date of composition. Both Cyrus Hoy and George Walton Williams have proposed that it was originally written around 1605 by Beaumont and Fletcher but extensively revised after 1625 by Massinger, who was largely responsible for the creation of the main plot in its present form

(Fletcher 1976: 3–11). The text we have is thus a palimpsest, the product of numerous revisions over a period of twenty or more years. An extreme example of the multi-layeredness of many plays of the period, it also replicates the form of ideology itself – combining residual and emergent beliefs in a construction that occludes the discrepancies and contradictions between them. Lucio's manhood is first awakened by his desire for Genovora, but he declares that his "heavenly love" for her is "the opposite to base lust" (5.2.46). Genovora rejects Lucio when he refuses to fight Lamorall, but then in 5.3 begs him to desist from fighting, even wishing (line 144) that time would go back a week when Lucio wouldn't have dared to fight; and the crude ideology of phallic violence is rejected at the end of the play where, having done its work, it can be occluded with the veneer of civilization. It is tempting to associate the coexistence of residual and emergent ideologies with different authors and different dates of composition, but this is not the only possible explanation. The playscript itself seems to be poised, like the audiences who saw it performed, between residual and emergent constructions of gendered identity, opportunistically invoking one or another as occasion required.

References and Further Reading

Barish, J. (1975). *The Antitheatrical Prejudice.* Berkeley: University of California Press.

Belsey, C. (1985). Disrupting Sexual Difference: Meaning and Gender in the Comedies. In J. Drakakis (ed.) *Alternative Shakespeares.* London: Methuen, 166–90.

Bentley, G. E. (1984). *The Profession of Player in Shakespeare's Time.* Princeton, NJ: Princeton University Press.

Berggren, P. S. (1983). "A Prodigious Thing": The Jacobean Heroine in Male Disguise. *Philological Quarterly,* 62, 383–4.

Bloom, H. (1998). *Shakespeare: The Invention of the Human.* New York: Penguin Putnam, Riverhead Books.

Bullough, V. L. and Bullough, B. (1993). *Cross Dressing, Sex, and Gender.* Philadelphia: University of Pennsylvania Press.

Callaghan, D. (2000). *Shakespeare Without Women: Representing Gender and Race on the Renaissance Stage.* London: Routledge.

Chambers, E. K. (1923). *The Elizabethan Stage,* Vol. 4. Oxford: Clarendon Press; rpt. 1951.

Comensoli, V. and Russell, A. (1999). *Enacting Gender on the English Renaissance Stage.* Urbana: University of Illinois Press.

Crewe, J. (1995). In The Field of Dreams: Transvestism in *Twelfth Night* and *The Crying Game. Representations,* 50, 101–21.

DiGangi, M. (1996). Queering the Shakespearean Family. *Shakespeare Quarterly,* 47, 269–90.

Dollimore, J. (1986). Subjectivity, Sexuality, and Transgression: The Jacobean Connection. *Renaissance Drama,* 17, 53–81.

Dusinberre, J. (1996). *Shakespeare and the Nature of Women,* 2nd edn. New York: St. Martin's Press.

Ferris, L. (1993). *Crossing the Stage: Controversies on Cross-Dressing.* London: Routledge.

Fisher, W. (2001). The Renaissance Beard: Masculinity in Early Modern England and Europe. *Renaissance Quarterly,* 54, 155–87.

Fletcher, J. (1976). *Love's Cure or, The Martial Maid, The Dramatic Works in the Beaumont and Fletcher Canon,* Vol. 3, ed. G. W. Williams. Cambridge: Cambridge University Press.

Garber, M. (1992). *Vested Interests: Cross-Dressing and Cultural Anxiety.* New York: Routledge.

Greenblatt, S. (1988). Fiction and Friction. In *Shakespearean Negotiations: The Circulation of Social Energy in Renaissance England.* Berkeley: University of California Press, 66–93.

Greenblatt, S., Cohen, W., Howard, J. E., and Maus K. E. (1997). *The Norton Shakespeare.* New York: W. W. Norton.

Harrison, W. (1968) [1587]. *The Description of England,* ed. G. Edelen. Ithaca, NY: Cornell University Press.

Henderson, D. E. (1997). A Shrew for the Times. In L. E. Boose and R. Burt (eds.) *Shakespeare: The Movie*. London: Routledge, 148–68.

Heywood, T. (1967). *The Fair Maid of the West Parts I and II*, ed. R. K. Turner, Jr. Lincoln: University of Nebraska Press.

Hic Mulier, or, The Man-Woman (1985) [1620]. In K. U. Henderson and B. F. McManus (eds.) *Half Humankind: Contexts and Texts of the Controversy about Women in England, 1540–1640*. Urbana: University of Illinois Press.

Hooper, W. (1915). The Tudor Sumptuary Laws. *English Historical Review*, 30, 433–49.

Howard, J. E. (1988). Crossdressing, the Theatre, and Gender Struggle in Early Modern England. *Shakespeare Quarterly*, 39, 418–40.

——(1994). *The Stage and Social Struggle in Early Modern England*. London: Routledge.

Jardine, L. (1983). *Still Harping on Daughters: Women and Drama in the Age of Shakespeare*. Brighton: Harvester Press.

Jones, A. R. and Stallybrass, P. (1991). Fetishizing Gender: Constructing the Hermaphrodite in Renaissance Europe. In J. Epstein and K. Straub (eds.) *Body Guards: The Cultural Politics of Gender Ambiguity*. New York: Routledge, 80–111.

——(2000). *Renaissance Clothing and the Materials of Memory*. Cambridge: Cambridge University Press.

Jonson, B. (1966). *Epicoene or The Silent Woman*, ed. L. A. Beaurline. Lincoln: University of Nebraska Press.

Laqueur, T. (1990). *Making Sex: Body and Gender from the Greeks to Freud*. Cambridge, MA: Harvard University Press.

Leach, C. (ed.) (1969). *The Two Gentlemen of Verona*. London: Methuen.

Levine, L. (1994). *Men in Women's Clothing: Anti-Theatricality and Effeminization 1579–1642*. Cambridge: Cambridge University Press.

Lucas, R. V. (1988). Hic Mulier: The Female Transvestite in Early Modern England. *Renaissance and Reformation*, n.s. 12, 65–83.

McLuskie, K. (1987). The Act, the Role, and the Actor: Boy Actresses on the Elizabethan Stage. *New Theatre Quarterly*, 3, 120–30.

Middleton, T. and Dekker, T. (1987). *The Roaring Girl*, ed. P. A. Mulholland. Manchester: Manchester University Press.

Orgel, S. (1996). *Impersonations: The Performance of Gender in Shakespeare's England*. Cambridge: Cambridge University Press.

Rackin, P. (1987). Androgyny, Mimesis, and the Marriage of the Boy Heroine on the English Renaissance Stage. *Publications of the Modern Languages Association*, 102, 29–41.

——(1993). Historical Difference/Sexual Difference. In J. R. Brink (ed.) *Privileging Gender in Early Modern England: Sixteenth Century Essays and Studies*, 23, 37–63.

Rose, M. B. (1988). Sexual Disguise and Social Mobility in Jacobean City Comedy. In *The Expense of Spirit: Love and Sexuality in English Renaissance Drama*. Ithaca, NY: Cornell University Press, 43–92.

Saeger, J. P. and Fassler, C. J. (1995). The London Professional Theater, 1576–1642: A Catalogue and Analysis of the Extant Printed Plays. *Research Opportunities in Renaissance Drama*, 34, ed. D. M. Bergeron.

Saslow, J. M. (1997). The Tenderest Lover: Saint Sebastian in Renaissance Painting: A Proposed Homoerotic Iconology for North Italian Art 1450–1660. *Gai Saber*, 1, 58–66.

Shapiro, M. (1994). *Gender in Play on the Shakespearean Stage: Boy Heroines and Female Pages*. Ann Arbor: University of Michigan Press.

Shapiro, S. C. (1987). Amazons, Hermaphrodites, and Plain Monsters: The "Masculine" Woman in English Satire and Social Criticism from 1580–1640. *Atlantis*, 13, 65–76.

Shepherd, S. (1981). *Amazons and Warrior Women: Varieties of Feminism in Seventeenth-Century Drama*. Brighton: Harvester.

Smith, B. R. (1991). *Homosexual Desire in Shakespeare's England*. Chicago, IL: University of Chicago Press.

Stokes, J. (1993). Women and Mimesis in Medieval and Renaissance Somerset (and Beyond). *Comparative Drama*, 7, 176–96.

Tiffany, G. (1995). *Erotic Beasts and Social Monsters: Shakespeare, Jonson, and Comic Androgyny.* London: Associated University Presses.

Traub, V. (1992). *Desire and Anxiety: Circulations of Sexuality in Shakespearean Drama.* London: Routledge.

Zimmerman, S. (1992). *Erotic Politics: Desire on the Renaissance Stage.* New York: Routledge.

7

The Homoerotics of Shakespeare's Elizabethan Comedies

Julie Crawford

One of the commonplaces of Shakespeare criticism is that the comedies end in marriage. This is not technically true: as one of the male suitors, Berowne, points out in *Love's Labour's Lost* (1594–5), "The ladies' courtesy / Might well have made our sport a comedy," but it does not: their "wooing doth not end like an old play: Jack hath not Gill" (5.2.874–6). In a number of other plays, such as *Twelfth Night* (1601–2), the marriage is deferred, or, as in *All's Well That Ends Well* (1602–3), threatened with divorce (see also Orgel 1996: 17; Shannon 2000: 186). Even for those plays which do end in marriage, plays are more than their endings, and the comedies' central concern with marriage allows a wide range of commentary on the institution and its workings. As a number of critics have pointed out, there is nothing "natural" about the marital heterosexuality which closes comedies; the marriage plots are often hurried, deferred, or anxiously enforced, "intersected" with homoerotic relationships, as in *A Midsummer Night's Dream* (1595–6), or existing alongside of them, as in *The Merchant of Venice* (1596–7) (DiGangi 1997: 62; Schwarz 2000; Pequigney 1992; Patterson 1999). Furthermore, as Laurie Shannon has recently argued, however normative heterosexual coupling may have been as hierarchy and means of social reproduction in the period, it contradicted the likeness topos at the center of positive ideas about union. In fact, the period's valorization of same-sex attraction and relations was so strong that the "ideological work of much comedy [was] less to celebrate or to critique marriage and its approach than to find a means to make it plausible or even thinkable in parity terms" (Shannon 2000: 186–7). Yet many critics accept the marriage ending as a central defining feature of comedy and posit a kind of compulsory heterosexuality or "heterosexual imperative" for the comedies (Green 1998: 380). This perceived telos thus guides our readings of the comedies as stories in which heterosexuality always triumphs, a reading which presumes that marriage is the same thing as heterosexuality. While most critics acknowledge the presence of homoeroticism within the comedies, especially in scenes of crossdressing, these moments of subversion or "holiday humor" are contained by, or within, the concluding "heterosexual" marriage; a three-hours' traffic of subversion and containment.

Yet "heterosexuality" is not an Elizabethan or early modern concept. Its current meaning, as a normative organization of sexuality into relationships between men and women, was contingent, both conceptually and etymologically, on the invention of the term "homosexuality" in the late eighteenth and early nineteenth centuries.[1] I interrogate the use of the term heterosexuality in order to highlight the second most important insight that queer scholarship on Shakespeare has offered us: Shakespearean comedies may often end in marriage, but they are not about heterosexuality. Marriage and heterosexuality are not the same thing, and the theoretical rigor that is brought to bear on studies of early modern homoeroticism – the questioning of terms and orders – is necessarily brought to bear on our understanding of heteroeroticism and marriage as well. As Valerie Traub has written, the homoerotics of Shakespearean comedy are most accurately perceived as "a cultural intervention in a heterosexually overdetermined field" (Traub 1992a: 118). At its best, queer scholarship has helped us to see the varied forms of affective relations and social alliances represented in the plays.[2]

Queer scholarship on Shakespeare offers us ways to see the social systems in which homoeroticism was present and to understand the erotic categories of an earlier culture. Following Michel Foucault, scholars have accepted that the Renaissance precedes modern regimes of sexuality, and to speak of "sexuality" in the period is a misnomer. In the premodern period sexuality was not understood as something that inhered in individuals, nor was it a defining marker, or maker, of identity. As Alan Bray puts it in his groundbreaking book *Homosexuality in Renaissance England* (1982), "to talk of an individual in this period as being or not being 'a homosexual' is an anachronism and ruinously misleading" (16). Beginning with Bray's book, scholars have attempted to understand the ways in which "homosexuality" worked in an era in which the homosexual – as an identity – and homosexuality – as a regime of sexual expression opposed to heterosexuality – did not exist. Unlike today, the early modern period recognized no homosexual minority, either oppressed or liberated. Yet as Gregory Bredbeck has pointed out, many formulations of historical difference assume "that unless we can find the subject as he is inscribed in our own language, then we cannot find him at all" (Bredbeck 1991: 43). A failure to examine homoerotic expression simply because our terms and orders did not apply to the early modern period is to tacitly accept that "the only sexuality that ever obtains is transhistorical heterosexuality" (Goldberg 1992: 6).

While the terms homosexual and heterosexual may have their roots in eighteenth- and nineteenth-century sexology and psychoanalysis, same-sex desire does not. As Valerie Traub points out, it is not the fact or presence of desire towards persons of the same gender that is culturally specific, but the meanings that are attached to its expression (Traub 1992a: 103). In fact, prior to codifications and normalizations of eighteenth- and nineteenth-century criminology, sexology, and psychology, same-gender desire was subjected to very little institutional regulation. As Jonathan Dollimore (1991: 26–7) points out, the absence of the autonomous or sexually disciplined self allows us to see a more complex relationship between law and desire and between dominant and deviant. Given that there was no separation between a homosexual minority and a heterosexual majority, sexual and erotic preferences were neither understood as distinct phenomena nor defined in opposition to one another. In a period without a fixed sense of sexual normalcy, norms may be produced but they are only temporarily dominant and always contestatory. Homosexuality, like heterosexuality, is neither essential nor constructed, but "provisional and context-dependent" (ibid: 32).[3] Yet at the same time as critics point to the openness of early modern eroticism and the instability of normative structures, it is equally important not to idealize the past as the free-play of polymorphous desires and to seek to find in the premodern period our "lost histories of perversion" (ibid: 22).

A portion of homoerotic criticism has focused on interrogating critics who presume that homoerotic relations are necessarily "disquieting," "unnatural," "humiliating," or (when between women) comic (Greenblatt 1988: 91; Howard 1988: 432; Adelman 1985: 81–2). A critique of these assumptions raises the question of historical accuracy – was homoerotic desire readily available as a source of humor and humiliation for Shakespeare's audiences? – but it is also a question of audience: to whom is male homoeroticism disquieting or desire between women funny? (Pequigney 1992: 206; Traub 1992a: 93). Homophobia was not necessarily a defining register of early modern homoeroticism, and early modern audiences did not necessarily identify only with heteroerotic desire. However, as Jean Howard (1994: 110) has argued, while there might not have been a subordinated sexuality in the same way as there was a subordinated gender, this does not mean that early modern culture did not exert pressure on the production and channeling of erotic energy. While Shakespearean comedies are certainly experimental in their eroticism, offering a range of possible pleasures, particular plays do privilege specific forms of erotic desire: some marginalize homoerotic attachments and privilege heterosexual closure (ibid: 111). In fact, according to some scholars, homophobia had indeed become a shaping force in erotic triangles by the end of the sixteenth century and may well figure in the representation of homoeroticism in Shakespeare's plays (Shepherd 1992; Patterson 1999: 28).

While care should be taken not to presume or erase historical homophobia, the specter of homophobia haunts criticism in other ways. A number of critics align themselves with Eve Sedgwick's "antihomophobic" critical practice, seeking in their criticism not to presume the pathology of homoeroticism. Yet there is a danger that in criticizing others' critical paradigms as homophobic – as when Jonathan Goldberg accuses some critics of "coming dangerously close to equating homosexuality and misogyny" (Goldberg 1992: 107, n.10) – we might actually limit or impede critical insights. The fear of the political implications of readings that are distasteful to us – that certain homoerotic dynamics are age-asymmetrical (conjuring up the specter of pedophilia), or that others are related to, if not the same thing as, misogyny – can shut down reading practices.[4] Committing to an anti-homophobic critical practice is important, but being aware of the political motivations of interpretive strategies applies both to those critics who ahistorically demonize homoeroticism, and to those who idealize it. The point of reading the homoeroticism in Shakespeare's comedies is neither to posit that Shakespeare was above homophobia, nor that he was victim to it, but rather to look at the ways in which Shakespeare's plays, like those of his contemporaries, reveal (an interest in) same-sex eroticism.

In order to grasp the varied meanings of early modern homoeroticism, we need to question the "epistemological certitudes" we bring to the study of premodern sexuality (Fradenburg and Freccero 1996: 9). For example, the late twentieth-century assumption that effeminacy was a sign of male homosexuality is patently untrue for the early modern period, when effeminacy was understood as the result of a man's excessive attention to women. Similarly, an assumption that homoerotic activity was considered deviant in the early modern period and therefore necessarily hidden or disguised, hinders our ability to recognize the extent to which homoerotic practices were a recognizable part of normal social relations. The search for an oppressed minority blinds us to the ways in which homosexual behavior served to empower certain men, not victimize them (Smith 1991: 12). Our assumption, tutored through late-modern homophobia, that male homosexuality is rigorously separate from homosociality is also a false one; as Alan Bray makes clear, many homosocial negotiations between men were done sexually. Ideally, these very differences help us to question our own assumptions about what homosexuality is: if it is not something that defines an individual, is it predicated on acts, desire, interactions? In the attempt to understand early modern homoeroticism – a term Valerie Traub uses to distinguish between legal and medical discourses of sodomy and tribadism, and the modern identificatory classifications of lesbian, gay, and homosexual (Traub 1992b: 69) – scholars have located several privileged sites in which it is most visible: sodomy, crossdressing, and certain recognized same-sex relations. I will turn briefly to the implications of each of these sites before offering some further rubrics through which we might recognize early modern homoeroticism as it appears in Shakespeare's comedies.

Sodomy

Sodomy became a key category for the study of early modern homoeroticism for several reasons. The legal deployment of sodomy in the late modern period is predicated on that of the early modern period, a fact which makes the specter of sodomy singularly significant for us. Sodomy was a charge leveled against those whose actions were considered anti-social – heretics, traitors, Catholics. The term sodomy was related to a range of acts which included, according to different texts and definitions, sexual relations between men and between women. According to Alan Bray, the term sodomy identified acts which occurred in stigmatizing contexts but which nevertheless went on in other contexts as part of their normative workings. Although Bray does not see sodomy and its attendant judgments as defining the limits of early modern male homoeroticism – persecutions for sodomy were actually very rare, while male homoeroticism was a defining feature of many central institutions – he does take physical sexual acts as the factual sign of male homosexuality in the period: for Bray, the homosexual is the sodomite. For Gregory Bredbeck (1991: 29), the sodomite, as the absolute

Other of social order, actually played a key role in the maintenance of social order. Yet for Bruce Smith (1991: 13–14), early modern legal proscriptions against sodomy were merely the *scientia sexualis* to the positive *ars erotica* of homoerotic desire in the visual arts and literature. While moral, legal, and medical discourses were concerned with stigmatized sexual acts, poetic discourses reveal the presence of homosexual desire. Like Smith, Valerie Traub (1992a: 64) points to the limits of depending on theology and law as evidence for female homoerotic activity, questioning whether the fact that no English woman was brought to trial under the sodomy statute meant that no women practiced such behaviors. Traub points to other texts – like gynecology and stage plays – for evidence of different languages of female homoerotic desire. Similarly realizing the limits of focusing on sodomy as a marker of early modern homoeroticism, Jonathan Goldberg uses the term "sodometries" to explain the relational structures which mediated between sodomitical and non-sodomitical forms of homoeroticism, the possible switch from friendship to sodomy which occurred through "the transgression of social hierarchies that friendship maintained" (Goldberg 1992: 119). The specter of sodomy always haunts the edges of male homoeroticism. Mario DiGangi questions the usefulness of sodomy as a marker of homoeroticism altogether, pointing out that the history of the persecution of sodomy is not the same thing as the persecution of homosexuality. Instances of condemnation of sodomy or tribadism do not signify the truth of a "whole system of homoeroticism any more than acts such as adultery suggest the truth of a whole system of "heterosexuality"; there were both orderly and disorderly forms of homoeroticism. Following Bray, Goldberg and DiGangi highlight the orderly forms of early modern male homoeroticism, from friendship and patronage to service. While the charge of sodomy certainly provides a vivid marker of stigmatized behaviors – including, but not limited to, same-sex erotic acts – it is by no means the dominant register of homoeroticism.

Crossdressing

Another central route to a critical recognition of the homoeroticism in Shakespearean comedies came through feminist criticism focused on the phenomenon of boy heroines, especially Rosalind as Ganymede, Portia as Balthazar, and Viola as Sebastian. Many critics pointed out that crossdressing highlighted the social construction of gender roles, suggesting that the differences between the sexes were a matter of costume and behavior rather than essence (Rackin 1987; Levine 1986; Howard 1988, 1994, 1998). For Phyllis Rackin, the boy heroine was an androgyne, a fusion of both sexes; for Michael Shapiro, she/he was a "figure of unfused, discretely layered gender identities – play-boy, female character, male persona" which were differently highlighted at different moments in the play (a reading in which conventional gender distinctions are preserved in their discrete layers (Shapiro 1994: 3)); and for Marjorie Garber (1991), the transvestite figure suggested a new gender category all its own. Working with poststructuralist and historicist ideas, feminists argued that during a period in which the family was in flux, so too were gender roles, offering sites of resistance and possibilities of new powers for women. Crossdressing comedies, with their "subversive reinscription of conventional gender roles," undermined the stability of these roles, offering us a glimpse of a "liminal moment" when gender definitions were open to play (Belsey 1988; Rackin 1987: 38). For Jonathan Dollimore, crossdressing is more accurately described not as transcendence of gender norms but as "transgressive reinscription" of the existing order, "an anti-essentialist, transgressive agency" which intensifies the instabilities in any normative system and reveals it as contestable (Dollimore 1991: 33, 298).

While some critics argue that Shakespearean comedies do not resolve the sexual ambiguity of the boy heroines, preserving their complex erotic appeal (Rackin 1987: 31; Smith 1992: 140), others evaluate the crossdressed boy heroine in male–female terms, and often within a heterosexual dynamic. While most boy heroines experience the broader male range of action, "contained" boy heroines serve the interests of a conventional sex–gender system, and "subversive" boy heroines teach men to be better husbands.[5] In these readings, crossdressing may allow women "on top," but they are still in a heterosexual position: the central dynamics, and erotics, occasioned by boy heroines are female–male ones. According to one interpretation, the boy heroine produces a dynamic in which male characters first fall in love with other "men," or mirror images of themselves, before they learn to love the non-masculine traits of women, a psychoanalytic model in which same-sex desire is understood as a rite of passage from homosexual adolescence to heterosexual manhood (MacCary 1985). While crossdressing produces homoerotic moments, these moments are temporary, dangerous, or comic, and inevitably subsumed to heterosexual closure.

Scholars have also considered the boy heroine in terms of his or her homoerotic appeal to the audience, not just to other characters. For Phyllis Rackin, the boy heroine, understood as an androgyne, provided an erotic appeal for all members of the audience. For others, the names the boy heroines assume, such as Ganymede and Sebastian, are homosexual prototypes, and the boy heroine – by both soliciting homoerotic dynamics and drawing attention to the "boy beneath" the layers of costume – is ultimately the object of male homoerotic desire. For Lisa Jardine, the ultimate effect of crossdressing and its resulting androgyny is to "kindle homosexual love in the male members of the audience" (Jardine 1989: 19, 17). Rosalind's claim that "boys and women are cattle of the same colour" attests to the truth that "the dependent role of the boy player doubles for the dependency which is woman's lot, creating a sensuality which is independent of the sex of the desired figure, and which is particularly erotic where the sex is confused (when boy player represents woman, disguised as dependent boy)" (ibid: 24). For Stephen Orgel, the ultimately male and male homoerotic nature of the early modern transvestite theatre was a way of dealing with the fear of female sexuality (assumed to be heterosexual), which was ultimately seen as more threatening than male homosexuality. Like women, boys were objects of desire for men, but unlike women, they did not threaten men with effeminacy (Orgel 1996: 26). Thus the all-male stage and the crossdressed boy heroine are ways of displacing the fears of women, and the female costume is a cover for the homoerotic body (ibid: 36).

Based on Philip Stubbes's oft-cited claim in *The Anatomie of Abuses* (1583) that after watching the performances of the transvestite theatre "every mate sorts to his mate, every one bringes another homeward or their way verye freendly, and in their secret conclaves (covertly) they play the Sodomits, or worse" (Stubbes 1973: 118, n.22 N8v), the male homoerotic response to the transvestite stage – both uncontrollably aroused and mimetic – has become a critical commonplace.[6] Far less attention has been paid to the responses of women, although, as Jean Howard points out, it is difficult to believe that men could have done all the looking in "the theatrical economy of gazes" (Howard 1994: 78). As members of the audience, women were not simply objects under patriarchy, they were subjects who exercised their judgment both economically and responsively. Yet while Stephen Orgel rightly considers women's erotic responses to the plays, he imagines them only in terms of heterosexual response, claiming that love matches and cuckoldry were "the two sides of the notion of liberty for women" (Orgel 1996: 37). It seems both remarkable and critically emblematic that in one of the most polymorphously erotic scenes in Shakespeare's comedies, the Epilogue in *As You Like It* (1599), when Rosalind promises that "If I were a woman, I would kiss as many of you as had beards that pleased me," no one has considered the idea that the beards which pleased her most might have been *no beards at all*. While it is acknowledged that the play ends with a renewed attack on the pretensions of erotic certitude and that Rosalind solicits a range of responses, the responses of women are presumed to be heteroerotic and those of the men homoerotic. Yet in this particular moment, Rosalind is addressing herself, coyly and homoerotically, to the women in the audience *as a woman*. While it is essential to introduce homoerotic considerations into scenes of crossdressing, it is equally important not to see them only as male. Rather than "really" being about men or male homoeroticism, crossdressing seizes upon contradictions, and the erotics of female characters crossdressing appealed not just to men but to women as well. The gaze which "objectifies" women, or sees them as objects of erotic desire, should not be "presumed male" (Bruster 1993: 22).

While many of Shakespeare's comedies do include verbal clues "that suggest a jokey but interested awareness of the boy's body beneath the woman's weeds" (Smith 1992: 137), Peter Stallybrass (1992) has drawn attention to the ways in which "the body beneath" is not an absolute ground of sexual difference, but a site of indeterminacy molded by the "almost magical properties of transvestism" and the prosthetic marks of gender (p. 76). Yet the ultimate basis of the male body has also been seen as the grounds for the male homoerotic nature of the early modern stage. Based on Thomas Laqueur's work on the early modern understanding of sexed bodies, Stephen Greenblatt argues that the early modern conception of gender as "teleologically male" finds its "supreme literary expression in a transvestite theatre" (Greenblatt 1988: 88). In this reading, crossdressing is ultimately about the emergence of male identity, and thus all sexuality has a homoerotic element (ibid: 92). While the condition of possibility for homoeroticism in Jardine and Orgel's reading is gender – understood as "feminine" in its dependent, asymmetrical dynamics – for Greenblatt the condition of homoerotic possibility is the sexed body. Jardine and Orgel argue that the transvestite theatre is "really" about male homoeroticism, and Greenblatt argues that it is really about men. Homoeroticism, almost invariably male, is presumed to rely on either gender or sex.

It is this final assumption that informs the work of Jonathan Goldberg and Valerie Traub. Both are critical of the fact that crossdressing has come to seem "the privileged locus of the representation of what gets called homosexuality in Renaissance drama" (Goldberg 1992: 115). To argue that boys and women are identical to each other, or that the less empowered or crossdressed male has a female position in homoerotic exchanges is to understand homosexuality as "a transvestite masquerade," a replay of heterosexuality without women (ibid: 111). Traub (1992a: 94) similarly points out that Jardine's argument that the erotic interest in the boy actor depends on his femininity reconstitutes the interaction as "implicitly heteroerotic." Assuming both effeminacy as a condition for homoeroticism, and a duality of activity and passivity as a necessary condition for all eroticism, such an argument posits that male–male interactions are the same thing as male–female ones. Traub points out that femininity and masculinity are gender terms, and that they are not the same thing as heterosexuality, an erotic term; Traub's invaluable point is that gender is not the sole determinant of eroticism or desire and that gender does not equal sexuality.[7] Gender anxiety is no more, and no less, constitutive of homoerotic desire than it is of heterosexual desire, and transvestism could theoretically engender heterosexual as well as homoerotic desires (ibid: 121). Rather than seeing gender as a product of clothing or as something sutured onto a body, both critics understand gender as the product of social relations, and both seek ways of locating homoeroticism which are not solely predicated on gender. As Traub insists, it is only because of the institutional character of heterosexuality – a relationship between two different genders – that gender has come to seem the sole determinant of arousal (ibid: 104). In fact desire is often motivated by differences *within* genders as well as those perceived to exist between them, and by other factors altogether, including age, religion, race, and power.

Homoerotic Relations

After sodomy and crossdressing, the situations and discourses most recognized as homoerotic are those which privilege same-sex relationships. Homoeroticism has been located in particular eras and locations: ancient Greece, as in *Troilus and Cressida* (1601–2), where the relationship of Patroclus to Achilles is analogous to that of *eromenos* and *erastes* (Smith 1992: 133); ancient Rome, a period in which the gender of the love object mattered less than class or age (Goldberg 1992: 69); and the timeless "golden world" invoked in *As You Like It*'s Forest of Arden with Duke Senior's homosocial Robin Hood-like band of "merry men" and "loving lords" (1.1.100–1, 115–16). But homoeroticism is also located in certain relationships, situations, and dynamics. For men, these relations included homosexual prostitution, male friendship and patronage, the patriarchal household – especially the relationships between masters and servants – the educational system, and the military (Bray 1994; Masten 1997; Stewart 1997; Smith 1991, 1992; Bredbeck 1991, 1992; Spear 1993;

Dollimore 1991).[8] Indeed, homoeroticism was so much a part of these relationships that it is possible for critics to "disappear it" into conventions like friendship (Goldberg 1992: 6). The homoeroticism in militarized relationships has similarly been dismissed as a convention; Robin Headlam Wells's sole note on homoeroticism in *Shakespeare on Masculinity* (2000) points out that the "idealized heroic love of brothers-in-arms" was a convention, and that many of the men who express erotic ties with other men are not homosexuals or even bisexual but "extravagantly, even compulsively, heterosexual" (ibid: 163). Regardless of this anachronistic – and too-protesting – use of terms, the fact that something is a convention does not, as Richard Rambuss points out, "make a discursive construct or a sentiment any less thick with significance" (Rambuss 1998: 1–2). The point is not that homoeroticism was not "really" present in conventional male relationships, but rather that it was not considered deviant or necessarily opposed to heteroerotic desire.

The comedies often reveal such male homoerotic dynamics at work: *Love's Labour's Lost* invokes the male homosocial nature of the academy, to which the male characters become "vow-fellows"; militarized homoeroticism – which Bruce Smith calls *masculus amor* – is one of the dominating themes of *Troilus and Cressida*; and a broad range of plays, including *Twelfth Night* – a play in which Jardine (1989: 33) points out that all the central relationships are those of eroticized service – suggest the homoeroticism of master and servant relationships. A number of plays also deal with the fine lines between acceptable homoeroticism and that which threatens social order. Many of these homoerotic dynamics, such as the personal service of male friends and retainers, were changing by the end of the sixteenth century, and as the legitimacy which protected these forms of homoeroticism decayed, they were opened to charges of sodomy (Bray 1994: 53). Arguably, this is a dynamic we see at work in *The Merchant of Venice*, a play in which Antonio's devotion to Bassanio seems "sadly outmoded" (Patterson 1999: 14).

While some institutions, such as education, the household, and the military, have received much critical attention for the sorts of homoerotic interactions they inspire, others, like religion, have not. Yet in a period in which religion, unlike sexuality, was a central defining feature of individuals, it is likely that religious beliefs and affiliations occasioned and facilitated homoerotic dynamics. For example, what is the significance of Proteus' promise to be Valentine's "beadsman" (*Two Gentleman of Verona*, 1.1.16–18) – a holy man engaged to pray for another – in a context in which same-sex Roman Catholic practices were tainted with the specter of sodomy? How is their same-sex loyalty related to the fact that heteroerotic desires in the play are often described as idolatrous?[9] What role does religious performance play in the disciplining of male behavior, including that which is potentially homoerotic? In *The Merchant of Venice* Gratiano's "skipping spirit" needs to be reformed lest he ruin Bassanio's chances at Belmont (2.2.173). He swears he will "put on sober habit" and "weare prayer books in my pocket," but not that night, "for we have friends / That purpose merriment" (2.2.178; 187). In this context, religion serves a disciplining role, but it is also perceived to be superficial rather than substantive. Finally, what are the connotations of the same-sex communities and religious retreats represented in the comedies? Portia invokes the monastery or convent when she tells the court that she has "breathed a secret vow / To live in prayer and contemplation, / Only attended by Nerissa here" (*Merchant of Venice*, 3.4.27–9) right before their profoundly homoerotic exchange about codpieces, and it is in the Widow Capilet's pilgrimage house – a refuge for women only – that Helena meets, and dowers, the virgin Diana. In addition to class and race, religion provides an understudied discourse through which to examine homoeroticism.

As the above discussion reveals, most scholarly attention to early modern homoeroticism has focused on male paradigms; female homoeroticism has fared less well. At worst, it is assumed not to exist at all, or, on occasion, seen only through the reviewers' heterosexist gaze which reads female–female homoeroticism as "really" for male pleasure and consumption.[10] According to one such interpretation, speeches like Helena's description of her relationship with Hermia as being "incorporate" like a "double cherry," while certainly inviting carnal imaginings, are erotic for the audience rather than the speaker (Bruster 1993: 11–13). We are assured, on the basis of no cited evidence, that eroticized female–female relations were either intended for third-party arousal, or were always open to erotic appropriation. The rhetoric of female objectification is assumed male, and female homoeroticism is wrested from the purview of women. Feminist insights about the determining power of the male gaze become both sexist and heterosexist when applied without exploration, denying female homoerotic desire in both speakers and audience members.

Yet there is a growing body of work which points to female homoerotic types and dynamics. Valerie Traub (1992b: 62) has examined the cultural and theatrical presence of the French female sodomite, English tribade, and theatrical "femme." Kathryn Schwarz (2000: 6–9) has drawn our attention to the figure of the Amazon, who, by exemplifying "female masculinity," troubles the relationship between sexed bodies and gendered acts and occasions diverse sexual possibilities and desires, and Theodora Jankowski (2000: 6) has focused on the virgin who either refuses marriage outright or "prolongs her virginity in an attempt to resist incorporation into the patriarchal sexual economy." Those characters whom Jankowski calls "queer virgins," such as *Measure for Measure*'s Isabella and *All's Well That Ends Well*'s Diana, not only resist the patriarchal binaristic marital model, but they enjoy bonds of friendship and affection which have erotic components (ibid: 6).

Another area in which female homoeroticism has recently received critical attention is in Queen Elizabeth's court. Not only were depictions of a woman with other women at the heart of the cult of Elizabeth, but Elizabeth's relationships with her female courtiers, the "semi-professional corps of women" who monitored access to her privy chamber, were often both exclusive and erotic (Berry 1989: 65; Brown 1999). The fact that Elizabeth joked that she should marry Princess Juana – a relationship in which she would play the husband's part – suggests the active presence of an imaginary of female homosocial and homoerotic alliance (Goldberg 1992: 41). Rather than being solely organized around the male homosocial and Petrarchan dynamics of male suitors for Elizabethan favor, the Elizabethan court also imagined female homoerotic possibilities. The queen was both Diana and the Petrarchan beloved, both surrounded by women and solicited by, and solicitous of, men. This recognition of the dual nature of the Elizabethan court should influence, I would argue, our interpretation of two of those Shakespearean comedies most explicitly associated with the queen, *The Merry Wives of Windsor* (1597, revised 1601), and *Love's Labour's Lost*. The former play concludes with Nan as "the Fairy Queen," a figure described by Pistol as a "radiant Queen" who "hates sluts and sluttery" (5.5.46). The play centers on the wives' humiliation of Falstaff – Elizabeth's favored character – but it is also a play about the alliance of two women, Mistress Page and Mistress Ford, who are so often together that one of their husbands makes a joke about them marrying each other (3.2.13–17). *Love's Labour's Lost* is even more complicated, with its topical allusions to the French court and the Duke of Alençon, who was, of course, a suitor for Elizabeth's hand, and an ending in which the Princess and her "ladies-in-waiting" defer, as Elizabeth so often did, the marriage offers of male suitors. While critics have often noted the male homosociality of the King of Navarre and his "vow-fellows," the homosociality and homoeroticism of the women's coterie has been less remarked upon.[11] Partially, I would argue, this lack of recognition is due to scholarly paradigms from outside of Shakespeare criticism which suggest that the exchange of love letters and sonnets – which make up a great deal of the action of the play – is not really about the women to whom they are sent, but rather about male homosocial, and homoerotic, relationships triangulated and cemented through those female figures (Marotti 1982). While the Princess and her waiting women attempt to socialize the men away from wooing simply "the sign of she" and into a more socially integrated role, they are also a coterie of literary and cultural critics who receive the men's letters, poems, favors and "in our maiden council rated them" (5.2.468–9; 779). When the King asks the ladies at the "latest minute" to grant them their loves, the Princess answers that it is a time "too short / To make a world-without-end bargain in" (5.2.786–7), a decision remarkably similar to Elizabeth's own. As in Queen Elizabeth's court, marriage is something to be constantly deferred, while women's coteries are maintained.

In addition to those dynamics long, or recently, recognized as occasioning female homoeroticism, are those dynamics which have been mined for their significance in male–male relations but rarely considered in female terms. One of these dynamics is the early modern practice of sharing beds. In *Much Ado About Nothing* (1598–9), for example, Beatrice informs Benedick that until the previous night – when heteroerotic machinations literally imperiled Hero's life – she had for the last "twelvemonth been her bedfellow" (4.1.45–7), and part of Celia's homoerotic description of her relationship with Rosalind includes the observation that "We still have slept together, / Rose at an instance, learn'd, play'd, eat together" (*As You Like It*, 1.3.69–70). While Traub has argued that such homoerotic female relationships as the one between Celia and Rosalind are part of a premarital past, Kathryn Schwarz points out that the telling of these stories gives them a prominent place in the narrative nonetheless, and, as I will argue later, they are not necessarily only premarital.[12]

A more prominent dynamic, long recognized as a site of male homoeroticism but not often considered for its possible female homoerotic connotations, is that between masters and servants. Several homoerotic exchanges between women and their waiting women occur during scenes of crossdressing in which the servant is making her mistress into a "man."[13] When Portia tells Lorenzo that she and her gentlewoman-in-waiting Nerissa are going to crossdress and enter a monastery, it gives rise to erotic joking between the two. Portia bets Nerissa that when they are "both accoutered like young men" she will "prove the prettier fellow of the two," and tells her that she has in mind "a thousand raw tricks of these bragging Jacks, / Which I will practice" (*Merchant of Venice*, 3.4.62). When Nerissa questions "Why, shall we turn to men?" Portia reprimands her, warning of the repercussions if she "wert near a lewd interpreter!" and then promises to tell her "all my whole *device*" – a term which itself solicits a "lewd interpretation" as a dildo – when they are together in the privacy of her coach (3.4.75–82).[14] Although critics often focus on the end-point of the disguises – Portia saving her man – the dressing itself, as a joint process between two women, has explicitly homoerotic connotations. There is a similar dynamic in *The Two Gentlemen of Verona* between a servant and her mistress. When Lucetta is dressing her mistress as a boy, she asks: "What fashion, madam, shall I make your breeches?" and when Julia responds: "Why e'en what fashion thou best likes, Lucetta," Lucetta avows that "You must need have them with a codpiece, madam" (2.7.49). Like the "device," the codpiece is associated both with the prosthesis or dildo and sexual license, which Lucio in *Measure for Measure* calls the "rebellion of a cod-piece" (3.2.109). When Lucetta criticizes men, Julia reprimands her and then tells her to "go with me to my changeroom / To take note of what I stand in need of," an erection/phallus joke which is not only about her lack as a man, but her erotic makings with her maid. While women were rarely prosecuted for tribadism or using illicit sexual devices – the "logic of supplementarity" which made female sodomy both possible and legally actionable (Traub 1992b: 67) – these sexual acts, while not marking the limits of female same-sex possibility, were nonetheless invoked in the comedies, and not only as a specter of horror.[15] Rather than simply highlighting Portia and Julia's phallic lack, puns about "devices" and "codpieces" provide an – not *the* – occasion for female homoerotic exchange.

Yet as Valerie Traub (ibid) has pointed out, the fact that the model of phallic imitation was favored by early modern legal and medical authorities – and determined as the grounds for punishment – does not delimit the ways in which women received erotic pleasure from one another.[16] As another model, Traub has pointed to the female "homoerotic pastoralism" of *As You Like It* and *A Midsummer Night's Dream* (ibid: 73).[17] In these plays homoeroticism is not initially occasioned by crossdressing or the subversion of gender roles, and "erotic virginity" is understood as a natural expression of love between women (ibid: 74; see also Jankowski 2000). Yet while the two pairs, Helena and Hermia and Celia and Rosalind, resist being "sundered," their homoeroticism is seen as elegiac, only granted significance after it has been rendered a thing of the past. But Traub's argument that the homoerotic desires of these female characters existed comfortably within the patriarchal order only until the onset of marriage gives too much credit to the restrictiveness, and heterosexuality, of marriage (Traub 1992b: 73). There is less of a sense that female homoeroticism endangers women's reproductive "performance" in these plays than a sense that the "twinning" or pairing of the women requires a new institutional instantiation for its continuation. The speed of Celia's marriage, as I will argue further below, is less an attempt to "heterosexualize" her, than a condition of her continued relationship with Rosalind and a fulfillment of her promise to make Rosalind her "heir." Traub argues that the drama suggests that if same-gender erotic practices could coexist with the marriage contract there would be little cause for alarm, but I would add that marriage itself was often precisely the enabling condition for its continuation (Traub 1992b: 78). This was true not just for "indivisible" pairs like Celia and Rosalind, but for age- and status-unequal relationships as well: female servants and waiting gentlewomen and their mistresses.

Although *The Merchant of Venice* has long been recognized for its homoerotic content, the critical focus on Antonio and Bassanio's relationship has occluded our recognition of another form of homoeroticism: the relation of service and dependence between two women. Belmont is an all-female community maintained through the interdependence of Portia and Nerissa. Nerissa's position in the household rarely varies with the male suitors; she is only asked to "stand all aloof" from Portia when Bassanio chooses his casket (3.2.42). Thus when Nerissa and Gratiano, the companions of Portia and Bassanio respectively, vow to marry each other – as Gratiano explains to Bassanio, "Your fortune stood upon the caskets there, / And so did mine too" (3.2.202) – Nerissa vows only to make the marriage if Portia "stand pleased withal" (3.2.209). She renegotiates her continuing relationship with Portia by means of – not in spite of – marriage. Similarly, in *Twelfth Night* Olivia, who "hath abjured the sight / And company of men" (1.2.41–2), is the sole head of her household, and her reign is fiercely defended by Maria, her waiting gentlewoman. Maria's role consists in maintaining her centrality in the household (Tvordi 1999: 22) and her position in the household is complex; at different points Sir Toby calls her "My niece's chambermaid" and "Penthesilea," a not-so subtle allusion to the Queen of the Amazons (1.3.49; 2.3.170). While Olivia's marriage allows her to maintain her own household and power (Jankowski 2000: 155), Maria's marriage to Sir Toby, Olivia's uncle, is less a heterosexualizing move than one which firmly entrenches her in the household. In both *The Merchant of Venice* and *Twelfth Night* the waiting gentlewoman, like the male beloved friend, is not excluded by marriage; rather than marking the end of the homosocial relationship, marriage gives it institutional continuation.

The Question of Marriage

Such scenes of institutional continuation bring this discussion of homoeroticism in Shakespeare's comedies (seemingly counter-intuitively) back to the question of marriage. While marriage is of central importance in the comedies, is it really the end – or "the other" – of homoeroticism? In fact, one of the reasons early modern homoeroticism was not threatening was because it was not defined in opposition to or as an impediment to marriage (Sedgwick 1985). Portia, who describes Antonio as the "bosom lover of [her] lord" (3.4.17), sees a homology between male–male and male–female loves (Pequigney 1992: 212), and in *The Two Gentlemen of Verona* Valentine uses the same language of Petrarchan love to refer to his male and female beloveds (Masten 1997). Yet there are also imaginative possibilities, such as certain Ovidian myths, in which male homoerotic desire actively disrupts marital (hetero)sexuality (DiGangi 1997: 31), and there are plays in which certain forms of male homoeroticism and homosociality clearly stand in distinction to heterosociality.

In *Much Ado About Nothing* Beatrice shows interest in, and gentle mockery of, Benedick's companions and monthly "new sworn brother" (1.1.65). Male–female desire stands in direct contrast to military homoeroticism; as Claudio puts it, "war thoughts / Have left their places vacant, in their rooms / Come thronging soft and delicate desires" (1.1.280–1). In *All's Well That Ends Well* the stakes of this opposition are higher. Helena's love for Bertram stands in contradistinction to his own allegiance to *masculus amor*, exemplified in his relationship with Parolles who calls Bertram "sweetheart," and tells him that "A young man married is a man that's marred" (2.3.294). Bertram vows that instead of marrying Helena he will go "to the Tuscan wars and never bed her," never spend "his manly marrow in her arms" (2.3.266–7; 279). Immediately after this avowal, he asks Parolles to "go with me to my chamber and advise me" (2.3.292). Aware of his feelings, Helena calls herself Bertram's "despiteful Juno," citing the story in which Jupiter abandons Juno for Ganymede, a foundational story of male homoeroticism (DiGangi 1997: 50). Yet Bertram's choices are not just men over women, they are also about social status and place: he goes "From courtly friends, with camping foes to live" (3.4.14). Near the end of the play, when Bertram is going to be reabsorbed into a courtly society – although by no means as a happily married man, which I will discuss below – Parolles recognizes that there is still a place for men like him in those very camps. "But I will eat and drink and sleep as soft / As captain shall," he vows: "There's place and means for every man alive . . . I'll after them" (4.3.321, 330).[18] In *All's Well That Ends Well* the militarized homosocial and homoerotic world is not destroyed or replaced by the play's marital economy, but it is marginalized and certainly does not hold the status it holds in tragedy.[19]

There is a similar dynamic in *The Two Gentlemen of Verona*, in which Proteus seemingly chooses heteroeroticism over his alliance with Valentine (in this case not a relationship of militarized homoeroticism, but one of gentlemanly emulation (Masten 1997: 38–9)).[20] Yet the play offers a surprise resolution to this seeming choice, and that resolution is marriage. Proteus' crime is that he betrays the terms of identification and triangulation with Valentine, not that he desires Sylvia. Valentine is reconstituted in a different male homosocial economy with the outlaws (whom he reintroduces to society as "reformed, civil, full of good, / And fit for great employment": 5.4.157–8), and it is Valentine who reconstitutes a triangle when he asks Proteus and Julia for their hands: "Come, come, a hand from either. / Let me be blest to make this happy close; / 'Twere pity two such friends should be long foes" (5.4.117–19). At the end of the play the marriages serve to recreate the triangulated economy of male emulation and identification, with and through the affections of women. As Valentine says to Proteus at the end of *The Two Gentlemen of Verona*, "our day of marriage shall be yours: / One feast, one house, one mutual happiness" (5.4.171–4).

Yet many of the dynamics in which marriage actually facilitates the continuation of homosocial and homoerotic relationships are predicated on precisely the relationship between homosociality and homoeroticism that facilitates male dominance. In *The Two Gentlemen of Verona* it is male bonds which are prioritized. In the rest of this essay I wish to turn to a different set of questions about marriage and the ends of homoeroticism, and these questions have to do with women. Do the plays' commitment of their heroines to marriage truly mark "the limits of their challenge to patriarchal ideology" (Howard 1994: 121)? When the heroine abandons her disguise does she really merely "dwindle . . . into a wife" (Belsey 1988: 187)? Feminists have recognized the extent to which the contest for meaning of the family in the sixteenth and seventeenth centuries momentarily unfixed the existing system of gender differences (ibid: 178, 190). But the unsettled "moment" has often been closed down by an uncritical acceptance of a historical model of the rise of "the restricted patriarchal nuclear family" which dictated that wives be "chaste, silent, and obedient" (Stone 1979). While these models have been questioned, much criticism is guided by the belief in a "sex–gender" system that is more restricted than history – or Elizabethan drama – suggests. Among these presumptions is the belief that marriage was necessarily opposed to homosexuality, and that it served as an endpoint to both women's agency and homoeroticism. If we accept the dominant historical model of the patriarchal family and see wives as chaste, silent, and obedient, we privilege prescriptive texts like marriage manuals over the evidence of plays, and historical paradigms over the evidence of women's lives: Margaret Hoby and Anne Clifford reading in their closets with other women; Mary Sidney and Mary Wroth's coteries of women readers being invited to share in the eroticism of sapphic allusions and female homoerotic desire.[21] Furthermore, if we project a modern definition of the heterosexual nuclear family back onto the Renaissance household, we ignore, as Mario DiGangi (1997: 23) has pointed out, the homoerotics of the household. DiGangi points to male retainers and servants, focusing on the desires of the patriarch for those other than his wife, but I would add the household presence of female servants, kin, and neighbors, the desires not only of wives but their cohorts. If we look at marriage as a form of alliance – related to, but not the same thing as, heterosexuality – we get a better sense of the range of affective, economic, authoritative, and erotic bonds that create marriage.

As I have already suggested, *The Merry Wives of Windsor* deals with the desires that a wife might have for someone other than her husband. The households in this play are not patriarchal and restricted; in fact the two wives, Mistress Alice Ford and Mistress Margaret Page, enter the play together and appear more often in each other's homes than not.[22] Master Ford's constant jealous fears that his "bed shall be abus'd" (2.2.292) has, I would argue, an extension into female homoeroticism. In 3.2 when Mrs. Page is on her way to Mrs. Ford's house, she sees Ford and asks if Mrs. Ford is at home. He responds that she is, and then makes an amazing observation: "I think if your husbands were dead, you two would marry." Mrs. Page's response recognizes and maintains the homoerotic implications of the joke even as it asserts her fidelity to marriage: "Be sure of that – two other husbands" (3.2.13–17). At the end of the play Mrs. Page invites everyone into the Page home to "laugh this sport o'er by a country fire" (5.5.241), but Ford's last line – the last line of the play – is that he "will lie with Mistress Ford."[23] His jealous marital exclusivity stands in (rather harmless) contrast to the collective nature of the Page household, but it is also informed by the idea of his wife marrying another woman, a specter which he himself has invoked. The substantive, and substantively vindicated, economy of *The Merry Wives of Windsor* is not, I would argue, marital; it is female homosocial. Moreover, it is a homosociality which threatens exclusivity and hints of homoeroticism, and while this fact incurs jealousy in one of the husbands, it is neither denigrated nor corrected.

While the homoerotic force of Celia and Rosalind's relationship has long been recognized – as Charles puts it, "Never two ladies loved as they do" and they are described as being like "Juno's swans . . . coupled and inseparable" (*As You Like It*, 1.1.113; 1.3.69) – it has often been determined to have an endpoint in marriage (Traub 1992a, 1992b; Tvordi 1999). Yet when Rosalind suggests that the differences in their estates necessarily separate them, Celia vows that as an only child ("You know my father hath no child but I, nor none is like to have") she will make Rosalind her father's heir, "for what he hath taken away from thy father perforce, I will render thee again in affection" (1.2.16–20). Although Celia may indeed resist Rosalind's heteroerotic interest in Orlando, telling her to "love no man in good earnest" and to "wrestle with [her] affections," the two women are not actually "sunder'd" in the play (1.2.25–6; 1.3.20; 1.3.95). Celia and Rosalind buy a cottage, pasture, and flock and for much of the play set up housekeeping (2.4.90),[24] and when the marriages are announced – the speed of Celia's has already been noted – Celia and Rosalind prepare for the ceremony together (5.4). At the end of the play, right after Duke Senior welcomes Celia as a daughter, he has all his lands restored to him and the inheritance Celia promised Rosalind at the beginning of the play is fulfilled (5.4.146, 160). Celia and Rosalind, whose relationship was once described as "dearer than the natural bond of sisters," actually do become more than sisters: marrying brothers and inheriting jointly. While many scholars have focused on the play's property exchanges between men, from primogeniture to marriage, *As You Like It* also focuses a great deal of attention on the property negotiations between two women, in which one woman promises to make another her heir. While feminist insights about marriage as a form of "traffic in women" between men have been crucially important, they have assumed the status of prescriptive explanations for all negotiations of alliance and desire, blinding us to the possibilities not just of women's resistance, but of their deployment of the marital institution for their own ends.

All's Well That Ends Well also features a marriage that enables female homosocial and homoerotic relationships to continue. Arguably, the play's central marriage is less a union between a man and a woman than a union between women. From the beginning of the play, the dominant relationship is that between the widowed Countess of Rossilion and her orphaned ward Helena, a gentlewoman whom she loves "entirely," and to whom she wants to give a lawful title (1.3.98, 100). While the Countess also loves her son – "my love hath in't a bond / Whereof the world takes note" (1.3.185) – she is anxious to make Helena call her not "mistress" but "mother." For her own part, as Helena tells the King, she wants to choose from "the royal blood of France / My low and humble name to propagate / With any branch or image of thy state" (2.1.197–9). The Countess's desire to give Helena a lawful title and Helena's desire to propagate her name find a happy meeting place in Bertram, the Countess's son. While we are used to seeing marriage as an institution through which men cement their bonds via a woman, in *All's Well That Ends Well* it is two women who cement their contacts through a man (whose desirability is also attested to by Helena's conventional protestations of love). If we expect marriage to end women's homosocial relationships, the play again surprises us. For not only does Helena obtain Bertram, and thus the Countess's promised title, but she also attains a second homosocial coterie of women in the widow Capilet, her daughter Diana, and her friend Mariana. It is Helena's gift of a dowry of three thousand crowns that enables Diana to stay out of the marriage market and inspires Diana to tell Helena "I am yours" (3.7.35; 4.4.29).[25] Diana's claim that she will "live and die a maid" (3.7.74) is not, as Theodora Jankowski (2000) points out, necessarily a vow that she will live a life without desire or eroticism; it is merely a vow that she will not marry a man. When the play is read with an awareness of the different forms of homosociality and homoeroticism, the happy ending of *All's Well That Ends Well* is not necessarily a heterosexual one; when Bertram attests to his loyalty to Helena at the end of the play, she replies that if he proves untrue, "Deadly divorce step between me and you!" (5.3.315). It is Helena's homosocial female alliances – cemented *through* marriage – that enable her position and prompt passions that promise longevity.

Editing, Directing, Performing

While a good-faith attempt to determine the historical meanings of early modern homoeroticism is essential for understanding the plays, it is also important to remember that plays have not come to us unmediated from their historical contexts. Editors, directors, and revisers are interested in homoeroticism as well. Stephen Orgel notes that during the scene in which Hymen presents Rosalind to her father so that he might marry her to Orlando, the Folio version reads that he "mightst ioyne his hand with his," whereas the third Folio is revised to read "her hand" (Orgel 1996: 32–3). In other words an editor "corrects" the gender that Rosalind's disguise as Ganymede leaves male. Laurie Osborne (1994) has drawn our attention to the ways in which Antonio's place at the end of *Twelfth Night* was "corrected" by late eighteenth-century performance editions of the play, precisely at a moment when there was a marked increase in persecutions of homosexuals and love between men would have been a very dangerous – and recognizable – subject for representation.

While many questions of the homoerotics of early modern staging and performance are unrecoverable, Mary Bly has drawn attention to the deployment of homoerotic puns in early modern plays, suggesting that in their reliance on "pun-understanders," puns "inscribe a place within early modern culture in which homoerotic double-talk is both erotic and celebratory, funny and profitable" (Bly 2000: 5). While Bly focuses on the performance repertoire of a specific syndicate which sought to exploit an identifiable group of men in early seventeenth-century London, her insight that homoerotic double-talk might have provided a temporary homoerotic fellowship – a very different three-hours' traffic – is provocative for the ways in which we understand the relationship between the performance of homoeroticism and its effects on its audiences. The same is true of contemporary performance, and while modern productions may not accurately or mimetically reveal what homoeroticism was like in Shakespeare's time, they can provide insight into the myriad homoerotic connotations of his plays. The camp homoeroticism deployed in "The Donkey Show" – a version of *A Midsummer Night's Dream* set in a disco and currently running in New York City – particularly in its use of such terms as "sweet bully Bottom," reveals the limits of privileging historical paradigms as the only way of grasping the homoeroticism of Shakespeare's comedies. While jokes about bottoms might be more specific to late modern forms of homoeroticism than early modern ones, playing with and highlighting homoerotic connotations is not itself ahistorical. Rather, it is a continuation of a practice in which theatre-makers solicited the responses of their audiences based on, among other things, allusions to contemporary imaginaries of erotic possibilities. Seeing these possibilities acted out and solicited undoubtedly provided a great deal of the pleasure of early modern theatre-going, much as it does today.

NOTES

1 On the origins of the terms "homosexual" and "heterosexual" and on the regulation of sexuality, see Foucault (1980), Weeks (1981, 1985), Halperin (1993), Boswell (1982/3), Greenberg (1988), and Katz (1990).

2 I use the term "queer" here to highlight an interest in same-sex eroticism that is not necessarily predicated on gay and lesbian identities. See Doty (1993) and Duggan (1995).

3 Dollimore (1991) suggests that the disruption of norms comes not from those with alternative identities, but from what he calls "reactive agency." Traub (1992a: 16) similarly looks at the "textual circulation of erotic energy" rather than trying to locate "homosexual" characters. She also sees theories of the unconscious as a helpful way of getting at the "possibility of erotic disruption," focusing on the "psychic mechanisms of condensation, displacement, introjection, projection, substitution, splitting and reversal" (ibid: 11).

4 There may be complicity between male homosociality and misogyny, but this is not necessarily so, nor does a defense of women necessarily have to be a defense of heterosexuality and a delegitimation of male–male relations. As Traub (1992a: 143) points out, we may want to find scenes in which the homoeroticism is playful, and untainted by association with patriarchy, but these are not the only scenes we should privilege in our scholarship. Homoeroticism can be complicit with dynamics which we might not want it to be, as when male homoerotic exchanges fuel exploitation or colonization.

5 For Jean Howard, Rosalind-playing-Ganymede-playing-Rosalind is the best educator of all (Howard 1988: 435).

6 Scholars have pointed out that antitheatrical texts, which often seem to presume that the transvestite theatre was irresistibly erotic, were neither descriptive documents nor evidence (Howard 1994: 22–3; Orgel: 1996: 6). Some viewers accepted boy actors playing women's roles as representations

of women, and others, like Mary Wroth, understood stage transvestism as insulating the stage from lustful feelings rather than arousing them (ibid).

7   Traub points to the difficulty, and limitations, of extracting an erotic vocabulary out of the polarities of gender: "Men desire women because their gender role positions them as active; men who desire men do so because they have taken up a feminized position in relation to other males; lesbians desire women in imitation of active male desire . . . All sexuality is engaged in a structurally heterosexual mode of operation based on the duality of passivity and activity" (Traub 1992a: 102).

8   Bray focuses on male relations of friendship and patronage, Masten on male literary collaboration, Spear and Dollimore on militarized homoeroticism. Alan Stewart focuses on "humanistically informed patronage relationships," locating sexuality not in acts but in social relations. His types are the "beating schoolmaster, cloistered monk, humanist bedfellow, closeted secretary" (Stewart 1997: xlv). Smith offers a range of paradigmatic male homosocial and homoerotic dyads, such as "Master and Minion" and "Combatants and Comrades." All of these critics focus solely on male homoeroticism.

9   When Proteus asks Silvia for her picture she refuses to be his "idol," telling him that it becomes his falsehood to "worship shadows and adore false shapes" (*Two Gentlemen of Verona*, 4.2.118, 127).

10 One critic describes the scene between Hermia and Helena as having "some of the potentially pornographic effects of female mud-wrestling," and suggests that many modern productions "not only presume the conventional comic view of violence between women but also rely on a sexual effect akin to the cinematic use of lesbian sex in pornography aimed at men" (Green 1998: 382). Another argues that the "'eroticism' in female–female eroticism is produced by characters but is not necessarily for them" (Bruster 1993: 2).

11 The exceptions are Dash and Jankowski.

12 Of course the idea that homoerotic relationships are adolescent – compare Valentine's claim that "I know [Proteus] as myself; for from our infancy / We have conversed and spent our hours together" (*Two Gentlemen of Verona*, 2.4.60–1) – can be read within a psychoanalytic model in which the adolescent bond necessarily gives way to heterosexual maturity (MacCary 1985; Adelman 1985). But, as Kathryn Schwarz notes about Helena and Hermia's homoerotic relationship: "If experience remains in the past, language does not, bringing bonds between women into a dramatic moment at which they intersect, rather than precede, the progress toward heterosexual consummation. Nostalgia for past pleasures, as it doubles and even displaces anticipation of the future, makes the erotic present a rather crowded place" (Schwarz 2000: 220). Here again, Shannon's comments about homonormativity are instructive.

13 Scholarship has often focused on the *result* of crossdressing – the shift to another identity and gender – and the erotic energy which subsequently circulates around the boy heroine (an eroticism, as we have seen, often understood as male homoeroticism). Yet the *process* of crossdressing itself often solicits female homoerotic desire.

14 Frankie Rubinstein's *Dictionary of Shakespeare's Sexual Puns* (1984) includes many entries on dildos, but they have received very little critical attention. See Orgel (1992).

15 In the course of a bawdy exchange about "pricks," when Boyet jokes to Margaret that he fears "too much rubbing," he may be invoking tribadism, a female–female sexual act whose translation is "to rub" (*Love's Labour's Lost*, 4.1.178).

16 As Traub points out, the fact that Viola calls herself a "monster" in her crossdressed disguise is not a summation of sixteenth- and seventeenth-century attitudes toward female homoeroticism, but an "expression of the *dominant* discourse on tribadism and sodomy" (Traub 1992b: 152). Yet while a critique of "a masculinist, scopic focus on genital sexuality" helps us to imagine more diverse female homoerotic possibilities, the answer is not necessarily to posit "a kind of desire and an economy of pleasure that is focused on the lovers' entire selves" rather than the bit between their legs (Jankowski 2000: 22). The idea of an economy of pleasure organized around lovers' "entire selves" is a model of mutuality and whole-person love which is also historically contingent rather than universal, and perhaps less applicable to the early modern period than other ways of understanding the modalities of erotic pleasure.

17   Traub (1992b: 80) argues that it is the "palpable 'femininity'" of these characters that has blinded us to the eroticism in their language of desire.

18   In another scene, Parolles reveals that he knows what one of the Lords does with his bedclothes (4.3.250).

19   According to Smith (1992), homoeroticism finds full transgressive expression only in the violent, political, and male world of tragedy.

20   Valentine triangulates his feelings for Proteus with those for Silvia, asking her to "entertain [Proteus] / To be my fellow-servant to your ladyship" (*Two Gentlemen of Verona*, 2.4.102). When Proteus in turn falls in love with Sylvia, he is unclear whether it is "mine eye, or Valentine's praise" that makes him love her, but he does in the end choose her over Valentine (2.4.195, 203–4).

21   On sapphism and female reading communities, see my "Sidney's Sapphics and the Role of Interpretive Communities," forthcoming in *English Literary History* (2002).

22   In one scene, when Ford tells his wife "Get you home, go," Mrs. Ford turns to Mrs. Page and asks, "Will you go Mistress Page?" (2.1.152, 155).

23   There is a subtle undercurrent of male homoeroticism in Master Page, who "has a marvelous infection to the little page" Robin, whom he later refers to as a "pretty weathercock" (2.2.115; 3.2.17). Interestingly, and unlike his counterpart Ford, Page expresses no jealousy about his wife's behavior, suggesting a greater sexual openness in their relationship. In contrast, Titania and Oberon's marriage is marked by conflicting homosocial desires, both of which center on the changeling boy. Titania tells Oberon that the boy's mother was a votress of her order, "And for her sake do I rear up her boy; / And for her sake I will not part with him" (2.1.123, 136–7). Oberon, however, wants the boy for a "Knight of his train" or to be his "henchman," both eroticized master and minion relationships (2.1.25, 121).

24   Their house-buying and homemaking is alluded to throughout act 3. On the homoerotic implications of this housekeeping, see Fisher (n.d.).

25   When the King tells Diana "Choose thou thy husband and I'll pay thy dower" (5.3.323), we know that she has already been provided with a dower, and, moreover, that it will keep her from having to marry.

References and Further Reading

Adelman, J. (1985). Male Bonding in Shakespeare's Comedies. In P. Erickson and C. Kahn (eds.) *Shakespeare's 'Rough Magic': Renaissance Essays in Honor of C. L. Barber*. Newark: University of Delaware Press, 73–103.

Belsey, C. (1988). Disrupting Sexual Difference: Meaning and Gender in the Comedies. In J. Drakakis (ed.) *Alternative Shakespeares*. London: Routledge, 166–90.

Berry, P. (1989). *Of Chastity and Power: Elizabethan Literature and the Unmarried Queen*. London: Routledge.

Bly, M. (2000). *Queer Virgins and Virgin Queens on the Early Modern Stage*. Oxford: Oxford University Press.

Boswell, J. (1982/3). Revolutions, Universals, Categories. *Salmagundi*, 58–9, 89–113.

Bray, A. (1982). *Homosexuality in Renaissance England*. London: Gay Men's Press.

——(1994). Homosexuality and the Signs of Male Friendship in Elizabethan England. *Queering the Renaissance*, 40–61.

Bredbeck, G. W. (1991). *Sodomy and Interpretation: Marlowe to Milton*. Ithaca, NY: Cornell University Press.

——(1992). Tradition and the Individual Sodomite: Barnfield, Shakespeare, and Subjective Desire. In C. Summers (ed.) *Homosexuality in Renaissance and Enlightenment England: Literary Representation in Historical Context*. New York: Harrington Park Press, 41–68.

Brown, E. M. (1999). Companion Me with My Mistress: Cleopatra, Elizabeth I and their Waiting Women. In S. Frye and K. Robertson (eds.) *Maids and Mistresses, Cousins and Queens: Women's Alliances in Early Modern England*. Oxford: Oxford University Press.

Bruster, D. (1993). Female–Female Eroticism and the Early Modern Stage. *Renaissance Drama*, 24, 1–31.

Dash, I. (1996). Single-Sex Retreats in Two Early Modern Dramas: *Love's Labor's Lost* and *The Convent of Pleasure*. *Shakespeare Quarterly*, 47, 4, 387–95.

DiGangi, M. (1997). *The Homoerotics of Early Modern Drama*. Cambridge: Cambridge University Press.

Dollimore, J. (1991). *Sexual Dissidence: Augustine to Wilde, Freud to Foucault*. Oxford: Clarendon Press.

Doty, M. (1993). *Making Things Perfectly Queer*. Minneapolis: University of Minnesota Press.

Duggan, L. (1995). The Discipline Problem: Queer Theory Meets Lesbian and Gay History. *GLQ: A Journal of Lesbian and Gay Studies*, 2, 179–91.

Fisher, W. (n.d.). Home Alone: The Place of Women's Desire in Shakespeare's *As You Like It*. Unpublished manuscript.

Foucault, M. (1980). *The History of Sexuality, Vol. I: An Introduction*. New York: Vintage.

Fradenburg, L. and Freccero, C. (eds.) (1996). Introduction. *Premodern Sexualities*. New York: Routledge.

Garber, M. (1991). *Vested Interests: Cross-Dressing and Cultural Anxiety*. London: Routledge.

Goldberg, J. (1992). *Sodometries: Renaissance Texts, Modern Sexualities*. Stanford, CA: Stanford University Press.

——(ed.) (1994). *Queering the Renaissance*. Durham, NC: Duke University Press.

Green, D. E. (1998). Preposterous Pleasures: Queer Theories and *A Midsummer Night's Dream*. In D. Kehler (ed.) *A Midsummer Night's Dream: Critical Essays*. New York: Garland.

Greenberg, D. F. (1988). *The Construction of Homosexuality*. Chicago, IL: University of Chicago Press.

Greenblatt, S. (1988). *Shakespearean Negotiations: The Circulation of Social Energy in Renaissance England*. Berkeley: University of California Press.

Halperin, D. (1993). Is There a History of Sexuality? In H. Abelove, M. A. Barale, and D. M. Halperin (eds.) *The Lesbian and Gay Studies Reader*. New York: Routledge.

Howard, J. (1988). Crossdressing, the Theater, and Gender Struggle in Early Modern England. *Shakespeare Quarterly*, 39, 418–40.

——(1994). *The Stage and Social Struggle in Early Modern England*. New York: Routledge.

——(1998). The Early Modern and the Homoerotic Turn in Political Criticism. *Shakespeare Survey*, 26, 105–20.

Jankowski, T. A. (2000). *Pure Resistance: Queer Virginity in Early Modern English Drama*. Philadelphia: University of Pennsylvania Press.

Jardine, L. (1989). *Still Harping on Daughters: Women and Drama in the Age of Shakespeare*. New York: Columbia University Press.

——(1992). Twins and Travesties: Gender, Dependency and Sexual Availability in *Twelfth Night*. In S. Zimmerman (ed.) *Erotic Politics: Desire on the Renaissance Stage*. London: Routledge.

Katz, J. N. (1990). The Invention of Heterosexuality. *Socialist Review*, 21.

Laqueur, T. (1990). *Making Sex: Body and Gender from the Greeks to Freud*. Cambridge, MA: Harvard University Press.

Levine, L. (1986). Men in Women's Clothing: Anti-Theatricality and Effeminization from 1579–1642. *Criticism*, 28, 121–43.

MacCary, W. T. (1985). *Friends and Lovers: The Phenomenology of Desire in Shakespearean Comedy*. New York: Columbia University Press.

Marotti, A. (1982). "Love Is Not Love": Elizabethan Sonnet Sequences and the Social Order. *English Literary History*, 49, 2, 396–428.

Masten, J. (1997). *Textual Intercourse: Collaboration, Authorship, and Sexualities in Renaissance Drama*. Cambridge: Cambridge University Press.

Orgel, S. (1989). Nobody's Perfect: Or Why Did the English Stage Take Boys for Women? *South Atlantic Quarterly*, 88, 1, 7–29.

——(1992). On Dildos and Fadings. *ANQ*, 5, 2–3, 106–11.

——(1996). *Impersonations: The Performance of Gender in Shakespeare's England*. Cambridge: Cambridge University Press.

Osborne, L. E. (1994). Antonio's Pardon. *Shakespeare Quarterly*, 45, 1, 108–14.

Patterson, S. (1999). The Bankruptcy of Homoerotic Amity in Shakespeare's *Merchant of Venice*. *Shakespeare Quarterly*, 50, 1, 9–32.

Pequigney, J. (1992). The Two Antonios and Same-Sex Love in *Twelfth Night* and *The Merchant of Venice*. *English Literary Renaissance*, 22, 2, 201–21.

Rackin, P. (1987). Androgyny, Mimesis, and the Marriage of the Boy Heroine on the English Renaissance Stage. *Publications of the Modern Languages Association*, 102, 29–41.

Rambuss, R. (1998). *Closet Devotions*. Durham, NC: Duke University Press.

Schwarz, K. (2000). *Tough Love: Amazon Encounters in the English Renaissance*. Durham, NC: Duke University Press.

Sedgwick, E. (1985). *Between Men: English Literature and Male Homosocial Desire*. New York: Columbia University Press.

Shannon, L. (2000). Nature's Bias: Renaissance Homonormativity and Elizabethan Comic Likeness. *Modern Philology*, 98, 2 (November), 183–210.

——(2002). *Sovereign Amity: Figures of Friendship in Shakespearean Contexts*. Chicago, IL: University of Chicago Press.

Shapiro, M. (1994). *Gender in Play on the Renaissance Stage: Boy Heroines and Female Pages*. Ann Arbor: University of Michigan Press.

Shepherd, S. (1992). What's So Funny About Ladies' Tailors? A Survey of Some Male (Homo-)sexual Types in the Renaissance. *Textual Practice*, 6, 1, 17–30.

Smith, B. R. (1991). *Homosexual Desire in Shakespeare's England: A Cultural Poetics*. Chicago, IL: University of Chicago Press.

——(1992). Making a Difference: Male/Male 'Desire' in Tragedy, Comedy, and Tragi-Comedy. *Erotic Politics*, 127–49.

Spear, G. (1993). Shakespeare's 'Manly Parts': Masculinity and Effeminacy in *Troilus and Cressida*. *Shakespeare Quartely*, 44.

Stallybrass, P. (1992). Transvestism and the 'Body Beneath': Speculating on the Boy Actor. *Erotic Politics*, 64–83.

Stewart, A. (1997). *Close Readers: Humanism and Sodomy in Early Modern England*. Princeton, NJ: Princeton University Press.

Stone, L. (1979). *The Family, Sex and Marriage in England 1500–1800*, abridged edn. New York: Harper and Row.

Stubbes, P. (1973) [1583]. *The Anatomie of Abuses*. Pref. A. Freeman. New York: Garland Publishing.

Summers, C. (ed.) (1992). *Homosexuality in Renaissance and Enlightenment England: Literary Representation in Historical Context*. New York: Harrington Park Press.

Traub, V. (1992a). *Desire and Anxiety: Circulations of Sexuality in Shakespearean Drama*. London: Routledge.

——(1992b). The (In) significance of 'Lesbian' Desire in Early Modern England. In S. Zimmerman (ed.) *Erotic Politics: Desire on the Renaissance Stage*. New York: Routledge, 150–69.

Tvordi, J. (1999). Female Alliance and the Construction of Homoeroticism in *As You Like It* and *Twelfth Night*. In S. Frye and K. Robertson (eds.) *Maids and Mistresses, Cousins and Queens: Women's Alliances in Early Modern England*. Oxford: Oxford University Press, 114–30.

Weeks, J. (1981). *Sex, Politics, and Society: The Regulation of Society Since 1800*. London: Longman.

——(1985). *Sexuality and its Discontents: Meanings, Myths and Modern Sexualities*. London: Routledge.

Wells, R. H. (2000). *Shakespeare on Masculinity*. Cambridge: Cambridge University Press.

Zimmerman, S. (ed.) (1992). *Erotic Politics: Desire on the Renaissance Stage*. New York: Routledge.

8

Shakespearean Comedy and Material Life

Lena Cowen Orlin

The scope of this chapter would seem less narrow were its title "Renaissance Comedy and Material Life." This is even though "material" is an adjective of multiple meanings, many of which have relevance as immediate for the study of Shakespeare as of his contemporaries. To remark just two of the ways in which the word is in active circulation in scholarly writing, Shakespeare's comedies are without question full of material objects, both called out as stage properties and referenced in dialogue. And the plays are of course key sites for the intervention of critics concerned to recover the material conditions that produced historical ideologies, institutions, subjectivities, and sexualities.

But the term "material *life*" has a specific valence in contemporary critical discourse, most often relating to what we might describe as the "everyday" life of "ordinary" people, and it is in this arena that Shakespeare's works appear to come up short. Because it is so perilous to attempt to delimit and recover a historical "ordinary," the word "material" is made to oblige for a range of interpretive objectives that find their readiest articulation in negative terms. These are concerns with subjects other than elite culture, high politics, structures of institutional power, and instruments of authority. They reflect interests in women as well as men, citizens rather more than courtiers, and production along with consumption. Recognizable symptoms of early modern material life may surface in Shakespeare's comic subplots, but they do not dominate the main actions of his plays as they do those of comedies written for the Renaissance stage by Thomas Dekker, Ben Jonson, Thomas Middleton, and others. The so-called "city comedies" of Shakespeare's fellow dramatists seem to seethe with the material life of Elizabethan and Jacobean London in a way that Shakespeare is said to have approached only in the tavern scenes of his history plays, *1* and *2 Henry IV*.

These distinctions between Shakespeare and his contemporaries have been underscored by habits of oppositional labeling. The city comedies of Dekker, Jonson, and Middleton are also called "realistic"; in contrast, Shakespeare's middle comedies are generally classed as "romantic." Lawrence Danson summarizes that "a Shakespearean comedy is a play which ends in betrothal, marriage, or the reunion and reconciliation of married couples" (Danson 2000: 61).

Long ago, Madeleine Doran pointed out that the categories of realistic and romantic comedies are not as mutually exclusive as our names for them can seem to suggest (Doran 1954: 148–51). On the one hand, one of the earliest and most important of the city comedies, Dekker's *Shoemakers' Holiday*, includes as a main action the love match of Rose and Lacy, and Middleton's *A Chaste Maid in Cheapside* features the courting couple Moll and Touchwood Junior as the only characters exempted from its satire. The list of romantic plots in "realistic" comedies could be indefinitely extended. At the same time, on the other hand, city life is richly represented in some of Shakespeare's "romantic" plays, like *The Merchant of Venice*, and also in a "problem" comedy, *Measure for Measure*. Still, Portia's formidable wealth and privilege and the Duke's dark experiment in civic order go to disqualify even these Shakespearean plays from membership in a grouping that includes *Shoemaker's Holiday* and *Chaste Maid* as works occupied with the common and quotidian. The city of "city" comedies is generally understood to be London, and the Continental settings of *The Merchant of Venice* and *Measure for Measure* seem to emblematize their distance from the material lives of those in Shakespeare's London audiences.

Finally, if Shakespeare has been understood to have produced anything closely resembling a city comedy, it is *The Merry Wives of Windsor*, with its cast of what look like urban citizens. Even this genre match is not a close one. Windsor is not London, nor is it even a city. We don't know what skills of huswifery and industry Mistresses Ford and Page practice, what trades Masters Ford and Page pursue, or how the Pages have accumulated wealth of sufficient magnitude to make their daughter a prize on the marriage market. Nevertheless, *Merry Wives* demonstrates its affinities with "realistic" plays by turning its back on the occupants of the royal castle we know to feature in its eponymous topography. It is unique among Shakespeare's comedies for its English setting. And the character who crosses all plot lines, Mistress Quickly, describes her work for Doctor Caius in vividly material terms: "I keep his house, and I wash, wring, brew, bake, scour, dress meat and drink, make the beds and do all myself" (1.4.89–91).[1]

Common generic distinctions are also confounded, this chapter argues, by the romantic plot of *The Merry Wives of Windsor*. The play may be at its most material in the storyline involving Anne Page and Master Fenton, an apparent paradox that has implications for all Shakespeare's middle comedies. The making of marriage – the one necessary ingredient of Renaissance comedies classed as romantic – was also a thoroughly material activity in the ordinary and everyday lives of members of Shakespeare's audiences. Our best evidence about how marriages were made in the early modern period comes from oral testimony taken in its church courts. In what follows, thus, the social and economic aspects of marriage are examined both in the courtship plot of *The Merry Wives of Windsor* and in court cases of broken betrothal. The chapter addresses the consequences of a material understanding of marriage for our reading of the strong women of Shakespeare's middle comedies and for the history of gender politics in early modern England. If the conventions of genre and the affective structures of our own culture have conditioned us to think of Shakespeare's comedies as "romantic," *Merry Wives* exposes the material life that nonetheless lies beneath.

"Romantic" Comedy in *The Merry Wives of Windsor*

The Merry Wives of Windsor is not often entertained in discussions of Shakespeare's great romantic comedies, for three reasons primarily. First, the play's incorporation of one of Shakespeare's most beloved characters, Sir John Falstaff, has preoccupied its readers. Georgio Melchiori begins the introduction to his edition of *Merry Wives* by stating flatly: "This is Falstaff's play." Historical evidence "leave[s] no doubt about it," Melchiori declares, pointing to the hierarchy of interest reflected both in the 1602 Stationers' Register entry for "*an excellent and pleasant conceited comedy of Sir John Falstaff and the Merry Wives of Windsor*" and also in the title of the 1602 Quarto, "A Most pleasaunt and excellent conceited Comedie, of Syr *Iohn Falstaffe*, and the merrie Wiues of *Windsor*" (Melchiori 2000: 1). It wasn't until the 1623 Folio that the play was printed with the short title by which it is now known. Even though the Folio serves for Melchiori's copytext, he continues to present the play as *Sir John Falstaff and the Merry Wives of Windsor*.[2] Paradoxically, the presence of the character Melchiori calls "the Falstafficon" (ibid: 101–2) has done damage to the play's critical reception. As Richard Helgerson puts it, *Merry Wives* has effectively been diminished by "its marginal relation to Shakespeare's great sequence of chronicle history plays" (Helgerson 2000: 60). Worse, as Anne Barton points out, there is a general sense that "the comedy itself constitutes a betrayal of Falstaff even worse than the one inflicted by Henry V" (Barton 1994: 70).

Only recently, feminist and materialist critics have found a second way of reading the play by redirecting the focus of their commentary from the fat knight to the merry wives. Through important essays by Helgerson, Ann Rosalind Jones, Rosemary Kegl, Natasha Korda, and Wendy Wall, among others, the play has enjoyed a dramatic elevation in critical esteem. The merry wives move Shakespeare into the interpretive territory of Dekker, Jonson, Middleton, and the dramatists of London life. Because they are generally more susceptible of vigorous Marxist and feminist readings, the wives are also more interesting to a current generation of critics than are Anne Page and her crew of suitors. Thus, Sandra Clark, who does not ignore the betrothal plot by any means, nonetheless states that the play is "concerned with marital relations rather than romantic love" (Clark 1987: 258).

While both Falstaff and the merry wives divert attention from the courtship of Anne Page, that storyline, also, third, bears its own share of responsibility for its relative obscurity in the critical tradition. It suffers by comparison to the romantic plots that Shakespeare executed with greater interest elsewhere, and to romantic leads of greater personal appeal. Such disinterest is of long standing; Anna Jameson did not include Anne Page among "Shakespeare's Heroines," for example. Helgerson points out that we never get to know these characters as we do others: "the principals are largely kept off stage and out of view. All the attention is given to the futile and misdirected efforts of the losers" (Helgerson 2000: 64). Barton attributes this obscurity to generic difference, suggesting that it is "not infrequently the fate of young lovers" in city comedies (Barton 1994: 80). Anne appears in three scenes and speaks twenty-eight lines (more or less, depending on the edition); many of these are innocuous half-lines. Fenton appears in four scenes and speaks ninety-four lines. Anne and Fenton are onstage together in only two scenes.

This may be sufficient evidence that the main interest of the courtship plot is not only not romantic in the way in which we usually understand the term, but also not characterologic. To approach plays in ways other than through character criticism is one of the more important agendas of current methods of literary interpretation. Another way of understanding the courtship of Anne Page and Master Fenton is in terms of its material, not its romantic meanings, and these are significant not only for our reading of *Merry Wives* but also for the illumination they shed on all Shakespeare's romantic comedies. Like *The Taming of the Shrew* and *The Merchant of Venice*, for example, *Merry Wives* features an impoverished young man seeking an heiress for a wife, but this play is even more forthcoming about the economic aspects of making a match in early modern England. Notably, the theme is pursued not only in the actions involving all Anne Page's suitors, Fenton and "losers" alike, but also in parallel through the "courtship" of the merry wives by Falstaff.

Thus, it is spelled out that were Anne Page to marry Slender he would maintain her "like a gentlewoman" during his lifetime and would ensure her potential widowhood with a jointure (amounting to £150 in the Folio and £300 in the Quarto). What inspires this generosity is the correspondingly specific information that Anne's grandfather has left her £700 and that she will inherit even more from her father; "she has good gifts" Slender says, debasing a term we more generally associate with intangible values (1.1.45–59). Fenton, who is equally well informed about Anne's many sources of attraction, "confesses" to her that his "first motive" in wooing her was her wealth. But Anne provokes him to go on to say, more lover-like, that "I found thee of more value / Than stamps in gold or sums in sealed bags."[3] He obliges her by continuing that he now "aims" at "the very riches of thyself" (3.4.13–18). In the event, Anne seems not at all discouraged by the degree to which Fenton's interest in her was and still is financial. She is true to her time in accepting composedly such advantages as she has. Falstaff, meanwhile, advances the theme of financial adventuring imperfectly disguised as romantic aspiration. He pursues Mistress Page as "a region in Guiana, all gold and bounty" (1.3.65–6) and Mistress Ford as "the key of the cuckoldly rogue's [her husband's] coffer" (2.2.260).[4]

As is true especially for *The Merchant of Venice*, *Merry Wives* is also concerned with the immediate costs of doing matrimonial business, monies that must be hazarded for the chance at greater gain. There are, for example, expenses associated with travel. In the course of Shallow's search for a suitable partner for Slender, the two men incur lodging expenses of which he complains (3.2.52). One of Mistress Page's plans for her unwelcome suitor is to prolong their flirtation until Falstaff is forced to pawn his horses to pay his own lodging costs (2.1.85–6). A second major category of expense is represented in tokens like the ring Fenton dispatches to Anne. Ford, disguised as

Brooke, only claims to have bought presents for Mistress Ford, but the fact that he does so in order to lend verisimilitude to his masquerade is sufficient indication that in such details the play accords with accustomed practice in contemporary courtships (2.2.188).[5] Finally, the suitors are also required to pay out fees to those who assist them. Thus, in order to secure a vicar for his clandestine wedding, Fenton promises to redeem the Host's losses in the scam involving the German duke, and he adds £100 more besides (4.6.4–5). "Brooke" pretends that he has proffered various fees and gratuities to learn what gifts Mistress Ford might want (2.2.189–90). Hard cash actually changes hands when he asks Falstaff to test his wife: "There is money: spend it, spend it, spend more, spend all I have" (2.2.221–2). Fenton also rewards Mistress Quickly for taking his ring to Anne Page (3.4.98).

All these economic exchanges presuppose another material condition of courtship in early modern England, which was its broadly social character. Ann Cook has importantly emphasized that *The Merry Wives of Windsor* is unique among Shakespeare's romantic comedies for its richly textured representation of those outside agents who involve themselves in the play's courtship plots (Cook 1991: 114).[6] Working in a different field of discourse, the records of early modern church courts, Diana O'Hara has also foregrounded the role intermediaries played in the conduct of betrothals. As she reports, intermediaries ascertained a potential partner's availability and possible interest, offered recommendations and advice in matchmaking, effected introductions, conveyed messages and delivered tokens as the courtship was engaged, gave material assistance, arranged clandestine meetings if not marriages, negotiated property arrangements in order to confirm commitments, and – of especial importance when promises were alleged and contested – served as witnesses to oral agreements (O'Hara 2000: 99–121).

Shakespeare himself played the role of intermediary in a betrothal case that came before the Court of Requests in 1612. At issue was a concord reached in 1604.[7] According to one servant in the Mountjoy household, the lodger Shakespeare was called upon to "persuade" another servant, Stephen Belott, to marry the Mountjoy daughter, Mary. Shakespeare apparently executed his rhetorical skills to good effect, for he reported back that Belott was amenable to the match – providing that Mary brought a sufficient marriage portion. Eight years later, at the time of the court case, Shakespeare did not remember the amount of the portion (Belott testified that it was £200) or the nature of the household furnishings and implements that were also promised. Sam Schoenbaum has observed that the depositions taken in Belott's subsequent suit, which probably involved the terms of the marriage settlement, "show the poet of humanity in the midst of human involvement with ordinary folk" (Schoenbaum 1981: 20). In this respect as in many others, Shakespeare was himself ordinary folk.

The large cast of intermediaries in *The Merry Wives of Windsor* is generously and comically redundant. Shallow, who has the opening lines of the play, uses the proprietary terms of the first-person plural in describing the attempted match of Slender and Anne Page ("We have lingered" in Windsor, he says, and "this day we shall have our answer": 3.2.52–4).[8] He also procures Mistress Quickly to command Anne Page's attention to Slender and then, in the event, does most of the wooing himself, telling Anne "my cousin loves you" and opening contractual negotiations. "He will maintain you like a gentlewoman," says Shallow, and "He will make you a hundred and fifty pounds jointure" (3.4.22–49). Based on Slender's income of £300 annually, this might have been expected to have been £100, so we may be intended to conclude that Shallow has contributed to the proposed jointure as well as with his gift to the Pages of a deer (1.1.73–4). As Simon Reynolds points out, when Shallow does step back, he nonetheless "remains hovering in the background, ideally positioned to witness anything that might be construed as a 'promise'" (Reynolds 1996: 318).

Only the Quarto allows Slender any direct courtship of Anne. By the time the text was reproduced in the Folio, Slender had lost his moments and come to be represented solely through the indirections of his intermediaries. The Folio adds to the Quarto the active assistance on Slender's behalf of Evans, who purveys information as to Anne Page's worth, introduces Slender to Anne, goes so far as to propose to duel on Slender's behalf against Caius, and, in yet another compounding instance of an intermediary recruiting an intermediary, solicits the further assistance of Mistress Quickly. Simple is also among the supporting agents as a messenger between Evans and Quickly.

The Host serves ineffectually as an intermediary for Caius – he says, malapropriately, "I will be thy adversary toward Anne Page" (2.3.85–6) – arranging the duel but also sending its opponents, harmlessly, to different sites. He is more helpful on behalf of Fenton, praising him to Page and securing the vicar. The parodic "courtship" of the merry wives also involves a crew of ancillary intermediaries: Pistol and Nym, carrying letters from Falstaff to the Mistresses Page and Ford; Simple, taking Falstaff a message from Slender, and Robin, furthering the wives' plot. Ford, to lend plausibility to his disguise as Brooke, pretends that he has consulted many fictional intermediaries and then makes Falstaff a kind of false intermediary himself when he bribes Falstaff to test his wife.

The most promiscuous of the intermediaries is, of course, Mistress Quickly. She is recruited by the wives to carry messages to Falstaff, who calls her Mistress Ford's "assistant, or go-between" (2.2.250; in the Quarto, she is "her spokes mate, her go between"). It is implied that Quickly's reward for this work is the promise of greater advantage in representing others of her agents in the courtship of Anne Page (2.1.142–51). In one key scene, Quickly asks Simple to tell Evans that she will speak to Anne on behalf of Slender, reassures Caius that she will be his advocate with Anne, and also accepts Fenton's coins to serve as his "voice" with her (1.4.144–5). When Shallow enlists Quickly to interrupt Anne Page and Fenton so that Slender can speak to Anne, she still has a word for Fenton, advising him, inasmuch as he has been unsuccessful with Page, to try his luck with Mistress Page (3.4.22, 75). Mistress Page says she will seek to know Anne's preferences, and Quickly boasts indefensibly, "This is my doing" (3.4.94). In a neat piece of sophistry, she concludes of her multiple roles as intermediary, "I will do what I can for them all three" (3.4.104).

If Quickly is the "universal advocate" of Cook's coinage (1991: 115), she is not as thoroughly ineffectual as has often been concluded. In act 3, scene 4, Fenton and Anne step aside to speak privately. Shallow, anxiously observing their colloquy, asks Quickly to intervene and "break their talk." Barton recognizes, as many other critics have not and as in fact the dialogue does not explicitly tell us, that we are to understand that Anne and Fenton have at that instant made their pledge to each other. Page drives Fenton away with words that are acutely ironic only if we understand the nature of their conversation: "I told you, sir, my daughter is disposed of." In other words, she has only just "disposed" of herself. (Later, Fenton will confirm this interpretation, saying that the couple has been "long since contracted": 5.5.217). When Quickly interrupts, however, Fenton is unable to seal their pledge with the ring he is poised to give Anne, and so he must instead hand it to Quickly (3.4.68, 98). With this, Quickly switches roles from Shallow's intermediary to Fenton's agent. She successfully completes the betrothal by effecting a tangible exchange that ceremonializes the binding promise of Fenton and Anne.

"The pursuit of Anne Page," Helgerson notes, "spins off plot, subplot, counterplot, by-plot at a vertiginous rate" (Helgerson 2000: 63–4). The sheer number of intermediary activities, operating at varying levels of detail and import, has led Cook to conclude that this is a main theme of the play and central to its social agenda. Reading across the interfaces of literary representation and historical practice, she argues that Shakespeare intended to demonstrate that "the whole system of courtship by committee" was "nonsense."[9] The parodic courtship of the merry wives by Falstaff is further evidence, for her, of how thoroughgoing Shakespeare's "comic critique" of the process is. Thus, "those who employ such methods" are punished in the end, she says, and Shakespeare makes clear his preference for one-on-one romance rather than committee involvement: "only honest, straightforward affection guarantees a happy, faithful marriage in this particular comic world" (Cook 1991: 115–16). This is of course to suppress the fact that Fenton acts by intermediaries, too, when required. So also, Rosemary Kegl writes that the play works "to assert the moral authority of companionate marriages" (Kegl 1994: 125), although in their two scenes together we have been given little evidence to characterize the relationship of Anne and Fenton as companionate. Onstage, there may be chemistry between the couple; in the reading, the most we can say is that Anne Page makes the best choice among the options with which the plot presents her.

As a historian working with the manuscript materials of the church courts, Diana O'Hara (2000) constructs her own case against the common practices of early modern intermediaries, arguing that many outside agents were meddlers, opportunists, and busybodies. Even those who were recruited, she states, could over-involve themselves and in various ways interfere with and exert pressure upon marriageable persons. This is, however, to exaggerate the effective power of intermediaries. Their interventions could be disorganized, confused, and occasionally contradictory in ways that Cook's terms – "system" and "committee" – tend to obscure. More often than not, church court cases brought forward instances in which one courting partner or another acted independently, changed his or her mind, reneged on what might have been interpreted to have been a promise, and successfully resisted advice or coercion.[10]

Had Anne been prevented from enacting her preference and had she been compelled instead to marry Slender or Caius, *The Merry Wives of Windsor* might in its own textual field have reinforced O'Hara's argument for social history. As it is, however, the play shows the conventional mechanisms of matchmaking to be supremely ineffectual. The play's mode of address is less polemical than comical, maximizing as it does all the chaotic potential for misdirections and self-delusions in a social custom that was undoubtedly at its most active and participatory in a village like Windsor (rather than a city like London). In this way, the plots, subplots, counterplots, and by-plots concerning the betrothal of Anne Page are in their first impact humorous. But their further and more important thematic effect is to establish with all the clarity of multiple contrasts that Anne Page makes her own choice despite the outside agents and their various interventions.

By setting in motion the diverse actions of so many intermediaries, *Merry Wives* thus places in the highest relief the agency and autonomy of its heroine. Our recognition of some of the deeper mythic structures of the romantic plot, however, make it inevitable that the resolution of the play is more often seen as a victory for Fenton over characters who have been called "losers." Instinctively, we respond to what may seem like a quest motif (and Peter Erickson (1987: 128) uses the very term in describing Fenton's "successful completion of his quest for Anne Page"), to some elements of the pattern of a damsel-in-distress (Cook (1991: 115) refers to Anne Page as a "besieged girl"), and to the folkloric resonances of the number three (Fenton is one of three suitors). Helgerson indicates that Anne "happily gives herself" to Fenton, but he also makes reference to Fenton's "victory" (Helgerson 2000: 62, 63). For Erickson this is Fenton's "triumph" (1987: 128), and Barton also terms Fenton "a victor" (1994: 88). Even Sandra Clark, who turns critical tradition on its head in saying that "Anne gets Fenton in the end," asserts that this is no consequence of that character's own actions. She is a "passive recipient," says Clark, while "Fenton is shown taking charge of the plotting which will ensure that true love wins out" (Clark 1987: 263–4).

To the contrary, it can be argued that Anne Page violates the rules in which her genre would seem to implicate her and, in Carol Neely's words, "has the last word on her marriage" and "chooses her own marriage partner" (Neely 1989: 220, 218). Such a position takes us back to the critical activity of act 3, scene 4, and to Barton's acute understanding that there Anne Page and Fenton make a promise that by the terms of early modern practice was considered legally binding. The scene opens with Fenton despairing of gaining the approval of Anne's father. "Alas," she responds, "how then?" How is the relationship to go forward? Fenton answers that "thou must be thyself," and this is what Anne from this point becomes: the representation of a self-defining subject. Fenton outlines all the reasons why Page objects to him: his rank, his impoverishment, his riotous youth, his bad companions, the impossibility that he could interest himself in Anne as anything other than "a property." Here Anne makes her test of him: "Maybe he tells you true." Fenton replies as she requires, speaking to the "very riches of thyself." Anne directs him to try again with her father but then, "If opportunity and humblest suit / Cannot attain it, why then – hark you hither" (3.4.1–21). She not only makes clear that she is willing to act in defiance of her father, but also takes the initiative in setting the scene for their private spousals.

When she and Fenton are interrupted by Shallow and Slender, she is crisp and authoritative with both. When Page again rebuffs Fenton, she asks her mother urgently, "do not marry me to yond fool." And when Mistress Page refers to a "better" suitor, Doctor Caius, Anne says bluntly: "I had rather be set quick i' th' earth, / And bowled to death with turnips" (3.4.81–6). These are the briefest of glimpses of Anne's decidedness of mind and strength of will. Shakespeare allows her so few lines that Slender's characterization of her as one who "speaks small" is apt. (As Simon Reynolds (1996: 319) points out, no creature of the play is made a weaker vessel than Slender, a "limb of Shallow," "no more than part of the Shallow estate," "himself loved by Shallow, and by 'father Page' . . . entirely as a property"). Anne is relatively silent, and she is also presumably chaste, but she is nonetheless thoroughly disobedient. If act 3, scene 4 has been frequently misread, so, too, has been act 4, scene 6. Because Fenton explains the masquerade at Herne's oak to the Host and rewards the Host to procure a vicar, the general presumption has been that he conceives the elopement plot.

Only Anne is in a position to have devised the scheme, however. First, she alone possesses knowledge of both Page's plan to have her "slip / Away" with Slender and also Mistress Page's counterplot for Caius to "shuffle her away" (4.6.23–4, 28). Second, she communicates this privileged knowledge to Fenton in a letter. Fenton's access to Anne is restricted, and the two are not in direct contact. Their only interaction at this stage comes in the one-sided form of Anne's correspondence. There, third, she may also give Fenton his assignment to find a vicar and a church. Hearing at third hand the news of planned events at Herne's oak, the Host asks Fenton laboriously, "Which means she to deceive, father or mother?" Fenton replies: "Both, my good host, to go along with me" (4.6.45–6). The two men understand Anne's intention to be the enterprising and determining force here. This is, as Fenton tells the Host, a letter "Of such contents as you will wonder at" (4.6.13).[11]

Thus, Anne Page can be understood to have disobeyed both of her parents to make her own marital choice. All evidences are that she initiates the elopement scheme. And she is, further, unique among the characters of her cast in never having been cozened or discomfited. If we read the ending of the play as a happy one, our reaction must be based in large part in trust that Anne Page knows her own mind. As a character of such agency and initiative, she is less unlike Shakespeare's other romantic heroines than has often been thought. But surely, it might be objected, this is to make *Merry Wives* even more a matter of romantic fantasy and even less relevant to its own material culture? Did the strong women of Shakespeare's middle comedies bear any relationship to the real-life women of the ordinary world of early modern England? In fact, in the records of early modern church courts, forceful and self-determining women are widely encountered.

Betrothal and Marriage in Early Modern Church Courts

There, for example, we meet Susan Herringham, whose courtship with Richard Vyne was said to have advanced materially when he sent her some tokens and she arranged a "merry" supper together (*Vyne contra Herringham* 1589: 271^v–274^r). After the meal, which featured two joints of meat Herringham had purchased for 8 pence, Vyne placed a ring on her finger. He asked her what she had to give in return. According to deponents in the case, Herringham said she had "nothing" except her own ring, and offered it to him. But then, "because it would not easily come off her finger, he had it not." Despite this somewhat discouraging turn of events, Vyne was nonetheless said to have persevered in his suit. In response, Herringham asked, first, for £20 for her child from a previous union; Vyne refused. Next, she suggested a house for her child to live in; Vyne agreed to lease the house she specified. Third, Herringham requested the lease of a second house for her own use should she outlive Vyne, and, fourth, she asked for a household's worth of furnishings; to both house and household he consented. "If this be all thou canst demand, give me thy hand," said Vyne, and, according to three witnesses, Herringham then made a promise of marriage.

Two of the witnesses were Richard Madder, a 53-year-old Dover husbandman, and Marie Madder, his 62-year-old wife; the supper took place in the hall of their house, and it was Marie who had delivered the tokens from Vyne and purchased the meat on Herringham's behalf. By Diana O'Hara's definition, the Madders were intermediaries in this courtship and were thus invested in its outcome. Shoemaker Thomas Harrison was called as the third witness to the betrothal. Herringham reportedly told mason Thomas Tadwell of her promise, too, although to Tadwell, in the first hint of trouble for the couple, she was said to have indicated that all was contingent upon the securing of her father's good will. On November 25, 1589 the four witnesses appeared before the Consistory Court of Canterbury when Vyne brought Herringham to court for having – despite this history and the Madders' interventions – defaulted on her promise. He sought to enforce what he claimed was their agreement; she had perhaps struck a better bargain elsewhere.

Susan Herringham's concern for her jointure was far from uncommon. The women of early modern church courts are generally depicted as cool-headed in negotiating their own economic security. Canterbury records also tell the story of a Widow Shurt, who was "fetched" by a man named Bradley to the house of his master and mistress about five miles from her home. Shurt and Bradley were described as having spent an afternoon talking alone together in the Thompsons' gallery. At about 5:00 p.m. Henry Thompson went up to learn the progress of the talks and gladly summoned his wife Dorothy to join him as a witness to a contract. Presumably the widow and the manservant had decided they could coexist happily enough, but Shurt had one remaining practical question: "where she should have a house to dwell in if it should please God that [Bradley] should die before her?" Because Bradley "had been a good and faithful servant," Thompson deposed, he further advanced his assistance to the couple by promising Bradley the lease of a house which would descend to Shurt if she were rewidowed. Again, the actions of these *in-loco-parentis* intermediaries failed along with the alleged betrothal (*Bradley contra Shurt* 1596: 135^r–138^r).

Even women younger and less experienced than Susan Herringham and the Widow Shurt negotiated aggressively. Susan Butler, for instance, wanted to lease a house and land near Sittingbourne in Kent, but, at 18 years of age, she was too young to do so on her own behalf. William Keble seized the advantage to say that he would be bound for the lease if she would act on her promise to marry him. Nonetheless she paused. According to witnesses, she required Keble to travel to Coventry "and fetch a testimonial that he the said Keble was not indebted and that he was free from all other woman" – that is, from promises to other women (*Cobb contra Butler* 1585: 3^v–4^r). In a similar vein, Martin Ingram reports a Wiltshire case from 1633. The marital negotiations of a widow had proceeded so far as to address the protection of her child's inheritance should she remarry. But the widow broke off discussions when she heard that her suitor, Thomas Eyres, "had ill-treated his first wife and was heavily indebted" (Ingram 1987: 199).

Church court depositions portray women who were skilled in manipulating all the languages of betrothal. As the case of Susan Herringham shows, one of these languages was material. Laura Gowing describes a 1574 case from London in which Jane Salisbury maintained a running tally of her exchange of tokens with William Lloyde. Unlike Herringham, who seized a material advantage in the circulation of rings, Salisbury was apparently anxious to keep a strict balance of exchange so as not even to appear to commit herself. Thus she preserved her own independence and power of choice (Gowing 1996: 161). Another of the languages of betrothal was gestural. Gowing also tells of a woman sued in 1579 by two men with competing claims. Ann Frier had contracted herself to Richard Robinson even though her father preferred Peter Richardson. At a betrothal dinner with Richardson, Frier proffered her left hand. She explained later that she did so with deliberation, having already given her right hand to Robinson. Her grandmother, however, perspicaciously demanded that Frier offer her right hand. Frier's temporizing strategies were not yet exhausted. She said shortly, "I take Peter," not, as she later made the case for her freedom from him, "I take him as my husband" (ibid: 144).[12] As this report suggests, the third language of betrothal was technical. In a Canterbury complaint brought by maidservant Susanne Woollet against William Saunders, it was emphasized that the couple had pledged themselves with words in the present tense, a legally binding terminology. Richard Crispe, who deposed that he had advised Saunders' disapproving father to give Woollet money and thus "make an end of the matter," clearly believed that the young maidservant had the technical knowledge to bring to the courts a compelling case for matrimonial enforcement (*Woollet contra Saunders* 1590: 73^r).

If there is any evidence that Susan Herringham was as biddable as contemporary ideology prescribed, it would seem to lie in the report that she sought her father's approval. Any courtship could be terminated for consent withheld by family or friends. Ingram describes marital negotiations brought to an end by "moral pressure," "threats of disinheritance," "blandishments," even physical coercion (Ingram 1987: 202). We might assume that women were more subject to such interventions, and certainly it is true that the particular type of intervention employed may have had a gendered valence. But in fact the phenomenon of familial intrusion in these matters generally showed a gender neutrality; both men and women were monitored by parents and by those acting *in loco parentis*. Here, as in other ways, *The Merry Wives of Windsor* rings true to social practice, with Slender as subject to supervision as is Anne.

Occasionally, split opinions among family and friends could create the sort of opportunity that Anne takes advantage of. Just as often, though, the issue of consent could be raised by one of the courting parties as a delaying tactic, an invention devised to prolong a pleasurable courtship or to avoid an unpleasant confrontation. Consent could be referenced as an invalidating condition, in order to forestall final commitment.[13] Women were fully as capable of this strategy of conditional betrothal as were men. Elizabeth I did not develop her legendary ability to manipulate the rituals of courtship in a cultural vacuum.

In a Canterbury case of 1602 brought against Margery Overye, the matter of familial approval is exposed as a pretext invoked to obscure other, self-profiting objectives. Thomas Launsfeild, having successfully wooed Overye, sought the assistance of her former master, Robert Austen, in securing her family's blessing. Austen testified that he did not proceed on Launsfeild's word alone; he first obtained confirmation from Overye herself that she was willing to marry this suitor. She reportedly assured him that she did "affect" Launsfeild and would "marry him before all the men in the world" and had "given her faithful promises in marriage to him." Austen warned her that she was unlikely to gain familial consent. This was not for any disapproval of Launsfeild but because Overye's marital portion was controlled by persons who would be unhappy to lose its benefits. Overye then declared hotly that she would marry Launsfeild "whether they would or no," and she was said to have told her father that she had made such promises that she could never go back. These words had a particular force. According to report, Overye's father yielded: "Therefore, I will not hinder them any longer but further them in their marriage" (*Launsfeild contra Overye* 1602: 131^r–132^v).

While all these cases show the legal authority of some early modern women's words and their empowering access to choice and self-determination, there remains, from a larger feminist perspective, the troubling issue of initiative. This is generally assumed to have been lodged solely in the hands of male suitors. Thus, Gowing suggests that in their "idiosyncratic but commanding mastery of [betrothal] conventions" and their ability to "evade, deny, or postpone" marital commitments, women could find a "special moment of self-definition and autonomy." Still, she points out that such moments occurred within a structure that "assigned to women the role of receiving, hearing, and responding to men's propositions" (Gowing 1996: 141, 144–5). While it is true that men retained agency in the vast majority of cases, there are also instances in these records in which women were said to have been the instigators of courtship and betrothal. Ingram reports a 1583 case in which maidservant Christian Veriat was described as having "paid a surprise visit on her lover." She "took it into her head to become contracted immediately . . . [and] would brook no . . . delay" in effecting a betrothal (Ingram 1987: 196–7). In Canterbury in 1598, a woman named Rebecca Odert was said to have stood in her father's yard making "signs" to John Jackson as he looked out at his lodging window. Sometimes she signaled that Jackson should write to her and sometimes she indicated that she had written him or sent him tokens. According to testimony, Odert was the first to promise that she "would never forsake the said Jackson while she lived." One day she and a (female) friend came unexpectedly to Jackson's door. She was invited in by Jackson's fellow lodger Stephen Stronge. When Jackson returned, it was said, he summoned five witnesses to a contract of marriage with Odert. By the time Jackson brought her to court, however, Odert had taken the name Simons, evidently having married another (*Jackson contra Odert alias Simons* 1598: 79ᵛ–85ʳ). Diana O'Hara cites a rare case in which one woman made compensation for such a change of heart: Joan Swift had a sow and pigs "which she would give to [Thomas Wood] conditionally that he would forsake her" (O'Hara 2000: 78).

The issue of initiative is, finally, a thoroughly subjective one. While church court depositions report women actively discouraging male advances or resisting claims and commitments, it is not in their nature to show us how often a woman subtly or overtly encouraged a man to open a process of courtship. Flirtation, not having legal force, was rarely at issue. But if these are matters of nuance and interpretation, a compelling matter of fact is that, as in the complaint lodged by Richard Vyne against Susan Herringham (and in every case discussed here except that made by Susanne Woollet against William Saunders), those who brought suit for matrimonial enforcement were more often men. Ingram confirms: "The prosecution of marriage contract suits was not the prerogative of either sex, but in most areas in this period male plaintiffs seem to have predominated" (Ingram 1987: 194). It may have been that men were more apt to bring complaints to the courts or were more optimistic about success there. In the event, as Ingram also notes, few such cases achieved endorsement for overturning an established marriage to reinstate a claimed betrothal. But the critical point is that the men who made such charges had to be willing to be shown publicly to have been manipulated by, rejected by, and bested by the women they brought to court – and still sought, generally in vain, to wed.

Domestic Patriarchalism in Theory

The cases brought in early modern church courts concerned "ordinary" women, not those in the social registers whose high-stakes property settlements required closely negotiated matches at younger ages. But depositions taken in these cases are, if anything, all the more surprising for their forceful representations of the very women we have imagined to have been most bound by contemporary exhortations to chastity, silence, and obedience. We would have expected such women to be those most disempowered by strict legal circumscriptions on the *feme covert*, and we would have thought them to be those most constructed by the culturally iconic "Patient Grissell" (whose princely husband married down). The betrothal narratives of the ecclesiastical courts do not fit the patterns of patriarchal oppression and repression that we have derived from our reading of sixteenth- and seventeenth-century sermons and conduct books.[14]

Admittedly, the bias of the church court records is towards those who bargained and those who felt betrayed; successful love matches would not have made their way to the church courts at all. And not all courtship narratives show us women who were as self-possessed as Herringham, offering a ring and then claiming to find it wedded to her own finger. Nonetheless, within their frame of reference, these records present us with women who more often than not appear to have had the upper hand in marriage negotiations.

It might seem that the only sure way to negotiate the differences between early modern ecclesiastical cases and our own patriarchal paradigms is to dismiss the church court depositions as false, misleading, or incomplete representations of events at issue. These they undoubtedly were – that is, they were certainly incomplete, and they were probably often false and misleading. So many cases pressed in these courts called out conflicting testimony that it is never possible to be certain of the truth of any one contested situation. Each party involved could tell a different truth, could have a motivation for presenting a partial truth, or could see advantage in inhabiting an untruth.[15] Depositions were mediated not only by these personal agendas and their self-censorships but, perhaps even more importantly, by legal procedures with their standards of evidence and by court scribes with their regularizing formulas. These set the parameters of the depositions, determined what questions were to be asked, and standardized the recording of all answers.

However, to proceed too far down the path of our own deconstructive strategies and interpretive skepticism is to render historiographically moot one of the most important bodies of evidence surviving to us from the early modern period. Church court depositions preserve at least something of the lost voices and material lives of the illiterate, the economically disadvantaged, and the politically disempowered. Witnesses include maidservants, laborers, widows, and craftspersons who otherwise left no individualized trace on the historical record. Their central narratives are based in appeals to common notions and prevailing logic. These represent constructs that are unfamiliar to us from the rhetoric of sermons and conduct books. But it is unimaginable that the prescriptive and legal discourses could have existed in perfect isolation, without impinging upon each other.

One interpretive challenge, then, is to find some way of understanding the coexistence of the competing bodies of textual evidence represented in patriarchal prescription and church court depositions. Such an undertaking is not unlike what might be engaged in any attempt to mediate between first-wave and second-wave feminist approaches to Shakespeare. First-wave feminism, perhaps best represented by Juliet Dusinberre's groundbreaking *Shakespeare and the Nature of Women* (1975), depicted Shakespeare as something of a proto-feminist in his creation of strong, articulate female characters as centers of interest, especially in his middle comedies. Second-wave feminism was more historicist in its recognition that Shakespeare could not escape being a man of his time. To establish the cultural norms and convictions of this time, scholars of the 1980s and 1990s turned often to the conduct books and sermons disseminating a patriarchal ideology that seemed to leave little room for Shakespeare's Rosalind, Olivia, Viola, and Beatrice. To begin to understand how such contradictory representations of women could have functioned concurrently in Shakespeare's works and in his culture, it is important to remind ourselves of the ideological underpinnings of sixteenth- and seventeenth-century domestic patriarchalism.[16]

The interest of the early modern state in the individual household was a matter, first, of its concern with general social order and, second, of its initiative in building a particular philosophical justification for its own power and authority. For the political order to be able to "naturalize" itself by analogy to the family, the family had first to be understood as a political organism. More, for the monarchy to succeed in justifying its own form, familial government had to be conceptualized as monarchic – that is, topped by a single head of household, always by general assumption male. Prevailing political theory could not allow for the conceptualization of a government shared jointly by husband and wife in the domestic sphere, because its analogous number in the political sphere would have been what Aristotle called aristocratic, shared, rule – inimical to monarchy.

The system of analogies was exploited not only for a conception of government but also for a theory of obligation. Just as with Aristotle, so, too, the Bible was cited selectively in the development of ideas of obedience. Again because of the needed emphasis on monarchic structures, the full meanings of the commandment to "Honour thy father and thy mother" could not be generally acknowledged (Exodus 20: 12). Especially critical to the hierarchization of gender in social theory was St. Paul's injunction to wives to "submit yourselves unto your own husbands, as unto the Lord. For the husband is the head of the wife, even as Christ is the head of the church" (Ephesians 5: 22–3). Although Paul referred only to domestic and doctrinal spheres, the ability of the political sphere to implicate itself in analogous structures meant that it could also cite Paul to cloak its own form in biblical, in effect divine, warrant. Patriarchal households and monarchic governments were thus thoroughly enmeshed in mutually justifying and naturalizing conceptualizations.

To understand these ideological mandates is to understand something of the cultural coercion of domestic patriarchalism. It is also to understand that, because the interest of the state was the household as a political unit, patriarchal dogma pertained to women even as Paul required, when they were wives – that is, when they assumed their roles in the constitutions of households. While it is true that patriarchalism worked by analogy to argue that children should be obedient to their parents and servants to their masters (and here the fifth commandment was a ready reference), in this aspect it was gender-neutral. Male and female children and servants were equally enjoined to obey parents, schoolteachers, clergymen, and masters. The philosophy was gendered only with respect to the political relationship inaugurated by marriage. To review just the titles of the most familiarly cited texts of patriarchal prescription is to be reminded that this was a literature for and about *married* persons:

The Commendation of MATRIMONY (Henricus Cornelius Agrippa von Nettesheim, 1526)
The Christian State of MATRIMONY (Heinrich Bullinger, 1541)
A Brief and Pleasant Discourse of Duties in MARRIAGE, called the Flower of Friendship (Edmund Tilney, 1568)
A Preparative to MARRIAGE (Henry Smith, 1591)
A Godly Form of HOUSEHOLD Government (John Dod and Robert Cleaver, 1598)

A Looking Glass for MARRIED Folks (Robert Snawsel, 1610)
A Discourse of MARRIAGE and Wiving (Alexander Niccholes, 1615)
A Bride Bush, or A Direction for MARRIED Persons (William Whately, 1616)
MARRIAGE Duties Briefly Couched Together (Thomas Gataker, 1620)
Two MARRIAGE Sermons: The Former, A Good Wife, God's Gift (Thomas Gataker, 1620)
A MARRIAGE Feast (William Bradshaw, 1620)
Of DOMESTICAL Duties (William Gouge, 1622)
A Care Cloth, Or a Treatise of the Cumbers and Troubles of MARRIAGE (William Whately, 1624)

An important feature of third-wave feminism has been the recognition that our interpretive attention to gender alone has been too gross: we need further to refine our work with attention to distinctions of nation, region, race, and class. Amy M. Froide has added to our roster of differences those of marital status. She demonstrates that at any given moment only about half the adult women in early modern England were wives: roughly 15 percent were widows, 30 percent were single, and the remaining 55 percent were married (Froide 1999: 237). By taking our notion of cultural convention from treatises such as those listed above, we have over-regularized the experiences of early modern women to those theorized for wives. We have subscribed to the formulation of women established as long ago as 1632 in *The Lawes Resolutions of Women's Rights*: "All of them are understood either married or to be married" (1632: 6). It cannot be overlooked that patriarchalism participated in a more general gender dynamic that restricted women's legal rights, their occupational horizons, and their social roles. But the long list of sermons and conduct books demonstrates that it was on married women that prescriptive energies were focused. *As a political theory*, patriarchalism was a contingent doctrine. It was inapplicable at any one time to as much as 45 percent of the female population of early modern England.

To put matters in their crudest terms, patriarchal tenets presented an ideology; church court depositions reported behavior. Clearly, it is not possible for one to have existed outside the other. But the effect of the scholarship of the past decades has been to imagine ideology as a preexisting cultural condition, in that our method has been first to reoccupy ideology and then to locate transgressions against it. As long as transgression is figured as a response to ideology, ideology assumes a powerful cultural primacy in our understandings. Our own preoccupation with transgression thus has worked to invest ideology with even more cultural authority than it may have possessed. If, however, we imagine beginning with the egg rather than the chicken in this unsequenceable nexus of cultural relationships, if we open our analysis with behavior in all its multivalence, then we, in effect, take behavior as the cultural condition which ideology must work to incorporate and against which ideology is coercively deployed. For the strategic purpose of rebalancing our notion of cultural conditions, we might reenvision patriarchalism as a phenomenon that was in many respects proactive but in others reactive.

Both patriarchal prescriptive literature and church court depositions were imaginative texts. The prescriptive literature represents cultural myth, in the sense that it projected upon society its own idealized view of how that society should be ordered. Depositions represent individual myth-making, in the sense that deponents shaped a story to suit a legal end. Inasmuch as the depositions purveyed a fiction that early modern society was willing to find legally tenable and fiscally binding, they might seem finally to have had considerable cultural purchase. Their representations of quick-thinking, self-determining, technically adept, tactically gifted women were legally credible, convincing, and effectual.

If it was the case that women had significant power during courtship, then those elements of patriarchal doctrine that were set in train with their marriages can be understood in part as responses to that power. In fact, their particular edge might be characterized as a kind of backlash. From this perspective, it is easier to see how hard · patriarchalism had to work to rein women back in for marriage and how unsusceptible many may have been to its strategies.

The Merry Wives of Windsor and Material Life

As a document in the history of gender relations in the early modern period, *The Merry Wives of Windsor* is arguably the most interesting of Shakespeare's comedies in that it represents not only the prerogatives exercised by women of marriageable age, but also the resistances maintained by some wedded women. Anne Page makes her match regardless of advice and interference, and the Mistresses Ford and Page are anything but silent and obedient.

For all the mystery cultivated in the "device" at Herne's oak – with characters "masked," "vizarded," and "enrobed" (4.6.39, 40) as elves, satyrs, the Queen of Fairy, and Hobgoblin – Anne Page executes her power of choice in a way that would have been broadly recognizable to those who testified in the cases of matrimonial enforcement that came before the church courts. Unlike the women described there, she takes advantage of fanciful comic confusion to elope; like many of them, however, she has multiple marital options and makes a selection among the alternatives. She is thus a kind of extroversion of everyday phenomena that, elsewhere in Shakespeare's canon, are transmuted even further through myth and fantasy. In others of Shakespeare's "romantic" comedies, women not only make their choices but also perform their own devices to enact them, the devices often involving exodus, crossdressing, and transgender role-playing.

In *Love's Labour's Lost*, for example, the Princess of France and her three ladies, making an embassage to Navarre, receive love-suits but forestall commitments for a year and a day, during which time Biron must satisfy Rosaline's terms of trial. In *A Midsummer Night's Dream* Hermia flees to the woods outside Athens rather than marry the man her father prefers for her and, in the end and with the aid of magical intervention, has her choice of Lysander. In *The Merchant of Venice* Portia hints to Bassanio about which casket he should choose to "win" her and then plays the role of a male law clerk to clear away the further impediments of his relational ties and obligations. In *Much Ado About Nothing* Beatrice deflects the provisional suit of Don Pedro, betroths herself to Benedick instead, and requires Benedick to avenge Hero before she will marry him. In *As You Like It* Rosalind gives Orlando her token of a necklace, dresses as a man for her exile in the forest of Arden, tutors Orlando in courtship, and stages her own mock betrothal and eventual wedding. In *Twelfth Night* Olivia rejects the advances of Orsino and makes her match with Cesario/Sebastian, while the cross-dressed Viola refuses a token from Olivia and eventually has her desire for Orsino. In *All's Well That Ends Well* Helen effects a medical miracle to win the power to select a husband, pursues her reluctant choice, and tricks him into consummating the marriage.

"Romantic" as these comedies are by generic systems of classification, they work fantastic elaborations upon what are at their essence common material circumstances in the making of early modern marriages. The plays show that the gender politics encountered in the records of the church courts resonated in early modern culture in ways figurative as well as literal. All Shakespeare's ornaments of plot and action are stratagems through which, in essence, the wills of his female characters are enacted. The wills of many "ordinary" women in early modern England seem to have been enacted, too, even without such journeys and disguises and literary ruses.

Shakespeare's romantic comedies do not often encourage their audiences to look beyond their endstage nuptial celebrations. *The Merry Wives of Windsor* is unusual for its companion plot involving the wives, the jealous husband, and the adulterous-minded Falstaff. Adultery is, however, one violation of patriarchal strictures the Mistresses Page and Ford do not entertain. Because the play instead celebrates their chastity, it has come in for harsh criticism from feminist scholars. Carol Thomas Neely, for example, argues that *Merry Wives* can accommodate "witty and mani-pulative married women who control all the men" (as well as "a remarkably cheeky and insubordinate daughter") only because "all its motifs function to protect the crucial possessions of the middle rank – money, land, and marital chastity" (Neely 1989: 218). Ann Rosalind Jones calls the power of Mistresses Page and Ford "tem-porary" because it does not destabilize models of "proper feminine behavior" (Jones 1998: 32).[17] These critics rightly understand the policing of wifely chastity as a hus-bandly interest, because so many of the implications of women's unchastity redound upon concerns of men's honor and property, as well as the patrilinear descent of possessions.

In characterologic terms, however, *The Merry Wives of Windsor* represents women as having their own interest in chastity. This might equally be understood as a concern for control of their own sexuality. It is unlikely that many of Shakespeare's readers would have found the play more ideologically pleasing had one or both of the wives allowed herself to have been seduced by Falstaff. His construction as a self-seeker, a fortune hunter, and a gull obviates any real contestation of this patriarchal dictate. Falstaff does not seriously test the wives' chastity, any more than Slender and Caius make Anne Page's choice a difficult one. Such are the evasions of comedy.

There is another way of reading the chastity of the merry wives, through early modern material life. Silence and obedience often had little real economic value. But the child born out of wedlock was a potential drain on parish resources, and the child of adultery within marriage threatened to divert private resources from a patrilineal inheritance structure. The church courts saw causes other than those concerned with matrimonial enforcement, notably including accusations of adultery, fornication, and bastard births. While cases of matrimonial enforcement were generally claims for personal damage, complaints about illicit sexuality were a matter for community policing and disciplining. On the subject of chastity, ideology may have seemed more coherent and more urgent, because it was sustained by the structures of material life.

So suggests *The Merry Wives of Windsor*. The play does not engage what was in fact the much-exampled female behavior of sex outside marriage. It works only to redefine the symptomatology of that behavior. The plot involving Anne Page disentangles the traditional triad of female virtues in that, while generally silent and undoubtedly chaste, she is far from obedient. The history of the merry wives also – and more explicitly – goes to dissociate both silence and obedience from chastity, to suggest that disregard of one or the other of the prescribed behaviors is not necessarily a marker for violation of the third. As Mistress Page says: "We'll leave a proof, by that which we will do, / Wives may be merry and yet honest too" (4.2.99–100). *Merry Wives* is not so radical as to allow infidelity in its married women. If the play has a social agenda, it is to propose that outspokenness and disobedience in women need not reflect on their sexual conduct.

This theme exposes some of the faultlines in contemporary social theory. There were others. By insisting that the household was a political institution, state ideology admitted only order and authority as concerns of householding. But early modern households were economic units as well, occupied with getting and spending. By and large, men did not marry in order to procure a political subject and women did not marry in order to acquire a political head. Through marriage, men and women established economic partnerships. As demonstrated in the matrimonial enforcement cases presented in the early modern church courts, most women brought marriage portions which provided needed capital in the inauguration of a household. Wives had important economic roles to play as well, not only running the household but also contributing to the family trade or craft. Among ordinary people, the household was more a corporation than a commonwealth. To secure basic necessities and achieve measures of comfort, husband and wife were required to share responsibilities in the way that Aristotle had termed "aristocratic." Households could never in practice operate as monarchically as ideology theorized.

Domestic patriarchalism was an imperfect political theory, with internal contradictions and imprecise analogies. But its problematics were engaged less in theory than in practice, and the cultural forces that most militated against some aspects of patriarchal ideology were not competing political ideologies. Instead, they were the economic demands of provision and production. The formation of marriage, the principal motive for every romantic comedy in the period, was a social and economic undertaking. As intimated by *The Merry Wives of Windsor*, what worked most forcefully against political ideology and domestic patriarchalism in early modern England was material life.

ACKNOWLEDGMENTS

I am grateful to the Dean and Chapter of Canterbury for the opportunity to have conducted research in the Canterbury Cathedral Archives and Library (hereafter, CCAL). Sections of this chapter were presented in seminars at the 28th Annual Meeting of the Shakespeare Association of America and the 29th International Shakespeare Conference at the Shakespeare Institute (both in 2000). I am grateful to Sandra Clark, Martin Ingram, Steven Mullaney, and, most especially, Loreen Giese for their responses and suggestions.

NOTES

1   My text is the Arden 3 *Merry Wives of Windsor*, edited by G. Melchiori (2000). For references to other plays by Shakespeare, I consult *The Norton Shakespeare Based on the Oxford Edition*, edited by S. Greenblatt, W. Cohen, J. E. Howard, and K. E. Maus.

2   One imagines a lively exchange between Melchiori and the Arden 3 general editors. Although the "traditional" name *The Merry Wives of Windsor* is preserved as the main title of the edition, Melchiori gives *Sir John Falstaff and the Merry Wives of Windsor* in introducing the playtext on pages 119 and 124. He insists that in the title of the Quarto and the Stationers' Register, "the original conception of this play is much more truly expressed" (p. xvii).

3   One of the ways in which the rival suitors serve the romantic plot is that Anne's marriage portion is established in the context of discussions among Slender and Shallow; it is not at the forefront in the courtship of Anne and Fenton.

4   Ford is concerned not only that his "bed shall be abused" and his "reputation gnawn at," but also that his "coffers" will be "ransacked" (2.2.277–8). Barton (1994: 79) refers to *Every Man Out of his Humour, The Phoenix, The Roaring Girl*, and *Westward Ho!* in pointing out that this is a common, cross-class theme of city comedy, with men of status seducing citizen wives in the interest of plundering merchant coffers. See also Hunter (1986: 4–5).

5   My understanding of courtship practices is based in Cressy (1997), Gowing (1996), Ingram (1987), O'Hara (2000), and also in private correspondence with Loreen Giese.

6   Simon Reynolds (1996: 315) also notes "Shallow's curious team approach to courtship." Peter Erickson (1987: 123) more acutely observes: "Neither the wives nor Fenton are shown to be superior moral beings," inasmuch as all "are implicated in the social system of plotting in which all the characters are engaged."

7   The Belott–Mountjoy Suit is usefully represented in Schoenbaum (1981: 20–39), which provides facsimiles and transcriptions as well as discussion.

8   For interesting speculation on Shallow's possible financial situation and economic concerns, see Reynolds (1996: 314–15).

9   One risk that *The Merry Wives of Windsor* does engage is that conventional reliance on intermediaries can allow for betrayal. Thus, Mistress Page threatens Robin: "have you been true to us?" "Ay," he replies; "My master knows not of your being here" (3.3.23–6).

10 My arguments with O'Hara are outlined in a review essay, "Rewriting Stone's Renaissance," forthcoming in the *Huntington Library Quarterly*.

11 Reynolds (1996: 317) seems to think Anne's letter is a thank-you note, written "presumably in response to his having sent a ring via Mistress Quickly."

12 In this context the George Wilkins play *The Miseries of Enforced Marriage* is interesting. As cited by T. G. A. Nelson, Young Scarborrow betroths himself to Clare but is then ordered to marry another woman. He says, "I haue no *hands* to take her to my wife" (Nelson 1998: 366; his emphasis).

13 Gowing (1996: 153–4) cites the 1576 case of a woman threatened by her suitor: "With no friends of her own there, verbal references to the authority of her kin are her only resource . . . enabling her to give in at the time, but to argue herself free from a binding contract later."

14 To some extent, this is to argue against a straw man – which is the interpretation we ourselves have built out of a literature that was both more varied and less culturally dominant than we have sometimes suggested.

15 Conflicting testimony is more common in cases dealing with issues other than courtship, such as testamentary cases. These other cases are useful reminders, though, of how misleading any one deposition can be.

16 This argument is made in more detail in Orlin (2000a), which should also be consulted for relevant bibliography.

17 See also on this subject Lawrence Danson (2000: 117), who recognizes the "superior power" of the women but says "the play's spirit is not progressive," and Peter Erickson (1987: 124), who describes how the play promotes "the redistribution of wealth upwards."

REFERENCES AND FURTHER READING

Barton, A. (1994). *Essays, Mainly Shakespearean*. Cambridge: Cambridge University Press.

Bradley contra Shurt (1596). CCAL MS X/11/5, fol. 135ʳ–138ʳ.

Clark, S. (1987). "Wives May be Merry and Yet Honest Too": Women and Wit in *The Merry Wives of Windsor* and Some Other Plays. In J. W. Mahon and T. A. Pendleton (eds.) *"Fanned and Winnowed Opinions": Shakespearean Essays Presented to Harold Jenkins*. London: Methuen, 249–67.

Cobb contra Butler (1585). CCAL MS X/11/1, fols. 3ᵛ–4ʳ.

Cook, A. J. (1991). *Making a Match: Courtship in Shakespeare and His Society*. Princeton, NJ: Princeton University Press.

Cressy, D. (1997). *Birth, Marriage and Death: Ritual, Religion, and the Life-Cycle in Tudor and Stuart England*. Oxford: Oxford University Press.

Danson, L. (2000). *Shakespeare's Dramatic Genres*. Oxford: Oxford University Press.

de Certeau, M. (1984). *The Practice of Everyday Life*, trans. S. Rendall. Berkeley: University of California Press.

de Grazia, M., Quilligan, M., and Stallybrass, P. (1996). Introduction. In M. de Grazia, M. Quilligan, and P. Stallybrass (eds.) *Subject and Object in Renaissance Culture*. Cambridge: Cambridge University Press, 1–13.

Doran, M. (1954). *Endeavors of Art: A Study of Form in Elizabethan Drama*. Madison: University of Wisconsin Press.

Dusinberre, J. (1975). *Shakespeare and the Nature of Women*. Basingstoke: Macmillan.

E., T. (1632). *The Lawes Resolutions of Women's Rights*. London.

Emmison, F. G. (1973). *Elizabethan Life: Morals and the Church Courts*. Chelmsford: Essex County Council.

Erickson, A. L. (1993). *Women and Property in Early Modern England*. London: Routledge.

Erickson, P. (1987). The Order of the Garter, the Cult of Elizabeth, and Class–Gender Tension in *The Merry Wives of Windsor*. In J. E. Howard and M. F. O'Connor (eds.) *Shakespeare Reproduced: The Text in History and Ideology*. New York: Methuen, 116–40.

Froide, A. M. (1999). Marital Status as a Category of Difference: Singlewomen and Widows in Early Modern England. In J. M. Bennett and A. M. Froide (eds.) *Singlewomen in the European Past, 1250–1800*. Philadelphia: University of Pennsylvania Press, 236–69.

Fumerton, P. (1999). Introduction: A New, New Historicism. In P. Fumerton and S. Hunt (eds.) *Renaissance Culture and the Everyday*. Philadelphia: University of Pennsylvania Press, 1–17.

Gibbons, B. (1968). *Jacobean City Comedy: A Study of Satiric Plays by Jonson, Marston, and Middleton*. Cambridge, MA: Harvard University Press.

Giese, L. L. (ed.) (1995). *London Consistory Court Depositions, 1586–1611: List and Indexes.* London: London Record Society.

Gowing, L. (1996). *Domestic Dangers: Women, Words, and Sex in Early Modern London.* Oxford: Clarendon Press.

Helgerson, R. (2000). *Adulterous Alliances: Home, State, and History in Early Modern European Drama and Painting.* Chicago, IL: University of Chicago Press.

Helmholz, R. H. (1974). *Marriage Litigation in Medieval England.* Cambridge: Cambridge University Press.

Houlbrooke, R. (1985). The Making of Marriage in Mid-Tudor England: Evidence from the Records of Matrimonial Contract Litigation. *Journal of Family History,* 10.

Howard, J. E. (1994). *The Stage and Social Struggle in Early Modern England.* London: Routledge.

Hunter, G. K. (1986). Bourgeois Comedy: Shakespeare and Dekker. In E. A. J. Honigmann (ed.) *Shakespeare and His Contemporaries: Essays in Comparison.* Manchester: Manchester University Press, 1–15.

Ingram, M. (1987). *Church Courts, Sex and Marriage in England, 1570–1640.* Cambridge: Cambridge University Press.

Jackson contra Odert alias Simons (1598). CCAL MS X/11/3, fols. 79^v–85^r.

Jones, A. R. (1998). Revenge Comedy: Writing, Law, and the Punishing Heroine in *Twelfth Night, The Merry Wives of Windsor,* and *Swetnam the Woman-Hater.* In G. M. Kendall (ed.) *Shakespearean Power and Punishment: A Volume of Essays.* Madison: Fairleigh Dickinson University Press; London: Associated University Presses, 23–38.

Kamps, I. (1995). Introduction. In I. Kamps (ed.) *Materialist Shakespeare: A History.* London: Verso, 1–19.

Kegl, R. (1994). *The Rhetoric of Concealment: Figuring Gender and Class in Renaissance Literature.* Ithaca, NY: Cornell University Press.

Korda, N. (2001). "Judicious Oeillades": Supervising Marital Property in *The Merry Wives of Windsor.* In J. E. Howard and S. C. Shershow (eds.) *Marxist Shakespeares.* London: Routledge, 82–103.

Launsfeild contra Overye (1602). CCAL MS X/11/4, fols. 131^r–132^v.

Leggatt, A. (1973). *Citizen Comedy in the Age of Shakespeare.* Toronto: University of Toronto Press.

Leinwand, T. B. (1986). *The City Staged: Jacobean Comedy, 1603–1613.* Madison: University of Wisconsin Press.

Manley, L. (1995). *Literature and Culture in Early Modern London.* Cambridge: Cambridge University Press.

Melchiori, G. (2000). Introduction. In G. Melchiori (ed.) The Arden Shakespeare: *The Merry Wives of Windsor.* Walton-on-Thames: Thomas Nelson and Sons, 1–117.

Mendelson, S. and Crawford, P. (1998). *Women in Early Modern England, 1550–1720.* Oxford: Clarendon Press.

Neely, C. T. (1989). Constructing Female Sexuality in the Renaissance: Stratford, London, Windsor, Vienna. In R. Feldstein and J. Roof (eds.) *Feminism and Psychoanalysis.* Ithaca, NY: Cornell University Press, 209–29.

Nelson, T. G. A. (1998). Doing Things with Words: Another Look at Marriage Rites and Spousals in Renaissance Drama and Fiction. *Studies in Philology,* 95, 351–73.

O'Hara, D. (2000). *Courtship and Constraint: Rethinking the Making of Marriage in Tudor England.* Manchester: Manchester University Press.

Orlin, L. C. (2000a). Chronicles of Private Life. In A. F. Kinney (ed.) *The Cambridge Companion to English Literature, 1500–1600.* Cambridge: Cambridge University Press, 241–64.

——(ed.) (2000b). *Material London, ca. 1600.* Philadelphia: University of Pennsylvania Press.

Pittenger, E. (1991). Dispatch Quickly: The Mechanical Reproduction of Pages. *Shakespeare Quarterly,* 42, 389–408.

Reynolds, S. (1996). The Lawful Name of Marrying: Contracts and Stratagems in *The Merry Wives of Windsor. The Shakespeare Yearbook,* 7, 313–31.

Roberts, J. A. (1979). *Shakespeare's English Comedy: "The Merry Wives of Windsor" in Context.* Lincoln: University of Nebraska Press.

Schoenbaum, S. (1981). *William Shakespeare: Records and Images.* New York: Oxford University Press.

Stretton, T. (1998). *Women Waging Law in Elizabethan England*. Cambridge: Cambridge University Press.

Vyne contra Herringham (1589). CCAL MS X/11/1, fols. 271ᵛ–274ʳ.

Wall, W. (1998). "Household Stuff": The Sexual Politics of Domesticity and the Advent of English Comedy. *English Literary History*, 65, 1–45.

Woollet contra Saunders (1590). CCAL MS X/11/2, fols. 42ᵛ–43ᵛ, 62ᵛ–63ᵛ, 73ʳ–74ʳ, 170ᵛ, 180ᵛ–181ʳ, 192ʳ–194ʳ.

9
Shakespeare's Comic Geographies
Garrett A. Sullivan, Jr.

This chapter focuses on specific Shakespearean geographies as they intersect with and illuminate key aspects of early modern culture. As considered here, geography is less a description of the physical landscapes and cultures of a particular region than a conceptual structure through which social and spatial relations are simultaneously materialized and represented, often in an idealized manner. In that different conceptual structures emerge at different times, geography is historical; in that more than one such structure obtains at any given moment, geography is multiple, most accurately referred to as "geographies." With Shakespeare's plays, geographies are also literary, and this chapter examines the ways in which the poetic geographies of the comedies are indebted to and emerge out of both literary and sociohistorical imperatives. The chapter first considers the comedies in light of what are commonly called the old and new geographies, then takes up the two critical schools that have dominated the study of geography in Shakespeare. After next discussing the importance of the ancient notion of the *oikumene* to Shakespearean comedy, the chapter analyzes three geographies central to a number of the comedies, those of hospitality, paternity, and flight. In doing so, it works to isolate some of what we might call the deep geographic structures of Shakespearean comedy.

In the last ten years, early modern studies has witnessed an explosion of interest in the interrelations of literature and geography, with foundational work being done by Richard Helgerson and John Gillies. While Helgerson's (1992) examination of the role of English atlases in early modern nation-formation has been highly influential, it is Gillies who has dealt most extensively and directly with Shakespeare, arguing for a view of the plays as enactments of "a dramaturgical version of the ancient poetic geographic economy of difference" (Gillies 1994: 25). The two critics approach the study of early modern geography from significantly different perspectives. Put somewhat schematically, Helgerson stresses the significance of the "new geography" for the construction of a land-centered conception of Englishness, whereas Gillies emphasizes the continued power of the "old geography" for the imaginative organization of space in Shakespeare. It is Gillies, then, who offers a direct answer to the question that writers have in one form or another been posing since Shakespeare's day: do his works place Shakespeare among the geographic "moderns"? If not, is he the willing heir to a geographic legacy more allegorical and poetic than scientific and objective? That is, is his work of a piece with the "old" geography or the "new"?

As typically defined, the "old" geography is marked by, in one cartographic historian's words, "the topography of myth and dogma" (Wilford 1981: 34), whereas the "new" is characterized by the desire both to render space accurately and to rationalize it. A positivist account of this distinction would recognize a difference between a false, poetic geography and a true, scientific one, and it would link the deployment of these terms to a teleological narrative in which the benighted old geography (associated with premodernity) gradually gives way to the enlightened new (associated with modernity). Such an account would seem to find much support in the history of Shakespeare's time. England in the late sixteenth and early seventeenth centuries is commonly understood as being on the cusp of geographic modernity. This period saw the production of some of the most important early achievements of English geography and cartography, most famously Christopher Saxton's atlas of England and Wales, with maps engraved between 1574 and 1579. Made possible by the deployment of newly sophisticated mathematical and surveying technologies, the production of Saxton's atlas is a milestone in the "accurate" representation of the land. Moreover, ideals of standardization and precision mobilized through innovations in these technologies played a small but significant role in the development of the spatiality of (early) modernity. In other words, Saxton's atlas can be seen as emblematizing and contributing to the emergence of geographic modernity. However, we should be leery about reading the subsequent history of that modernity back into the moment of its inception. Moreover, the maps contained within Saxton's atlas resonate with an "old" geography that, given its continued affective and imaginative weight, is misunderstood if considered either merely vestigial or greatly attenuated in its force.

The conflict between old and new geographies is gestured toward in Ben Jonson's famous scoffing reference to Shakespeare's "Bohemian shore." As reported by William Drummond, Jonson complained that "Shakespeare in a play brought in a number of men saying they had suffered shipwreck in Bohemia, where there is no sea near by some 100 miles." For Jonson, Shakespeare's geographic illiteracy is of a piece with what the former perceives to be the latter's more general under-educatedness, manifested in Jonson's description of Shakespeare in the prefatory matter to the First Folio as having "small *Latine*, and lesse *Greeke*." The terms of Jonson's disparagement seem very much our own; the adducement of a Bohemian shore in *The Winter's Tale* is routinely read by critics as a gaffe on Shakespeare's part. However, this "error" appears as such from the perspective of the new geography and its ideal of geographic accuracy. Indeed, it is easy to see how Shakespeare's reference is an extremely effective dramatic one. The Bohemian shore is first and foremost distant and strange: a fairy-tale strand upon which a royal infant is left to the mercy of the elements, and her carrier is devoured by a bear. For "Bohemia," read remote and foreign; for "shore," think of the liminality that a coast encodes. The passage from the realm of the familiar to that of the dangerously alien is suggested by and encapsulated in Shakespeare's "Bohemian shore," and in this regard the geographic reference is both precise and effective.[1] If Jonson's querulous comment voices imperatives associated with the new geography, in Shakespeare's text we see the old in vital action. Both geographies coexist in the early modern period, and from the perspective of that period it would be distortive to mark too hastily one as vigorously "emergent" and the other as feebly "residual." Indeed, the very terms "old" and "new" inject a certain view of the future into the early modern present; they bespeak the false inevitability of a specific temporal unfolding recognized only through hindsight. In addition, they give to Shakespeare's dramatically effective geographical reference a hint of both benightedness and belatedness, his "Bohemian shore" representing the kind of error that will supposedly disappear in the brave new world of modern geography. This is not to read Jonson and Shakespeare, or the different forms of comedy with which each is aligned, as emblematic of geographies new and old.[2] It is instead to recognize that both geographies are operational in the early modern period, even as the principles expressed in the new geography are used to denigrate all that is associated with the old.

Significantly, the distinction between the old geography and the new finds its analogue in two kinds of scholarly work on Shakespeare and early modern drama. Referring to "critical literature on the drama's use of . . . literary or legendary or mythological or archetypal geographies," John Gillies notes that "Such writing is generally uninterested in 'real' geography. The guiding assumption is that literary geography means one thing and 'real' geography another" (Gillies 1998: 21). The opposition Gillies draws is underdeveloped, but he is distinguishing here between what I will refer to as "archetypal" and "particularist" geographic criticisms. For the comedies, the best example of the first school is Northrop Frye's *A Natural Perspective* (1965), in which Frye posits a "green world" to which Shakespeare's comic protagonists temporarily retreat. As the term suggests, the "green world" is no particular place; it is a symbolic site of regeneration in which the social conflicts experienced by the characters in the world from which they have fled (Athens in *A Midsummer Night's Dream*, for example, or the court of Duke Frederick in *As You Like It*) are quasi-magically resolved.[3] The second school offers no clear *locus classicus*. However, it represents the current dominant approach to Shakespeare and geography, and for this reason, I will now take it up in some detail.[4]

If the archetypalists ignore the particularity of dramatic locations in favor of reading them as imprecisely defined symbolic spaces ("green" or otherwise), the particularists attend closely to the sociohistorical significance of such locations.[5] In doing so, they might take up the history of a particular city and/or its people, or focus on the broad cultural associations evoked in the audience through references made to an entire country; they might examine Italy's political, economic, or social history, or consider the representation of a loosely defined "Italian Other." Often there are specific representational problems that need to be addressed: does "Verona" stand in for Italy or a generic city therein, or does it have for Shakespeare its own particular civic resonances? But this problem pales before another that all particularist criticism on the comedies needs to consider: when does a city like Venice stand for itself, and when is it, say, an analogue for London? Is it appropriate to bring a location's history to bear on Shakespearean representations of that location when those representations may have much to do with England and little to do with Italy?[6] If not, how do you know precisely when it is not appropriate, and how do geographical references work in such an instance? What do we do with examples of "real geography" that finally do not seem so real?

The above example of Bohemia suggests one of the ways in which real geography works in Shakespeare: as a suggestive (if imprecise) indicator of foreignness. More specifically, the real and symbolic are intertwined and interanimating. A different kind of example is to be found in *The Two Gentlemen of Verona*, in which Verona is twice mentioned when Milan is meant – and in which Valentine seems to have gone well out of his way in order to make an unnecessary sea journey from the former to the latter (3.1.81; 5.4.130; 1.1.53–4). Shakespeare does not concern himself here with either geographic accuracy or consistency; what matters most is that these locales are both foreign and both traveled between, and the idea of a sea voyage only increases our sense of the journey as a significant and at least potentially perilous one.[7] On other occasions, however, Shakespearean geography takes on a greater precision. The obvious comic examples are Windsor and Venice; *Merry Wives* is peppered with enough references to the town for the play to offer proleptic echoes of Jacobean city comedy in its geographic specificity,[8] while *Merchant* presents us with a Venice much more fully realized than is either Verona or Milan in *Two Gentlemen*. Partly because of Shakespeare's "realistic" representation of Venice, it is this location more than any other (excepting Rome, which is not very important to the comedies) that has generated sustained critical interest.[9] However, *Merchant* also provides an intriguing counter-example in Belmont, the fairy-tale home of Portia, an affluent orphan pursued by Bassanio. Indeed, Belmont and Venice seem like antithetical locales until one considers the extent to which Belmont's mythological landscape – it is "Colchos' strond, / And many Jasons come in quest of her [i.e., Portia, metaphorized as the golden fleece]" (1.1.171–2) – is inseparable from the Venetian economic dealings that underwrite Bassanio's pursuit of Portia, as well as Lorenzo's of Jessica. Insofar as it is an international nexus of economically motivated activity – "the four winds blow in from every coast / Renowned suitors" (1.1.168–9) who seek Portia and her wealth – Belmont resembles Venice, that famous hub of worldwide trade. Moreover, it is in Belmont that Antonio's ships are restored to him (5.1.275–6), and thus it is where his status as Venetian merchant is reaffirmed. Even in the comedy most given over to geographic realism, we locate a fairy-tale (if not a "green") world whose operations interpenetrate those of the Venetian "real" one. Geographies actual and mythic, just like those "new" and "old," overlap and inform one another.

What, then, does all of this suggest about Shakespearean geography? The above paragraph might seem to suggest the limits of the particularist approach and hint at the strengths of an archetypal one. This is not quite right, however. For one thing, many particularists remain keenly aware of the limits of the most literal-minded version of their work. A good example of this awareness is to be found in a brief and insightful essay by Manfred Pfister, who argues against what he calls the "Shakespeare and Italy" school of criticism, suggesting that it gives us much information about Italy without satisfactorily showing how that information might illuminate the plays.[10] Pfister asserts instead that

> The underlying opposition of England and Italy . . . provides a spatialized model for basic and culture-specific value oppositions constructed across (border) lines such as northern versus Mediterranean, Protestant versus Catholic, nature versus artifice, authenticity versus sophistication, plebeian versus middle class versus aristocratic, land versus trade, country versus city, male versus female, etc. etc. And the underlying cross-cultural oppositions between England and Italy, between the site of performance and the sights arranged in the fiction, are modulated and varied in the smaller-scale spatial oppositions set up within the plays. (Pfister 1997: 300)

This version of particularism both avoids the pitfalls of the narrow application of "real" information to Shakespeare's plays and recognizes the significance of broad categories of sameness and otherness to the geographic logic of a play. At the same time, it is emphatically not a form of Fryean archetypalism; in lieu of the opposition between dehistoricized conceptions of court and green world, we find pairings of specific socio-historical categories arranged so as to acknowledge that England is always the first term. (After all, Pfister reminds us, we are dealing in Shakespeare's plays less with Italian history than with English cultural conceptions of Italy.) Most intriguing is the assertion that large cross-cultural oppositions are echoed and reinflected, "modulated and varied," in "smaller-scale spatial" ones. Of course, it is possible to reverse the priorities expressed in this formulation – to see that the "smaller-scale" oppositions do in some ways determine the forms that larger cross-cultural oppositions take. More precisely, oppositions large and small mutually inform the terms of each other's representation. National or civic geographies are generated in Shakespeare's comedies through – sometimes entirely in terms of – geographies of kinship, allegiance, and home.

In claiming this, I am developing further and modifying the insightful work of Gillies, who uses Giambattista Vico's conception of "poetic geography" as a point of entry into Shakespeare's plays:

> Vico supposes that the archaic image of the Greek *oikumene* – a word which suggestively combines the senses of 'world' and 'house' – predates and prescribes the earliest known formulation of its geography in Herodotus. In other words, the imaginative form of the *oikumene* controls its factual geographic content. Instead, therefore, of supposing that the Greeks formed the image of their world . . . from their commerce with that world, Vico supposes that the essential *oikumene* began in Greece itself. In the beginning, then, the Greek image of the "world" was literally bound by their geographic "home." Then, as further geographic knowledge became available, the symbolic architecture of the *oikumene* was simply exported or extrapolated to accommodate it. (Gillies 1994: 5)

While this formulation might suggest the installation of a timeless geographic structure – a symbolic architecture "simply" exported or extrapolated – Gillies's model is simultaneously transhistorical and culturally and temporally constituted: while the poetic geography is "paradigmatic for any geography which differentiates between an 'us' and a 'them,'" it also "accomodates ever more specific and diverse geographic information" (ibid: 6–7, 6).[11] At the same time, what is underdeveloped is a sense of how the inherited structure of the poetic geography, especially the concept of the *oikumene*, can be understood as being responsive to the sociocultural pressures of a given historical moment as well as being reinflected by them. One era's *oikumene*, both "world" and "house," is not the same as another's: indeed, the term need not have *any* conceptual purchase at a given historical moment, although it does in Shakespeare's day.[12] Put differently, the poetic geography that early modern culture inherits should be viewed less as a stable intellectual legacy that defines the terms of dramatic spatial representation than as a potent but malleable conceptual resource in engagement with which early modern spatial imperatives are represented, idealized, contested, and/or reimagined.

The conceptual interpenetration of "house" and "world" is repeatedly suggested in Shakespeare's comedies. Consider a stock comic situation that Shakespeare developed on a few occasions: the entrance of a stranger into a strange land.[13] In *The Comedy of Errors*, for instance, a befuddled Antipholus of Syracuse reports that

> They say this town is full of cozenage:
> As, nimble jugglers that deceive the eye,
> Dark-working sorcerers that change the mind,
> Soul-killing witches that deform the body,
> Disguised cheaters, prating mountebanks,
> And many such-like liberties of sin:
> If it prove so, I will be gone the sooner. (1.2.97–103)

Dromio of Syracuse later unknowingly echoes his master when he asserts of Ephesus that "This is the fairy land. O spite of spites, / We talk with goblins, owls, and sprites!" (2.2.188–9). The traveler confronted with such wondrous behavior later suffers a modified reprise of it, but this time the focal point is the house. Antipholus S. is browbeaten into taking dinner with his "wife," Adriana, and his entrance into a house that only others recognize as his leads to his articulation of his displacement: "Am I in earth, heaven, or in hell? / Sleeping or waking? mad or well advised? / Known unto these, and to myself disguised!" (2.2.211–13). The irony is that this house is where Antipholus (of Ephesus) should be most at home; he is disguised to himself because the property others claim is his, which emblematizes the *oikumene* that should ground his sense of identity, is unrecognizable to him.[14] This example of his dislocation has cosmic and theological overtones ("Am I in earth, heaven, or in hell?"); "world" and "house" are interpenetrated here, the household geography intertwined with that of both country and cosmos in the service of the representation of one character's strong sense of displacement.

A similar example of displacement from home and country is to be found in *The Taming of the Shrew*; in this instance, a traveler passing from Pisa to Padua enters a land not of seeming sorcerers and witches but of the apparently insane. Vincentio is struck speechless by Katherine's references to him as a fair maid, and Hortensio wonders if her address "will make the man mad" (4.5.35) – as mad as Kate's speech suggests she already is (41).[15] This comic situation, in which the fact of his traveling opens Vincentio up to the refiguration of his identity by others (not only as "fair maid" but as Petruchio's "loving father": 4.5.60), is slightly modified in a subsequent scene in which Lucentio's serving men insist that Vincentio is masquerading as Lucentio's father. What prompts this insistence is Vincentio's attempt to gain admittance to his son's house, where he plans to offer hospitality to his traveling companions: "You shall not choose but drink before you go. / I think I shall command your welcome here, / And by all likelihood some cheer is toward" (5.1.10–12). However, Vincentio is denied entry when those in the household claim that they do not know him. This does not lead Vincentio to the posing of cosmic questions ("Am I in earth, heaven, or in hell?"), but to his insistence that others have betrayed him; the difference between the two responses emerges out of the different social positions of the characters, Vincentio being a patriarch while Antipholus S. is "like a drop of water / That in the ocean seeks another drop" (1.2.35–6). That being said, taken together these two moments from *Taming* offer a variation on the theme adduced in *The Comedy of Errors*: a traveler's encounters with an alien culture represented both at regional and house-hold levels. In each of the plays, the traveler passes outside his own *oikumene*, and these scenes stage comically the collision between one world (view) and another. At the same time, the movement of comedy will take us from collision to integration: Antipholus of Syracuse discovers his twin and weds Adriana's sister, Luciana, while both Lucentio and Bianca lay claim to Vincentio's fatherhood in a ritual of repentant obeisance (5.1.99–106). Links between the two worlds are forged, and for the trav-eler the strange land is integrated into his own *oikumene* – is in a sense "domesticated" – by the formation of new, as well as the discovery of old, blood alliances. Indeed, the strangeness of that land is eradicated with the revelation of such alliances, suggest-ing a geography in which regional difference is subordinated to household and blood relations that are both primary and determining.

What we have seen, then, is that issues of alienation and identification are worked out through the representation of relations between conceptually intertwined regions and households. Such is typical of Shakespeare's comedies, so much so that the geog-raphy of these plays is to a great extent that of certain basic conceptual structures and the patterns of action which those structures enable and with which they are associated. In what follows I will focus on the geographies of hospitality, of paternity, and of flight. These geographies are neither timeless nor static; indeed, the dramatic mobilization of each bespeaks its potency for and engagement with its particular historical moment. In addition, each geography overlaps with one or more of the others, just as they inter-sect with the geographies of region and household that have already been touched upon. Through focusing on these structures, we will begin to come to terms with a comic geography that is sometimes new and old, and is both particular and archetypal – just not quite in the way that these descriptors have usually been taken to mean.

Geography of Hospitality

We have seen that Vincentio had hoped to offer Petruchio and Katherine "some cheer" from the house to which he was immediately thereafter denied admission. Similarly, Antipholus of Ephesus brings guests to his house to offer them "A table-full of welcome" (3.1.23) only to be debarred entrance. Enraged, Antipholus E. seeks to break into his own house, at which point he is warned by Balthazar that in doing so he "war[s] against [his] reputation, / And draw[s] within the compass of suspect / Th' unviolated honor of [his] wife" (86–8) – this because they have discovered that Adriana entertains another man within. Were he to embark upon the public action he intends, Antipholus E. would bring dishonor on his wife, and thereby enter into combat with his own reputation. Thus, his frustrated impulse to hospitality almost brings Antipholus E. to do violence to his own public persona. The comic force of this scene lies in the way in which two important forms of patriarchal performance – first of hospitality and second of control over one's wife – come into conflict. This conflict occurs around a specific space, with the denial of physical access to the house encoding the overturning of normal relations: the head of the household is literally shut out. That this is not a narrowly domestic matter is made plain in Balthazar's above lines, which attest to the public implications of Antipholus E.'s attempted actions. As he puts it a few lines later: "Now in the stirring passage of the day / A vulgar comment will be made of it [i.e., your attempt to break in]" (99–100). In early modern England (as in Shakespeare's Ephesus), household matters are never simply that, as they are intertwined with broader civic and state affairs in a way that confounds any anachronistic notion of the relation between "public" and "private." This is one reason why hospitality is such a crucial ideological issue for the Renaissance English.

Hospitality to both the poor and to one's peers was a highly visible marker of aristocratic identity. Moreover, hospitality and housekeeping were synonymous in early modern culture, and the former obviously both had implications for and necessarily grew out of the practice of the latter. Indeed, while the extravagant performance of generosity raised the possibility of a debilitating profligacy, hospitality as an ideal spoke not only to the proper management of the household, but to the broadly beneficial social effects of that management. Hospitality both attested to and advanced the health of the polity. That being said, Shakespeare wrote at a moment in which the significance of hospitality was undergoing a transformation:

> By the later sixteenth century this image of an elite given in honor to open hospitality, but not excessively so, began to yield to alternative patterns, especially those produced by growing mobility and the growth of London. Both Court and City played an increasing role in the experience of the nobility and many of the gentry, and perceptions of a civil society encouraged new ideas of social separation. It became questionable if the honor code required even the semblance of hospitality, since no reputation was to be gained from the plaudits of the multitude. (Heal 1990: 391–2)[16]

Despite such historical changes, hospitality is a crucial concept in Shakespeare's work;[17] it continues to have force for him even during the period of its attenuation, and, as the above example suggests, the practice of hospitality generates a geography of its own. In *The Comedy of Errors* this geography centers upon the threshold to Antipholus E.'s house, with the frustration of hospitality taking the form of refused admittance.

Another interesting example is *Much Ado About Nothing*, in which Leonato's hospitality offered to the returning warriors is both a precondition and the backdrop for all of the action of the play. Moreover, just as Leonato is both Governor and head of household, so are Messina and his home largely collapsed into one another.[18] For Don Pedro to "com[e] this night to Messina" (1.1.2) is for him to arrive at Leonato's house, where he seems to stay for the length of the play. Also, the arrangement of the marriage between Claudio and Hero can be seen as an extension of Leonato's hospitality, a view underscored by the familiar notion of the father "giving away" his daughter (e.g., 2.1.270–1). Claudio's later repudiation of his fiancée, then, entails and is described as the returning of this gift as damaged goods, a "rotten orange" (4.1.21–30, esp. 30). (It also suggests Leonato's failure as a manager of his own household, as he is putatively unable to regulate the actions of his daughter.) Significantly, Claudio's shaming requires his later acceptance of Leonato's "niece" as his bride. While his willingness to do so necessarily troubles our sense of Claudio as a romantic lead, it also restores the relations of hospitality that he had earlier ruptured. The form that this restoration takes – Claudio's willing acceptance of Leonato's choice as his bride – makes plain the extent to which these relations are first and foremost male homosocial ones, consolidated here through the traffic in women. While this play is unusual in that it transpires in a single region, we again see the formation of blood alliances between representatives of two worlds, and in this case hospitality enables the forging of these links.

Other comedies could be discussed here; *Love's Labour's Lost*, for instance, is structured around the King of Navarre's having "sworn out house-keeping" (2.1.103), a practice that leads to his denial of entrance into the city of the Princess of France and her entourage. Swearing off hospitality shapes the geography and the action of the play, in which the men maintain their vow to keep women from the court by themselves traveling to the ladies' tents. What links this comedy to the two preceding ones is the centrality of hospitality to Shakespeare's construction of the play's geography. Certainly one could say more about Navarre or Messina or Ephesus as specific locales – numerous critics have – but in and across these plays it is the geography of hospitality that most engages Shakespeare's imagination and that provides a structure for significant aspects of the dramatic action.

Geography of Paternity

Much Ado makes plain the significance of male homosocial relations to the logic of comedy. Of course, the play marks an interesting variation on a traditional theme, as there is no *senex* figure impeding the central love match.[19] Certainly, other Shakespearean comedies feature such a character – think of Egeus in *A Midsummer Night's Dream* – but it is also the case that fathers frequently play a more positive role in Shakespearean comedy. Indeed, they often function as the means by which disparate worlds are brought together; fathers can bridge the gap between one city or region and another and thereby enable the romantic match that will finally forge blood alliances between prominent families of disparate geographic origins.[20]

As we have seen, Petruchio claims Vincentio as his father shortly after meeting him upon the road to Padua. In his first appearance on stage, Petruchio stresses that his present actions and identity have been shaped by the death of his biological father: "Antonio my father is deceased, / And I have thrust myself into this maze, / Haply to wive and thrive as best I may" (1.2.52–4). This maze is metaphorical, referencing as it does Petruchio's efforts to "seek [his] fortun[e] farther than at home" (49), but as it turns out the maze is also, broadly, Padua itself and, more narrowly, the Minola household. In addition, if his entrepreneurial voyage is prompted by Antonio's death, it is also advanced by his father's identity. Petruchio announces that "I know [Katherine's] father though I know not her, / And he knew my deceased father well" (1.2.99–100). The utility of this knowledge is made plain in the next scene, in which Petruchio's announcement of his father's identity to Baptista leads the latter to say: "I know him well, you are welcome for his sake" (2.1.70). This welcome is an important precondition for Petruchio's wiving and thriving, and it is enabled through the operations of a network of fathers.[21]

The working assumption in the exchanges just mentioned is that character is legible through paternity. This assumption is both represented and ironized in *The Two Gentlemen of Verona*, in which the Duke of Milan attempts to ascertain the nature of Proteus' character by first asking Valentine questions about the character of Proteus' father: "Know ye Don Antonio, your countryman?" (2.4.51). The Duke's subsequent interrogation of Valentine is designed by Shakespeare to reveal to the audience Valentine's false impression of his friend's merits; his catalogue of Proteus' virtues, which emerges out of the positive account of Antonio's character that Valentine offers the Duke, stands in ironic contrast to Proteus' shape-shifting throughout the play. Here, then, character is not grounded in paternity, but this is a deliberate inversion of the norm in Shakespeare; Proteus' very name attests to the inutility in his case of traditional ways of reading character. More typical is Sebastian's shorthand delineation of his character through a glancing reference to his father, "that Sebastian of Messaline whom I know you have heard of" (*Twelfth Night*, 2.1.15–16). The final clause tacitly attributes Sebastian Sr.'s widespread reputation to his exemplary virtue, and what is meant to be communicated to both Antonio and the audience is that the son follows in his father's footsteps.

What unites these three examples is not only their interest in the relationship between paternity and character; it is also that in each case the articulation of that relationship works to overcome geographic difference. In each example, the discussion of paternity comes as a male character passes into a new city or country; that character's entrance into an alien land is managed through the mediating force of paternity.[22] Indeed, the reputations of fathers transcend geographic boundaries in ways that enable the forging of new alliances, including marriage. In Shakespearean comedy, then, regional difference is both negotiated and functionally erased through cross-regional links between fathers. It is worth stressing that in each of the examples just adduced, at least one father is either absent or dead; the son depends upon the reputation his father has established, but he is not merely a representative of an older generation. Shakespeare's comedies stage the formation of new homosocial relations while attesting to the groundedness of these new relations in an older social (or reputational) network of men.

From the perspective of the homosocial relations taken up here, then, the "real" geography of the plays is not tremendously important as such; it is as the sociospatial grid through which such relations are worked out that geography matters most. This grid is historically inflected insofar as it is in engagement with the patriarchal social relations that predominate in early modern England. Such engagement is often critical. For instance, Shakespearean comedy is suspicious of arranged marriage; in general, it champions love matches and is reproving of extreme examples of the homosocial regulation of affective relations. This view is significant when one considers the importance of arranged marriage in early modern English society. However, the precise role of arranged marriage varied across classes, being most important and prominent among aristocrats. Moreover, the importance of compatibility and affection between husband and wife was increasingly touted, especially in Protestant marriage manuals; by the mid-seventeenth century, few writers would advocate the overriding importance of paternal design for a given marriage match. How, then, do we map onto this variegated and shifting historical situation the comedies' particular emphasis on the geography of paternity? If Shakespeare opposes coercive forms of arranged marriage, paternity nevertheless undergirds relations in the play; he does not repudiate (although in a number of places he does interrogate) the homosocial underpinnings of marriage. For these reasons we must consider the relationship between play and history with great care. As Ann Jennalie Cook (1991) has shown, it is notoriously difficult to situate the comic representation of love matches in clear relation to the social history of early modern England. Just as the plays offer a symbolically inflected rather than a narrowly "real" geography, so do they exist in a complexly mediated relationship to the realities of early modern courtship and marriage. Arguably the most important mediating force is genre, for the geography and the social relations of the comedies emerge not only out of Shakespeare's engagement with social history, but also through his adoption and modification of received generic matter. This is true not only in the case of marriage. To use an example from the geography of hospitality, the presence and centrality of the house in *Comedy of Errors* reveals that play's debt to Plautine new comedy (Coulter 1919: 71–2), even as the house's importance lies in its activation of an early modern emphasis on and interest in hospitality. The main point is simple: the geographies of Shakespeare's plays attest not only to their engagement with the details of social history, but also to their status as generic artifacts. These geographies emerge at the intersection of received literary discourses and contemporary historical phenomena.

Geography of Flight

One of the most obviously generic patterns of the comedies is that of the passage from a constraining social environment to a more liberating one (and then, in the form either of staged or projected action, back again). It is this movement that lies at the heart of Frye's influential postulation of a green world to which the comic protagonist(s) travel. What revisionists of Frye have noted, however, is that this movement is in fact seldom represented in the comedies.[23] The episodes that best enact this pattern are to be found in characters' journeys to the forests of Arden and Mantua (in *As You Like It* and *Two Gentlemen of Verona*), as well as to the woods near Athens (in *A Midsummer Night's Dream*). These are the strongest examples of green worlds in the comedic canon. But what exactly do these green worlds look like? How would one define the geography of these spaces, and how is this geography related to the social relations of the play? To answer these questions, and also to consider the geography of flight in Shakespeare's comedies, I will focus on the forests of *As You Like It* and *A Midsummer Night's Dream*.[24]

Martha Ronk (2001: 255) has commented that "The Forest of Arden seems in one's memory to dominate *As You Like It*." While this is so, Shakespeare's forest is overdetermined in a way that makes a precise accounting of its different spaces difficult to produce. To some degree, this overdetermination is licensed by early modern definitions of the forest, which, as the *OED* makes plain, could contain not only trees and undergrowth but pasture (1.a). At the same time, the word often connoted not the pastoral but the wild; it suggests an "uncultivated waste, a wilderness" (*OED* 3). In a different register, the forest was a site of princely prerogative. That is, forests were often woodland spaces set aside for royal hunting (*OED* 2); their beastly inhabitants were preserved in order to be destroyed later by the monarch and members of her retinue. What is striking about the forest, then, is that it has its own multifarious geography, both physical and symbolic. As princely hunting ground, the forest is an extension of the court, a status that gives added force to courtly Petrarchisms that construe the lover as hunter and the beloved as elusive hunted. In addition, the forest is either untamed or cultivated (or both), wilderness or pasture. Insofar as each of these spaces implies its own social geography, the forest can be host to courtiers, country folk, and savages. It can connote both civility and barbarism.

In *As You Like It* Shakespeare assumes and expands upon the multiplicity of the forest's meanings. The Forest of Arden is first introduced as a kind of pastoral ideal; the banished Duke Senior lives there, and "many young gentlemen flock to him every day, and fleet the time carelessly as they did in the golden world" (1.1.109–11). The forest, then, initially answers to the description of a kind of prelapsarian pastoral *otium*, but it also functions as an alternative court to which many men travel, a point negatively made by the Duke himself in his famous comparison of "these woods" with "the envious court" (2.1.1–17, esp. 3–4). That the men "live like the old Robin Hood of England" (1.1.108–9) also makes plain the potential threat they pose to the rule of Duke Frederick, who is indirectly construed through this reference to Robin Hood as the evil King John of British folklore. The forest-as-court of Duke Senior emblematizes right rule, and its pastoral overtones work to reinforce this.

If for some the forest resembles a golden world, for others it appears to be a wilderness. Orlando initially threatens Duke Senior and his men because he thinks Arden a "desert inaccessible": "I thought that all things had been savage here" (2.7.110, 107). The dangers posed by passing through this wilderness are articulated by Rosalind and Celia, whose fear of thieves and assailants prompts their donning of disguises (1.3.102–34). However, just as Duke Senior transforms banishment into his entrance into a world in which he can find "good in everything" (2.1.17), so do Rosalind and Celia turn this wilderness into an opportunity: "Now go in we content / To liberty, and not to banishment" (1.3.133–4). Even Orlando comes to see the forest in different terms: the "melancholy boughs" (2.7.111) of the trees in this "desert inaccessible" will soon bear his writings. Indeed, the question posed at the outset of one of his poems, "Why should this a desert be?" (3.2.119), suggests how the meaning of the forest has for Orlando begun to undergo a transformation.

These examples suggest how multiple the forest is in Shakespeare's play, simultaneously golden world and barren desert. In addition, they show how characters in this play imaginatively and willfully shape the forest in terms suited to them, as in Celia's "To liberty, and not to banishment." The geography of the Forest of Arden, then, is a malleable and symbolic one. It is not simply a green world into which these characters enter, for we witness, most clearly in the cases of Rosalind and Orlando, the ways in which the forest is *constructed* as a symbolically potent site by the play's characters. Moreover, these constructions are obviously dependent upon and necessitated by the flight or banishment of Orlando, Celia, and Duke Senior. The geography of the forest is largely defined in relation to what they have left behind; both the forest's dangers and its allures are shaped in terms of the strictures and imperatives of the world(s) from which these characters have fled and to which, after the end of the fifth act, they will presumably return. At the same time, this geography is an historical one in that *As You Like It* obviously draws upon period conceptions of the forest. In doing so, though, the play modifies those conceptions in order to construe the forest first and foremost as a site of both banishment and liberty.

A Midsummer Night's Dream offers us something slightly different – a space that is less forest than wood. In contrast to the forest in *As You Like It*, the wood's location is more or less precisely delineated: we are twice told it stands just outside of Athens, either a league or a mile (1.1.165; 1.2.90–2). Also, it does not serve as the destination for those who leave the city, at least not in the same way as the Forest of Arden does. Hermia and Lysander intend to pass through this wood on their way to his aunt's house; the actors use it as a rehearsal space for a play to be performed for the duke's nuptials in Athens; and the wood is both the staging ground for the faeries' revels and for Oberon's transformations of numerous characters. It is the transformative nature of this space that is most important: the wood is where rude mechanicals become Pyramus and Thisbe, Bottom becomes an ass, and the male lovers, at least as each is defined in terms of the object of his desires, become other than what they had previously been.

Even before the introduction of either magic or playmaking into *A Midsummer Night's Dream*, the wood's significance as a transforming agent is suggested by Hermia in conversation with Helena:

> And in the wood where often you and I
> Upon faint primroses were wont to lie,
> Emptying our bosoms of their counsel sweet,
> There my Lysander and myself shall meet,
> And thence from Athens turn away our eyes
> To seek new friends and stranger companies.
> Farewell, sweet playfellow. (1.1.214–20)

While it is first described as the location for past female intimacy, the wood soon signifies as the site of a future heterosexual assignation. This means that while it is a transitional space between a world of restriction, represented by Egeus, and one of amatory fulfillment, the wood is also the site of a same-sex friendship cast in retrospective terms.[25] It is where Hermia once went in order to share "counsel sweet" and where she will soon go to elope with Lysander. In addition, the wood both marks and makes possible a broader shift in social relations: Hermia somewhat callously says goodbye to a "sweet playfellow" and prospectively embraces "new friends and stranger companies." In eloping with Lysander she is radically modifying her *oikumene*; she will refigure her identity through both marriage and her formation of or insertion into new social relations outside the city. The wood, then, is both the edge of home and the border of a world that grounds identity. Moreover, the liminality of this space is represented by the transformations that occur there.

While the above lines suggest the perceived metamorphic function of the wood, Hermia's transformation has begun before she travels there, and early indications of it also manifest themselves in terms of a relation to place. Shortly before first alluding to the wood, Hermia discusses how her love for Lysander has affected her and her relation to her home city: "Before the time I did Lysander see, / Seemed Athens as a paradise to me. / O, then, what graces in my love do dwell / That he hath turned a heaven into a hell!" (1.1.204–7). Love has transformed Hermia's *oikumene* from within, thereby shifting the coordinates of her place-centered sense of identity. For Hermia the wood can be seen less as a magical space than as the site onto which a partly accomplished and partly wished-for metamorphosis is projected. Much as Rosalind turns her banishment into liberty, Hermia rejects Athens (in the persons of Duke Theseus and her father, Egeus) only after it has refused her desires (e.g., 1.1.117–21). For the fleeing lover, the wood is important for the part it plays in that rejection. While each of the two spaces is overdetermined to such a degree that a complete analysis of either is impossible, *As You Like It*'s forest and *A Midsummer Night's Dream*'s wood are linked by the fact that each is largely defined by its shifting symbolic relation to the "civilized" world outside of which it stands.

As with the geographies of paternity and hospitality, the physical worlds of these two comedies are shaped less in terms of geographical "fact" than in accordance with

the representation of specific sets of social relations and practices that are both literary and historical in origin. As we have seen, Shakespeare has been criticized for the
form this representation takes, and not only in his day. Anne Barton, for instance,
adopts a Jonsonian view when she places "Jonson's meticulously created urban worlds,
usually contemporary London, more or less thinly disguised, against those of a man
who insisted upon ruralizing even his cities (Athens or Messina, Milan and Tyre)"
(Barton 1983: 159).[26] Barton's complaint is that Shakespeare's geography just isn't
accurate, especially in contrast with Jonson's "meticulously created urban worlds."
What I have tried to show, however, is that Shakespeare's geography answers to a set
of dramatic and cultural imperatives that, when properly understood, render evalua-
tions such as Barton's anachronistic and misleading. The irony is that it is the geographies of the dramatist often described as our contemporary that appear to be so
alien, and it is his rival, who is far less frequently understood as "one of us," who leads
the charge of the anachronists with his grumbling about geographic verisimilitude.
What this should remind us is that any geography, old or new, does not entirely represent its era. Indeed, it is the interplay of such different geographies that hints at
what a variegated and diverse thing any given "era" finally is, including our own.
Additionally, we have seen that Shakespeare's works break down false oppositions
between archetypalism and particularism, and that the geographies of the comedies
are ones in which early modern social relations are both staged and modified. These
geographies usually represent period practices and concerns in a heightened or idealized way, and thus constitute Shakespearean fantasies of early modern social life that
manage relations both inside and beyond the *oikumene*. In this regard, the Bohemian
shore, or many of the similar "gaffes" to be found in the comedies, shows that
Shakespeare feels right at home with what may seem unfamiliar to us: geographies
that are at once poetic and historical, archetypal and particular.[27]

ACKNOWLEDGMENT

I would like to thank Linda Woodbridge for her helpful feedback.

NOTES

1   "The remoteness and lack of precision was probably the point: when Ben Jonson and others laughed
    at Shakespeare for setting a scene of *The Winter's Tale* on the sea-coast of Bohemia, they were drawing
    a mistaken equation between the dramatic location and the actual, land-locked middle-European
    country. The point of such settings was not to place the play in terms of topographical reality but
    to remove any overt application to English current affairs: "'Bohemia,' or 'Sicily,' or 'Iberia,' really
    means 'elsewhere'" (Wiggins 2000: 112).
2   The dramatist most frequently associated with the new geography is Marlowe, whose indebtedness
    in the *Tamburlaine* plays to Abraham Ortelius's atlas *Teatrum Orbis Terrarum* (1570) was first
    recognized long ago; see Seaton (1924).

3   As Frye puts it, the green world has a "miraculous and irresistible reviving power. [It is associated with] dream, magic and chastity or spiritual energy as well as fertility and renewed natural energies" (Frye 1965: 142–3). The continued influence of Fryeian archetypal criticism is felt in books such as that of Roberts (1991).

4   There are numerous recent essays and collections devoted to geographic issues in Shakespearean comedy, most taking Italy as their focus, as that country is the setting for many of the plays. Examples include Gillies and Vaughan (1998); Klein and Marrapodi (1999); Levith (1989); Marrapodi et al. (1997); and Relihan (1997).

5   Particularist criticism tends to focus on one location in one or more plays, whereas archetypal critics usually discuss a number of plays in light of a seemingly characteristic place and/or practice. I point this out because in composing this essay I have come to recognize the limitations of particularist criticism when it comes to accounting for patterns that emerge across multiple plays. At the same time, by enacting a method both "literary" and "real" (to return to Gillies's terms), I have tried to sidestep some of the limitations of archetypal criticism.

6   Manfred Pfister says of Shakespeare's plays with Italian settings, the "scene is England almost as much as Italy, as they carefully mingle English and Italian local color. Or, to put it less metaphorically, they superimpose the spatial context of the performance – the theatre and the London and England of performers and audience – with that of the fictional Italian setting" (Pfister 1997: 300).

7   "Shakespeare delighted in the diversity of the Italian city-states, the movement and interaction from one community to another, often subject to the quasi-epical intervention of their civic dynasties" (Levin 1997: 22). On the significance of sea journeys (and international mercantile activity) to Shakespeare, see Cohen (2001).

8   There has been much recent criticism on *Merry Wives* and the history and geography of Windsor. See, for example, Marcus (1991); Kegl (1994); and Helgerson (2000, esp. pp. 57–76).

9   See, for instance, Gillies (1994: 122–37); Levith (1989: 12–39); McPherson (1990); Platt (2001); and Sohmer (1999). Venice is the only Italian city to which Levith devotes an entire chapter.

10   Pfister (1997: 295) cites McPherson and Levith as examples of this school.

11   It is worth noting that while the poetic geography helps illuminate the spatial logic of the comedies, with the exception of *The Merchant of Venice* these plays have no significant role in Gillies's study.

12   It is of course simplistic to suggest that conceptions of either world or house are monolithic at any given historical moment. On multiple early modern "worlds," see Greene (2000). In what follows, I attempt to map out certain aspects of Shakespeare's geographic "world," assuming not only that "a world is a symbolic construction that exists in statements about it and responses to it" (ibid: 10), but that that world emerges out of the representation of specific spaces and practices.

13   In addition to the two plays taken up here, one can also consider *Twelfth Night*, which modifies many themes and situations found in *The Comedy of Errors*.

14   On the relationship between property and identity, see De Grazia (1996) and De Grazia (2000).

15   Of course, Antipholus of Syracuse is taken for a madman by some of the Ephesians (e.g., 4.3.76–91). A similar ascription of madness is made to Vincentio in the second scene from *Taming* discussed here (e.g., 5.1.63–4).

16   See also Palmer (1992). This paragraph is adapted from a discussion of hospitality in Sullivan (1998: esp. 177–80).

17   This is true not only in the comedies. Consider *Macbeth*, for instance, and its representation of violated hospitality, both in the murder of Duncan and in the disruption of Macbeth's feast by Banquo's ghost.

18   The world of Dogberry and the town watch stands as the most significant exception to this.

19   The play toys with the possibility of Leonato taking up this role, however, as he is an early if misinformed advocate of another suitor, Don Pedro, for his daughter. The *senex* figure frequently prefers another man over his daughter's favorite.

20   What is striking, though, is how often they serve in this capacity while also being either absent or dead.

21 It is worth pausing over what it means to *know* here. It is certainly possible that Baptista and Antonio were acquainted with one another, but Petruchio also refers to knowing Baptista when he means only that he has heard about him. In these lines, personal knowledge of characters is difficult to distinguish from reports that have circulated about them. No clear lines are drawn between "knowing" and "knowing of." In this context, the reputation of a character has as much force as personal acquaintanceship with him.

22 See also *All's Well That Ends Well*, 1.2.19–51, for a related example.

23 Hawkins (1968: 64–5) points out that only four comedies – *Two Gentlemen*, *A Midsummer Night's Dream*, *Merchant*, and *As You Like It* – answer to this pattern, and not always in the central action of the play. However, I would argue that *Merchant*'s Belmont figures in a very different way than do the forest spaces in the other plays; for this reason, I would not group it with the other locations.

24 I am excluding *Two Gentlemen*'s forest of Mantua from this discussion because it is comparatively underrepresented.

25 See Traub (1992) for a discussion of marriage and the abandonment of eroticized same-sex relations by female dramatic characters.

26 One might point out that Barton's distinction between rural and urban seems too absolute, as examination of period views of London and its suburbs can attest.

27 It is important to note that the dramatic geographies discussed above are dependent upon and emerge out of at least two other early modern geographies: those of the city and of the stage itself. For a discussion of *locus*, *platea*, and the geography of the stage, see Weimann (1978). On the significance of (many of) the theatres being located in suburban "liberties," see Mullaney (1988).

References and Further Reading

Barton, A. (1983). Shakespeare and Jonson. In K. Muir, J. Halio, and D. J. Palmer (eds.) *Shakespeare, Man of the Theater.* Newark and London: University of Delaware Press and Associated University Presses, 155–72.

Cohen, W. (2001). The Undiscovered Country: Shakespeare and Mercantile Geography. In J. E. Howard and S. C. Shershow (eds.) *Marxist Shakespeares.* London: Routledge, 128–58.

Cook, A. J. (1991). *Making a Match: Courtship in Shakespeare and his Society.* Princeton, NJ: Princeton University Press.

Coulter, C. C. (1919). The Plautine Tradition in Shakespeare. *Journal of English and Germanic Philology*, 18, 66–83.

De Grazia, M. (1996). The Ideology of Superfluous Things: *King Lear* as Period Piece. In M. de Grazia, M. Quilligan, and P. Stallybrass (eds.) *Subject and Object in Renaissance Culture.* Cambridge: Cambridge University Press, 17–42.

——(2000). Weeping for Hecuba. In C. Mazzaio and D. Trevor (eds.) *Historicism, Psychoanalysis and Early Modern Culture.* New York: Routledge, 350–75.

Frye, N. (1965). *A Natural Perspective: The Development of Shakespearean Comedy and Romance.* New York: Columbia University Press.

Gillies, J. (1994). *Shakespeare and the Geography of Difference.* Cambridge: Cambridge University Press.

——(1998). Introduction: Elizabethan Drama and the Cartographizations of Space. In J. Gillies and V. M. Vaughan (eds.) *Playing the Globe: Genre and Geography in English Renaissance Drama.* Madison, WI: Fairleigh Dickinson University Press, 19–45.

Gillies, J. and Vaughan, V. M. (eds.) (1998). *Playing the Globe: Genre and Geography in English Renaissance Drama.* Madison, WI: Fairleigh Dickinson University Press.

Greene, R. (2000). A Primer of Spenser's Worldmaking: Alterity in the Bower of Bliss. In P. Cheney and L. Silberman (eds.) *Worldmaking Spenser: Explorations in the Early Modern Age.* Lexington: University Press of Kentucky, 9–31.

Hawkins, S. (1968). The Two Worlds of Shakespearean Comedy. *Shakespeare Studies*, 3, 62–80.

Heal, F. (1990). *Hospitality in Early Modern England.* Oxford: Clarendon Press.

Helgerson, R. (1992). *Forms of Nationhood: The Elizabethan Writing of England.* Chicago, IL: University of Chicago Press.

——(2000). *Adulterous Alliances: Home, State, and History in Early Modern European Drama and Painting.* Chicago, IL: University of Chicago Press.

Kegl, R. (1994). "The Adoption of Abominable Terms": The Insults that Shape Windsor's Middle Class. *English Literary History,* 61, 253–78.

Klein, H. and Marrapodi, M. (eds.) (1999). *Shakespeare and Italy.* Lewiston, NY: Edwin Mellen Press.

Levin, H. (1997). Shakespeare's Italians. In M. Marrapodi et al. (eds.) *Shakespeare's Italy: Functions of Italian Locations in Renaissance Drama,* revd. edn. Manchester: Manchester University Press, 17–29.

Levith, M. J. (1989). *Shakespeare's Italian Settings and Plays.* New York: St. Martin's Press.

McPherson, D. C. (1990). *Shakespeare, Jonson, and the Myth of Venice.* Newark: University of Delaware Press.

Marcus, L. S. (1991). Levelling Shakespeare: Local Customs and Local Texts. *Shakespeare Quarterly,* 42, 168–78.

Marrapodi, M. et al. (eds.) (1997). *Shakespeare's Italy: Functions of Italian Locations in Renaissance Drama,* revd. edn. Manchester: Manchester University Press.

Mullaney, S. (1988). *The Place of the Stage: License, Play, and Power in Renaissance England.* Chicago, IL: University of Chicago Press.

Palmer, D. W. (1992). *Hospitable Performances: Dramatic Genre and Cultural Practices in Early Modern England.* West Lafayette, IN: Purdue University Press.

Pfister, M. (1997). Shakespeare and Italy, Or, The Law of Diminishing Returns. In M. Marrapodi et al. (eds.) *Shakespeare's Italy: Functions of Italian Locations in Renaissance Drama,* revd. edn. Manchester: Manchester University Press, 295–303.

Platt, P. G. (2001). "The Meruailouse Site": Shakespeare, Venice, and Paradoxical Stages. *Renaissance Quarterly,* 54, 121–54.

Relihan, C. (1997). Erasing the East from *Twelfth Night.* In J. G. MacDonald (ed.) *Race, Ethnicity, and Power in the Renaissance.* Madison, WI: Fairleigh Dickinson University Press, 80–94.

Roberts, J. A. (1991). *The Shakespearean Wild: Geography, Genus and Gender.* Lincoln: University of Nebraska Press.

Ronk, M. (2001). Locating the Visual in *As You Like It. Shakespeare Quarterly,* 52, 255–76.

Seaton, E. (1924). Marlowe's Map. *Essays and Studies by Members of the English Association,* 10, 13–35.

Shakespeare, W. (1969). *The Complete Works,* gen. ed. A. Harbage. Harmondsworth: Penguin Books.

Sohmer, S. (1999). Another Time: The Venetian Calendar in Shakespeare's Plays. In H. Klein and M. Marrapodi (eds.) *Shakespeare and Italy.* Lewiston, NY: Edwin Mellen Press, 141–61.

Sullivan, G. A., Jr. (1998). *The Drama of Landscape: Land, Property, and Social Relations on the Early Modern Stage.* Stanford, CA: Stanford University Press.

Traub, V. (1992). The (In)significance of Lesbian Desire in Early Modern England. In S. Zimmerman (ed.) *Erotic Politics: Desire on the Renaissance Stage.* London: Routledge, 150–69.

Weimann, R. (1978). *Shakespeare and the Popular Tradition in the Theater: Studies in the Social Dimension of Dramatic Form and Function.* Baltimore, MD: Johns Hopkins University Press.

Wiggins, M. (2000). *Shakespeare and the Drama of His Time.* Oxford: Oxford University Press.

Wilford, J. N. (1981). *The Mapmakers.* London: Junction Books.

10

Rhetoric and Comic Personation in Shakespeare's Comedies

Lloyd Davis

Most Feelingly Personated

As Maria, Sir Toby, and Sir Andrew plan their gulling of Malvolio in *Twelfth Night, or What You Will*, they urge each other on, and whet the audience's appetite, by recapping their motives. They have just been requested to "separate" their misdemeanors from themselves,[1] a reprimand that is the final straw. Maria, who cannot evade or ignore Malvolio in the same way that the others can, seems especially incensed. For her the steward is "a time-pleaser, an affectioned ass that cons state without book and utters it by great swathes; the best persuaded of himself, so crammed, as he thinks, with excellencies, that it is his grounds of faith that all that look on him love him" (2.3.132–5). Yet Malvolio's self-regard is not only his most irksome trait, it also offers the best way to get at him: "on that vice," Maria plots, "will my revenge find notable cause to work" (2.3.135–6):

> I will drop in his way some obscure epistles of love, wherein by the colour of his beard, the shape of his leg, the manner of his gait, the expressure of his eye, forehead, and complexion, he shall find himself most feelingly personated. (2.3.138–41)

Even Sir Andrew senses something is up, but it takes Sir Toby to spell it out for his friend and the audience:

> *Sir Toby.* He shall think by the letters that thou wilt drop that they come from my niece, and that she's in love with him.
> *Maria.* My purpose is indeed a horse of that colour.
> *Sir Toby.* And your horse would now make him an ass. (2.3.146–9)

The characters' delight at the scheme winds audience and readers up, and while Shakespeare makes us wait a medium-length scene (itself an interesting one, as Viola and Orsino continue to circle around each other's emotions, sharing in the self-delusion that is going around), it is worth it "for the love of mockery [and] in the name of jesting" (2.5.16–7), when Malvolio next enters and we watch his antagonists watch his swelling self-fantasy.

The trick that is being played relies on Shakespeare staging characters' responses to the weaknesses of one another's personalities. It exemplifies Sir Philip Sidney's definition that comedy inheres in "imitation of the common errors of our life" (Sidney 1963: 23) and is the sort of stunt that features in humorous texts across all periods. Audience and characters are complicit, and comic suspense lies largely in the extent of Malvolio's deception. Maria describes his new appearance at the end of act 3, scene 2, and we finally get to view or imagine it two scenes later. His entry is one of those moments when the written text cannot really do justice to the impact that a crazily dressed, strutting, and smiling Malvolio has in practically all productions. It's a show-stopper. What director and actor could miss the chance of playing it up, a moment of revenge against antitheatrical crusaders from all periods which reveals their own self-dramatizing drives – the pompous steward demeans himself, fulfilling the genre he opposes. The uproar provoked visually is intensified by the social and psychical release in this classic instance of what Freud called the "tendentious joke," where the three parties involved – joker(s), audience, and object of the joke – play out rebellion against authority and the sidestepping of repression (Freud 1963: 97–105).

If reading or hearing the scenes cannot fully convey their hilarious visual potential, it does highlight the humor's verbal dimensions. Of course, the language Shakespeare uses is very funny – the epithets that Maria, Toby, and Feste fire off against their victim, for instance, or Malvolio's own stuffy pronouncements and, what's worse, his erotic musings. But the lines also disclose the way in which a number of linguistic practices are central to the antagonism between Malvolio and the rest. A haughty oratorical manner seems to be the hub of his affectation: he "cons state without book and utters it by great swathes." Malvolio's method of rote learning and reciting speeches repeats one of the key routines of Tudor classrooms.[2] In attributing this trait to the steward, Shakespeare shows the way that lessons learnt at school might be embodied and deployed later in life. In the words of Roger Ascham, "excellency in learning . . . is a marvelous jewel in the world" (Ascham 1888: 29), one to be wielded as well as worn. Malvolio uses language to cow others and establish his status in Olivia's household over and against theirs. He tries to structure these social relationships through a rhetorical bearing; yet as Maria insinuates, he is less than successful with everyone except Malvolio. He is "best persuaded of himself," the object of an eloquence that molds and presents his identity but convinces him alone of its reality. Aristotle states pithily in the *Rhetorica* that a statement is persuasive "because there is somebody whom it persuades" (Aristotle 1971: 1356b28). Malvolio's words attain the minimal level, attracting that lone "somebody" needed for persuasion to occur.

The terms Maria uses and their comic success suggest the great extent to which rhetorical concepts were integrated in dramatic and social discourse in Shakespeare's time. Rhetoric was of course a staple of grammar school education as well as being part of dramatic training for apprentice players. The famous classical works on philosophy and rhetoric were widely available in Latin (including Ficino's translation of Plato's dialogues), and were discussed in popular English works such as Elyot's *The Governor*, Sidney's *Defence of Poesie*, Bacon's *Advancement of Learning*, and a growing number of vernacular handbooks and guides. In many ways, Shakespeare and his contemporaries lived in a rhetorical culture (Altman 1978; Thomson 1997; Vickers 1988; Platt 1999; Hutton 2000; Trousdale 2000). One of the most significant ways that rhetoric was understood and practiced in the period was in relation to ethics, which connected personal values to civic and communal ones. Language is conceived as central to relations between self and others, persuading them to accept the roles and actions one undertakes and that they might adopt. In this context, Maria's evoking of personation is most suggestive: it captures a rhetorical sense of selfhood and identity often implicit in early modern characters' interactions. It reveals that now conventional ideas of character and characterization might not immediately correspond to early modern notions. As Peter Thomson notes, a rhetorical understanding of character as much as the conditions of scripting and production meant that Shakespeare and other playwrights were not trying "to create a gathering of subjectivities – what later criticism would call 'characters'" (Thomson 1997: 324–5; cf. Burns 1990). They were aiming to realize *personation*, whereby one person can represent another, either someone else or a different version of him- or herself. The effects of personation can encompass accepting, or rejecting, the persona assumed by neighbors and friends, by players onstage, or by leading public figures, including the sovereign.

"He shall find himself most feelingly personated." Maria's words envisage processes of perception, emotion, language, and theatricality that exemplify the interaction between rhetoric and identity. Malvolio will discover a masculine self in the language someone else has used to depict him, a language close to what he would use and would like others to use about him, which seems to confirm his own words. But the self he will find won't be directly or physically present. It will be "feelingly personated," caught up in the emotive exchanges and investments that he and others have in the persona being represented.

Maria hits on a perfect rhetorical strategy for bringing Malvolio down: fit him with a character that he already believes is completely his. Her letter amounts to what Thomas Wright, in his 1604 book *The Passions of the Mind*, might call "a tale well told in Rhetorical manner (flexibility of voice, gestures, actions or other oratorical persuasions)" (Wright 1986: 161), graphically recreating Malvolio's manner and expression. Little wonder he "find[s] himself most feelingly personated." For the dual sense of identity, which oscillates between self and others' perceptions (and that other characters in *Twelfth Night*, most notably Viola, work overtime to reconcile), appears complete, in a synthesis of affect shared with Olivia. Maria's letter reproduces the tropes and desires of Malvolio's speech and thought but attributes them to the figure they seek to address. Yet just as he feels he finds himself, Malvolio loses himself, as it were. (Olivia's earlier comment, "you are sick of self-love, Malvolio" (1.5.77), suggests that this fate was always in store.) In many ways, the humor derives from staging the simultaneous success and failure of personation. Shakespeare applies and undermines the rhetorical practices on which his drama relies.

The episode magnifies the struggles of all the characters to speak about themselves in ways that they and others can approve. In this respect, the play's subtitle, *What You Will*, suggests the many facets of rhetoric and personation being explored. On the one hand, it asserts a degree of control over desires, intentions, and their results – a confident "What you will!" On the other, it implies the failure of attempts to perform or will anything, in spite of "your" will or desires – a hesitant "What you will?"; a resigned "Whatever happens happens." *Twelfth Night* juxtaposes these contradictory tendencies as strikingly as any early modern play. The preoccupation of each character with role-playing – even the "natural," Feste, is ready to "dissemble myself in't" (4.2.4) when required – underscores the way in which deliberate construction of self-identity is a recurrent practice in Shakespearean drama. The centrality to this practice of language and rhetoric, especially when the latter is taken to include a full range of "oratorical persuasions," suggests the significance of traditions and concepts of personation to Shakespeare's work. While the essays in this volume illustrate many significant aspects of Shakespeare's comedies, at times it can seem, in Geoffrey Hartman's terms, as though "the locus of the dramatic action" in the plays "were the effect of language on character" (Hartman 1985: 43).

Nonetheless, as the preceding discussion of Maria's success and Malvolio's failure has suggested, the relationship between the comic plays and rhetorical personation is complex and paradoxical. Wayne Rebhorn contends that rhetorical readings frequently "aim to locate the presence of rhetorical figures or structures in a literary work, thereby identifying it implicitly or explicitly as a simple continuation or repetition of material one finds in rhetoric manuals" (Rebhorn 1995: 296). At best, this kind of approach struggles to consider those charged moments in Shakespeare's drama when tropes and topoi are pushed to question or break any norm that a manual or handbook might illustrate (though it has also been recognized that such examples are themselves often quite slippery).[3] As Marion Trousdale has recently noted, "in its rhetorical figures" early modern discourse "is almost never single-voiced" (Trousdale 1997: 140). Shakespeare's texts exemplify this multi-voiced capacity, nowhere more so than in dramatizing the possibilities and limits of personation. In staging the breakdowns and complications in persona with which characters grapple, the plays both reiterate and question key traditions of Western rhetoric. The comedies in particular are produced and informed by the rhetorical history of personation even as they rewrite and restage it.

The nexus between rhetoric and ethics – between a good style and a good character or *ethos* – is central to all positive accounts of rhetoric and poetics from Plato on. The question comic personation recurrently poses is whether this link might be tenuous, simplistic, or even nonexistent. In the sequence of eleven comedies he wrote probably between 1592 and 1602, Shakespeare again and again returns to this question; that earnest ethical topos of rhetorical discourse is the paradoxical starting point for the plays' surprises and inversions. Christy Desmet observes that "as his career progresses Shakespeare begins to reflect on rather than simply use his repertoire of rhetorical strategies" (Desmet 1992: 61); in addition to this reflexive interest and an increasingly complex treatment of related issues, the various comedies explore the different contexts where the ethics and rhetoric of personation come into conflict. Across these plays Shakespeare shows that the implications of personation are entwined with many important social institutions and cultural practices. In this respect, personation is always "inter-personation"; personae are neither monadically circumscribed nor self-consistent.

Hence the humor of comic personation can disrupt the rhetorical tradition's ethical agenda and its emphasis on individual ethos. It represents a potential crisis because it focuses sharply and quizzically on the main reason for studying and practicing rhetoric as distinct from sophistry – that the goal of the perfect orator is to "be a good man" (Quintilian 1969: 1.Pref.9). Shakespeare's comedies challenge this maxim and its confidence in *vir bonus*. For this reason he stands implicated in Aristotle's charge in the *Rhetorica* that comic poets are "in a manner slanderers and gossips," who make fun of others (Aristotle 1971: 2.6.20). But the sophistication of his plays' rhetoric and personation – along with their comic success – merits and confirms Quintilian's admission that comedy's "contribution to eloquence may be of no small importance, since it is concerned with every kind of character and emotion" (Quintilian 1969: 1.8.7). Shakespeare realizes that comic personation is central to the tradition it paradoxically subverts.

Rhetoric, Comedy, Personation: Plato to Puttenham

Plato's criticisms of sophistry can be interpreted, somewhat against the grain, as a description of transgressive humor. The possibility of such an anti-Platonic reading arises in a number of the dialogues but is particularly apparent in the attack made in the dialogue simply called *Sophist*. This figure is identified as "one of those whose province is play" (Plato 1985: 235a), and his resistance to dialectical examination is summed up in a kind of non-definition: "the Sophist has appeared in so many guises that for my part I am puzzled to see what description one is to maintain as truly expressing his real nature" (ibid: 231b–c). The sophist embodies a series of guises or personae rather than a single identity, and such multiplicity makes him antithetical to the ethical–rhetorical program that Plato articulates here and in other dialogues such as the *Gorgias* and *Phaedrus*.

Plato uses the sophist to signify the prospect that truthful expression and real nature might not exist; but rather than accept that possibility as a norm, he chooses to condemn it and the figure that embodies it. In a related way, and a little earlier on, the dialogue attempts to explain the basis of false reasoning in order to exclude it from the realm of authentic philosophy: "When a person supposes that he knows, and does not know; this appears to be the great source of all the errors of the intellect" (ibid: 229c). Presumed knowledge, multiply changing guises – despite or perhaps because of their exclusion from the categories of truth and nature, these are the facets of personation on which Malvolio's deception and self-deception depend. Shakespeare's plays consistently probe the ambiguous role of humor in the serious business of personation. Indeed, because of its capacity to support or undercut ethical values, from the classical period on comedy is often treated as a significant but problematic rhetorical mode. Writers on rhetoric seem uncertain whether they can responsibly enjoy comedic discourse, carefully prescribe its techniques and effects, or critique it. In drawing his comic personae, Shakespeare takes full advantage of these problems. Before turning to the plays and characters themselves, the tradition of comic personation he is working with and against can be examined.

In discussions of rhetoric and poetics later in the classical period, the explicitly ethical concerns of Socrates and Plato tend to give way to explanations of what makes for effective speech and presentation. In the *Rhetorica* Aristotle declares that "The foundation of good style is correctness of language" (Aristotle 1971: 1407a18–19), and that it is important to "give the impression of speaking naturally and not artificially" (ibid: 1411b23). Though Aristotle's approach is specific and functional, the moral tenor of his predecessors' judgments remains in the preference for correctness, good style, and naturalness over artificiality. Quintilian reiterates these values throughout the *Institutio Oratoria* in his emphasis on propriety, or "calling things by their right names" (Quintilian 1969: 3.2.1): "those words are best which are least far-fetched and give the impression of simplicity and reality" (ibid: 8.Pref.22–4). Repeatedly such stylistic observations are underpinned by moral distinctions and terms.

In *De Poetica* Aristotle extends these oppositional concepts to the basic notions of dramatic character: "The objects the imitator represents are actions, with agents who are necessarily either good or bad" (Aristotle 1971: 1448a1). The erringly hybrid figures crucial to dramatic comedy do not easily fit into this ethical–rhetorical scheme. In the *Ars Poetica* Horace adopts a similar perspective. He bases the key criterion for characterization explicitly on notions of realism rather than on ethical binaries; yet the moral subtext of personation remains: "If it is an untried theme you entrust to the stage, and if you boldly fashion a fresh character, have it kept to the end even as it came forth at the first, and have it self-consistent" (Horace 1978: 125–7); "you must note the manners of each [individual's] age, and give a befitting tone to shifting natures and their years" (ibid: 156–7). The emphasis on self-consistency and fittingness intertwines ethical and stylistic virtues. As is discussed below, English rhetoric handbooks later address these issues under the term "decorum."

Some classical rhetoricians are keen to explain what makes comedy work. The anonymous *Rhetorica ad Herennium* lists eighteen ways an orator can cause an audience to laugh (and most are funny):

> . . . a fable, a plausible fiction, a caricature, an ironical inversion of the meaning of a word, an ambiguity, innuendo, banter, a naivety, an exaggeration, a recapitulation, a pun, an unexpected turn, a comparison, a novel tale, a historical anecdote, a verse, or a challenge or a smile of approbation directed at some one. (*Rhetorica* 1968: 1.6.10)

In book two of *De Oratore* Cicero offers a long discussion of various aspects of comedy, including a similar catalog of verbal witticisms (1967, 2.61.250ff). He distinguishes two types of wit, one related to facts and the other to words. The second entails saying "something pointed in a phrase or reflection" (Cicero 1967: 2.60.244). The first combines anecdote and mimicry, narrative and drama, in a kind of "continuous irony ... wherein the characters of individuals are sketched and so portrayed ... they are found out in some fault sufficiently marked to be laughed at" (ibid: 2.60.243). The greatest comic effects are produced through combining both types of wit (ibid: 2.61.248). Cicero regularly aims to elevate rhetoric above drama – "orators ... are the players that act real life," he claims pointedly (ibid: 3.56.214)[4] – but in linking the two kinds of humor he foretells the basic rhetorical ingredients of Shakespeare's comic success and dramatic comedy more generally.

Most notably, Cicero suggests that comic discourse, and hence serious discourse too, is flexible and mobile. Where Horace decrees that "A comic subject is not susceptible of treatment in a tragic style" (Horace 1978: 81), Cicero develops a more subtle, context-sensitive understanding of both modes:

> But remember this, that whatever subjects I may touch upon, as being sources of laughing-matters, may equally well, as a rule, be sources of serious thoughts. The only difference is that seriousness is bestowed austerely and upon things of good repute, jesting upon what is a trifle unseemly, or, so to speak, uncouth; for example, we can, in identical terms, praise a careful servant, and make fun of one who is good-for-nothing ... In fact all kinds of remarks are derived from identical sources. (Cicero 1967: 2.61.248–9)

The reversibility of comic discourse, the use of the same words to praise or mock, reveals its potential for surprise and controversy. It leads Cicero to warn that comedy calls for "most careful consideration" (ibid: 2.58.237), and that "restraint ... above all else, must be practised in jesting" (ibid: 2.59.238) so as to "distinguish an orator from a buffoon" (ibid: 2.60.247). At the same time, his acknowledgment that humor and seriousness are not intrinsically opposed but are related to audience expectations ("repute") and to stylistic inflection ("identical terms") opens the way for some of the more specific accounts of comedy and personation offered in early modern English rhetoric and comic drama. Many classical attitudes to comedy and rhetoric are developed in sixteenth-century works on poetics and rhetoric. In particular, the emphasis on propriety and naturalness of style and persona is reviewed in relation to the various types and effects of comedy.

Towards the end of *The Defence of Poesie* Sidney follows Horace in calling for the separation of tragic and comic characters and plots. He attacks their mingling "with neither decencie or discretion" (Sidney 1963: 39). He echoes Ciceronian caution in calling for comedy to be measured and restrained, producing not immoderate laughter at "sinful things" but "delightfull teaching which is the ende of Poesie" (ibid: 41). The notion of delight raised here represents humor in harmony rather than conflict with its social milieu. That position is developed by one of Sidney's great admirers, Abraham Fraunce, in *The Arcadian Rhetorike*. As the title suggests, Fraunce discusses rhetoric in rather benign terms; tropes are given positive interpretations, often supported by quotations from *The Arcadia*. His treatment of *Ironia* is a case in point: "a Trope, that by naming one contrarie intendeth another. The speciall grace whereof is in iesting and merie conceipted speeches. This trope continued maketh a most sweet allegorie . . . for then it is apparent that wee speake but iestinglie, and not as wee thinke" (Fraunce 1950: 10). Irony's potentially tendentious reversals of meaning, as highlighted by Cicero, are not addressed. Fraunce prefers to envisage a harmonious discursive world. His account of *Prosopopoia*, or rhetorical personation, focuses in Horatian manner on reconciling language, identity, and cultural order:

> A fayning of any person, when in our speach we represent the person of anie, and make it speake as though he were there present: an excellent figure, much vsed of Poets, wherein wee must diligentlie take heede, that the person thus represented haue a speach fit and conuenient for his estate and nature. (Ibid: 85)

In this particular rhetorical and poetic realm, the function of personation is to confirm individual and social roles for the audience's edification and enjoyment.

Henry Peacham's view of rhetoric and personation in *The Garden of Eloquence* is in general agreement with Fraunce's, but at times his tone is less idealistic. In the Dedicatory Epistle, Peacham insists on the valuable, aesthetic effects of the power of speech: "wisedome appeareth in her beauty, sheweth her majestie, and exerciseth her power, working in the mind of the hearer partly by a pleasant proportion, and as it were by a sweet and musical harmonie, and partly the secret and mightie power of perswasion." The final phrase can be read as signaling the "interplay of rhetoric, power, politics" (Rebhorn 1995: 297) at work in Renaissance conceptions of eloquence. In parts of his work Peacham does raise the antagonistic dimensions of rhetorical discourse, for example the tropes *Sarcasmus*, "a bitter kinde of mocke, or dispytefull strumpe, vsed of an enemy" (Peacham 1971: sig.Diii), and *Diasirmus*, "when we delude the reasons of our aduersaryes, and so by scoffing, debase their authority" (ibid: sig.Diiii). Yet Peacham's overall position is again to conceive eloquence as socially affirmative. One example he develops in some detail is tied closely to personation: "*Mimisis*, an immitation of speech, whereby we counterfeit not only what one sayd, but also vtteraunce and gesture, immitating euery thing as it was" (ibid: sig.Giiii). Peacham goes on to emphasize the attention to detail with which Mimisis can be presented, making discourse enjoyable and profitable for the audience:

> To rehearce a wise mans words, and to immitate his modest manners, causeth great attentiuenesse, and bringeth much delectation to the hearers . . . to heare any saying immitated hansomely, doth very much delight and please the hearer, some be so excellent in this kind of counterfeiting, that they are able to make a wyse mannes sayinges better, and a fooles much worse. (Ibid: sig.Giiii)

Even where folly is imitated the goal remains didactic, underlining rhetoric and personation's constructive functions. In Fraunce and Peacham's handbooks the nexus of ethics, rhetoric, and comedy is approved and reinforced.

Other writers in the period consider rhetoric less positively, with an eye to its potential to misrepresent ideas and persons. In *The Advancement of Learning* Francis Bacon adapts Platonism's anti-sophistic stance to his paradigm of social and intellectual development. Extravagant rhetoric – "the first distemper of learning, when men study words and not matter" (Bacon 1969: 30) – can jeopardize the entire project: "the great sophism of all sophism being equivocation or ambiguity of words and phrase, specially of such words as are most general and intervene in every inquiry" (ibid: 152). At one level, Bacon's concern is heuristic – he fears the undermining of conceptual development and clarification. At another, it is entwined with reservations about the nature of people's minds: "false appearance . . . [is] imposed upon us by words . . . although we think we govern our words . . . yet certain it is that words, as a Tartar's bow, do shoot back upon the understanding of the wisest, and mightily entangle and pervert the judgement" (ibid: 154–5). Bacon could be describing Malvolio's experience, the reflexive deception of reason and emotion that his own talk produces. Bacon's use of "pervert" evokes a sense of the serious ethical dilemmas that rhetoric can trigger. He seeks to prescribe "the duty and office of rhetoric" and so control its impact on character and the passions: it should "apply reason to imagination for the better moving of the will" (ibid: 168). By subjecting eloquence to reason, Bacon would order personation and the way that language constructs and influences its audience.

In this respect Bacon's view of rhetoric can be compared to Ben Jonson's formal opinions on language in *Discoveries*. Jonson's comedies reveal widely diverging images of disordered and centered characters; at times he seems to enjoy the former's license and to question the latter's controlling motives. In *Discoveries*, however, Jonson is adamant that language reflects, if not causes, corrupt "manners and fashions": "It imitates the publicke riot" (Jonson 1925–52: 593). What Jonson means by imitation is difficult to pin down, but the notion that language is relatively autonomous probably comes closest to his sense of its distinctiveness from and complicity with prevailing mores. Like Bacon and Thomas Wright, Jonson affirms deep links between language, identity, and the mind: "It springs out of the most retired, and inmost parts of us, and is the Image of the Parent of it, the mind. No glance renders a mans forme, or likenesse, so true as his speech" (ibid: 625). He also acknowledges the liability of reason to be undermined by passions, those "spirituall Rebels [that] raise sedition against the understanding" (ibid: 564). Jonson endorses unity among style, topic, and persona, with words "to be chose according to the persons wee make speake, or the things wee speake of" (ibid: 621). In this system, dramatic character and events are normatively oriented. A "festive" model of comedy is endorsed, one which "ends happily in the return of a repressive order characterized by a wise and tolerant acceptance of individual waywardness" (Bristol 1985: 32). The complex of stylistic, cultural, and ethical opinions reproduces a rhetoric of personation where excess is regarded as anomalous and temporary rather than socially transgressive or suggestive.

Sidney, Fraunce, Peacham, Bacon, and Jonson share a relatively consistent attitude towards the importance of "rhetorical norms" for evaluating and depicting character. William J. Kennedy sums up this perspective: "The rhetorical act thus generates a dramatic interest in how the speaker clings to a certain role, shifts to another, moves through a succession of them, or enacts two or more opposing ones simultaneously, and how he squares or fails to square these roles with his moral selfhood" (Kennedy 1978: 5). In this conception, it is possible for a figure not to fulfil rhetorical–ethical norms but personation, even if comically disrupted, remains normatively oriented. There are significant degrees of variation from this position in some early modern texts and some modern interpretations. Personation can encompass social and personal conflict, and its comic modes might suggest ethical discord.

In *The Passions of the Mind* Thomas Wright agrees with Jonson (who wrote a prefatory sonnet for the text) on language's capacity to reveal and mirror hidden passions – "in words as in a glass may be seen a man's life and inclination" (Wright 1986: 166) – but he is also drawn to consider extreme situations where norms of character for speakers and audiences might no longer pertain: "men in great pain or exceeding pleasure can scarce speak, see, hear, or think of anything which concerneth not their passion" (ibid: 128). He suggests undertaking "a certain secret survey of men's speeches to see if we may discover some more hidden passions" (ibid: 166), and notes the persuasive power of emotive rhetoric: "if once they can stir up a Passion or Affection in their Hearers, then they have almost half persuaded them" (ibid: 90). In such cases, Wright spells out a wide scope for rhetorical personation in terms of interaction, self-representation, and analysis. His focus is less on endorsing standards for verbal style and social conduct than on representing and examining the array of unstable meanings and behavior that the passions can generate. Wright's exploration of links between style and conduct could be considered a sign of early modern rhetoric's integrated conception of personation: "The unity of rhetoric as a system is seen in the connections it makes between language and feelings: it moves from psychology to style (or *elocutio*) and back again, offering a coherent model of how language can influence behavior" (Vickers 1982: 135). Yet it is also possible to interpret at least sections of Wright's work as revealing moments when coherence, unity, and system break down, and the unpredictability of personation's meanings and effects comes into play. In this light, Wright's text suggests more radical dimensions of humor in relation to both identity and social order than festive comedy would allow.[5]

Two final examples of early modern discussions of personation and comedy reinforce this awareness of comedy's risky edge. In *The Art of Rhetorique*, the period's standard rhetorical text (Trousdale 2000: 625), Thomas Wilson does not claim to be able to explain laughter,[6] but he does emphasize the aggressive dimensions of humor:

> it appeareth that they which vtterly can be pleasaunt, and when time serueth can giue a merie aunswere, or vse a nipping taunt, shall be able to abashe a right worthie man, and make him at his wittes end, through the sodaine quicke, and vnlooked frumpe giuen. I haue knowne some so hitte of the thumbes, that they could not tell in the world, whether it were best to fight, chide, or to goe their way. And no maruaile: for where the iest is aptly applied, the hearers laugh immediately, and who would gladly bee laughed to scorne? (Wilson 1909: 135)

Wilson's strange idea of the *pleasantness* of these combative encounters challenges the delights of "arcadian" rhetoric discussed above. His sense of humor has targets in sight:

The occasion of laughter, and the meane that maketh vs mery . . . is the fondnes, the filthines, the deformitie, and al such euill behauiour, as we fee to be in other . . . Somtimes we iest at a mans bodie, that is not well proportioned, and laugh at his countenance, if either it be not comely by nature, or els he through folly can not well see it. (Ibid: 136)

No one is completely spared. Though "notable euill liuers, and heinous offenders . . . pitifull caitifes, and wretched beggers" are not to be "taunted, or iested withal," this is because "euery one thinketh it a better and a meeter deede, to punish naughtie packes then to scoffe at their euil demeanour: and as for wretched soules or poore bodies, none can beare to haue them mocked . . . except they foolishly vaunt them selues" (ibid: 137). There are social means other than humor for dealing with these minority groups. And while those "honest of behauiour" or "generally wel beloued" should not be "made any laughing stockes," all can be spoken to "as their good wits shal giue good cause" (ibid). Wilson's account of comedy establishes in-groups, "we, vs, euery one," and outsiders; the former can enjoy and use humor to dominate the latter, as well as decide on which "good cause" can bring humor into play in order to dominate. As will be seen in a number of Shakespeare's plays, being able to judge when meanings and personae should be deemed comically integrated or excluded from the main public group constitutes considerable control in any interaction.

If Wilson's treatment of comedy and eloquence reveals social power intertwined with the use of humor, George Puttenham's discussion of tropes is sharply conscious of specific moments and effects when humor is used. At times Puttenham reaffirms the notion of an arcadian rhetoric whose function is to keep its audience content; his *Arte* aims for "the fashioning of our makers language and style to such purpose as it may delight and allure as well the mind as the ear of the hearers" (Puttenham 1936: 137). He also endorses the reciprocity between language and persona, noting that many have "called style, the image of man for man is but his mind, and as his mind is tempered and qualified, so are his speeches and language at large" (ibid: 148). These kinds of reciprocal effect motivate his "own purpose, which is to make of a rude rhymer, a learned and a Courtly Poet" (ibid: 158), and they reach a climax in his discussion when "the courtier becomes a living trope; he actually incarnates the verbal figure Puttenham personifies as The Courtier" (Montrose 1983: 440). In this perspective, the happy outcomes at which Puttenham's rhetoric is directed involve courtly success and individual advancement. Arcadian humor promises a social and ethical payoff.

With such goals in mind, personation requires great caution, as the courtier turns words from their "own right signification, to another not so natural" (Puttenham 1936: 178).[7] The major concern lies in not offending social and verbal decorum, which Puttenham labels *decency*, a "lovely conformity, or proportion, or convenience between the sense and the sensible" (ibid: 262). Decency initially seems to entail conforming to prevailing standards of discourse and conduct. In this light, it can become a key element in self-improvement that leads to social success: "every man may decently reform by art, the faults and imperfections that nature hath wrought in them" (ibid:

287). Decorous self-personation can bring public rewards. It exemplifies the workings of festive comedy, where individual and social motives are mutually satisfied. But Puttenham's courtly sensitivity alerts him to the fact that decency is highly contingent:

> our speach asketh one manner of *decency*, in respect of the person who speaks: another of his to whom it is spoken: another of whom we speak: another of what we speak, and in what place and time and to what purpose. (ibid: 263)

The multiple factors carry an increased chance of the failure of decency. In such breakdowns lie grounds not only for personal disappointment but also for comedy. Puttenham explains that people laugh due to the *indecency* or lack of decorum in what they encounter: "in every uncomeliness there must be a certain absurdity and disproportion to nature" (ibid: 291). The explanation disregards various causes of comedy that other rhetoricians adumbrate (such as witty puns). Instead, it highlights the way that disruptions to supposedly natural routines and troubles in everyday exchanges are central to comedy. Puttenham goes on to add that "uncomeliness" can also be realized by "the opinion of the hearer or beholder to make the thing ridiculous" (ibid). His alertness to potential friction between speaker and audience turns rhetorical interaction into a social drama in which personation is inevitably interpersonal, dependent on others' responses. Everyone, on occasion, might find him or herself "a little o'erparted" (*Love's Labour's Lost*, 5.2.574) and subject to judgment. Here Puttenham discloses the strategic dimensions of conduct and dialogue that comic personation exposes and explores.

The main topics and features of rhetorical discourse from Plato to Puttenham – eloquence and ethics, wit and characterization, arcadian oratory, humor and power, the contingency of decorum – are all reproduced in Shakespeare's plays, which use language "to work through the social and ethical exigencies of ordinary life" (Bristol 2000: 93). Of course, Shakespeare's plays do contain set oratorical pieces that envoice noble personae and stir the passions; yet they also include less overtly striking speeches in which identities and relations between speakers and audiences are set up and tested. Indeed, some of the most interesting and amusing moments of his comedies are staged when cultural, personal, and rhetorical norms give way to ethical contradictions and conflicts. At these moments, readers, audiences, and characters are surprised to find that the language they rely on to talk to and about themselves, the one bequeathed by rhetorical tradition, often ends up saying more, or less, than they might mean.

Great Persuasion

In act 4, scene 4 of *The Two Gentlemen of Verona* the main female figures meet for the first time. Julia is disguised as Sebastian and is delivering a message from her faithless lover, Proteus, to his new beloved, Silvia. Through Proteus' scheming, Valentine, Silvia's own lover and Proteus' erstwhile companion, has been banished. The

crisscrossed network of love and friendship is already complicated and grows more so
as Sebastian tells Silvia a tale of "Julia," forsaken by Proteus. A sequence of personations is set in train, as Julia displaces her identity and emotion onto her "mistress,"
with the double aim of portraying Proteus' fickleness and moving Silvia against him:

> . . . my poor mistress, movèd therewithal,
> Wept bitterly; and would I might be dead
> If I in thought felt not her very sorrow.
> *Silvia.* She is beholden to thee gentle youth.
> Alas, poor lady, desolate and left.
> I weep myself to think upon thy words. (4.4.162–7)

Julia had previously lamented that in this role she must "prove false traitor to myself"
(4.4.98), but her words evade doing so. Because she is disguised, she is still able to
envoice her own experience and identity. Silvia's pathic or emotive response bears out
Julia's feelings and confirms her own nature – "A virtuous gentlewoman, mild, and
beautiful," Julia sums up (4.4.172). This sequence of personations is in the vein of
arcadian rhetoric. The empathy between both characters seems delightful, especially
in contrast to the competitive exchanges between the two (and more) gentlemen that
have taken place since the opening scene. It is a "festive" dialogue that suggests the
ethics of friendship.

   The audience is also alert to another layer of personation and intention that runs
through the dialogue. Sebastian's tale is not false but it is expedient: "I hope my
master's suit will be but cold, / Since she respects 'my mistress'' love so much"
(4.4.173–4). Unaware of the dialogue's full context, Silvia finds herself personated by
it, set up to assume a certain emotive and personal response. This other dimension is
more competitive than arcadian. It reflects the play's depiction of male rivalry and
suggests that such rivalry moves out to affect and influence others. Julia's comment
reinforces the audience's distance from the touching narrative Sebastian recounted.
The wit of the episode thus emerges from the contrast between the delight of the dialogue and its diverse effects of personation, in which Silvia and Julia simultaneously
enact different relationships to themselves and to each other. The interplay between
their identities and connections, along with the different levels of understanding
accessible to characters and audience, complicates the modes of personation that are
being staged. The scene illustrates the way that dramatic discourse relies on and
exploits the split between audience and characters' understanding. Where Platonism
finds this split disconcerting, since it suggests unethical manipulation of identity for
persuasive effect, Shakespeare uses it to explore different comic possibilities in the
rhetoric of personation.

   Such possibilities feature in episodes when characters speak to themselves, using a
"rhetoric of self-address" to convey a sense of sincere revelation (Newman 1985: 21).
Earlier in *Two Gentlemen*, Julia reflects on her words and actions, highlighting the gap
between persona and speech, when she hands back to Lucetta Proteus' unread letter,
"maids in modesty say 'No' to that / Which they would have the profferer construe

'Ay'" (1.2.55–6). After Lucetta returns, Julia immediately begins to equivocate again. She can reflect on her conduct, and the contradictory ways in which she feels it necessary to present herself, but not alter it. Where Lucetta experiences a wilful mistress, audience and readers can observe the limitations of Julia's sense of self at this point in the action. In *The Merry Wives of Windsor* Ford has a series of speeches where he declares it necessary and justified to watch his wife; initially, he sees it as honest work, "labour well bestowed" (2.1.207), that fits his citizen role. After listening to Falstaff's boasts, however, he angrily believes his position is warranted, "God be praised for my jealousy!" (2.2.271–2). The more earnest he becomes, the further his companions and the audience drift from his sense of justified outrage.

The rhetoric of self-address in these scenes reveals a disjunction between how speakers aim to personate themselves and the effects they realize for others, onstage and off; a "rivalry between ego and persona in the construction of subjectivity" (Freedman 1991: 35). In *Twelfth Night*, having realized that Olivia has fallen for Cesario, Viola notes the way such complications exceed anyone's control: "O time, thou must untangle this, not I. / It is too hard a knot for me t' untie" (2.2.39–40). Her instrumental role in the mix-up doesn't grant any mastery over the way relations and identities develop. In *A Midsummer Night's Dream* the novice actors' guesses about how their audience will respond (act 3, scene 1) reflect a wider uncertainty over the impression performances can create. It comes to a point when Bottom wakes from his dream, still discussing cues and entries as though performance can be entirely scripted, only to be mystified by the personations he thinks he recalls: "Methought I was – there is no man can tell what. Methought I was, and methought I had – but man is but a patched fool if he will offer to say what methought I had" (4.1.202–4). His bewilderment exemplifies an air of lost or unknowable selfhood that recurs throughout the comedies and which contests the ethical focus of traditional rhetoric.

Bottom can never guess that his "translation" was part of Oberon's scheme to assert authority over Titania. But the larger frame for "Bottom's Dream" exemplifies the way that the involvement of others – as observers, addressees, or interlocutors, each guided by their own motives – penetrates most acts of personation in Shakespeare's plays. A relatively meek figure such as Jessica in *The Merchant of Venice* sharply feels the moral pressure of such "inter-personation." In farewelling Lancelot, she creates an impression of sincerity not only by voicing her regret that he is leaving but also by criticizing her father and house. The tension between the first- and third-person pronouns in the lines "what heinous sin it is in me / To be ashamed to be my father's child! / But though I am a daughter to his blood, / I am not to his manners" (2.4.15–18) underwrites the inner "strife" between blood and manners that she experiences. Jessica feels that deep-seated parts of the identity she is endowed with are no longer compatible. Her struggle to forgo them is intensified by doubts over whether her new identity will be genuinely taken up by Lorenzo. Until, and even as, they elope, she cannot be completely sure of his character and intentions, and what they might mean for her own: "Who are you? Tell me for more certainty . . . For I am much ashamed of my exchange" (2.6.26, 35). Jessica's shame has many levels: most obviously, her crossdressed garb, but more poignantly the exchange of faith and community she has entered into. For the moment her new role is guaranteed only by the ducats with which she gilds herself, thereby joining the transactions between identity and materiality that all characters in the play try to negotiate to their advantage. The humor in Jessica's anxiety emerges through a festive reading of her movement from the marginal group to the mainstream. The comic aspects of personation in this case seemed to depend on accepting broader social practices and perspectives.

The Comedy of Errors careers through the complications of inter-personation. All the twins must grapple with identities foisted on them with little regard for what or whom they would like to say they are (or are used to saying). Self-personation seems foreclosed in the ongoing "disjunction between personal and communal accounts of one's identity" (Freedman 1991: 79). As Viola also discovers in *Twelfth Night*, such dilemmas can quickly spin out to ensnare most of the other characters. The comic note in *Errors* is of near-desperation, as everyone tries to mediate and talk about oneself in response to surprising accounts of unknown identities and relationships. At one point, Luciana lectures Antipholus of Syracuse on his "husband's office" (3.2.2) to Adriana. Even if he can't fulfill it, she exhorts, he should pretend: "Look sweet, speak fair, become disloyalty . . . Be secret-false" (3.2.11, 15). She commends deception so long as Adriana might enjoy her social role: "Comfort my sister, cheer her, call her wife" (3.2.26). For once Antipholus gets into the spirit of misrecognition; he would embrace it, but not quite as Luciana intends. He tries to turn this new identity into a way of winning her:

> . . . Would you create me new?
> Transform me, then, and to your power I'll yield.
> But if that I am I, then well I know
> Your weeping sister is no wife of mine,
> . . . far more, to you do I decline. (3.2.39–44)

Antipholus plays the attributed identity against his now shaky sense of selfhood and tries to open up new roles for Luciana and himself. She finds her own identity re-cast and hurriedly exits. Dromio's tense catechism – "Do you know me, sir? Am I Dromio? Am I your man? Am I myself?" (3.2.73–4) – responds to a similarly unforeseen coupling with Nell the kitchen maid. He flips between inner and outer reference points of identity ("your man," "myself") in an attempt to locate where he might stand.

Even the most self-assertive characters can be surprised to find that they are subject to the pressures of "inter-personation." The initial confrontation between Katherine and Petruccio in *The Taming of the Shrew* can be read in such terms (2.1.180ff.). Petruccio prepares by running through his tactics – he aims to contradict each speech act of Katherine's with one of his own, thereby affirming his rhetorical sway over her. Audience anticipation builds up, and when he makes the first move by renaming her "Kate" it seems that Petruccio's script will prevail. Katherine of course rejects her new name and they proceed to test each other using word play, insults, slaps, and force. Throughout the exchange they strive to impose not only their own discursive and physical identities but also the persona they want the other to have. The way they personate themselves depends on what they can do to and with the other's words and identity. When his original tactics cannot overcome Katherine, Petruccio finally changes tack and invokes Baptista's paternal authority: "setting all this chat aside, / Thus in plain terms: your father hath consented / That you shall be my wife" (2.1.260–2). Given this support, and the additional backing he gains as Baptista, Gremio, and Tranio enter to see what has happened (all banking on his success), Petruccio can indeed claim "It were impossible I should speed amiss" (2.1.275).

The encounter underscores the reciprocity of personation but also its competitive nature. One character's gain is another's loss, and the humor derives from the relentless pace at which the duo score against each other. The scene is also decisive in widening the significance of personation from individual and interpersonal speech to the cultural settings in which such speeches occur. This move draws out the tensions between the aims of the characters – their sense of what they mean and aim to achieve in their speech – and what the people and social codes around them will let them mean. The kind of sensitivity to context and feedback that Puttenham notes in the humorous effects of "indecency" – the potential readiness of observers to see absurdity in any "disproportion to nature" – suggests numerous ways in which personation is influenced by social practices and discourse, even as characters try to affirm their independence or determine the nature of the relationships they have with those around them.

Family relationships are a key factor in personation in Shakespeare's plays. Characters frequently assess and negotiate identity in relation to kinship ties. In his speech at the beginning of *As You Like It*, Orlando aims to define his view of proper family ties, especially the respect and status he believes due from his brother. The old servant Adam names the dual strains of Oliver's identity that impinge on Orlando, "my master, your brother" (1.1.22), for the older brother's mastery extends over the younger. The struggle to impose and resist personae is waged directly through the names and titles they use to address each other – a sequence of testy "sirs," followed by "boy," "elder brother," "villain," and "villein" (1.1.25–48). The "sirs" in particular convey animosity in the guise of respect, as they debate their relative roles:

> *Oliver.* Know you before whom, sir?
> *Orlando.* Ay, better than him I am before knows me. I know you are my eldest brother,
> and in the gentle condition of blood you should so know me. (1.1.36–9)

In appealing to their shared blood, Orlando invokes the bond and institution that are used against him. Oliver's ensuing account to the wrestler Charles, encouraging him not to hold back when he fights Orlando, exploits this tension in familial discourse: "it is the stubbornest young fellow of France, full of ambition . . . a secret and villainous contriver against me his natural brother" (1.1.121–3). Later a transformed Oliver describes his actions as "unnatural" (4.3.123), yet the readiness with which Charles accepts such "brotherly" speaking (1.1.131) suggests that at least in part characters understand family relationships and identities in terms of animosity as much as love. Celia's attempt to cheer Rosalind when the next scene begins likewise mixes family love and hatred: "If my uncle, thy banished father, had banished thy uncle, the Duke my father, so thou hadst been still with me I could have taught my love to take thy father for mine" (1.2.7–9). Celia's notion of "teaching" herself to love shows the deep changes to character forced by family circumstances. Again, Orlando finds himself first repudiated by Duke Frederick on account of his family – "I would thou hadst told me of another father" (1.2.196) – and later welcomed by Duke Senior for the same reason (2.7.194–9). Family is destiny, or close to it.

The force of inter-personation, which Jessica feels in *The Merchant of Venice*, is also part of the onus of family rhetoric. Portia is subject to it through the patriarchal lottery: "so is the will of a living daughter curbed by the will of a dead father" (*Merchant*, 1.2.21–2). *A Midsummer Night's Dream* opens with Egeus seeking to impose his authority on Hermia – "she is mine," he bluntly states (1.1.97). Adriana conceives the apparent breakdown of her marriage to Antipholus of Ephesus as the dissolving of both their identities:

> I am not Adriana, nor thy wife . . .
> How comes it now, my husband, O how comes it
> That thou art then estrangèd from thyself? –
> Thy "self" I call it, being strange to me
> That, undividable, incorporate,
> Am better than thy dear self's better part.
> (*Comedy of Errors*, 2.2.112–23)

In each case, and whether in support or opposition, the characters conceive the weight of family ties upon their autonomy. Comic suspense and surprise result as they struggle with an institution which both provides and denies their identity.

Family bonds are perhaps the most conspicuous case of social practices influencing personation in Shakespeare's comedies, but there are many other instances. The kind of ethical purity that Platonism sought in rhetoric and self-presentation seems foreclosed by the sheer density of roles and discourse that weaves in and around characters' speech. At one level the impact of social situations is manifest as intended identities and courses of action speedily unravel when circumstances alter. *Love's Labour's Lost* shows the four lords' desperate efforts to keep up with events. In act 4, scene 3 each reveals their lovelorn passion and then hides to watch another do the same. The King steps forth to reprimand Dumaine and Longueville for breaking "faith and troth" (4.3.139). Biron then trumps them all. He mocks their performances as "a scene of fool'ry" (4.3.159), and claims the moral high ground: "I am betrayed by keeping company / With men like you, men of inconstancy" (4.3.175–6). Yet he too falls with the arrival of Jaquenetta and Costard bearing his own letter to Rosaline. None escapes the inconsistency between their intended and actual roles: "Let us once lose our oaths to find ourselves," advises Biron to everyone's relief (4.3.335). Impressive pronouncements – Armado might call them the "Sweet smoke of rhetoric!" (3.1.54) – are made then undercut as soon as circumstances thwart or spark passion.

Biron predicted all of this when he first signed the schedule, "Necessity will make us all forsworn . . . For every man with his affects is born" (1.1.147–9), but none can forestall it. As Thomas Wright (1986: 179) affirmed, "internal conceits and affections" complicate people's external actions and words, disclosing aspects of identity not perceived by the subject, let alone others, till events put them in play.

Love's Labour's Lost closes with the ladies compelling the lords to recast themselves and their language before they meet again. In this view, personation is mutable but also motivated; it can be improved, "decently" reformed in Puttenham's phrase, through one's own efforts. Similar opportunities are offered in other plays: Portia and Nerissa use the ring-trick to impress on Bassanio, Graziano, and Antonio the significance of the newly married state. The most developed version comes in *As You Like It*, when Rosalind, in the guise of Ganymede, guides Orlando to reform his language and conduct as "Signor Love" (3.2.266–7). Rosalind regards Orlando's manner as self-love and criticizes the romantic clichés through which he misperceives the nature of his and others' emotions – "in all this time there was not any man died in his own person, videlicet, in a love-cause" (4.1.82–3), she literally counters one of his avowals. Rosalind's success is part of the play's overall arcadian mode, best summed up by Amiens's praise of Duke Senior's ability to "translate the stubbornness of fortune / Into so quiet and so sweet a style" (2.1.19–20). In other plays, however, characters are often shown to have less capacity to "translate" the discourse they use. Cultural values speak through and personate them, and festive synthesis, though often invoked generically in a happy ending, seems unlikely.

From the opening lines of *The Merry Wives of Windsor* intense pressure is placed on everyone to use a shared language. Falstaff and his followers disrupt the group through their unaccustomed, exaggerated speech, the corollary of their disorderly designs on the wives and money of Windsor. The initial dispute between Shallow and Falstaff centers on who said what, while Slender's empty, erring repetitions of his uncle absurdly magnify the way a communal group endows its members with the sense of what they can say and should do, regardless of whether they understand it:

> *Slender.* . . . if you say "marry her," I will marry her. That I am freely dissolved, and dissolutely.
> *Evans.* It is a fery discretion answer . . . His meaning is good.
> *Shallow.* Ay, I think my cousin meant well. (1.1.210–15)

Evans reinterprets the words Slender used and Shallow is not sure what he really meant; nevertheless, the community permits certain verbal license to insiders. Such acceptance is balanced by the scope to impose some kind of punishment or mockery on discursive outsiders, as in the Host's practical joke on Evans and Dr. Caius, inciting them to a duel before averting it: "Let them keep their limbs whole, and hack our English" (3.1.66–7). Characters such as the Host and Mistress Quickly are central to the way the community functions because they mediate talk and information between others. Fenton tries to work through both of them to gain access to Anne Page, and in each case he uses verbal imagery to secure support: "Let me have thy voice in my behalf" (1.4.137); "Yet hear me speak" (4.6.3). His success is registered not only in marrying Anne but in having the Pages accept his redefinition of their actions: "this deceit loses the name of craft, / Of disobedience, or unduteous title" (5.5.203–4).

This community holds that the way someone speaks (or writes) justifies their place and treatment. But it is not only outsiders or newcomers who feel the pressure. Master Ford himself constantly adverts to what his neighbors will say about him. He is painfully conscious that he has no identity other than that attributed to him: "Who says this is improvident jealousy . . . I shall not only receive this villainous wrong, but stand under the adoption of abominable terms" (2.2.254–60). Hence Ford is fixated on Page's response to Falstaff, since they are rivals for the same kind of socially respected persona. He envisages triumph in "divulg[ing] Page himself for a secure and wilful Actaeon, and to these violent proceedings all my neighbours shall cry aim" (3.2.36–7). Page justifies Ford's concern – "trust me, we'll mock him," he conspires with Evans and Caius (3.4.194); yet even he, along with Shallow and Evans, tries to dissuade Ford from seeking public affirmation of his cuckoldry. Such is Ford's commitment to the group perspective that he implores derision. He wants to become a "saying": "let me for ever be your table-sport; let them say of me, 'As jealous as Ford, that searched a hollow walnut for his wife's leman'" (4.2.141–3). His frenzied conduct discloses selfhood unable to recognize itself except in terms of an internalized communal discourse. Public personation rules in Windsor.

Though a main role such as Master Ford vividly concentrates the effects of public personation, the discursive contexts affect everyone's identity. Shakespeare alternates focus between major and minor figures to show the widespread consequences for personation generated by communal discourse. As noted earlier, Petruccio's success in *The Taming of the Shrew* relies on a group of male figures who, despite their own rivalries, are prepared to endorse and reiterate what he says. In *The Merchant of Venice* the words of minor figures crucially reveal the material values that inform characters' sense of themselves. Salerio and Solanio eagerly revise Antonio's sadness in terms of financial concerns. The readiness with which they do so shows that the metaphor of personal–financial value is naturalized throughout Venice. Though Antonio denies such explanations, he still speaks its ambivalent register – "I thank my fortune for it" (1.1.45). From this point on, almost all personal references carry materialist inflections, as characters debate each other's worth. The fundamental ethical puzzle of what makes a "good" man is translated into a question of credit; having social advantage over someone is conceived as a winning wrestling hold, physical ascendancy as material ascendancy; lovers' commitments are guaranteed and traded by rings. At crucial moments in the plot, minor characters rehearse a chorus of shared sentiments, "the plain highway of talk" (3.1.10), to situate events all the more securely in the materialist framework – before Jessica elopes with Lorenzo (2.6.1–19), when Bassanio's ship departs (2.8), while pondering Antonio's situation (3.1), or when the trial scene commences. In this last scene, as Shylock enters the Duke begins: "let him stand before our face. / Shylock, the world thinks – and I think so too" (4.1.15–16); the royal "we" is less in effect here than a single public voice, ready to confront the alien.[8]

As the case falls rapidly away from Shylock, Graziano's exclamations sound the force-ful voice of the triumphant majority, eager to penalize outsiders who disrupt its codes but willing to collaborate in resolving disputes among its own, as occurs in the final scene, when Portia, Bassanio, and Antonio are reconciled.

Shylock's fate exemplifies Thomas Wilson's explanation of humor in *The Arte of Rhetorique*. Comedy becomes a weapon through which a social group polices its members, punishing offenders, testing and rewarding members. In this conception, comic personation is closely linked to the operation of power and violence. When the Duke in *The Two Gentlemen of Verona* discovers Valentine's plan to elope with Silvia he immediately asserts discursive authority to repersonate the courtier, "base intruder, over-weening slave" (3.1.157), and banishes him. The Duke eventually reverses this identity and retitles him "Sir Valentine" (5.4.142). In *The Taming of the Shrew* the struggle over personation waged between Petruccio and Katherine is framed by the Lord's power to "practise on" Sly's identity (Induction, 1.32) and that of his page, Bathol'mew. (Previously, with the same imperious air, the Lord ordered two of his dogs to be coupled (Induction, 1.14); he initially labels Sly a beast and swine.) The power to determine others' identities rests not only in making overt commands, but in leading followers to accept the personae imposed on others and on themselves – the two huntsmen have little option but to concur with the Lord's plan for Sly and respond with flat statements that echo his own (Induction, 1.38–9), while Barthol'mew is told "from me, as he will win my love, / He bear himself with hon-ourable action" (Induction, 1.105–6). Accepting how a powerful figure characterizes someone else effectively settles one's own persona (at least for the time being and in that context).

Much Ado About Nothing offers an extended treatment of these issues. It shows that a community's personal discourse is for better or worse organized through defi-nitions of character and conduct provided by its ruling figures, Don Pedro and Don John. In the first half of the play, characters are led into love through the words of others. Marriage is the constant theme of conversation in Messina – "Thus goes every-one to the world," observes Beatrice (2.1.278–9). Don Pedro woos Hero on Claudio's behalf, and then organizes the others "to bring Signor Benedick and the Lady Beatrice into a mountain of affection th' one with th' other" (2.1.318–19). All the characters accept that heterosexual lovers are constrained not only by the way they speak of themselves and of each other but also by the way others speak of them. Benedick can scoff at the transformation in Claudio's language: "He was wont to speak plain and to the purpose . . . now he is turned orthography" (2.3.16–18); yet he takes seriously what the other men say about Beatrice's feelings for him: "This can be no trick. The conference was sadly borne" (2.3.196–7). For all her earlier sarcasm, Beatrice is similarly swayed by what she hears about Benedick: "I / Believe it better than reportingly" (3.1.116–17).

In this context, where affections and characters are overwhelmingly molded by what people say, it is little surprise that some characters are immediately ready to repeat Don John's slander against Hero; "So will you say," he confidently predicts of Claudio and Don Pedro (3.2.113). Leonato asks: "Would the two princes lie?" (4.1.151), searching for any remnant of the consensus that had bound almost everyone together. Discursive community has been fractured by the all-important words of authority. Beatrice can attack these words as lies and bitterly denounce their supposedly "proper saying" (4.2.306); nonetheless, they compel everyone to accept or deny them and the personae they impose. They take over the way in which the community talks about itself and its members. The rest of the action focuses on revealing the rhetorical circumstances through which Hero could be characterized as "but the sign and semblance of her honour" (4.1.31), in order to restore her "maiden truth" (4.1.163). Ironically, it is Dogberry's jumbled speech that leads to the restoration of consensual discourse. But most strikingly it is the subjection of everyone's sexual and ethical personae to what Beatrice calls "great persuasion" (5.4.94) – the persuasiveness of the great and the significance of persuasion – that is staged.

> Now to tell you in plaine words, what laughter is, how it stirreth and occupieth the whole body, how it altereth the countenance, and sodainly brasteth out that we cannot keepe it in: let some mery man on Gods name take this matter in hand: for it passeth my cunning. (Wilson 1909: 135)

Thomas Wilson's inability to explain the workings of laughter is an ironic admission, for like other rhetoricians from his time and earlier, he is most interested in explaining the workings of humor. Comedy exemplifies the artful use of language and the construction of personae that lie at the heart of rhetorical practice. The early modern period's notions and styles of comedy were wide-ranging – from festivity and arcadian happiness, to nuanced wit, to aggressive reproof and violent abuse. Shakespeare's plays combine these various types of humor with the traditional rhetoric of comedy. They represent personae whose speech is filled with the humorous tropes and verbal ticks that rhetoricians were keen to classify. More significantly, the plays use the comic genre to reiterate and reassess major points about social relations and ethical identity that rhetorical discourse had always sought to explain and define. They explore the links among festive comedy, arcadian rhetoric, and edifying norms; they relate comic personation to both decorum and transgression; and they stage the pressures between inter-personation and individualization, idiosyncratic humor and communal power, self-knowledge and subjection. Shakespeare's comedies both continue and challenge the history of rhetorical personation by revealing the paradoxes and contradictions of its serious premises.

NOTES

1 *Twelfth Night* 2.3.87. All references to Shakespeare's plays are to the editions in the *Norton Shakespeare* and will be included parenthetically in the text.
2 For important discussions of pedagogy and rhetoric in England through the sixteenth and seventeenth centuries, see Altman (1978), Halpern (1991), Bushnell (1996).
3 Discussions of George Puttenham's rhetoric have frequently focused on its paradoxical treatment of tropes and their cultural value; see Montrose (1983), Attridge (1986), Parker (1987), Davis (1993).

4 Cf. Quintilian's brusque reminder: "I am not trying to form a comic actor, but an orator" (11.3.181).

5 Influential accounts of comedy's radical implications at both psychological and social levels are offered in Freud's essay on humor, in relation to the ego's struggle "against the unkindness of the real circumstances" (Freud 1953–74: 163), and in Bakhtin's (1968) discussion of grotesque realism, degradation, and the carnivalesque suspension of social hierarchy. Cf. Bristol (1985), Stallybrass and White (1986).

6 See Wilson (1909: 135). The passage in question is quoted at the end of this essay; in it Wilson echoes quite closely Cicero's remarks in *De Oratore* (Cicero 1967: 2.58.235).

7 Puttenham follows many of the examples offered by Richard Sherry in *A Treatise of the Figures of Grammer and Rhetorike* (1555).

8 Similarly in the Duke's later judgment against Shylock, "thou shalt see the difference of our spirit" (4.1.363).

REFERENCES AND FURTHER READING

Altman, J. B. (1978). *The Tudor Play of Mind: Rhetorical Inquiry and the Development of Elizabethan Drama.* Berkeley: University of California Press.

Aristotle (1971). *De Poetica* and *Rhetorica.* In W. D. Ross (ed.) *The Works of Aristotle*, Vol. 11. Oxford: Clarendon Press.

Ascham, R. (1888). *The Schoolmaster.* London: Cassell.

Attridge, D. (1986). Puttenham's Perplexity: Nature, Art, and the Supplement in Renaissance Poetic Theory. In P. Parker and D. Quint (eds.) *Literary Theory / Renaissance Texts.* Baltimore, MD: Johns Hopkins University Press, 257–79.

Bacon, F. (1969). *The Advancement of Learning.* In *The Advancement of Learning and New Atlantis.* Oxford: Oxford University Press.

Bakhtin, M. M. (1968). *Rabelais and His World*, trans. H. Iswolsky. Cambridge, MA: MIT Press.

Barber, C. L. (1959). *Shakespeare's Festive Comedies: A Study of Dramatic Form and Its Relationship to Social Custom.* Princeton, NJ: Princeton University Press.

Bristol, M. D. (1985). *Carnival and Theater: Plebeian Culture and the Structure of Authority in Renaissance England.* New York: Methuen.

——(2000). Vernacular Criticism and the Scenes Shakespeare Never Wrote. *Shakespeare Survey*, 53, 89–102.

Burns, E. (1990). *Character: Acting and Being on the Pre-Modern Stage.* Basingstoke: Macmillan.

Bushnell, R. (1996). *A Culture of Teaching: Early Modern Humanism in Theory and Practice.* Ithaca, NY: Cornell University Press.

Cicero (1967). *De Oratore*, 2 vols, trans. E. W. Sutton and H. Rackham. Cambridge, MA: Harvard University Press.

Davis, L. (1993). *Guise and Disguise: Rhetoric and Characterization in the English Renaissance.* Toronto: University of Toronto Press.

Desmet, C. (1992). *Reading Shakespeare's Characters: Rhetoric, Ethics, and Identity.* Amherst: University of Massachusetts Press.

Fraunce, A. (1950). *The Arcadian Rhetorike*, ed. E. Seaton. Oxford: Blackwell.

Freedman, B. (1991). *Staging the Gaze: Postmodernism, Psychoanalysis, and Shakespearean Comedy.* Ithaca, NY: Cornell University Press.

Freud, S. (1953–74). Humour. In J. Strachey (ed.) *The Standard Edition of the Works of Sigmund Freud*, Vol. 21. London: Hogarth.

——(1963). *Jokes and Their Relation to the Unconscious*, ed. J. Strachey. New York: W. W. Norton.

Halpern, R. (1991). *The Poetics of Private Accumulation: English Renaissance Culture and the Genealogy of Capital.* Ithaca, NY: Cornell University Press.

Hartman, G. (1985). Shakespeare's Poetical Character in *Twelfth Night*. In P. Parker and G. Hartman (eds.) *Shakespeare and the Question of Theory*. New York: Methuen, 37–53.

Horace (1978). *Satires, Epistles, and Ars Poetica*, trans. H. Rushton Fairclough. Cambridge, MA: Harvard University Press.

Hutton, S. (2000). Platonism, Stoicism, Scepticism and Classical Imitation. In M. Hattaway (ed.) *A Companion to English Renaissance Literature and Culture*. Oxford: Blackwell, 44–57.

Jonson, B. (1925–52). *Timber: Or, Discoveries; Made upon Men and Matter*. In *Ben Jonson*, Vol. 8. Oxford: Clarendon Press.

Kennedy, W. J. (1978). *Rhetorical Norms in Renaissance Literature*. New Haven, CT: Yale University Press.

Montrose, L. A. (1983). Of Gentlemen and Shepherds: The Politics of Elizabethan Pastoral Form. *English Literary History*, 50, 415–59.

Newman, K. (1985). *Shakespeare's Rhetoric of Comic Character: Dramatic Convention in Classical and Renaissance Comedy*. New York: Methuen.

Parker, P. (1987). *Literary Fat Ladies: Rhetoric, Gender, Property*. London: Methuen.

Peacham, H. (1971). *The Garden of Eloquence*, ed. R. C. Alston. Menston: Scolar Press.

Plato (1985). *Sophist*. In H. Cairns and E. Hamilton (eds.) *The Collected Dialogues*. Princeton, NJ: Princeton University Press.

Platt, P. G. (1999). Shakespeare and Rhetorical Culture. In D. S. Kastan (ed.) *A Companion to Shakespeare*. Oxford: Blackwell, 277–96.

Puttenham, G. (1936). *The Arte of English Poesie*, ed. G. D. Willcock and A. Walker. Cambridge: Cambridge University Press.

Quintilian (1969). *Institutio Oratoria*, 4 vols, trans. H. E. Butler. London: William Heinemann.

Rebhorn, W. A. (1995). Petruchio's "Rope Tricks": *The Taming of the Shrew* and the Renaissance Discourse of Rhetoric. *Modern Philology*, 92, 294–327.

Rhetorica ad Herennium (1968). Trans. H. Caplan. Cambridge, MA: Harvard University Press.

Shakespeare, W. (1997). *The Norton Shakespeare: Based on the Oxford Edition*, ed. S. Greenblatt, W. Cohen, J. Howard, and K. E. Maus. New York: W. W. Norton.

Sherry, R. (1555). *A Treatise of the Figures of Grammer and Rhetorike*. London: Richard Tottell.

Sidney, P. (1963). *The Defence of Poesie*. In A. Feuillerat (ed.) *The Prose Works of Sir Philip Sidney*, Vol. 3. Cambridge: Cambridge University Press.

Stallybrass, P. and White, A. (1986). *The Politics and Poetics of Transgression*. London: Methuen.

Thomson, P. (1997). Rogues and Rhetoricians: Acting Styles in Early English Drama. In J. D. Cox and D. S. Kastan (eds.) *A New History of Early English Drama*. New York: Columbia University Press, 321–35.

Trousdale, M. (1997). Reading the Early Modern Text. *Shakespeare Survey*, 50, 135–45.

——(2000). Rhetoric. In M. Hattaway (ed.) *A Companion to English Renaissance Literature and Culture*. Oxford: Blackwell, 623–33.

Vickers, B. (1982). On the Practicalities of Renaissance Rhetoric. In B. Vickers (ed.) *Rhetoric Revalued: Papers from the International Society for the History of Rhetoric*. Binghamton, NY: Center for Medieval and Early Renaissance Studies, 133–41.

——(1988). *In Defence of Rhetoric*. Oxford: Clarendon Press.

Wilson, T. (1909). *The Arte of Rhetorique*, ed. G. H. Mair. Oxford: Clarendon Press.

Wright, T. (1986). *The Passions of the Mind in General*, ed. W. W. Newbold. New York: Garland.

11

Fat Knight, or What You Will: Unimitable Falstaff

Ian Frederick Moulton

No man is more dangerous than he that with a will to corrupt hath the power to please. (Samuel Johnson)

If Falstaff were running the world, it would be like the Balkans. (W. H. Auden)

We all like Old Jack. (Maurice Morgann)

If ever a subject was in need of a breath of fresh air, it is the study of Falstaff, Shakespeare's most renowned comic character. A figure of monumental excess, Falstaff invites hyperbole.

For example, he is said to be:

fat-witted
a fat-kidneyed rascal
a fat-guts
a fat rogue
a fat paunch
a fat deer
a fat villain
a fat fool
a fat man
a gross fat man
an old fat man
the old boar
the town bull
woolsack
a foul-mouthed man
sweet beef
Jack
Sack-and-Sugar Jack

lean Jack
blown Jack
poor Jack
chops
no starveling
a gummed velvet
Sir John Paunch
a rascal
an oily rascal
a whoreson impudent embossed rascal
a whoreson obscene greasy tallow-keech
a whoreson round man
a villain
claybrained guts
a bed-presser
a horse-breaker
a huge hill of flesh
a devil
a trunk of humors
a bolting hatch of beastliness
a stuffed cloak-bag of guts
an old white-bearded Satan
a villainous abominable misleader of youth
a natural coward

And that is just what his friends call him.

His critics have been much kinder: to them he is "unimitable" (Johnson 1973: 204); "a man of birth and fashion, bred up in all the learning and accomplishments of the times; – of ability and Courage equal to any situation" (Morgann 1972: 208); "a man of genius" and "no coward" (Bradley 1909: 263, 266); "a being overflowing with an inexhaustible fountain of life and humanity" (Bailey 1916: 149–52); "a god who does for our imaginations very much what Bacchus and Silenus did for those of the ancients" (Dover Wilson 1961: 128); "ageless in his exuberance . . . sublime" (Bloom 1998: 298–9). He is both "a real presence" and "beyond our last thought" (ibid: 313). Not a bad trick for a stuffed cloak-bag of guts.

My goal is not to sum up Falstaff – a thankless task that has been undertaken many times, most successfully by Samuel Johnson, who managed to describe Falstaff without sentimentalizing him, idealizing him, or disapproving of him. Instead, I want to focus on some of the issues Falstaff raises. Everyone insists he is attractive, but what is the nature of his attraction? Do we respond to the same things in Falstaff that Shakespeare's original audience did? And what is this quintessential comic character doing in a history play?

Comedy and History

Falstaff appears in three plays: the histories *Henry IV* parts one and two, and the comedy *The Merry Wives of Windsor*. While the relative dates of the plays cannot be determined precisely, it is fairly clear that Falstaff was first introduced in *1 Henry IV*, and that his popularity not only ensured him a prominent part in that play's sequel, but also in *Merry Wives*. In the *Henry IV* plays, Falstaff, a corrupt and dissolute knight, serves as a surrogate father to the young prince Hal who, estranged from his real father, Henry IV, seeks a political education by immersing himself in an urban world of taverns, brothels, and petty crime. Hal's relation to Falstaff is affectionate but confrontational, and is marked by increasing tension as Hal moves closer to assuming the responsibilities of rulership. When after his father's death Hal becomes King Henry V, he publicly rejects and humiliates Falstaff, who shortly thereafter dies of what some say is a broken heart. Falstaff's death is reported in some detail in *Henry V*, a play in which it seems Falstaff was meant to be a major character, but for artistic or practical reasons Shakespeare chose instead to kill him off.

In *The Merry Wives of Windsor* Falstaff appears in a completely different context, though he is still surrounded with some of the minor characters who accompany him in the *Henry IV* plays. Here Hal is barely mentioned, and Falstaff spends his time plotting ways to seduce two respectable Windsor housewives – more to get their money than for any sexual motive. The wives (who are not the least bit tempted) decide the best way to drive him away is to play along with him in order to shame him in various ways – including dumping him into the Thames in a basket of filthy clothes, compelling him to dress as an old woman, and having him soundly beaten. They finally agree to meet him in the woods at night, thus setting the stage for a public shaming in which the would-be seducer is pinched and tormented by the town's children dressed as fairies. At the play's conclusion, the fat knight admits defeat and all is forgiven.

While the *Henry IV* plays are well-integrated with each other and events occurring in the first are carefully referred to in the second, *Merry Wives* contradicts the *Henry* plays on many points of detail. It seems clear that while Shakespeare was willing to build a comedy around Falstaff, he was not concerned to connect the world of that comedy closely with the very different world depicted in the histories. This difference in the world of the plays is echoed by a difference in Falstaff's social role and dramatic significance: in the histories, Falstaff is corrupting aristocratic virtue and must be banished; in comedy, he is corrupting middle-class morality and may be redeemed.

While other Shakespearean characters appear in more than one play, Falstaff is the only major character to appear in more than one *type* of play. Critics have often attempted to distinguish the Falstaff of the *Henry IV* plays from that of the *Merry Wives*, arguing that in the history plays Falstaff has a dignity and almost philosophical weight that he lacks in the comedy. We will shortly address these claims in detail, but at this point it is worth noting that although the history plays reveal his full complexity, there is no doubt that Falstaff is a character most at home in comedy. He brings an anarchic, comic energy to the *Henry IV* plays that is entirely absent from any of Shakespeare's other histories. Though Shakespeare's art thrives on the mixing of genres and frequently challenges generic norms, Falstaff remains magnificently out of place in the *Henry IV* plays. Whatever the play's title, when Falstaff is on stage, you're watching a comedy.

The juxtaposition – or collision – of comedy and history deepens the significance of both genres. Comic fooling gains a serious undertone when set against the harsh realities of power politics; and power politics become ironic, if not ridiculous, when confronted with parody and laughter. In the midst of a great tetralogy which seeks to define the nature of ideal kingship and good government, Falstaff represents a negation of everything both Henrys are striving for. His parodic energy operates as a solvent, dissolving the bonds of honor, honesty, and service upon which the feudal monarchy is based. And yet Falstaff's comic energy is crucial to the movement in the second tetralogy from the courtly reserve of Richard II to the populism of Henry V – from Richard's idealism to Henry's pragmatism. Richard II is imprisoned in rituals of kingship which isolate him from his people. Henry V, educated by Falstaff, learns to appeal to the common man (and woman) while manipulating them for his own purposes.

What We Can Learn from Falstaff

What exactly is it that Falstaff teaches Hal? William Empson argued that Falstaff is a good tutor for a Renaissance prince because he is both nationalistic and Machiavellian (Empson 1986: 56–7). At first glance this seems an odd idea: Falstaff is too selfish to care about his nation and too "gross . . . open, [and] palpable" to be Machiavellian. And yet Falstaff has always been associated with a certain bluff, witty, drunken Englishness – at his death, after all, Mistress Quickly confidently predicts that he is in "Arthur's bosom" (her mistake for Abraham's bosom). And though Falstaff may appear obvious, he is a very slippery character. One thing Hal learns from him is how to lie with impunity.

One tends to think of Machiavellian characters in Shakespeare as being evil schemers like Richard III, Iago, or Edmund. But although Falstaff's Machiavellianism is comic, not tragic, his scheming and general amorality are everywhere apparent. His famous catechism on the subject of "honor" is not only a rejection of social hypocrisy; it is also a rejection of all ideology beyond self-preservation, of any value which cannot be measured on a scale of physical comfort:

Well, 'tis no matter; honour pricks me on. Yea, but how if honour prick me off when I am come on? How then? Can honour set-to a leg? No. Or an arm? No. Or take away the grief of a wound? No. Honour hath no skill in surgery, then? No. What is honour? A word. What is in that word 'honour'? What is that 'honour'? Air. A trim reckoning! Who hath it? He that died o' Wednesday. Doth he feel it? No. Doth he hear it? No. 'Tis insensible then? Yea, to the dead. But will it not live with the living? No. Why?

Detraction will not suffer it. Therefore, I'll none of it. Honour is a mere scutcheon. And so ends my catechism. (*1 Henry IV*, 5.1.129–39)

This is Falstaff clearing his mind of cant – as Dr. Johnson famously admonished Boswell, in social life one often has to say false and stupid things, but one should never make the mistake of believing them (Boswell 1965: 1235). Falstaff lives in an aristocratic society structured by codes of honor, but he can clearly see the harsh physical realities (he that died o' Wednesday) that honor sugar-coats. This clear perception, especially valuable on the foggy battlefield at Shrewsbury, is perhaps Falstaff's most admirable characteristic – and it is eminently Machiavellian.

Like Machiavelli's Prince, Falstaff's awareness of cant makes him a master of its use. What is the Gadshill robbery and its aftermath if not a lesson on the power of cant? When the Prince confronts Falstaff with evidence of his cowardice during the robbery, everyone present knows Falstaff is lying, and yet he is so shrewd a rhetorician that no one can hold him to it. Pretending that he fled only because he recognized Hal and "the lion will not touch the true prince" (*1 Henry IV*, 2.5.250), Falstaff gives Hal a master class in cynicism and political manipulation. Falstaff does not believe in reverence for the true prince, but when he pretends he does Hal cannot contradict him, because to do so would be to deny the very myth which keeps him in power. Here Hal learns from Falstaff the Machiavellian lesson that political power does not rest on the natural order, but on rhetoric and mythology. Hal knows this already in his first soliloquy in which he brags of his ability to "falsify men's hopes" (1.2.189), but his inability to counter Falstaff's lies about Gadshill shows that he has not yet learned how to put his Machiavellian theory into practice. Despite his temporary loss of face, however, he is a good pupil, and learns quickly.

Banishing Plump Jack

Though Hal's time with Falstaff gives him crucial lessons in political behavior, and although he has a certain fondness for his fat mentor, Hal has little compunction about casting Falstaff off when his usefulness has passed. Henry V's public rejection of Falstaff at the end of *2 Henry IV* is one of the most famous scenes in all drama – in part because it is unclear what we are to make of it. On one level, Henry's action is unsurprising – he has been hinting that he will cast off his low companions since his first appearance on stage in *1 Henry IV*. Moreover, it's clearly the "right" thing to do – Falstaff is corrupt and self-serving, and ought not be given the political power he craves.

Moreover, Henry's rejection of the wild companions of his youth was part of his legend, a legend which Shakespeare adapted, but did not invent. In *The Famous Victories of Henry the Fifth*, an anonymous contemporary play dealing with the same material, Henry turns on his companions in much the same way Shakespeare's Henry does on Falstaff:

> I prethee Ned, mend thy maners,
> And be more modester in thy tearmes . . .

> Ah Tom, your former life greeves me,
> And makes me to abandon & abolish your company for ever
> And therefore not upon pain of death to approach my presence
> By ten miles space; then if I hear well of you,
> It may be I will do somewhat for you,
> Otherwise looke for no more favour at my hands,
> Then at any other mans: And therefore be gone. (740–58)

As usual, Shakespeare takes his material to levels of complexity and emotional power undreamed of in his sources. For unlike the analogous characters banished in the *Famous Victories*, Falstaff is charming and funny, and we don't want to see him banished. To make matters worse, Henry's manner is unexpectedly harsh – much harsher than the corresponding passage from *Famous Victories*. Rather than expressing regret at the necessity of sending Falstaff away, Henry chastises him like a Puritan preacher:

> I know thee not, old man. Fall to thy prayers.
> How ill white hairs becomes a fool and jester!
> . . .
> Make less thy body hence, and more thy grace.
> Leave gourmandizing; know the grave doth gape
> For thee thrice wider than for other men.
> Reply not to me with a fool-born jest.
>   (*2 Henry IV*, 5.5.45–53)

The difference in tone is crucial. Not only is the speech much harsher than its counterpart in *Famous Victories*, it is much harsher than any previous speech of Henry to Falstaff. Henry has always complained of Falstaff, but never before from such a height of moral indignation.

The scene is so dramatically powerful because it plays on the difference between reality and theatre: in "real life" we would not want Falstaff to have the laws of England at his commandment; in the theatre we want him on any terms. From at least the time of *Richard III* Shakespeare was well aware that morally corrupt characters were often the most compelling. Of course, when it comes to moral corruption, Falstaff is not in the same league as Richard; Falstaff may be wicked, but as Dr. Johnson points out, he never kills anyone. As well, being old, fat, and desperate for attention, Falstaff is a potential object of sympathy in a way Richard could never be. If we hate seeing Falstaff rejected, it's because we have stopped laughing at him and started to pity him.

To a certain extent, our feelings about Falstaff will depend on our feelings about his protégé Henry V. Writing in the eighteenth century, Samuel Johnson finds nothing to complain of in Henry: in consorting with Falstaff "his sentiments are right, though his actions are wrong." In general, "he is great without effort and brave without tumult." Shakespeare does make a point of sometimes showing Henry in a less than flattering light: provoking a foreign war to distract attention from domestic troubles; hanging his old chum Bardolph for petty theft; and massacring his prisoners in a fit of rage.

Nonetheless, Shakespeare may well have intended Henry, with all his faults, to stand as a portrait of the ideal monarch: "the mirror of all Christian kings" (*Henry V*, 2.1.6).

Whether Henry is a good king is debatable, but since Johnson wrote in 1765 monarchy is not what it used to be. Many of us would not admire a good king even if we bumped into him joking with the louts at our local bar. As a young man choosing between dangerous fun and adult responsibility, Henry remains compelling. As a prince-in-training, his frustration with the burden of ceremony is unlikely to move many twenty-first-century readers deeply. We like Henry when he seems democratic – good old Hal hanging out with drunks, bartenders, whores, and thieves. We find him harder to take when he is what God and Shakespeare have destined him to be – a king. Henry remains a fascinating character, but if we no longer believe that our political leaders have been chosen for us by divine providence there will always be something alienating and even academic about Henry. And the further we get from early modern notions of the divine providence attendant on kings, the more harshly we are likely to judge Henry's rejection of Falstaff. God's anointed may have an obligation to tell "the old white-bearded Satan" to get behind him, but if we see Henry as a manipulative and skillful politician, we are less likely to approve.

It is not hard to *understand* why Falstaff should be rejected (of course vice is attractive). But though we may see the moral logic behind Henry's decision, it is hard to *feel* that he has done the right thing. Falstaff's rejection is powerful because it pits our judgment against our sympathy. As Johnson shrewdly recognized, the glory of Falstaff is to be bad and attractive at the same time.

No Respect

Falstaff's faults – his lying, his cowardice, his ill-treatment of the Hostess, his corrupt misuse of the powers granted him in wartime – ought not to be whitewashed in order to make him more admirable. Like Hal, Falstaff is a morally ambiguous character, and Shakespeare goes to great lengths to show us just how serious Falstaff's corruption is. He is not simply a loveable rogue who sweet-talks money out of less loveable rogues. When a rebellion erupts that threatens not only the peace of the kingdom but the life of his beloved Hal, Falstaff reacts first by raising an army of financially comfortable men who all pay him off to get out of military service. He then forces into service the sickest and poorest and weakest people he can find, and when battle comes, he leads them to a place where they are sure to be killed. It is even suggested that Falstaff profits financially from his men's deaths, for he leaves their names in the muster book so they will continue to draw pay (which he pockets) after their death (*2 Henry IV*, 3.2.125). Anyone who thinks Falstaff is loveable should watch the "recruiting" scene from Orson Welles's *Chimes at Midnight*, in which Welles delivers the repeated line "Prick him," with the same cool arrogance as Charles Foster Kane firing his only friend Jed Leland.

Not only does Falstaff have a pitiless disregard for the lives of the men he impresses, he also lets down his friend Hal, providing him with an army which is militarily useless. Shakespeare encourages us to laugh at Falstaff's abuse of power, especially during that recruiting scene in *2 Henry IV*. But just as he does not disguise Hal's occasional cruelty, he clearly shows the consequences of Falstaff's vicious opportunism. Taken together, Hal and Falstaff provide us with a searching exploration of the morality of charisma – our willingness to forgive the faults of those we admire.

Unlike many of Falstaff's admirers, Shakespeare himself is careful never to idealize or sentimentalize his fat knight. The mix of comedy and pathos which makes Falstaff so compelling is best summed up in the Hostess's famous description of his death:

> Nay, sure he's not in hell. He's in Arthur's bosom, if ever any man went to Arthur's bosom. A made a finer end, and went away an it had been any christom child. A parted ev'n just between twelve and one, ev'n at the turning of the tide. For after I saw him fumble with the sheets, and play with flowers, and smile upon his fingers end, I knew there was but one way. For his nose was as sharp as a pen, and a babbled of green fields. "How now, Sir John?" quoth I, "what man? Be o' good cheer." So 'a cried out, "God, God, God," three or four times. Now I, to comfort him, bid him a should not think of God; I hoped there was no need to trouble himself with any such thoughts yet. So a bade me lay more clothes on his feet. I put my hand into the bed and felt them, and they were cold as any stone. Then I felt to his knees, and so up'ard and up'ard, and all was cold as any stone. (*Henry V*, 2.3.11–23)

This remarkable passage is at once a vividly detailed description of a sick man's death, a meditation on mortality which equates a dying old man to a newborn child, and a bawdy joke. The pathos of the passage is there for all to see, and is only heightened by Mistress Quickly's malapropisms; ridiculous in other contexts, here her verbal confusion is deeply touching. A little less obvious to modern readers is the pun on "stone" – Elizabethan slang for "testicle." It tells us much about Shakespeare's attitude towards Falstaff that even on the sad occasion of the great man's death he cannot refrain from one last joke at the fat knight's expense. The final indignity for Falstaff is not Hal's rejection, but Mistress Quickly groping up his legs to see how cold his stones are. However much Shakespeare might have loved his greatest comic creation, he refuses, even at the end, to give him any respect.

This attitude is significant, for it contradicts a general trend in writing about Falstaff to take him very seriously indeed. There is, indeed, a marked tendency in critics to compare Falstaff to Hamlet, as if to give Plump Jack some *gravitas* by associating him with the melancholy Dane. The fact that no one would ever dream of doing the reverse, praising Hamlet on the grounds that he is as complex a creation as Falstaff, reveals a persistent cultural tendency to value the tragic over the comic, and a desire to "elevate" the comic by demonstrating its deep seriousness. Shakespeare, it seems, knew Falstaff better than that.

Parallels

Dr. Johnson says Falstaff is "unimitable," and in a way he's right. There is no other character quite like Falstaff. But that does not mean that he exists in a vacuum. He is the heir of several venerable dramatic traditions: the *miles gloriosus* or bragging soldier of classical comedy; the Vice of medieval morality plays; the fool and jester of Elizabethan entertainments. He may have no rival in Shakespeare, but he certainly has relatives – characters who are in some respects different from Falstaff, but fulfill many of the same dramatic functions. Falstaff's appeal may resist definition, but comparing him to these analogous figures lets us see more clearly the qualities that make him unique.

Harold Bloom (1998: 117) says that "only an idiot would compare" *Twelfth Night's* Toby Belch with Falstaff – one assumes he means "equate," but let it go. The defensive tone is enough of a giveaway: like Sir John, Sir Toby is a drunken, dissolute aristocrat who throws his weight around, gulls his companions of their money, and flirts with the middle-aged women who bring him sack. Unlike Falstaff, he never questions aristocratic values or codes of conduct. And he takes his own honor very seriously indeed.

There is also Parolles, the braggart and coward of *All's Well That End's Well*. Like Falstaff, Parolles corrupts the youth of good character who associate with him. And like Falstaff he is the object of an elaborate practical joke designed to reveal his cowardice. Like Falstaff, he is publicly shamed and rejected. And like Falstaff he is supremely resilient in defeat, proudly declaring: "simply the thing I am will make me live. Being fooled, by foolery thrive! There's place and means for every man alive" (4.3.336–42). But for most of the play Parolles has none of Falstaff's self-awareness; he is a fashion-monger and opportunist who is incapable of laughing at himself. Besides, Parolles is a young man, and has none of the pathos of age which is fundamental to Falstaff's appeal. Both Parolles and Sir Toby fall far short of Falstaff because they never question themselves. They mock the world but take themselves seriously.

Falstaff's wry self-awareness has led some critics to see him as a sort of Elizabethan Socrates – a "philosopher of Eastcheap" driven to question the received truths of his society, who is ultimately cast out and destroyed by the hypocritical state. Although Shakespeare's direct knowledge of Socrates from either Plato or Xenophon is likely to have been minimal, he would certainly have been aware of popular stories and notions regarding Socrates. He may also have been familiar with Montaigne's many references to Socrates in the *Essays*, though these were not published in English until 1603, several years after the Falstaff plays were written. Given his fondness for Plutarch, it is likely that Shakespeare's primary source on Socrates was Plutarch's *Life of Alcibiades* (Goodman 1985).

Like the comparison of Falstaff to Hamlet, one may suspect that the equation of Falstaff and Socrates is designed largely to give Plump Jack a dignity which he would otherwise lack. In many ways, of course, Falstaff and Socrates are utterly dissimilar – Falstaff wouldn't have much time for the idea of the good, nor would he be interested in designing an ideal republic or living a life of austere simplicity. For that matter, given that Hal ends up being the "star of England" (*Henry V*, Epilogue), *he* is a poor fit with the traitor Alcibiades. Falstaff resembles Socrates mostly as being a supposed corrupter of aristocratic youth – a charge he, like Socrates, indignantly denies. One well-known story about Socrates which Shakespeare passes up is that of his having a pisspot emptied on his head by his shrewish wife Xanthippe – a colorful possibility of revenge for either the Hostess or Mistress Ford.

Any possible analogy between Falstaff's rejection and Socrates' death sentence collapses when one tries to imagine Falstaff voluntarily drinking hemlock. But, oddly enough, Falstaff *was* modeled on a martyr: as the editors of the Oxford Shakespeare are keen to point out, in the earliest versions of *1 Henry IV*, Falstaff was not called Falstaff, but Oldcastle, as is the corresponding character in the *Famous Victories*. In their first scene together, Hal even calls him "my old lad of the castle" (*1 Henry IV*, 1.2.37). The reference is to the historical Sir John Oldcastle, a Lollard and a knight who served Henry IV in several campaigns, but was ultimately imprisoned and charged with heresy. Oldcastle escaped and attempted to lead an armed rebellion against Henry V, but was captured and executed in 1417. By the late sixteenth century Oldcastle had come to be seen by many in Shakespeare's England not as a rebel and a heretic, but as a proto-Protestant martyr, one of the Puritan "saints" celebrated in Foxe's *Acts and Monuments*.

The Epilogue to *2 Henry IV* protests that Falstaff is not Oldcastle, and it seems that Shakespeare was forced to change the character's name due to pressure from Oldcastle's descendants, in particular William Brook, Lord Cobham, who served as Lord Chamberlain in 1596–7 – very probably the period when *1 Henry IV* was first staged. As Lord Chamberlain, Cobham was in charge of the licensing of all plays, so he would have been in an excellent position to protect his ancestor's reputation.

Why did Shakespeare choose to portray a Protestant martyr as a dissolute and worldly knight? It has been remarked that much of Falstaff's speech, especially in *1 Henry IV*, draws ironically on biblical language, and he often echoes and parodies the tone and rhythms of a preacher. He makes frequent promises to "repent" (*1 Henry IV*, 3.3.3–9), and claims to have lost his voice "hallowing and singing of anthems" (*2 Henry IV*, 1.2.172). Kristen Poole (1995) convincingly relates Falstaff to contemporary stereotypes of dissolute Puritans – especially those generated in the satiric pamphlets associated with the Marprelate controversy of the early 1590s. Prior to the Restoration, negative views of Puritans were of two kinds: the first, still familiar to us, was the dour, preachy Malvolio. The other, odd to us, but common in England in Shakespeare's time, was to see Puritans as carnivalesque figures of riot, who used scripture to justify free love, lawlessness, and disrespect for established authority. As Oldcastle, Falstaff parodies the first of these stereotypes and embodies the second. When he speaks of his "vocation" – a term Puritans used to describe their call to godliness – he is referring to stealing (*1 Henry IV*, 1.2.92–3); when he speaks of inspiration, he is talking about sack and sherry. And as many commentators have pointed out, his seeming death and comic recovery on the field of Shrewsbury is a parody of the resurrection, in which he is "born again," just as dishonest and self-serving as ever.

Shakespeare's representation of an unruly Oldcastle may serve as an indication that by the 1590s a substantial portion of the population might have seen Oldcastle as a dangerous extremist rather than as a Puritan martyr. In any case, the fact that Falstaff was originally intended to be Oldcastle puts Hal's rejection of him in a new light. Audience members who knew their history would have not only expected Oldcastle to fall out with Henry V, but to lead a rebellion against him and to be executed by him. Although Henry hangs Bardolph for robbing a church, Falstaff gets off much more gently – and treason is never one of his faults. A character called Oldcastle might have been reasonably expected to be far more antagonistic. While we tend to see Henry's treatment of Falstaff as too harsh, the original audience might have expected much worse on both sides of the relationship.

Practical Concerns

It has often been remarked that Shakespeare's genius was not so much for inventing characters as for transforming them. Romeo, Juliet, Cleopatra, Hamlet, Othello, Macbeth – all of these existed in other versions before Shakespeare brilliantly re-defined them and adapted them to his uses. More than any other Shakespearean character, Falstaff is marked by the practical conditions of the theatre which created him. His appearance in *1 Henry IV* created a demand for the character which sustained two other plays – *2 Henry IV* which, despite some new thematic concerns, is structurally a repetitive sequel to the earlier play – and *The Merry Wives of Windsor*, a comedy which places Falstaff and his companions in a completely different generic context.

At the end of *2 Henry IV* an Epilogue, possibly spoken by the actor who played Falstaff, announces that "if you be not too much cloyed with fat meat, our humble author will continue the story with Sir John in it," but famously Shakespeare did not keep his promise: Falstaff does not appear in *Henry V*; instead, we hear that ludicrous yet touching account of his offstage death from Mistress Quickly. Many critics have speculated that Shakespeare changed his mind about introducing Falstaff into *Henry V* because the celebration of Henry's morally ambivalent heroism could not withstand the corrosion of Falstaff's acid wit. There is some justice to this reasoning, but Falstaff's absence may also have been provoked by a change in the personnel of Shakespeare's company: Will Kempe, in all likelihood the original Falstaff, may well have left the company between the production of *2 Henry IV* and *Henry V* (Dover Wilson 1961: 124). Despite Falstaff's vaunted universality, it may have been that staging Falstaff without Kempe would have been as unthinkable as making a sequel to *Casablanca* without Humphrey Bogart.

Perhaps it is the contingent nature of Falstaff, and Shakespeare's obvious concern to milk the character, that has provoked critics such as John Dover Wilson to insist repeatedly that there is a "real" Falstaff who appears only in *1 Henry IV*. The Falstaff of *2 Henry IV* is a less pleasant and more offensive variation; the Falstaff of *The Merry Wives* is an imposter, a "pseudo-Falstaff" (Dover Wilson 1961: 4–5; Bloom 1998: 315). Critics uncomfortable with the evidence of Shakespeare responding to the marketplace thus create an ideal Falstaff, untouched by commerce and vulgar popularity.

It is true that different sides of Falstaff's character come out in each of the plays in which he appears. In *1 Henry IV* Falstaff is most powerful and memorable, partly because he is so deeply woven into the texture of the play. He is given the perfect foil in Hotspur, who is a compelling character in his own right. Hotspur is young, rash, serious, passionate, noble, and ambitious. Falstaff is old, slow, comic, cynical, corrupt, and lazy. Hal, in different ways, is learning from both men, and Shakespeare stresses the relations between the three characters at the battle of Shrewsbury, where Hal stands momentarily between the dead body of Hotspur and the seemingly dead body of Falstaff, and eulogizes them both, recognizing that he is their heir as well as his father's (*1 Henry IV*, 5.4.95–109).

In *1 Henry IV* Falstaff is not only the opposite of Hotspur, he is also a parodic mirror of Hal's father King Henry, presiding over the misrule of Eastcheap as Henry presides over his rebellious and unruly kingdom. Falstaff's role as Hal's second father is most apparent when he and Hal take turns impersonating Henry in the common room of the Boar's Head tavern, a performance remarkable not only for the way it suggests the theatricality of political power but also because it marks one of Falstaff's few unselfish gestures (2.5.340–1). He plays the king to help Hal, so that his friend (and future patron?) will be able to turn aside his father's wrath when they meet. A foil to Hotspur and a parody of monarchy, Falstaff is not only the most entertaining and witty character in *1 Henry IV*, he is also the most resonant and thought-provoking.

Dover Wilson is right to note that Falstaff is represented differently in *2 Henry IV* than he is in part 1. In *2 Henry IV* Falstaff is almost entirely separated from Hal – which helps prepare audiences for his banishment at the end of the play. In part 1 Hal appears in every scene Falstaff does; in part 2 they share only one scene. Not only are the characters moving apart physically, they are also increasingly morally distant from each other. Falstaff's actions and motives in part 2 are more obviously self-serving. Unpleasant issues dealt with lightly in part 1, such as Falstaff's refusal to pay the Hostess and his manipulation of his military command for personal gain, are dwelt on at length in part 2. Falstaff's scenes and speeches in part 2 are modeled on those in the earlier play, and in each case a comparison of the two reveals how much Plump Jack is diminished. In part 1 Falstaff speaks cogently against the foolishness of killing and dying for the sake of honor. In part 2 he is reduced to praising drunkenness as a source of inspiration. In part 1 he is revealed as a clever liar after the Gadshill robbery; in part 2 he is revealed as an impotent old man in his encounter with Doll Tearsheet. Perhaps most importantly, in part 1 he is given his greatest moment – playing the king and shrewdly defending himself to Hal in an eloquent speech which is both tongue-in-cheek and deadly serious:

> If sack and sugar be a fault, God help the wicked. If to be old and merry be a sin, then many an old host that I know is damned. If to be fat be to be hated, then Pharaoh's lean kine are to be loved. No, my good lord, banish Peto, banish Bardolph, banish Poins, but for sweet Jack Falstaff, kind Jack Falstaff, true Jack Falstaff, valiant Jack Falstaff, and therefore more valiant being, as he is, old Jack Falstaff,
> Banish him not thy Harry's company,
> Banish him not thy Harry's company.
> Banish plump Jack, and banish all the world. (2.5.428–38)

There is no corresponding moment in part 2, only the moment when the new King Henry – now the Lord's anointed – banishes the world in pursuit of his divine destiny.

In *Merry Wives* Falstaff is somewhat less wicked than he is in *2 Henry IV*, but he is also much less shrewd than in *1 Henry IV.* His motives are purely monetary, and he is gulled repeatedly – not only is he tricked time and again by the Wives, he also fails to see through Ford's fairly transparent disguise as Master Brook. Though the *Merry Wives* has always been a popular play, many of Falstaff's more ardent worshippers dismiss it out of hand. Not Verdi, though, who used the play and its Falstaff as the basis for the crowning achievement of his career and one of the greatest of all comic operas.

The Perils of Popularity

It is clear that Falstaff was popular with Shakespeare's original audience – why else would Shakespeare have featured him in three plays, and promised his appearance in a fourth? He seems to have been popular with readers as well as spectators: the Quarto of *1 Henry IV*, the first play Falstaff appears in, was reprinted seven times before the appearance of the First Folio in 1623. And while there are few records of performance of Shakespeare's plays before the closing of the theatres in 1642, a commendatory verse by Leonard Digges, prefacing a 1640 collection of Shakespeare's poetry, asserts that Falstaff is one of Shakespeare's most popular characters (Munro 1932: I, 457).

After the reopening of the theatres in the 1660s, Falstaff's popularity continued unabated. *Merry Wives* and *1 Henry IV* were staged frequently in the early years of the Restoration, and have been performed steadily ever since. Falstaff's popularity in the Restoration extended to readers as well as spectators: he is featured prominently on the title-page illustration of a 1672 volume entitled *The Wits or Sport Upon Sport* – a collection of comic excerpts from popular plays dating back to the 1590s. *The Wits* opens by reprinting almost all of the Falstaff scenes from *1 Henry IV* under the title "The Bouncing Knight or, the Robbers Rob'd" (Kirkman 1672: sig. C1r). The *Henry IV* plays were never more popular than in the first half of the eighteenth century: in the period 1700–50 there were at least 220 London performances of part 1 and at least 80 of part 2 (Child 1946: xxxv). And Samuel Johnson (1973: 204) maintained that no plays of Shakespeare were more frequently read.

Falstaff became a figure of controversy only in the later eighteenth century. In his 1765 edition of Shakespeare, Johnson offered a perceptive reading of the character, but for Johnson there is nothing problematic about Falstaff: he is a contemptible figure, but one who is witty and self-aware enough to be entertaining rather than disgusting. Johnson admires Falstaff's high spirits, but contends that he is dangerous precisely because he is entertaining: "neither wit nor honesty should think themselves safe with such a companion when they see Henry seduced by Falstaff."

The process of rehabilitating Falstaff began with Maurice Morgann's 1777 *Essay on the Dramatic Character of Sir John Falstaff.* Morgann, a Welsh gentleman and sometime civil servant, was driven to literary criticism because he could not accept the common opinion that Falstaff was "an absolute coward." Morgann argues at length that Falstaff is a man of character and a great soldier. Whatever one thinks of his argument, Morgann's approach is significant on two counts. First, since Falstaff is celebrated and popular, Morgann assumes that he must be fundamentally good and admirable. Morgann is troubled that although "we all like *Old Jack* . . . by some strange perverse fate, we all abuse him, and deny him the possession of any one single good and respectable quality" (Morgann 1972: 10). How can we like such a contemptible man? Since Morgann cannot imagine that a reasonable spectator could be attracted by "deformity of character" it naturally follows that Falstaff's character must not really be deformed. One wonders what similar logic would do for Richard III – more deformed in every way than Falstaff – and also one of Shakespeare's most popular characters.

Second, though Morgann is aware that Falstaff is a literary creation which exists within a certain dramatic tradition, he also assumes that there is a "real" Falstaff, an ideal Falstaff who transcends his manifestations in print and on the stage. For Morgann, Falstaff is not so much a character to be interpreted, as a person to be vindicated:

> His ill habits, and the accidents of age and corpulence, are no part of his essential constitution; they come forward indeed on our eye, and solicit our notice, but they are second natures, not *first*; mere shadows, we pursue them in vain; *Falstaff* himself has a distinct and separate substance. (Ibid: 212)

It is amazing to think that Falstaff's fatness has, in some sense, nothing to do with him – especially since the plays themselves focus on it obsessively. Upon reading Morgann's essay, Johnson remarked, "Why sir, we shall have the man come forth again; and as he has proved Falstaff to be no coward, he may well prove Iago to be a very good character" (Boswell 1965: 1213 n.1).

Johnson's glib dismissal belies the enduring appeal of Morgann's argument. Falstaff arouses a bizarre passion among his defenders. John Dover Wilson's contention that "Falstaff has become a kind of god in the mythology of modern man" (Dover Wilson 1961: 128) seems ludicrously hyperbolic, and yet it is neither an exceptional view nor the most extreme claim made on the fat man's behalf. Criticize "plump Jack" and your membership in the human community is put in doubt. In his popular survey of Shakespeare's plays, Harold Bloom (1998) argues passionately that "when we are wholly human, and know ourselves, we become most like either Hamlet or Falstaff" (ibid: 745), and suggests several times that Falstaff ought to be worshipped as a god (ibid: 4, 306). As recently as 1989 a study appeared which seriously equated Falstaff not only with Silenus and Father Christmas, but also with Krishna, Merlin, and Loki, the Norse god of mischief (Marshall 1989). Falstaff is a wonderful character, but why is he being deified? No one in the plays dreams of seeing him in this worshipful manner. And is there any character in Shakespeare more devoted to the physical world and material pleasures?

A Natural Gentleman

It is odd that Shakespeare's most successful figure of misrule appeals most strongly to his most conservative readers – those who insist most forcefully that Shakespeare's work is universal and transcendent, the finest expression of a Christian humanism which lies at the heart of "Western" culture. How is it that these guardians of enduring values are so attracted by one of the most famous reprobates in literature? Perhaps it has to do with who Falstaff is: he is not just *anyone* living free of restrictions – he is a fat old man from the ruling class living free of restrictions. Falstaff appeals to cultural elitists partly because he is himself a member of the elite. He appeals to middle-aged male critics because he is a middle-aged male wit. His rebellion against convention has no whiff of revolution about it – he is asserting his right to live a life of complete selfishness, and makes no excuses about it.

And this is why the same critics who attribute superhuman powers of artistic judgment to Shakespeare cannot bear the thought that Falstaff appears not only in the *Henry IV* plays but also, in a different key, in *The Merry Wives of Windsor.* They may love the fat knight's antics in Eastcheap, but they are not so happy when Sir John is foiled by common townsfolk. They laugh when Falstaff abuses Mistress Quickly, but are outraged to see him outwitted by Mistress Page and Mistress Ford. Most of all, they cannot accept that wise philosophical Falstaff, who debunks honor and celebrates drunken energy, should be revealed in Merry Wives as a money-grubbing cad who tries (unsuccessfully!) to seduce other people's wives for profit.

Falstaff's class position is crucial to his character. As William Empson remarked: "Falstaff . . . is a picture of how badly you can behave, and still get away with it, if you are a gentleman – a mere common rogue would not have been nearly so funny" (Empson 1935: 102–9). And as Samuel Johnson noted disapprovingly, Falstaff's treatment of social inferiors is particularly predatory: "he is always ready to cheat the weak, and prey upon the poor" (Johnson 1973: 205). The image of him from the title page of *The Wits* shows him as a smug cavalier holding an enormous glass and cheerfully ignoring the entreaties of the distraught, half-crazed Hostess.

Mother Prat

Falstaff's social position – a corrupt knight rather than dissolute commoner – is also crucial to understanding his significance to Shakespeare's original audience. In the context of the 1590s, Falstaff embodies a particular cultural anxiety: the weakening of aristocratic English manhood in the face of foreign military threats (Moulton 2000: 70–9). It has often been pointed out that the vogue for English history plays corresponded almost exactly to the period of the war with Spain between 1588 and 1603. One of the things Shakespeare's histories are responding to is a concern about the ability of England to withstand a foreign war with a much stronger continental power. Can England put aside its civil quarrels and unite against external enemies? Is English manhood strong enough to defeat the foreign threat? *Henry V* provides a powerful answer in the affirmative, but that answer is not possible as long as Falstaff is on stage. Running around the Shrewsbury battlefield with a bottle of sack instead of a pistol may seem like good fooling to us, but at a time of national crisis such jokes are not necessarily funny. Plump Jack personifies all the vices that moralists worried were sapping the native vigor of English manhood: disrespect for authority, lack of piety, overindulgence in sensual pleasure, a propensity to equivocate on moral issues, and a tendency to mock old virtues. Falstaff puts a pillow on his head and parodies the king; he misuses his military authority for his own profit; instead of keeping the peace, he robs travelers on the highway (for fun!); he talks back publicly to the Lord Chief Justice; and he is actively attempting to corrupt the heir to the throne.

The perceived weakness of English manhood was often seen in terms of effeminacy – through indulgence in soft pleasures, English men were becoming unmanned. Effeminacy in early modern England was a complex and sometimes contradictory concept. There was no particular association of effeminacy with homosexual behavior; instead, men were thought to become effeminate by spending too much energy in sex with women, as well as giving too much attention to women or by indulging in "womanly" activities (Moulton 2000: 27–9). Much was made of courtiers who spent their time dancing and writing poetry rather than fencing and riding. In *1 Henry IV* we have a perfect confrontation between the manly and effeminate in Hotspur's story of the foppish courtier who came to the battlefield to demand his prisoners (1.3.28–69).

Thus, masculinity is another field in which Hotspur and Falstaff can be seen as complete opposites: Hotspur is so manly he prefers his horse to his wife, whereas Falstaff is constantly losing his horse and dislikes fighting. Falstaff's name says it all. Some critics nod knowingly as they point out the similarity between "Fall-staff" and "Shake-spear" (Bloom 1998: 273). Could Plump Jack be a self-portrait? Unlikely, and not least because of the opposing connotations of the two names: Fall-staff (or False-staff) suggests flaccidity and lack of virility, Shake-spear the opposite.

Effeminacy in early modern England was often understood physically as well as psychologically: womanly men would have womanly bodies. And Falstaff's body is repeatedly described in feminine terms. While the bodies of effeminate young men are said in the period to be soft and smooth, Falstaff's body is almost maternal in its swollen plenitude. W. H. Auden remarked that Falstaff resembles "a cross between a very young child and a pregnant mother" (Auden 2000: 111). Similarly, Valerie Traub (1992: 56–9) has explored the notion that Falstaff's stuffed and surfeited body is not only grotesque, but in some sense feminine and maternal. Imagery effeminizing Falstaff's body is particularly prevalent in *2 Henry IV*, in which he compares himself to "a sow that hath overwhelm'd all her litter but one" (1.2.11–12), and laments: "My womb, my womb, my womb undoes me" (4.3.18–22). In *1 Henry IV* he compares his sagging flesh to "an old lady's loose gown" (3.3.3). Traub (1992) goes on to argue that such images suggest that Falstaff is as much a surrogate mother as a father for Hal. (Note that Hal's actual mother is utterly absent from the plays – not staged and never once referred to.) But these oddly feminine qualities of Falstaff also point to his failure to live up to codes of aristocratic masculinity and military virtue. After his brawl with the significantly named Pistol in *2 Henry IV*, Mistress Quickly worries that Falstaff has been wounded, and voices her concern in terms which suggest both castration and the sexual penetration of Falstaff's body: "Are you not hurt i' th' groin?" she asks, "Methought he made a shrewd thrust at your belly" (2.4.187–8).

In the *Henry IV* plays femininity is almost entirely elided; there are few female characters, and all are in subordinate roles (Howard and Rackin 1997: 160–85). When feminine characters do appear, they are associated with military weakness – Hotspur worries that his wife will keep him from his horse (*1 Henry IV*, 2.4); Mortimer's Welsh bride keeps him in Wales and away from Shrewsbury (3.1.200–19); Doll Tearsheet and the Hostess prey on men, weakening them sexually and, it is suggested in the final scenes of *2 Henry IV*, even killing them (5.4). If Falstaff is feminine, it is in his grotesque denial of masculine virtue and vigor. When England needs its noblemen to be as fit and avid for combat as "greyhounds in the slips / Straining upon the start" (*Henry V*, 3.1.31–2), Falstaff is fat, lazy, and dangerously idle. One could not find a more effective image combining sloth, filthiness, selfishness, and horror of the feminine than the one Falstaff chooses for himself – a sow eating her own piglets. No wonder he is excluded from Hal's (and Shakespeare's) "band of brothers."

It is worth noting in this context that Falstaff's "boundless physical vitality" is not particularly sexual. As a figure of Vice and Misrule, he is vaguely associated with sexual misbehavior, and the Boar's Head tavern where he lives seems to double as a brothel. But although Mistress Quickly describes Falstaff (and most of the other male characters) with a series of unintended sexual *double entendres* (*2 Henry IV*, 2.1.12 etc.), no one in any of the plays finds him sexually attractive. Even in *Merry Wives*, where he plays the seducer, Falstaff is never sexually aggressive. It is clear that he is wooing Mistresses Ford and Page for their money, not their sexual favors (1.3.59–64).

Again it is useful to contrast him with Richard III – that other corrupt, yet attractive, Shakespearean grotesque. Richard, like Falstaff, is "not shaped for sportive tricks," and yet as his brutal scene with Lady Anne reveals, he is terrifyingly adept at seduction. Richard is in many ways an excessively masculine character, and while he has no shred of affection in him, he is more than willing to use sexual aggression as a means to power. There are some creepy parallels here with Falstaff's pupil Hal, who ends his career of conquest by sweet-talking a French princess. But nothing could be further from Falstaff than Richard's lean reptilian charm. If Richard is a parody of masculine aggression, then Falstaff is a parody of effeminate passivity. As his scene with Doll in *2 Henry IV* makes clear, Falstaff is impotence itself, and the punishments he suffers in *Merry Wives* are those generally meted out in early modern England to impotent men or unruly women: he is ducked in a stream, dressed as an old woman, beaten, and crowned with cuckold's horns.

Fashion

Critics often proclaim that Falstaff is immortal – that he responds to fundamental aspects of human nature, and thus will always appeal to the better sort of readers and theatregoers. In some sense, this seems true – after all, the role has been popular for 400 years. And yet on the occasions that I have taught *1 Henry IV* I have noticed that many of my students don't have a particularly strong response to Falstaff. Though engaged with the play and with Shakespeare in general, they don't get Falstaff. Or, rather, they don't get him like Harold Bloom says they should. Perhaps they aren't fully human . . . How could they resist Shakespeare's comic masterpiece? Bloom doubts that academics other than himself have sufficient breadth of experience to evaluate Falstaff (Bloom 1998: 281). Perhaps this is true, but college students tend to be fairly familiar with Falstaff's milieu: drinking, pub life, casual sex, and minor criminal activity are not alien to many young adults. Why don't they love Falstaff? Why aren't they, like Hal, looking for dissolute and manipulative old men to serve as surrogate fathers?

Well, for one thing, Falstaff is a poor fit with contemporary youth culture. Since the 1950s heyday of Elvis Presley, James Dean, and the young Brando, rebelliousness in Western popular culture has been firmly associated with youth. The last great Falstaff on film was Orson Welles, in a low-budget (but brilliant) production made in the mid-1960s – an odd contemporary of Bob Dylan's *Like a Rolling Stone* and Jimi Hendrix's *Are You Experienced.* Even at the height of Vietnam, Falstaff's drunken rejection of military honor failed to touch a nerve.

The recent boom in big-budget Shakespeare films started with Kenneth Branagh's *Henry V* (1989), which begins – as the play does – by getting rid of Falstaff so that we can focus on the energetic young king. The other Shakespeare projects that got funded in the 1990s almost all focused on young characters coming to terms in different ways with adult responsibilities and adult love: Hamlet, Romeo and Juliet, Beatrice and Benedick, Viola, Olivia, and Orsino. Even the blood and guts of *Richard III* and *Titus Andronicus* were more inspiring to filmmakers than Plump Jack. The witty and Academy Award-winning *Shakespeare in Love* (1998) drew on *Romeo and Juliet*, the sonnets, and *Twelfth Night* – Eastcheap was notable by its absence; there was no witty, cantankerous old man giving young Will helpful advice about Life. The exception that proves the rule was *My Own Private Idaho* (1991), a film starring Keanu Reeves and River Phoenix as slackers and gay prostitutes, which incorporated rewritten scenes from *1 Henry IV* into a modern storyline set in the grunge rock culture of the Pacific Northwest. There is a "Falstaff character" in the film, but he has little of Plump Jack's wit or charisma. He is a good deal younger than Falstaff, and has about as much in common with him as the Oldcastle character in *Famous Victories* does.

Scholarly attention in the last twenty years or so has also tended to focus on Hal at Falstaff's expense. Influential work by Stephen Greenblatt and other New Historicist critics has had relatively little to say about Plump Jack, concentrating instead on issues of kingship and public performance raised by Hal's transformation into Henry V. Despite Valerie Traub's work on the effeminacy of Falstaff's body, he has also been relatively neglected by the recent boom in gender studies. Attempts to reinterpret Falstaff and Hal's relationship as homoerotic (Goldberg 1992) run up against Falstaff's fundamental lack of sexual energy. And Falstaff's upper-class status and utter selfishness have ensured that Marxist critics searching Shakespeare for signs of social subversion have gone elsewhere – to Jack Cade in *2 Henry VI* rather than Jack Falstaff in *2 Henry IV.*

Shakespeare may be for all time, but Falstaff clearly does better at some times than others. Does the current lack of interest in Falstaff portend the end of Western

Culture? Probably not. It may suggest instead that any character broad enough to have truly universal appeal would also be bland and generalized – more Mickey Mouse than Plump Jack – and Falstaff is anything but bland. Falstaff's richness as a character comes directly from his historical specificity – his mock-Puritan rhetoric, his capons and bottles of sack, his immersion in the street slang of a city vanished four hundred years ago. Sack and sugar, his favorite drink, is not only long out of fashion, its very name is so unfamiliar that it requires a footnote.

Falstaff's philosophic weight – his championing of the flesh over the spirit, of the self over society, of pleasure over sacrifice – only gains from its serious engagement with a series of specific issues, such as the nature of divine rulership, which were of great interest to Shakespeare's audience but which have long since ceased to matter. If *we* value Falstaff's rejection of honor, his parody of monarchy, his disrespect for the Lord Chief Justice, it is because we apply these attitudes to a far different set of cultural circumstances than Shakespeare ever imagined. If that's not a living tradition, what is?

REFERENCES AND FURTHER READING

Auden, W. H. (2000). *Lectures on Shakespeare*, ed. A. Kirsch. Princeton, NJ: Princeton University Press.

Bailey, J. (1916). A Note on Falstaff. In I. Gollancz (ed.) *A Book of Homage to Shakespeare*. Oxford: Oxford University Press, 58–62.

Bloom, H. (1998). *Shakespeare: The Invention of the Human*. New York: Penguin Books.

Boswell, J. (1965) [1791]. *Life of Johnson*. New York: Oxford University Press.

Bradley, A. C. (1909). The Rejection of Falstaff. In *Oxford Lectures on Poetry*. London: Macmillan, 247–78.

Child, H. (1946). The Stage History of King Henry IV. In J. Dover Wilson (ed.) *The First Part of the History of Henry IV*. New York: Cambridge University Press.

Dover Wilson, J. (1961). *The Fortunes of Falstaff*. New York: Cambridge University Press.

Empson, W. (1935). *Some Versions of Pastoral*. London: Chatto and Windus.

——(1986). Falstaff. In D. B Pirie (ed.) *Essays on Shakespeare*. New York: Cambridge University Press, 29–78.

The Famous Victories of Henry the Fifth (1962). In G. Bullough (ed.) *Narrative and Dramatic Sources of Shakespeare*, Vol. 4. New York: Columbia University Press, 299–343.

Goldberg, J. (1992). Desiring Hal. In *Sodometries: Renaissance Texts, Modern Sexualities*. Stanford, CA: Stanford University Press, 145–75.

Goodman, A. (1985). Falstaff and Socrates. *English*, 34, 97–112.

Greenblatt, S. (1988). Invisible Bullets. In *Shakespearean Negotiations: The Circulation of Social Energy in Renaissance England*. Berkeley: University of California Press, 21–65.

Howard, J. and Rackin, P. (1997). *Engendering a Nation: A Feminist Account of Shakespeare's English Histories*. New York: Routledge.

Johnson, S. (1973) [1765]. Johnson on Shakespeare. In J. Wain (ed.) *Johnson as Critic*. Boston, MA: Routledge and Kegan Paul, 149–252.

Kirkman, F. (ed.) (1672). *The Wits, or Sport upon Sport*. London. (Wing W3220)

Marshall, R. (1989). *Falstaff: The Archetypal Myth*. Longmead, UK: Element Books.

Morgann, M. (1972) [1777]. An Essay on the Dramatic Character of Sir John Falstaff. In D. A. Fineman (ed.) *Shakespearean Criticism*. Oxford: Clarendon Press.

Moulton, I. F. (2000). *Before Pornography: Erotic Writing in Early Modern England*. New York: Oxford University Press.

Munro, J. (ed.) (1932). *The Shakespeare Allusion Book: A Collection of Allusions to Shakespeare from 1591 to 1700*, 2 vols. Oxford: Oxford University Press.

Poole K. (1995). Saints Alive! Falstaff, Martin Marprelate, and the Staging of Puritanism. *Shakespeare Quarterly*, 46, 1, 47–75.

Rackin, P. (1990). *Stages of History: Shakespeare's English Chronicles*. Ithaca, NY: Cornell University Press.

Traub, V. (1992). *Desire and Anxiety: Circulations of Sexuality in Shakespearean Drama*. New York: Routledge.

12

Wooing and Winning (Or Not): Film/Shakespeare/Comedy and the Syntax of Genre

Barbara Hodgdon

After Judi Dench's fairy-godmother-like Queen Elizabeth names Shakespeare the poet of true love, enabling him to join the Lord Admiral's Men, *Shakespeare in Love* (John Madden, 1998) ends by rhyming paired images – Will Shakespeare writing Viola's name and her first line in *Twelfth Night* on a blank page and Viola de Lesseps's solitary figure, walking on an expansive beach. Madden, however, had filmed an alternative ending in which Viola, meeting an Indian chief and his squaw, asks: "What country, friends, is this?", to which the chief replies: "This is America, lady." Apparently Madden had also wanted to have Manhattan's skyline rise (magically, digitally) in the distance, but only Viola's encounter with Native Americans survives (film's equivalent of foul papers?). As I write, not only does imagining the image-ghost of Manhattan's skyline (with the WTC Towers prominent) seem particularly resonant but, especially given the film's critical and commercial success, Madden's joke hints that America's cinematic marketplace has replaced the English Rose.

Shakespeare in Love offers a perfect example of fitting the public's desires to Hollywood's priorities, of finding a common ground where, as Rick Altman argues, the audience's ritual values coincide with Hollywood's ideological ones (Altman 1999: 207). Raising the bar for the phantom genre of Shakespeare films considerably, its success also depends on exploiting a tension between "authenticity" and accessibility, on its ability to appeal to multiple groups of spectators and to serve them diversely. Each of the films I want to consider – two *Midsummer Night's Dreams* (Adrian Noble, 1996; Michael Hoffman 1999), *Twelfth Night* (Trevor Nunn, 1996), *Love's Labour's Lost* (Kenneth Branagh, 2000), *10 Things I Hate About You* (Gil Junger, 1999), and (briefly) *The Merchant of Venice* (Nunn, 2001) – negotiates that tension between authenticity (or textual reverence) and accessibility somewhat differently and with differing degrees of success. No one set of mixing instructions governs them all; rather, they inhabit a spectrum ranging from filmed Shakespeares to Shakespeare films. What happens, I want to ask, to that already peculiarly flexible genre called Shakespearean comedy when it couples with cinema? What, if any, sorts of liaisons do these comedies make

with established or emergent film genres and how does such hybridization and cre-
olization energize viewers' pleasure?

Genre Games

A recent *New Yorker* cartoon bearing the tag line "I don't mind if it's Shakespearean
as long as it's not Shakespeare" neatly marks the differing force of a film that bears a
linear relation to an "original" and one which, placing "Shakespeare" in adjectival
relation to the substantive "film," travels toward cinema, currently the principal
means for conveying Shakespeare's cultural authority in a mass-mediated age.
Simplistically put, more Shakespeare means filmed theatre. Relying heavily on
medium or long shots and infrequent cuts, filmed Shakespeares tend to preserve the
integrity of action within a scene, reserving close-ups either to privilege a psychology of "character" and an actor's performance, as with Henry Goodman's extraordinary Shylock in Nunn's *Merchant*, or to confront and reveal what the playtext intuits
but half buries, as when the camera isolates the jeweler's balance sinking under the
yarmulke and tsitsith Shylock discards before leaving the courtroom. Less Shakespeare,
on the other hand, not only regularly plays fast and loose with textual–theatrical signs
(to the distress of purist critics, for whom Shakespeare remains a more potent signifier than film) but goes beyond narrative integrity to engage Shakespeare – and his
cultural authority – lightly, on a different level, Here, Shakespeare's image pasted
inside Mandella's school locker offers a perfect icon for his near-closeted status in *10
Things I Hate About You*: evoking the text-king, the film also escapes his residual
tyranny by situating itself in relation to several mass-media genres, among them the
TV sit-com (which shares a Shakespearean pleasure in the primacy of talk) and the
chick flick, viewing staples for the Leonardo DiCaprio-does-Romeo generation Baz
Luhrmann's *William Shakespeare's Romeo + Juliet* (1996) brought (sighing and weeping)
to the multiplex.

In playing the genre game, filmed Shakespeare or Shakespeare film may matter,
but what matters even more is how particular examples burr onto other film genres
and recycle their strategies. Borrowing its autumnal palette and emphasis on social
detail from Merchant–Ivory films, *Twelfth Night* crosses Nunn's neo-Brechtian materialist theatre practice with a nostalgia for "deep England," a lost world view.
Hoffman's *Dream* exhibits a similar nostalgia for a Victorian past (also the current
period of choice for stage Shakespeare, preserving a sense of historical distance while
also seeming vaguely familiar), though its Tuscan setting even more securely ties it
to Kenneth Branagh's *Much Ado About Nothing* and to the Branagh formula, what Janet
Maslin calls "pot-luck Shakespeare": "pick a travel agent's dream setting, cast attractive actors no matter what, give an outrageous costume party, and hope for the best"
(Maslin 1999: B1). Given their focus on women in love, *Twelfth Night* and Hoffman's
Dream – both called "feminist" by media critics – fall (almost but not quite) into the
category of women's films, differentiating them from *10 Things*, a teen film energized
by high-concept marketing. And in the era of made-for-TV film, Nunn's *Twelfth Night*

and Noble's *Dream* have aired on premium channels; Nunn's *Merchant* more recently, on PBS's Masterpiece Theatre.

Another way to play the genre game would be to situate these films along a spectrum from high to mass culture. But even here, what is high and what is mass culture changes: genres are not transhistorical (witness Northrop Frye's famous definitional drift away from traditional literary categories) but time-related, a point most obvious in Branagh's *Love's Labour's Lost*'s attempt to re-genrify Shakespeare's play by kidnapping 1930s Hollywood musicals – *Top Hat, Swing Time, Follow the Fleet*, and *Shall We Dance?* among them. As *Love's Labour's* also illustrates, cinematic literacy, the ability to recognize intertextual quotations as well as their transformations and transcodings, is necessary to activate a film's generic potential, even to admire what might be called Shakespearean spin, for after all, Shakespeare himself was the Great Recycler. Noble's *Dream*, for instance, not only cites *E.T.* and *The Wizard of Oz* but also latches onto a library of children's classics – *Alice's Adventures in Wonderland, Peter Pan, Mary Poppins*, and *The Lion, the Witch, and the Wardrobe* – rebranding his stage production for a wider audience. Hoffman's *Dream* casts a wider net, mixing Verdi, Bellini, and Gustave Moreau with memories of silent cinema's spectacle scenes and Max Reinhardt's 1935–6 *Dream* as well as constructing a fairyland café whose habitués (their make-up by Paul Engelen, who designed *Star Wars: The Phantom Menace*) recall those of that "wretched hive of scum and villainy," the Cantina at Tatooine's Mos Eisely Spaceport in George Lucas's *Star Wars*. Even *10 Things* poaches on other territories: Heath Ledger models Patrick Verona on Richard Burton's Petruchio, and his stadium serenade of Kat Stratford raids Astaire–Kelly routines (*10 Things* 2000: 8, 13).

What is true of all genres – that they look different to different audiences, serve diverse groups diversely, and represent a site of struggle and cooperation among multiple users – also applies to this group of comedies. Spectators with a vested interest who seek to be led back to a relatively stable object or origin – a phenomenon that occurs only with a culture's major building blocks, such as Shakespeare – may resist the kinds of generic hyphenations I have been describing. Thus, both filmed Shakespeares and Shakespeare films look one way to a spectator who reads only for a Shakespearean generic economy, but rather differently to a viewer who is less tied to its rules than to those of popular or mass-culture genres, where tastes and decisions take on other colorations and contours. Moreover, although genre once depended on *constituted* communities made up of spectators attuned to its syntactic elements and constitutive moments, now genre anchors *constellated* communities, brought together along generational lines. In a mass-mediated world, where presence has gone the way of Walter Benjamin's aura, genres serve as stand-ins for an *in praesentia* community, as a vehicle of lateral communication. Even in a media marketplace where Shakespeare has some currency, branding a film with his name does not ensure its box-office prowess; rather, what counts is its ability or inability to define and find an audience – and a genre – which together can form such a community (Altman 1999: 99, 189). To explore how this latest explosion of "Shakespearean" comedies recycles what Howard Hawks's *Bringing Up Baby* calls "the love impulse," counting on spectator memory to work their generic magic and searching for generational or cross-generational appeal, I turn now to particular films and to the distinctive consuming and consumable pleasures each puts on offer.

Little Boy Lost

Adrian Noble's *Dream*, made in association with British TV's Channel 4 and ostensibly conceived to extend the stage life of his 1994 Royal Shakespeare Company production, is haunted by a desire to recuperate the play's late nineteenth-century afterlife as a children's fairy tale. The film is situated within a web of borrowings, beginning with Noble's theatrical original, which raided Peter Brook's famous 1970 "white-box" production, substituting baggy trousers for Asian pajamas, translating Titania's scarlet ostrich-featherbed into a huge pink umbrella and the fairies' trapezes into green ones. Superimposing another layer of dreaming, Noble adds a silent chorus, a pajama-clad boy (Osheen Jones) who works to attract audiences of films such as *Home Alone*, with which it intersects tangentially (Burt 1998: 3), and *The Indian in the Cupboard* or *E.T.*, which it cites (twice), as the workmen bicycle to the forest and as Bottom and Titania (the boy in a side-car) motorcycle toward consummation, both journeys silhouetted against a huge digitized moon. But rather than opening out the theatrical performance, as many filmed Shakespeares do, Noble's *Dream* closes in the spacious, red-hued "blank page" which allowed its performers room and scope. Flattening out the highly stylized set, which appears overtly two-dimensional, the film registers equally stylized costumes – Theseus/Oberon's Oscar Wilde-like dressing gown and all the characters' fantastically feathered wigs – as artificial imports from another medium. Although individual performances – Desmond Barrit's monumental Bottom, Barry Lynch's sly, earthy Puck – survive the transfer, the film not only aches for its absent stage life but, because the boy dreamer also tropes an absence – that of a Barrie-esque nursery-world of antique fables and fairy toys – it seems caught between Brook's modernist "empty space" (the realm Herbert Blau (1982: 7) marks as "consciousness itself") and a disappeared Victorian past. Aptly characterized by one critic as "a wild children's party where clowns in garishly coloured costumes do their turns nonstop and shout their lines at top volume over the hubbub of the little ones" (*Evening Standard* 1996), this curiously postmodern cocktail, a Freudian-dreamer star-child at its center, offers an exaggerated case of how changeling boys cause critical (and cinematic) trouble.[1]

Against a star-studded black sky, the camera tracks across clouds, zooms down to a window and travels through it to pan around a nursery, picking up a toy theatre, a rocking horse, stuffed animals, and a clock saying "Happy Hours" before closing on a copy of Arthur Rackham's *A Midsummer Night's Dream* next to the boy's sleeping figure. But no (arguably) innocent Rackham-esque fairies come to life; instead, the boy witnesses a series of primal or pseudo-primal scenes: "Now, fair Hippolyta . . ." keys a close-up of him looking through a keyhole to see Alex Jennings's Theseus kiss Hippolyta (the gorgeously sexy Lindsay Duncan) and the lovers' dilemma; once they leave for the wood, he falls (like Alice) down the vortex of a rabbithole calling

"Mummy," popping up through a chimney pot to hear the workmen planning their play. Bottom takes him along to the forest where, seeing himself as a turbanned changeling boy enclosed in a bubble (borrowed from *The Wizard of Oz*), he puzzles at his alter-image. Conjuring up the fairies (doubled with the workmen and costumed to parody their real-life attire), he vies with Oberon for control of the figures in his toy theatre (itself an echo of Ron Daniels's 1982 RSC staging), levitates Hermia from sleep, and watches Titania and Bottom copulate in the umbrella, now become a boat skidding across the moonscape's glittery surface. As morning breaks, a fast track links him with Oberon and Puck, seated on door-pedestals which rise from the floor during the lovers' quarrel. Simply the most active dreamer in the forest, he pushes the moon into view for Titania and Oberon to gaze at and, after Bottom wakes, turns stage-manager, closing one door on the forest and opening another onto the final wedding banquet and the play, staged in the toy theatre, now grown huge.

Dreamer, voyeur, included spectator (similar to Young Lucius in Julie Taymor's *Titus*, itself recalling Jane Howells's BBC-TV *Titus Andronicus*), changeling boy, sur-rogate for Oberon, Puck, Bottom (and, arguably, Noble himself): the boy occupies such a dizzying array of subject positions that deciphering his appearances in this intertextual mélange takes precedence over narrative. Blurring the boundaries between real and fictional characters – and between the genres of childhood initia-tion, fairy tale, and comedy – his presence works to make dreaming coincide with rather than run parallel to the everyday court world. But does one more layer of imag-ining matter? Mary Ellen Lamb has explored how Shakespeare's *Dream* staged a con-frontation between a "low" popular culture of old wives' tales, folklore, and fairy tales and the "high" culture of the early modern schoolroom where, through instruction in classical learning, male children were weaned away from the childhood culture asso-ciated with women and socialized as masculine subjects (Lamb 2000). Not only do her insights pertain to reading the boy's presence in Noble's film, but they also align with Bruno Bettelheim's pseudo-Freudian trajectory, which entails the child relin-quishing infantile dependency on the mother in order to achieve an independent exis-tence (Bettelheim 1977). Noble's "happy ending," however, chooses other means of allaying and resolving separation anxiety.

Watching the play from a balcony, the boy applauds each performer, grows sad at Bottom's and Thisbe's deaths. After zooming in on a clock (as Theseus mentions the time), the film cuts to the boy, again calling "Mummy," and another cut links him briefly to Hippolyta before a sequence of quick shots, moving from stage to backstage spaces, details the play's layered ending. As Oberon mentions the blots of nature, the boy appears in close-up; lifting him up, Oberon gives him – dreamer, Indian boy, and Bottom, fused – to Titania. Then, following his epilogue, Puck leads the boy back onto the stage where, borne aloft by Bottom, he is passed to Theseus, who sets him down amid the entire cast, all posed for a curtain-call tableau. Given the boy's calls for "Mummy" (which result in various Daddys), one might expect an interpolated scene where, Bottom-like, he tries to explain his dream; instead, like Judy Garland's Dorothy, he finds himself surrounded with those he loves. Whereas Brook found in Shakespeare's play a "hidden dream of sex and love," Noble's film intuits another, more overtly sentimental secret: that the theatre company constitutes both family and home. If, at its finale, Noble's film seems, like many contemporary American films, to take undue trouble to reconstruct both, each is, as Salman Rushdie writes, "anywhere, and every-where, except the place from which we began" (Rushdie 1992: 57).

Getting to the Bottom of Love; or, A Man's Own Affair

"From the greatest storyteller of all time – a romantic comedy": this tag from the trailer for Hoffman's *Dream* tellingly marks its attempt to ride on *Shakespeare in Love*'s coattails by crossing Shakespeare with a popular film genre. Bowing to the current cultural rage for cinematic updates of Henry James, its Victorian milieu was shot in Montepulciano, Italy (James's favorite Tuscan town) by a director whose recent films include *One Fine Day* (a comedy romance) and *Restoration* (a period drama). For added luster, the film comes equipped with impeccable credits: production design by Luciana Arrighi, Oscar nominee for *Howard's End* and *Remains of the Day*; costumes by Gabriella Pescucci, Oscar winner for Martin Scorsese's *Age of Innocence*; its fairy kingdom built on the "Fellini Stage" at Rome's Cinecitta Studios. Emulating Branagh's avowedly commercial strategy of surrounding himself with media celebri-ties, its casting – Rupert Everett (Oberon), Calista Flockhart (Helena), Kevin Kline (Bottom), Michelle Pfeiffer (Titania), and Stanley Tucci (Puck) – not only shamelessly addresses a wide variety of spectators but also creates tensions between actors' known images and their roles. Perhaps most obvious with Pfeiffer, costumed as Everyman's (Pre-Raphaelite) fantasy, or with Everett's half-nude lounging Oberon, inviting both heterosexual and homoerotic gazes, the phenomenon peaks with Flockhart, whose TV Ally McBeal, caught between a pop-feminist careerism and her desire for Mr. Right, almost perfectly syncs up with Helena as well as with Hoffman's central trope, "Love makes fools of us all." Such combinations of star presence and character allow spec-tators to align themselves with screened identities, which brings them pleasure and pride. As Altman writes, "Thorsten Veblen was right about the Leisure Class. What he could not forsee was the extent to which we strive to join a class whose other members are only imagined" (Altman 1999: 193). Searching to find something for everyone, this *Dream* sells what it can, attempts to appeal to all markets – even, in a prerelease campaign, to middle- and high-school students, through materials circu-lated by Youth Media International Ltd. that invite them to engage with plot, char-acter, imagery, theme, Shakespeare's attitudes to love, and the differences between theatre and film, as well as offering teachers an opportunity to win a "Midsummer Trip to Hollywood," including a behind-the-scenes tour of 20th Century Fox Studios, and prizes (the *Brittanica* CD multimedia edition, soundtrack CDs, autographed posters) for their schools.

From its opening sequence – where servants prepare a sumptuous *al fresco* banquet in the Villa d'Este gardens, the camera lingering on painterly still-lifes of ripe fruits and gorgeous flowers – Hoffman's *Dream* stakes its appeal (Bottom-like) on the consumable pleasures associated with travelogue films. Overseeing the preparations,

Theseus (David Strathairn) plucks a white rose for Hippolyta (*Braveheart*'s Sophie Marceau) – like Hermia (Anna Friel), dressed to look like a John Singer Sargent portrait (Rothwell 2000: 51). Everything not only seems perfectly in place but perfectly placed to evoke the 1890s connection advertised in the first title card: "Necklines are high. Parents are rigid. Marriage is seldom a matter of love." But as Hippolyta reacts to Theseus' treatment of Hermia by slapping his cheek, leaving him wrong-footed, this *Dream* hints that its period milieu covers a sexual politics with one foot in Shakespeare and the other more firmly placed in the late twentieth century. Although the film remembers Hippolyta's gesture when, after waking the (nude) lovers, Theseus rides aside with Hippolyta and (silently) consults her before announcing that all couples will marry, that interpolated moment constitutes its only sign that women's voices might influence patriarchal prerogatives. Elsewhere – at least in its treatment of the young women's desires – Hoffman's film positions women along a good girl (Hermia)/bad girl (Helena) continuum that participates in a politics of feminist backlash endorsed by Shakespeare, who after all, saw to it that every "Jill" did find sexual bliss with her desired "Jack." The narrative requires it, and Hoffman makes good on it, most expressly in a fantasy ending that cuts between the paired lovers lying in romantically appointed beds, awed at the twinkling Tinker-bell lights which, like the digitized butterflies fluttering through the opening sequence, bless their unions.

Yet however much Hoffman details the lovers' adventures in a wood "lit like a Little League night game" (Winter 1999: 121) and populated by assorted nymphs, satyrs, centaurs, and Medusa-like figures (modeled on Etruscan deities), where a family of dwarves who steal from Theseus' kitchens supply Titania's fairies with an antique phonograph and Victor Red Seal Records (pool-toys which pump operatic arias into Titania's bower), and where Puck wobbles ("Look how I go . . .") from one frame to the next on Helena's bicycle, he is less interested in their dreams than in Bottom's. A grown-up clone of Noble's changeling boy, Kline's Bottom stands at the film's center, and his liaison with Titania, as Courtney Lehmann argues, transforms the film from "romantic comedy" into the more serious genre of "masculine romance manqué," in which sociosexual anxieties regarded as trivial in the feminized genre of romance are inflected with "the status, dignity and decorum of canonical drama" (Lehmann 2002). Indeed, the film's backstory raises questions about exactly whose bottom – the character's, Kline's, or Hoffman's – is being brought into play in this re-genrifying move. Speaking of Bottom as a dreamer, actor, and pretender who "clings to delusions of grandeur because he has no love in his life," Hoffman imagined a love story between him and Titania – desiring "to love simply, unconditionally, in a way the politics of her relationship with Oberon made impossible" – which would give his film an "emotional spine": their "struggle with love and pride, and their simple, if brief, discovery of each other, felt like a gift." Initially cast as Oberon, Kline at first rejected the idea of playing Bottom but then phoned Hoffman, having devised a way that he could play Oberon, Bottom, and Theseus. Writes Hoffman, "He'd already begun his work. He was Bottom volunteering to play Thisbe, the Lion, the Wall – everything" (Hoffman 1999: vii–viii).

Having set up the plot's opening moves, Hoffman focuses on his hero. To the strains of *La Treviata*'s *brindisi*, the camera pans a market square and discovers Bottom, dressed in a spanking white suit and straw bowler, seated at an outdoor café table – a wannabe bon vivant, looking remarkably (and intentionally) like Marcello Mastroianni. Tipping his hat, he exchanges admiring glances with several women, but as the camera picks up another woman stalking the square (her Italian phrases conveniently subtitled "Where's my husband? Where's that worthless dreamer?"), he shies away. After performing for his fellow-amateurs and the crowd, Bottom is publicly humiliated: red wine gets dumped on his pristine clothes, the women he'd flirted with laugh at him, and when he returns to his dark, barren rooms, his wife (that stalking figure) again appears, giving him a disgusted look that further deflates him. Borrowing Shakespeare's infamous shrew for perhaps fifteen seconds of film time, Hoffman traps Bottom's pseudo-Petruchio in a loveless marriage with Everyman's nightmare, the castrating bitch. The (impeccably Victorian) answer to this dilemma, of course, is as old as the profession Hoffman evokes by turning Titania's fairy bower into a bordello-like love nest: the Other Woman, embodied in a figure who, encompassing the age-old virgin/whore dichotomy, will give him not only what he needs but what he wants. Wives may be one thing, the film teaches, but male fantasy rules in Titania's roost, rewarding Bottom for his frustrating marriage by giving him a "wife" who exceeds his most potent dreams and staging him at the center of an interlude which wraps infantile desire together with moments of soft-porn erotic play, tying it all up with flowery bows – and with Pfeiffer's Titania, operating at high sexual voltage.

Following his transformation into an ass (Kline's donkey ears and furry cheeks permit him to remain "himself" rather than vanish behind an ass head, thus enhancing the possibility for spectators to share his sensual experiences), Bottom exchanges glances with his fantasy queen in a sequence of shots recalling his earlier gaze at the women in the square. Just before the pair have sex, Titania "takes Bottom's hairy hand [and] places it on her milk-white breast . . ."; embracing him, she suddenly "steps away and looks down . . . at Bottom's privates [laughing] with fascinated delight". . . . "Roll[ing] on top of her soft donkey love, [she] throws her head back in ecstasy . . . [and] moans" – not, rather obviously, the sexual neophyte Hoffman had imagined (Hoffman 1999: 59–60). Accompanying these erotic rites, *Casta Diva* ("chaste goddess") from Bellini's *Norma* further counterpoints and ironizes the moment. Like Titania, Norma is the high priestess of a forest cult of virgins; presumed to be a virgin herself, she has actually borne her lover two sons, and the revelation of her double life precipitates the opera's tragedy. Distinctly privileged, their right-royal fantasy is this *Dream*'s centerpiece, to which all returns and through which the rest gets filtered. Later, as Oberon watches this scenario replayed through insistently cut-in point-ofview shots which accentuate how Hoffman consistently shoots Pfeiffer's Titania as completely open to the fabled male gaze, he seems to get ideas of how he himself (Kate-like?) might learn from it. In this film, sexual pedagogy is everybody's business. And indeed, *Casta Diva* bleeds over from Titania's bower to underlay a high-angle shot of the royal fairy couple, "new in amity," processing into the distance before turning into twinkling lights.

As Bottom wakes, the camera moves in as the bower ratchets down, spilling him out; now dressed in his own clothes, he finds a tiny replica of Titania's feathery bower: inside it is a miniature of the golden crown she gave him, which he puts in his pocket. Later, after his triumph as Pyramus (nearly eclipsed by Flute's moving performance as Thisbe), after the three couples receive the fairies' blessings, and after the workmen, medals around their necks, celebrate their good fortunes, the film cuts to Puck, speaking his epilogue in the town square. His look up to a window keys a mid-shot of Bottom, holding the tiny fairy circlet: gazing out from his window, he sees a sky filled with twinkling lights, one especially bright – and then, they disappear. In close-up, Puck shrugs as the camera slowly pulls away from his solitary figure. Hoffman's script, however, gives Bottom an even more bathetic finale in which, as the Tinker-bell light assumes Titania's form, the pair "look at each other with great curiosity. She reaches out her hand and touches the windowpane. He opens it. Then, reaching for his hand, she takes the little fairy crown . . . and slips it onto his finger, like a wedding ring. She smiles a little sadly, fades, and is gone. Bottom is left smiling too. His eyes fill up with a strange kind of joy" (Hoffman 1999: 114). If these temptations to excess tip Hoffman's *Dream* toward suggesting that, while marriage is *supposedly* "Juno's crown," "true" weddings exist only in fantasy, that idea nonetheless inflects the film's closing moves. Cut in to Puck's epilogue, Bottom's tail piece, with its "magical" fantasy, lies beyond the aristocratic lovers' fairy blessings, which remain safely enclosed within its final sequence. That both the lovers and Bottom share a visitation of tumbling fairy lights works to pull their fantasies into alignment, but Bottom's return to his bleak marriage also suggests that only the few – and only aristocrats – live sexually fortunate lives. Recalling the legend of *Dream*'s original performance for a noble wedding, how might Hoffman's film read were it screened, say, at a contemporary bridal dinner?

Double Your Pleasure

Describing *Twelfth Night* as "a strange mixture of poignant romance, broad comedy and subtle melancholy," Nunn writes of his desire "to make the content of the play more real, less stylized, so that the extremes are seen in a real social context . . . We can't get off the hook by dismissing it as an improbable comedy." Although it is no surprise to hear that "Shakespeare seems to be playing with the attraction of woman in man and man in woman," Nunn's comments on mixed genre and on the social real – his trademark as a theatre director – offer a useful gloss on the "staging" of his film (*Screening* 1996: 1–2). Handsomely shot, this *Twelfth Night* shares the travelogue aura of Hoffman's *Dream*, but differs from it in that its combination of canonical text and quintessentially English landscape produce a version of "nation" not unlike that of heritage films such as *Remains of the Day* or Peter Greenaway's more stylized *The Draughtsman's Contract*; moreover, its emphasis on class hierarchy also recalls Masterpiece Theatre's much-beloved *Upstairs, Downstairs* (see Higson 1993). Framing its action in the interiors and gardens of a country house, the film's most obvious debt is to Chekhov's hermetic, hot-house worlds; given its intense visual detail, *mise-en-scène* becomes a supporting actor. Unlike Hoffman's *Dream*, Nunn's *Twelfth Night* knows precisely what it is – an up-market cultural product, its bid for a market-share resting securely on Shakespearean authenticity and on its distinguished cast of performers. Some – Helena Bonham Carter (Olivia), Nigel Hawthorne (Malvolio), and Ben Kingsley (Feste) – are familiar to art-house audiences: Bonham Carter from a series of heritage films as well as Zeffirelli's *Hamlet*, Hawthorne from *The Madness of King George III*, Kingsley most notably from *Gandhi*. Identified primarily as stage actors – Imogen Stubbs (Viola), Toby Stephens (Orsino), Mel Smith (Sir Toby), Richard E. Grant (Sir Andrew), Imelda Staunton (Maria), Nicholas Farrell (Antonio) – others (Stubbs in particular) are making cross-over appearances from theatre to film, another sign of how this *Twelfth Night*, despite its claims on a cinematic real, shadows its theatrical "original."

The film opens with a prologue that cues spectators to read sexual disguise as a parlor charade: costumed as veiled "oriental" houris, Viola and Sebastian perform "O Mistress Mine" for a shipboard audience, revealing their "real" gender (Sebastian plucks off Viola's moustache; she fails to remove his real one) just as storm and shipwreck threaten. In the aftermath, following Viola's attempt to drown herself, she hides from Orsino's soliders in a cemetery where, watching Olivia visit *her* brother's grave, she hears of Orsino. Explaining her physical and psychic vulnerability, this justifies her transformation into Cesario, seen through close-ups of body parts: a hand picks up scissors, locks of hair fall to the floor; unlacing her corset, she buttons up trousers, stuffing them with a sock, binds her breasts and does up her shirt; picking up the false moustache she had worn earlier, she swaggers off – a self-constructed "man" – towards a distant castle. If both sequences clarify, even over-narrate, plot elements that Shakespeare's play merely brushes in, winking at coherence and convention, the pains Nunn takes to establish Viola's sexual disguise as disguise exhibit considerable anxiety about keeping gender in place. Although the video jacket promotes the film as "Wittier than *The Birdcage* and more fun than *To Wong Foo*," given the riskier gender-bending of films such as *The Crying Game*, *M. Butterfly*, and *Orlando*, Nunn's overt efforts to link gender to appropriately sexed bodies seem both theatrically and cinematically tame, as though fearing to disturb the film's prevailing realism.[2]

Just as Branagh's *Much Ado* takes form as a cinematic love-letter to Emma Thompson's Beatrice, Nunn's film puts Imogen Stubbs's Viola center-stage, but with an important difference. For, although the camera repeatedly closes in on her gaze to reveal her point of view, that produces a near-melodramatic excess which, as in Chekhov, dramatizes her inability to speak directly. Simultaneously desiring subject and desired object (and thus a kind of double stand-in for Nunn himself), her Cesario/Viola often appears estranged from her role, generating the sense that she is "outside" the narrative, a late twentieth-century (Brechtian) performer. When, acting as Orsino's embassy, she first encounters an Olivia who not only more fully inhabits her part but whose "character" takes life from a candle-lit sitting-room-shrine that expresses her melancholic self-absorption, Stubbs's liminal status as observer rather than participant works to defuse any hints of gender transgression, muting the potential for homoerotic play. Although the film stages body-jokes and "put-on" male performances that threaten to expose her identity and her desire for Orsino – she starts away from a fencing instructor's hand on her breast, punches Orsino in fake cama-raderie as he puts an arm around her shoulders, sneaks a look at his nude body as she scrubs his back – only in the "patience on a monument" speech do Stubbs and "Viola" fuse, moving Orsino to look again. Reassuring spectators that the "right" bodies indeed will couple to ensure "happy ending," that moment also points forward to the film's final negotiation between Stubbs's dissembling "comedian" and "Viola": there, attired in a gorgeous ball gown, she joins the other couples in a gala dance that, turning her into an icon of perfect femininity, frames her figure between two "dress-up" occasions, the one a sham, the other "for real" (Hodgdon 2001).

Although Nunn's *Twelfth Night* may hesitate to flaunt gender-bending, it fully exploits film language: nearly every edit serves narrative coherence, and he keeps the film moving by following its characters' travels in tracking shots that take full advantage of location shooting and by cross-cutting in a way that not only clarifies the relations between plot and subplots but charges them with intensified significance. One sequence in particular illustrates the film's tonal complexity, its ability to convey the performance of painfully repressed desire that lies at its center. Built around the most haunting of *Twelfth Night*'s songs, "O Mistress Mine," the opening's signature, it serves tropes of "character" as well as community. It begins with a drunken Sir Toby and Sir Andrew crashing through a cold frame into the kitchen garden and then appearing in the kitchen where Feste and Maria join them. As they become more boisterous, the film cuts to a pince-nezed Malvolio, reading *Amour* in his rooms, and then to Orsino, asking Cesario/Viola, seated at the piano, for "that old and antique song." As she picks out the melody, it bleeds over a cut to the kitchen, where, at Sir Toby's request, Feste takes it up on his accordion; detailing the others' muted reactions in mid-shots, the film cuts to Olivia in bed ("O stay and hear, your true love's coming") and then to Cesario/Viola and Orsino, playing cards by candlelight. Back in the kitchen, as Feste sings "What is love? 'Tis not hereafter," the camera picks up Maria, listening intently, her gaze fixed on Sir Toby; then, Orsino's remark that "women are as roses" and Cesario/Viola's sad response, "To die, even when they to perfection grow," key a cut to Feste's "What's to come is still unsure." All those in the kitchen join Feste for the song's concluding lines, "In delay there lies no plenty . . . Youth's a stuff will not endure," and a high-angle shot briefly links them further before the inter-cutting quickens, picking out individuals, showing Sir Toby and Maria together and, in separate shots, Cesario/Viola and a smiling Orsino, then isolating (in turn) Sir Andrew, Feste, and Sir Toby. Following Malvolio's appearance and the plot to gull him, the film constructs a coda to this ensemble, a string quintet with three extra instruments. Posed at the foot of the staircase, Maria, Sir Toby, and Sir Andrew hesitate, not wanting the evening to end; finally, as Maria turns to leave, Sir Toby almost follows her up the stairs but instead bids her "Good night, Penthisilea," sniffs, and looks away ("She's . . . one that adores me"). As Andrew muses, "I was adored once too," the film cuts to Maria in mid-close-up, nearly in tears, and then to Viola: unbinding her breasts, she gazes at her reflection in the mirror and removes her moustache

("Disguise, I see thou art a wickedness . . . How will this fadge"); looking at her brother's photograph, her "As I am man . . . As I am woman" keys a cut-in shot of Olivia in bed ("What thriftless sighs shall poor Olivia breathe?"), and Viola blows out her candle.

Playing fast and loose with scenic integrity, the sequence functions as a "Definition of Love," a gift from the film to the play via a Chekhovian middle term that, taking "What's to come is still unsure" as its mantra, shows couples without coupling, expresses dilation and delay, desires that remain unspeakable in excess, even as it points towards the film's multiple endings. Like Hoffman's *Dream*, its closing sequences set up a contrast between the unfortunate and fortunate in shots that are the cinematic equivalent of theatrical exits: keyed by Feste's omniscient perspective and accompanied by his final verses, Sir Andrew drives off in a carriage, Sir Toby and Maria in another, Antonio and Malvolio walk through the gates in driving rain; then, having safely dismissed these outsiders, the film concludes with tableau-like shots of couples dancing out their world-without-end bargains. In voice-over (film's most powerful speaking position), the last verse of Feste's epilogue bleeds over to his figure, seated on a bluff overlooking the sea: speaking "And we'll strive to please you every day," he becomes the "whirligig of time," wheeling off down the sunset hillside, his laughter echoing in the wind. If that laugh seems expressly designed to cue cinema spectators' pleasure, Nunn's carefully composed finale also points back irrevocably towards the theatre to mark his film as a substitute for the Shakespearean (or Chekhovian) *Twelfth Night* he has never staged.

It's Show Time!

Harley Granville-Barker opens his 1926 preface to *Love's Labour's Lost* by remarking: "Here is a fashionable play; now, by three hundred years, out of fashion . . . It abounds in jokes for the elect . . . [and even] a year or two later the elect themselves might be hard put . . . to remember what the joke was" (Granville-Barker 1965: 1). Writing just as modernism had become an established aesthetic, Granville-Barker anticipates the collapse of historical signs, fashions, and styles into the "blank parody" now associated with postmodernism.[3] Moreover, his comments offer a trenchant gloss on Branagh's film of *Love's Labour's Lost*, his latest attempt to reinvent himself – and Shakespeare – as popular auteurs, this time by piggy-backing onto the Golden Age American musical. Initially, one could imagine that synchronizing *Love's Labour's* with musical comedy just might work: both, after all, are highly artificial; both are courtship-oriented; and neither makes a major investment in "character," relying instead on the patterned alternation, confrontation, and parallelism between male and female leads and/or groups. Yet, as with *New York, New York*, a pastiche of classical musicals and Scorsese's themes and obsessions filtered through a loose musical framework which – even with the star presences of Liza Minnelli and Robert De Niro – didn't sell, *Love's Labour's* met with box-office failure: notably, it is the only Branagh film lacking simultaneous publication of a screenplay.[4] Put simply, both time and timing were out of joint. In the 1930s, musical comedy was mass culture; now, however, the Fred Astaire–Ginger Rogers team as well as Gene Kelly have danced their way upwards. And since the musical is no longer "base, common and popular," *Love's Labour's* not only finds itself at odds with Branagh's self-proclaimed populist impulses,[5] but its combination of two high-culture genres limits its attempt to re-genrify Shakespeare (He sings! He dances!) and to make his play speak to contemporary audiences through nostalgic time-travel and the back-to-the-future lure of reanimating past conventions of generic syntax, style, and fashion.

Trademarked as "a romantic musical comedy," the film is prefaced with an image resembling posters for 1930s films and a series of stills identifying actor and role before opening onto the grainy black-and-white footage of "Navarre Cinétone News" (raiding newsreels via *Citizen Kane*) showing four bomber jackets labeled "Bad Boy" (Berowne), "The King", "Duke" (Dumaine), and "Lucky" (Longaville) to mark the men as war heroes who (according to Branagh's voice-over) have "cast off their military uniforms, while world events still allow, [to] devote themselves to a rigorous three years of study." In so locating its historical moment, the film also situates itself as an example of what Peter Donaldson calls media allegory – that is, by making media history a central part of the reworkings of the text, it recasts Shakespearean metatheatricality as cross-media critique (Donaldson 2002). Exactly how the conventions of musical comedy rub against Shakespeare is almost immediately apparent. As the King (Alessandro Nivola) requires his companions to sign their three-year oaths and Branagh's Berowne segues into the George Gershwin–Desmond Carter "I'd Rather Charleston," the juxtaposition of Gershwin's melodic line to Shakespeare's verse reveals just how *slow* iambic pentameter sounds in relation to the song's crisp lyrics. Despite the reliance of both Shakespeare's text (here, heavily cut: only about 70–75 percent remains) and song on stressed end rhymes, the pace of delivery as well as the pace of editing seem at odds, the one "in swing time," the other plodding beside it. Even the lovers' barbed exchanges sound limp when set beside Carter – or Cole Porter or Irving Berlin – and Patrick Doyle's overly insistent score, hyping the romantic mood between musical numbers, further leeches out any remaining tension.

That distinction also reveals just how hard the film has to work to integrate song-and-dance numbers into the narrative. In a musical, music is privileged beyond its usual means of signification as background score, entering into a process through which it comes to stand for personal and communal joy and, in particular, for the mythic values associated with coupling and courtship. By convention, the musical's style turns on a series of dissolves which exploit the interpenetration of different spaces, characters, images, and sounds. While *every* film does not make a direct link between this continuity and the coupling process, the musical clearly derives its model, as Altman writes, "from the interpenetration of space, pyschology, and name implied by the biological act of sexual intercourse and the social institution of marriage that consecrates it" (Altman 1987: 109). And in the musical, the verbal wit which substituted for sexual scenes denied representation by the Hays Office censors in, say, the genre of screwball comedy, gets displaced by dance: dance is symbolic love-making, and the couple who can dance together stay together. Here, however, two systems – verbal wit and dance – are doing double work, resulting in redundancy: double consumption; double play. When, for example, the lovesick Berowne's "And when love speaks, the voice of all the gods / Make heaven drowsy with the harmony" shifts to "Heaven, I'm in heaven . . . ," the opening line of Irving Berlin's "Cheek to Cheek," the song (a hymn to pleasure) then introduces a shot in which all the men (magically) float up to a planetarium-like ceiling adorned with golden orbs. This, in turn, leads into a further sequence where, in top hats and tails, the men dance with their chosen ladies in one of the film's many "big" numbers, most of which are captured in wide, shallow shots that string out all four couples across the width of the screen (Jays 2000: 54–5). As Altman argues, such excesses in the narrative system – "unmotivated events, rhythmic montage, highlighted parallelism, [and] overlong spectacle" – alert spectators to "the existence of a competing logic, a second voice," functioning as a kind of "explosion" which momentarily disturbs the film's equilibrium (Altman 1987: 345–6).

Just as Granville-Barker marks *Love's Labour's* as "abound[ing] in jokes for the elect," Branagh's film is obsessed with in-jokes, one-offs, and the details of its own stylish surfaces – the right cigarette lighters, martini glasses, café-table lamps, scarlet lipsticks, garden-party hats, golden bathing costumes (for the Esther Williams–Busby Berkeley-inspired rhythmic swimming sequence), and captivating gowns which make it look cut from the pages of a long-ago *Vogue*. From its studio-constructed autumnal Oxbridge milieu, in which the women's vibrantly color-coded costumes introduce technicolor punctuation marks and also serve to identify the paired couples, to the (obviously fake) moon floating in the sky as the Princess and her ladies go up the lazy river in very British punts (borrowed from Cambridge and hung about with "oriental" lanterns), the paper bag covering Jacquenetta's head, the girlish pajama party (the Princess clutching her teddy bear), the replay of old Woody Allen jokes (*Annie Hall's* cocaine sneeze), and the orchestra's white Harpo Marx wigs: no cliché has been forgotten, each "set of wit" gets visual punch. When Berowne calls love "as mad as Ajax" the camera picks up Ajax's bust, Cupid's arrow piercing his helmet; as Berowne continues – "it kills sheep" – the film cuts to a (stuffed) sheep keeling over. Seated at the bar, whiling away time before the ladies appear, the King flips olives into his mouth, *à la* Katharine Hepburn in *Bringing Up Baby*; Branagh's Berowne sports a neat moustache that makes him look remarkably like Laurence Olivier, with whom he was once so strongly identified; later, Alicia Silverstone's Princess imitates the scratchy squeaks of Jean Hagen's Lina Lamont in *Singin' in the Rain*; for Berlin's "Let's Face the Music and Dance" the usual aping of Hermes Pan routines gives way to Bob Fosse and *Cabaret* as masked men dressed in silken muscle shirts dance with Cyd Charisse-like partners amid swirling sexy-red smoke. As Costard, Nathan Lane produces a fake-flower bouquet and trails of colored scarves for the Princess; misdelivering the letter, he whips out a rubber chicken (the capon): vaudeville comic turns, birthday-party tricks hoary with age. Later, as master of ceremonies for "The Masque of the Seven Worthies," his rendition of Berlin's "There's No Business Like Show Business" seems, on the one hand, perfectly attuned to the moment – and to Branagh's desire to marry Shakespeare to the sheer pleasure of entertainment – and, on the other, oddly disjunctive, since the show itself never appears, except in fragments (billed as "Night of 1,000 Stars") on yet another Cinétone Newsreel. Timothy Spall's fantastically Daliesque Don Armado represents even more of a time-bound curiosity. Modeled on the campy European gigolos played by Erik Rhodes who pursued Ginger Rogers in *Top Hat* and *The Gay Divorcee* (O'Hogan 2000), his performance of Cole Porter's "I Get a Kick Out of You" in an outrageous Spanish accent is filmed as a kind of promotional video in which, costumed variously in a proper bowler, a dressing gown, as a Mafia don, and (finally) in a dueling rig, "character" gets folded into costume – and into presentational mode, the film's signature trope.

However much it inevitably results from the demands of keeping four couples, as well as other character-ensembles, simultaneously in focus, this presentational style not only pulls people into lines – the women in their punts, the couples taking places for a dance, the country people marching dutifully from left to right to get offscreen, making way for the next routine – but also, despite either the occasional use of a circling camera (one of Branagh's trademarks) or of reaction shots that bow to the dialogue, makes the seams between Shakespeare's narrative and the musical all too visible. Moreover, the primary convention on which the musical depends – the notion that *everyone* is a skilled dancer or musical performer – falls by the wayside for, with the exception of Adrian Lester's Dumaine, Branagh's amateur Fred and Gingers are far from accomplished. Although Branagh claims that he was "happy to accept – even encourage – a certain rawness in the singing and dancing provided it came from a very clear sense of who the people were" (Press book 2000, n.p.), as in Peter Bogdanovich's *All For Love*, the idea of singing in one's own voice and dancing one's own dances contributes in part to the film's failed box-office appeal. In a sense, *Love's Labour's* has, like many of Shakespeare's plays, a multiple textuality – in this case, the video print and the DVD version. In the print scanned for video, the line-up dance numbers drop the couples at either ends, which often means that Lester (the best dancer and the only black man) gets left out. Furthermore, the DVD contains not only a "featurette" of Branagh's cast hamming it up – in fifteen outtakes, fluffs, or missteps followed by moments of corpsing that function as a partial documentary of the making of *Love's Labour's* – but also four filmed scenes that ended up (mostly) on the cutting-room floor. Among these are two "shows": the Muscovite "masque," with the men (badly) disguised as "Russians," and the Masque of the Nine Worthies, perhaps the most notable omission, especially since, as with *Dream's Pyramus and Thisbe*, its showcase of amateur performances is anticipated throughout. Presumably, including it on DVD marks it both for the consumption of Shakespearean-users and to prove, or improve, Branagh's Shakespearean credentials, but leaving it out of release prints seems a wise choice, for as the camera captures individual moments of misperformance, they occur in an interruptive, jangled rhythm – one thing after another – that simultaneously goes against the grain of the film's *musical* performances (as well as its syntax of genre) and shows them up as equally amateur. Perhaps more significant, however, is that the Nine Worthies Masque and its (failed) attempt at creating an imagined community took up too much screen time – time that the film chooses to invest in re-genrifying the play's finale through the musical.

Famously, the closing moves of Shakespeare's play – from Marcade's arrival, bringing news of the Princess's father's death forward – deny comedy's final constitutive moment, delaying the possibility of triumphant coupling for a year: as Berowne remarks, "that's too long for a play." But not for Branagh's film, which chooses to inter-weave (and dramatize) the anti-generic signs of Shakespeare's play with the syntax of musical comedy. At once its most original and most derivative move, *Love's Labour's* negotiates its ending in various stages, and by articulating "history" through its sim-ulacra. As the couples part in moments reminiscent of *Brief Encounter*, the film inter-cuts their farewells, Gershwin's "They Can't Take That Away From Me" linking them together even as it privileges Berowne and Rosalind, the only pair allowed a linger-ing kiss. The song bleeds over into an airport departure where, the women wrapped in furs, the men in trenchcoats, the film takes spectators back to *Casablanca*'s famous ending, but since it appears simply as a kind of cinematic mirage, not only are the sexual energies of the citation somewhat diminished (four couples rather than a charged triangle), but its politics dissolve into a moment of cinema history. As a series of waves or glances from the airborne women in the plane's windows to the men below articu-late the couples' final farewells, the play's last words – "You that way, we this way" – appear as sky-writing, measuring the extent to which Shakespeare's language operates as a kind of ghostly vapor trail for this, the first of the film's several endings.

Having (almost) paid its Shakespearean debts, *Love's Labour's* then turns to its other generic obligations by (arguably) constructing something like the finale of the most famous anti-musical, *All That Jazz*, which concludes with unsuccessful open-heart surgery (articulated as a big production number) and fantasy sequences of death and dying – a musical which reveals comedy dying of self-inflicted wounds. Just as refer-encing *Casablanca* cues spectators to recall the events of World War II, the film con-tinues its nostalgic time-travel through media history by representing that war in a montage of scenarios shot (again) in grainy black-and-white newsreel footage – not incidentally, book-ending the narrative. Berowne appears in a field hospital, tending the wounded, gazing at Rosalind's photograph; Costard, suitcase of tricks in hand, is in the trenches; the Princess and her waiting women are led away to internment; the smiling King, Dumaine, and Longaville appear as fighter-pilots; Armado and Moth have been taken prisoner; Boyet becomes allied with the French resistance; and Nathaniel and Holofernia, attired in air-raid helmets, "Dig for Victory." Curiously enough – and especially given contemporary evocations of national "unity" – the sequence looks like overt media propaganda for Benedict Anderson's imagined com-munity. But what is also striking here is a blatant (all too Shakespearean?) gender and class stereotyping that marks the French as feminized, passive victims and shows the British male aristocrats engaged in heroic exploits, saving civilization for ensuing gen-erations.[6] Finally the couples, reunited on the occasion of VE Day, join a street cele-bration that now includes the entire cast; as they raise their glasses to toast one another, the black-and-white footage turns to color and, in voice-over, Branagh's Berowne marks the moment with "And when love speaks, the voice of all the gods / Make heaven drowsy with the harmony," driving home the Shakespearean message, endorsed by the musical's syntax, of mythic consummation, transcending time.

How might spectators translate these tropes into the genres' and the culture's master themes? That's certainly on offer here, though what becomes obvious is that, in this collision between genres, one doesn't serve the other all that well. For one thing, having *Love's Labour's* characters re-enter history not only seems strongly inappropriate to Shakespearean comedy but also to the musical, for the latter's premise is that plot is sufficient to overcome time; denying it altogether, it remains locked in an eternal realm, beyond history. Achieved through a collection of fantasy signifiers of history, Branagh's ending elides the losses of the war, circulates a feel-good fairy tale, resolves global politics through troubling the syntax of genres noted primarily for solving the culture's merry war with the institution of marriage. Tellingly, that ending does not cite what is perhaps the most famous image of VE Day to which it had access: the photograph of an American sailor kissing a girl in Times Square. What that absence reveals is that, in this distinct clash between a quintessentially English text and a quintessentially American genre, Branagh's "romantic musical comedy" is a form of squatting on another's, far from neutral, territory. Much like *Henry V's* MacMorris, *Love's Labour's* seems, at its close, poised to ask: "What ish my nation?" For, having used up the syntax of the musical to make an "American" film, Branagh then discards that identification and, by making history disappear into a series of ever-receding media referents, recolonizes as British both genre and nation.

Somewhat Shakespeare: *Shrew*-ing Around

"How Do I Loathe Thee? Let Me Count the Ways" and "Romeo, Oh Romeo, Get Out of My Face" read advertising tags for Gil Junger's *10 Things I Hate About You*, his entry into High-School Shakespeare, a genre driven in part by late twentieth-century teenage commodity culture. Marking the misanthropy of the film's heroine, Kat Stratford (Julia Stiles, teen-Shakespeare's poster girl),[7] both lines point to how the film uses (and uses up) Shakespeare. Borrowing *Shrew's* narrative trajectory, touching base with some obligatory scenes and character clues, the film indicates his presence through a (mostly) submerged chain of floating signifiers that occasionally rise to the surface, as when David Krumholtz (future MBA and Hortensio figure) gives Kat's friend Mandella a "Renaissance" prom dress and, costumed as Shakespeare, markets himself as the Bard of her obsessions. Working Shakespearean literacy into its sophisticated, hip script (by Karen McCullah Lutz and Kirsten Smith), *10 Things* draws its primary literacy from the TV sit-com: filmed in short takes, its fast pace depends, much like Nunn's *Twelfth Night*, on various modes from shtick and physical comedy to verbal wit and serious drama, offering a range of performative possibilities well suited to the "supposing" behaviors endemic to adolescents' domestic and sexual politics. Beginning with Junger himself, known primarily as a TV director, the film relies on such sit-com veterans as Joseph Gordon-Levitt (Cameron James, the Lucentio figure) and Larisa Oleynik (Bianca), already coupled on *3rd Rock From the Sun*, Michael Eckman (David Krumholtz), Allison Janney (Ms. Perky, the guidance counselor), Walter Stratford (Larry Miller), and Daryl "Chill" Mitchell (Mr. Morgan, the English teacher). Evoking the adage that if Shakespeare were alive today he'd be writing sit-coms, *10 Things* cannily exploits the cross-referencing familiar to TV audiences, where characters from one program appear on others, creating a dense textual network similar to the performative crossings available in repertory theatre's cross-casting strategies.

Shot at Tacoma's castle-like Stadium High School, the film imagines itself in Seattle, known for its music scene, which not only becomes a story point but also, given the strong juxtaposition between narrative and soundtrack, marks *10 Things* as a high-concept film – marketing features that can be accentuated and extended within its social appropriation (Press book 12, 14; Wyatt 1994: 39–44). Here, although soundtrack occasionally comments on image (as in *American Graffiti*), it more often leads the action by interpreting images, as in the film's opening. In a VW convert-ible, Bianca and her friends bop to the Barenaked Ladies' rendition of "One Week" (familiar from Mitsubishi commercials); beside them in a battered car, Kat turns up the volume on Joan Jett's chick-metal "Bad Reputation" ("I don't give a damn about my reputation" precisely fitting her feisty "shrew-ness"). As in *The Graduate*, songs are integrated directly into the narrative, providing character information as well as (here) enunciating the difference between Bianca and Kat. Moreover, by having vintage-rock songs from the late 1970s and 1980s "covered" by late 1990s indie-rock bands, the soundtrack creates a double verisimilitude that anchors the film to two periods, offering some spectators a nostalgic return to "the way they were" in high school, others an up-to-the-minute sound.[8] More significantly, the songs framing the film take Kat from Jett's "Bad Reputation" to "I want you to want me" (a Cheap Trick release covered by Letters to Cleo), voicing her metamorphosis from perfidious "shrew" to potential girlfriend.

Those critics who faulted *10 Things* as having "the artistic integrity of a Pop Tart" (Matthews 1999: 56) raise the perennial question of the relation between verbal lan-guage and cinematic performance: unless a film pays complete homage to Big Willy, Shakespeare's text (so the argument goes) loses performative force. Yet in expecting a more radical treatment of the play's taming trajectory, most also were caught in a double bind between "more Shakespeare" but "less *Shrew*." Choosing the latter route, *10 Things* re-genrifies the conventions of Shakespeare's comedy of remarriage (Cavell 1981) to suit the comedy of adolescent dating culture, reshaping *Shrew* to conform with obligatory highlights of the high-school genre's socialization scenarios detailing life in classroom and cafeteria, on the athletic field, at a drunken party (where Kat gets trashed, turning "normal" teen behavior into an anti-spectacle), and at the prom, which occupies a pivotal position, the occasion for a series of revelations and rever-sals. Like *Shrew*, *10 Things* turns on suitors getting access to Bianca by paying Patrick Verona (Heath Ledger, alias Petruchio) to date Kat, but differs from it by introduc-ing a "villain," teen-model Joey Donner (Andrew Keegan), obsessed with his self-image: a potential sexual threat to Bianca, he also is responsible for Kat's antipathy to men (she confides to Bianca that he deflowered her in ninth grade). Yet although the plot takes place "between men," since Kat is more of an obstacle to her sister than to the guys, the film amplifies the relation between the Stratford sisters, turning Kat into a substitute mother who, confronting Bianca's desire to conform, tells her: "You don't always have to be what they want you to be," and goes to both party and prom as much to permit Bianca to lead a "normal" life as to satisfy her own desires. Indeed, Bianca's metamorphosis – partially articulated in a riff on Lucentio's language lesson where Cameron helps her with French – parallels her sister's, taking her from Joey, who just wants sex, to Cameron, who wants to be her boyfriend: becoming *like* Kat, she knees Joey at the prom, avenging her sister.

Overall, adolescents not only run the show but have a more realistic and intelligent take on the tenuous truce between the sexes than the (largely impotent) adults, who inhabit a shadow-world fraught with fantasies and cultural anxieties (Zacherek 1999: 21). Mr. Chapin, the not-so-bright soccer coach, eyes Kat lustfully (she flashes her breasts at him, allowing Patrick to escape detention study-hall); Ms. Perky, Bianca's grown-up clone, writes romance novels on her laptop but needs Kat to supply a synonym for "pulsating member" ("tumescent"); Mr. Morgan counters Kat's objection to the "oppressive patriarchal values that dictate our education" by referring to his own race and class; and Kat and Bianca's father, a beleaguered obstetrician, requires Bianca to put on a pregnant belly before going out, warning her: "No drinking, kissing, body-piercing, tattoos, or ritual animal slaughter."

10 Things, however, focuses primarily on Kat and Patrick's story, using the pair to stage an exposé of teenage mores and peer pressures. As in Hoffman's *Dream*, Bianca and Kat serve the virgin/whore trope – Bianca, the "totally pure" virgin (and hence desirable) vs. Kat the "heinous bitch," within popular idiom, synonymous with feminist or femi-nazi (she listens to alternative punk and reads *The Bell Jar*) and with not being afraid to speak her mind (Mr. Morgan calls her "Miss-I-have-an-opinion-about-everything"). Playing light and easy with these connotations through witty, acerbic dialogue, the film also marks Patrick as an outsider, a new-boy-in-school with a rumored outlaw past. Although their eventual coupling – solidified late in the narrative by a paintball fight that evokes the Kate–Petruchio wooing scene's traditional farcical knockabout (borrowing from screwball comedy the notion that the couple who fight together belong together) – picks up *Shrew*'s discomfortable taming strategy by suggesting that Patrick brings out the best in Kat, it not only gentles *Shrew*'s more oppositional tactics but emphasizes that their relationship comes from a shared recognition that it's all right to go against the grain. As Patrick puts it, to Kat's surprise: "I say do what you want to do."

Like *Shrew*, *10 Things* end-loads its narrative with a spectacular speech – here, one set up not by Patrick but by Mr. Morgan, who assigns students the task of rewriting a Shakespearean sonnet which, as it turns out, does double duty. On the one hand, the usually surly Kat doesn't resist because rewriting Shakespeare is precisely what she – and the film – are about; on the other, her public classroom performance, as in Shakespeare's play, voices the film's ideological investment:

I hate the way you talk to me
And the way you cut your hair,
I hate the way you drive my car,

I hate it when you stare.
I hate your big dumb combat boots
And the way you read my mind.
I hate you so much it makes me sick,
It even makes me rhyme.
I hate the way you're always right,
I hate it when you lie.
I hate it when you make me laugh,
Even worse when you make me cry.
  I hate it when you're not around and the fact that you didn't call;
  But mostly I hate the way I don't hate you, not even close, not even a little bit,
    not even at all.

Focusing on the very features the film has privileged – talk, clothes, behaviors – Kat's sonnet considerably qualifies Kate's "submission," and Stiles's extraordinary stillness, her ability to register feeling with a subtle look or gesture, astonishes both the class and Patrick before, broken-hearted but still resistant, she rushes from the room. Just as Kate's speech is the perfect expression of *Shrew*'s marital prerogatives, *10 Things*, taking a cue from *Dead Poet's Society*, reads Shakespeare as the pedagogue of relationships, a mediatory voice (or anti-voice) capable of fashioning or refashioning the self – and, ultimately, the culture.

For what *10 Things* teaches is that something like "true friendship" sustains the dating process. If the film is not precisely a full-scale critique of bourgeois teen culture – wearing the right clothes, belonging to the right cliques – it is also not a critique of patriarchal ideology. Indeed, patriarchy turns out to be benevolent on several fronts: Kat's father reveals that he has sent Sarah Lawrence a check that will ensure her admission; Patrick presents her with a Fender Strat guitar, enabling her desire to reinvent herself by forming an angry-girl band. Tellingly, both moves turn on money exchanges, Patrick's gift on commodity culture. Although attracted to each other, their lives are not dominated by that attraction; Kat is free to go off to college and/or to play her music. And by affirming that individual freedom trumps "normal" teen culture, it's quintessentially American: in some sense, Kat and Patrick behave like Western gunslingers, standing alone and unafraid, defying conventions. Moreover, just as Shakespeare becomes a floating chain of signifiers, so does "romance," drifting away from the contexts of its production. Although that particular chain of signifiers may continue to serve patriarchal interests (how could it not?), it does so less because of any precise connection (thus avoiding the stigma of false consciousness) than because ideological structures always tend to affirm the status quo (Shumway 1995: 398–9). Significantly, *10 Things* neither talks down to its audience nor puts scare quotes around its romantic twists and turns, and perhaps that's its final "lesson," for at the close, as the camera leaves Kat and Patrick, booming up to a high-angle shot that integrates them into the bustling high-school community, the film ends by focusing on Letters to Cleo, playing atop the school's castle-like tower, to privilege the idea of *performance* which undergirds both Shakespeare's play and *10 Things*.[9] Significantly, too, leaving *Shrew* behind frees all of the film's couples from marriage promises, permitting an ambiguous ending consonant with the alternatives to social structures that the film has explored. Genre, one might say, makes all the difference.

Once More, From the Top

At this moment of global crisis, Americans have turned less to high culture (or Shakespeare) for images that will express themselves than to mass culture, to extra-theatrical events, real-world performances: the firemen raising the flag amid the ruins of the World Trade Center's towers, for example, evoked the photograph of six soldiers raising the flag on Iwo Jima's Mount Suribachi in February 1945 (Marling 2001: 1). Always disappearing before our eyes, cinema responds to a psychic need to rehearse for loss, invites us to reassess our relations to grief and mourning (Hodgdon 2002). Given recent events which remind us, as Philip Larkin (1964) writes, "What will survive of us is love," perhaps comedy's equivalent for Aristotle's tragic catharsis rests in a kind of mnemonics of delight, reperformances of joy. With that in mind, it seems fitting to replay some fragments from these comedies: Adrian Lester's limber body and liquid voice putting Gene Kelly moves on "I've Got a Crush on You" in *Love's Labour's*; or Heath Ledger's Patrick Verona in *10 Things*, mike in hand, serenading Kat with Frankie Valli's "Can't Take My Eyes Off Of You" from the stadium bleachers; Nigel Hawthorne's Malvolio reading trashy romances in his dressing gown or, in the letter scene, nuzzling between a nude statue's breasts; and Sam Rockwell's Thisbe who, sweeping off his wig to regender himself male as he laments Pyramus' death, brings to Hoffman's *Dream* "the brief homoerotic shimmer of the possibility that a man had feared the loss of his beloved Bottom" (Masten 2001: 8). Or, at the very end of Nunn's *Merchant*, Gabrielle Jordan's Jessica, remembering her father by repeating her part in a text they had previously shared, "A woman of valour who can find" (*Esheth Chail*),[10] lines traditionally spoken by husband and wife on Sabbath Eve: "She doeth him good and not evil / All the days of her life." Good deeds all, intimations of love for a naughty world.

NOTES

1 Thornton Burnett makes an intriguing, if somewhat strained, argument for reading the boy as a "floating phallus."
2 On the film's pull between theatre and cinematic realism, see McNab (1996), Osborne (forthcoming), and Burt (1998).
3 On postmodernism's defining features, see Jameson (1991).
4 See, for instance, Grant (2000) and *Daily Express* (2000).
5 As outlined in Branagh (1989).
6 See Wray (2002) for an intriguing reading of the film and its connections to Branagh's history as a "domestic auteur."
7 Stiles plays Ophelia in Michael Almereyda's *Hamlet* and Desi in Tim Blake Nelson's *O*.
8 My thanks to Elizabeth A. Deitchman for this information.

9 As do the out-takes appearing after the film's credits where, as on *Love's Labour's* DVD, a series of
   scenarios shows the cast playing alternative versions of their roles that bring to the surface the frank
   sexuality that high-school comedy excludes.
10 From Proverbs 31:10.

REFERENCES AND FURTHER READING

Altman, R. (1987). *The American Film Musical.* Bloomington: Indiana University Press.
——(1999). *Film/Genre.* London: British Film Institute.
Bettelheim, B. (1977). *The Uses of Enchantment: The Meaning and Importance of Fairy Tales.* New York:
   Random House.
Blau, H. (1982). *Take Up the Bodies.* Urbana: University of Illinois Press.
Branagh, K. (1989). *Beginnings.* New York: W. W. Norton.
Burt, R. (1998). *Unspeakable Shaxxxspeares: Queer Theory and American Kiddie Culture.* New York: St.
   Martin's Press.
Cavell, S. (1981). *Pursuits of Happiness.* Cambridge, MA: Harvard University Press.
Daily Express (2000). Ken's Labour's Lost on the Bard. 30 January, 39.
Donaldson, P. S. (2002). Cinema and the Kingdom of Death: Loncraine's *Richard III. Shakespeare Quarterly,*
   special issue on film.
Evening Standard (1996). A Party in Pyjamas. 28 November, n.p.
Grant, S. (2000). Video. *Sunday Times: Culture,* 27 August, 27.
Granville-Barker, H. (1965). *Prefaces to Shakespeare,* Vol. 4. Princeton, NJ: Princeton University Press.
Gristwood, S. (2000). What is this thing called *Love's Labour's Lost? Guardian,* 27 March, 12–13.
Higson, A. (1993). Re-presenting the National Past: Nostalgia and Pastiche in the Heritage Film. In
   L. Friedman (ed.) *British Cinema and Thatcherism.* London: University College London Press, 109–29.
Hodgdon, B. (2001). Shakespeare and Gender Disguise. In A. Leggatt (ed.) *The Cambridge Companion to
   Shakespeare's Comedies.* Cambridge: Cambridge University Press.
——(2002). Reincarnations. In P. Aebischer, N. Wheale, and E. J. Esche (eds.) *Re-(Con)Textualizing
   Shakespeare.* Forthcoming.
Hoffman, M. (1999). *William Shakespeare's A Midsummer Night's Dream.* New York: Harper Collins.
Jameson, F. (1991). *Postmodernism or, The Cultural Logic of Late Capitalism.* Durham, NC: Duke University
   Press.
Jays, D. (2000). Review of *Love's Labour's Lost. Sight and Sound,* April, 54–5.
Lamb, M. E. (2000). Taken by the Fairies: Fairy Practices and the Production of Popular Culture in *A
   Midsummer Night's Dream. Shakespeare Quarterly,* 51, 277–312.
Larkin, P. (1964). An Arundel Tomb. *The Whitsun Weddings.* London: Faber and Faber, 45–6.
Lehmann, C. (2002). Crouching Tiger, Hidden Agenda: How the Renaissance and Shakespeare are Taking
   the Rage Out of Feminism. *Shakespeare Quarterly,* special issue on film, Fall.
Love's Labour's Lost (2000). Press book. Miramax Films.
McNab, G. (1996). Review of *Twelfth Night. Sight and Sound,* November, 60.
Marling, K. A. (2001). Salve for a wounded people. *New York Times,* 14 October, section 2, 1, 29.
Maslin, J. (1999). A *"Dream"* of Foolish Mortals. *New York Times,* 14 May, B1, 24.
Masten, J. (2001). Authorship in Love. Unpublished Shakespeare Association of America seminar paper.
Matthews, P. (1999). Review of *10 Things I Hate About You. Sight and Sound,* July, 55–6.
O'Hogan, A. (2000). *Daily Telegraph,* 31 March, 27.
Osborne, L. E. (forthcoming). Cutting Up Characters in Trevor Nunn's *Twelfth Night.* In C. Lehmann
   and L. Starks (eds.) *Spectacular Shakespeare: Critical Theory and Popular Cinema.* New Jersey: Associated
   University Press.
Rothwell, K. S. (2000). Shakespeare Goes Digital. *Cineaste,* 25, 3, 51–2.
Rushdie, S. (1992). *The Wizard of Oz.* London: British Film Institute.

Screening Shakespeare: Twelfth Night (1996). London: Film Education.

Shumway, D. R. (1995). Screwball Comedies: Constructing Romance, Mystifying Marriage. In B. K. Grant (ed.) *Film Genre Reader II.* Austin: University of Texas Press, 381–401.

10 Things I Hate About You. (2000). Press book, Touchstone Pictures.

Thornton Burnett, M. (2000). Impressions of Fantasy: Adrian Noble's *A Midsummer Night's Dream.* In M. T. Burnett and R. Wray (eds.) *Shakespeare, Film, Fin de Siècle.* London: St. Martin's Press.

Winter, J. (1999). Review of *A Midsummer Night's Dream. Village Voice,* 44, issue 19, 121.

Wray, R. (2002). The Singing Shakespearean: Kenneth Branagh's *Love's Labour's Lost* and the Politics of Genre. In P. Aebischer, N. Wheale, and E. J. Esche (eds.) *Re-(Con)Textualizing Shakespeare.* Forthcoming.

Wyatt, J. (1994). *High Concept: Movies and Marketing in Hollywood.* Austin: University of Texas Press.

Zacherek, S. (1999). There's Something About Teenage Comedy. *Sight and Sound,* December, 20–2.

13

The Two Gentlemen of Verona

Jeffrey Masten

> The most fruitful method of studying the works of Shakespeare is that which views them in the chronological order of their production.
>
> Edward Dowden (1874)

How do we start, at the very beginning? How, that is, do we read what may be the first play Shakespeare wrote? This is one of the questions raised by *The Two Gentlemen of Verona*, now often considered the earliest of Shakespeare's plays, and printed as such in several influential complete-works editions, including the 1986 Oxford edition and the 1997 Norton edition on which it is based.[1] To ask this question is to contemplate where we begin with Shakespeare, how the terms in which we begin matter to the study not only of this early play, but of those that follow, and how we conceptualize the very idea of a writing career for a playwright in the theatre of Shakespeare's era.

I

"Love and a bit with a dog, that's what they like," says the theatrical manager Philip Henslowe in the recent film *Shakespeare in Love*, as he describes to a young William Shakespeare, in the midst of a performance of *The Two Gentlemen of Verona*, what Renaissance audiences desire to see in a play (Norman and Stoppard 1998: 18). No less formidable a critic than Queen Elizabeth I seems to agree with the mercenary Henslowe in the film: his comment is precipitated by Elizabeth commending *Two Gentlemen*'s player-dog ("Well played, Master Crab") and throwing him a sweetmeat: "*the dog wolfs it down. Everyone applauds*," reads the film's screenplay.

Though *Two Gentlemen* is only seen in brief snippets in *Shakespeare in Love* (it is background action and noise to what the film presents as the more pressing problem of Shakespeare's writing block), the film is nevertheless the strongest – and certainly the most widely circulated and viewed – recent construal of the place of this play in

Shakespeare's writing career. Indeed, perhaps precisely *because* the play only appears in the film's interstices, this framing of the play within a larger, romanticized narrative of Shakespeare's writing career is all the more powerful – hardly noticed by viewers on their way toward a compelling retelling of the writing of *Romeo and Juliet* and what the film presents as the beginning of Shakespeare's writing career in earnest. As such, the film replays and builds upon a familiar literary-critical narrative of Shakespeare's writing career and the place of *The Two Gentlemen of Verona* within it.

Nevertheless, given that the film posits a *new* beginning for Shakespeare's career – a beginning-again with *Romeo and Juliet* to replace the false start of *Two Gentlemen* – we should pause to notice what is at stake in this substitution and rewriting. *Shakespeare in Love* in effect portrays *Two Gentlemen* as the last of Shakespeare's plays to fail to register "the very truth and nature of love," to quote the terms of the queen's wager (Norman and Stoppard 1998: 95). Within the film's construal of the Shakespearean career, this truth is, instead, the accomplishment of *Romeo and Juliet*, and "the very truth and nature of love" becomes, through what the film portrays as the effect of that play in its first performance on stage, very carefully sutured to *heterosexual* love. The remainder of Shakespeare's career, in the seductive narrative that concludes the film, will become the playwright's attempt to repeat and reconstitute – to write back into being – that performance of *Romeo and Juliet*, a moment of ostensible authenticity in theatrical performance that had momentarily linked representation (the love between the characters Romeo and Juliet) and reality (the love between Lady Viola and Shakespeare, a woman acting with a man onstage).

Within this admittedly powerful and seductive scheme, *The Two Gentlemen* – as it is seen in glimpses and dismissed by Henslowe – comes by default to stand for the ostensibly unrealistic and artificial earlier plays. Unlike *Romeo and Juliet*, *Two Gentlemen* becomes in the film's retrospect the province of apparently unrealistic boy actors in women's roles (a conflict, as the film presents it, between what is represented on stage and *how* it is represented, by boys). Shakespeare's ostensible immaturity as a writer, pre-*Romeo*, is simultaneously linked in the film with the apparently immature representational practices of the Renaissance stage, which, the film implies, Shakespeare will ever-after attempt to write beyond or outside. "You will never age for me, nor fade, nor die," says the film's Shakespeare, bidding Viola farewell at film's end. "Write me well," she replies, and the film's new writing career resumes with *Twelfth Night* (Norman and Stoppard 1998: 153). Constructing a new history for the birth of realism in Renaissance drama and performance practice, the film leaves *Two Gentlemen* in the past, where it is understood to be both artificial and strangely mongrelized: "love and a bit with a dog" (ibid: 18). Henslowe's formulation leaves *The Two Gentlemen of Verona* almost in the shadow of bestiality.[2]

It is not my intention in this essay to question the idea that *The Two Gentlemen of Verona* is one of the first plays Shakespeare wrote – though it is probably worth noting with Gary Taylor, Stanley Wells, et al. (1997: 109) that "the play could belong to any year in the decade before [Francis] Meres mentioned it" in his 1598 listing of Shakespeare's early work. What I rather seek to examine – and what *Shakespeare in Love* provides convenient shorthand for – are, first, the critical categories that have attached themselves to *earliness* in reading Shakespeare's career and thus to this often ignored play. And, second, once we have noticed the ideological freight of those critical categories – the frames into which they put this play – I seek to return to the powerful career narrative outlined by *Shakespeare in Love* in order to see other possibilities. If the film promulgates two beginnings for Shakespeare's career (the false start of love and dogs, and the new beginning of "the very truth and nature of love"), we might instead, working against the powerful grain of this film and the criticism on which it is based, view the road not taken in this film and its presentation of Shakespeare's career. What happens, I will ultimately ask, when we view *Two Gentlemen* not as the degraded remnant of Shakespeare's immature, earliest writing practice, and read it, instead, as articulating a different frame for that career?

II

Our mindes have jumped so unitedly together, they have with so fervent an affection considered of each other, and with like affection so discovered and sounded, even to the very bottome of each others heart and entrails, that I did not only know his, as well as mine owne, but I would (verily) rather have trusted him concerning any matter of mine, than my selfe.

Montaigne, "Of Friendship" (1892)

What if the very truth and nature of love is located elsewhere – not, or not only, between a Romeo and a Juliet, but between, say, two male friends named Proteus and Valentine? "Cease to persuade, my loving Proteus," Valentine says, in the first line of *The Two Gentlemen of Verona*,[3] and the play thus begins in the midst of a conversation between the two "loving" friends of its title, with Proteus attempting to "persuade" Valentine to remain with him, rather than depart for the emperor's court. "Wilt thou be gone? Sweet Valentine, adieu," comes Proteus' reply (1.1.11). This opening dialogue places at center stage the relationship of the two friends, a relationship the play eventually gives a significant history of dialogue and *non*-separation; once arrived at court, Valentine describes the history of the friendship to the Duke: "I knew him as myself; for from our infancy / We have convers'd, and spent our hours together" (2.4.57–8). To *converse*, in sixteenth-century English, meant both to speak together (as it does now) but also to dwell together (*OED*; Masten 1997b: 358–60), and Valentine here thus gives to this friendship a history of sustained dialogue and intimate association. The audience's knowledge of the two gentlemen of the play's title is no different: the play, like the lives Valentine describes, has begun in mutual conversation; the friends have been speaking together, dwelling together on stage, from their first entrance – from line 1 and the play's infancy.

Valentine describes his friend within the familiar vocabulary of Renaissance friendship; for a Renaissance audience or reader, the words "I knew him as myself" would immediately associate this friendship with a long line of theorists of male friendship, stretching back to the classical authorities Aristotle and Cicero, and including

Renaissance writers like the French essayist Michel de Montaigne, and English fiction writers like Philip Sidney, Edmund Spenser, and John Lyly, among many others.[4] Montaigne, whose essay "De l'amitié" ("Of Friendship") circulated widely in French before being published in a popular, reprinted English translation beginning in 1603, wrote of male friends:

> In the amitie I speak of, [the friends] entermixe and confound themselves one in the other, with so universall a commixture, that they weare out, and can no more finde the seame that hath conjoyned them together. If a man urge me to tell wherefore I loved him, I feele it cannot be expressed, but by answering; Because it was he, because it was my selfe. (Montaigne 1892: 202)

Like many of the other contemporaries of Shakespeare who wrote of this love between friends, Montaigne relies upon friendship's classical heritage, citing Aristotle's definition:

> All things [are] by effect common betweene [friends]; wils, thoughts, judgements, goods, wives, children, honour, and life; and their mutuall agreement, being no other than *one soule in two bodies*, according to the fit definition of Aristotle, they can neither lend or give ought[5] to each other. (Ibid: 205; my emphasis)

This, then, is the dialogue, the conversation, in which Shakespeare's two gentlemen engage at the beginning of the play, a dialogue that can only loosely be labeled such, since, as Montaigne and Shakespeare both suggest, this is a duologue between two persons who are one – who already know each other as themselves: "they can neither lend or give aught to each other." Proteus suggests as much as when he imagines, in lines we have already begun to examine, the persistence of the pair's "mutual agreement," their commonality:

> Wilt thou be gone? Sweet Valentine, adieu;
> Think on thy Proteus, when thou (haply) seest
> Some noteworthy object in thy travel.
> Wish me partaker in thy happiness,
> When thou dost meet good hap; and in thy danger
> (If ever danger do environ thee)
> Commend thy grievance to my holy prayers,
> For I will be thy beadsman, Valentine. (1.1.11–18)

Though the play will complicate this formulation, Proteus here projects the men's hours spent together into a *future* of nonseparated separation, as the "partaker in [Valentine's happiness]" even during his travels. Not only does Proteus describe himself as Valentine's ("think on *thy* Proteus"), but, through repetition, Proteus' persistent "thy's" become, in effect, "ours." All things – including themselves, including self-possession – are in common between them.

Perhaps the most difficult challenge facing a modern reader or audience of *Two Gentlemen* is assimilating (or even *seeing*) the play's insistence, in its beginning and in its closing moments, on the intensity of mutual affection between adult male friends, a relation the play describes repeatedly as "love," the same word it uses to describe affection between men and women. At least since the early twentieth century, critics of the play have tended to confront this issue by denigrating the value the play places on male friendship. In his influential 1921 edition, Arthur Quiller-Couch treats the play as part of a medieval and Renaissance tradition that

> had a fashion with Friendship: a literary convention of refining, idealizing, exalting it out of all proportion, or at any rate above the proportion it bears, in our modern minds, either to love between man and woman or to parental love. (Quiller-Couch 1921: xv)

In the 1969 Arden edition, Clifford Leech sees the play as both mocking and participating sympathetically in what he terms "the Friendship Cult" (Leech 1969: lxxiv). In the critical terms these critic–editors use, we can see an attempt to undercut the importance of friendship in the play, by establishing it as an artificial "fashion" or "convention" – even to suggest that it exists at the extreme margin of Renaissance culture as a "cult." (In 1969 the word "cult" might have lent friendship a sense of either/both the primitive – an "early" formulation that Leech implies Anglo-American culture has now progressed beyond – or/and the delusional (*OED*).) But as the list of Renaissance writers cited above suggests, and as historians of sexuality have begun convincingly to demonstrate, friendship was neither a mere "fashion" or "convention" nor a cult, but at the very center of English social structure (Bray 1994). Or, more precisely, reading the conventions of friendship, in *Two Gentlemen* and elsewhere, helps us to see the ways in which it is *no more nor less* a "fashion" or "convention" than the conventions that describe and inscribe cross-sex courtship and marriage in this culture. Indeed, however inadvertently, Quiller-Couch's slight historical hesitation (Renaissance friendship is "out of all proportion, or at any rate *above the proportion it bears, in our modern minds*") may point readers of *Two Gentlemen* precisely toward a historical reevaluation of languages of affection. What *are* the proportions of kinds of love in *Two Gentlemen*? What is the very truth and nature of love in this play? This is a question the play takes up, and its apparent answer in the final scene, as we will see, is one of the reasons for modern critics' unease with the play.

I have emphasized the language of male–male affection in *Two Gentlemen* because I think it is possible for modern readers and audiences, trained to think of comedies as about cross-sex marriage, to glide over its intensities in reading and performance. But as I have also suggested, the play also portrays love between men and women, and Valentine's opening line gestures in both directions; "Cease to persuade, my *loving* Proteus" posits both a beloved friend Proteus and a Proteus who is loving a woman, Julia: "affection chains thy tender days / To the sweet glances of thy honour'd love," Valentine notes (1.1.3–4). Similarly, the "*sweet* glances" of Julia are echoed in Proteus' reply to his friend ("*Sweet* Valentine, adieu"), and in Valentine's similar address to his friend as he departs for court later in the scene: "*Sweet* Proteus, no; now let us take our leave" (1.1.56; my emphasis). "Parting is such sweet sorrow," say another pair of lovers, Romeo and Juliet (2.2.184),[6] and in *Two Gentlemen* the reverberations of the affectionate word "sweet" across same-sex *and* cross-sex pairs can serve to remind us, first, that we may need to recalibrate the categories of affection in Renaissance culture; second, that the language of affection moves frequently among and across these categories in this play; and third, that a character's engagement with these categories is often simultaneous, in a way that our modern reliance on the mutually exclusive categories of hetero- or homosexuality makes difficult to see. Montaigne too cites the multiplicity and simultaneity of Renaissance affections: "these two passions," he writes of "affection toward women" and male–male "amitie," "entred into me in knowledge one of another, but in comparison never" (Montaigne 1892: 199, 200).

With Montaigne, and with Quiller-Couch, we will necessarily return to this comparison/proportion in the play's ending, for in the interim *Two Gentlemen* places the demands of same-sex friendship in conflict with the demands of cross-sex courtship. It does so, however, precisely *through* the structuring rhetoric of male friendship and its emphasis on commonality, identicality, and interchangeability ("it was he . . . it was my selfe"). Taking this discourse as its starting point, the play asks: if two men are so alike, if all is common between them, will they not also desire the same woman? And in that sense, is the very truth and nature of cross-sex love the product of the identicalness and emulation inherent in friendly love?[7]

Proteus' two soliloquies in act 2 take up this very question, asking both where his desire for Valentine's beloved Silvia comes from, *and* discussing his two "passions"[8] (to use Montaigne's terms) in an identical vocabulary:

> Is it mine eye, or Valentinus' praise,
> Her true perfection, or my false transgression
> That makes me reasonless, to reason thus?
>
> . . .
>
> Methinks my zeal to Valentine is cold,
> And that I love him not as I was wont:
> O, but I love his lady too-too much,
> And that's the reason I love him so little. (2.4.192–202)

The speech shows Proteus unable fully to distinguish his own passions from Valentine's – thus showing his identicalness to Valentine again, as the repetition of "too-too" (also audible as "two-two") may emphasize. Simultaneously the speech puts Proteus' two "loves" in contention and turns on the currency of that word to describe both relationships. Even the word *zeal*, which to a modern audience or reader will seem a primarily religious term, relates the speech to the intensity of Proteus' language of love, since in this period zeal also meant "ardent love or affection; fervent devotion or attachment (to a person or thing)" (*OED*). (As Elizabeth Charlebois (2000) has shown, the etymologically similar *zeal* and *jealousy* are closely associated and not fully distinguished in Shakespeare's era, in a way that may remind us of Proteus as a zealous "beadsman" (= one who prays) for his friend in the opening dialogue.)

Here, in becoming like Valentine in his desire for Silvia, Proteus has lost his "zeal" or affection for his friend, and in his next solo speech he again compares his loves, in strikingly parallel formulations:

> To leave my Julia, shall I be forsworn;
> To love fair Silvia, shall I be forsworn;
> To wrong my friend, I shall be much forsworn.
> And ev'n that power which gave me first my oath
> Provokes me to this threefold perjury.
> Love bade me swear, and Love bids me forswear.
> O sweet-suggesting Love . . . (2.6.1–7)

The inversion of the syntax in the speech's third line (shall I/I shall) and the addition of an intensifier ("*much* forsworn") seems to privilege the bonds of friendship. (In the original printed text of the play the point is even more emphatic, since the First Folio places question marks after each of the first two lines, but not after the third (Shakespeare 1623: TLN 930–2).) Even as Proteus' speech continues to demonstrate the overlapping languages of love, it also puts pressure on the ideas of friendship we have seen outlined in Montaigne: "I cannot leave to love," Proteus says,

> and yet I do;
> But there I leave to love, where I should love.
> Julia I lose, and Valentine I lose;
> If I keep them, I needs must lose my self;
> If I lose them, thus find I by their loss:
> For Valentine, myself: for Julia, Silvia.
> I to myself am dearer than a friend . . . (2.6.17–23)

Proteus' speech relies upon but inverts the principles of Renaissance friendship. In making himself "dearer than a friend," Proteus double-crosses the friend who is supposed to be "as individuate as man from himself," to quote an English conduct-book description of friendship (Braithwait 1630: 293). Losing his friend, he claims to find himself: "I cannot now prove constant to myself, / Without some treachery us'd to Valentine" (31–2). Yet for all his revisions of friendship's language, Proteus nevertheless grounds his betrayal of his friend in the language of friendship; like the previous soliloquy, this one turns on the use of a single term in the languages of both kinds of love: "Valentine I'll hold an enemy, / Aiming at Silvia as a sweeter *friend*" (29–30; my emphasis). This line shows the way in which friendship and courtship – love between men and between men and women – are constantly merging into and substituting for one another in this play, and, though they would seem to be most at odds in Proteus' betrayal of Valentine for Silvia, even here they cannot be entirely differentiated. Abandoning Valentine ("Sweet Valentine, adieu"), Proteus chooses Silvia as a "sweeter friend" – and so becomes *more like Valentine*.

The culmination of this tension is this disturbing final scene – disturbing to modern audiences and readers because it stages the attempted rape of Silvia by Proteus, but further disturbing to twentieth-century critics for the way in which it resolves or concludes the tensions between Proteus' two loves. In a way to which we will return, this conclusion, further, disturbingly marks the effective end of Silvia's role and voice in the play, with implications that extend to other female characters (Julia, Lucetta). In this final scene, as Proteus attempts to rape Silvia, Valentine intervenes and vows never again to trust him, calling him a "ruffian" and a "common friend" (an oxymoron within the class-specific rhetoric of gentlemanly friendship) (5.4.60, 62). But when Proteus begs forgiveness, Valentine relents, pronouncing himself "satisfied" with Proteus' "repentance." And then, surprisingly, at least to modern eyes (that is, let us say, eyes like Quiller-Couch's that anticipate the correct proportion of marital to friendly love at least in our modern era), Valentine proceeds to give his beloved Silvia *back* to the repentant rapist from whom he has just saved her, in a couplet spoken to Proteus: "that my love may appear plain and free, / All that was mine in Silvia I give thee" (82–3).

Valentine's statement, I would suggest, has been shocking and disturbing to modern readers and audiences in part because it seems straightforwardly to value same-sex male bonds over cross-sex desire; the speech may be seen as the resumption of the disrupted conversation between men that begins the play, and seems to allow, in the play's ending, the folding of marriage into the context of male friendship – rather than, as we might now conventionally expect, vice versa. In this moment, in exchange for Proteus' "ransom" of "hearty sorrow" for his transgression, Valentine receives Proteus back as "honest," meaning both "trustworthy" and "chaste" (5.4.74–8). Further, in the doubly resonant syntax of his resonant couplet, Valentine seems both to give Proteus all that he owns in Silvia (that is, he gives Silvia *to* Proteus) *and* to transfer all his love for Silvia to Proteus: "that my love [to you, Proteus,] may appear plain and free, / All that [love that] was mine in Silvia I give thee."

To a modern audience accustomed to a sex/gender system that clearly designates cross-sex marriage as more important than same-sex friendship and furthermore sees same-sex and cross-sex affection as linked to mutually exclusive categories of identity, Valentine's valuation of his love of Proteus over his love of Silvia is unexpected, and has struck many critics and directors of the play as simply erroneous. ("Commentators have struggled to explain these lines away," Leech (1969: 116) summarizes, and numerous solutions to what has been viewed as the problem of these lines have been proposed: they have been reassigned to other characters, or emended, or taken as evidence that Shakespeare didn't write parts of the play, or didn't write these particular lines.) Quiller-Couch, faulting Valentine, wittily remarked of his forgiving couplet that "there are, by this time, *no* gentlemen in Verona" (Quiller-Couch 1921: xiv), and he attributed the lines to another "botch[ing]" playwright (or playwrights) who attempted to rewrite Shakespeare's original scene.

It is worth noting, however, that earlier in the scene the play seems to side with Valentine's assumptions about the value and relation of friendship and love, and, ironically, it is Proteus who articulates the position now taken by modern critics. As Proteus attempts first to woo Silvia and she labels him "counterfeit to thy true friend" (an untrue likeness of his second self), Proteus remarks: "In love, / Who respects friend?" (5.4.53–4). "All men but Proteus," says Silvia (54), who seems to speak here almost with the voice of Montaigne in a passage we noted earlier:

these two passions [are] entered into me in knowledge of one another, but in comparison never: the first [= friendship] flying a high, and keeping a proud pitch, disdainfully beholding the other [= affection for women] to passe her points farre under it. (Montaigne 1892: 200)

The play constructs in advance, then, through the privileged voice of Silvia, a world in which – for "all men," even, by the last lines of the play, Proteus – friendship seems elevated over marriage and, in the play's resolution, containing it.

Once Julia in boy's clothing has been rediscovered and reunited with Proteus, once Silvia has been reassigned once again to Valentine, the play concludes as it began, in a conversation between the two gentlemen (newly reinstated as "gentlemen" by the Duke). The play's last lines, spoken by Valentine to Proteus, only further emphasize the enclosure of marriage within friendship, as Valentine seems to emphasize the rejoining of the two friends as much as their marriages with Julia and Silvia: "our day of marriage," he says to his friend, "shall be yours, / One feast, one house, one mutual happiness" (5.4.170–1). Although the middle of the play had staged these as mutually exclusive alternatives that (nevertheless) employ the same affectionate vocabularies, in the play's concluding lines, gentlemanly friendship is restored *through* (not at the cost of) marriage to women. No longer "too-too" or "two-two," here the friends are repeatedly, mutually reunited – one marriage, if not one soul, in two bodies, all things in common between them, to quote Montaigne again: "wils, thoughts, judgements, goods, [and almost] wives . . ." "*One* feast, *one* house, *one mutual* happiness." Raising the question of just who is being coupled in these final lines, the play seems also massively to complicate any simply, modern heterosexual notion of "the very truth and nature of love."

III

In this brief reading of *Two Gentlemen* I have attempted to recontextualize, to bring back to visibility, the intensity of relations between men that frame it. We might think of this as a problem of cultural translation, in which the word "friend" – so seemingly clear and familiar to us as a word we still use today – is something of a "false friend," a word seemingly cognate between Shakespeare's English and our own, but which has been drained of much of its Renaissance meaning and power in the intervening centuries. This is to say, on the one hand, that such a reading of this play is not accomplished simply by restoring a sense of the interplay between the play, its historical contexts, and its intertexts; it is also a function of taking the glossing of the play (a matter usually relegated to editors of editions – the Bonds, Leechs, Quiller-Couchs) – into our own hands. For, as I have suggested, in this context (perhaps in *every* context), it is not only the difficult or obsolete words that require editorial commentary, but, perhaps even more urgently, the seemingly familiar words *friend, zeal, sweet, love, marriage* – even *one* in a world where two can be one. The modern, commonsense, only apparently transparent meanings of these words (a necessarily partial list) must be unseated and resituated, for each of these terms exists, in earlier English, within and across different networks of meaning and they imply potentially different social structures and relationships in this period.

Bringing male–male relationships in particular back to visibility, insisting that our reading of the play take account of and attempt to "translate" the intensity of their terms, requires care, however, since it is also crucial to notice the exclusions that these terms and relations entail. Like most contemporaneous descriptions of male friendship, for example, the play presents its negotiations of male relations almost entirely within a strictly upper-class context – these are two *gentle*men of Verona, not "common" friends – and the ending of the play emphasizes the reintegration of Proteus and Valentine into the circle of gentlemen at court, with the Duke explicitly reinstating Valentine's gentlemanly title: "Sir Valentine, / Thou art a gentleman, and well deriv'd, / Take thou thy Silvia, for thou hast deserv'd her" (5.4.143–5). Even the outlaws Valentine befriended in the forest turn out to be worthy of reintegration into gentlemanly society at play's end, "endu'd with worthy qualities . . . reformed, civil, full of good, / And fit for great employment" (5.4.151–5), where "great" denotes both value and social class. The language of equality and identicality in the discourse of friendship – what Montaigne calls "the perfect union and agreement, which we here require" – produces a structure that keeps cross-class relations at a distance.[9]

Further, we would not want to fail to register the misogyny that accompanies the privileging of male friendship in this culture – explicitly in Montaigne, who bars women from friendship with men, saying that they lack the "conference and communication" required of male friendship, defined as a relationship of equals (Montaigne 1892: 200), and who doesn't even contemplate the possibility of female–female friendship.[10] This exclusion takes a more muted form in the play, but, significantly, the play presents the attempted rape as Proteus' transgression against Valentine, not Silvia, and Silvia speaks no lines thereafter, seemingly becoming a voiceless piece of particularly mobile property: "Take thou thy Silvia." This is to say: a reading that restores a more fully contextualized history of sexuality to the play – a history, in this case, of male–male affect that exists simultaneously with and "above" male–female marriage – will not necessarily also present liberatory potential for women characters.

At the same time, the play does present at least two potential avenues of resistance and critique to the privileged model of male friendship I have outlined. First, Proteus' clownish servant Launce's comic monologues (dialogues?) with his dog Crab take up and parodically rewrite both male–female relations in the play *and* the idea of the male friend as an indistinguishable second-self, particularly in act 2.3: "I am the dog. No, the dog is himself, and I am the dog. O, the dog is me, and I am myself. Ay; so, so" (2.3.21–3). The comedy of the speech either suggests that persons really *are* differentiatable, whatever Montaigne might say, and Launce should be able to distinguish himself from a cross-breed dog; or, more subversively (and possibly at the same time), it illustrates the way in which the discourse of friendship is potentially *mobile* in this culture, able to be transmitted, however accidentally, from master to servant and deployed in a new way that here mixes up species. (While deeply attentive to differences among categories, Launce's monologue is a complicated mixing, and mixing up, of kinds and species: mother, father, sister, cat, Jew, stone, shoe, hat, maid, man, dog.)

A second lens for resisting and critiquing male friendship is offered, somewhat ambivalently, through the role of Julia, who spends part of the play dressed as the young man Sebastian. On the one hand, if the rape–repentance–forgiveness scene is the mechanism by which Proteus offends against his friend and then is reunited with him, the character Julia provides, alternatively, an onstage observer who comments on the falseness of Proteus' actions in relation not only to Valentine but also to herself. Dressed as a male page, she observes and glosses the scene as Proteus serenades Silvia: "He plays false . . . so false that he grieves my very heart-strings" (4.2.57–60).[11] This moment (like all moments involving boy actors playing women characters playing young men on the Renaissance stage) is a complex one; the play here offers up for its audience an *onstage* audience to Proteus' performance, a figure who, because dressed as and referred to as a young "man" (4.2.54), but also understood to be a woman, gives the audience several identificatory positions from which to view Proteus' multiple falsehoods. (That is, the play stages the figure of both a young man and a woman whose heart-strings "grieve.") Further, it is Julia/Sebastian who, in the last scene of the play, reroutes Proteus' desires after Valentine forgives him and gives him Silvia. Julia's presentation of the "wrong" ring at this climactic moment has the effect of discovering the Julia-identity in the Sebastian clothes (5.4.90–9); and makes it possible that, with the friends already reunited, the women of the play will also get *their* desires in marriage.

I call the resistance the figure of Julia provides "ambivalent," however, because, at the same time that she manipulates the play's ending via the ring plot to bring the lovers back together within the bounds of friendship, the fact that she remains in men's clothes through the end of the play also has effects that may return it to a predominantly male focus. Valentine brings Proteus and Julia ceremonially together after the moment of her discovery:

> Come, come; a hand from either;
> Let me be blest to make this happy close:
> 'Twere pity two such friends should be long foes. (5.4.115–17)

The play here stages a version of the traditional marriage ceremony (complete with the priest Valentine's coupling couplet and Proteus and Julia each effectively responding "I do" in reply (5.4.118–19)). But Valentine's phrase "two such friends" here (with Julia, again, still dressed as Sebastian) may visually and rhetorically have produced for its Renaissance audience *another* kind of ceremony, a friendship-ritual historian Alan Bray (2003) has uncovered, performed at the threshold of the church and called the "handfast." This ceremony joined two men in mutual friendship; its chief visual symbol was two joined hands.[12] Iconographically and rhetorically, the play thus again raises the question of what it couples in its endings.

The difficulty of reading Julia's resistance is further elaborated in the conversation between the Duke, Valentine, and Proteus in the play's final lines, as the play places

Julia (once again as Sebastian) within yet another configuration of Renaissance affection (that of adult men for younger men). With the Duke unaware of Julia's gender and identity – already known to the audience and previously disclosed to most of the characters – Valentine seemingly offers "Sebastian" up to the Duke (and thus to the play's audience) as an object of this other kind of male–male admiration: "What think you of this page, my lord?"

> *Duke.* I think the boy hath grace in him, he blushes.
> *Val.* I warrant you, my lord, more grace than boy.
> *Duke.* What mean you by that saying? (5.4.163–5)

This moment of gazing at Sebastian recalls Proteus' earlier command to "Look to the boy" at the moment of his/her swoon (5.4.84), and, though promised, the answer to the Duke's question is deferred beyond the end of the play, leaving an audience, too, perhaps to wonder at the meaning of this "saying" (if not boy, is this figure a man? a woman?) and at the meaning of a character who is made to wear the resonantly homoerotic name of St. Sebastian alongside her own through the end of the play.[13] The very truth and nature of love in this play – and the "One feast, one house, one mutual happiness" in which it concludes – may thus, in this simultaneously ceremonial and deferred end, be trebly complicated.

IV

Now, what does extraordinary growth imply?

Edward Dowden (1874)

In its depiction of *The Two Gentlemen of Verona*, *Shakespeare in Love*, I have suggested, builds upon earlier critical construals of Shakespeare's early writing, its value, and its place in the canon. As Margreta de Grazia (1991) has shown, this mode of examining Shakespeare's career, the authorial–developmental model, begins in the eighteenth century with Edmond Malone, but owes much to the late nineteenth-century critic Edward Dowden, who wrote in his 1877 Shakespeare "primer":

> The most fruitful method of studying the works of Shakespeare is that which views them in the chronological order of their production. We thus learn something about their origin, their connection to the mind of their creator, as that mind passed from its early promise to its rich maturity and fulfillment. (Dowden 1877: 32)

Dowden's conception of Shakespeare study – a theory expounded in his influential *Shakspere: A Critical Study of His Mind and Art* (1874) and circulated widely in that much-reprinted volume and in the primer volume, itself frequently republished in England and the United States in the late nineteenth and early twentieth centuries – has, even after a century and more, retained a strong influence on the way we conceptualize reading, performing, editing, and filming Shakespeare (de Grazia 1991: 25). Perhaps more than most plays, *The Two Gentlemen of Verona* has suffered under this developmental model; within a rubric that posits historical change at the level of the individual artist and conceptualizes that change in terms of development, progress, and maturity. *Two Gentlemen*, as *Shakespeare in Love* makes clear, has been viewed as workmanlike and immature – the product of Shakespeare's "apprenticeship" and his "first experimentation with romantic comedy" (Bevington 1992: 75). It is nevertheless useful to cast a critical eye on the circularity of the logic that demotes *The Two Gentlemen of Verona* in the implicitly upward trajectory of Shakespeare's works: as critical statements, "it falls early in Shakespeare's career, and so it is a bad play" often shades imperceptibly into "it is a bad play and so it falls early in Shakespeare's career." In this sense, the notion of "maturity" in later Shakespearean drama – a feature built into the larger critical model – may seem to require and indeed to call forth the ostensible insufficiencies of the early plays. A conception of "rich maturity," to return to Dowden's terms, may not just follow but also *produce* a support-ing notion of "early promise"; indeed, the very metaphor of the *"fruitful* method" seems to imply a trajectory of organic growth that the perceptive critic or reader will proceed to harvest.

We will return momentarily to the developmental, organic model of Shakespeare writing, but I want first to notice how, within such a paradigm, the earliness and ostensible prematurity of *Two Gentlemen* has become linked to other critical categories that the reading of the play I have offered makes especially legible.

Let's look at two examples – one interested in the formal properties of *Two Gentlemen*'s poetic verse, the other concerned structurally with the plot of the play and its resolution. Though both examples are drawn from early twentieth-century criti-cism of the play, each represents views that have persisted in later critical discussions and editions. Discussing the versification of *Two Gentlemen* in relation to Shakespeare's subsequent career, R. Warwick Bond writes, in his 1906 Arden edition:

> There can be no doubt that [Shakespeare's] progress from thinness to compression and
> pregnancy, from exactitude and rigidity to irregularity and fluidity, corresponds to a
> growth in readiness and fecundity of suggestion that overpowers attention to metre.
> (Bond 1906: xiii)

In Bond's conception, the early Shakespearean verse of *Two Gentlemen* is conceptual-ized as "thin," "exact," and "rigid" compared to the density (the simultaneous "com-pression and pregnancy") of later plays. The Shakespearean canon as a whole is conceptualized as moving away from *Two Gentlemen* and toward "readiness and fecundity." Comparing the writing in some scenes of the play even to other early Shakespeare plays, Marco Mincoff likewise describes *Two Gentlemen*'s writing as "flat and apparently imitative" (Mincoff 1976: 174–5).

Working at a very different level of analysis, that of the play's plot structure, Quiller-Couch (in his influential 1921 Cambridge Shakespeare edition quoted earlier) finds the play's final scene so "dramatically inconsistent" (p. xiv) that he hypothesizes

Shakespeare must have written an earlier version that was, for reasons now unavailable to us, discarded in the theatre and revised by others into the version we now have. Though Shakespeare's hypothetical, original version of the scene doesn't exist in the text we now read (the 1623 Folio text, on which all subsequent editions are based), Quiller-Couch argues that Shakespeare wrote "something which, if theatrically ineffective, was better, *because more natural*, than the text allows us to know" (p. xix). (In Quiller-Couch's fantasy, the hypothesized but nonexistent Shakespearean ending would not so devalue marital love.) Analyzing the plot more recently, Stanley Wells likewise links the apparent deficiency of the play to its "failure to devise a plot which will enable characters conceived within the conventions of romantic love to behave in a manner compatible with these conventions" (Wells 1963: 166).[14]

These two types of critical approaches to *Two Gentlemen*, different as they are, employ particularly resonant categories to devalue the play and (thus? also?) place it early in Shakespeare's career. Is the verse of the play "imitative" or "pregnant"? Is the play at one with, or at odds with, the conventions of romantic comedy? As far afield as it might seem from the intricacies of dating Shakespeare's early plays or from the terms of mainstream Shakespearean criticism, recent critical work on theories and histories of sexuality – the work of "queer theory" – helps us cast a critical eye on these categories and their relation to Shakespearean "earliness." As Judith Butler, Eve Kosofsky Sedgwick and others have argued, late nineteenth- and early twentieth-century Anglo-American culture has often conceptualized homosexuality as the "artificial" counterpart to the "naturalness" of heterosexuality, and indeed as the artificial "copy" produced through parodic imitation of a heterosexual original (Butler 1991; Sedgwick 1990). Queer theory can thus help us see the ways in which the very mode of writing attributed to *Two Gentlemen* – flat, imitative, unnatural; exact and rigid in its unreality; ungenerative in its non-pregnancy – shares a terminology with which *modern* culture has described homosexuality (Butler 1991; Edelman 1994). Deploying (however inadvertently) still more categories associated with modern homosexuality, Bond goes so far as to refer to the play's verse's "markedly dissolute character," and it is difficult not to hear in his repeated description of the "weakness" of the play's "end-stopped habit" some suggestion that the very verse of the play is somehow sodomitical (Bond 1906: xiii). (Quiller-Couch's construal is more complex still, for rather than simply derogating early Shakespeare as unnatural, Quiller-Couch first separates Shakespeare from the play: it is the extant early *text* that is unnatural in its conclusions.)

Lest these connections seem far-fetched, we should notice that, in its desire to get beyond the career-stage for Shakespeare it represents through *Two Gentlemen*, this is a set of connections the plot of *Shakespeare in Love* underlines by romanticizing and privileging its *opposite*. It aligns authorial originality (Shakespeare writing alone at a desk), heterosexual passion (Shakespeare's relationship with Viola de Lesseps), and the production of subsequent plays like *Romeo and Juliet*; on the other side of the cusp the film places between these two plays – between early and later – lie, correspondingly, writer's block, sexual dysfunction, *The Two Gentlemen of Verona*, and boy actors in women's roles.

In this context, it is worth noting that many of the critics I have cited – Dowden, writing in the 1870s and thereafter, Bond in his 1906 Arden edition, Quiller-Couch in his 1921 edition – were conceptualizing the meaning and canonical place of *Two Gentlemen* during precisely the period in which, recent historians of sexuality have argued, Anglo-American culture was articulating the language (and separability) of homo- and heterosexuality and their cultural meanings (Halperin 1990; Sedgwick 1990; Chauncey 1994). This is to say: not only does the discourse used by the critics to describe this play resonate with questions of sexuality that are themselves taken up, as I have argued, in quite another way by the play; this way of *describing* the play (its significance in the Shakespearean chronology, its verse, its plot) emerges at a particularly important cultural and historical moment. The critical discourse (and, I am suggesting, the dismissal of this play) is historically contingent. If, for Mincoff, "imitative" writing is bad, in *Two Gentlemen*, imitation and emulation (of other gentlemen) are precisely the *valued* terms, as when Panthino advises Antonio to send Proteus to court:

> There shall he practice tilts and tournaments,
> Hear sweet discourse, converse with noblemen,
> And be in eye of every exercise
> Worthy his youth and nobleness of birth (1.3.30–3)

Imitation, doubling ("I knew him as myself"), emulation, copying: far from being derided in Renaissance culture, as we have seen, these are condoned as the very tenets and practices of gentlemanly friendship. In Shakespeare's culture this valuation of imitation extends to writing as well: "To be sure your stile may passe for currant, as the richest alloy," Henry Peacham instructs in his conduct book *The Compleat Gentleman*: "imitate the best Authors as well in Oratory as History" (Peacham 1622: 44). Peacham's rhetoric is literally about *value* (he puns on chronological and monetary currency); here the imitative style is both up to date *and* valuable, not devalued, "early," or pre-mature. Similarly, at the level not of verse-writing but of plot, we might see the historical contingency of structural analyses that view the plot of *Two Gentlemen* as an "apprentice" attempt at romantic comedy, a "failure" to produce characters who can act "compatibly" with "the conventions of romantic love" (Wells 1963), or as a play "destructive of the relationships of the characters as they have been developed" (Barton 1974: 143). These construals, too, may rely on an ahistorically heterosexual notion of this comedy. As we have already had occasion to see, the question of how (or what) these characters develop, and of just who is joined in the play's concluding couplings, has multiple answers. Whose day of marriage shall be whose? What if the conventions of love(s) the play explores are multiple?

V

In the authorial–developmental growth model, Shakespeare begins with a failed or merely proleptic apprenticeship in romantic comedy, overthrows this for the "very truth and nature of love" and the beginning of the writing career in earnest in *Romeo and Juliet*, ascends through history plays to the heights of tragedy, emerges into the familial "reconciliation" that is often said to characterize the final plays now known as romances, and, following another such reconciliation, bids farewell to the stage in *The Tempest*, seen in this influential model as the last and self-consciously valedictory play of his career.[15] *The Tempest* as last play, with Prospero (read autobiographically as Shakespeare) drowning his book, has persisted as the final play in this career narrative,[16] even though *The Winter's Tale* may have been written later (Orgel 1987: 63–4), and despite the several Shakespeare plays that clearly follow *The Tempest* chronologically: the history *Henry VIII*, the lost play *Cardenio*, and the tragicomedy *The Two Noble Kinsmen*.

A different model of the career might, however, notice that last title, *The Two Noble Kinsmen*, and might remark that Shakespeare apparently began *and ended* his career writing not about a nearly omnipotent magician–scholar in retirement, but about male friends in pairs: two gentlemen, two kinsmen. This is the frame of the chronology as we now believe we know it; this is, if our metaphor must be "growth," a preoccupation Shakespeare never outgrew. It may be that there is no way to characterize an authorial career free of the preoccupations of critics and what they (we) currently see as valuable or central to the career. Still, seeing the persistence of male friendship and its constantly renegotiated relation to cross-sex marriage in Shakespeare's writing – from a modern perspective that begins from a vantage point made possible by modern homosexuality and its historians/theorists, while cautiously not simply *reproducing* that modern constellation in the texts of the past (Halperin 1990: 2) – gives us a rather different model of the Shakespearean career and its ostensible trajectory.

Once we see that Shakespeare's career is framed by friendship plays, we may more thoroughly see friendship as not simply a frame – a border, a beginning and an end – but a *framework*, a texture present throughout the plays. We might ask, for example, emending Wells's structural/conventional terms of analysis, how "characters conceived within the conventions of [*friendship's*] love" persist in the plays, and how the conventions of friendship interact, across the canon, with other kinds of conventions and generic frameworks.[17] This is true of the comedies – to take the obvious examples, the intense friendship of Bassanio and Antonio in *The Merchant of Venice*, and the friendship of Antonio and Sebastian in *Twelfth Night* ("Antonio, O my dear Antonio! / How have the hours rack'd and tortur'd me, / Since I have lost thee!" (5.1.218–20) says Sebastian at the moment of their reunion/reconciliation). Both of these pairs, not incidentally, are related, through the etymological thread of the name Sebastian/ Bassanio, to Julia's chosen name in *Two Gentlemen*.[18]

Though the conventions of friendly love will, as my analysis of *Two Gentlemen* has suggested, need to be recalibrated in relation to the generic preoccupations of comedy (the question of which couples, comprised of which genders, sleep with each other is also at issue in the concluding lines of *Merchant*), the persistence of friendship hardly ends there. In the history play *Henry V*, for example, a differently framed notion of the Shakespearean career gives renewed prominence to Lord Scroop, "the man that was [Henry's] bedfellow" (2.2.8), who, in his attempted betrayal, is denounced by Henry for crimes against not only England but also friendship:

> But O,
> What shall I say to thee, Lord Scroop, thou cruel,
> Ingrateful, savage, and inhuman creature?
> Thou that didst bear the key of all my counsels,
> That knew'st the very bottom of my soul,
>
> . . .
>
> O, how hast thou with jealousy infected
> The sweetness of affiance! (2.2.93–7, 126–7)

Henry here announces his (former) "affiance" with Scroop, a word that denotes in this period not only their intimacy and/or "affinity," but also the kind of ceremonial joining entailed in the friendship ritual Bray has uncovered, resonating with another of the *OED*'s period definitions for the word: "The pledging of faith; solemn engagement; esp. the plighting of troth between two persons in marriage, a marriage contract." This play, in overthrowing this friendship, may suggest that, in early modern culture, gentlemen are encouraged to have friends from whom they are indistinguishable (and Henry's rhetoric, citing "the very bottom of [the] soul," recalls features of Montaigne's discussion), but the situation is more complex for kings – as all readers of Christopher Marlowe's *Edward II* will recognize.

The intensities of friendship are, to take a final example, no less present in Shakespearean tragedy, as Hamlet and Horatio's initial greeting onstage witnesses, in emphasizing their interchangeability:

> *Hor.* Hail to your lordship!
> *Ham.* I am glad to see you well.
> Horatio – or I do forget myself.
> *Hor. The same*, my lord, and your poor servant ever.
> *Ham.* Sir, my good friend – I'll *change that name* with you.
> (1.2.160–3; additional emphasis mine)

Remembering Horatio, Hamlet remembers (doesn't forget) himself, and exchanges the name of friend with his friend. "Give me that man / That is not passion's slave," Hamlet later says to his friend, "and I will wear him / In my heart's core, ay, in my heart of heart, / As I do thee" (3.2.71–4). This is the only relationship, one might say, that survives the devastation at the end of *Hamlet*; at the moment of his death, Hamlet again references the pair's interchangeability and friendly love, asking Horatio to live on in order to speak with his voice:

> If thou didst ever hold me in thy heart,
> Absent thee from felicity a while,
> And in this harsh world draw thy breath in pain
> To tell my story. (5.2.346–9)

(Fortinbras may have Hamlet's "dying voice," but it is Horatio who speaks with it.)
At the moment of Hamlet's death, it is Horatio who bids him adieu, in terms that,
however familiar to us, are nevertheless remarkable in their language of affection:
"Now cracks a noble heart. [Hamlet's? Horatio's? both?] Good night, sweet prince, /
And flights of angels sing thee to thy rest!" (5.2.359–60). Horatio's prayer for his
friend eerily recalls the farewell that begins *Two Gentlemen*: "Sweet Valentine, adieu,
/ Think on thy Proteus, . . . / and in thy danger / (If ever danger do environ thee) /
Commend thy grievance to my holy Prayers."[19]

VI

O sweet-suggesting Love . . .

I have been noting the persistence of intense male friendship throughout Shakespeare's
writing career at the level of character, but, as I hope my examples and analysis may
already have begun to suggest, there is another way to think about this persistence
or framework, through a discursive approach to friendship in Shakespeare's writing
career. Concentrating on friendship as a discourse or syntax of affective relations is
more critically generative in allowing us to see the potential *mobilities* of friendship's
effects across Renaissance culture (and across kinds of people/characters), and, unlike
"character" as a rubric, it is attuned to the very *permeability* of the person/character in
friendship contexts. I thus want to conclude by considering alongside these characters (or actually *producing* and invigorating them) the language of male affection as a
structuring vocabulary – or at least one "keyword" in it. "Sweet prince," "Sweet
Valentine," "Sweet Proteus," the "sweeter friend," the "sweetness of affiance" – each
of these examples relies upon a rhetoric of "sweetness" as a marker of these relationships' intensity across the Shakespeare canon. "Sweetness," as a language of affect, is
remarkably mobile in the period (within Shakespeare, it is deployed between men and
between men and women, as we saw in *Two Gentlemen*, and, in other plays, between
women as well), but it is a language I think we are especially apt to overlook or regard
as merely "metaphorical" in relation to men's friendships. Glossing 2.4.149 in *Two
Gentlemen*, Leech writes: "The use of 'sweet', absolutely, as a form of address between
man and man on equal terms, is rare in Shakespeare" (Leech 1969: 41), yet the
evidence belies him. Whether as an adjective ("Sweet Valentine," "Sweet Bassanio,"
"Sweet prince," "Sweet Palamon" in *Two Noble Kinsmen*) or in an "absolute" "form of
address" that cannot be separated from such adjectival uses, *sweet* (with words like
converse, conversation) forms a part of the syntax of affective male relations. ("*Hor.* Here,
sweet lord, at your service. / *Ham.* Horatio, thou art e'en as just a man / As e'er my
conversation cop'd withal": 3.2.53–5.)

There is not space in this essay fully to explore the dynamics of friendship's sweetness in Shakespeare's plays or in early modern culture more generally, but, re-
glossing and resituating this word, it is important to note that "sweet" is closely
related to Greek verbs for "to rejoice" and "to please," and to Latin "*suāvis* . . . sweet,

suādēre to advise (properly, to make something pleasant to)" (*OED*). "Sweet" is thus connected etymologically to *suade* (an early modern verb meaning "persuade") and to *suave* (a word still with us), which meant in early modern English, "Pleasing or agreeable to the senses or the mind; sweet." Though the *OED* sees these connections in the dim etymological past of these words, the linking of persuasion and sweetness is ubiquitous in English around 1600. In the late sixteenth and early seventeenth centuries, Campion, Middleton, Dekker, Shakespeare, Jonson, Tourneur, and Massinger, to name a few, all use the phrase "sweet persuasion(s)," or the words in similar close proximity to each other, and this connection has been a feature of the Shakespearean evidence already quoted: "Cease to persuade, my loving Protheus," says "sweet Valentine." "Sweet Bassanio," reads Antonio's letter to his friend in *Merchant*, "if your love do not persuade you to come, let not my letter" (3.2.315–22). Although this is an argument that remains to be worked out in more detail, I think that the "persuasion" that often accompanies "sweets" in friendship discourse is about (in Montaigne's terms) "entermixing and confounding," the making of two into one, "one soul in two bodies." To conceptualize the friend as "sweet" imagines the friend as a food that literally becomes a (pleasant) part of the body, wearing him in the heart's core.[20] The sweetness of the friend registers the susceptibility *to* the friend that comes as a part of the very truth and nature of this love, as these texts define it. Like eating, sweet persuasion figures the doubling, imitative interaction of the self with the other, here defined (as we noted above) as an incorporated second self.[21]

Shakespeare was himself taken to be just such a sweet reincorporation of another person; in 1598 Francis Meres wrote, in the very text that helps us to date *Two Gentlemen* as an early play: "the *sweete* wittie soule of *Ouid* liues in *mellifluous* & *hony-tongued Shakespeare*, witness his *sugred* Sonnets among his *priuate* friends" (Meres 1598: 1844; additional emphasis mine). This final use of *sweet* may serve as a reminder that as critics we must move, ultimately, outside the authorial/career model (whether developmental or otherwise framed), to notice the ways that Shakespeare himself (where "self" is of course precisely the idea under scrutiny) is susceptible to, the product of, and the reinscriber of, others' "sweet persuasion." Meres's early Shakespeare has another soul (Ovid's) in his heart of heart: he reads, imitates, absorbs, incorporates other words, other texts, other theatrical performances; they are instrumental, persuasive, and they persist throughout "his" career (which is also, in this model, continuous with Ovid's). On the one hand, this is true of the "sources" that inform his career-long return to and rewriting of friendship's syntax, from *Two Gentlemen* to *Two Kinsmen*. On the other hand, Shakespeare's susceptibility, persuadability, incorporation of the other that becomes the writing self, is potentially also a model for the collaboration that writes *Two Noble Kinsmen*, where Shakespeare writes with John Fletcher. Indeed, these two different "hands" come together in this play, as Shakespeare and Fletcher write of their source-text, Chaucer, wishing "To his bones sweet sleep" (1.Prol.29). (Goodnight, sweet source.)

Tracing this particular rhetoric – which is in part the syntax of male relations in this period, though *not only that* – must in the end serve to remind us that the Shakespeare career is coextensive with, persuaded by, other careers, other texts, other writings, a career not organically grown but "entermixed and confounded." Is the early Shakespeare of *The Two Gentlemen of Verona* potentially mid-Marlowe, or late Lyly, which is to say, also very late Ovid?[22] "Sweete prince I come," says Gaveston in the opening lines of *Edward II* (c. 1593); "these, these thy amorous lines / Might have enforced me to have swum from France" (Marlowe 1967: 1.1.6–7). Following his valentine to court like a Proteus ("There shall he . . . / Hear sweet discourse, converse with noblemen"), Gaveston then proceeds to describe himself through the same Ovidian text (the story of Hero and Leander) cited in the opening lines of *Two Gentlemen*.

Following out such *discursive* connections (and there are of course many, many more) may show us – in contradistinction to Dowden, following one "mind [as it] passed from its early promise to its rich maturity and fulfillment" – the importance of finding other, less securely individuated, more complexly collaborative models for understanding the production of writing[23] in the culture where Shakespeare read, wrote, conversed – models that may alter our sense of the pre-"maturity," significance, and resilience of *The Two Gentlemen of Verona*.

NOTES

1   For an overview of critics' attempts to date the play, see Taylor, Wells, et al. (1997: 109).
2   On the significance of dogs in Shakespeare, see Garber (1998).
3   All references to *The Two Gentlemen of Verona* are to act, scene and line numbers in Leech (1969) and appear parenthetically in the text.
4   See the friendship of Pyrocles and Musidorus in Sidney's *Arcadia*; Book IV of Spenser's *Faerie Queene* (subtitled "of Friendship"); Lyly's *Euphues*.
5   *Ought* (noun) = "aught, anything whatsoever," property; but perhaps with a further resonance of *ought* as "obligation." See *OED*, *ought* and *aught*, spelled interchangeably in the period.
6   All references to plays by Shakespeare other than *Two Gentlemen* are to act, scene, and line numbers in Evans et al. (1974).
7   On "mimetic desire" in the play, see Girard (1989).
8   The rhetoric of dual passions is also available, for example, in Shakespeare's sonnet 144.
9   As I have argued elsewhere, the play may "mystify or sidestep tensions in sixteenth- and seventeenth-century England over social mobility – over whether gentlemen were *born* (ancestrally derived) or *made*" at "a time when the boundary between gentlemen and common men was increasingly fluid and contested" (Masten 1999: 212–13). See also Whigham (1984) and Lindenbaum (1975).
10 On female friendship, see Traub's (1994) classic article, Traub (2001), and Shannon (2002: 84–9, 95–8).
11 That musical discourse should be the discourse of both female companionship (Julia and Lucetta, scene 1.2) and of female critique of male behavior, which "jars so" (4.2.65), requires further study.
12 For another possible "handfast" moment, see Orlando and Ganymede's rehearsal of marriage in *As You Like It* 4.1.
13 On the homoerotic resonance of the name "Sebastian" in Renaissance drama, see DiGangi (1997: 20, 167), and Howard (1992: 175, 188).
14 See also Barton (1974: 143).
15 On the developmental model as also a generic progression, see de Grazia (1991: 24–5) and the table of contents, for example, in Evans et al. (1974).

16   On the implications of *The Tempest* as final play, see Masten (1997a: 107–12). This career narrative has also been the subject of a film: Peter Greenaway's *Prospero's Books* (1991).
17   See Goldberg's suggestive prolegomena for a study of friendship across the Shakespeare canon (Goldberg 1992: 142–3).
18   See DiGangi (1997), Howard (1992).
19   As Derrida (1997) emphasizes, there is a persistent elegiac thread to friendship discourse, from the classical period onward.
20   On the significance of sugar in early modern culture, see Fumerton (1991), Hall (1996), and Wall (2002).
21   Again, this discourse is not by any means limited to men, though this is one place that I think it must be made visible through critical and editorial emphasis. For an example of its mobility across our modern sexual categories see, in addition to the evidence already cited in *Two Gentlemen*, the conclusion of *Merchant*, with Bassanio's address to his "Sweet doctor," Portia (5.1.284).
22   Similar questions were asked of "Late Shakespeare" on a panel of that name at the Shakespeare Association of America meeting (Minneapolis 2002), by panelists Gordon McMullan, Suzanne Gossett, and Howard Marchitello.
23   For accounts of Renaissance playwrighting that emphasize the writer's intersection with the culture, see, most influentially, Greenblatt (1988). For accounts of the predominantly non-individuated and collaborative nature of Renaissance playwrighting, see Bentley (1971), Hirschfeld (2000), Masten (1997b), and Orgel (1981).

REFERENCES AND FURTHER READING

Barton, A. (1974). Introduction: *The Two Gentlemen of Verona*. In G. B. Evans et al. (eds.) *The Riverside Shakespeare*. Boston: Houghton Mifflin, 143–6.
Bentley, G. E. (1971). *The Profession of Dramatist in Shakespeare's Time, 1590–1642*. Princeton, NJ: Princeton University Press.
Bevington, D. (1992). Introduction: *The Two Gentlemen of Verona*. In D. Bevington (ed.) *The Complete Works of Shakespeare*, 4th edn. New York: HarperCollins, 75–7.
Bond, R. W. (1906). Introduction. In *The Two Gentlemen of Verona*. London: Methuen, ix–xliii.
Braithwait, R. (1630). *The English Gentleman*. London: John Haviland [for] Robert Bostock.
Bray, A. (1994). Homosexuality and the Signs of Male Friendship in Elizabethan England. In J. Goldberg (ed.) *Queering the Renaissance*. Durham, NC: Duke University Press, 40–61.
——(2003). *The Friend*. Chicago, IL: University of Chicago Press.
Butler, J. (1991). Imitation and Gender Insubordination. In D. Fuss (ed.) *Inside/Out: Lesbian Theories, Gay Theories*. New York: Routledge.
Charlebois, E. (2000). The Jealous Zealot: Faith, Desire, and Epistemology in English Renaissance Drama. Unpublished Ph.D. dissertation. Evanston, IL: Northwestern University.
Chauncey, G. (1994). *Gay New York: Gender, Urban Culture, and the Making of the Gay Male World 1890–1940*. New York: Basic Books.
de Grazia, M. (1991). *Shakespeare Verbatim: The Reproduction of Authenticity and the 1790 Apparatus*. Oxford: Oxford University Press.
Derrida, J. (1997). *Politics of Friendship*, trans. G. Collins. London: Verso.
DiGangi, M. (1997). *The Homoerotics of Early Modern Drama*. Cambridge: Cambridge University Press.
Dowden, E. (1874). *Shakspere: A Critical Study of His Mind and Art*, 3rd edn. New York: Harper and Brothers.
——(1877). *Shakespeare*. Literature Primers series. London: Macmillan.
Edelman, L. (1994). *Homographesis: Essays in Gay Literary and Cultural Theory*. New York: Routledge.
Evans, G. B., et al. (eds.) (1974). *The Riverside Shakespeare*. Boston: Houghton Mifflin.

Foucault, M. (1980). *The History of Sexuality, Vol. 1: An Introduction*, trans. R. Hurley. New York: Vintage. (Original work published 1976.)

Fumerton, P. (1991). *Cultural Aesthetics: Renaissance Literature and the Practice of Social Ornament*. Chicago: University of Chicago Press.

Garber, M. (1998). Shakespeare's Dogs. In J. Bate et al. (eds.) *The Selected Proceedings of the International Shakespeare Association World Congress, Los Angeles, 1996*. Newark: University of Delaware Press, 294–313.

Girard, R. (1989). Love Delights in Praises: A Reading of *The Two Gentlemen of Verona*. *Philosophy and Literature*, 13, 231–47.

Goldberg, J. (1986). Shakespearian Characters: The Generation of Silvia. In *Voice Terminal Echo: Postmodernism and English Renaissance Texts*. New York: Methuen, 68–100.

——(1992). *Sodometries: Renaissance Texts, Modern Sexualities*. Stanford, CA: Stanford University Press.

Greenaway, P. (Dir.) (1991). *Prospero's Books*. Miramax Films.

Greenblatt, S. (1988). *Shakespearean Negotiations: The Circulation of Social Energy in Renaissance England*. Berkeley, CA: University of California Press.

Hall, K. (1996). Culinary Spaces, Colonial Spaces: The Gendering of Sugar in the Seventeenth Century. In V. Traub, M. L. Kaplan, and D. Callaghan (eds.) *Feminist Readings of Early Modern Culture: Emerging Subjects*. Cambridge: Cambridge University Press, 168–90.

Halperin, D. M. (1990). *One Hundred Years of Homosexuality and Other Essays on Greek Love*. New York: Routledge.

Hirschfeld, H. (2000). Collaborating across Generations: Thomas Heywood, Richard Brome, and the Production of *The Late Lancashire Witches*. *Journal of Medieval and Early Modern Studies*, 30, 340–74.

Howard, J. E. (1992). Sex and Social Conflict: The Erotics of *The Roaring Girl*. In S. Zimmerman (ed.) *Erotic Politics: Desire on the Renaissance Stage*. New York: Routledge.

Leech, C. (ed.) (1969). *The Two Gentlemen of Verona*. The Arden Shakespeare. London: Methuen.

Lindenbaum, P. (1975). Education in *The Two Gentlemen of Verona*. *Studies in English Literature*, 15, 229–44.

Marlowe, C. (1967). *Edward the Second*, ed. W. Moelwyn Merchant. London: Benn.

Masten, J. (1997a). *Textual Intercourse: Collaboration, Authorship, and Sexualities in Renaissance Drama*. Cambridge: Cambridge University Press.

——(1997b). Playwrighting: Authorship and Collaboration. In J. D. Cox and D. S. Kastan (eds.) *A New History of Early English Drama*. New York: Columbia University Press, 357–82.

——(1999). A Modern Perspective. In B. Mowat and P. Werstine (eds.) *The Two Gentlemen of Verona*. New York: Washington Square Press and Folger Shakespeare Library, 199–221.

Meres, F. [1598] (1974). *Palladis Tamia*. In G. B. Evans et al. (eds.) *The Riverside Shakespeare*. Boston: Houghton Mifflin, excerpt 1844–5.

Mincoff, M. (1976). *Shakespeare: The First Steps*. Sofia: Bulgarian Academy of Sciences.

Montaigne, M. de (1892). *The Essays of Montaigne*, trans. J. Florio. London: David Nutt. (Original work published 1632.)

Norman, M. and Stoppard, T. (1998). *Shakespeare in Love: A Screenplay*. New York: Hyperion.

Orgel, S. (1981). What is a Text? *Research Opportunities in Renaissance Drama*, 2–4.

——(1987). Introduction: *The Tempest*. Oxford: Oxford University Press, 1–87.

Oxford English Dictionary online (2002). Oxford: Oxford University Press.

Peacham, H. (1622). *The Compleat Gentleman*. London: Francis Constable.

Quiller-Couch, A. (1921). Introduction. In A. Quiller-Couch and J. Dover Wilson (eds.) *The Two Gentlemen of Verona: New Cambridge Shakespeare*. New York: Macmillan, vii–xix.

Sedgwick, E. K. (1990). *Epistemology of the Closet*. Berkeley: University of California Press.

Shakespeare, W. (1623). *Mr. William Shakespeares Comedies, Histories, & Tragedies*. London: Isaac Iaggard and Ed. Blount.

Shannon, L. (2002). *Sovereign Amity: Figures of Friendship in Shakespearean Contexts*. Chicago: University of Chicago Press.

Taylor, G. and Wells, S., et al. (1997). *William Shakespeare: A Textual Companion*. New York: W. W. Norton by arrangement with Oxford University Press.

Traub, V. (1994). The (In)Significance of "Lesbian" Desire. In J. Goldberg (ed.) *Queering the Renaissance*. Durham, NC: Duke University Press, 62–83.

——(2001). The Renaissance of Lesbianism in Early Modern England. *GLQ: A Journal of Lesbian and Gay Studies*, 7, 2, 245–63.

Wall, W. (2002). *Staging Domesticity: Household Work and English Identity in Early Modern Drama*. Cambridge: Cambridge University Press.

Wells, S. (1963). The Failure of *The Two Gentlemen of Verona*. *Shakespeare Jahrbuch*, 99, 161–73.

Whigham, F. (1984). *Ambition and Privilege: The Social Tropes of Elizabethan Courtesy Theory*. Berkeley: University of California Press.

14

"Fie, what a foolish duty call you this?" *The Taming of the Shrew*, Women's Jest, and the Divided Audience

Pamela Allen Brown

A common view about *The Taming of the Shrew* is that changing attitudes about women have made it impossible to enjoy what once gave pleasure to all (Garner 1988: 106, 117). This view ignores signs that neither time's passage nor the rise of feminism made the play provocative. Although *Taming* was frequently staged from its first recorded performance in 1594 to the closing of the theatres (Haring-Smith 1985: 7–8), it does not follow that universal applause fueled this demand. Like Lina Wertmuller's *Swept Away* or David Mamet's *Oleanna*, Shakespeare's comedy was tailor-made to split spectators into factions. This essay situates the play in a field of popular comic texts to show that Shakespeare radically altered the shrew tradition in order to make some women playgoers targets rather than sharers in the comedy, fomenting dissension and debate as well as laughter.[1]

Some of the best-known studies of early female spectatorship have focused on whether and how playwrights sought to please or placate women (Orgel 1989: 8; Gurr 1987: 149; Levin 1989: 168–73).[2] *Taming* plays by a different set of rules, making it germane to ask what would have set their teeth on edge. Certainly the play is a virtual catalog of male offenses in the eyes of early modern women, including the violence of drunken rogues and despotic husbands, the predatory greed of fortune hunters, the callousness of fathers who auction off daughters without their consent, the abrogation of wives' customary rights to food and clothing, and the noxiousness of being lectured by a reincarnation of Griselda. At the same time, the play offered a tempting spectacle to women who might applaud the Marlovian nerve of a Petruchio or revel in the shaming of a scold. In this way the play divided men from women, and women from women.

As Barbara Freedman has pointed out, the play has deeply split its critics, too, creating a virtual stalemate in interpretation. One camp maintains that original audiences would have taken Kate's final lecture as an incontrovertible statement of God's truth, leading to comic resolution; another reads the same lines as deeply ironic and subversive, in a farce rife with games and role-playing; and yet another sees the play as offering a delightful lesson in the humanizing, transformative power of love (sum-marized in Freedman 1991: 119–21). Interpreters tend to homogenize the play, striving to fix its meaning without regard to women's reactions, even though the play offered women absolutely no "indication of a comfortable, egalitarian compromise" as other comedies and merry tales about marital conflict normally did (Thompson 1988: 18). The best work on the play attempts to situate it within the textual, social, and economic discourses that shaped women's lives. Scholars have read *Taming* alongside conduct books, sermons, and polemics about marriage and wife-beating, laws and rituals against shrews and scolds, economic evidence about enclosures and new com-modity forms, and stories and plays about shrews and shrew-taming, including the much-disputed Quarto *Taming of a Shrew* (Dolan 1996; Boose 1991, 1994; Newman 1991; Korda 1996; Wayne 1985; Marcus 1992). My reading grows out of this flour-ishing branch of feminist *Shrew* criticism, but I choose to place the shrew's meta-morphosis in an intertextual field of ballads and jests accessible to all women as part of the world of cheap print and oral culture. I am most interested in narratives that expose the rarely acknowledged conflict between women who grovel too much – and the women who hate them. In my view, the tamed Kate has never been a self-actualized wife displaying her own "spirit, wit, and joy" (Neely 1985: 219), but a performing object fashioned to be deliberately, confidently offensive.

To make this case I have sought out familiar, deeply ingrained topoi that ensured that the comic action would be understood by audiences at all ranks and levels of lit-eracy and education. Women came to the theatres as participants in a common culture rife with traditional forms of satire, mockery, jest, and clowning. These experiences shaped the mental worlds of women who saw *Taming of the Shrew* and determined the play's horizon of meaning on the stage for which it was created. I follow a course sug-gested by Andrew Gurr, who maintains that the "hermeneutics" of theatre "depends as much on the audience's state of mind as it does on the author's and the players' expec-tation of what, mentally, their audience will be prepared for. That 'mindset' is a con-sequence of the mental furniture the Shakespearean playgoer might have been equipped with," including his or her education, prejudices, and expectations (Gurr 1987: 6).[3] Proverbs, merry tales, and ballads, as social historians have argued, provide limited but valuable access to some of the more common modes of thought and belief that make up this mindset, while jokes and laughter are especially useful in illuminating "areas of structural ambiguity" in society (Thomas 1977: 77), including ideologies of gender.[4] Such seemingly trivial texts as ballads and jests were important to women because they provided them with language with which to weigh their options and form narratives about their experience (Wiltenburg 1992: 50; Gowing 1996: 231–62).

While *Taming* is often read as promoting a patriarchalism no one would think of challenging, its one-sidedness is deliberately divisive. A husband's *absolute* sovereignty was never accepted without question as part of everyday gender relations; in fact, conduct manuals, sermons, court records, and popular literature show that the proper degree of subordination was a constant topic of debate (Dolan 1996: 4–5).

According to Ann Thompson, the play also flies in the face of a jest and novella tradition promoting mutuality in marriage; in Boccaccio and Chaucer, tales about a husband's triumph over a wife are quickly countered with stories about a wife's victory over her mate. Because its spectacle of wifely submission is so uncompromising and disturbing, *Taming* has "probably been played straight less often than any other play in the canon" (Thompson 1988: 18). Moreover, the play turns its back on a flourishing comic culture that featured incorrigible, anarchically appealing shrews and viragoes who often acted in league with other women (Wayne 1985; Brown 2002). In popular texts and plays, jesting women attack marriage as a prison, castigate fortune-hunting suitors and tyrannical husbands, and mock any woman who makes herself a spectacle of submission. Playgoers familiar with this rich street literature would find ample precedents there should they decide to shout Petruchio and his admirers down, applaud Bianca and the Widow, or hiss at Kate's unseemly conversion.

Playgoing was a far less passive endeavor than it is today. Audiences were used to voicing their pleasure or dislike, engaging in laughter and applause or hisses and shouts of abuse, and women "were certainly capable of reacting in numbers and vocally to what they saw on stage" (Gurr 1987: 44–6, 57). Women who went to the theatre regularly included citizens' wives, marketwomen, prostitutes, and servants; aristocratic women attended in smaller numbers (ibid: 55–63). Simply by venturing into the theatres they showed they were not cowed about strictures governing female deportment, but perhaps the most striking fact about female playgoers is how stubbornly they ignored dire warnings about the dangers of theatre itself. As Jean Howard has observed, we should not assume that women were abashed or silenced, rather than energized or emboldened, by their transgressive position within audiences (Howard 1994: 78, but see Findlay 1999: 133). Antitheatricalist divines assured them they'd be ogled, pawed, and bewhored, perhaps even abducted, yet they kept going. Such determined playgoers seem capable of discerning the actual risks, and weighing them against the histrionic polemics of antitheatricalism. Something kept them coming to the theatres, but their motives for taking in a play like *Taming of the Shrew* must have varied as much as their differences in status, wealth, and education.

Once a woman paid to enter the theatre she was entitled to judge the performers and the playwright, along with everyone else, male and female, rich and poor, learned and illiterate, servants and citizens. For the actors who confronted these heterogeneous audiences, it was a rare play that could please all sectors all the time. Dealing with antipathy and even violence from the audience was an occupational hazard. Apprentices and laborers in particular were given to gate-crashing, calling for changes in the play, rioting, and even tearing theatres apart. Joining some disturbances were fishwives and applewives, working women whose bodies formed a highly audible, mobile, and visible challenge to the theory of women's enclosure and subjugation. Faced with an unruly sea of heads in which gender and other markers of identity were explosively mixed, players and writers had to take an aggressive course – striving not merely to please spectators, but to commandeer emotions through what Frank Whigham has aptly called "seizures of the will" (Callaghan 2000: 162; Whigham 1996: 1, 18).

The Taming of the Shrew uses two principal strategies for seizing control: bait and switch, and divide and conquer. The Induction sets the audience up for one kind of play then quickly substitutes another, grabbing the attention of spectators who expect something quite different. When Christopher Sly and the Hostess tumbled onstage in the first productions of *Taming of the Shrew*, they played to men and women who had seen similar scenes in their own neighborhoods, where deadbeats and alewives were chronic opponents, as they were in jests, ballads, and jigs (Clark 1983: 83–4, 87; Jayne 1966: 47). If women's "prejudices" were stirred by the brawl, they were most likely aimed against the loud-mouthed vulgarian who claims descent from "Richard Conqueror." The alehouse haunter was a butt of satire in chapbooks, jigs, ballads, and plays, often castigated by wives who blast drunkards as whoring wastrels who starve their families and bring home venereal diseases.[5] Before running off to fetch the thirdborough, the alewife challenges Sly to pay for broken glasses, producing a quick sketch of Sly's drunken idiocy and absurd pretensions. The officer never arrives, but judgment by the audience begins at once, with the Hostess seizing the role of righteous, though shrewish, judge.

When the Lord arrives he instantly sweeps away the prosaic law of the neighborhood, exploiting Sly's stupor to impose a law of his own. His elite jest demands that the audience forget the familiar and homely alehouse flyting it has just seen. Acting as his own Master of the Revels, he hires a band of players for his trick, but casts his page Barthol'mew in the crucial role of Sly's new wife, a fascinating choice. The Lord has professionals at hand yet chooses an amateur, explaining "I know the boy will well usurp the grace, / Voice, gait, and action of a gentlewoman" (Induction 2.137–8),[6] lines that seems to aim a satiric dart at the sodomitical leanings of foppish lords who are connoisseurs of erotic paintings, fine wine, and pages with a talent for usurping the woman's part. After this sophisticated Italianate frame has been jerked into place, the audience quickly receives a fairly pointed warning that it had better attend to the "comonty" with sharper wits than Sly's, who longs for it to be over after the first scene. The ale of the opening has been replaced with the wine of the Lord's play, and if the audience prefers ale it will have to go without, like Sly.

As if to offer a substitute, the gender and class reversals and erasures in the Lord's house greatly multiply and complicate the available range of spectatorial pleasures, especially for women watching. The Induction (which could be retitled "Instruction to the Auditors") informs them that a powerful pleasure-seeker has hired a boy to play "Kate" in order to amplify his practical joke against Sly. Whether wild or tame, this shrew is a crossdressed and rehearsed work of masculine artifice – just like the "Lady Wife" Barthol'mew, who also mouths what his Lord and master wants him to say. The play does not invite women to side with Kate, who is depicted as more scold (and woman-hater) than shrew. Instead, the play entices women to engage in a mix of fantasy and identification – initially, at least, they may admire the skillful Latinate witplay of Bianca or gaze with erotic delight at the boy actor flirting and intriguing with Lucentio; at the same time they are also free to admire the brute energy of a Petruchio or the class-transgressive theatricality of a Tranio.

Even in these early scenes, however, there are signs that the party is going to be a short one for women, who are invited in to the feast, then abruptly told to "behave." While the sexual and social registers rapidly shift in the dizzying Induction, the audience barely notices that it, too, has been placed under the management of a fantasy patron. After abducting Sly and altering his identity, the Lord employs actors who instruct the commoner how to behave as a proper auditor should. One should use the correct generic term ("comedy," not "comonty"). One should mark the action, which requires more attention than a holiday gambol or trick. And one should certainly not expect sexual gratification during or after the play. These lessons prefigure the taming to come, but they also bear an uncanny resemblance to the constant complaints aimed at women playgoers – who were singled out as naturally lustful and most susceptible to theatre's sexual allure, and scorned for going to plays to see and be seen, rather than to learn and understand.[7]

The Induction defers gratification for the audience as well as for Sly. By the time they saw the first scene in Padua, spectators would have been impatient to meet the Shrew they'd been promised. Expectation, prejudice, and performance tradition all played their part in creating this demand. The starring virago might be modeled on Socrates' choleric Xantippe, familiar from jests, or Uxor of the Flood plays, or Tom Tyler's pugilistic wife Strife. Or she might be the thick-skinned, unkillable shrew of jest books and ballads: the wife who never stops crossing her husband, even when he tries to drown her (Dolan 1996: 325). If death overtakes her, she lives on in hell, cast as the devil's dam. Soon she is hounding the devil himself, whom she beats to a pulp or terrifies with her flyting (*An Excellent New Ditty*: 335–6). We are supposed to recoil at her image, but her vulgar strength exerts a powerful fascination, displaying a grip on subjectivity as worthy of our interest as "Kill Claudio" or "I am Duchess of Malfi still."

Soon after Katherine makes her entrance, it becomes clear she is no arch-shrew. She claims to have no interest in marrying but soon whines for a husband (2.1.31–6), unlike other anti-marriage maids, such as Julia of Dekker, Chettle, and Haughton's *The Pleasant Comodie of Patient Grissill*, or the many wives and maids who praised the single life in street ballads. When Petruchio lies to Baptista that she has privately agreed to wed, she does not say a word. She never tries to escape her fate through trickery or flight (unlike Anne Page of *Merry Wives* or Hermia of *Midsummer*) or through suicide, faked or real (unlike Juliet of *Romeo and Juliet* or Moll Yellowhammer of *Chaste Maid in Cheapside*). Once she is married, she does nothing that would gain her credentials as a strong shrew in the jesting tradition known to the audiences of the play. Unlike the boisterous wife in the sixteenth-century ballad *A Merry Jest of a Shrewd and Curst Wife Lapped in Morel's Skin* (quoted in Dolan 1996: 257–88), she doesn't scold her husband, beat him, or hound him with curtain lectures. She has no gossips or sympathetic kin, so cannot plot with them against him. Despite her billing as Padua's most famous shrew, Kate caves in under pressure that appears cruel and unusual to us, but may have seemed rather minor to women used to hearing about the protracted tortures strong shrews endured in jests and ballads. If Kate turns out to be a *weak* shrew, how did the play persuade anyone of Petruchio's unique skill in engineering her transformation to "a second Grissel"?

The answer lies in the play's realignment in mid-stream from a battle of the "madly mated," in which the wife stands a fighting chance, to an exhibition weighted outrageously toward men onstage and in the audience. To accomplish this turnaround, the play evokes and then erases a longstanding native performance tradition in which a female clown – not a male shrew-tamer – held center stage. The virago who cast the longest shadow over English stage shrews was Noah's Wife ("Uxor"), who had delighted audiences for two hundred years. In the great pageant cycles, the Flood plays starred this dauntless termagant, who provided "the oldest native comic role for women" and whose much-anticipated appearance in the play was "a dramatic tradition" that was "familiar and loved" (Bradbrook 1958: 134; Marx 1995: 110; also Wayne 1985: 161–4). As a clown, her main function was to rouse laughter through outrageous displays of defiance against the hapless Noah. She performed close to the audience, often making direct appeals to women watching, ridiculing Noah and urging all wives to show their husbands who was boss. In the Chester Flood play she joins her "good gossips" for a last tipple as the waters rise, and insists that they be saved. For his part, Noah calls on husbands in the crowd to join him in wishing their wives were dead, so they might enjoy peace and quiet. The couple falls about the ears in a slapstick bout, and Noah gets the worst of it. Uxor sits on him vaunting merrily, while he groans that she's breaking his back. Now it's her turn to ask women watching to join her in wishing all husbands dead. Finally Noah and his sons pummel her and drag her onto the ark. When she is finally afloat, she accepts the Flood as divine punishment against sinning humankind. But it is God's will, not Noah's, that tames her (Marx 1995: 110; Lumiansky and Mills 1974: 52).

Uxor continued to influence stage representations of shrews, from Strife in *Tom Tyler and His Wife* to Adriana in *Comedy of Errors*. When Petruchio drags Kate offstage from her own wedding, the physical business ensured at least an echo of the famous fisticuffs of the Flood plays. But the echo has grown quite faint. Kate abuses the bound Bianca more than she does Petruchio. Unlike Uxor or Strife, Kate defers to her male opponent in crucial ways after landing just one blow, and without making any appeal to the women in the audience. Contemporary playgoers were thus denied a deeply ingrained performance tradition: seeing a shrew without a brawl might have been like seeing Kemp without a jig. Such an aporia demands a compensatory spectacle. *Taming* replaces the acrobatic dustup between a "woman on top" and her milksop husband with the very different pleasure of seeing a zany fortune-hunter perform his talky taming act on a balky bride.

Petruchio displaces Kate as the prime spectacle in the play as soon as he enters. He is a king of shreds and patches: his vigor and rhetoric seem borrowed from Tamburlaine, his boastfulness from *commedia's* Capitano, and his carnivalesque wedding antics from native clowns and jesters, such as Tarlton and Scogan. Although he controls the theatrical pleasure from then on, upstaging Kate, the stage tradition of connubial warfare from the old Flood plays has not completely vanished, at least on the male side. In the manner of Noah bantering with his male audiences, Petruchio invites men in the theatre to amplify his merry misogyny: "He that knows better how to tame a shrew, / Now let him speak. 'Tis charity to show" (4.2.179–80) – a speech custom-tooled to raise the hackles of women excluded from, and targeted by, his appeal.[8] Jesting culture indicates that men debated "how to tame a shrew" so often, and thought it such an impossible feat, that they would have been primed to take

Petruchio up on his challenge. (When Sir John Harington read the Quarto version of the play, the ironic moral he gleaned from it was a variant of the old saw "Every man can tame a wife save he that has her.")[9]

Petruchio's bluster works as a wedge that completes the work of splitting the audience. Brusque, confident, he enlists the complicity of men and challenges women to cross him at their peril. Right away he announces his intentions to marry for money. As he is governed solely by "gold's effect," rich old widows and ugly shrews alike are fair game. His first exchange with Hortensio places everyone on alert that he is "a fortune-hunting rascal," as Lisa Jardine (1989: 60) succinctly puts it; but the message would have sounded a far louder warning to women listening in 1590s London. At home, back in the neighborhood, women were constantly called on to scrutinize their neighbors and to participate in the local dramatics of surveillance and control. They were likely, therefore, to bring this experience to the theatres as part of their "mental furniture."[10] As the "chief judges" of proper behavior in communities, women bore the prime responsibility for policing marital matters (Gowing 1996: 123). The most important decision in most women's lives, the choice of a husband, was usually reached after extended negotiation and inquiry by her family and female friends. Whether maid, wife, or widow, a female spectator would have been trained to look for signs of venality in any suitor with designs on a maid with a fat dowry.

Popular ballads and jests reinforced that message. Ballad narrators advised women about choosing a partner, and warned them to steer clear of wooers whose sole objective is to "wive it wealthily" (1.2.76). Although created and sold largely by men, such ballads were usually written in the personas of women, addressing them directly, and women and girls of all social levels and occupations bought and sang them. Hawked at theatre doors, alehouses, markets, and street corners, ballads were cheap and ubiquitous, with 3–4 million copies circulating in England by the late 1590s (Watt 1991: 11, 42). A woman's low literacy would not bar her access to ballad culture, because she could hear them sung or read aloud, and she could sing them herself afterward. For these reasons, ballads offered "female speaking positions" in a far more immediate way than did the all-male stage or in the mostly male-authored texts of official and literary culture (Smith 1999: 200; Wiltenburg 1992: 50).

Like writers of controversy pamphlets, ballad authors often wrote on both sides of an issue, in the alternating voices of men and women. Because ballad audiences often joined in and sang along, they functioned as participants as well as consumers, invited to take an active part in the performance and the debate it could foster. The miniature dramas of dialogue and "answer" ballads capitalized on gender divisions in audiences to create what Wurzbach calls "a kind of discussion forum" (Wurzbach 1990: 97); the ballads cuing these debates are full of back-and-forth mockery and insults by men and women. Ballad writers and authors of attacks on women often joked that only "galled jades," or choleric, shrewish and whorish women, took umbrage at misogynist squibs (Kennedy 2000: 25–8), but some ballads in women's voices roundly attacked men who proved themselves to be lying lovers or brutal, drunken, and impotent husbands.

Many "counsel ballads" offer up advice by wives who gave up their freedom to men who were after their money. Martin Parker's *The Married Womans Case* warns maids about "quarreling coxcombes" who indulge themselves while starving their wives, making them "leape at a crust." In *The Cunning Age* a remarried widow finds out too late that her husband is a bankrupt fraud: "Oh woe is me, Cousin, that ever 'twas done, / A beggarly slave my affection hathe wonne; / He brag'd of his riches, whereof he had none." In *A Fairing for Maids* the female presenter offers caveats about fortune hunters and praises the single life, while a group of women in *The Married wives complaint, Or the Hasty Bride repents her bargain* trade tales of woe about husbands who beat them and waste their marriage portions on drink and gambling.[11]

Monitory texts like these shaped the mental worlds of women playgoers, whose suspicions would have been stirred by Petruchio's bold declaration "wealth is burden of my wooing dance" (1.2.63). Placed on the alert, they would have watched closely for signs of violence, gambling, lying, and profligacy. They would not have long to wait. Petruchio roars like a sailor, guzzles his wine, cuffs a priest, and lays huge wagers. He also lets a horse fall on his bride, starves her, and denies her clothes. Most tellingly, he avers he has plenty of money, but shows little evidence of it: before the wedding, he boasts about going to Venice to buy Kate "rings, and things, and fine array," but never produces them (2.1.342). He takes his bride on a worthless horse to a cold house full of "ragged, old, and beggarly" servants (4.1.130). After he abuses the tailor about Kate's new gown, he slyly passes the bill to Hortensio and asks him to pay it (4.3.169). Hortensio obeys without a word of protest, only too pleased to help. Here and later, Hortensio is rather too obviously a surrogate for the men in the audience who are eagerly assisting in the fantasy of control beyond their means.[12]

Just before his first encounter with Kate, Petruchio brags that he is "rough and woos not like a babe" (2.1.133). He never shows signs of dependency or doubt, unlike the Noahs and Tom Tylers of stage tradition, while Kate seems a petulant girl flailing wildly in words, rather than the stage and jest book shrew who was a past hand at flyting. As Linda Bamber puts it, "The dialectic between the two is unequal because Kate represents the Other very feebly" (Bamber 1982: 33). Petruchio rudely flouts her express wish to be called Katherine, naming her Kate a dozen different ways; but she does not answer his challenge by renaming *him*. The insults she does come up with do not faze him. Petruchio turns her mocks against her without breaking a sweat, showing up their "wit battle" as deliberately anomalous and irritatingly unequal.

One might assume that early modern Englishmen always painted themselves as superior to women in such skirmishes; but jest books and comedies do not bear out this assumption. Among all the misogynist japes are many examples of women squelching their male opponents. Women playgoers would have been well versed in comic proverbs that deflate men's cocksureness, such as *better a shrew than a sheep* and *sauce for the goose is good for the gander*. Through oral culture and cheap print, especially merry tales and songs, they would have known such famous jesting viragoes as Long Meg of Westminster, Mother Bunch, and the Wife of Bath, who had an afterlife as a ballad heroine who pointed out the moral flaws of biblical authorities, including Paul himself (*Wanton Wife of Bath*: 214). A few of Shakespeare's spectators might have read or heard the recently published *Jane Anger, her Protection for Women* (1589), the first addition to the *querelle* in an Englishwoman's voice, which protests the double standard and bristles with satire and jokes against men (Travitsky 1984: 258, 263–6; Woodbridge 1984: 63–6).

Kate simply does not measure up to jesting women in this tradition. Her sense of timing – the *sine qua non* of comic delivery – is noticeably sketchy. Compare the scattershot ineffectuality of Kate's beast-pun, "Asses are made to bear, and so are you" (2.1.195) with the aplomb of "a stately dame [who] was a notable good huswife," in a story from Bacon's *Apophtheghmes new and old* (1626). Once when Sir Walter Raleigh was a guest at the lady's country estate, he rose early and overheard her say to a maid who took care of the swine, "Is the piggie served?" Afterward she descends "in great state to the great chamber," where Raleigh and other gentlemen are seated. "Madam," says Raleigh, thinking to put her to the blush, "Is the piggie served?" She answers, "You know best, whether you have had your breakfast" (305). Mouth-shutting humor was not the sole property of "stately dames." In another jest, a "Countrywoman" relieves herself by the side of the road. Two men pass by and one taunts her, asking why she doesn't cackle over her newlaid egg. She answers, "so I would have done too, my friend, but that I feard such a knave as thou art, would have stollen my egge. Yet to save your longing, take one mouthfull, and be gone." The story ends with the biter bitten and the woman on top: "The Countrywoman went laughing away, hee not having a word to reply" (*Pasquils jests*, 1629: sig. C).

My point is not that *Taming*'s women playgoers heard exactly these jokes, but that they are representative of jest types that were familiar from the oral and print byways of popular culture. Ballads and jest books demonstrated that skill at jesting was not restricted to any one class or gender, and that even the lowliest servant, whore, or crone could wield the scourge of laughter against a tormenter. As one merry book warned, "the greatest reputed wit for quipping, may be graveled by a wit more sharp, though less esteemed" (*Politeuphuia*, 1598: 158). The danger to a man's *amour propre* was taken seriously in this highly oral and theatrical culture. Jesting well was no trivial pursuit, and being laughed at a pain to be avoided at all costs. Rhetoricians imitated Cicero and Quintilian in giving advice to readers about when and how to fire off witty ripostes and anecdotes, providing copious examples. A fierce antagonism, rather than a desire to make merry, motivates most of the jests in the handbooks. Thomas Wilson and George Puttenham warned readers to study and practice jesting to arm themselves against the inevitable taunts, fleers, and flouts that flesh is heir to. For the less literate, including women, jesting skill could be acquired through the ear and eye. Jesting could provide a woman with brief moments of social power, and a potent form of self-defense – especially when she was accosted by an aggressive suitor wielding sexual innuendoes and frontal attacks, as Petruchio does in his first meeting with Kate.

Kate's futile attempts at mastery invoke well-worn subtypes of women's jesting. In the famous "scornful maid" topos, a maiden puts down a lovesick wooer, usually by countering Petrarchan raptures with pithy insults that deflate his pretensions and manhood. This category of jesting had a practical use: early modern women often endured years-long periods of courtship, during which they were expected to "scorn, jeer and generally discourage the advances of a suitor" (Mendelson and Crawford 1998:

117). Ballads about comic wooing were legion, often presented as ludicrous dialogues between country bumpkin and pert maid. This well-worn comic format underlies Kate's sneer that she is "too light for such a swain as you to catch" (2.1.200), but Petruchio denies her the straight lines she needs for this kind of jesting, and his compliments are tardy, barbed, and insincere: "For thou art pleasant, gamesome, passing courteous, / But slow in speech, yet sweet as springtime flowers" (238–9). If Kate were truly quick in speech, she might have squelched his clichéd compliments, just as "a scoffing Lady" does in one jest. When the lady calls her suitor's wit "very pretty," her victim asks "why so?" She answers, "Because all that is little is pretty" (Hickes 1671: 12). Kate also might have zeroed in on Petruchio's venality in courting her for her fortune, a common topic in anti-suitor jest. In one story a maid grows sick and tired of her suitor's greedy interest in her father's fine mare, which he visits each time he comes to woo. She breaks it off, but he returns later to try again. She pretends not to recognize him, but he protests his renewed passion. She looks down coldly from her window and replies: "I crie you mercie, for that now I well remember you; you are he that cam'd a Wooing to my fathers Mare."[13]

Taming's wooing match moves quickly to the field of innuendo and bawdry, a risky discourse for real women, but one at which many women excel in the jesting literature. Kate tells Petruchio to beware her waspish sting, and he says he'll pluck it out. She answers: "Ay, if the fool could find where it lies" – a suggestive riposte (208). Then she retreats, insisting a wasp's sting lies in its tongue, but Petruchio names its tail. Trapped, she is offended, and turns to leave. He counters with "What, with my tongue in your tail?" and Kate erupts in fury, striking him (213–15). The gender connotations of Petruchio's archaic obscenity have changed over time. In the early modern period any jest-variant on "kiss my arse" was a weapon of last resort, used to infuriate and silence an obnoxious victim because it was assumed to create a feeling of shameful disgust. In jest books more women than men resort to this scatological barb, turning the strong pudeur that fills misogynist jest against their male opponents. Even the great Tarlton cannot produce a riposte when a woman broaches the taboo subject. In "How a Maid drave Tarlton to a Non-Plus" from *Tarltons Jests*, the great clown meets "a wily Country wench, who gave him quip for quip: Sweetheart (saies hee) I would my flesh were in thine. So would I Sir (saies shee) I would your nose were in my, I know where, Tarlton angred at this, said no more, but goes forward."[14] As this jest suggests, laughter always possesses an ambiguous duality and a dangerous fickleness: the same joke can arouse disgust and pleasure, just as the same play can be repugnant to some and delightful to others. Petruchio's sally may have brought forth groans from some in the audience, but shouts of laughter from others. In playing the shrew, he shows himself willing to shock and offend by appropriating the shrew's most devastating weapon.

But Kate is not through yet. In the final bout she tries to get Petruchio on the hip by attacking his virility. Women in the jesting literature, from ballads to jigs to comedies, revel in hitting men below the belt, using as many puns as they can muster. Gossips quip that a childless husband named Angel is "a grain too light"; another husband who has given his wife no children "can add and he can subtract, but he cannot multiply" (*A Banquet of Jests* 1639: 213; 1633: 175). Shrews gather to bewail their husband's loglike inertia and minuscule genitalia (*A Talk of Ten Wives*, 1530: 29–33). Kate draws on this tradition as she insults Petruchio's potency (calling him "withered," "no cock of mine," "craven," and "jade") and piles on epithets that cut against his masculine honor and status ("no gentleman," "coxcomb," "such a young one"). He dodges these verbal bullets, providing a reassuring performance for men who bore the heat of women's examination, and their jests, back home in the courts of neighborhood judgment. His technique probably appeared clever to those with little wit to begin with. In a linguistic equivalent to banging drums to drown out a woman's speech (in the manner of jester-tamer Richard III), he denies her any standing to jest with him, and miss-takes every one of her statements. It is like a tennis match in which one player wields a bazooka instead of a racket. If this play were in essence a game, as many astute observers have argued, then Kate would be a player. The aggravating fact is that she is not.

Kate's wooing and wedding stage her scandalous demotion from jester to puppet, robbing her of words and agency and severing her connection with the female audiences who were traditional allies of the battling stage shrew and the jesting gossip-shrew.[15] I am aware that my analysis cuts against most feminist readings by seeing Kate as a figure who would annoy some women rather than inspire identification or sympathy. But there is very little within the play that would prompt early modern women to pity a woman who beats her sister, mocks her father, says not a word when she is betrothed against her will, and hasn't the wit to vex a suitor or revenge herself on a tyrant husband.[16] Their expectations would have run in a different direction altogether. A shrew was supposed to provide laughter, not tears. Companionable shrews in the gossips' literature inspire their weaker friends to revolt against their hated husbands, in tippling rounds punctuated by laughter. Such a wife is distinct from the scold who quarreled with husband, neighbors, and servants alike, attracting opprobrium in the jesting literature geared to reinforcing "neighborhood."

As signaled by Kate's lack of allies, she is more scold than shrew.[17] Padua is dying to be rid of her. When Petruchio abducts her from her own wedding party, no one tries to stop them. Baptista chuckles at his good fortune: "Nay, let them go – a couple of quiet ones!" Bianca coolly observes that her sister "being mad herself, is madly mated," while Gremio predicts that time will reveal truth: "Petruchio is Kated" (3.2.229, 233–4). These reactions may have led audiences to expect at long last what the title promised: an extended brawl between a "swearing Jack" and a roaring shrew. But like the Lord who tantalizes Sly with a "Lady wife" who is no lady, the play has something else in store. Its novelty lies not only in the absence of blows but in the surgical removal of the female jesting subject from its discursive field – thereby denying satisfaction to audience members who were led to expect at least a mad mating, if not a Kating.

The "taming school" will merely complete the process of converting Kate into a performing object. From the wedding to the play's end the maleness of the comedy intensifies, reinforced by Petruchio's hostile all-male staff and the arrival of Hortensio to gawk pruriently at Kate's breaking. Cut off from aid, Kate doesn't make any more jokes, but takes them on the chin. Women watching are no longer invited to choose between subject positions, or to alternate between fantasy and critique, but are forced to peer in at an all-male laboratory with one experimental animal. Some may have felt lively concern for the beleaguered, hungry bride, even a frustrated urge to assist her as they would an abused neighbor. Their sympathy may have been muted, however, by the seductive display of food and finery, the lack of any visible beating, and the location inside Petruchio's house far from Padua, where Kate's wails cannot reach her neighbors' ears. Female neighbors were expected to step in first when other women stood in danger of serious harm, but most interventions occurred only when noisy beatings disturbed the peace (Gowing 1996: 217–19, 230–1; Amussen 1988: 123).

By the end of the play, Kate is being compared to an obedient child (" 'Tis a good hearing when children are toward" (5.2.186)), having vacated her crucial clown's role and leaving a gap that is never filled. Women onstage and off have lost their standing as players in the working out of the jest-within-a jest. Bianca and the Widow fight a rearguard action, taking up the oppositional stance of the shrew and providing a final chorus of revulsion against the gestures and rhetoric of Kate's submission. Some women who disliked Kate may have enjoyed her comeuppance and hissed the other wives' insubordination; but the actions and words of Bianca and the Widow, though few, may have served to cue those playgoers who have been left cold by Petruchio's great feat and Kate's irritating devolution from clown to mouthpiece.

In short, *Taming*'s division of women spectators accommodated those who felt a surge of power at Petruchio's success and isolated those affronted by it. Petruchio's jester-like intransigence and confident machismo seem engineered to neutralize distaste for the play's raw anti-feminism. As Carol Clover points out, both male and female spectators engage in cross-gender identification (Clover 1992: 20, 43, 54). Sadism and voyeurism play their part in spectatorial pleasure for women as well as men; Bruce Smith observes that "in asking questions about women and staged violence, we need to distinguish . . . three possibilities: women as objects, women as subjects, and women as subject/objects." At times women may have "read themselves as perpetrators of violence," taking pleasure in seeing others humiliated and punished onstage (Smith quoted in Callaghan 2000: 184 n.12). In their own neighborhoods, women took part in disciplining other women for transgressions ranging from scolding to incontinence, providing a possible model for female responses to Kate and her taming. Class differences may have played a further role in splitting the audience: Kate is wealthy and foreign in addition to being a shrew, attributes that may have further reduced her appeal, especially for poorer women.[18]

By the play's final scenes, any grounds for female identification with Kate have narrowed to the vanishing point. As promised, Petruchio has transformed his unruly bride into "a second Grissel," a marvel for all to gape, or gripe, at (2.1.289). The miraculous cure is fraught with irony because utterly passive wives were not universally admired (Brown 2002: ch. 6). Women in plays, jests, and ballads call any wife who caters to her husband's most absurd whims – as Kate does in the sun–moon scene of 4.1 – a "tame fool" whom wiser women should shun (*The Womens Sharpe Revenge*, sig. K4r–v).

Faced with the metamorphosed Kate, Bianca and the Widow size her up and find her a fool and a turncoat. Most important, they utterly refuse to take her as a model. The two women form an alliance in a common cause, while Kate shows what she really is under her new "Grissel" garb: one of the boys. When Kate takes off her cap and stamps on it, the Widow exclaims: "Lord, let me never have a cause to sigh / Till I be brought to such a silly pass!" Bianca bursts out in fury: "Fie! what a foolish duty call you this?" (5.2.127–9). Although Kate has returned from taming school with her rhetorical claws out, ready to school other wives, they are having none of it.

> *Petruchio.* Katherine, I charge thee tell these headstrong women
>   What duty they owe their husbands.
> *Widow.* Come, come, you're mocking. We will have no telling.
> *Petruchio.* Come on, I say, and first begin with her.
> *Widow.* She shall not. (5.2.134–9)

The reaction of Bianca and the Widow (one can almost see them plugging their ears) is the *expected* female reaction to the Griselda gospel that Kate proceeds to inflict on them – and on unwilling auditors. Early modern women were constantly pressured to imitate patient Griselda, despite the fact that they found her intensely irritating. In the tale told and retold by Boccaccio, Petrarch, and Chaucer, poor but virtuous Griselda is so obedient that her husband, a Marquis, decides to test her by taking away her babies and lying that he is going to have them killed. She never complains or even sheds a tear, so her husband finally relents; she is reunited with her children and achieves great fame. In her study of street literature in England and Germany, Joy Wiltenburg observes that "authors of both countries noted that this story annoyed real-life women, who had no intention of following Griselda's example; but it was recommended to them nevertheless" (Wiltenburg 1992: 93). Chaucer, for one, was quite aware that his Clerk's tale would infuriate wives, as its mocking envoy makes plain. In popular texts women show a clear distaste for her story, which they call an anachronism, a throwback to the bad old days "when women had not the wit to know their libertie," scoffs a woman in a pamphlet about tale-swapping fishwives (*Westward*: sig. C4v). Other women bluntly term her foolish – "a ninnie pobbie fool," as the Welsh shrew Gwenthyan puts it in *Patient Grissill*.

In advice literature promoting the Griselda gospel, shrews burst in to denounce Griselda stand-ins. As with any dialogue, the danger of such a method is that readers may hear a dissonant fiction that they prefer over the model. An exchange from Robert Snawsel's *A Looking Glass for Married Folks* (1610) assumes that wives who try to proselytize, spreading the doctrine of submission, will provoke the wrath of other women. In this excerpt, the Griselda type is Eulalie, who is lecturing Xantippe on how to treat her husband, while Margery eavesdrops:

> *Eulalie.* This course I also took: if at any time he came drunken home, I would not then for anything have given him a foul word, but would cause his bed to be made very soft and easy, that he might sleep the better, and by fair speeches get him to it.

Margery. Here are fetters for the legs, and yokes for the necks of women! Must they crouch in this manner to their currish and swinish husbands? If I had such a one, and he behaved himself like a swine, so I would use him like a beast.
Eulalie. I had thought we had been rid of your company.
Margery. I stood behind, and heard you so long, that I could no longer hold my peace. Are you a woman, and make them such dishclouts and slaves to their husbands? Came you of a woman, that you should give them no prerogative, but make them altogether underlings? (Quoted in Dolan 1996: 190)

As if to cut off any possible challenge from a vigorous voice like Margery's, *Taming of the Shrew* loads the dice even here. Unlike Margery, who stays to listen and fight, Bianca and the Widow leave the room when the jesting turns bitter, only to be dragged back to hear Kate abuse their ears. Their debate skills are certainly inferior to Margery's, and their antipathy to Kate brief, peevish, and inchoate. After Kate delivers her sheep's sermon the shrews fall silent, frustrating any women auditors looking for a less repressible surrogate in the face of this attack aimed directly at them. Although many have attempted ingenious recuperations of the scene, it is difficult to gainsay Wayne's blunt assessment: "Kate's words offer little to the women in her audience that they can adopt without compromising their integrity" (Wayne 1985: 173). If Kate's words are offensive to women, then her actions – dragging in the other wives, stamping on her cap, offering to let Petruchio walk on her – amount to outright insult. Records of litigation and evidence about oral culture and popular satire provide ample proof that many women rushed to defend themselves when their integrity was compromised (Fox 2000; Gowing 1996). Made bold by their transgressive presence within the theatres, assured of their right as paying customers to criticize, female playgoers had absolutely no reason to endure the hateful sight of a "Lady Wife" slavishly putting her hand beneath her husband's foot.

The theatrical history of *Taming* suggests that women did not endure it. Like a taunting ballad in the voice of a husband, met with an answer ballad from a wife's point of view, the play prompted the only sequel in the Shakespearean corpus: John Fletcher's *The Woman's Prize, or the Tamer Tam'd* (1611), which was staged during years in which Shakespeare's play was still being performed at the Globe, at the Blackfriars, and at court (Haring-Smith 1985: 8). Possibly some women playgoers enjoyed comparing the old Petruchio and the new one, who is out-maneuvered and out-jested at every turn by his new wife Maria and her army of gossips. The new play offers women everything the old play denied them: strong shrews, female alliances, group action, gossips' jokes and songs, festive rituals, exuberant anti-masculinist mockery, and female control of marital sex and household space. The superabundance of women's jesting indicates how rigidly it was suppressed in the older play. Fletcher creates a Maying, Hocktide, and Horn Fair all in one, holiday revels that were specially defined by the participation of women. Most important, he revives the more level playing field of Uxor and Noah, in which the neighborly shrew keeps her gossips, her dignity – and her audience. Kate loses all, which was her function as Petruchio's tamed fool. By "reading as a woman," many feminists have read Kate as a victim who requires our sympathy and whose words demand respect. Early modern women were not likely to have made that mistake.

NOTES

1 I would like to thank Jean Howard, Melinda Gough, and Sasha Roberts for their comments on earlier drafts of this essay.

2 Orgel famously stated that the "success of any play was significantly dependent on the receptiveness of women" (Orgel 1989: 162). Some critics argue that women's desires were neither homogeneous nor easily read; others point out that women and their tastes were often the target of stage satires that showed little sign of catering to them. Jean Howard (1994: 73–9) maintains that as paying customers women disrupted patriarchal authority and disturbed playwrights by making them judges of plays. Dympna Callaghan (2000: 139–65) rejects most accounts of female spectatorship for reproducing early modern fantasies about women as uncritical, credulous, and hysterical. Laurie E. Osbourne (1991: 507) suggests that women wielded power as spectators *despite* the scathing satire directed against them by playwrights. Linda Woodbridge (1984: 252) maintains that women's angry rejection of misogynist drama curtailed the production of shrew-baiting plays during and after the *Hic Mulier* year.

3 Such an integrated approach is needed, he says, because scholarly speculations about the reactions of women playgoers rely uncritically on highly biased comments about women's motives and behavior, and misuse the scarce evidence that is available. Gurr restricts himself to judgments based on the reading practices of playgoers, however, thus focusing on a literate minority subgroup restricted to fewer women than actually attended. My view is that common culture, available to both women and men, and at any stage of literacy, offers a more inclusive source for assessing the expectations and prejudices of playgoers.

4 See especially Fox (2000) on oral culture, Sharpe (1986) on plebeian marriage, and Gowing (1996) on slander and defamation; they deftly employ many kinds of popular comic texts to assess the mental worlds of non-elites, including women.

5 Examples include *The Women's Sharpe Revenge* (1640), *Pasquils Palinodia* (1619), and Thomas Heywood's *Philoconothista, or the Drunkard, Opened, Dissected, and Anatomized* (1635).

6 All references to *The Taming of the Shrew* are from the Bevington edition in Dolan (1996).

7 My argument is based on Callaghan's thesis that "the fantasy of female spectatorship" brought into implicit relation the ignorant plebeian and the "ideal spectator," the impressionable gentlewoman (Callaghan 2000: 142, 160).

8 Kate addresses the audience once in *Taming of A Shrew* (77: ll.40–2) but not at all in *Taming of the Shrew*. The much-abused Quarto has a sharper Kate and more jesting by women. For example, after Kate gives her final lecture, her sister Emelia is rebuked by her husband with "I say thou art a shrew." He gets in reply a tart "Thats better than a sheep" (108: 59–60). See Marcus's (1992) trenchant argument about the gender politics of suppressing links between the two texts, esp. pp. 184–91.

9 "For the shrewd wife, reade the booke of taming a shrew, which hath made a number of us so perfect, that now every one can rule a shrew in our country, save he that hath her." From Harington's *The Metamorphosis of Ajax* (1596), quoted in Marcus (1992: 190).

10 I set out this argument at greater length in *Better a Shrew than a Sheep* (Brown 2002). Findlay (1999: 133) has come to similar conclusions about the link between women's roles as judging neighbors and as theatregoers, commenting that audiences could act as a "censoring community."

11 *Pepys Ballads* no. 74, *Pepysian Garland* no. 42, *Douce Ballads* 2, 144b, quoted from an unpublished essay by Sandra Clark, "The Economics of Marriage in the Broadside Ballad." I would like to thank Sandra Clark for allowing me to read and quote her work.

12   Some popular texts give free rein to authoritarian male fantasies, but these dreams can also draw
      scorn. In a satire on drunks, tavern-haunting husbands instruct each other how to master their
      wives: "And let all scolds be damn'd as deep as hell; / Abridge her maintenance, and from her backe
      / Pull her proud clothes, for they doe make her swell." This prompts the narrator's contempt:
      "And thus in divellish counsell there they sit, / Til of Sherry they have drowned their wit" (*Pasquils
      Palinodia*: 8). For an intriguing argument that *Taming* itself should be read as anti-masculinist satire,
      see Kahn (1977).

13   From a commonplace book at the Huntington Library, HM 1338, ca. 1635, 70r.

14   *Tarltons Jests* (London, 1611), n.pag. For examples in the same mode see *Pasquils jests*, including
      "An old Gentlewoman's answer to a flowting Gentleman," "Of a young gentleman that would have
      kissed a mayd with a long nose," "A merry answer to a merry question," and "A Milk-maides answer
      to a scoffing Companion."

15   Strife in *Tom Tyler*, for example, has gossips who bind her wounds when she is beaten; when she
      gets her revenge, they celebrate with her, singing a carol that invites the audience to join in. Shrews
      in ballads often address themselves to neighbors, wives, and maids who are listening.

16   The strongly conservative nature of neighborhood judgment suggests that women spectators would
      not have felt much pity for Kate. Making a similar point about domestic tragedies, Findlay (1999:
      133) argues that "even female spectators would have been unlikely to give unequivocal support to
      rebellious wives or daughters."

17   Scolding was legally actionable in the courts, but shrewishness was not (Dolan 1996: 288). The
      distance between the two terms, and the frequent mildness of "shrew" in use, is apparent in the
      proverb "a shrew profitable may serve a man reasonable," which would not be said of a scold.

18   Callaghan makes a similar point about Heywood's comedies: "no doubt citizens' wives, applewives,
      and fishwives identified with Heywood's female characters and enjoyed a spectacle of female power,
      but those same women might equally have enjoyed the spectacle of the humiliation of an aristo-
      cratic woman" (Callaghan 2000: 148).

REFERENCES AND FURTHER READING

Amussen, S. D. (1988). *An Ordered Society: Gender and Class in Early Modern England*. Oxford: Blackwell.

Bacon, F. (1626). *Apophthegmes new and old*. London.

Bamber, L. (1982). *Comic Women, Tragic Men: A Study of Gender and Genre in Shakespeare*. Stanford, CA: Stanford University Press.

A Banquet of Jests. Or Change of Cheare (1639). London.

Boose, L. E. (1991). Scolding Brides and Bridling Scolds: Taming the Woman's Unruly Member. *Shakespeare Quarterly*, 42, 179–213.

——(1994). *The Taming of the Shrew*, Good Husbandry, and Enclosure. In R. McDonald (ed.) *Shakespeare Reread: The Texts in New Contexts*. Ithaca, NY: Cornell University Press, 193–225.

Bradbrook, M. (1958). Dramatic Role as Social Image: A Study of *The Taming of the Shrew*. *Shakespeare Jahrbuch*, 94, 134.

Brown, P. A. (2002). *Better a Shrew than a Sheep: Jesting Women in the Dramas of Early Modern Culture*. Ithaca, NY: Cornell University Press.

Callaghan, D. (2000). "What is an Audience?" *Shakespeare Without Women: Representing Gender and Race on the Renaissance Stage*. London: Routledge.

Clark, P. (1983). *The English Alehouse: A Social History 1200–1830*. Harlow: Longman.

Clark, S. (1998). The Economics of Marriage in the Broadside Ballad. Unpublished essay.

Clover, C. J. (1992). *Men, Women, and Chain Saws: Gender in the Modern Horror Film*. Princeton, NJ: Princeton University Press.

Dekker, T. (1953). *The Dramatic Works of Thomas Dekker*, 3 vols., ed. F. Bowers. Cambridge: Cambridge University Press.

Detmer, E. (1997). Civilizing Subordination: Domestic Violence and *The Taming of the Shrew*. *Shakespeare Quarterly*, 48, 273–94.

Dolan, F. E. (ed.) (1996). *The Taming of the Shrew: Texts and Contexts*. New York: Bedford/St. Martin's Press.

An Excellent new Ditty; Which proveth that women the best warriors be, / For they made the Devill from earth for to flee (ca. 1607–31). In W. Chappell and J. Ebsworth (eds.) (1866–99) *The Roxburghe Ballads*, 9 vols. Hertford: Stephen Austin and Sons, I: 335–6.

Findlay, A. (1999). *A Feminist Perspective on Renaissance Drama*. Oxford: Blackwell.

Fox, A. (2000). *Oral and Literate Culture in England 1500–1700*. Oxford: Clarendon Press.

Freedman, B. (1991). *Staging the Gaze: Postmodernism, Psychoanalysis, and Shakespearean Comedy*. Ithaca, NY: Cornell University Press.

Garner, S. N. (1988). The Taming of the Shrew: Inside or Outside the Joke? In M. Charney (ed.) *'Bad' Shakespeare: Revaluations of the Shakespeare Canon*. Rutherford, NJ: Fairleigh Dickinson University Press, 105–19.

Gowing, L. (1996). *Domestic Dangers: Women, Words, and Sex in Early Modern London*. Oxford: Clarendon Press.

Gurr, A. (1987). *Playgoing in Shakespeare's London*. Cambridge: Cambridge University Press.

Harbage, A. (1941). *Shakespeare's Audience*. New York: Columbia University Press.

Haring-Smith, T. (1985). *From Farce to Metadrama: A Stage History of The Taming of the Shrew, 1594–1983*. Westport, CT: Greenwood Press.

Hickes, W. (1671). *Oxford Jests*. London.

Hodgdon, B. (1992). Katherina Bound; or, Play(Kating) the Strictures of Everyday Life. *Publications of the Modern Languages Association*, 107, 538–53.

Howard, J. E. (1994). *The Stage and Social Struggle in Early Modern England*. London: Routledge.

Huston, J. D. (1976). "To Make a Puppet": Play and Play-Making in *The Taming of the Shrew*. *Shakespeare Studies*, 9, 73–87.

Jardine, L. (1989). *Still Harping on Daughters: Women and Drama in the Age of Shakespeare*, 2nd edn. New York: Columbia University Press.

Jayne, S. (1966). The Dreaming of the Shrew. *Shakespeare Quarterly*, 17, 41–56.

Kahn, C. (1977). *The Taming of the Shrew*: Shakespeare's Mirror of Marriage. In A. Diamond and L. R. Edwards (eds.) *The Authority of Experience: Essays in Feminist Criticism*. Amherst: University of Massachusetts Press, 84–100.

Kehler, D. (1986). Echoes of the Induction in *The Taming of the Shrew*. *Renaissance Papers*, 31–42.

Kennedy, G. (2000). *Just Anger: Representing Women's Anger in Early Modern England*. Carbondale: Southern Illinois University Press.

Korda, N. (1996). Domesticating Commodities in *The Taming of the Shrew*. *Shakespeare Quarterly*, 47, 109–31.

Levin, R. (1989). Women in the Renaissance Theater Audience." *Shakespeare Quarterly*, 40, 165–74.

Lumiansky, R. M. and Mills, D. (1974). *The Chester Mystery Cycle*. London: Early English Text Society/Oxford University Press.

Marcus, L. (1992). The Shakespearean Editor as Shrew-Tamer. *English Literary Renaissance*, 22, 177–200.

Marx, W. G. (1995). The Problem with Mrs. Noah: The Search for Performance Credibility in the Chester *Noah's Flood* Play. In J. A. Alford (ed.) *From Page to Performance: Essays in Early English Drama*. East Lansing: Michigan State University Press, 109–26.

Mendelson, S. and Crawford, P. (1998). *Women in Early Modern England*. Oxford: Clarendon Press.

Neely, C. T. (1985). *Broken Nuptials in Shakespeare's Plays*. New Haven, CT: Yale University Press.

Newman, K. (1991). *Fashioning Femininity and English Renaissance Drama: Women in Culture and Society*. Chicago: University of Chicago Press.

Orgel, S. (1989). Nobody's Perfect: Or Why Did the English Stage Take Boys for Women? *The South Atlantic Quarterly*, 88, 7–29.

Osbourne, L. E. (1991). Female Audiences and Female Authority in *Knight of the Burning Pestle*. *Exemplaria*, 3.2 (October): 491–517.

Pasquils jests and Mother Bunches Merriments (1629). London.

Pasquils Palinodia, and His progresse to the taverne . . . (1619). London.

Politeuphuia. Wits Commonwealth (1598). London.

Rackin, P. (2000). Misogyny Is Everywhere. In D. Callaghan (ed.) *A Feminist Companion to Shakespeare.* Oxford: Blackwell, 42–58.

Shapiro, M. (1993). Framing the Taming: Metatheatrical Awareness of Female Impersonation in *The Taming of the Shrew. Yearbook of English Studies,* 23, 143–66.

Sharpe, J. A. (1986). Plebeian Marriage in Stuart England: Some Evidence from Popular Literature. *Transactions of the Royal Historical Society,* 5th series, 36, 69–90.

Smith, B. R. (1999). *The Acoustic World of Early Modern England: Attending to the 0-Factor.* Chicago: University of Chicago Press.

A Talk of Ten Wives on their Husbands' Ware (1530, rpt. 1871). In F. J. Furnivall (ed.) *Jyl of Breyntford's Testament . . . The Wyll of the Devyll and his Last Testament, a Talk of Ten Wives on their Husbands' Ware.* London: Taylor.

The Taming of a Shrew (1594, rpt. 1957). In G. Bullough (ed.) *Narrative and Dramatic Sources of Shakespeare,* vol. 1. London: Routledge; New York: Columbia University Press.

Tarltons Jests (1611). London.

Thomas, K. (1977). The Place of Laughter in Tudor and Stuart England. *Times Literary Supplement,* January 21, 77–81.

Thompson, A. (ed.) (1988). "Introduction." *The Taming of the Shrew.* Cambridge: Cambridge University Press.

Travitsky, B. (1984). The Lady Doth Protest: Protest in the Popular Writings of Renaissance Englishwomen. *English Literary Renaissance,* 14 (autumn), 255–83.

The Wanton Wife of Bath (ca. 1613). *Roxburghe Ballads,* VII: 213–15.

Watt, T. (1991). *Cheap Print and Popular Piety, 1550–1640.* Cambridge: Cambridge University Press.

Wayne, V. (1985). Refashioning the Shrew. *Shakespeare Studies,* 17, 159–87.

Westward for Smelts, Or the Water-mans Fare of mad-merry Western wenches (1620, rpt. 1978). Ed. H. M. Klein. Hildesheim: Gerstenberg Verlag.

Whigham, F. (1996). *Seizures of the Will in Early Modern English Drama.* Cambridge: Cambridge University Press.

Wiltenburg, J. (1992). *Disorderly Women and Female Power in the Street Literature of Early Modern Germany and England.* Charlottesville: University of Virginia Press.

The Womens Sharpe Revenge . . . performed by Mary Tattle-well, and Joane Hit-Him-Home (1640). London.

Woodbridge, L. (1984). *Women and the English Renaissance: Literature and the Nature of Womenkind, 1540–1620.* Urbana: University of Illinois Press.

Wurzbach, N. (1990). *The Rise of the English Street Ballad, 1550–1650.* Cambridge: Cambridge University Press.

15

The Comedy of Errors and The Calumny of Apelles: An Exercise in Source Study

Richard Dutton

The main sources of *The Comedy of Errors* are familiar friends, possibly too familiar to receive the attention they warrant: Shakespeare drew the main plot of twins separated at birth from the *Menaechmi* of Plautus (possibly consulted in part in William Warner's translation); further material, including the addition of a second set of twins, from the same playwright's *Amphitruo*; and lesser details from such works as George Gascoigne's *Supposes*, John Lyly's *Mother Bombie*, and John Gower's *Confessio Amantis*. The usual narrative of all this is of Shakespeare fleshing out, humanizing, and Christianizing these disparate materials. That is what we find, for example, in T. W. Baldwin's repeated attentions to the play, including his exhaustive *On the Compositional Genetics of "The Comedy of Errors"* (1965), or more succinctly in R. A. Foakes's Arden edition.[1]

Christianizing is an important element in the process, associated with Shakespeare's translation of the action from Epidamnus, in Plautus, to Ephesus. The hint for this may have come from the tale of Apollonius of Tyre in Gower, but if so the dramatist built extensively on this to incorporate most of the biblical resonances of Ephesus (mainly associated with St. Paul in the Acts of the Apostles and his Epistle to the Ephesians) into his story.[2] So much so that, as Joseph Candido puts it in one of the shrewder and more imaginative studies of Shakespeare's use of his sources: "one could easily argue that Shakespeare's play is at least as much Pauline as it is Plautine" (Candido 1990: 221). As Donna Hamilton succinctly summarizes: "Ephesians includes statements on the need to maintain a hierarchical relationship between master and servant and husband and wife, and instructions to 'Put on the whole armour of God that ye may be able to stand against the assaults of the devill'; in Acts, Ephesus is a place where evil spirits abound" (Hamilton 1992: 64).[3] It will be readily apparent how much these themes inform the play that Shakespeare wrote. So Glyn Austen, in an explicitly Christian reading of the play, has no difficulty in suggesting that "Shakespeare's primary reason for shifting the setting from the Epidamnum of his Plautine source to Ephesus would have been to capitalize on the proverbial quality of the latter as a disordered society" (Austen 1987: 58).

So far so good. But traditional accounts both of the sources and of the change of location leave a good deal that is not explained about the play and its origins, late in the 1580s or early in the 1590s.[4] Donna Hamilton's is the one attempt to relate these matters fully to the religious tensions of the immediate period, taking the play to be an allegory of church politics at a time when the Church of England was reacting intemperately to criticism from nonconformists (Hamilton 1992: 59–85). I want to propose a different context, however, one suggested by a hitherto overlooked source which carries with it a considerable freight of Reformation baggage. In adapting Plautus, Shakespeare changed the name of the principal twins from Menaechmus (admittedly a mouthful in English) to Antipholus – or "Antipholis" as it appears twice in the First Folio text, the only early witness. What does the name mean, and where did Shakespeare find it? It is instructive here to follow T. W. Baldwin's exhaustive labors on this, as on so many other features of the play, since he got very close to the answer but failed to recognize it because (I suggest) it did not square with what he wanted or expected to find.

Unable to identify a specific source for Antipholus, Baldwin examined a variety of options, concluding that it is the type-name of a lover, deriving from the Greek feminine Αντιφιλα (Antiphila: "worthy of devotion"). In arguing this, Baldwin considered – only to reject – Henry Cunningham's suggestion that Shakespeare's usage parallels that of Philip Sidney and William Camden, who both use the name "Antiphilus":[5]

> Quite evidently also, Shakespeare did not get Antipholis, Antipholus, from the correct Latin transliteration Antiphilus of Sidney, as Cunningham suggested. In the *Arcadia*, "*Erona* irreligious gainst Loue, must loue the base *Antiphilus*" as punishment, since this Antiphilus lived a "false-harted life, which had planted no strong thought in him, but that he could be vnkind". This Antiphilus is "vnkinde", anti love.
>
> Also Camden dubs Ralph Brooke, who had attacked him, Antiphilus, "mihi iugulum petit iste Antiphilus"; this here cutthroat Antiphilus! Brooke had been "anti", against or in opposition to "philus", a calumniator, as Camden repeats. These Antiphili of Sidney and Camden certainly do not represent Shakespeare's idea; they are anti, whether it be in Antiphilus, Antipho, etc.[6]

And this line of thought has largely been adopted by recent editions, though R. A. Foakes is properly circumspect: "Antipholus appears to stem from the Greek 'Antiphilos,' listed as a proper name for a lover in H. Estienne (Stephanus), *Thesaurus Graecae Linguae* (1572), but we do not know where Shakespeare found it."[7] This is very reasonable if we assume that the play is essentially a romantic comedy. But in fact romantic love, while considerably more prominent an issue than it is in Plautus, remains a secondary theme in the play. Whatever warmth there ever was between Antipholus of Ephesus and his wife, Adriana, has cooled a good deal by the time of the play. And while Antipholus of Syracuse seems attracted for a time to her sister, Luciana, Shakespeare cannot be bothered even to confirm if this leads to a marriage at the end of the play. It is the same-but-not-the-same pairing of the two sets of twins which is at the heart of the play, not their romantic attachments: they serve only as catalysts to the main action.

In this blinkered conviction that Shakespeare was really concerned with romantic comedy, Baldwin failed to appreciate that Antipholus in fact derived from what in the Renaissance was one of the most famous essays of classical antiquity: Lucian's περι του μη ραιδιῶσ πιστευιεν διαβοληι, best known by its name in Latin translation, *Calumnia non temere credendum*, "On not believing rashly [or: being too quick to put faith] in slander." This was evidently where Sidney and Camden also found the name, though as we shall see there are reasons for supposing that Shakespeare found it directly in Lucian. There were several translations of the essay in the fifteenth and sixteenth century, both into Latin and into various European vernaculars. Though there was, apparently, no complete translation into English, it was widely drawn on, notably by Sir Thomas Elyot in his influential *Book of the Governor* (1531), which contains a chapter "Of Detraction and the ymage therof made by the painter Apelles." Most famously, it was translated into Latin in 1518 by the humanist scholar, biographer, and friend of Martin Luther, Philip Melanchthon. This version was reprinted many times, often collected together with other translations of Lucian by Erasmus and Sir Thomas More — by far the best selling of all their works throughout the sixteenth century.

The essay *Calumnia* was particularly famous, as Elyot's title indicates, because it contained a detailed description of a painting on the theme of slander by Apelles, the greatest artist of classical antiquity. The painting had long been lost, but in the Renaissance a number of artists, including Botticelli, Raphael, Mantegna, Dürer, Breugel, and Rubens, attempted to recreate Apelles' masterpiece from Lucian's account.[8] Of particular interest from our perspective is the section of the essay which explains how Apelles came to paint his masterpiece, spurred on by the experience of being slandered himself:

> I should say, however, that Apelles of Ephesus long ago preempted this subject for a picture; and with good reason, for he himself had been slandered to Ptolemy on the ground that he had taken part with Theodotas in the conspiracy in Tyre, although Apelles had never set eyes on Tyre and did not know who Theodotas was . . . Nevertheless, one of his rivals named Antiphilus, through envy of his favour at court and professional jealousy, maligned him by telling Ptolemy that he had taken part in the whole enterprise, and that someone had seen him dining with Theodotas in Phoenicia. (Lucian 1913–67: 363)

Apelles was born in Colophon, but spent part of his working life in Ephesus, and this is where Lucian locates him. This passage thus appears to be the only instance outside of Shakespeare which brings together the town of Ephesus with the name "Antiphilus" (Αντιφιλοσ in the original Greek). This in itself – given Shakespeare's adoption of Ephesus as his setting, in defiance of his other sources – creates a strong prima facie case for its having been where he found it. But there are, as we shall see,

other aspects of the essay which also relate closely to the play, and they suggest why
Shakespeare might have found it so apposite for his purposes.

Slander

There are features of the story as Lucian tells it which show that it cannot be true in
its entirety: the ruler to whom Apelles is said to have been slandered was not even
born before the painter died. Moreover, this Antiphilus is otherwise unknown: his
name, which may well therefore be fictional, is a cognomen in the essay for a
slanderer, "'vnkinde', anti love," as in the forms Baldwin cites from Sidney and
Camden. It would be ironic to the point of sarcasm if it was also to be understood "as
a proper name for a lover." There are, rather, compelling grounds for supposing that
Shakespeare associated "Antipholus" with slander in this way. One of the primary
consequences of the presence of Antipholus of Syracuse in Ephesus is the inadvertent
chain of slanders which he unleashes on his brother, his brother's wife, and his
brother's creditors. Shakespeare draws attention to it by making it the subject of a
sustained passage by the merchant Balthasar, warning Antipholus of Ephesus against
actions which will all too easily destroy reputations:

> Herein you war against your reputation,
> And draw within the compass of suspect
> Th' unviolated honour of your wife.
>
> . . .
>
> If by strong hand you offer to break in
> Now in the stirring passage of the day,
> A vulgar comment will be made of it;
> And that supposed by the common rout
> Against your yet ungalled estimation,
> That may with foul intrusion enter in,
> And dwell upon your grave when you are dead;
> For slander lives upon succession,
> For e'er hous'd where it gets possession. (3.1.86–106)

This offers a disinterested perspective on a concern with honor and reputation which
is common to all the principal characters. The issue is never simply whether they are
honorable or virtuous, but whether they are thought to be so, whether public gossip
accounts them so: the power of words alone to rob them of something which is
intimately part of their own identity. So Adriana berates a bemused Antipholus of
Syracuse, believing him to be her husband (and so, in a Pauline sense, her flesh, herself):

> How dearly would it touch thee to the quick,
> Shouldst thou but hear I were licentious?
> And that this body, consecrate to thee,
> By ruffian lust should be contaminate? (2.2.130–3)

Similarly, doubts about financial probity challenge reputation as closely as do imputations of sexual impropriety, as we see in Antipholus of Ephesus' quarrel about the chain of gold:

> *Antipholus of Ephesus.* You gave me none; you wrong me much to say so.
> *Angelo.* You wrong me more, sir, in denying it.
>   Consider how much it stands upon my credit.
>   . . .
>   This touches me in reputation. (4.1.66–72)

Later, Angelo acknowledges the reputation Antipholus has enjoyed hitherto, in words that pointedly conflate money and public estimation:

> Of very reverend reputation, sir,
> Of credit infinite, highly belov'd,
> Second to none that lives here in the city;
> His word might bear my wealth at any time. (5.1.5–8)

If the text never quite rises to the eloquence of Cassio's lament in *Othello* for his reputation, it is nevertheless shot through with the same concern.

Adriana unwittingly compounds her husband's loss of reputation simply by telling (as she thinks) the truth:

> O husband, God doth know you din'd at home,
> Where would you had remained until this time,
> Free from these slanders and this open shame. (4.4.63–5)

And Angelo similarly takes him (or, in fact, his brother of Syracuse) to task for so endangering both of their reputations:

> Signior Antipholus, I wonder much
> That you should put me to this shame and trouble,
> And not without some scandal to yourself (5.1.13–15)

Scandal and slander are etymologically and conceptually cognate (see *OED* under "Slander"), different public manifestations of ruined reputation, of lost honor. These are among the deepest concerns of the play.

The Comedy of Errors is a play about identities and selfhoods: the collision of two long-separated pairs of identical twins undermines the comfortable, conventional certainties the four of them have enjoyed about themselves and their places in the world. For the twins are not only physically indistinguishable, they also share the same names – socially, the signifiers by which identity and individuality are primarily conferred. The uneasy farce which this generates may be understood as figuring forth a number of deep-seated psychological insecurities, which in this play are to be resolved in the reconstruction of the lost nuclear family – unlike the action of most of Shakespeare's

Elizabethan comedies, where resolution at least notionally lies in the construction of new families by marriage.[9] As part of this *regressive* process there is an important sense in which the two Antipholuses (like the two Dromios) *are* the same person, are undifferentiated versions of the same selfhood. Or, as the Duke puts it: "One of these men is *genius* to the other" (5.1.332).

In that identity lie the seeds of slander and scandal: in simply existing as they do, *they* as it were slander *himself*. By being in the same place, and being the-same-but-not-the-same, Antipholus of Syracuse repeatedly (if unwittingly) slanders Antipholus of Ephesus, giving rise to a scandal in which his brother denies receipt of a precious object and fails to pay his debts. At the same time he compounds a sexual slander which Antipholus of Ephesus has largely brought upon himself, with some assistance from Adriana's jealousy: that he is shunning her and being unfaithful. Adriana puts the worst construction on her husband's tardiness, which Antipholus of Syracuse tends to confirm by denying her and lavishing his attentions on Luciana. Conversely, Adriana's refusal to admit her true husband for lunch prompts him to imagine *her* cuckolding *him*, so giving rise to a mirror image of the scandal in which she had supposed *him* unfaithful to *her*. Even worse, Antipholus of Ephesus takes this as grounds for misbehaving himself, supping with the Courtesan at the Porcupine and taking her ring (easily construed by slander as a sexual favor), promising the gold chain or carcanet commissioned for his wife in return. When the Courtesan believes that he will neither give her the chain nor return her ring, she resolves to get even by forging the only *deliberate* slander in the play:

> My way is now to hie home to his house,
> And tell his wife that, being lunatic,
> He rush'd into my house and took perforce
> My ring away. (4.3.89–92)

It is a moot point whether Adriana would have preferred her husband proved a lunatic or an adulterer. In all of this, slander has the force of nightmare, giving life and credibility ("credit") to the deepest fears and insecurities about social, financial, mental, and sexual integrity, before it is banished by truth in the form of the Abbess/Mother.

Although the theme of slander (as instigated by an Antiphilus in Ephesus) is what most compellingly links Shakespeare's play with Lucian's essay, there are other suggestive details. One is the repeated likening of both Dromios to asses, culminating in this exchange:

> *Antipholus of Ephesus.* Thou art sensible in nothing but blows, and so is an ass.
> *Dromio of Ephesus.* I am an ass indeed; you may prove it by my long ears. (4.4.25–8; see also 2.2.199, 3.1.15)

Of course the Dromios are the butts of much of the comedy, and the likening of fools to asses is commonplace, even proverbial. Yet a prominent feature of Lucian's account of Apelles' picture, and its many Renaissance imitations, is that the man who hears the slander (commonly referred to in translations as a judge or prince) has asses' ears: "On the right of it sits a man with very large ears, almost like those of Midas, extending his hand to Slander while she is still at some distance from him" (Lucian 1913–67: 365). By the same token, the choice of Luciana as the name of a character for whom there is no parallel in Plautus is intriguing in the context of the debt I suppose to Lucian. The name clearly has associations with the Latin "lux," light, and its traditional Christian associations with truth, so this may be coincidental. But both in Lucian and in the visual tradition, Truth herself is the antithesis of Slander, counterbalancing on one side of the composition the man with the large ears on the other. For someone alert to the parallels, the play seems repeatedly to recall features of the famous essay.

Religion

Outside the confines of Plautine farce, where is slander – and most particularly *self-slander* – a pressing issue? In the context of the play Shakespeare crafted, it is in matters of religion: the whole dimension opened up by the translation of the action to Ephesus. The slander of Antiphilus against Apelles, according to Lucian, was political, that he had conspired against the ruler, Ptolemy. But in Counter-Reformation England there could be no distinction between what Queen Elizabeth herself linked as "matters of religion or of the governaunce of the estate of the common weale."[10] The interest of Melanchthon, Elyot, and other humanists in Lucian's essay was partly stylistic, but more urgently a matter of its moral teaching, which readily translated into the religious/political sphere:

> In the preface to the Latin versions, dedicated to Frederick III, Elector of Saxony, Melanchthon spoke of the elegance of Lucian's style, the vividness of the account of Calumny found in it, and the seriousness of the moral prescriptions Lucian set down. Calumny is a pestilential vice, so he wrote, one so pervasive that even a wise prince like Frederick would be well advised to be on constant guard against its workings. (Cast 1981: 95)

In a pioneering study which shows how this theme relates both to the integrity of the humanist artist and to religious controversy, Fritz Saxl (1936) traced it through various pictorial representations in the early sixteenth century, and most particularly in a woodcut adopted by Marcolini da Fortì as a trademark for his publishing house in Venice, eventually known as the *Bottega della Verità*. This "shows Truth rising from an abyss towards Heaven, while Saturn in the person of an old man with an hourglass takes her by the arm to save her from the danger of falling back into the pit and at the same time from the onslaught of a creature with a dragon's tail who pulls her tail and beats her with snakes" (Saxl 1936: 199). This combines "the Greek idea that Truth must be brought up from the depths, and the Latin that Saturn is the father of Truth," while the creature can be identified as *Calumnia*. This extension of the basic theme, that Truth is the child of Time, brings it into association with one of the most celebrated of the Renaissance allegories, the traditional Calumny of Apelles. The design is, in fact, essentially a modified *Calumnia Apellis*. According to Lucian, Calumny drags her victim by the hair into the presence of the Unwise Judge, and Truth stands in the background, raising her eyes towards Heaven. In Marcolino's *impresa* there is no Judge. Of all the base figures of Lucian's account, only Calumny remains; and it is no mere mortal, but Truth herself, who is the object of attack. Time comes to her aid in her affliction. (p. 200)

Saxl suggests that the theme was particularly espoused by Marcolino's associate, Pietro Aretino:

> For him old Lucian's fable was no mere antique tale, the sport of fashionable erudition. It [i.e., the vindication of truth] was, on the contrary, an essential canon of his creed; and the basic theme of the classical account – that the courts of princes are the seats of Calumny, where to speak honestly is to invite indignity, and truth and repentance follow slowly – is in no small degree a factor in the literary life of Aretino. (p. 201)[11]

For Aretino and other such humanist commentators, "Time conquers Calumny; Time is the deliverer of Truth from persecution and oppression, and in the end brings honour and reputation" (ibid).

But Marcolino's *impresa* clearly also relates to religious themes. It bears the motto *Veritas filia Temporis* (Truth, the daughter of Time) and Saxl shows that this entered Renaissance circulation in association with a parallel woodcut in "William Marshall's *Goodly Prymer of Englyshe*, issued just at the time of Henry VIII's breach with Rome . . . The drawing stands for the liberation of Christian Truth (as seen by Protestant reformers) from her captivity under the monster of Roman hypocrisy" (p. 203). The whole motif became deeply embedded in Reformation controversy, and employed by Protestants and Catholics alike, as in the case of Hieronymus Lauretus, who in his compilation of the *Forest of Allegories* (1570) considers heretics as slanderers whose false accusations are their dogmas. This almost certainly explains why Philip Melanchthon should have been drawn to translate Lucian's essay: few texts would more convincingly marry his classical erudition (he became a Professor of Greek at the age of 18) with his Lutheran convictions. As Jean Michel Massing relates:

> En 1538 Eoban Hess commence son apology de Melanchthon, un long poème écrit à la demande du réformateur, par une description de la peinture d'Apelle; dans son analyse, il conclut que la calomnie est le pire des maux, surtout dans les controverses religieuses. Hess attaque viollement les bulles papales contre Luther mais la finalité du poème est de défendre Melanchthon de ses détracteurs qui l'avaient accusé de compromision. (Massing 1990: 146)[12]

Massing also shows how the theme of the overthrow of Slander/Heresy can be read into the way emblemists like Hadrianus Junius and Geoffrey Whitney skillfully brought together pictures and texts on the theme of truth:

Quelques emblèmes présentent les figures de la Calomnie integrées dans une scène plus complex. Junius et Whitney les on reprises dans leur allégories du Temps révélant la Vérité (*Veritas filia temporis*). Ce motif et cette maxime . . . ont été influents pedant tout le XVIe siècle, surtout dans les controverses religieuses et la propagande politique anglaise. (ibid: 99–100)[13]

Once we understand that the Calumny of Apelles is a text/motif that was readily understood as a metaphor for religious heresy, we are better placed to comprehend the nature of the multiple "slanders" which Shakespeare locates in Ephesus. Yet these are only fully intelligible in relation to that specific location and its resonances. Some of these we have already noted, all deriving ultimately from the Bible: demons and witchcraft (the Greek for slander is διαβολη, whence "diabolic"), disorder, the proper relationship between husbands and wives (Kinney 1988). But we need also to consider post-biblical resonances which attached to Ephesus, specifically those which associated the town with the Virgin Mary, and the town's significance in Shakespeare's own day.

The links of Ephesus with the Virgin Mary were particularly strong, since many believed she went to live there with St. John after the death of Christ, and that she died (or, as some would say, was received into heaven) there:

> Jerusalem's claim to Mary's grave was disputed. Other scholars assert that the Virgin died at Ephesus, where the Council of 431 proclaimed her *Thetokos*, and where she lived in John's care after the Crucifixion. The tradition of John's stay in Ephesus is very strong, and Jesus' recommendation of Mary to his keeping offers weighty support for the argument that she lived with him. (Warner 1976: 87–8)

There was a compelling theological sequence to this account in that in pagan antiquity Ephesus was closely associated with the virgin goddess Diana, whose temple there was (and is) famous. As Anne E. Mather puts it: "fervor for the local Diana of the Ephesians gave way very quickly to equally deep devotion to Mary" (Mather 1992: 91; quoted in Markidou 1999: 86). Marina Warner glosses this further: "There could be, therefore, a chain of descent from Hippolyte to Diana to the Virgin, for one tradition holds that Mary was assumed into heaven from Ephesus, where she spent the last years of her life, and where St. Thomas, according to the legend, received her heavenly girdle as proof" (Warner 1976: 280).[14]

It is difficult to believe that Shakespeare's original audiences did not associate the Diana/Virgin traditions of Ephesus with the Abbess and the Priory which are the focal point of the play's resolution. This seems all the more likely when we also consider the contemporary associations of the place, which made any such Christian presences highly unlikely. By the late sixteenth century Ephesus was one of the ancient and revered Christian sites which had fallen to the Ottoman Turks, a shame which was felt across divided Christendom, as we see for example in John Foxe's *Book of Martyrs*, which carefully lists such losses (Foxe 1583: 760).[15] The Plautine and biblical derivations of the play inevitably focus our attention on the classical past, as if the action takes place (if we have to date it at all) up to fifteen hundred years before Shakespeare wrote.

But there are good reasons for supposing that it would have been received as a contemporary tale. When Dromio of Syracuse is "find[ing] out countries" in Luce/Nell, his master asks him "Where America, the Indies?" (3.2.112/13, 131) – the only direct reference in the whole of Shakespeare to the continent unknown in classical times. Yet the name of the Duke of Ephesus, Solinus (only voiced in the opening line), surely reminded audiences either of Suleiman the Magnificent or of his successor Selim or Selimus II, Sultan of Turkey until his death in 1574.[16] Inasmuch as Shakespeare allows us to be specific at all, we are in modern times, in a land probably ruled by the Muslim Turks, and this gives substance to the otherwise inexplicable enmity between Christian Syracuse (cf. Antipholus of Syracuse avers "as I am a Christian," 1.2.77) and Ephesus, which is so strong as to condemn Egeus to death simply for being in the wrong place and requires Antipholus and Dromio of Syracuse to keep secret their origins.[17] In such a context, it is all the more surprising that the resolution of the play should hinge on the discovery of a palpably Christian Abbess and Priory.

We should beware, however, of being too simplistic in our understanding of how the Turk registered on the Elizabethan consciousness. While the whole of Christendom feared the westward progress of the Ottoman Empire, not effectively blocked until the sea-battle of Lepanto in 1570 (the context in which *Othello* is situated), England actually cultivated diplomatic and trading links with Constantinople, primarily to counterbalance the growing sway across Europe and the Mediterranean of the Catholic Habsburg powers.

Indeed, if we examine the very context in Foxe's *Book of Martyrs* where the loss of Ephesus to the Turks is recorded, we find some interesting equations being drawn. A running headline in the 1583 edition is "Prophesies of the Turke and the Pope, which of them is the greater Antichrist" (pp. 765–6). Foxe tries to suggest a link between the adoption of the doctrine of transubstantiation in 1215 and the rise of the Ottoman Turks shortly thereafter (sidenote, "The tyme of Transubstantiation. The tyme of the Turkes", p. 768); and there is a developed comparison between the Turks and the pope:

> Now in comparing the Turke with the pope, if a question be asked whether of them is the truer or greater Antichrist, it were easy to see and judge, that the Turke is the more open and manifest enemye against Christe and hys Church. But if it be asked, whether of them two hath bene the more bloudy and pernitious adversary to Christe and his members: or whether of them hath consumed and spilt more Christian bloud, he with sword, or this with fire and sword together, neither is it a light matter to discerne, neither is it my part here to discusse, which doe onely write the history, and the Actes of them both. (Ibid: 773)

But we can reach our own conclusions! From a zealous Protestant perspective, Roman Catholicism and Turkish Islam both constitute aggressively alien and implicitly similar Others.

The similarities are such, in fact, that it is commonly possible for Catholic and Turk to be interchangeable signifiers in the early modern period, and that I suggest is what is at work in *The Comedy of Errors*. Ephesus is both the modern town under the Turkish yoke, and the town traditionally associated with the Virgin Mary, so central to Roman Catholic Christianity. So the Syracuse/Ephesus divide in the play is not only that between Christian and Turk; it is also that between Protestant and Catholic. And once that discourse is activated, the allegory of two sets of identical and identically named twins slandering each other simply by being in the same place is easily decoded. In that Counter-Reformation world, identities and allegiances depended as never before on inscrutable inner faith, in a way that generated suspicion, mistrust, and false understandings. Antipholus slandered his brother Antipholus, perhaps unwittingly, to the ass-eared Dromio, while Repentance and Truth lagged far behind. The parallels with the often paranoid 1950s Cold War, with its nights of the living dead, give modern generations some idea of what it must have been like. It is particularly chilling in this context to remember T. W. Baldwin's suggestion (so much more compelling than his explanation of "Antipholus") that the sentence of death hanging over Egeon throughout the play would have reminded theatregoers at the Curtain or Theatre of the execution of William Hartley, a seminary priest, hard by in Finsbury Fields in 1588. Egeon is only ever so named at the end of the text. Solinus first addresses him as "Merchant of Syracusa" (1.1.3), and in the First Folio speech-prefixes invariably identify him as "Merchant" (in a play full of merchants) or "Father": "merchant" was the code-term, as the authorities well knew, by which the Jesuits at large in England referred to each other. The "merchant" under threat of death is a potent reminder throughout the play of the utterly malign force of religious slander.

This is not the place to speculate about what, if anything, this tells us about Shakespeare's own faith. It is not immediately apparent that people from Syracuse are more admirable than those from Ephesus, or vice versa. On the contrary, the pressures of the play are towards inclusiveness rather than vindictive exclusion. In particular, they move towards the reconstruction of the original nuclear family of Egeon and Emilia, their sons and their servants; the differences located in the relationships of the Antipholi with the sisters Adriana and Luciana are doubtless important, but they are secondary in the context of that life-saving regression to the primary unit. The fact that this process is conducted under the aegis of the Abbess/Mother, so redolent of the Virgin Mary in Ephesus, perhaps points us towards the Catholic faith as the vehicle of redemption. But it is more psychologically compelling in this context that the Catholic was the Old Faith, the faith of an undivided Christendom, where brother did not slander brother just by what he believed, or was thought to believe, or where he lived. The errors of the play are wanderings – literal, theological, and slanderous; the comedy lies in a magical regression to a state where they no longer exist.

ACKNOWLEDGMENTS

This chapter was commissioned to appear in *Religion and the Arts*, ed. Dennis Taylor. Reproduced by permission of the editor.

I am happy to acknowledge that it was in the course of reading Michael Frayn's splendid novel, *Headlong* that I first came across the associations between Lucian, Apelles, Antipholus, Ephesus, and slander. Some of the work for this essay was done during a month's fellowship at the Huntington Library in 2001, travel for which was paid for by the British Academy: I am extremely grateful to both institutions.

NOTES

1   Baldwin also addressed these matters in his edition of the play for Heath's American Arden Shakespeare and *Small Latine & Lesse Greeke*. See Foakes (1962) "The Sources" (xxiv–xxxiv). All references to the text, unless otherwise noted, are to this edition.

2   Foakes (1962) reproduces the key biblical passages in an appendix (pp. 113–15).

3   Hamilton (1992) reads the play as a parodic commentary on contemporary ecclesiology, the "errors" or wanderings of the Church of England between the Catholicism of Rome and the ever more extreme Protestantism of the Puritans, largely on the associations of Ephesus as the place where Paul had appointed Timothy to a position in the church (1 Timothy 3ff.): whether that position was as a bishop, as traditional Episcopalians claimed, or as an evangelist preacher, as Presbyterians and other Puritans claimed, was matter of fierce debate in the late sixteenth century.

4   The terminal dates for the play are usually taken to be 1589 and 1593, the period of the French civil war from which Henri of Navarre emerged as Henry IV, which seems to be alluded to at 3.2.120–2.

5   Between Greek, Latin, and English forms, any of these names – Antipholus, Antipholis, Antiphilos, and Antiphilis – might well be interchangeable in sixteenth-century usage.

6   Baldwin (1965: 100–1), citing Cunningham (1907: xxix); Philip Sidney's *Arcadia* (1590), pp. 159r, 231v; and William Camden, *Britannia* (1600), *Ad Lectorem*, at end, p. 4.

7   Foakes (1962: 2, n.1). Foakes, publishing a few years before *Compositional Genetics*, here follows Baldwin's version of things in *Shakespere's Five-Act Structure* (1947: 695–6). They cover similar territory. A more recent but improbably random suggestion about the derivation of Antipholus is that of Elizabeth Truax (1992: 35): "Shakespeare created the name Antipholus by combining the name Pholus, a centaur mentioned by Ovid in *Metamorphoses* XII.306, with 'anti', the antipathy between Syracuse and Ephesus which is so important to the intrigue of the play." Quoted in Markidou (1999: 70).

8   The tale of the Renaissance rediscovery and transmission of Lucian's essay, and the paintings it inspired, has been told in detail by David Cast (1981) and Jean Michel Massing (1990).

9   For different psychoanalytic readings of the play see MacCary (1978) and Freedman (1980).

10 Proclamation of May 16, 1559 to mayors and other local officials on the licensing of plays; cited in Chambers (1923: IV, 263).

11 Repentance, a haggard old woman, stands between Calumny and Truth in Lucian's essay and paintings based on it.

12 "In 1538 Eoban Hess begins his apology for Melanchthon, a long poem written at the request of the reformer, with a description of the Apelles painting; in his analysis, he concludes that slander is the worst of evils, above all in religious controversies. Hess violently attacks the papal bulls against Luther, but the ending of the poem is concerned to defend Melanchthon from his detractors, who had accused him of compromising himself." (My translation)

13 "Several emblems present figures of Calumny integrated in a more complex scene. Junius and Whitney reprised them in their allegories of Time revealing Truth (*Truth the Daughter of Time*). This motif and this maxim . . . were influential throughout the whole of the sixteenth century, above all in the religious controversies and English political propaganda." (My translation)

14 Even accounts of the Virgin Mary's death in Jerusalem often want to preserve the link with Ephesus. For example, "Now it happened that John was preaching in Ephesus when suddenly there was a clap of thunder, and a shining cloud picked him up and whisked him to Mary's door" (De Voragine 1993: 78).

15 Ephesus (Efez) is, of course, still in modern Turkey.
16 Solinus is actually the name of a third-century Roman geographer, and it is far from clear why
    Shakespeare used it except that his book, commonly known as *Polyhistor*, dealt with the Eastern
    Mediterranean.
17 I am indebted to Vassiliki Markidou's unpublished doctoral thesis, *Shakespeare's Greek Plays*, for this
    perspective on the sixteenth-century associations of Ephesus.

References and Further Reading

Austen, G. (1987). Ephesus Restored: Sacramentalism and Redemption in *The Comedy of Errors*. *Literature and Theology*, 1, 54–69.

Baldwin, T. W. (ed.) (1915). *The Comedy of Errors*. Heath's American Arden Shakespeare. London.

——(1931). *William Shakespeare Adapts a Hanging*. Princeton, NJ: Princeton University Press.

——(1944). *William Shakespere's Small Latine & Lesse Greeke*, 2 vols. Urbana: University of Illinois Press.

——(1947). *Shakespere's Five-Act Structure*. Urbana: University of Illinois Press.

——(1965). *On the Compositional Genetics of "The Comedy of Errors."* Urbana: University of Illinois Press.

Candido, J. (1990). Dining Out in Ephesus: Food in *The Comedy of Errors*. *Studies in English Literature*, 30, 217–41.

Cast, D. (1981). *The Calumny of Apelles: A Study in the Humanist Tradition*. New Haven, CT: Yale University Press.

Chambers, E. K. (1923). *The Elizabethan Stage*, 4 vols. Oxford: Clarendon Press.

Cunningham, H. (ed.) (1907). *The Comedy of Errors*. London: Arden Shakespeare.

De Voragine, J. (1993). The Assumption of the Virgin. In W. G. Ryan (trans.) *The Golden Legend: Readings on the Saints*, 2 vols. Princeton, NJ: Princeton University Press, vol. 2, 77–97.

Foakes, R. A. (ed.) (1962). *The Comedy of Errors*. London: Methuen.

Foxe, J. (1583). *The ecclesiasticall histories, conteining the acts and monuments of martyrs . . . Newly recognised and inlarged by the author*. London: printed by John Day. [i.e., the 1583 edition of *The Book of Martyrs*, consulted at Lancaster University Library]

Freedman, B. (1980). Egeon's Debt, Self-Division and Self-Redemption in *The Comedy of Errors*. *English Literary Renaissance*, 10, 360–83.

Hamilton, D. B. (1992). *Shakespeare and the Politics of Protestant England*. Hemel Hempstead: Harvester Wheatsheaf.

Kilroy, G. (n.d.). Paper, Inke and Penne: The Literary *Memoria* of the Recusant Community. Unpublished research paper.

Kinney, A. (1988). Shakespeare's *Comedy of Errors* and the Nature of Kinds. *Studies in Philology*, 85, 25–52.

Lucian (1913–67). Slander. In A. M. Harmon (ed. and trans.) *Lucian*, 8 vols. Cambridge, MA: Harvard University Press, vol. 1: 359–93.

MacCary, W. T. (1978). *The Comedy of Errors*: A Different Kind of Comedy. *New Literary History*, 11, 525–36.

Markidou, V. (1999). *Shakespeare's Greek Plays*. Unpublished doctoral thesis: Lancaster University.

Massing, J. M. (1990). *Du Texte à l'image: la calomnie d'apelle et son iconographie*. Strasbourg: Presses universitaires de Strasbourg.

Mather, A. E. (1992). The Virgin Mary: A Goddess. In C. Olson (ed.) *The Book of the Goddess. Past and Present: An Introduction to Her Religion*. New York: Crossroad, 80–96.

Saxl, F. (1936). Veritas filia Temporis. In R. Klibansky and H. J. Paton (eds.) *Philosophy and History: Essays Presented to Ernst Cassirer*. Oxford: Clarendon Press, 197–222.

Truax, E. (1992). *Metamorphosis in Shakespeare's Plays: A Pageant of Heroes, Gods, Maids, and Monsters*. Lewiston, NY: Edwin Mellen Press.

Warner, M. (1976). *Alone of All Her Sex*. London: Weidenfeld and Nicolson.

16

Love's Labour's Lost

John Michael Archer

The critical adventures of *Love's Labour's Lost* might serve as an allegory for developments in the profession over the last thirty years, especially where the treatment of Shakespeare's comedies is concerned. In differing ways, Terence Hawkes (1973), influenced by Walter Ong, and William C. Carroll (1976), working within established literary history, inaugurated the discussion of language as an unstable bond between words and things in the play. Somewhat later, Malcolm Evans (1985, 1986) developed Hawkes's concern with spoken language into a poststructuralist analysis of writing's invasion of speech in both the lovers' and the pedants' scenes. Keir Elam (1984), meanwhile, had extended the literary–historical concern with classical rhetoric and hermeticism into a thorough semiotic reading of the play. The "language" work of the 1970s and 1980s soon gave way to feminist studies of gender and, to a lesser degree, sexuality. Katherine Eisaman Maus (1991) asserts that theorists had neglected the role of gender in the language-games of the text and their legal basis. Patricia Parker (1993, 1996: 30–2) discusses its complex network of puns on gender, class, and male–male sexuality. Mark Breitenberg (1996: 128–49) takes up masculinity and Eve Sanders (1998: 48–55) female literacy in the play.

More recently still, critics have turned to what Walter Cohen calls the "national and racial ambivalence" of *Love's Labour's Lost* (Cohen 1997: 737). Without losing sight of language and sexual difference, I want to focus on these terms. What is the difference between nation and race? What justifies their differentiation? How do they modify ambivalence, and who is the object of their ambivalence? I suggest that if we look closely at *Love's Labour's Lost* and the social text that surrounds it we will discern a range of overlapping categories of subjectivity that will help us place race and nation amid language, gender, and sexuality. I will begin by examining the developing sense of the nation as an imagined political community that lies behind the play's light but verbally complex comedy. Language acquisition and print culture are related to this category. Citizenship, ethnicity, and economic belonging form another cluster of referents, particularly surprising ones given the play's mixed reputation as if anything an excessively courtly and aristocratic entertainment. Current work on "blackness," however, has already shown how color circulates in intricate ways throughout *Love's Labour's Lost*. I would add that race cannot be understood apart from the play's obsession with abstruse learning, in which the discoveries of the moderns compete with the knowledge of Graeco-Roman and biblical antiquity. Religion figures in the image of antiquity as well: at the end of the play, references to Judaism confound ethnic and theological anti-Semitism, and may indirectly signify Catholicism. The figure of the Jew intimates bodily irregularity and ethnic difference to complete the scapegoating mechanism that gives the play its familiar comic structure.

My attention to current critical interests has projected an unexpected itinerary indeed for a rereading of *Love's Labour's Lost*, Shakespeare's most courtly and cerebral comedy. Yet this path suits the play's well-known mixture of recondite knowledge and topical reference; to expand its field of allusion to the ways people do and don't fit in is to confirm our sense of this inconclusive play's abiding concerns and anxieties. In further refining the ways "nation" modulates "race" in the period, I hope to suggest categories for further work on *Love's Labour's Lost*, the comedies, and early modern drama at large – ethnicity, citizenship, religion, and the neglected sphere of antiquity.

Love's Labour's Lost begins with the formation of a male aristocratic community dedicated to "fame" and the immortality it offers, an honor that will "make us heirs of all eternity" (1.1.1–7).[1] The King of Navarre and his three followers, Berowne, Dumaine, and Longaville, are conquerors who war against their own affections (1.1.8–9). Like the four pious young noblemen of Anjou in Pierre de la Primaudaye's *The French Academie*, who retire to study together during a break in the wars of religion, these French-speaking scholars have exchanged arms for letters (Primaudaye 1586). Neither of these communities is primarily a national one, but both are defined in military and strategic terms that prepare the way for national discourse: the men of Anjou contemplate the threatened breakup of their sovereign's domains, while Navarre's followers are soon reminded of the Princess of France's embassy to reclaim Aquitane (1.1.135). Shakespeare may be mocking the unintentionally absurd seriousness of Primaudaye's academy in his "little academe" (1.1.13). Berowne, who tauntingly recalls the news about the Princess's visit, resists signing on at first, particularly to the article about not seeing a woman during the three-year retreat (1.1.37, 80–3). He calls Longaville's provision that women caught within a mile of court lose their tongues "A dangerous law against gentility" (1.1.127) – not gender, for class, manners, and reputation are more important than women for both Berowne and the King.

Primaudaye's dialogue contains lengthy and thoroughly conventional praise of male friendship, but Shakespeare is wryly aware of male–male eroticism's threat to reputation from the start of his play (Primaudaye 1586: 136–48). The word "academe," as modern editors realize, immediately brings to mind what Sidney's historian calls "the dangerless Academy of Plato," far from battle, but redolent of the "abominable filthiness" authorized in *Phaedrus* or *The Symposium* (Shakespeare 1998: 113–15; Sidney 1973: 105, 128). Plato's *Symposium*, part of the play's humanist inheritance along with

Erasmus and Rabelais, who reverenced it, promises that men will produce progeny in beauty by giving birth to ideas and laws that last forever. The frosty Berowne is accused of nipping the first-born infants of the spring, to which he replies: "Why should I joy in any abortive birth?" (1.1.101, 104). As Patricia Parker has shown in detail, the opening scene's obsession with what, and who, comes after and before initiates the play's chain of scatological and ultimately sodomitical references (Parker 1993, 1996: 20–1, 30–2). When Armado's letter on the "obscene and most preposterous event" (1.1.235) is read aloud, we recognize another member of the male community of academicians (is the event Costard's following Jaquenetta, as Parker suggests, or his preceding Armado with her, or the preposterous sexual act itself?). Of course, Armado is included only for "recreation," as a comic butt, "One who the music of his own vain tongue / Doth ravish like enchanting harmony" (1.1.164–5). But Armado's linguistic extravagance seems the extension rather than the antithesis of the courtier's repetitive word-play. The traveler of "tawny Spain" (1.1.171) is an outlander like the approaching Princess, and his masculine tongue is a permissible substitute for the female tongue whose threatened excision marks the symbolic boundaries of the student body. Throughout the play, as we will see, Armado uses his tongue to claim intimacy with his highness the King while demonstrating intimacy with the lowly Moth. Navarre's academy is haunted at the outset by intimations of transgressive male sexuality, including sodomy, and its implications for social hierarchy. The play struggles, often pleasurably, to distance its courtiers from anxieties about male–male intimacy. It does so in part by scapegoating Armado and other masculine figures on the margins who are linked with urban and national rather than courtly definitions of belonging and identity.

Holofernes the local schoolmaster is the other prime example of irregular masculinity. His initial judgment on Armado, passed to his still more ineffectual friend Nathaniel the curate, will introduce us to city and nation as displaced settings for the play. The Spaniard is "too affected, too odd, as it were, too peregrinate," or too much of a wanderer or foreigner:

> I abhor such fanatical phantasimes, such insociable and point-device companions, such rackers of orthography, as to speak "dout" *sine* "b", when he should say "doubt", "det" when he should pronounce "debt": d, e, b, t, not d, e, t. He clepeth a calf "cauf", half "hauf"; neighbour *vacatur* "nebour", neigh abbreviated "ne". This is abhominable, which he would call "abominable". It insinuateth me of insanie. (5.1.13–14, 16–25)

This is a very funny and very puzzling passage. Holofernes believes that in certain words letters like "b" and "gh," unsounded in Shakespeare's time as in ours, are to be pronounced, according to orthography (or "ortagriphie" in both the First Quarto and the Folio). The schoolmaster may be saying that Armado wants to rack or distort spelling by omitting letters like "b" or "gh" on the page, but it is more likely that Armado implicitly tortures orthography by enunciating words as if they were written phonetically. As Keir Elam explains, Holofernes' terms are borrowed from contemporary manuals in the lively debate over English spelling instruction and reform (Elam

1984: 262–3). Hart (1569) and Bullokar (1580) would invent new characters in order paradoxically to simplify spelling by, among other things, removing superfluous letters; Mulcaster (1582) and Bales (1590) wished merely to regularize the status quo in both spelling and pronunciation (for a survey, see Goldberg 1990: 190–207). Holofernes' position is unique, however: he would both spell and pronounce letters that common idiom elides, partly, one suspects, to restore plausible derivations like "debt" from Latin *debitum*, and false but credited ones like "abominable" from *ab homine*. He is a pedantic fool, but the satire registers a palpable uneasiness over the dual influences of writing and print on an oral culture.

Holofernes' own name probably derives from Rabelais' Thubal Holofernes, who taught the young Gargantua to copy his texts in Gothic script before the invention of printing (Rabelais 1955: 70). John Drakakis has very usefully related Holofernes' rant to Benedict Anderson's concept of print capitalism and its creation of national consciousness (Drakakis 1997: 229–30). According to Anderson, print languages

> created unified fields of exchange and communication below Latin and above the spoken vernaculars. Speakers of the huge variety of Frenches, Englishes, or Spanishes, who might find it difficult or even impossible to understand one another in conversation, became capable of comprehending one another via print and paper. (Anderson 1991: 44)

To read this a little differently from Drakakis: print made the national possible by preserving the local, by allowing dialect, and I would suggest accent as well, to coexist with a standardized, visual monolect. It is significant that the object of the schoolmaster's scorn is a foreigner, or a "stranger" to use the common Elizabethan word. One odd thing about Armado is that he has mastered his second language – he may be verbose and silly, but he knows enough not to pronounce the l in "calf," whatever his stage accent was like. Armado's case is doubly odd in comparison with the stereotypical Spaniard of sixteenth-century English theatre, who is usually so proud that he refuses to speak the audience's tongue at all (Hoenselaars 1992: 46, 64). Holofernes' extreme conservatism in pronunciation and spelling reflects misgivings about the potential inclusiveness of the new world of print culture. In her recent overview of print's relation to *Love's Labour's Lost*, Carla Mazzio notes that Edmund Coote's handbook *The English Schoole-Maister* of 1596 offered instruction to foreigners, women, and servants, all of whom may be found on the fringes of Navarre's academe (Mazzio 2000: 203; see also Sanders 1998: 49).

Attention to strangers, or "aliens" as they were also called, is actually well-attested in English language manuals, particularly spelling manuals. In *An Orthographie* John Hart directs his method toward "vnlearned naturall English people" and "Secondly for straungers or the rude countrie English man," an awkward redoubling that nevertheless couples strangers with "foreigners," as English subjects born outside London were called by the city's residents (strangers include the Welsh and Irish as well; Hart 1569: 4 recto–verso). William Bullokar – whose scorn for silent b, l, and gh caught Elam's eye – promises in his subtitle an "easie and speedie pathway to all Straungers, to vse our language, heeretofore very hard vnto them." In the text, Bullokar observes that strangers condemn English as barbarous and without order or sensibility. He seeks to correct this false impression by concentrating on pronunciation, omitting superfluous characters and including a chart of English sounds that are hard for aliens to pronounce (Bullokar 1580: 1, 19, 38). On the other side of the debate, Peter Bales suggests a technique for rote learning of spelling as it is, to help English speakers, "and partlie for the benefit of Straungers," although he hedges in the final poem on his triple system of shorthand, spelling, and calligraphy: "Swift, true, and faire, together ioyne in one: / (My Countrymen) to profit you alone" (Bales 1590: E1 recto, R3 recto). Bales's ambivalence may have the same source as Holofernes' exasperation with Armado. The unified, silent supra-vernacular of English print culture admitted aliens to the national culture. Moreover, passable spelling and pronunciation according to emerging urban standards may have helped some strangers or their offspring to pass for English in ways that were not welcome to all. It is true that complaints against aliens often concerned their self-seclusion from English society rather than assimilation to it, but many strangers did blend in with their surroundings (Pettegree 1986: 303–5). Fears about passing often accompany accusations of aloofness and divided loyalty: this is a paradox that many members of minority groups have had to face in different eras. Hart had already employed an unsettling analogy along these lines, precisely when decrying the preservation of superfluous letters in pedantic spellings that commemorate the non-English derivation of certain words:

> it is even as we would not have any straunger to be conversant, nor dwell amongst us, though he be a free Denison, . . . except (of a certaine fond curiositie) he should weare continually some mark, to be knowen whence he is, I think, to thend we should be able to know thereby how to refuse him when some of us listed. (Hart 1569: 15 verso)

By the end of the sixteenth century some Londoners might have welcomed such marks on strangers, just as Holofernes would mark alien derivations in the pronunciation of words.

Frances Yates told part of the story in claiming long ago that opposition to French and Flemish foreign-language teachers had found its way into both anti-alien feeling and *Love's Labour's Lost* in the early 1590s.[2] Rioting by London apprentices in June 1595 was partly about economic competition from strangers, mostly in the cloth trade. While it is difficult to believe that rivalry over French lessons played a role in the unrest as Yates seems to suggest, strangers learning English rather than English speakers learning French or Italian may have been a source of worry for the dissidents. In May 1593 one in a long series of "libels" or protest statements had been posted on the Dutch Church, beginning:

> Ye strangers y[t] doe inhabite in this lande
> Note this same writing doe it vnderstand
> Conceit it well for savegard of your lyves
> Your goods, your children, & your dearest wives.[3]

The stress on strangers understanding or noting the writing may be an ironic touch in the Dutch church libel. In complaining about alien merchants and unregulated artisans, the rhyme typically accuses Protestant immigrants of religious hypocrisy and cowardice in escaping persecution for profiteering in London. The surviving copy of the entire libel links it with the French church, probably a mistake for the nearby Dutch congregation, although French, Flemish, and Dutch people were often confused. The verses also compare the ravenous aliens to Jews, as James Shapiro (1996: 185) has pointed out. The May posting is significant, since it recalls the "Ill May Day" riots against strangers of 1517.

Yates (1936) links 1593 and 1595 to *Love's Labour's Lost* by citing the conclusion of this exchange about Costard and Jaquenetta from the start of Act 3:

> *Armado.* Warble, child, make passionate my sense of hearing.
> *Moth.* [Sings] Concolinel.
> *Armado.* Sweet air! Go, tenderness of years, take this key, give enlargement to the swain, bring him festinately hither. I must employ him in a letter to my love.
> *Moth.* Master, will you win your love with a French brawl?
> *Armado.* How meanest thou? Brawling in French? (3.1.1–9)

Yates finds rioting against French speakers in Moth's French dance or *bransle* (ibid: 66). Historians now doubt that rioting took place in 1593, but unrecorded scuffles or disturbances could have occurred (Archer 1991: 1–9). I think the allusion to "brawling" in this sense holds. "Concolinel" may have been heard by some in the audience as the beginning of a French song ("Quand Colinelle": Shakespeare 1998: 3.1.3 n.). Moth's reply also adds a commercial touch whose anti-alien connotation has not been remarked: "No, my complete master; but to jig off a tune . . . with your hat penthouse-like o'er the shop of your eyes" (3.1.10, 15–16). Armado's love is set out in the windows of his eyes; his hat is the awning that typically sheltered tradesmen's wares. In London non-citizens were forced by law to erect lattices in their windows as well, to prevent their goods from being seen in the street (Archer 1991: 134). But citizen merchants displayed their products freely, especially along Goldsmith's Row in Cheapside, a vista of aristocratic consumerism Boyet seems to recall in his description of the love-struck King's solicitation of the Princess:

> Methought all his senses were locked in his eye,
> As jewels in crystal for some prince to buy;
> Who, tendering their own worth from where they were glassed,
> Did point you to buy them along as you passed. (2.1.241–4)

Elsewhere in the play love's merchandise is showcased lower down on the male anatomy. Overhearing Longaville say he will tear up his poem during the sonnet eavesdropping scene, Berowne quips: "O, rhymes are guards on wanton Cupid's hose: / Disfigure not his shop" (4.3.55–6). Guards are embroidery on hose or barriers before a house; the disfiguring of Cupid's shop glances at rioting against shopkeepers as well as the way love poetry covers up, and calls attention to, wanton desires.

The confusion of erotic metaphors with the language of buying and selling reaches its climax when the men, having abandoned their vow to avoid women, woo the ladies in Russian disguise (5.2.157–264). The commercial promise of the Muscovy Company of merchant adventurers is evoked or mocked in this scene. There was no Russian community in London, and as I will show below the strangeness of the false Muscovites belongs to a more academic order of ethnicity than the references to France and the Low Countries. Nevertheless, intimations of actual immigration figure in an episode mostly taken up with courtly love-games far from the urban streets. Katherine plays a typical match in her covert identification of the masked "Long(a)ville": "sir, I *long. / . . . . 'Veal'*, quoth the Dutchman" (5.2.244, 247; my emphasis). Such syllabic punning is characteristic of the empty circulation of signifiers that make and unmake masculine aristocratic identity in the court scenes (Breitenberg 1996: 135–6). But the subsequent teasing of Longaville as a horned calf headed for the butchery of cuckoldom partly depends upon the popular link between the Dutch and gluttony. Because he pronounces English "well" as "veal," the Dutchman condemns himself through what comes out of his mouth, like Longaville. Dutch *viel* also means plenty, as it does in Dekker's *The Shoemaker's Holiday*, where Lacy disguises himself as a Dutch artisan and a Dutch sea-captain has "veale ge drunck."[4]

Marston's *The Dutch Courtesan* is a somewhat later play which features a Dutch accent, and in its citizen *milieu* we also find the explanation for another nonce reference to the Muscovite disguise. Mistress Mulligrub, a vintner's wife, advertises herself as well as his wares in the shop: "though my husband be a citizen and's cap's made of wool, yet I ha' wit and can see my good as soon as another" (Marston 1976: 3.3.27–9). After the lords leave, Rosaline says "Well, better wits have worn plain statute-caps" (5.2.281). Sumptuary laws apparently mandated that apprentices and citizens wear simple woolen caps on occasion (Shakespeare 1956: 5.2.281 n.). Rosaline's remark flatters a large part of the public theatre audience by contrasting the courtiers' aristocratic goings-on with the practical wit of the citizenry, whose civic language the scene often echoes. Holofernes' pageant of the Nine Worthies, which parallels the Muscovite masque on the popular level of adventure plays and urban spectacle (as Meredith Skura has pointed out), is directly related to citizen culture (Skura 1993: 88–95, 89 n. 9). Carroll (1976: 233) describes Richard Johnson's "The Nine Worthies of London" of 1592, in which representatives of the Grocers and other companies took the Worthies' places. As Judas Maccabaeus, the schoolmaster is mercilessly flouted by the lords for a face as rigid as his pronunciation:

> *Berowne.* Saint George's half-cheek in a brooch.
> *Dumaine.* Ay, and in a brooch of lead.
> *Berowne.* Ay, and worn in the cap of a tooth-drawer. (5.2.611–13)

We do not know what the audience made of the courtiers' cruelty. Holofernes' exercise in a citizen mode is clearly inadequate, however, and the insults culminate in his association with the lowly tooth-drawer. Caps entail status once more, since the badge on the cap indicates the wearer's occupation; the tooth-drawer with his leaden brooch was evidently the lowest of the low, perhaps a vagrant or mountebank who aped one mark of the citizen's identity (Shakespeare 1956: 5.2.610 n.). The citizen audience is invited to join in the scapegoating of its failed member, or employee. Furthermore, the schoolmaster is hooted off stage as "Monsieur Judas," a natural title from the French Boyet, perhaps, but redolent of Londoners' disdain for would-be monsieurs from northern Europe (5.2.624). Holofernes, who is seen policing the borders of correct pronunciation at the start of act 5, has become assimilated to the "peregrinate" outlandishness he attacked in Armado.

I will return to the Muscovites and Worthies in discussing the general categories of race and antiquarian knowledge that overlie specific images of ethnicity in *Love's Labour's Lost*. Holofernes' ambiguous status – he is both native and strange, a school "master" and a servant – is also part of the urban atmosphere of the play. "He teaches boys the hornbook" (5.1.44), as Moth says, and the use of this word for the horn-covered ABC that served as a primer establishes his school as English in character despite the Navarrese setting of the action. "Do you not educate youth at the charge-house on the top of the mountain?" Armado asks Holofernes. The mountain is from a colloquy by Erasmus, but the phrase "charge-house" has defied explanation (5.1.75–9 and Shakespeare 1998: 230 n.). I think the simplest interpretation, initially offered by Theobald, is the best – that the school is supported at someone's charge, which would make it an endowed school like most others (Shakespeare 1904: 221–2). There were several ways of becoming the master of an endowed school in Elizabethan England. Schools were often sponsored by various livery companies or trades, and membership in a company was the normal prerequisite for London citizenship. But Holofernes' inseparability from Nathaniel the "parish curate" (5.2.532) hints that he has been hired to run an endowed school administered by the parish.

The parish had become the basic unit of local government in many parts of Tudor England, particularly in London. The parish vestry, a board of citizens, nominated the officials that the roughly corresponding ward appointed, such as constables (Archer 1991: 82–92, 68). Nathaniel, Holofernes, and Constable Dull, three characters constantly linked in the subplot, thus intimate the microcosm of the parish, the most familiar division of city administration to the London audience. The same would hold true for many a country village, and Shakespeare further asks us to transport the parish to his imaginary Navarre, which seems split between the King's court and a countryside inhabited by Jaquenetta and the "swain" Costard with little room for civic culture in between (5.1.119). Nevertheless, London lives in the language the characters speak rather than the action they present, and London constituted the most complete example of how police, education, and religion operated together on the neighborhood level. London was also the setting of the public theatres where this array of local ideological apparatuses might be subjected to public scorn.

Shakespeare's contribution to *Sir Thomas More* is the *locus classicus* for the citizen–alien opposition in his works, and a glance at its relation to *Love's Labour's Lost* will round off my discussion of the comedy's urban context. The setting, Ill May Day itself, is ominous, but the crisis begins with an amusing complaint about the strangers' introduction of outlandish vegetables into England:

Lincoln. . . . our infection will make the city shake, which partly comes through the eating of parsnips.
Clown. True, and pumpions together.[5]

Pumpions are pumpkins, like the "gross wat'ry pumpion" that Falstaff memorably represents to Mrs. Ford; the fat knight is also called "this Flemish drunkard" (*The Merry Wives of Windsor*, 3.3.41, 2.1.23). The unhealthy, watery, and alien qualities of the pumpkin lie behind Costard's description of his role in the Worthies show: "I am, as they say, but to parfect one man in one poor man – Pompion the Great, sir" (5.2.500–1). These are the only instances of the word in Shakespeare. The poor man will be reduced to a pumpion by the pedants' outlandish display; as Costard gets the name "Pompey" right a few lines later it is likely the swain is making an ortho-graphically adjusted joke that the apprentices would appreciate. When More himself steps forth to face down the rioters in the history play, they demand "the removing of the strangers, which cannot choose but much advantage the poor handicrafts of the city." More tells the apprentices that if they succeed they will in effect have taken the King's place, "Authority quite silenc'd by your brawl" (Add. 2.70–1, 78). "Brawling" is not uncommon in Shakespeare, but the use of the word to designate the century's archetypal anti-alien revolt strengthens the possibility that "French brawl" in *Love's Labour's Lost* is a pointed allusion.

More brings his lengthy pacification to an end by asking the rioters to imagine themselves in exile among a barbarous nation that would "Spurn you like dogs, and like as if that God / Owed not nor made not you. . . . / This is the strangers' case" (Add. 2.135–6, 139). In *Love's Labour's Lost* the Princess questions Armado's faith using similar, if gentler, terms:

Princess. Doth this man serve God?
Berowne. Why ask you?
Princess. 'A speaks not like a man of God his making. (5.2.522–4)

Although the phrase is proverbial, its contexts in both *Sir Thomas More* and *Love's Labour's Lost* suggest that it could take on an anti-alien meaning at a time when lin-guistic, ethnic, and religious differences were often joined.[6] Armado obligingly throws in an unfortunate Spanish phrase (*fortuna de la guerra*) four lines later. Of course, stranger communities in London were Protestants from France or Holland, not Spaniards; most of them had been driven out of their homelands by Catholic Spain. Yet in the *More* fragment Shakespeare includes Armado's country in his list of exilic places: "Go you to France or Flanders, / To any German province, Spain or Portugal" (Add. 2.127–8). Spaniards count as aliens even though there were few of them in England, for a general category of the alien or ethnic Other was developing, which current criticism provisionally names "race" and associates with "black" or dark skin color.

As a traveler from "tawny" Spain, Armado is half-way between European alienness and African blackness. Costard calls him "Dun Adramadio," and he twice compares himself to King Cophetua, a legendary ruler from Africa, in his love for the beggar-maid Jaquenetta (4.3.195; 1.2.104–5, 4.1.66). Jaquenetta's pregnancy by Armado, which seemingly provokes Costard to violence, has an air of miscegenation about it that mostly comes from anti-alien sentiment but may also reflect the developing anxieties of a chromatic racism (5.2.668; on fears of intermarriage and mixed children, see Pettegree 1986: 289). Rosaline, "A whitely wanton with a velvet brow" and "pitch-balls" for eyes (3.1.191–2), also represents some kind of mixture of colors. At the start of his defense of dark beauty in 4.3, Berowne claims "Of all complexions the culled sovereignty / Do meet as at a fair in her fair cheek" (ll.230–1). "Complexion" denotes the combination of bodily humors, and thus skin tone as well, as the paradoxical pun on "fair" indicates. As Peter Erickson argues, the paradoxical element in Berowne's apology for Rosaline's "black as ebony" appearance (line 243) partly undoes it: his praise of the impossible is a rhetorical display born of competition among men. Kim F. Hall links rhetorical display to economic competition and the way women and blackness are each made into commodities, differently revalued and traded by white men. As both critics show, the defense of blackness also expresses male ambivalence toward women in general (Erickson 1993: 519; Hall 1995: 90–1). Moth's reply to Armado's curious question about the "complexion" of Samson's love underlines this point: she was "Of the sea-water green, sir" (1.2.80). A certain antiquarian fascination attaches to the Thomas Browne-like inquiry into the color (as it turns out) of the Philistine Delilah – but she was neither black nor white, Moth says, only "green" or pathologically concupiscent in Elizabethan medical terms, as some felt all women were. Jibes about excessive sexual desire lie behind Katherine's taunting of Rosaline for her "beauty dark" in 5.2 and Rosaline's rejoinders (ll.20–45). Most discussions of race in the play dwell on 4.3; the way desire and blackness create rhetorical rivalry among women as well as men needs more critical attention.

The other episode that has received critical notice is the entry of blackamoor musicians with the disguised Lords in the Muscovite or Russian "masque" (5.2.157 SD; Erickson 1993: 519; Hall 1995: 13; Shakespeare 1998: 14). It used to be thought that this stage direction was influenced by the Gray's Inn Revels of 1594–5, in which an imaginary Russian ambassador recounts a battle against "Negro-Tartars" and brings in captives (Shakespeare 1956: 142 n.; Shakespeare 1998: 64). I have suggested elsewhere that the similarity may be due to a common source in the little-known but persistent early modern association between Russia and dark skin color. The linkage of blackness with the frozen north – another example of paradox – takes several forms, among them the blackness of flesh burnt by the sun or branded to denote enslavement. Branding, burning, and Muscovy figure in Sidney's *Astrophil and Stella*; slavery was a well-known feature of Russian society from the travel narratives, and Sidney made use of it to trope love-service to a mistress in a manner that clearly influenced the Muscovite's speeches in *Love's Labour's Lost*. For all its comic ineptitude, the Lords' Russian disguise also masks the memory of white slavery and the symbolic blackening of white identity at a time when the triangular slave-trade had finally replaced Eastern Europe with Africa as the primary site of enslavement. Anxieties about the loss of identity are only partly subsumed in the familiar Petrarchan discourse of the masculine self's diminution in love (Archer 1998). Whiteness as well as blackness is placed in question by *Love's Labour's Lost*, and the interplay among citizenship, alienage, and an emergent national consciousness helps us to see how this is so.

The blackamoors and Muscovites recur to another pair of submerged categories in the play, the opposition between antiquity and modern knowledge. When the Lords withdraw into their "little academe" their study is presumably directed toward the classical world that produced the original Academy, and perhaps toward the Bible as well. Yet Navarre also says they will be "Still and contemplative in living art," the *ars vivendi* of the philosophers, but also the practical arts of living in the present (1.1.14). The moderns, it was often said, had bettered the ancients through travel and the discovery of lands unknown to them. In Navarre's academy, however, the contribution of Armado, that "refined traveller of Spain," is to be a minor distraction. He is "A man in all the world's new fashion planted"; the coupling of "world" with "new," and the world "planted," suggest news of the new world and its Spanish plantations or colonies as well as other fashionable pieces of geographical lore (1.1.161–2). After the Lords' conversion to the pursuit of love, new-fangled or modern knowledge in Armado's mode suddenly predominates. In the eavesdropping scene their sonnets accrue the far-fetched metaphors of fair suns and Ethiopians that later punctuate the Russian interlude (4.3.66, 115). The choice of Muscovite disguise can itself be read as an attempt to impress the ladies through a display of fantastic knowledge, the knowledge of the New Geography of the Old World that counterpoised Africa and its blackamoors at one extreme with Russia on the other (Archer 1998: 167). Berowne repents his disguise by linking "Russian habit" with "speeches penned" and "Figures pedantical" (5.2.401–8). The same sort of geographical pedantry was sent up by the law students of Gray's Inn in their revels of 1594–5, as we have seen. Despite claims about its Scythian or Sarmatian antiquity, Russia was a topical example of novelty because of Ivan the Terrible's apparent courtship of Mary Hastings (1583), the Muscovy Company (founded 1584), and Giles Fletcher's travel book *Of the Russe Commonwealth* (1591).

The pedants' pageant of the Nine Worthies unknowingly answers the Lords' masque of the Muscovites. It partly restores the play's image of learning to the sphere of antiquity, albeit the very late antiquity limned by the medieval order of things. "For it is notoyrly knowen thorugh the unyversal world that there been nine worthy," as Caxton wrote in his preface to *Le Morte Darthur* (1485), "that is to wete, thre Paynyms, thre Jewes, and thre Crysten men" (Malory 1990: cxliii). As an encyclopedic device, the Worthies united the classical world with the Bible, and both of these versions of antiquity with the recent chivalric Christian past in a prelude to the ancients–moderns debate. The triplets were as follows: Hector, Alexander, Julius Caesar; Joshua, David, Judas Maccabaeus; Arthur, Charlemagne, Godfrey of Bouillon. Godfrey, a crusader who conquered Jerusalem, was often replaced with a local prince or hero in the frequent renditions of the device down to Shakespeare's time (Carroll 1976: 229–35). The pedants of Navarre alter the traditional order in drastic but not unprecedented ways, with results that rival the Muscovites in ridiculousness. "We are shame-proof," Berowne says, "and 'tis some policy / To have one show worse than the

King's and his company" (5.2.510–11). But the acceleration of the comedy's scapegoating machinery does not drown out its criticism of the courtiers' modern geographical pedantry.

As to the professional pedants and their helpers, their set of Worthies only makes
it to five, and throws the tradition seriously out of balance by presenting four rather
than three classical figures against one biblical hero. Pompey replaces his conqueror
Caesar in the person of Costard's Pompion, Alexander remains from the customary
grouping, Hercules is added out of nowhere, and Hector is retained, coming along
after Judas Maccabaeus (5.2.543–670). The classical foursome matches the "mess" or
group of four Muscovites (5.2.361), emphasizing the parallel with the Lords but also
serving to isolate the Hebrew, or rather Jewish, component as supernumerary for
reasons I will address later. What is left out of the procession of Navarrese Worthies
is not as important as what is retained or added, but considering the omissions will
bring us back to print culture, the nation, and the way Love's Labour's Lost is a small
part of the legacy that the Nine Worthies bequeathed to English culture.

William Kuskin (1999) on Caxton shows how the fourteenth-century printer
used the Christian set of heroes, Charlemagne, Godfrey, and especially King Arthur,
to consolidate a literate community through the three relatively inexpensive editions
he named after them (ibid: 511–24). The Worthies declined from serious treatment
in the new medium of print to popular pageantry, increasing burlesque, and "the
painted cloth" (5.2.571) of demotic mechanical reproduction during the century after
Caxton (Carroll 1976: 232–3). By the 1590s they certainly lent themselves to the
exact combination of popular festivity and affected learning we see in Love's Labour's
Lost: in Nashe's The Unfortunate Traveller a Wittenberg orator greets the Duke of
Saxony with Latin tags and comparisons to "all the Nine Worthies" (Nashe 1972:
291). The nine would continue to inspire civic pageants and apprentice adventure
plays into the seventeenth century. Such a reputation would seem to nullify late
medieval attempts to build national consciousness on a small scale through a common
print language and a sharable hero like Arthur. In Love's Labour's Lost the memory of
Arthur survives only in the passing allusion to "Queen Guinevere of Britain" cuckolding him (4.1.122).

Nevertheless, the pedants' performance retains some of the civic–popular thrust of
medieval pageantry while reminding us of the source of the play's concern with print
culture. Kuskin describes Queen Margaret's entry into Coventry in 1456, in which
each Worthy swore a loyalty oath to the royal visitor. In England the tradition was
less about fame than the display of sovereign power over the subject, yet in the towns
the subjects were also citizens. The Nine Worthies of Coventry "organize the social
body by visibly locating authority in the royal figure, while simultaneously demonstrating that this authority is constructed through the participation of the entire community." A display of loyalty to authority, the performance also "differentiates the
various members of the community who make that authority possible." A short time
later, print would assume something like this differentiating yet unifying role (Kuskin
1999: 515, 524). The Coventry entry did not influence Love's Labour's Lost, yet the
pattern it exemplifies may live on in Holofernes' insistence that the Worthies will

best answer the call to entertain the Princess, a royal guest (5.1.101–10). Costard–Pompey, "the best Worthy," is proud to say: "I here am come by chance, / And lay my arms before the legs of this sweet lass of France" (5.2.556, 550–1). There is a lot of reason to agree with William Carroll's judgment that the theatre audience should not follow the Lords in mercilessly mocking moments like this (Carroll 1976: 88). The Nine Worthies allow the humble performers to pay tribute to authority while displaying their own rough-cut knowledge of antiquity and its relation to popular Christian history and the contemporary construction of power. They are eager to please and not a little foolish, but our laughter is quickly compromised by the Lords' cruelty and disavowal of their own risible attempts at courtship through more topical conceits.

In the Coventry entry Queen Margaret is shown slaying a dragon after the Worthies' oath. The ruler was often made a tenth worthy in such pageants, and there was also a medieval tradition of nine female Worthies, mostly figures from Asian antiquity like Semiramis. In John Ferne's 1586 dialogue *The Blazon of Gentrie*, however, the women Worthies are recast in classical, Jewish, and Christian triplets like the men. This form remained influential in England, where Judith was featured as a biblical Worthy despite the Protestant rejection of the apocryphal books (McMillan 1979: 129–31). Judas Maccabaeus from the more stable male grouping was also from the Apocrypha, of course, and it is tempting to assume that the similarity in their names, both of which recall the land of Judah and the naming of the Jews, is partly responsible for her inclusion.

Shakespeare's choice of the name "Holofernes" may reflect more than Rabelais' pre-printing press tutor. The biblical Holofernes was Judith's enemy, and H. R. Woudhuysen suggests that his decapitation by Judith lies somewhere behind the ladies' cutting short of the Lords' wooing (Shakespeare 1998: 42). Woudhuysen's Arden edition also includes a wonderful photograph of a cap brooch depicting Judith with Holofernes' head to illustrate the brooch reference in the Judas Maccabaeus scene (ibid: 25). Holofernes the schoolmaster plays this Worthy, so the picture is apposite, and it also brings to mind the complex parallelism that lies behind the episode. In the Geneva Bible's Book of Judith, a marginal note to the display of Holofernes' head at 14:1 refers to 2 Maccabees 15:31, where Judas Maccabaeus displays the head of Nicanor, another foreign oppressor (Geneva 1969: 414 verso, 473 verso). Judith and Judas both decapitate the enemies of the people. The circularity is dizzying: Holofernes plays Judas, who beheaded a biblical villain very like the Holofernes who was beheaded by Judith. He is really his own enemy, an alien to himself and his community, and this is exposed to the female gaze of the Princess and her women. It is the male courtiers, however, who distance their own failure with the ladies by revealing that the schoolmaster's Judas Maccabaeus is a fraud, a Nicanor or Holofernes indeed or, as is made explicit, a Judas Iscariot (5.2.590–1).

The Lords' expulsion of Judas Maccabaeus from the stage is the climax of the scapegoating process, although it is not the final word on success and failure in the play. Popular notions about a multicultural antiquity resolve themselves into a Jewish scapegoat in a faint preview of the penultimate action of *The Merchant of Venice*.

Although a biblical leader, Judas Maccabaeus came along very late, almost as a transitional figure to the New Testament and its Jews; the Geneva Bible follows Calvin's reading of Daniel 11:34 in repeating that Maccabaeus was only a "little help" to the people, an inadequate hero relegated to the Apocrypha by Protestants (Geneva 1969: 364 recto; Calvin 1948: 330–1). There is also the matter of his name:

> *Holofernes.* . . . *Judas I am.*
> *Dumaine.* A Judas!
> *Holofernes.* Not Iscariot, sir.
>   *Judas I am, ycleped Maccabaeus.*
> *Dumaine.* Judas Maccabaeus clipped is plain Judas. (5.2.589–93)

"Judas" is spoken thirteen times in the play, "Jude" twice; the name appears only a few times in other Shakespeare plays. Holofernes' hero is "Not Iscariot," but "clipped" he is revealed to be a typical Jew, that is, circumcised: Nashe calls Jews "foreskin clippers," and 1 Maccabees 1:16 decries an operation to undo circumcision, according to the Geneva Bible's note (Nashe 1972: 351; Geneva 1969: 450 recto; Shapiro 1996: 265 n.74). "Ycleped" and clipped, Judas Maccabaeus is named and unnamed or reduced to a type at once, as the jokes about his being "outfaced" show (5.2.617).

Subsequent jokes about endings take on the dominant scatological tone of the play. Why does "sweet Jude" stay on stage? "For the latter end of his name," Dumaine guesses, but not for "Maccabaeus" according to Berowne: "For the ass to the Jude? Give it him. Jud-as, away!" (5.2.620–2; "Judas" in Q, "Iud-as" in F). To Parker's argument that very dense punning on anality occurs throughout this exchange, I would add the Christian association of Jews with excrement and finally with sodomy that Jonathan Gil Harris has conclusively traced in early modern England (Parker 1993: 468; Harris 1998: 79–88). The association is in fact a key one: in this scene, the members of the little academe attempt to displace the taint of anality onto Holofernes and the other would-be Worthies in a manner that goes back to Greek Old Comedy but which uses modern anti-Jewish stereotyping. Sodomitical wordplay clusters around the pedants earlier in the comedy, and just before Judas' speech Holofernes presents Moth as Hercules, who killed Cerberus the "canus" and strangled serpents in his – there is some suspense before the rhyme – "manus" (5.2.583–5).[7] Moth is much admired by Costard, who calls him "My sweet ounce of man's flesh, my incony jew" (3.1.133). The word "incony" means something like "precious," but it rhymes with "cuny," a slang word for the female genitalia. It has a connotation of sexual luxuriousness in *Love's Labour's Lost*: Costard refers later to "incony vulgar wit" in a passage that ends with praise of Moth (4.1.141). In the first passage Costard asks "What is the price of this inkle?" or ribbon, and this word carries over the "inc" sound and chimes with "ingle," or catamite. Moth as "jew" recalls Armado's epithet for him, "tender juvenal" (1.2.8); in *A Midsummer Night's Dream* we have "Most brisky juvenal, and eke most lovely Jew" (3.1.95). Juvenal was the satirist most associated with scatology, catamites, and Jews.[8] "Incony jew": the play of syllable and signifier in *Love's Labour's Lost* links Jews with sodomy long before Hercules and Judas Maccabaeus make their appearance.

Armado is Moth's master, of course, and the Spaniard is persistently linked with anal imagery, in a manner that implicates the King as well as his page. "For I must tell thee it will please his grace," he claims, "sometime to lean on my poor shoulder and with his royal finger thus dally with my excrement, with my mustachio" (5.1.94–7). At the end of the play, as he leaves for Jaquenetta's service, Armado tells the King: "I will kiss thy royal finger" once more, as if to remind us of the professed intimacy Navarre has tried to shrug off (5.2.870). Armado was apparently slated to perform Judas Maccabaeus in the initial proposal for the Worthies scheme (5.1.118–19).[9] As a Spaniard, he might also have been associated with Jewish *conversos*, giving the portrayal even more point. As it is, his turn as Hector allows him to rebuke the taunting Lords with a literal-minded declaration that he is not the role he plays: "Sweet Lord Longaville rein in thy tongue . . . The sweet war-man is dead and rotten" (5.2.653, 657). Facing Costard's challenge over Jaquenetta's pregnancy, Armado refuses to fight in his shirt because he "goes woolward for penance" since living in Rome, an allusion that links him to hidden Catholics rather than secret Jews (5.2.705–8).

Yet Catholics were often lumped together with Jews because of both groups' supposedly literalistic adherence to law and ceremony. In justifying his friends' oath-breaking in the play's central speech, Berowne uses a theological metaphor to set them apart from such strict observers:

> It is religion to be thus forsworn,
> For charity itself fulfils the law,
> And who can sever love from charity? (4.3.337–9)

Again, these lines might come from *The Merchant of Venice*: a new testament has arrived to supplement and supplant the old. In leaving their oath to the academe and its laws behind, the Lords enter a new dispensation of heterosexual "love." The pedants are cast as spiritual Jews who remain immersed in the strict letter, useless knowledge, excremental self-absorption, and sodomy that their betters have abandoned. One male community based on learning and language has been scapegoated for the anxieties of another.

How successful is the scapegoating device? Hector, as we have seen, follows the disgraced Judas and talks back to the aristocrats. Moreover, the Princess supports him, the initial sign perhaps of her resistance to Navarre's final romantic gambit (5.2.662). After Marcade arrives to cut the gambit short with news of the French king's death, the Princess rejects the Lords' overtures as "a merriment" before the ladies impose their famous penances (5.2.778). Promises are made, but they violate comic temporality – a year and a day are "too long for a play," and love's labors seem lost for all intents and purposes (5.2.867). Armado recalls the "royal finger" as he introduces "the dialogue that the two learned men have compiled, in praise of the owl and the cuckoo? It should have followed in the end of our show" (5.2.870–6). These songs of Hiems and Ver, winter and spring, return us to the pedants' pageant; they dwell on the cuckoldry destined for men who do marry in time, and lock the characters into an endless cycle of seasonal and linguistic play. As Mazzio (2000: 198) demonstrates, vocabulary lists in language manuals often featured seasons and the flowers associated with them like these songs do. Even as comic scapegoating partly fails on the level of representation, then, the language of the play remains the language of town life and its anxieties about linguistic difference. In canvassing some major categories of identity in *Love's Labour's Lost*, I have tried to show how the language of the play, more than its courtly "content," is bound to the worlds of print and citizenship that preoccupied its London audience. These worlds provide material contexts for urban-centered notions about nation and race that the play's language channels along with its literal depiction of a fictional Navarre divided between court and country.

NOTES

1   All references to the play, unless otherwise noted, are from Shakespeare (1998).
2   Yates (1936: 60–1). Many of her specific conclusions linking characters to historical personages are less helpful.
3   Freeman (1973: 50). The poem is signed "per. Tam-berlaine," and as Freeman points out this may have led to the implication of Marlowe and Kyd in the libel.
4   Shakespeare (1956: 5.2.247 n.).
5   *Sir Thomas More* Add. 2.13–16, in Shakespeare (1997). References to Shakespeare's plays other than *Love's Labour's Lost* are to this edition.
6   The examples in Tilley (1950: M162) suggest that the proverb mainly pertains to class and religious differences. Tilley does not cite the *More* passage. Rosalind uses the proverb in asking about her secret admirer in *As You Like It* 3.2.205, and later to mock Jaques for traveling to strange lands (4.1.36).
7   For the earlier wordplay see almost all of 4.2 and 5.1, including references to Holofernes' relations with his boy and girl students. In the recent Kenneth Branagh movie musical, the "problem" of Nathaniel's fondness for the pedant is resolved because Holofernes has become "Holofernia."
8   "Inkle" itself might come from a Dutch word for "single" (Shakespeare 1904: 101), another reflection of alien influence on cloth manufacture. It is also linked homophonically to "ink," printing, and blackness in the play (1.1.236, 5.241). On Jews and the Roman satirist, see Juvenal (1974: 148, 266, 276).
9   In the First Quarto and the Folio Holofernes tells Nathaniel that the presenters will be "Joshua, yourself; myself, and this gallant gentleman [Armado], Judas Maccabaeus" (5.1.118–19 and textual note). Shakespeare (1998) solves the crux by removing "myself, and." I suggest that "David" may have preceded these words, meaning that Holofernes was originally David, Nathaniel Joshua and Armado Judas. The Jewish Worthies, all played by the pedants, would thus have been emphasized in the original scheme; Joshua, in any case, was clearly there.

REFERENCES AND FURTHER READING

Anderson, B. (1991). *Imagined Communities: Reflections on the Origin and Spread of Nationalism*, revd. edn. London: Verso.
Archer, I. (1991). *The Pursuit of Stability: Social Relations in Elizabethan London*. Cambridge: Cambridge University Press.
Archer, J. M. (1998). Slave-Born Muscovites: Racial Difference and the Geography of Servitude in *Astrophil and Stella* and *Love's Labor's Lost*. In J. Gillies and V. M. Vaughan (eds.) *Playing the Globe:*

Genre and Geography in English Renaissance Drama. Madison, NJ: Fairleigh Dickinson University Press, 154–75.

Bales, P. (1590). *The Writing Schoolemaster*. London: Thomas Orwin.

Breitenberg, M. (1996). *Anxious Masculinity in Early Modern England*. Cambridge: Cambridge University Press.

Bullokar, W. (1580). *Bullokars Booke at large, for the Amendment of Orthographie for English speech*. London: Henrie Denham.

Calvin, J. (1948). *Commentaries on the Book of the Prophet Daniel*, vol. 2, trans. T. Myers. Grand Rapids, MI: William B. Eerdmans.

Carroll, W. C. (1976). *The Great Feast of Language in Love's Labour's Lost*. Princeton, NJ: Princeton University Press.

Cohen, W. (1997). *Love's Labour's Lost*. In S. Greenblatt (gen. ed.) *The Norton Shakespeare*. New York: Norton, 733–8.

Drakakis, J. (1997). Afterword. In J. J. Joughin (ed.) *Shakespeare and National Culture*. Manchester: Manchester University Press, 326–37.

Elam, K. (1984). *Shakespeare's Universe of Discourse: Language-Games in the Comedies*. Cambridge: Cambridge University Press.

Erickson, P. (1993). Representations of Blacks and Blackness in the Renaissance. *Criticism*, 35, 499–527.

Evans, M. (1985). Deconstructing Shakespeare's Comedies. In J. Drakakis (ed.), *Alternative Shakespeares*. London: Methuen, 67–94.

——(1986). *Signifying Nothing: Truth's True Contents in Shakespeare's Texts*. Athens, GA: University of Georgia Press.

Freeman, A. (1973). Marlowe, Kyd, and the Dutch Church Libel. *English Literary Renaissance*, 3, 44–52.

Geneva (1969). *The Geneva Bible: A Facsimile of the 1560 Edition*. Madison: University of Wisconsin Press.

Goldberg, J. (1990). *Writing Matter: From the Hands of the English Renaissance*. Stanford, CA: Stanford University Press.

Hall, K. F. (1995). *Things of Darkness: Economies of Race and Gender in Early Modern England*. Ithaca, NY: Cornell University Press.

Harris, J. G. (1998). *Foreign Bodies and the Body Politic: Discourses of Social Pathology in Early Modern England*. Cambridge: Cambridge University Press.

H[art], J. (1569). *An Orthographie*. London: William Seres.

Hawkes, T. (1973). *Shakespeare's Talking Animals: Language and Drama in Society*. Totowa, NJ: Rowman and Littlefield.

Hoenselaars, A. J. (1992). *Images of Englishmen and Foreigners in the Drama of Shakespeare and His Contemporaries*. Rutherford, NJ: Fairleigh Dickinson University Press.

Juvenal (1974). *The Sixteen Satires*, trans. P. Green. Harmondsworth: Penguin Books.

Kuskin, W. (1999). Caxton's Worthies Series: The Production of Literary Culture. *English Literary History*, 66, 511–51.

McMillan, A. (1979). Men's Weapons, Women's War: The Nine Female Worthies, 1400–1640. *Mediaevalia: A Journal of Medieval Studies*, 5, 113–39.

Malory, T. (1990). *Works*, vol. 1, ed. E. Vinaver. Oxford: Clarendon Press.

Marston, J. (1976). *The Dutch Courtesan*. In R. A. Fraser and N. Rabkin (eds.) *Drama of the English Renaissance, Vol. 2: The Stuart Period*. New York: Macmillan.

Maus, K. E. (1991). Transfer of Title in *Love's Labor's Lost*: Language, Individualism, Gender. In I. Kamps (ed.) *Shakespeare Left and Right*. New York: Routledge, 205–23.

Mazzio, C. (2000). The Melancholy of Print: *Love's Labour's Lost*. In C. Mazzio and D. Trevor (eds.) *Historicism, Psychoanalysis, and Early Modern Culture*. New York: Routledge, 186–27.

Mulcaster, R. (1582). *The First Part of the Elementarie*. Facsimile edn. Menston: Scolar Press.

Nashe, T. (1972). *The Unfortunate Traveller and Other Works*. Harmondsworth: Penguin Books.

Parker, P. (1993). Preposterous Reversals: *Love's Labor's Lost*. *Modern Language Quarterly*, 54, 435–82.

——(1996). *Shakespeare from the Margins: Language, Culture, Context*. Chicago: University of Chicago Press.

Pettegree, A. (1986). *Foreign Protestant Communities in Sixteenth-Century London.* Oxford: Clarendon Press.

Primaudaye, P. de la (1586). *The French Academie*, trans. T. B[owes]. London: Edmund Bollifant.

Rabelais, F. (1955). *The Histories of Gargantua and Pantagruel*, trans. J. M. Cohen. Harmondsworth: Penguin Books.

Sanders, E. R. (1998). *Gender and Literacy on Stage in Early Modern England.* Cambridge: Cambridge University Press.

Shakespeare, W. (1904). *Loues Labour's Lost*, ed. H. H. Furness. New Variorum Edition of Shakespeare. Philadelphia: J. B. Lippincott.

——(1956). *Love's Labour's Lost*, ed. R. David. The Arden Edition of the Works of William Shakespeare. London: Methuen.

——(1997). *The Riverside Shakespeare*, 2nd edn., gen. ed. G. B. Evans. Boston, MA: Houghton Mifflin.

——(1998). *Love's Labour's Lost*, ed. H. R. Woudhuysen. The Arden Shakespeare. Walton-on-Thames: Thomas Nelson.

Shapiro, J. (1996). *Shakespeare and the Jews.* New York: Columbia University Press.

Sidney, P. (1973). *An Apology for Poetry or The Defense of Poesy*, ed. G. Shepherd. Manchester: Manchester University Press.

Skura, M. A. (1993). *Shakespeare the Actor and the Purposes of Playgoing.* Chicago, IL: University of Chicago Press.

Tilley, M. P. (1950). *A Dictionary of the Proverbs in England in the Sixteenth and Seventeenth Centuries.* Ann Arbor: University of Michigan Press.

Yates, F. A. (1936). *A Study of Love's Labour's Lost.* Cambridge: Cambridge University Press.

17

A Midsummer Night's Dream

Helen Hackett

"Whatever pleases in the world is a brief dream": Elizabeth Carey and *A Midsummer Night's Dream* as Wedding-Play

Was *A Midsummer Night's Dream* written to celebrate a particular wedding? First proposed in the nineteenth century, this intriguing idea has divided Shakespeareans along battle-lines. On one side are those who read the fairies' departing blessing as spoken across the boundary of performance, bestowed upon a real couple in a real house about to consummate their real marriage:

> Now until the break of day
> Through this house each fairy stray.
> To the best bride bed will we,
> Which by us shall blessèd be,
> And the issue there create
> Ever shall be fortunate. (5.1.392–7)[1]

A favored possibility is the marriage in 1596 of Thomas Berkeley to Elizabeth Carey, granddaughter of the Lord Chamberlain, who was patron of Shakespeare's playing company, the Lord Chamberlain's Men. David Wiles has shown how references to time and astrology in the play correspond with the date of this wedding, and has set *A Midsummer Night's Dream* in the context of Renaissance epithalamia and entertainments (Wiles 1993). On the other side are those who point out that there is no record of the *Dream*'s having been performed at a wedding, and that the only contemporary account of the Carey–Berkeley wedding makes no mention of any play-performance (Smyth 1883: 395). Beyond this, opponents of the wedding theory seem disturbed by the idea of Shakespeare writing for an aristocratic patron, and for a specific occasion, as somehow elitist and diminishing as opposed to the supposed excitement and wide appeal of the commercial stage (e.g., Shakespeare 1967: 12–14; Wells 1991; Shakespeare 1995: 111–12; Williams 1997: 1–18, 263–5).

Some illuminating work has explored the territory between the two positions. What if the fact that *A Midsummer Night's Dream* is a masterpiece – the one thing which everyone agrees upon – is precisely the result of its being a dual-purpose play, designed by Shakespeare both to appeal to courtly tastes at the wedding of his noble patron's granddaughter, and to run successfully to paying playhouse audiences (Young 1966; Montrose 1995)? The *Dream* is unlike most of Shakespeare's other plays in that it has no single principal source, yet certainly any attempt to list the derivations of its diverse components – dream-vision, sparring courtly lovers, fairies both regal and rustic, a man transformed into an ass, bathetic farce – quickly becomes encyclopedic. Besides Chaucer's *Knight's Tale*, Plutarch's *Life of Theseus*, the French romance *Huon of Bordeaux*, Reginald Scot's *Discoverie of Witchcraft*, Apuleius' *Golden Ass*, and Ovid's *Metamorphoses* – all excerpted by Bullough (1966: I, 367–422) – one could add Chaucer's *Legend of Good Women* and *Merchant's Tale*, the story of Balaam's ass in the Bible (Numbers 22), Seneca's *Hippolytus*, Robert Greene's *James IV*, John Lyly's *Endimion*, folk-tales of erotic encounters with the Fairy Queen, Spenser's *Faerie Queene*, entertainments for Elizabeth I at Kenilworth in 1575 and Elvetham in 1591, folk-rituals of maying and midsummer, dream-lore both popular and academic . . . and more. Yet the experience of watching or reading the play is very far indeed from suffocation under a heap of erudition or archaic folklore. David Young's argument is persuasive, that, whether because of an aristocratic commission or merely personal artistic ambition, in this play Shakespeare self-consciously took a step forward in his art, and did so by means of astonishing, unshowy inclusiveness and "the wedding of elements previously considered incompatible" (Young 1966: 33). In this metaphorical, aesthetic sense the *Dream* is certainly a marriage-play.

One argument for connecting *A Midsummer Night's Dream* with the Carey–Berkeley wedding lies in the bride's interest in dreams, as attested to by a recently discovered manuscript. In 1593 Elizabeth Carey's father, Sir George Carey, closed a letter to his wife from the court at Windsor with his blessing for "Bess," their cherished daughter and only child, and a postscript, apparently for Bess's information, listing "games in court." These include "dremes and interpretations of them," "going to the wood with letters," and "awakings at theyr mistres name, and shewinge the causes whi, or sleepinge and likewise shewinge cause wherfor" (Duncan-Jones 1998: 171). Other evidence confirms Elizabeth's special interest in dreams. The following year, Thomas Nashe, a client of the Careys', dedicated to her his treatise on dreams and apparitions, *The Terrors of the Night* (1594). The *Dream* is packed with echoes of *Terrors*, so much so that it qualifies as a neglected source for the play (Tobin 1992).[2] Later, probably in around 1610–11, when Elizabeth Berkeley was recently widowed, her employee Henry Stanford wrote to her that he had traveled to London to confirm her personal motto with Clarencieux Herald, and had chosen for her, from Petrarch, "Quanto piace all mondo e breue sogno" – "whatever pleases in the world is a brief dream" (Duncan-Jones 1999: 312).[3] *A Midsummer Night's Dream* fits readily into a pattern of Elizabeth Carey's known personal interest in dreams, and the dedication to her of texts which complimented her by catering to this enthusiasm.

One obvious objection to the Carey–Berkeley wedding as the occasion for *A Midsummer Night's Dream* is its date, February 19, very distant from midsummer. A play's title need not fix it to a particular date or season: *Twelfth Night* contains hardly any references to winter or Christmas-tide revels, but does have some to midsummer madness and to May games.[4] However, *A Midsummer Night's Dream* tends to be experienced by audiences and readers as an intensely summery piece. One solution might lie in earlier plans for Elizabeth Carey's marriage. Before she was contracted to Thomas Berkeley, her father undertook protracted negotiations for a match with William Herbert, son of the earl and countess of Pembroke. This fell through in the autumn of 1595 when an introductory meeting between the young couple had the unfortunate outcome of William Herbert's "not liking" his proposed bride (Hannay 1990: 159). It has often been suggested that the context for the first seventeen of Shakespeare's Sonnets, which urge a beautiful young man to marry and procreate, may have been a Herbert family commission arising from frustration at William's repeated stalling in marriage negotiations in the mid- to late 1590s (Shakespeare 1997b: 55–6). It is possible that *A Midsummer Night's Dream* was originally commissioned for a hoped-for Carey–Herbert wedding planned for the summer of 1596, by which time William Herbert would have been the slightly more marriageable age of 16, and there would have been plenty of time for settling the financial and legal aspects of the contract. The Careys were still expecting their daughter to marry Herbert as late as October or November 1595; they were evidently highly displeased by the breakdown of this plan, and moved swiftly, by December, to tie up a betrothal to Berkeley, no doubt to spare their beloved daughter the humiliation of hanging around as rejected goods (Smyth 1883: 395; Chambers 1930: I, 567). All of this might well have occasioned the February wedding performance of a play originally envisaged as for a summer date.

Two Votaresses

Among the many verbal resonances between Nashe's *Terrors of the Night* and *A Midsummer Night's Dream* is Nashe's remark that "In *India* the women verie often conceiue by diuells in their sleepe" (Nashe 1910: 359). In her reading of the *Dream* Margo Hendricks (1996) has explored the Elizabethan iconography which associated India both with the supernatural and with boundless female sensuality and fecundity. This is clearly the shared context for both Nashe's statement and Shakespeare's description of Titania's Indian votaress:

> His mother was a vot'ress of my order,
> And in the spicèd Indian air by night
> Full often hath she gossiped by my side,
> And sat with me on Neptune's yellow sands,

> Marking th' embarked traders on the flood,
> When we have laughed to see the sails conceive
> And grow big-bellied with the wanton wind,
> Which she with pretty and with swimming gait
> Following, her womb then rich with my young squire,
> Would imitate, and sail upon the land
> To fetch me trifles, and return again
> As from a voyage, rich with merchandise.
> But she, being mortal, of that boy did die;
> And for her sake do I rear up her boy;
> And for her sake I will not part with him. (2.1.123–36)

As observed by Louis Montrose, this votaress is set against another votaress in the play: the "imperial vot'ress" described by Oberon to Robin, whose evasion of Cupid's arrow caused the "little western flower" to become a love-charm (Montrose 1986: 74–5, 82–3):

> That very time I saw, but thou couldst not,
> Flying between the cold moon and the earth
> Cupid, all armed. A certain aim he took
> At a fair vestal thronèd by the west,
> And loosed his love-shaft smartly from his bow
> As it should pierce a hundred thousand hearts.
> But I might see young Cupid's fiery shaft
> Quenched in the chaste beams of the wat'ry moon,
> And the imperial vot'ress passed on,
> In maiden meditation, fancy-free. (2.1.155–64)

This imperial votaress is clearly Elizabeth I: the idea of her as a "vestal" devoted to virginity, her association with empire, her identification with the moon, and indeed in itself the visionary quality of her depiction all invoke the standard conventions of 1590s panegyric of the queen (Hackett 1995: ch. 6; 1997: ch. 2). The insertion of this royal encomium may be another connection with the Carey–Berkeley wedding. Opinions vary as to the likelihood of Elizabeth's having made the river journey from Richmond, where she was then resident, to Blackfriars, where the wedding took place, to attend the wedding (Chambers 1930: I, 359; Wiles 1993: 139). However, even if she was not there in person to hear this passage, "the Queen had to be evoked in her absence as in her presence," as David Wiles has pointed out (ibid: 121). The reason for doing so on this occasion was not merely that she was the godmother of both bride and groom, but that the bride's family were among her closest connections: Henry Carey, the bride's grandfather, as son of Mary Boleyn was certainly Elizabeth's cousin and possibly her half-brother by Henry VIII. The familial intimacy is marked by the fact that Elizabeth Carey was endowed with her royal godmother/cousin/aunt's Christian name. If there was one court wedding the queen was likely to attend, this was it. Even if she did not actually do so as things turned out, in their preparations the Careys and their players may have felt it prudent to provide for the possibility that she would grace them with her presence. Moreover, the inclusion of a passage of iconic celebration of the queen would function, whether she was physically present or not, as a flattering acknowledgment of the Careys' royal blood and the fact that this was in a sense a "royal" wedding. She is here as an emblem of the Careys' lineage, like a regal symbol on a coat-of-arms.

Another phenomenon of 1590s royal panegyric, however, was that it frequently inscribed within its extravagant praises darker tones of criticism and dissent. This was especially so when the moon-image was deployed: on the one hand it could connote heavenly radiance, the chastity and divinity of Diana, and endless self-renewal, but on the other it had a dark side and could connote mutability and supposed female irrationality and fickleness, traits which Elizabeth's younger and politically frustrated male courtiers increasingly attributed to the ageing queen (Hackett 1995: ch. 6; 1997: ch. 2). In *The Faerie Queene* this aspect is personified by Belphoebe and her capricious and unfair treatment of Timias/Ralegh (IV. vii–viii). Meanwhile, in Shakespeare's treatment of the queen as lunar deity, not far below ostensible celebration is considerable ambivalence about the inviolability and unbodiliness of the "wat'ry moon." As she glides ethereally across and out of the scene, her chastity seems ghostly, deathly, and sterile; after all, Theseus has already threatened Hermia with living

> a barren sister all your life,
> Chanting faint hymns to the cold fruitless moon
> . . . earthlier happy is the rose distilled
> Than that which, withering on the virgin thorn,
> Grows, lives, and dies in single blessedness. (1.1.72–8)

He has presented this as a fate equivalent to death (1.1.65). As a whole, this is a play which emphatically celebrates youth, desire, and marriage: "quick bright things" and the processes by which "Jack shall have Jill" (1.1.149, 3.2.461). The Indian votaress may be dead, her subversive all-female male-mocking alliance with Titania consigned to the past, but in the word-picture which offers her to us her vitality, fecundity, and downright fleshliness seem far more in keeping with the world and spirit of the play than do the intangible "maiden meditations" of her imperial counterpart. The "imperial votaress" passage strikes a delicate balance between necessary allusion to the bride's regal relation, and the repudiation of virginity appropriate to a marriage-play.

"The ill affected wombe": Titania as Hysteric

Somewhere between the queenly imperial votaress and the sensual Indian votaress stands the figure of Titania. Jonathan Bate accounts for the imperial votaress passage as a kind of prophylactic, keeping at bay the otherwise hard-to-resist identification of Titania with Elizabeth (Bate 1993: 140–1). Besides Spenser's *Faerie Queen*, first published in 1590, Elizabeth had also been associated with the Fairy Queen in entertainments on her progresses, such as the one at Elvetham in 1591 (Wilson 1980: 115). Clearly it would not be a good idea to be seen to be representing her as an unruly wife requiring humiliation by means of an erotic encounter with an ass-headed weaver. Nevertheless, Elizabethan iconography and allegory rarely proceeded by simple one-for-one identification, but much more often by complex layerings and encodings of meaning which could mobilize what Annabel Patterson has called "functional ambiguity" (Patterson 1984: 18). While acknowledging Shakespeare's care to avoid any direct sense that Titania "is" Elizabeth, we need not rule out Louis Montrose's (1986) reading of Titania's fate as expressive of a felt need to curtail female power; indeed, deflection of personal identification is precisely what enables Shakespeare to deliver sentiments about the dangers of unbridled female autonomy.

However, if like Elizabeth, or a nightmare version of Elizabeth, in her volatile "feminine" style of rule, Titania is clearly no Virgin Queen. Her sensuality is no less than that of her pregnant votaress. There has been debate as to whether or not Titania and Bottom actually have sex (Swander 1990: 92–108; Sutherland and Watts 2000: 137–42). There are strong clues, however, in the fact that Titania is first awoken by Bottom singing a "Cuckoo" song, implying that Oberon is about to be cuckolded (3.1.123–9); and in Titania's later rhapsody as she embraces Bottom in her bower and banishes her attendants:

> So doth the woodbine the sweet honeysuckle
> Gently entwist; the female ivy so
> Enrings the barky fingers of the elm.
> O how I love thee, how I dote on thee! (4.1.41–4)

This may merely elaborate upon how she will "wind thee in my arms" (line 39), and it is also a variation upon a conventional emblem of the ideal married couple (Shakespeare 1995: 4.1.42–3 n.), but it is hard to miss the phallic and copulative overtones.

Yet this sensuality is precisely what is absent from Titania's marriage, as is its natural fruit, a child. Titania signally lacks the riches which her Indian votaress triumphantly flaunted in her swelling womb. It does not take an excessive leap of the imagination to see Titania's adoption of the Indian boy not only as a tribute to the memory of her dead friend, but also as compensation for the fact that her union with Oberon is childless. Moreover, Bottom seems to provide her with not only a substitute lover but also a substitute child. Montrose has written of "all those desires to be fed, scratched and coddled that render Bottom's dream recognizable to us as a parodic fantasy of infantile narcissism and dependency" (Montrose 1995); but we can just as easily place the emphasis upon Titania's opportunity to indulge in a fantasy of maternity.

Quite who is at fault for the childlessness of the royal fairy marriage remains unspecified in the play. Titania declares that she has forsworn Oberon's bed, but justifies this as punishment for his infidelities (2.1.61–73). Most medical writers of the period acknowledged that the causes of infertility could lie in the physiology of either the wife or the husband, but nevertheless tended to place most blame upon disorders of the womb and the complex relation of that mysterious organ to the feminine temperament (Rueff 1637: 11–12, 14, 20ff[5]; Gélis 1991: 15). Titania closely fits most Renaissance definitions of a hysteric, a sufferer from womb-sickness. For Reginald Scot, all women were liable to hysterical symptoms through their mere possession of female anatomy: he explains that the reason why witches are more often women than men is because women "have such an vnbrideled force of furie and concupiscence naturallie, that by no meanes is it possible for them to temper or moderate the same." They are provoked by "euerie trifling occasion," and this is exacerbated "by meanes of their pernicious excrements, which they expel. Women are . . . monethlie filled full of superfluous humors, and with them the melancholike bloud boileth" (Scot 1584: 278–9). Possessing a womb made women more prone to disease: the physician John Sadler wrote that, when he researched and considered all female medical complaints, "I found none more frequent, none more perilous then those which arise from the ill affected wombe"; all the other organs are affected by it, and "there is no disease but may procede from the evill quality of it" (Sadler 1636: sigs. A4v–A5r; Rousseau 1993: 122). In particular, lack of sexual intercourse was thought to cause retention and accumulation of the female seed combined with a lack of health-giving moisture in the womb, resulting in derangement, volatility, and an unquenchable sexual appetite which was a threat to social order (Rousseau 1993: 105, 112, 118–19, 137; Maclean 1980; Lemay 1992: 131–5).

A childless woman like Titania was locked into a vicious circle: her female body was believed to make her innately emotionally turbulent, yet it was understood that this very emotional turbulence could in turn harm the reproductive functioning of the female organs. To cure barrenness, John Sadler advised that "Excesse in all things is to be avoyded; lay aside all passions of the minde . . . as adverse to conception" (Sadler 1636: 121). Yet barrenness itself, according to the author of *Aristotle's Master-Piece*, "daily occasions discontent, and that discontent creates difference between Man and Wife, or by immoderate grief frequently casts the Woman into one or other violent Distemper" – a fairly accurate depiction of the state of Oberon and Titania's marriage (*Aristotle's Master-Piece*, 1684: 78).

The idea that Titania needs curing not only of unruliness but also of barrenness is supported by the identity of the fairies in attendance in her bower as she frolics with Bottom. They include Peaseblossom, whose "father," peascod, was associated with love and sexuality in folk-magic, partly because of the verbal inversion of the term cod-piece – a cod was a bag of seeds (Reynolds and Sawyer 1959: 518; Savage 1923: 341). The sexual connotations become clear if we consider the description of the pea-plant in a herbal of 1597: "the cods be long, round *Cilindri forma*; in which are contained seedes" (Gerard 1974: 1044). Mustardseed, meanwhile, was valued as a folk-remedy for its heat: a woman seeking to conceive was advised to eat such "good, hot foods" (Stannard 1999: ch. 4, p. 67; Lemay 1992: 140). Among other benefits, mustard "prouoketh appetite," "prouoketh the tearmes" (i.e., menses, understood to be necessary to conception – see below), and "raiseth women sick of the mother out of their fits" (Gerard 1974: 190). Midsummer's Eve was a favored time for the most efficacious gathering and application of such herbal stimulants (Stannard 1999: ch. 4, p. 194, ch. 7, p. 67; Reynolds and Sawyer 1959: 513, 516, 517).

Both human conception and its failure were routinely understood in both medical books and folk-beliefs of this period in terms of the sowing and cultivation of crops and fruit (Rueff 1637: 1–2, 5–7; Gélis 1991: 4–5, 36, 38–9, 45, 222, 270). We find this reflected throughout Shakespeare's works. Thus in the first seventeen sonnets, the ones which urge a young man to procreate, appears the question "where is she so fair whose uneared womb / Disdains the tillage of thy husbandry?" (Sonnet 3, lines 5–6; see note in Shakespeare 1997b), along with much other imagery of the seasons: "let not winter's ragged hand deface / In thee thy summer" (Sonnet 6, lines 1–2). In other works by Shakespeare we find Agrippa's succinct description of Cleopatra's fruitful relationship with Julius Caesar – "He ploughed her, and she cropped" (*Antony and Cleopatra*, 2.2.234) – and Lucio's report to Isabella regarding her brother and his mistress:

> as blossoming time
> That from the seedness the bare fallow brings
> To teeming foison, even so her plenteous womb
> Expresseth his full tilth and husbandry.
> (*Measure for Measure*, 1.4.40–3)

Conversely, infertility was understood and explained in terms of failed harvests and displaced seasons. One popular early modern manual of women's health, *The Birth of Mankinde*,[6] accounts for barrenness as an imbalance of humors in the womb, which is too cold, moist, hot, or dry (see also Lemay 1992: 135–7). It illustrates this "by a familiar example of sowing of corne":

> For if it be sowen in ouer cold places . . . where the sunne doth not shine, in these places the seed or graine sowen, will neuer come to proofe, nor fructifie . . .
> And further, as concerning ouermuch humiditie, if ye sow your graine in a fen or marsh and waterie ground, the seed will perish thorough the ouermuch abundance of water, which extinguisheth the liuelinesse and the naturall power of the graine and seede.
> (Roesslin 1598: 189)

All of this sheds light upon Titania's description of the disorder in the seasons which has resulted from her quarrel with Oberon. Floods and "contagious fogs" have meant that

> The ox hath therefore stretched his yoke in vain,
> The ploughman lost his sweat, and the green corn
> Hath rotted ere his youth attained a beard.
> The fold stands empty in the drownèd field,
> And crows are fatted with the murrain[7] flock.
> The nine men's morris is filled up with mud,
> And the quaint mazes in the wanton green

> For lack of tread is undistinguishable.
> . . . hoary-headed frosts
> Fall in the fresh lap of the crimson rose. (2.1.93–108)

This is almost certainly a topical allusion to the poor summers and failed harvests of the mid-1590s, as many scholars have recognized (e.g., Chambers 1930: I, 360; II, 99–100). In a highly Ovidian play, it is an Ovidian-style aetiological myth, explaining natural phenomena by means of a quarrel between tempestuous gods. At the same time, however, the topical allusion functions as a means of speaking about Titania's own barrenness, at once caused by and causative of her marital strife. Figures of masculine physical force – the ox and the sweaty ploughman – waste their efforts; likewise, according to one medical handbook, "If the Womb be defective in attracting the Seed ejected, Men frequently labour in vain" (*Aristotle's Master-Piece*, 1684: 85–6). "The childing autumn" has been aborted; instead, Titania and Oberon are the "parents and original" of a "progeny of evils" (2.1.112, 117, 115). In these latter lines Titania seems to accuse herself and her spouse not only of barrenness but also of creating metaphorical monstrous births. Throughout, the pattern of correspondence works in two directions simultaneously: Titania and Oberon have caused sterility and monstrosity in nature, but this sterility and monstrosity are in turn images of the fairy couple's marital and parental failure.

Titania's speech here is also a negative variation upon a conventional topos in entertainments for Elizabeth I. As the queen spent her summers progressing around the countryside of her realm, speeches and pageants would compliment her with having brought simultaneous spring and harvest; or, as autumn began to set in, with having extended the summer by her presence (Wiles 1993: 2). The figure of Summer in Nashe's *Summer's Last Will and Testament*, 1592, explained that

> Eliza, England's beauteous Queen,
> On whom all seasons prosperously attend,
> Forbad the execution of my fate,
> Until her joyful Progress was expired.
> For her doth Summer live and linger here. (Wiles 1993: 4)

At Elvetham in 1591, a visit which began on September 20, a greeting oration declared that:

> Thee, thee (sweet Princes), heav'n, and earth, and fluds,
> And plants, and beasts, salute with one accord . . .
> No seedes now feare the biting of the woorme;
> Nor deere the toyles; nor grass the parching heat;
> Nor birds the snare; nor come the storme of haile. (Wilson 1980: 105)

Like a fertility goddess, or the sun itself, the queen bestows natural harmony and perpetual summer wherever she goes; only when she departs does autumn descend, as evoked in the farewell oration from the same entertainment:

> Autumn, with his withered wings,
> Will bring in tempest, when thy beames are hence . . .
> Leaves fal, grasse dies, beasts of the wood hang head,
> Birds cease to sing, and everie creature wailes.

This speech has the repeated refrain, "For how can Summer stay, when Sunne departs?" Fortuitously, it appears that a "great raine" did indeed begin to fall as Elizabeth reached the gates of the estate (Wilson 1980: 116–17).

Titania will directly echo this familiar regal iconography when she tells Bottom that "The summer still doth tend upon my state" (3.1.146). However, her earlier speech of the disordered seasons is a precise inversion of such celebrations of the cosmic influence of monarchy. Instead of prolonging summer, female rule in *A Midsummer Night's Dream* has blighted summer. It has done so because it constitutes unruliness, subversiveness, resistance of proper submission to the male. Meanwhile, the best the imperial votaress can do is drift past and out of the scene, leaving a little western flower purpled in her wake, having become the love-charm which will wreak erotic havoc. The fact that Elizabeth's bestowal of perpetual summer by her mere presence is nothing more than a complimentary fiction, in stark contrast to the actual failed harvests and social hardships of the mid-1590s, is exposed by subtle means yet with unmistakable clarity.

Why Wait Four Days? The Moon and Menstruation

Early modern thinking about conception also has bearing upon the opening lines of the play. Why must Theseus and Hippolyta wait four days and four nights for their wedding? Theseus is clearly impatient for consummation:

> O, methinks, how slow
> This old moon wanes! She lingers my desires
> Like to a stepdame or a dowager. (1.1.3–5)

As Duke of Athens he can presumably have his wedding whenever he likes. Part of the answer clearly lies in the need to wait for a new moon: it was believed that this was an auspicious time for a wedding, and that marriage under a waning moon was imprudent (Thomas 1971: 297, 620). In fact all activities which involved growth, from new enterprises to breeding animals and cultivating crops to cutting hair, were regarded as best carried out under a waxing moon, while a waning moon was a good time for cutting nails, blood-letting, or any other tasks where one would wish effusion or regrowth to be retarded (Digges and Digges 1576: ff. 17v, 18v, 26v; Dariot 1583?: sigs. F1r, F2r; Heydon 1603: 184–6, 425; Opie and Tatem 1989: 260–4; Simpson and Roud 2000: 244). Works such as Leonard Digges's very popular *A Prognostication Euerlastinge* offered guidance and tables for choosing the right day in the moon's cycle for all such activities.[8]

If trivial bodily chores must be carefully timed in accordance with the moon's phases, this was obviously even more crucial for consummation of a marriage. Just as a new moon was beneficial for sowing crops, so also it was beneficial for human conception (Gélis 1991: 38–9, 271). Such analogical thinking was intensified by the belief, inherited from Aristotle, that the menstrual cycle coincided with the lunar cycle, and that most women had their periods at the end of the lunar month (Lemay 1992: 71–2, 89; Heydon 1603: 425; *Aristotle's Master-Piece*, 1684: 48–9, 50–3; Shuttle and Redgrove 1978: 65, 155, 180–1, 192; Gélis 1991: 14; Rousseau 1993: 111). Indeed, some still believe this today, and according to the authors of *The Wise Wound* the scientific jury is still out on the matter (Shuttle and Redgrove 1978: 65, 155–9, 192; Gray 1994: 66–7, 69–70, 73). The time of the dark moon and of menstruation was associated with sleep, dreams, and the occult (Shuttle and Redgrove 1978: 65, 103, 154, 225; Gray 1994: 72–3); and the fourth quarter of the moon which led into it was cold and moist, "rotting humid things," corresponding to Titania's description of recent meteorological conditions (Lemay 1992: 71–2, 87–8).

The moon was considered "feminine, of the night, and fleugmatick" (Dariot 1583?: sig. B3v). As *A Midsummer Night's Dream* opens, the bride-to-be indeed seems serenely in tune with the steady yet ungovernable progress of the moon – "Four nights will quickly dream away the time" (1.1.8) – while Theseus restlessly opposes himself to a stale, female moon, "Like to a stepdame or a dowager," who is "withering out" his "revenue" of virility (1.1.5–6).[9] One of the functions of Hippolyta's swift rejoinder is to smooth away the provocative implication that Elizabeth as "old moon" makes her courtiers similarly frustrated through her age and indecisiveness. At the same time, it indicates that the couple are waiting for the right time in the menstrual as well as the lunar cycle for their hymeneal "solemnities" (1.1.11). Sadler advised that "The aptest time for conception is instantly after the monthes be ceast, because then the wombe is thirsty and dry, apt to draw the seed, and also to retaine it" (Sadler 1636: 120). Such careful timing might be especially necessary in the case of an Amazon like Hippolyta: a life of excessive physical exertion placed a woman at risk of barrenness, "as is recorded of the Amozonites, who being active, and alwayes in motion, had their fluxions very little, or not at all" (Sadler 1636: 15). Jacob Rueff concurred: "Among women . . . they which are over man-like, are not so apt for generation . . . For these women almost universally, doe want the issuing forth of the Termes at their due seasons" (Rueff 1637: 14).[10] It was well understood that menstruation was necessary for conception, "even as the trees which doe not blossome and send forth flowers . . . doe not fructifie, nor bring forth fruit" (ibid: 11).

The idea of menstruation is present in the play in a train of imagery of empurpling by blood: this is the change also undergone by the milk-white flower which becomes the love-charm, and the mulberries spattered with Pyramus' blood.[11] These images primarily present themselves as figurations of hymeneal bleeding: the flower is "purple with love's wound" (2.2.167), and Bottom/Pyramus garbles his lines to lament that "lion vile hath here deflowered my dear" (5.1.286). Nevertheless, especially in view of the insistent prevalence of moon-imagery throughout *A Midsummer Night's Dream*, menstrual bleeding is another closely related form of female bleeding which we may detect in these images of empurpling. It must not be forgotten that "flowers" was a common term for menstrual blood (Roesslin 1598: 190–1; Rueff 1637: 11 and passim; *Geneva Bible*, 1969: ff. 52v–53r, Leviticus 15; Gélis 1991: 10). Moreover, the flower which Oberon uses as the antidote to the love-charm has often been identified as mugwort or St. John's Wort. The uses of this herb included rituals of love-divination on Midsummer's Eve, and treatment of female infertility caused by an overly cold and moist womb; but it was also used to ease menstrual pains and to induce regular menstruation, and it emitted a blood-like reddish-purple and reputedly magical juice if squeezed (Rueff 1637: 20–6, 50, 111–12; Gerard 1974: 946; Reynolds and Sawyer 1959: 517; Opie and Tatem 1989: 269, 336–7; Gélis 1991: 11, 23, 29; Shakespeare 1995: 4.1.72n.; Simpson and Roud 2000: 238–9).

Menstrual blood was regarded, going back to Pliny and Leviticus, as defiling and blighting anything with which it came into contact (*Geneva Bible*, 1969, Leviticus 15, ff. 52v–53r; Lemay 1992: 75; Opie and Tatem 1989: 247; Gélis 1991: 13–14; Simpson and Roud 2000: 233). Copulation with a menstruating woman would not only harm the male member, but might produce a child who was red-haired, birthmarked, leprous, or sickly and short-lived (Lemay 1992: 77, 88–9; Sadler 1636: 11; Gélis 1991: 14–15; Simpson and Roud 2000: 76, 234). Worse than this, it could result in the growth of an unformed lump of flesh in the womb which would either cause an obstruction or emerge in a travesty of birth: such growths were called "moles" or "molas," or "moon-calves" (*OED*, mooncalf 1.a.; Guillimeau 1612: 13; Sadler 1636: 125; Rueff 1637: 137–8, 142). Even worse again, sex during menstruation was regarded as the principal cause of monstrous births (Paré 1982: 5; Gélis 1991: 263–4). Ancient authorities on this could be cited, including scripture: "menstruous women shal beare monstres" (*Geneva Bible*, 1969: f. 395v, II Esdras 5: 8; Paré 1982: 5; Simpson and Roud 2000: 234). The near-homophony between "menstruous" and "monstrous" probably reinforced the association. It was regarded as a divine punishment upon the parents for their excessive lust: Ambroise Paré, author of *On Monsters and Marvels*, attributed monstrous births with animal features – such as horns, feathers, or hooves – to the fact that parents who copulated during menstruation were themselves "like brutish beasts, in which their appetite guides them, without respecting the time, or other laws ordained by God and Nature" (Paré 1982: 5). The author of *Aristotle's Master-Piece* blames monstrous births upon men who

> rashly marry or run upon their Wives without any due regard to their menstrual courses, or the Wombs cleansing itself to the Season of the year, or the Moon or Suns progress through the Coelestiall Signs . . . let Man, who is indued with a rational Soul, and ought above all other Creatures to have dominion over his appetite and affection, consider how cruel he is to his posterity that brings such mischief upon them. (*Aristotle's Master-Piece*, 1684: 48–9, 50–3)

Theseus' sexual record, according to mythology, and as alluded to in the *Dream* (2.1.77–80), was far from the restraint and self-control prescribed here. His impatience at the opening of the play is entirely in character with this; but it seems also that in taking a wife and aspiring to conceive an heir he is mindful of the need to do things properly. As we are constantly reminded through the play, weddings are "solemnities" to be conducted with order and ritual as well as festivity. Hippolyta seems almost to be tutoring Theseus in this in the opening lines of the play, but by the day of his wedding he has learned his lesson well and it is he who repeatedly uses the term (1.1.11, 4.1.87, 133, 184, 5.1.360). Many of Shakespeare's original audience would have been aware, from their Ovid and Seneca, of the proof that Theseus and Hippolyta did perform their conjugal rites sensibly and seasonably, in the person of their son, the extraordinarily beautiful and gifted Hippolytus.[12] Waiting for the wedding night until the right phase of both the lunar and menstrual cycles is congruent with the fairies' blessing, as that night is reached at the end of the play, whereby "the blots of nature's hand / Shall not in their issue stand" (5.1.400–1). This might have carried special force at the Carey–Berkeley wedding: Thomas Berkeley's head and neck had been cast awry by an injury in his teens, so the fairies' lines function to reassure the bride and her family that the disability is not hereditary. Like Theseus and Hippolyta, Thomas and Elizabeth Berkeley would come to rejoice in the physical evidence that they had timed and performed their conjugal rites well: John Smyth's Berkeley family history records that "The fruits of the marriage appeared by the birth of Theophila their daughter . . . the 11th of December, 42 weeks and two daies next after their mariage, Anno 1596" (Smyth 1883: 396).

Bestiality

As we have seen, Paré attributed monstrous births with animal features to the animalistic unregulated lust of their parents. The other chief explanation for such births was copulation with actual beasts; medical writers asserted that this occurred and could produce offspring, and gave anecdotal examples (Paré 1982: 5–6; Rueff 1637: 160; Gélis 1991: 265–6). Theseus, of course, was famous not only for his sexual intemperance, but also as the vanquisher of just such a monstrous birth, the Minotaur, a bull-beaded man who was the progeny of the lustful Pasiphae and a bull. Bottom – half-man, half-ass – looks like a comic version of the Minotaur, and like the offspring of such a bestial union. He is consistently referred to in the play as a monster, beginning with Quince's aghast exclamation, "O monstrous!" (3.1.99, and 3.2.6, 377). At the same time, Titania's infatuation with him recalls Pasiphae's bestial mating. From the first plotting of his revenge, Oberon wishes upon her not just attraction to any old passing bumpkin, but specifically lust for a beast. He hopes her first waking gaze will be upon "lion, bear, or wolf, or bull, / On meddling monkey, or on busy ape" (2.1.180–1) – the bull, of course, a precise allusion to Pasiphae. Again, as he anoints her sleeping eyes, he wishes upon her passion for "ounce, or cat, or bear, / Pard, or boar with bristled hair" (2.2.36–7).

Where Titania seems to compensate for her lack of a child by adopting the Indian boy and then by infantilizing Bottom, Oberon seeks to punish her with exactly the sort of union which would produce a monstrous birth, meeting her desire for motherhood with a horrific travesty. As retribution for Titania's refusal to him of her sexual attentions, Oberon degrades her to the basest level of subhuman lust. Even before she sets eyes on Bottom, he has been the subject of a bawdy bestial innuendo: his transformation occurs as he misses his cue from Flute/Thisbe, and that repeated cue-line from Thisbe praising her lover is that he is "As true as truest horse that yet would never tire" (3.1.90, 97).

Just as tragic possibilities hover around the borders of this comedy (see below), so beasts and the troubling forces they embody are often invoked but not fully seen. Helena, unloved and unprotected in the wild wood, at once risks being devoured by wild beasts, suffers beast-like cruelty including a threat of rape from Demetrius, and feels herself to be as repulsive as a bear or monster (2.1.214–30, 2.2.100–2). Imaginary bears are mentioned no fewer than six times (2.1.180, 2.2.36, 100, 3.1.104–6, 4.1.112, 5.1.22). The lion is not just the comical creature in the performance of *Pyramus and Thisbe*, but also, somewhere in the distance, the "hungry lion" who roars as the newly wedded couples take to their beds (5.1.362). The worries of the mechanicals that their lion will frighten the ladies indicate an implied savagery not only of physical violence but of untamed sexuality – remember that, in Bottom's malapropism, the lion "deflowers" his dear (5.1.286). Incidental remarks about this lion invite us to contemplate the borders between the human and the animal: "let not him that plays the lion pare his nails, for they shall hang out for the lion's claws" (4.2.35–7; this from the newly restored Bottom, who knows something about the proximity of man and beast); and "Here come two noble beasts in: a man and a lion" (5.1.215–16). Altogether, the play makes us well aware of the potentially animalistic aspects of human nature, especially in the form of sexuality. Hairiness is an emblem of this: Titania might fall for a "boar with bristled hair" (2.2.37) and actually does fall for the ticklishly hairy Bottom (4.1.24–5, 50); Flute/Thisbe, trying to kiss Bottom/Pyramus, unwittingly utters bawdy innuendoes as he/she kisses only the wall's hole and hairy stones (slang for testicles; 5.1.189–200). Hairiness, denoting a bestial sexuality unregulated by reason, must be made safe, laughed at, and dispelled in order to progress towards the order of marriage and well-planned procreation.

"Two of both kinds makes up four"

The four days and nights of nuptial delay are among several sets of four in the play: four Athenian Lovers; Theseus and Hippolyta, and Oberon and Titania as two more linked couples forming a foursome; four named fairy-attendants upon Titania and Bottom. Four may be said to be the governing number of the play just as it is the governing number of Book IV of *The Faerie Queene*; and, as Alastair Fowler has shown in relation to that work, its symbolic resonance is that of the Pythagorean number of concord and of marriage (Fowler 1964: 24–5, 37, 48). Just as the irreconcilable conflict of Lysander and Demetrius over Hermia is resolved by the redirection of Demetrius' desire towards Helena, forming a stable tetrad of two marriages and two friendships, so Spenser resolves Cambell and Triamond's conflict over Canacee by introducing Cambina, forming an identical tetrad in which "all alike did loue, and loued were" (*FQ* IV.iv.52). Amyas, Placidas, Aemylia, and Paeana are brought into alignment as yet another tetrad of "paires of friends in peace and setled rest" (*FQ* IV.ix.17). The simultaneous symmetries and parallels within the tetrad correspond to balance and harmony between the four elements, and thereby to the cosmic harmony ordained by God (*FQ* IV.x.35).

Spenser writes of the personification of Concord:

> strength, and wealth, and happinesse she lends,
> And strife, and warre, and anger does subdew:
> Of litle much, of foes she maketh frends,
> And to afflicted minds sweet rest and quiet sends. (*FQ* IV.x.34)

This is very much the mood in which *A Midsummer Night's Dream* ends. The journey from act 1 to act 5 is one from disharmony to harmony, from tragic potential to comic resolution, making "concord of this discord" (5.1.60). The Hippolyta of act 1 has been won by the sword; she disagrees – politely? combatively? – with her betrothed in the opening lines, and remains enigmatically and perhaps resentfully silent until his anxious enquiry "what cheer, my love?" (1.1.122; see McGuire 1985: 1–18). By her wedding-night she has been converted to address her spouse affectionately as "my Theseus," just as the reformed Titania, on awaking from her curative enchantment, immediately turned to "My Oberon" (5.1.1, 4.1.75; see McGuire 1985: 16). Hermia and Helena are threatened with death and rape and systematically demolish their much-vaunted "schooldays' friendship" when it competes with their heterosexual desires (3.2.202), but they too emerge unscathed as restored friends and contented wives. Act 5 helps us to measure how far we have traveled from the problems of act 1 by returning to some of them in neutralized form, especially in the inset performance by the mechanicals, wherein Shakespeare's choice of story emerges as no arbitrary one. Thisbe's blood-stained mantle may be understood as a prettifying reminiscence of Hippolyta's inconvenient menstruation with which we began;[13] while Pyramus and Thisbe at once fulfill the tragic fate of doomed loves as described by Lysander and Hermia in act 1, and save Lysander and Hermia themselves from this tragic outcome. Moreover, the play converts the projected tragedy into a guise not only safely fictional but indeed ludicrously farcical. All dangers have been dispelled.

The ending of the play feels so very right and joyful not only because it is snatched from the jaws of potential tragedy, but also because of the ultimate happy coincidence between female desires and the preservation of the patriarchal order. Again this may be related to early modern thinking about fertility. Sadler wrote that a chief cause of barrenness was "compeld copulation; as when parents enforce their daughters to have husbands contrary to their liking, therein marrying their bodies but not their hearts, and where there is a want of love, there for the most part is no conception" (Sadler 1636: 108–9). Again,

> Another Natural Cause of Barrenness is, want of Love between Man and Wife; Love is
> that Vital Principle that ought to animate each Organ in the Act of Generation, or else

'twill be but spiritless and dull; for if their Hearts be not united in Love, how should their Seed unite to cause Conception. (*Aristotle's . . . Midwife*, 1700: 129; see also Lemay 1992: 132)

A woman would not conceive if she received "little or no satisfaction . . . in the act of Copulation" (*Aristotle's Master-Piece* 1684: 79). Egeus and Theseus must sanction the marriage of Hermia to Lysander, but equally Hippolyta and Titania must be educated into loving wifehood, for all these unions to produce the fortunate issue foretold in the fairies' blessing. The tensions surrounding the depiction of courtship and marriage in the course of the play might seem to make it less than suitable material for an entertainment at an actual wedding; but its suitability lies in the comprehensiveness, and joyousness, with which those tensions are ultimately resolved, and the deftness whereby forces of female desire are at once accommodated and subdued.

The Femaleness of the Themes of the *Dream*

Yet even if women are to some degree quelled, this remains a play in which femaleness is very much to the fore. This exploration has tried to show how significant are early modern beliefs and superstitions about the female body in both the plot and the language of the play. Extending this, the themes of the *Dream* correspond almost exactly with most of the key terms of early modern thought about the nature of women. Consider, for instance, Ian Maclean, in his survey of *The Renaissance Notion of Woman*, writing without any reference to *A Midsummer Night's Dream*. He observes the persistence of Aristotelian ideas of female inferiority, grounded in "the metaphorical association of woman with mother earth, nutrition, fruitfulness and the fluctuations of the moon"; and notes that "Imagination is thought to be stronger in women because cold and moist objects are subject to metamorphosis." In the eyes of Renaissance physiologists, "all mankind is in a process of continual change linked to age and health; but in this process woman changes more, and more often, and within a shorter space of time." In a play about metamorphosis, therefore, and transformative forces of dream, love, imagination, and magic, it is inevitable that women should have prominence. Maclean summarizes: "two external forces are said to act on the uterus: the moon and the imagination" (Maclean 1980: 44, 42, 46, 41). G. S. Rousseau in his study of early modern hysteria pursues similar enquiries: "Why was Renaissance woman thought to be so influenced by the moon and so possessed of the devil?" (Rousseau 1993: 111). The moon, the occult, change, the imagination – all of these are the key images and themes of *A Midsummer Night's Dream*, and all of them belonged in some sense in the province of women.

Reginald Scot scoffed that Robin Goodfellow and other nocturnal spirits were merely nonsense with which "in our childhood our mothers maids have so terrified us" (Bullough 1966: I, 396). Nashe's *Terrors of the Night* also locates dismissively in childhood a foolish pleasure in hearing "aged mumping beldams as they sat warming their knees over a coal scratch over the argument [i.e., the meaning of a dream] very curiously" (Nashe 1910: 163). The two characters in *A Midsummer Night's Dream* who have the profoundest sense that a dream might be a revelatory, transformative experience are the proletarian, uneducated, dull-witted Bottom (4.1.198–215), and Hippolyta, tamed yet still demurring from her husband's rationalism and impatience:

> But all the story of the night told over,
> And all their minds transfigured so together,
> More witnesseth than fancy's images,
> And grows to something of great constancy;
> But howsoever, strange and admirable. (5.1.23–7)

Just as Caliban is a brute yet has the most lyrical sensibility of all the characters in *The Tempest* (3.2.130–9), so here the disenfranchised, mechanicals and women, stand in alliance as those most open to the inexplicable and poetic.

In the case of women, this is not unconnected to the emphasis upon fertility which I have traced through the play: conception can bear a double-meaning, of the body but also of the mind (Sacks 1980). Medical writers understood the fetus to be formed out of the shapeless matter of the menses in the womb, fertilized by the semen, but were undecided between Galen's view that the semen and menses mingled jointly to become the substance of the fetus, and Aristotle's view that the semen became a spiritual force which worked upon the matter of the menses to give them human shape. The language used to describe the Aristotelian theory is well worth noting in relation to *A Midsummer Night's Dream*. Jacob Rueff wrote:

> *Aristotle* saith, that the Termes of the woman, are a prepared matter, of the whole Feature [i.e., fetus], although it be crude and indigested, which is form'd & fashion'd by the seed of man, received into it, the same seed being turned into vitall spirit, which like a workman, doth proportion and fashion this matter. (Rueff 1637: 9)

Think of Theseus' description of how the imagination, like the womb, "bodies forth / The form of things unknown," while the poet's pen, like the penis, "Turns them to shapes, and gives to airy nothing / A local habitation and a name" (5.1.14–17). Compare again a commentary on *De Secretis Mulierum*, described by its recent translator as "a widely circulating epitome of the sixteenth-century view of women" (Lemay 1992: 2):

> philosophers say that the male seed has the same relationship to the female menses as an artificer does to his work. For just as a carpenter alone is the efficient cause, and the house is the effect, in that he alters and disposes the matter of the house, so the male seed alters the female menses into the form of a human being. (Lemay 1992: 64)

The poet, the craftsman like Quince the carpenter and his fellows, the bridegroom who hopes to be a father – all of these alike are engaged in making and shaping. In one sense this reduces the bride and prospective mother to the status of mere matter to be worked upon; but it also recognizes her power to generate matter, and her consequent necessity to the act of creation, and thereby likens the female to imagination itself. Shakespeare offers to Elizabeth Carey, or perhaps some other bride, or any mother-to-be, the not inconsiderable compliment of comparison with the visionary powers of the mind from which his art grows.

ACKNOWLEDGMENTS

This essay has been much improved by the invaluable feedback of Katherine Duncan-Jones, Steve Hackett, Margaret Healy, Chris Laoutaris, and Neil Rennie. Its remaining deficiencies are of course entirely my own responsibility.

NOTES

1   All references to A Midsummer Night's Dream are to Peter Holland's World's Classics edition (Oxford: Oxford University Press, 1995).
2   Even more verbal correspondences can be added to those listed by Tobin.
3   This is the last line of the opening sonnet of the Canzoniere.
4   3.4.52, 127, in The Norton Shakespeare, ed. Stephen Greenblatt et al. (New York: Norton, 1997a). All further references to works by Shakespeare other than A Midsummer Night's Dream are to this edition unless otherwise specified.
5   In second sequence of page numbering.
6   Thirteen editions of English translation 1540–1634; STC 21153–64.
7   A plague of livestock. See Bible, 1934: Exodus 9: 3.
8   Fifteen editions 1555–1626, incl. 1592, 1596; STC 435.35–435.63.
9   Such fiscal language was often applied to semen, e.g., Othello 4.3.86.
10 In second sequence of page numbering.
11 In Ovid – though they are not specifically mentioned in the mechanicals' performance. See Bullough (1966: I; 406–9).
12 He nevertheless met a tragic end: Ovid (1916: XV.497–546); Seneca (1966).
13 Jean Paris (1975: 136–7) thinks it is evident that Hippolyta is menstruating.

REFERENCES AND FURTHER READING

Aristotle's Compleat and Experienc'd Midwife (1700). Trans. W. S.
Aristotle's Master-Piece, Or The Secrets of Generation Displayed in All the Parts Thereof (1684).
Barber, C. L. (1959). Shakespeare's Festive Comedy: A Study of Dramatic Form and its Relation to Social Custom. Princeton, NJ: Princeton University Press.
Bate, J. (1993). Shakespeare's Ovid. Oxford: Clarendon Press.
Bible, The Geneva (1969). Facs. Intro. Lloyd E. Berry. Madison: University of Wisconsin Press. (Original work published 1560.)
Bible, The Holy (King James Bible) (1934). London: Odhams. (Original work published 1611.)
Bloom, H. (ed.) (1987). Modern Critical Interpretations: William Shakespeare's 'A Midsummer Night's Dream'. New York: Chelsea House.
Bullough, G. (1966). Narrative and Dramatic Sources of Shakespeare, vol. 1. London: Routledge.
Calderwood, J. L. (1992). Harvester New Critical Introductions to Shakespeare: 'A Midsummer Night's Dream'. Hemel Hempstead: Harvester Wheatsheaf.

Chambers, E. K. (1930). *William Shakespeare: A Study of Facts and Problems*, 2 vols. Oxford: Clarendon Press.

Dariot, C. (1583?). *A Breefe and Most Easie Introduction to the Astrologicall Iudgement of the Starres*. Trans. F. Wither.

Digges, L. and Digges, T. (1576). *A Prognostication Euerlastinge of Righte Good Effecte*.

Duncan-Jones, K. (1998). *Christs Teares*, Nashe's "forsaken extremities." *Review of English Studies*, n. s., 49, 194, 167–80.

——(1999). Bess Carey's Petrarch: Newly Discovered Elizabethan Sonnets. *Review of English Studies*, n. s., 50, 199, 304–19.

Fender, S. (1968). *Studies in English Literature no. 35: 'A Midsummer Night's Dream'*. London: Arnold.

Fowler, A. (1964). *Spenser and the Numbers of Time*. London: Routledge.

Garber, M. B. (1974). *Dream in Shakespeare: From Metaphor to Metamorphosis*. New Haven, CT: Yale University Press.

Gélis, J. (1991). *History of Childbirth: Fertility, Pregnancy and Birth in Early Modern Europe*, trans. R. Morris. Cambridge: Polity Press. (Original work published 1984.)

Gerard, J. (1974). *The Herball or Generall Historie of Plants*. Facs. Amsterdam: Theatrum Orbis Terrarum. (Original work published 1597.)

Gray, M. (1994). *Red Moon: Understanding and Using the Gifts of the Menstrual Cycle*. Longmead, Dorset: Element.

Guillimeau [Guillemeau], James [Jacques] (1612). *Childbirth: or, The Happy Deliverie of Women*. Trans. from French.

Hackett, H. (1995). *Virgin Mother, Maiden Queen: Elizabeth I and the Cult of the Virgin Mary*. Basingstoke: Macmillan.

——(1997). *Writers and Their Work: 'A Midsummer Night's Dream'*. Plymouth: Northcote House.

Hannay, M. P. (1990). *Philip's Phoenix: Mary Sidney, Countess of Pembroke*. Oxford: Oxford University Press.

Hendricks, M. (1996). 'Obscured by Dreams': Race, Empire, and Shakespeare's *Midsummer Night's Dream*. *Shakespeare Quarterly*, 47, 37–60.

Heydon, C. (1603). *A Defence of Iudiciall Astrologie*.

Kott, J. (1988). Titania and the Ass's Head. In B. Taborski (trans.) *Shakespeare our Contemporary*. London: Routledge, 171–90.

Lemay, H. R. (1992). *Women's Secrets: A Translation of Pseudo-Albertus Magnus's 'De Secretis Mulierum' with Commentaries*. Albany: State University of New York Press.

McGuire, P. C. (1985). *Speechless Dialect: Shakespeare's Open Silences*. Berkeley: University of California Press.

Maclean, I. (1980). *The Renaissance Notion of Woman*. Cambridge: Cambridge University Press.

Montrose, L. A. (1986). *A Midsummer Night's Dream* and the shaping fantasies of Elizabethan culture: gender, power, form. In M. W. Ferguson, M. Quilligan, and N. J. Vickers (eds.) *Rewriting the Renaissance: The Discourses of Sexual Difference in Early Modern Europe*. Chicago, IL: University of Chicago Press, 65–87.

——(1995). A Kingdom of Shadows. In D. L. Smith, R. Strier, and D. Bevington (eds.) *The Theatrical City: Culture, Theatre and Politics in London, 1576–1649*. Cambridge: Cambridge University Press, 68–86.

Nashe, T. (1910) [1594]. *The Terrors of the Night*. In R. B. McKerrow (ed.) *The Works of Thomas Nashe*, vol. 1. London: Sidgwick and Jackson, 339–86.

Opie, I. and Tatem, M. (eds.) (1989). *A Dictionary of Superstitions*. Oxford: Oxford University Press.

Ovid (1916). *Metamorphoses*, Books IX–XV, trans. F. J. Miller. London: Heinemann.

Paré, A. (1982). *On Monsters and Marvels*, trans. J. L. Pallister. Chicago, IL: University of Chicago Press. (Original work published 1573.)

Paris, J. (1975). *Univers parallèles I: Théâtre*. Paris: Éditions du Seuil.

Paster, G. K. (1993). *The Body Embarrassed: Drama and the Disciplines of Shame in Early Modern England*. Ithaca, NY: Cornell University Press.

Patterson, A. (1984). *Censorship and Interpretation: The Conditions of Writing and Reading in Early Modern England*. Madison: University of Wisconsin Press.

——(1989). Bottom's Up: Festive Theory. In *Shakespeare and the Popular Voice*. Oxford: Blackwell, 52–70.

Reynolds, L. A. and Sawyer, P. (1959). Folk Medicine and the Four Fairies of *A Midsummer Night's Dream*. *Shakespeare Quarterly*, 10, 513–21.

Roesslin, E. (1598). *The Birth of Mankinde, Otherwyse Named the Womans Booke*. Trans. T. Raynalde.

Rousseau, G. S. (1993). 'A Strange Pathology': Hysteria in the Early Modern World, 1500–1800. In S. L. Gilman et al. *Hysteria Beyond Freud*. Berkeley: University of California Press, 91–221.

Rueff, James [Jacob] (1637). *The Expert Midwife*. Trans. from Latin.

STC. Pollard, A. W. and Redgrave, G. R. (1976–91). *A Short-Title Catalogue . . . 1475–1640*, 3 vols., 2nd edn. London: Bibliographical Society.

Sacks, E. (1980). *Shakespeare's Images of Pregnancy and Birth*. Basingstoke: Macmillan.

Sadler, J. (1636). *The Sick Womans Priuate Looking-glasse Wherein methodically are handled all uterine affects, or diseases arising from the Wombe*.

Savage, F. G. (1923). *The Flora and Folk Lore of Shakespeare*. London: J. Burrow.

Scot, R. (1584). *The Discouerie of Witchcraft*.

Seneca (1966). *Phaedra*. In E. F. Watling (trans.) *Four Tragedies and Octavia*. Harmondsworth: Penguin Books.

Shakespeare, W. (1967). *The New Penguin Shakespeare: 'A Midsummer Night's Dream'*, ed. S. Wells. Harmondsworth: Penguin Books.

——(1979). *The Arden Shakespeare: 'A Midsummer Night's Dream'*, ed. H. F. Brooks. London: Routledge.

——(1995). *World's Classics: 'A Midsummer Night's Dream'*, ed. P. Holland. Oxford: Oxford University Press.

——(1997a). *The Norton Shakespeare*, ed. S. Greenblatt et al. New York: Norton.

——(1997b). *Shakespeare's Sonnets*, ed. K. Duncan-Jones. The Arden Shakespeare. London: Thomas Nelson.

Shuttle, P. and Redgrove, P. (1978). *The Wise Wound: Menstruation and Everywoman*. London: Gollancz.

Simpson, J. and Roud, S. (2000). *A Dictionary of English Folklore*. Oxford: Oxford University Press.

Smyth, J. (1883). *The Berkeley Manuscripts: The Lives of the Berkeleys*, ed. Sir John Maclean, vol. 2. Gloucester: Gloucester and Bristol Archaeological Society.

Stannard, J. (1999). *Herbs and Herbalism in the Middle Ages and Renaissance*. Aldershot: Ashgate.

Sutherland, J. and Watts, C. (2000). *Henry V, War Criminal? and Other Shakespeare Puzzles*. Oxford: Oxford University Press.

Swander, H. (1990). Editors vs. Text: The Scripted Geography of *A Midsummer Night's Dream*. *Studies in Philology*, 87, 83–108.

Thomas, K. (1971). *Religion and the Decline of Magic*. London: Weidenfeld and Nicolson.

Tobin, J. J. M. (1992). Nashe and Shakespeare: Some Further Borrowings. *Notes and Queries*, 237, 309–12.

Wells, S. (1991). *A Midsummer Night's Dream* Revisited. *Critical Survey*, 3, 1, 14–29.

Wiles, D. (1993). *Shakespeare's Almanac: 'A Midsummer Night's Dream', Marriage and the Elizabethan Calendar*. Cambridge: D. S. Brewer.

Williams, G. J. (1997). *Our Moonlight Revels: 'A Midsummer Night's Dream' in the Theatre*. Iowa City: University of Iowa Press.

Wilson, J. (1980). *Entertainments for Elizabeth I*. Woodbridge: D. S. Brewer.

Young, D. P. (1966). *Something of Great Constancy: The Art of 'A Midsummer Night's Dream'*. New Haven, CT: Yale University Press.

18

Rubbing at Whitewash: Intolerance in *The Merchant of Venice*

Marion Wynne-Davies

On January 10, 1564 John Shakespeare, in his capacity as a borough chamberlain, recorded that during the previous year Stratford-Upon-Avon Corporation had paid a group of workmen 2 shillings to whitewash the walls of the old Guild Chapel. This commission had not been intended, however, to fulfill decorative or restorative purpose, since the accounts note that the money was "payd for defasyng ymages in ye chappell" (Savage and Fripp 1921–2: 1, 128).[1] The Corporation had finally agreed, four years after the accession of the Protestant Elizabeth I, to remove all visible traces of Catholicism, and so the walls, with their bright depictions of saints and miracles, were disfigured alongside the destruction of rood-loft and stained glass. Yet the very term used to describe the workmen's activities reveals a covert reluctance. For while "defasyng" might well signify the Protestant bishops' desire to blot out the memory of Catholicism, just as the images of the old faith were being blotted over with paint, at the same time the verb suggests another interpretation. To deface also means to discredit, and in the mid-sixteenth century the term developed a spiritual connotation whereby "defacers" were identified with heretics. Given their reluctance to undertake the work, it is probable that from the point of view of the Stratford-Upon-Avon Corporation and its chamberlain, John Shakespeare, the "defasyng" of their Catholic Guild Chapel amounted to a discrediting of the true faith, if not to a heretical act.

Nor was the Stratford Corporation alone in its reluctance to efface the pictorial memorials of the old faith in the face of Puritan zeal, although it was rather slower than other townships to commission the work (Hughes 1997: 97). For example, Eamon Duffy describes how

> Both the bishops and their Puritan critics were especially aware of the potent influence of what they called the "monuments of superstition," the physical remnants of Catholic cult which represented both a symbolic focus for Catholic belief, a reminder of the community's Catholic past and its corporate investment in the old religion, and a concrete hope for its ultimate restoration. (Duffy 1992: 582)

However, as Duffy goes on to explain, by simply painting the sacred images, communities could appear to accept Protestant prohibitions while at the same time retaining their "reminder of" and "investment in" Catholicism, since "the reversibility of whitewashing was an established fact" (ibid: 283). The title of this essay, "Rubbing at Whitewash", draws upon an anecdote recounted by Duffy about how the congregation at Chichester, when confronted with the whitewashed image of the passion, simply rubbed at the paint in passing until the picture was as bright as before. As such, the process of rubbing at whitewash corresponds to the act of disclosure. And so ineffectual was the "defasyng" process in Stratford that four hundred and fifty years after the images in the Guild Chapel were whitewashed the old script is still discernible. It seems that the restoration of 1804 was the primary cause of the damage we see today, although the current glossy lemon decoration cannot have helped (Honan 1999: 426; Davidson and Alexander 1985: 76). Certainly, when William Shakespeare returned to Stratford in the mid-1590s to undertake the purchase of New Place he might easily have crossed Chapel Lane and reminded himself of the half-concealed representations. In his youth Shakespeare would have been very familiar with the Guild Chapel and its attached buildings, since he would have attended school in the Guild buildings and might well have attended classes in the Chapel itself (Bloom 1914: 277).[2] In addition, as a Corporation official, John Shakespeare would have had ready access to the Guild's precinct, and, given the accumulating evidence for the Catholicity of the Stratford Shakespeares, it is highly likely that John would have made William aware not only of the whitewashed images, but also of what they signified to a family who continued to veil the external signifiers of its faith.[3]

Still, in 1597 when Shakespeare returned to Stratford, his wealth and status assured locally through the occupation of a spacious and well-situated house, he was no longer a boy immersed in the affairs of a small rural town, or a known participant in the covert intrigues of the midlands' recusant network. Indeed, for critics Shakespeare's faith has proved as protean as his sexuality, and this essay makes no claim to identify new "evidence." However, when the increasing accumulation of historical material is gathered, reconfigured, and placed alongside texts, interesting and provoking collisions are becoming increasingly inevitable (Wilson 1997; Dutton 1998). First, it has long been accepted that in 1597 Shakespeare was in Stratford, setting up home opposite the old Guild Chapel. Moreover, in addition to any general curiosity, he would have had business at the Guild, since in purchasing New Place he had inadvertently become immersed in legal wrangling over the rightful ownership of the deeds. Second, the half-visible images in the Chapel have remained only partly covered through the centuries, having been described by various county and town historians. On his return to Stratford, therefore, Shakespeare would have seen, alongside the Doom and other legends of the Holy Cross, the story of St. Helena and her victory over the Jews, visible through its veil of whitewash.

The story of St. Helena was popular in England, since she was said to have been the daughter of King Coel of Colchester ("Old King Cole"), although her renown derived from being the mother of Constantine and, more significantly, the discoverer of the true cross. There are a number of variants, but the story basically recounts how St.

Helena travels to Jerusalem and, with the forced aid of a Jewish man, finds where the cross has been concealed. Although there are three crosses, the true one is revealed when it is used to bring a dead man or girl back to life, and St. Helena returns triumphant. The most significant variant in England occurs in the medieval poem *Cursor Mundi*, a spiritual history of the world. In the section on St. Helena she is asked to adjudicate the case between a Christian goldsmith and a Jewish usurer. Since the Christian is unable to pay back his debt, the Jew demands that "he sulde yield of his awen flesse" and carries a "sharp grundin knife in hande" in order to exact the penalty. Of course, Helena points out that the Jew is allowed only "flesse" and informs him that if he takes "a drope of blode" the "wrange is [th]ine." When the Jew hears that his punishment will be to lose all his "catel" (goods) and to have his tongue cut out, he agrees to show St. Helena where the cross has been hidden. The continental St. Helena narrative of finding the true cross is thus linked in the *Cursor Mundi* with a common folk motif of the flesh-bond (Halio 1993: 17). In both sequences the idealized Christian woman defeats the Jew in order to uncover the symbol of spiritual truth, thereby ensuring the propagation and continuation of the true faith in God.

The poem, originally written in a northern dialect, was given a new lease of life in the fifteenth century when a "southern" version was produced somewhere in the east midlands. There were at least nine manuscripts and it is conceivable given the date and location of these works that Shakespeare might have seen them. Indeed, Shakespeare's possible knowledge of the *Cursor Mundi* has been established for some time; for example, Furness cited it in 1888 (Furness ca. 1916: 313–14). On the other hand, the St. Helena story was well established in medieval and early Tudor popular imagination, and a comparison between the possible narrative source and the visual image in Stratford-Upon-Avon proves informative. Over 135 churches were dedicated to St. Helena and pictorial representations of the story of the true cross were common. The wall paintings in the Stratford Guild Chapel participated, therefore, in a well-known narrative tradition that merged word with image for the faithful. The choice of the legend as a subject for representation was appropriate for Stratford since the Guild was dedicated to the holy cross (its full title being, The Guild of the Holy Cross), and the images depict the whole narrative, of which St. Helena's discovery is an essential part. Restoration work was undertaken at the Guild Chapel in 1804 and it was after this that the images were described in print by R. B. Wheler and replicated in a series of plates by Thomas Fisher made between 1807 and 1836 (Wheler 1806: 92–103; Fisher and Nichols 1838). Subsequent "restoration" work has defaced the wall paintings far more effectively than John Shakespeare's whitewashing and so we are fortunate that textual and pictorial evidence exists, enabling us to reconstruct the Helena sections. Wheler describes how on the north side of the Chancel walls,

> The Empress Helena was represented bearing the cross in her arms, and touching it with the body of a female, lying in a coffin; an attendant carried the other two crosses . . . men, dogs, trees and beasts, filled up the landscape. The pair of paintings beneath, represented other parts of the same history, and in point of *time* precede the last described picture . . . [these were] the setting out of Helena . . . entirely obliterated . . . where

Helena may supposed to have been drawn, seated on a white horse; her crown only and part of the horse remained: there were four attendants on horseback, and before them went two men, blowing singularly shaped trumpets . . . behind them was seen a church, and other public buildings (part of a town) . . . the adjoining compartment, represented Helena attended, among others by a person of consequence, denoted by a hawk upon his fist; she was addressing a man in a supplicatory posture, who seemed just liberated from a prison, at the door of which stood a keeper, with a key in his hand . . . In the background of the picture was represented the finding of the three crosses . . . the lower compartment . . . [showed] the newly discovered cross . . . Helena knelt beside the altar . . . [while] angels, playing on musical instruments, appeared in a corner of the picture. (Wheler 1806: 102–3; ellipses denote my own abbreviation)

In addition, from Fisher's illustrations it is possible to identify the kneeling man from the inscription beneath: "Here seynte Helyn examyneth the J . . . for ye Holy Cross . . . Julius Cyryacus . . . where hete was" (Bloom 1914: 265; ellipses denote words that were already illegible at the time of Fisher's work).

The Guild wall paintings represent Helena as a late fifteenth-century lady with the appropriate accoutrements of her class, who is situated in the pastoral and civic settings redolent of early modern art, while the inscriptions verify the Jewish identity of the supplicant. Thus, if Shakespeare did know the *Cursor Mundi* it would have functioned primarily as a reinforcement of his already extant knowledge of the story through the pictures on the wall of the Guild Chapel. Moreover, we know that those half-concealed images would have been particularly interesting to the playwright during his 1597 return to Stratford, because during that year he was almost certainly composing *The Merchant of Venice*.

The Merchant of Venice is customarily dated after August 1596 when the Spanish ship, the *San Andrés*, had been captured by the English fleet and was renamed the "Andrew," and as such explaining the allusion to "my wealthy Andrew dock'd in sand" (1.1.27);[4] and dated before 1598 when references to the play were made in Francis Meres's *Palladis Tamia* and in the *Stationer's Register*, September and July 1598 respectively. These dates correspond to the purchase of New Place, which would have entailed a number of visits to Stratford. Certainly we can judge that the Shakespeare family had settled into their new home by February 1598 at the latest (Honan 1999: 236).

The correspondence between Shakespeare's comedy and the St. Helena story will have been immediately apparent when reading the précis of the *Cursor Mundi* passages and the description of the holy cross wall paintings. In a simple analogy, therefore, Portia may be equated with St. Helena, Antonio with the Christian Goldsmith, and Shylock with the Jew. The trial scenes are similar and certain passages bear a light comparison. So that as the *Cursor Mundi* depicts the Jew with a "sharp grundin knife in hand," so Gratiano asks Shylock: "Why dost thou whet thy knife so earnestly?" (4.1.121). And as St. Helena warns the Jew not to shed "a drope of blode" so Portia informs Shylock that if he lets fall "One drop of Christian blood, thy lands and goods / Are . . . confiscate" (4.1.306–7) (Morris 1877–92: III, 1226–35). Yet the phrases are commonplace and provide no concrete textual proof that Shakespeare worked with the medieval poem itself. The wall-painting Helena similarly parallels Portia, in terms of rank, "fair" appearance, and shift from country to city, and the defeated "Julius Cyryacus," or Judas Iscariot, is reminiscent of Shylock at the close of the court scene. What is clear, therefore, is that Shakespeare knew the legend of St. Helena and that he chose to use the narrative and some characterization in *The Merchant of Venice*. Moreover, by placing the lack of a certain textual source of the St. Helena story alongside Shakespeare's unquestionable knowledge of the wall paintings in the Guild, his visit to Stratford in 1597, and the dating of *The Merchant of Venice* (1596–7), the Chapel's pictorial version emerges as the most likely source.[5] Yet if Shakespeare drew his knowledge, or at least a reminder, of the St. Helena legend from the walls of the Guild Chapel, the images and the narrative they expounded would have come inextricably bound up with more recent concerns about the true cross and the faith it espoused.

To begin with, the pictures Shakespeare would have seen in 1597 were not bright and clear, but "defasyed" with the semi-transparent whitewash of a pro-Catholic town corporation, under whose orders his father had acted thirty-three years before. In these circumstances the legend of St. Helena would inevitably have taken on a different, covert, signification. Just as the early Jews had supposedly hidden the true cross, so the sixteenth-century Protestants in their attempts to obliterate Catholicism had ensured that the symbols of the old faith were covered over. Thus, St. Helena becomes a symbol of the true Catholic faith and its feminized church, which has been hidden beneath the whitewash, just as the true cross was buried beneath Calvary. And in both cases the concealment acts as an impetus to disclosure. The true cross will inevitably be uncovered by divine intervention in the form of St. Helena, and, in parallel, the image of the saint must be perceived through the veil of paint, thereby promising a final discovery in which the true faith of Catholicism will be restored. It was precisely the confluence of the revelatory process and religious oppression that made St. Helena's story a suitable allegory for the post-Reformation Catholic Church. The discovery of the true cross thus divinely predicts the triumph of the true faith of Catholicism.

For Shakespeare, whose father had twice appeared on the recusancy rolls in 1592, and who still counted a number of known Catholics among his acquaintances and family, the significance of the "defasyng" for those who were still sympathetic to the old faith could not but have been apparent. It is unsurprising, therefore, that alongside the incorporation of the St. Helena narrative into *The Merchant of Venice* Shakespeare also persistently incorporates contemporary Catholic discourse. The allusions are well known; for example, Peter Milward lists the general references that may be associated with Catholicism. These include the use of the word "holy" in conjunction with the body of the church; praying at wayside crosses; kneeling before Mary; devotion to the saints; prayers for the souls of the deceased; the mass linked to confession and penance; and the last sacrament (Milward 1973: 24–42; 1997).[6] However, in order to place these thematic signifiers within the material circumstances of *The Merchant of Venice*'s production, it is necessary to look at the play's Catholic discourse in conjunction with the St. Helena legend's specific associations with late sixteenth-century Stratford's adherence to the old faith.

The first scene of the play immediately offers two allusions. First, in attempting to interpret Antonio's sadness, Salerio suggests that he might be concerned about his economic ventures:

> Should I go to church
> And see the holy edifice of stone
> And not bethink me straight of dangerous rocks,
> Which touching but my gentle vessel's side
> Would scatter all her spices on the stream . . . (1.1.29–33)

At a pictorial level, Salerio simply points out the material similarity between the "stone" of the church and coastline "rocks," but by describing the "edifice" as "holy" the speech evokes a Catholic adjectival use, commonly mocked by Protestants. Moreover, the equivalence of a church and disaster or wreckage must have appeared at least unusual in a Christian society, which was more used to interpreting the church as a symbol of salvation. And this is particularly true when used in conjunction with the sea passage as a metaphor for humankind's journey through life. Yet Salerio, in his attempt to empathize with Antonio, perceives the church as dangerous, and in expounding his theory he employs a Catholic adjectival formulation. Of course, Antonio denies such cares and the witty debate about the cause of the merchant's melancholy persists until he and Bassanio are left alone. It is within the security of their close friendship that the second use of Catholic terminology is introduced, as Antonio interrogates Bassanio about the "lady . . . / To whom you swore a secret pilgrimage" (1.1.119–20). As Jay O. Halio points out, "Religious imagery was commonplace for lovers" and Bassanio makes comparable use of classical allusions alongside the Christian ones when he refers to "Jason" and the "golden fleece" (1.1.172, 170; Halio 1993: 109). Yet there is no internal narrative reason for Antonio to suggest that Bassanio's wooing of Portia must be "secret." One of Shakespeare's source texts, Il Percorone, has an equivalent concealed quest suggesting that a redundant vestige of that narrative might remain in the play. On the other hand, linked to Salerio's image of the dangerous "holy edifice," a "secret pilgrimage" to the lady of Belmont begins to appear reasonable. On one level, the Venetian Christians simply employ expected Catholic terminology, but at the same time, the spiritual concerns of late sixteenth-century England begin to emerge. Faith, and particularly a faith with Catholic sympathies, becomes a possible source of danger, necessitating secrecy and covert acts of worship.

The opening of the subsequent scene in Belmont encompasses expectations of perfection in terms of character, narrative, and spiritual allusion, and along with the other idealizations constructed by Bassanio, any Catholic significations are quickly deconstructed by Portia's down-to-earth prose. The lady of Belmont is no ardent saint, nor is she on a quest to discover the true cross. Rather, Portia recognizes her own fallible human state as she responds to Nerissa's injunctions: "If to do were as easy as to know what were good to do, chapels had been churches, and poor men's cottages princes' palaces" (1.2.12–14). Merchant (1967: 169) notes that "the term [chapels] was also used for an outlying chapel of a principal church or monastery. Compare its use in Stratford for the Guild Chapel" (Merchant 1967: 169). Thus Portia not only undercuts any romantic idealization of herself, but also belittles her spiritual antecedent, St. Helena, in her whitewashed position on the chapel wall, and goes on to point out that "it is a good divine that follows his own instructions" (1.2.14–15). The desired significations, of both spiritual and romantic love, appear to be distanced from the actualities of Portia's estate, thereby creating, at the beginning of the play, a slippage of meaning and understanding that serves to divide Belmont from Venice. The alternate worlds of the play begin, therefore, to suggest a series of dualities that persist until the final harmonious resolution in a triumphant Belmont.

An analysis of the play's dialectics has become routine practice, setting up a panoply of opposites: location, gender, race, faith, class, sexuality, economics, as well as an array of moral epithets. Thus Venice is a city inhabited by men, whose diverse races and faiths reflect the heterogeneity of a mercantile port, whereas Belmont is a secluded country house ruled over by a white Christian noblewoman. In Venice the expediency of trade demands a certain mixing of social classes and a coexistence with other marginal identities, such as Antonio's possible homoerotic attachment to Bassanio. In Belmont money and lands are inherited and marriage is the only foreseeable destiny for Portia, whose beauty and wealth appear to confer moral virtues, just as Shylock's race and faith seem to condemn him to the role of villain. But this is, inevitably, a reductive analysis of the play's thematic dichotomies and a number of important analyses have focused upon these arguments in order to uncover the fragile nature of such easy divisions. Earlier criticism often accepted the dualities unquestioningly, interpreting Portia as "the heroine of a romance story [who] is fair, noble, maiden, [and] an only daughter who loves simply and unquestioningly," or deciding that the play was neither "anti-Jewish" nor informed by racial prejudice.[7] While some critics always questioned such assumptions, Auden's essay in *The Dyer's Hand* (1963) being a case in point, it was not until the 1990s that academic interpretations of the play determinedly investigated the play's forefronting of prejudice in its various forms. An insightful example of this more challenging approach may be seen in Jim Shapiro's important contribution, *Shakespeare and the Jews*, that offers as one conclusion:

> Racist fantasies continue to compel belief because they tap into some of the deepest fears people have of "turning" – especially of physical, sexual, or religious transformation. Dig deep enough and one discovers that the affirmation of cultural identity too often rests upon the slippery foundations of prejudice and exclusion. (Shapiro 1996: 227)[8]

Shapiro's findings are echoed by a number of present-day critics who have excavated the "prejudice" and "fears" that inform the dialectics in *The Merchant of Venice*. Karen Newman sees Portia's role as challenging early modern gender conventions and "pervert[ing] authorized systems of gender and power" (Newman 1987: 133), while Alan Sinfield argues that "the early modern organization of sex and gender boundaries was different from ours, and the ordinary currency of that culture is replete with erotic interactions that strike strange chords today" (Sinfield 1996: 176–7).[9] The acknowledgment of the play's openness to questions of gender and sexuality is paralleled by similar critical debates over the discourses of economics, class, the law, and postcolonialism, in which dominant ideological positions are seen to be either undermined or ultimately reinforced. The recent focus upon the problem of reading questions of race/racism into an early modern play by present-day readers has brought a much-needed self-awareness of our own discomfort in discussing issues of prejudice.[10] While recognizing our own subject position, however, John Drakakis asserts that to ignore such issues leads to a "disseminating of [the play's] prejudices" and that, rather, we need "To acknowledge that such prejudices are the products of a determinate history whose partial and horrifying solutions cannot, and should never be allowed to, exert a permanent claim on our own historically constituted sensibilities" (Drakakis 1998: 209). Drakakis's essay is immersed in its own theoretical ethos – cultural materialism – and is self-aware of the economics of its own production, yet its warning to be aware of and alert to racial and religious prejudice has a wider signification.

Thus, Shapiro's much-needed analysis of the anti-Semitism in *The Merchant of Venice* uncovered a history of prejudice against the Jews in medieval and early modern Europe for a readership/audience constructed by its knowledge of the twentieth-century Holocaust. And Portia's flippant racist dismissal of the black Prince of Morocco – "Let all of his complexion choose me so" (2.7.79) – can no longer be heard without incurring an awareness of present-day racist attitudes. These prejudices are apparent to us because we live with them; they are as Drakakis points out part of "our own historically constituted sensibilities." There is, however, evidence of yet another aspect of intolerance in the play and one that precipitated a more immediate and real danger in late sixteenth-century London and the south midlands. A wealth of critical prose has been spent trying to determine which Jewish and black people Shakespeare could have known and, with more cause, how these people would have been treated given their obvious difference from the dominant social groups. While the dangers of being black or wearing "Jewish gaberdine" should not be dismissed, during the late sixteenth century the clearest, almost everyday, acts of prejudice were against Catholics. Being Catholic might not have been as obvious as being black or Jewish, but if detected it could be more dangerous. Although the Protestant state fluctuated in its readiness to persecute, monetary and physical punishments against those whose spiritual whitewash had not proved sufficiently opaque were known throughout England and Wales. The area surrounding Stratford-Upon-Avon was no exception and the influx of Jesuits in the early 1580s provoked increasingly harsh measures against those persisting in their Catholic practices. For example, in 1583 John Somerville, who was a distant relative of Mary Arden, was implicated in a Catholic plot to assassinate Elizabeth I and was executed at Tyburn, and a *Hore beate Mariae* was discovered that had been given to him by his sister, Elizabeth Somerville.[11] Thus, those terms, phrases, gestures, and belongings that had been commonplace to the Catholic faith became, particularly after the 1580s, signifiers of danger.

The Merchant of Venice is replete with such allusions; those in scenes 1 and 2 have already been identified as suggesting a material threat or disillusionment. With the entrance of Shylock in scene 3 the pervasive nature of prejudice and its dangers becomes more apparent. For example, Shylock appears simply to reject a dinner invitation from Bassanio, yet the combination of terms he uses – "I will not eat with you, drink with you, nor pray with you" (1.3.32–3) – overlays the social division with a disturbing sacramental reading. Similarly, the comic sequences with Launcelot Gobbo, while apparently consisting of light banter, suggest the recusancy of the countryside and its adherence to the old terms, as Old Gobbo invokes "God's sonties" (saints; 2.2.42). Later Launcelot refers to "Ash Wednesday" (2.5.24–7), a reference that initially seems inconsequential, until compared with the overt Easter references in act 5 (Gnerro 1979: 101–2). The Gobbos thus reminds us that while language may be whitewashed with the seeming nonsense of the clown, Catholic phrases and ceremonies refused to be defaced from popular memory. But the dangers of Catholicism are apparent not only in the urban streets of Venice, but also in the seemingly idyllic setting of Belmont.

The idealization of Portia is a critical commonplace, and at the center of the play her perfections become associated with a Catholic discourse. The Prince of Morocco appears to adopt the terminology of courtly convention when he refers to Portia as "this shrine, this mortal breathing saint" (2.7.40). However, a "shrine" is a reliquary containing a remembrance of a dead saint, whereas Portia's vocal and visible presence at the temple affirms her as "mortal" and "breathing." As such, the lady of Belmont seems to be worshiped in decease as much as in a live immediacy and this inevitably promulgates a disruption of the assumed romantic discourse. The use of the word "shrine" in this context, therefore, undercuts the commonplace parallel of spiritual and secular love, allowing a slippage of meaning. As an indeterminate object of faith, Portia in her half-dead/half-alive state signifies disturbing questions rather than courtly certainties, and consequently the play's Catholic allusions are foregrounded as a source of disquiet within the Belmont scenes. Morocco does not mistake the meaning of the noun "shrine" (as some critics believe); instead, his words suggest one of the play's dichotomies, in which negated signifiers of faith are simultaneously shown to be extant. But such revelations inevitably incurred risks.

Morocco, the Prince of Arragon, and Bassanio face "hazard[s]," in that when they agree to undertake the choice of caskets they must swear "Never to speak to lady afterward / In way of marriage" (2.1.41–2). And even this folktale-like prohibition provokes questions about social custom, legitimacy, and sexual practice that are particularly apposite for a play that continually focuses upon racial difference. It is, however, the scene in which Bassanio chooses, that his love for Portia is represented as dangerous, through the extended metaphor of torture.

> *Bassanio.*   Let me choose,
> For as I am, I live upon the rack.
> *Portia.* Upon the rack, Bassanio? Then confess
> What treason there is mingled with your love.
> *Bassanio.* None but that ugly treason of mistrust,
> Which makes me fear th' enjoying of my love, –

There may as well be amity and life
'Tween snow and fire, as treason and my love.
Portia. Ay, but I fear you speak upon the rack
Where men enforced do speak any thing.
Bassanio. Promise me life, and I'll confess the truth.
Porta. Well then, confess and live.
Bassanio.   'Confess and love'
Had been the very sum of my confession:
O happy torment, when my torturer
Doth teach me answers for deliverance! (3.2.24–38)

Within fifteen lines the lovers use the word "rack" three times, "confess" four times, and also refer to "confession" and "enforced do speak." They mention "treason" and "fear" twice each, while also noting "mistrust," "torment," and "torturer." Admittedly, in the same passage Portia and Bassanio proclaim their love (four times) and foresee that the "truth" will lead to "deliverance," but the weight of the lines is decisively towards torture, fear, and confession. Inevitably the passage has produced a complex array of editorial annotation to explain why two romantic lovers should invoke such negative emotions. John Russell Brown in the Arden edition, M. M. Mahood in the Cambridge edition, and W. Moelwyn Merchant in the Penguin edition suggest that there is an allusion to Roderigo Lopez, a Jewish physician who had professed to be Christian (Brown 1955: 78, xxiii; Mahood 1987: 114: Merchant 1967: 190).[12] Originally Lopez had come from Portugal, and he was executed in 1594 for his part in a plot to poison Don Antonio, a claimant to the Portuguese throne, and Elizabeth I. Certainly, Lopez had been tortured on the rack, an operation that had produced the expected "confession," but his fate was hardly uncommon. However, an interest in any possible Jewish connections that the play might display has sometimes led editors and critics to overlook other possible allusions. The scenes in Belmont, therefore, while constantly negotiating with the Venice sequences through parallels of image, theme, and vocabulary, cannot be read as using source material in exactly the same way. It is one thing to represent Shylock as tortured and confessing, in which a reference to Lopez would infer a deeply anti-Semitic signifier, but it is quite another if the white, Christian aristocrat Bassanio claims, even in metaphor, to be on the rack. Conjunctions between the trial and casket scenes are certainly possible, yet the words "rack," "confess," and "love" occur in Belmont and must also, therefore, be read in the quasi-spiritual context of Bassanio's "secret . . . pilgrimage" to the "shrine."

It is possible to reread Bassanio's casket scene as part of the play's Christian allegory by concentrating upon the idea of love and deliverance. In a useful guide, *Shakespeare's Christian Dimension* (1994), Roy Battenhouse anthologizes seven essays that address *The Merchant of Venice* and commonly agree on Bassanio's role as an everyman figure. In parallel, Antonio is recognized as Christ-like, sacrificing himself in order to allow Bassanio to live and gain the ideal salvation offered at Belmont. And J. A. Bryant's essay argues that Portia may be identified as "Christ's divine nature" in parallel to "Christ's physical nature" as represented by Antonio (Battenhouse 1994: 74). Thus, although Bryant makes no reference to the torture trope, Bassanio's "love" for Portia as Christ's divine nature may indeed be seen to lead to "deliverance" in heaven. Barbara Lewalski looks more closely at the casket sequences (again there is no specific reference to the rack), interpreting the narrative as "everyman's choice of paths to spiritual life or death," and relating them to the trial scene where Portia becomes "the Virgin Mary [who] intercedes for man by appealing to the Mercy of God" (Lewalski 1962: 80–1). The combination of Christian allegory and the image of the rack would, of course, have been familiar in the late Elizabethan era when men and women were commonly tortured and executed for their faith. Or, more accurately, for an active pursuance of their Catholic faith.

During the 1580s and 1590s a succession of Jesuits and seminary priests were placed on the rack, supposedly to obtain a confession of their treasonable intent against the queen in her position as head of the church. The subsequent judgment invariably condemned them to be hanged, but cut down before they died so that their genitals could be cut off and their bowels removed and burned before them. The sufferings of the more famous Catholic martyrs, such as Edmund Campion in 1581 and Robert Southwell in 1595, would have been well known, but there were regular religious executions at Tyburn. Moreover, some of them had connections to Stratford and would have been known to John and William Shakespeare. These men included Thomas Cottom, the brother of the Stratford schoolmaster (1582); Edward Arnold and John Somerville who were related to the Arden family (1583); and William Debdale, one of William Shakespeare's school fellows (1586). In the light of this political context, the words used by Bassanio and Portia to describe their unfulfilled desire – rack, treason, confess, love, and deliverance – must be reread, for Belmont is not merely a Christian ideal, it may also be a place of Catholic sanctuary.

To begin, by presenting Portia as a cross between a saint, possibly St. Helena, and the Virgin Mary in her role as intercessor for the sinful mortals, in England in the mid-1590s, *The Merchant of Venice* must encompass a Catholic context, and one that semi-idealizes the old faith. Further, by portraying Bassanio as an everyman figure on a secret pilgrimage to this saint's shrine, during which journey he invokes the image of torture, but a "happy torment" that will lead to "deliverance," the courtly lover begins to look suspiciously like a recusant. But this is a long way from identifying Bassanio with one of the Catholic martyrs from Stratford or elsewhere. No such close allegory exists and no *clef* is necessary to understand the way in which recurrent events of the Elizabethan spiritual world are played out through the text and on the stage. One clear pointer to the way in which Shakespeare invokes a more complex and much wider interpretation of late sixteenth-century Catholicism may be seen in the insistent use of the words "confess" and "confession." Interestingly, the editors Halio and Brown point out that the lovers invert the common proverb "Confess and be Hanged" when they align confession with life and love (Halio 1993: 166; Brown 1955: 78). Yet within the Catholic system of belief it is precisely through confession and contrition that spiritual life and the love of God may be attained. Thus, for a committed Elizabethan Catholic, confession and contrition were essential, because it was only by confessing their mortal sins, repenting of them and undertaking penance that they could receive absolution and receive communion. And this was particularly true when associated with death, the last sacrament, or being hanged for your faith. Thus Bassanio may indeed be fearful, knowing that his own acts of treason or sin must be confessed in order to attain the ideal of Christian mercy as represented by Portia. Such a general Catholic interpretation corresponds with the numerous allusions to confession and the sacrament that recur throughout the Shakespearean canon, from the early plays such as *Romeo and Juliet*, through the more complex plays like *Measure for Measure*, to the late romances of *Cymbeline* and *The Winter's Tale* (Milward 1973: 30–1). Yet at the same time the vocabulary of torture used by both lovers opens the lines to a more specifically located discourse in terms of both time and place.

It is important to remember that, when Bassanio speaks of the "rack . . . treason . . . mistrust . . . fear . . . torment and torturer," the words invoke not only the rarefied experience of the martyr, but also the everyday fears of the entire recusant population of late sixteenth-century England. The recusancy rolls give us some idea of the extent of open opposition to the Protestant church, but covert adherence to the old faith would have been much more extensive. While the whitewash of conformity remained in place an inner belief was relatively safe, but after the early 1580s' Jesuit mission an atmosphere of betrayal and suspicion became both prevalent and extensive. Shakespeare's father is a telling example. The records of his recusancy, the loss of his civic roles, and his increasing monetary problems are well-documented, yet the full extent of his Catholic sympathies remains concealed (Brownlow 1989; Honan 1999: 39, 354–6; Wilson 1993: 468–72). And that is precisely the point. In late sixteenth-century England an open declaration of faith verged on the suicidal. Only those who were prepared to die for their faith, like Campion, or those too inexperienced to know better, like Debdale, would have openly courted the perils of the torturer and the rack. The Catholic everyman would, like John Shakespeare, have whitewashed over the symbols of his faith. It is highly likely therefore, particularly given the tenacity of a faith that had claimed single tenure within Britain a generation earlier, that a late sixteenth-century audience would have been conversant with the concepts in, and threatening realities of, Bassanio's casket speech.

The Merchant of Venice is a play about the way in which a visible exterior may conceal a different and more valuable interior, about the way in which prejudice produces the marginalization and persecution of certain racial and religious groups, and about the way in which harmony and redemption might be engineered. While being a comedy, in that a final resolution is achieved, the play questions the reconciliation of the dichotomies and prejudices that have been raised in the first four acts. Moreover, these divisions exist at such a materially threatening interface that the awareness of actual reprisals manipulates the audience and readers into a position of historical self-awareness, in which religious and/or racial prejudice are fatally entwined with death and destruction. But still the play insists upon a comic resolution: Bassanio wins Portia, Antonio's life is saved, they all return to a Belmont in which the harmony of the spheres attempts closure upon the unpleasantness of the trial scene in Venice. Even in the court scene, although it ends with Shylock as a broken man about to convert to Christianity, there is no loss of life, no physical mutilation, and no particularly exacting monetary penalty either. Audiences and readers seem to be expected to accept an idealized ending, which given the expectations of the genre they are happy to comply with, but at the same time it remains impossible to ignore the impact of Shylock and the trial scene. This problematic resolution has been the source of critical debate, with directors and critics varying between continued irresolution and the successful containing of marginalized elements. Those analyses which have identified a Christian allegory veer more towards a harmonious end. But given the way in which the play undercuts a timeless spiritual allegory, uncovering the sharp divisions of Catholic and Protestant convictions in the late sixteenth century, the neat resolutions of Belmont need to be reexamined.

The first three acts of *The Merchant of Venice* shift between Venice and Belmont, but acts 4 and 5 are set respectively in the two locations, thereby conferring by contrast an atmosphere of relief, calm, and security onto Portia's country house. It is no surprise, therefore, that the final sequence opens on an idyllic setting, with Lorenzo and Jessica affirming their love in the moonlit gardens. This is affirmed within the play's Christian allegory, as Lewalski (1962: 83) concludes: "Belmont . . . figures forth the Heavenly City." And the overall spiritual tone is emphasized by biblical references, such as the candle seen by Portia and Nerissa:

> That light we see is burning in my hall:
> How far that little candle throws his beams! (5.1.89–90)

which recalls the allusion to Christ in Matthew 5: 16, "Let your light so shine before men." The emphasis upon Christ's resurrection is also noted by Mark L. Gnerro, who points out that,

> Although Shakespeare casts the love duet (and many of the speeches following it) into the language of classical allusiveness, there is a pervasive strain of imagery drawn from the Easter liturgy, specifically from the vigil for Holy Saturday, suggesting Shakespeare was aiming to show religious grace inspiring natural goodness and reconciliation. (Gnerro 1979: 101)

In particular, Gnerro points out that the use of the anaphora "In such a night . . ." at the beginning of the lovers' responses to one another, closely resembles the repetition of "Haec nox est" in the preface to the Easter Saturday mass in which the paschal candle represents the rebirth of light into the world at Christ's resurrection. Yet Gnerro wonders "how Shakespeare came by this phrasing from the liturgy of the Catholic Church" (ibid: 102). There are, however, other more accessible Catholic referents in the scene. For example, Portia has informed the household that she has "breath'd a secret vow, / To live in prayer and contemplation" with Nerissa in a "monast'ry" (3.4.27–8 and 31), although of course the audience knows that in reality they have disguised themselves as men and undertaken a more material salvation of Antonio. In act 5 this fake narrative is repeated when Stephano informs the moonlit lovers that

> My mistress will before the break of day
> Be here at Belmont, – she doth stray about
> By holy crosses where she kneels and prays . . .
> [accompanied by]
> None but a holy hermit and her maid. (5.1.29–31, 33)

These actions are precisely the practices that the Protestant church was trying to stamp out. While the monasteries had been disbanded in the 1530s, the physical remains of Catholicism, including wall paintings and holy crosses, remained concealed ready to be taken out again if circumstance allowed it, as became starkly apparent during the Northern uprising of 1569 (Duffy 1992: 583). If, therefore, within the romance narrative Belmont represents an ideal pastoral world, while in the broad spectrum of Christian allegory denoting a spiritual salvation, a similar vision should recur within the allusions to contemporary religion. Read within these parameters, Belmont comes to symbolize the fabric of the Catholic church, in which Latin liturgy is recalled, just as the nuns and hermits are evoked by Portia's fabricated narrative. Moreover, as Easter becomes the expected climax within the Christian allegory, so here the resurrection may encompass the return of the true faith, the rediscovery, as it were, of the true cross. But it remains a nostalgic vision. The house is never entered and, above all, Belmont and its lady are not the perfect visions of the Catholic church and the Virgin Mary seen in the old miracle and morality plays.

Portia is, therefore, in some ways a saint, even St. Helena or the Virgin Mary, but in other ways her own prejudices and ready acknowledgment of her mortal flaws undercut any such spiritual idealism. Belmont might well, from one angle, look like the heavenly city, a pastoral haven, or even a convent, but from another perspective it seems disturbingly similar to Venice with its intolerant social codes and open disparagement of difference. Yet there are several anomalies in the description of Venice and its laws, which make the Italian city sound more like a midland town. For example, Shylock refers to the "charter" and "freedom" of Venice, and it has been noted that while this is an inaccurate formulation for a sovereign state, it is quite acceptable for a town like Stratford-Upon-Avon. Indeed, Stratford had gained its charter in 1553 when the supposedly Protestant Corporation took over the administration of the town from the Catholic Guild, an act that led, of course, to the whitewashing of the images in the Guild Chapel. In addition, the trial scene formulates a debate, not of Italian law, but of the growing "conflict between the Tudor common law and the mitigating equity of the Chancery courts" (Honan 1999: 258). In other words, the case could be decided either upon statute or precedent, or upon a plea of conscience, natural justice and mercy. Shakespeare had reason to understand the distinction, since in 1597 his parents took a ten-year-old case concerning a property claim to the Chancery court (Mahood 1987: 17). And if Shylock and Antonio meet on the Rialto, did they have their counterparts on the Clopton Bridge? It is tempting to identify the honorable Antonio with John Shakespeare; after all, both were merchants, both had "argosies" that failed, and the convictions (faith and friendship) of both led them into mortal danger. Moreover, John was a glove-maker and Portia demands Antonio's "gloves" from him (4.1.422), and as a known recusant John might well have considered himself, along with Antonio, as "a tainted wether of the flock" (4.1.114), a metaphor inappropriate for Antonio, but a commonplace to the Stratford wool-trader. Yet any allusion to John Shakespeare in the play is as uncertain as his faith, for while he might have been a merchant, he was also a usurer.[13]

In 1570 John Shakespeare was twice accused of breaking the usury laws and was subsequently fined. It is now acknowledged that the seemingly harsh moral attitudes to usury in Elizabethan England were, in practice, unworkable (Leinward 1999; Edelman 1999). It was as impossible for a nobleman to sustain an outward show of wealth without borrowing, as it was for the wool trade to function without credit. Usury was a fact of late sixteenth-century life and whatever censorious tracts and racist condemnations were published, those in business continued to lend money and charge interest. A contemporary audience would have been fully conversant with such pragmatic decisions and this compounds our understanding of Shylock as a sympathetic character, whose human pleas exert immense theatrical power. Moreover, by combining the recently uncovered spiritual information about John Shakespeare, together with the idea of usury and the play's Catholic allegory, a more complex understanding of the religious prejudice to which Shylock is subject becomes apparent. For Shylock may be seen to represent, not only a Jew with the consequential and extensive racial and religious discrimination inevitably implied (although that in itself would be enough), but also a focus for all religious intolerance. When he invokes the sacrament at the beginning of the play, "I will not eat with you, drink with you, pray with you" (1.3.32–3), when he calls upon his "oath in heaven" sworn upon "our holy Sabbath" (4.1.224 and 36), and when he finally crumples at his enforced conversion, "I pray you give me leave to go from hence, / I am not well" (4.1.391–2), Shylock's representative power expands to include a more complex array of religious difference. And when he reminds Antonio that he has been called "misbeliever" and been spat upon (1.2.106–7), the actuality of religious and racial persecution must be recognized as dangerously pervasive and insidiously persistent.

In the play Shylock is referred to as the "Jew" and in criticism he has been called the Devil and a Puritan. It would be a further reductive simplification to add "Catholic." Intolerance, in all its forms, feeds upon ready and unsophisticated identifications, and upon the pigeonholing of difference as a prelude to marginalization, repulsion, and attack. *The Merchant of Venice* explores these social mechanisms through the multiple discourses of race, religion, class, gender, and sexuality, thereby exposing the ideological investment in difference for a range of audiences. Thus, anti-Semitism in a post-Holocaust age, and racial prejudice alongside an acknowledgment of slavery and the human rights movement, must be recognized as different from, but allied to, the persecution of Catholics by the early modern Protestant church and state. It is hardly surprising that *The Merchant of Venice* provokes uncomfortable reactions, and it will continue to do so as long as racial and religious intolerance perverts the course of justice, denies mercy, and promotes the death and destruction of those who simply happen to be different.

NOTES

1 I am indebted to Honan's (1999) informative biography throughout this essay, although my explanation of "defasyng" differs somewhat from his. In addition, I should like to thank Michael Wood for the useful and informative comments made on this essay.

2 Bloom points out that the Chapel was used as a schoolroom after the dissolution of the Guild in 1553 and was still being used for this purpose in 1628, despite several attempts to revert to religious use only (Bloom 1914: 277).

3 The question of whether Shakespeare was Catholic or had Catholic sympathies has been focused upon increasingly over the last ten to fifteen years. Thus Richard Dutton wrote in 1989: "Fascinating as such possibilities are, they remain a tottering edifice of speculations. Perhaps Shakespeare *was* born a Catholic and perhaps secretly he adhered to the old faith" (Dutton 1989: 7). Whereas ten years later Park Honan was able to assert confidently that "a nucleus of Catholics lay near the centre of his [Shakespeare's] early acquaintanceship" (Honan 1999: 80). No unquestionable evidence has yet emerged as to William Shakespeare's faith or his time in the Catholic Hoghton household near Lancaster, but the pro-Catholic sympathies of his close and extended family, as well as his companions in Stratford, is now fully proved. I am grateful to Richard Dutton for his insightful and helpful comments on Shakespeare's faith.

4 All references are to the Arden Shakespeare edition (Brown 1955).

5 M. D. Anderson suggests that the Stratford Guild might even have performed a St. Helena play (Anderson 1963: 202–3). This seems to me quite likely since the Guild held its feast and procession in May and, although not corresponding with St. Helena's saint's day, May 3 is the date on which the "Invention of the Cross" is celebrated. This means that Shakespeare might have seen a St. Helena pageant, but the speculative nature of such an unproven hypothesis relegates the material definitively to a footnote.

6 Richmond Noble and Naseeb Shaheen provide useful biblical references from the play and also prove that Shakespeare was fully conversant with Protestant texts, such as the Book of Common Prayer and the Geneva Bible (Noble 1935: 161–9; Shaheen 1999). Shakespeare may have displayed knowledge of Catholic images and spoken verse in the play, but his textual referents are Protestant, a predictable conclusion given the period of his education and employment, as well as the common Catholic church background of his age.

7 The first two quotations come from Brown's Arden edition (Brown 1955: xlvii, xxxix). The description of Morocco in Halio's Oxford edition fails to consider race as an important element in the portrayal of the prince's character (Halio 1993: 34). I have not quoted M. M. Mahood's initial sentence in his description of "Some attitudes and assumptions behind the play," but it is worth adding in this footnote: "The Kenyan writer Karen Blixen once told the story of *The Merchant of Venice* to her Somali Butler, Farah Aden, who was deeply disappointed by Shylock's defeat. He was sure the Jew could have succeeded, if only he had used a red-hot knife. As an African listener, he had expected a tale about a clever trickster in the Brer Rabbit tradition; Shylock let him down. We can be as far off-course as Farah in our reading of the play if we do not pay some heed to the attitudes of its first audience" (Mahood 1987: 8). The contradictory discourses present in just four sentences, with their combination of patriarchal imperialism and postcolonial self-awareness in an edition that offers important scholarly insights into the play, serves to reinforce Mahood's own warning about being "off-course."

8 Martin D. Yaffe's *Shylock and the Jewish Question* (1997) is another useful source, although Yaffe's tendency to pursue harmonious readings does not concur with the analysis here.

9 See also Belsey (1991) and Patterson (1999).

10 See particularly Loomba and Orlin (1998) and Macdonald (1997). An important distinction between race in terms of appearance and race as genealogical inheritance is made by Elizabeth A. Spiller (1998).

11   Domestic State Papers Elizabeth, Vol. I, no. 55, 7/11/1583. For a recent account of how Shakespeare
     alludes to Somerville in another play, see Martin (2000), where he points out that the positive
     representation of Somerville in the play suggests a pro-Catholic reading.
12   Halio in the Oxford edition of the play is more circumspect, observing only that the "rack" was an
     "instrument of torture used . . . to stretch someone out cruelly until he or she confessed" (Halio
     1993: 165).
13   For a discussion of the comparability of Shylock and Antonio see Tanner (1999), in which Tanner
     sets "Antonio the sodomite" alongside "Shylock the usurer."

REFERENCES AND FURTHER READING

Anderson, M. D. (1963). *Drama and Imagery in English Medieval Churches*. Cambridge: Cambridge
    University Press.
Battenhouse, R. (ed.) (1994). *Shakespeare's Christian Dimension*, Bloomington: Indiana University Press.
Belsey, C. (1991). Love in Venice. *Shakespeare Survey*, 44, 41–53.
Bloom, J. H. (1914). *Shakespeare's Church*. Stratford-Upon-Avon: Shakespeare Press.
Brown, J. R. (ed.) (1955). *The Merchant of Venice*. London: Methuen.
Brownlow, F. W. (1989). John Shakespeare's Recusancy: New Light on an Old Document. *Shakespeare
    Quarterly*, 40, 186–91.
Bryant, J. A. (1961). Bassanio's Two Saviours. In R. Battenhouse (ed.) *Shakespeare's Christian Dimension*.
    Bloomington: Indiana University Press, 71–6.
Coyle, M. (ed.) (1998). *New Casebooks: The Merchant of Venice*. London: Macmillan.
Davidson, C. and Alexander, J. (1985). *The Early Art of Coventry, Stratford-Upon-Avon, Warwickshire*.
    Kalamazoo, MI: Medieval Institute Publications.
Drakakis, J. (1998). Historical Difference and Venetian Patriarchy. In M. Coyle (ed.) *New Casebooks: The
    Merchant of Venice*. London: Macmillan.
Duffy, E. (1992). *The Stripping of the Altars: Traditional Religion in England c. 1400–c. 1580*. New Haven,
    CT: Yale University Press.
Dutton, R. (1989). *William Shakespeare: A Literary Life*. London: Macmillan.
——(1998). Shakespeare and Lancaster. *Shakespeare Quarterly*, 49, 1–21.
Edelman, C. (1999). Which is the Jew that Shakespeare Knew: Shylock on the Elizabethan Stage.
    Shakespeare Survey, 52, 99–106.
Fisher, T. and Nichols, J. G. (1838). *Ancient allegorical, historical and legendary Paintings . . . on the walls
    of the Chapel of the Trinity, belonging to the Gilde of the Holy Cross at Stratford-upon-Avon*. London: J. G.
    Nichols.
Furness, H. H. (ed.) (ca. 1916). *The Merchant of Venice: A New Variorum Edition*. Philadelphia, PA:
    Lippincott.
Gnerro, M. L. (1979). Easter Liturgy and the Love Duet in *MV* 5.1. In R. Battenhouse (ed.) *Shakespeare's
    Christian Dimension*. Bloomington: Indiana University Press, 100–2.
Halio, J. L. (ed.) (1993). *The Merchant of Venice*. Oxford: Clarendon Press.
Honan, P. (1999). *Shakespeare: A Life*. Oxford: Oxford University Press.
Hughes, A. (1997). Building a Godly Town: Religious and Cultural Divisions in Stratford-Upon-Avon.
    In R. Bearman (ed.) *The History of an English Borough: Stratford-Upon-Avon, 1196–1996*. Stroud: Sutton
    Publishing, 97–109.
Leinwand, T. B. (1999). *Theatre, Finance, and Society in Early Modern England*. Cambridge Studies in
    Renaissance Literature and Culture 31. Cambridge: Cambridge University Press.
Lewalski, B. K. (1962). Allegory in *The Merchant of Venice*. In R. Battenhouse (ed.) *Shakespeare's Christian
    Dimension*. Bloomington: Indiana University Press, 76–83.
Loomba, A. and Orlin, M. (eds.) (1998). *Post-Colonial Shakespeare*. London: Routledge.

Macdonald, J. G. (1997). *Race, Ethnicity and Power in the Renaissance.* London: Associated University Presses.

Mahood, M. M. (ed.) (1987). *The Merchant of Venice.* Cambridge: Cambridge University Press.

Martin, R. (2000). Rehabilitating John Somerville in *3 Henry VI. Shakespeare Quarterly*, 51, 332–40.

Merchant, M. M. (ed.) (1967). *The Merchant of Venice.* Harmondsworth: Penguin Books.

Milward, P. (1973). *Shakespeare's Religious Background.* London: Sidgwick and Jackson.

——(1997). *The Catholicism of Shakespeare's Plays.* Tokyo: The Renaissance Institute, Sophia University.

Morris, R. (ed.) (1877–92). *Cursor Mundi.* London: Kegan Paul.

Newman, K. (1987) Portia's Ring: Unruly Women and the Structures of Exchange in *The Merchant of Venice.* In M. Coyle (ed.) *New Casebooks: The Merchant of Venice.* London: Macmillan, 117–38.

Noble, R. (1935). *Shakespeare's Biblical Knowledge.* London: Society for the Promotion of Christian knowledge.

Patterson, S. (1999). The Bankruptcy of Homoerotic Amity in Shakespeare's *Merchant of Venice. Shakespeare Quarterly*, 50, 9–32.

Savage, R. and Fripp, E. I. (1921–2). *Minutes and Accounts of the Corporation of Stratford-Upon-Avon and Other Records 1553–1620.* Oxford: Oxford University Press.

Shaheen, N. (1999). *Biblical References in Shakespeare's Plays.* Newark: University of Delaware Press.

Shapiro, J. (1996). *Shakespeare and the Jews.* New York: Columbia University Press.

Sinfield, A. (1996). How to Read *The Merchant of Venice* Without Being Heterosexist. In M. Coyle (ed.) *New Casebooks. The Merchant of Venice.* London: Macmillan, 161–80.

Spiller, E. A. (1998). From Imagination to Miscegenation: Race and Romance in Shakespeare's *The Merchant of Venice. Renaissance Drama*, 29, 137–64.

Tanner, T. (1999). *The Merchant of Venice. Cambridge Quarterly*, 41, 76–99.

Wheler, R. B. (1806). *History and Antiquities of Stratford-Upon-Avon.* Stratford: J. Ward.

Wilson, I. (1993). *Shakespeare, the Evidence: Unlocking the Mysteries of the Man and his Work.* London: Headline.

Wilson, R. (1997). Shakespeare and the Jesuits. *Times Literary Supplement*, December 19, 1997, 12.

Yaffe, M. D. (1997). *Shylock and the Jewish Question.* Baltimore, MD: Johns Hopkins University Press.

19

The Merry Wives of Windsor: Unhusbanding Desires in Windsor

Wendy Wall

I would all the world might be cozened, for I have been cozened.

Falstaff (4.5.88–9)

I know not which pleases me better, that my husband is deceived, or Sir John.

Mistress Ford (3.3.264–5)

Shakespeare in Love: a recent Academy Award-winning film narrating the story of the bard's rising fame bore this curious title. Why would the producers choose to introduce a revered English writer in this manner? Why, if not to fulfill the audience's desire to see an icon of Western culture humanized into acting perhaps imprudently when caught in the throes of passion? To show the grand master susceptible to emotions seemingly at odds with the controlled genius attributed to him? This title prompts me to reflect on the "fortnight anecdote" told about Shakespeare's *The Merry Wives of Windsor*, which describes the play as commissioned by Queen Elizabeth. Devised in 1702 by John Dennis and embellished in 1709 by Nicholas Rowe, this legend attributes a desire to the queen similar to that driving the title of the film: Elizabeth is said to have been so eager to see the detached Falstaff in love that the bard was ordered to scribble out a play in a mere two weeks.

Despite its apparently fabricated account of the play's origin, the fortnight legend says something useful about *The Merry Wives of Windsor*; for it addresses both the messy textual state of the play and one of its central thematic concerns; in particular, it touches on the way that disorderly passions can unsettle measured behavior and the ideologies supported by that behavior. Shakespeare's only English comedy has long been seen as the story of financial and marital crises in a small town, with an aristocratic intruder attempting to seduce wives while rival suitors vie for the daughter of a rich businessman. Part farce and part citizen comedy, the play is distinguished by its inventory of English middle-class practices, its relocation of the beloved Falstaff from the realm of history to a new milieu, and its plethora of topical references. *Merry*

Wives has also sparked an unresolved discussion about whether it was written for a royal occasion and why it exists in two versions of very different lengths – the 1602 Quarto (reprinted in 1619) and the 1623 Folio. Imagining the queen's whimsy as prompting a hastily written play seemingly resolves editorial problems, explains textual loose ends, and makes the work clearly occasionalist. In rooting the play in the expenditure of female mirth and in a woman's desire to control a man, the anecdote also extends themes within the play to envelop the story of its making. But the legend ignores the fact that the playwright would have pointedly refused to satisfy the queen, since the Windsor Falstaff is in love only with money.

Merry Wives does present Falstaff playacting the part of "being in love," however, in a moment showing the attractions of unruly desire. In this scene, the townspeople arrange for Falstaff, dressed in horns as local ghost Herne the Hunter, to rendezvous with Mrs. Ford. Falstaff comments on his disguise by fantasizing himself a mythological virile god to be sacrificially slaughtered in sexual glory:

> Now, the hot-blooded gods assist me! Remember, Jove, thou wast a bull for thy Europa; love set on thy horns. O powerful love, that in some respects makes a beast a man; in some other, a man a beast . . . When gods have hot backs, what shall poor men do? For me, I am here a Windsor stag, and the fattest. (5.5.2–6; 11–13)

While we might read this passage as Falstaff's attempt to put the best possible spin on his ridiculous costume, we also note his obvious delight in being adorned as an emblem of both male virility and impotence. Describing himself as godlike and bestial at the same moment, caught in a moment of confident glory while a fat stag ripe for the kill, Falstaff holds forth the pleasure of masquerade. The unreadability of his position – as divine or animalic – feeds into his fantasy of a metamorphic and labile identity. This scene serves as the final reprimand to Falstaff's ongoing dream of plenitude, which he persistently expresses in terms of financial conservatism and imaginative license; he plans to become rich by feigning love and transforming wives into foreign ports to which he can trade freely (1.3.64–8). Though the play hints that Falstaff might best see himself as the mythic hunter Actaeon, whose prohibited desires were self-destructive, he seems instead gratified by his ability to become an abundant beastly god and "poor" mortal. The pleasures of a mercurial theatricality become visible at a moment ostensibly designed to target inappropriate behavior. Imagining himself "in love," Falstaff reveals fantasies that should, in the traditional reading of the play, be corrected by a shaming ritual designed to mock someone all dressed up with nowhere to go.

This denouement marks the third time that Falstaff suffers for his presumption and the only moment in which citizens – rather than simply wives – submit him to a public sport. Critics have identified early modern shaming rituals, such as the skimmington, as the proper context in which to read this scene and the play as a whole. The skimmington was a folk ceremony designed to correct an inversion of gender hierarchy in the home, namely by having a brow-beaten husband struck with a skimming ladle. G. K. Hunter argues that *Merry Wives* similarly uses ritual to effect social norms: "Bourgeois life proceeds by cajoling and joking and watching out for one another's pettinesses and aggressions, bearing with such excesses but pushing them all the time back towards the middle position" (Hunter 1986: 11). Indeed, it has become a critical commonplace that *Merry Wives* celebrates middle-class moderation and lauds a community built around the protection of property. According to this view, Windsor's financial and sexual crises are resolved through shaming rites and a marriage that reinstitutes conformity based largely on civility, thrift, moderation, and discretion. These values are given gendered and political valences, for the play affirms female domestic authority and middle-class ethics over and above an aristocratic male drive for power, while rooting national identity in bourgeois domestic life. This inter-pretation is predicated on a teleological structure (transgression, mortification, expi-ation) and a clear sense of which desires are licensed by the community.

Yet in the play's conclusion, shame is not possessed solely by one character, for soon after Falstaff is made to look foolish by fake fairies, the Pages discover that they have been tricked by their daughter. The prodigal Fenton lectures the Pages on their "shameful" attempts to marry their daughter against her will; and the main targets of satire in the play, Mr. Ford and Falstaff, mock non-idiomatic speakers of English as the true outsiders. Although Falstaff has supposedly learned humility, he goads the Pages in ways that reveal his glee that supposedly medicating wounds have spread to the moral doctors: "I am glad, though you have ta'en a special stand to strike at me, that your arrow has glanced" (5.5.231–2). At the moment that he should renounce fantasies of excess and instead gird his desires, Falstaff imagines social reparation as governed by somewhat uncontrollable arrows which glide off an object without deliv-ering the full effect of the blow ("glance," *OED* 1a). The final scene thus raises the question of whether the play endorses a middle-class civility founded on harnessing unruly passions. If moral correction is dependent on the production and delivery of shame to the right parties, does shame get directed "properly"? Or does it instead get dispersed among people who revel in the emotional and personal elasticity afforded by spectacle? Instead of singling out one offender who learns to adjust his behavior to fit community standards, I argue, the final ritual illuminates the town's investment in theatrical forgery and in shared humiliation. As it constructs national identity within middle-class norms, *Merry Wives* marks *resistances* to this production, for it dis-sects the sometimes uncivil emotions – mirth, aggression, pretense, and shame – that stray outside the bounds of moderation.

Keeping this theme in mind, let's return to consider the conditions under which the fortnight legend was generated. After Dennis's adaptation of *Merry Wives* flopped, he appealed to the impeccable dramatic taste of the legendary Queen Elizabeth as well as the faults she unwittingly instilled in the play. Elizabeth's longing for a spectacle of passion and her supposed satisfaction with the outcome substitute for Dennis's shameful failure. But in citing the queen's extravagant eagerness to rush the play into production, the legend hints at the vulnerability of a woman unable to control her impulses just at the moment that it lauds the accomplishments of the measured queen. Her stamp of approval for the play is also the sign of its – and possibly her – defi-ciency, since its "incomplete" status invites future playwrights to claim and to alter the text. Indeed this popular anecdote inscribes the unhusbanded queen as the object of her own fantasy; for she herself, like the bard or Falstaff in love, is seen in retrospect as a figure whose evidently human desires pleasurably strain against her iconic status. Transferring shame, immoderately expending passion, and appropriating property: the crossover between *Merry Wives'* themes and the story of its origins helps to explain why the fortnight anecdote has become the lens through which critics and editors have read the play for centuries even though it has no factual basis.

Yet the image of the playwright writing furiously at the behest of a patron obscures something that both *Merry Wives* and *Shakespeare in Love* acknowledge: the thoroughly commercial nature of theatre. With cash-flow problems, identity confusion, and script fiascoes haunting performance at every turn, the film pairs the instability of passion with the equally precarious economics of show business. *Merry Wives* similarly tells a story of a wooing *inextricable* from finance. In fact the play's narrative of adulterous desire, jealousy, and romance is saturated in the language of domestic management, as it investigates what might be called an affective husbandry. During the early modern period, the term "husbandry" pertained not only to being a spouse, but also to the careful management of resources, the monitoring of saving and spending, and the constitution of a household as a unit of production and consumption (Markham 1631; Tusser 1573). Though not presenting an amorous Falstaff, *Merry Wives* shows this character from the Henriad taking on the role of domestic and sexual invader by combining business with pleasure. The result is a set of scenes in which domestic economy sets the stage for the experiences of characters as they express anger and pleasure. Elsewhere in Windsor, suitors compete for heiress Anne Page in a plot that culminates in transvestite brides and a disrupted household. Investigating the uneasy relationship of desires to early modern discourses about husbandry thus leads us to reconsider the social norms that the play endorses. What does being merry, ashamed, vindictive, or theatrical have to do with the conflicting accounts of the "ideological work" that critics have attributed to this play?[1]

I

The problem of the play's dating and of its existence in two widely divergent early editions remains a point of debate among scholars. *Merry Wives* may have been performed as early as 1597, perhaps in conjunction with a court appearance, but most scholars date the play between 1598 and 1600. The earliest evidence of the play's existence comes from the 1602 Quarto, *A Most pleasaunt and excellent conceited Co-medie, of syr John Falstaffe, and the merrie Wiues of Windsor*, which runs roughly half the length of the 1623 Folio version. Since most scenes in the Quarto in which Falstaff and the Host appear are consistent with the Folio, critics have speculated that the actors playing these characters generated the short version as a "memorial reconstruction" (Daniel 1881; Greg 1910).[2] Earlier scholars had argued instead that the Quarto was written by Shakespeare but revised for later performances, or that it constituted an abridged version of the play for provincial touring (Roberts 1979: 1–40). Pointing to the Folio's allusions to Elizabeth's chivalric honor society, some critics suggest that the play was presented at the 1597 Order of the Garter ceremony, at which Shakespeare's patron Lord Hunsdon was installed. But this argument remains speculative, since internal evidence about the play's celebration of the court, as we shall see, is ambiguous. Despite notable differences between the two variants, to which I will return, both tell a story that focuses on gender and on middle-class domestic practice.

Set among largely prosperous householders in a town, *Merry Wives* inventories domestic spaces (coffers, closets, bakehouses), objects (hodge-pudding, venison pasties), and practices (laundering, distilling, physic). Mistress Quickly freely itemizes her chores when introducing herself as servant to Dr. Caius: "I may call him my master, look you, for I keep his house; and I wash, wring, brew, bake, scour, dress meat and drink, make the beds and do all myself" (1.4.88–92); and the two wives repel Falstaff's advances by transmuting him into the objects of housewifery: fat puddings, candle wax, and cooking grease. Moral ordering becomes a form of housework, as the wives take up and extend their roles as cooks, doctors, and launderers. "I think the best way [for revenge] were to entertain him with hope till the wicked fire of lust have melted him in his own grease," Mrs. Ford declares (2.1.64–6). Falstaff's disruptions of Windsor notably cannot be resolved by the Justice of the Peace, parson, or even local prominent businessmen. Instead that task falls to housewives and, secondarily, to local citizens who take up their cause as they subject Falstaff to a housecleaning orchestrated by fairies interested in pinching "slutty" maids (5.5.47).

Merry Wives is also identified as *domestic* in its concern with national affiliation. Shakespeare's only comedy located in England and only play set in contemporary England seemingly creates a thick description of everyday life filled with neighborly squabbles, town feasts, wandering bears, wise women, ghost stories, Cotswold games, and the allure of the nearby court. Peppered with Welsh and French dialects, the play pairs sexual transgressions with assaults on the English tongue. Mistress Quickly, for example, mistranslates and sexualizes a Latin lesson designed to initiate boys into proper English masculinity (Parker 1991; Pittenger 1991); and Pistol interprets Falstaff's seductions as wanting to "translate" Mrs. Ford "out of honesty into English" (1.3.46). By the conclusion, however, the valences of this translation are reversed: the scene of powerfully chaste women laundering corruption gives way to a public attempt to manage faulty speakers of the native language. Redrawing power divisions in terms of nationality and ethnicity, Ford substitutes foreigners for merry wives: "I will never mistrust my wife again, till thou art able to woo her in good English," he tells Evans (5.5.134–5). *Merry Wives* thus represents a national community protected by a constant patrol of linguistic, social, and sexual improprieties; the village constitutes a domestic home front relentlessly claimed by citizens (Wall 2001).[3]

Underscoring the message delivered by Mrs. Page – "Wives may be merry and yet honest too" (4.2.96) – critics observe that the women use their domestic authority to inject agency into the Renaissance conception of idealized womanhood. Unlike Petruchio who tames his wife to conventional standards, Falstaff is bested by wives whose judgments are validated by the community. Carol Thomas Neely argues that

Merry Wives departs from the teleological marital conventions of romantic comedy; it is "the Shakespearean play in which women's power is most persistent and least contained and in which their status is most like that of Stratford women" (Neely 1989: 217). Other critics demonstrate the play's studied exploration of masculine anxieties as well as the early modern linkage between folklore, social ritual, and gender roles (Parten 1985; Cotton 1987). By revising the skimmington to punish sexual presumption rather than gender inversion, the play allows women to control the very techniques for social regulation that validated gendered hierarchies. But since the wives may only dabble with rituals if resolutely chaste and since they ultimately relinquish their regulatory power to citizens, they elasticize their position as objects trafficked between men only to reinforce, in many ways, the structures enabling that trafficking (French 1981: 106–10). Counterbalancing its critique of flawed masculinity with an affirmation of traditional womanhood, the play suggests that husbands have no need to be tyrannical precisely because citizenly women patrol themselves in just the way that bourgeois society dictates; that is, part of the "ideological work" done by the play is its reassurance that manipulative women protect good husbandry (Clark 1987: 263; Korda 2001).

Now primarily designating marital roles, the terms "husband" and "wife" suggested a vocation in the early modern period. The outpouring of classical and contemporary estate guides, cookbooks, and conduct manuals reveal a concerted attempt to rehabilitate domestic practice and make people of rank take interest in the cultivation of land (McRae 1992; Thirsk 1967). Due to the shift from feudal to wage labor and the shrinkage of large households, elite property owners were forced to develop efficient methods in order to keep their estates. In the wake of increased urbanization and specialized production, the economy enlarged to include the rise of the "middling sort" (Leinwand 1993). Implying that aristocratic consumption was a moral and national failure, manuals such as Thomas Tusser's 1573 *Five Hundred Points of Good Husbandry*, Barnabe Googe's *The Whole Art and Trade of Husbandry*, and Gervase Markham's *English Husbandman* and *English Housewife* sought to champion England's anti-courtly character. Women at all points on the social spectrum were urged to embrace the role of "good wife," which fused virtue with industry (Cahn 1987: 11–32; Ezell 1987: 36–61). These guides made domestic *oeconomia* a touchstone for marking the "proper" definitions of social groups (Hutson 1994).

The discourse of husbandry is central to *Merry Wives*. Near the end of the play, the Host discusses Fenton's plot to trick the Pages by eloping with Anne: "Well, husband your device" the Host advises him, his pun indicating that Fenton should take extraordinary care in his plan to wed (4.6.51). What Fenton has proposed is a financial deal with the Host that requires a careful division of labor; they must act as deliberate managers in creating a spectacle or "devise" to effect a marriage. Yet the meaning of husbandry is obviously being stretched, since Fenton's elopement threatens the dowry he needs and since he pays the Host to create a diversion that will disrupt the Page household; that is, Fenton has hardly absorbed the advice provided in guidebooks. The Host's choice of the term "device" also reminds the audience of the Welsh parson's earlier plan for assuaging dissension in the town: "It is petter that friends is

the sword, and end it," Evans states, "and there is also another device in my prain
. . . There is Anne Page, which is daughter to Master Thomas Page, which is pretty
virginity" (1.1.39–43). His unsuccessful plan to resolve Slender's loss of status by
pushing him toward a beneficial marriage raises the question of whether such devices
can indeed be well-husbanded.

Throughout the play characters assess their emotions and actions in terms of
economy. When considering whether or not to bribe Falstaff to seduce his wife, Ford
concludes: "If I find her honest, I lose not my labour; if she be otherwise, 'tis labour
well bestowed" (2.1.227–9). In conjuring up this decidedly odd schema to express a
jealousy discouraged in conduct manuals, Ford draws upon the vocabulary of the good
householder. Tellingly the "labour" he thinks not lost is that of disguise and identity
switching, since testing his wife's honesty requires that he give up his role as husband
and transform into his feared evil twin, the thief of domestic sexuality and property.
Self-loathing here inhabits the discourse of sound judgment and financial moderation.
Falstaff similarly appropriates the language of fiscal responsibility when he hatches a
plot to feign love:

> I'll make more of thy old body than I have done. Will they yet look after thee? Wilt
> thou, after the expense of so much money, now be a gainer? Good body. I thank thee.
> Let them say 'tis grossly done; so it be fairly done, no matter. (2.2.133–8)

Having spent his time being wasteful, he now seeks to be a "gainer," this expanse signified by his supervised large girth. But he also plans to use his body efficiently
("fairly" if "grossly") in a scheme to recompense for his expenditures. Falstaff imaginatively doubles himself into both manager and goods, making his deficiencies into
a sign of deserving. Punning on his corporeal excess, he delights in mocking *oeconomia*: "I am in the waist two yards about, but I am now about no waste: I am about
thrift" (1.3.38–40). *2 Henry IV* offers a similar pun: "Your means are very slender and
your waste is great," reprimands the Chief Justice. "I would it were otherwise, I would
my means were greater and my waist slenderer," replies Falstaff, pointing to his bur-
geoning belt (1.2.140). Following the tenets expressed in Shakespeare's first sonnet,
the Windsor Falstaff decides that one can "mak'st waste in niggarding"; he therefore
decides not to economize at all but instead to seek a brand of husbandry that will
allow him to substitute for other husbands. Since "waste" also referred to a girdle used
to hem in a midsection, Falstaff's plan to be about "no waste" appropriately bears the
secondary meaning of *not* reining in extravagance. After Falstaff's punishment, Mrs.
Page tellingly uses the word "waste" in its legal meaning, as an unauthorized act of
damage by a tenant: "he will never, I think, in the way of waste attempt us again"
(4.2.198–9). Mrs. Page effectively translates Falstaff's parodic discourse about entrepreneurial thrift into a legal metaphor emphasizing self-ownership.

While critics have recognized ways which domestic management pervades the play's
representation of social and sexual crises, they often see the play as a lesson about
putting the house in order. What this reading leaves unaddressed are the passions
within Windsor that drive and confuse the play's didacticism, mainly by undercutting

pragmatism, civility, and moderation. Ford provides a case in point, since he is an overly invested husband in multiple ways: he has an unfounded fear of his own cuckoldry and he oversupervises his household. When impersonating Brook, he outlines a plan to have Falstaff bed his wife as a prologue to his own attempts, a plan that even Falstaff finds contrary: "Methinks you prescribe to yourself very preposterously," with "preposterously" signifying things inverted or errant (2.2.231). Falstaff's amazement that Brook should want his beloved seduced by another unmasks riven desires within Ford; instead of merely testing his wife, he courts her sullying and his confirmation as failed husband. Ford also relishes "tortur[ing]" his wife (3.2.36), and hysterically responds to the sight of the laundry- or buck-basket by conflating gratification and humiliation: "Buck? I would I could wash myself of the buck! Buck, buck, buck! Ay, buck; I warrant you, buck, and of the season, too, it shall appear" (3.3.145–7). In his diatribe, Ford converts dirty laundry into the horned deer that figures both his sexual vulnerability and the virility of his overly lusty rival. Horns come to signify a rutting beast as well as a shameful lack of control over household goods and persons. As such, his desire to "wash himself" of the buck only suggests a counterproductive trap: given his own domestic metaphors, he can't win by eliminating the buck (sexual potency) or embracing it (humiliation). Looking to laundry tubs for evidence of his losses and finding instead an expansive identity, Ford displays a perverse fantasy of wastefulness. Even his friend Mr. Page reprimands him: "are you not ashamed? What spirit, what devil suggests this imagination?" (3.3.198–9).

Ford's "fantastical humors" (3.3.158) are evidenced by his odd relationship to household property, for he imagines his wife's infidelity as a failure of domestic labor. "There's a hole made in your best coat, Master Ford!" he exclaims to himself. "This 'tis to be married; this 'tis to have linen and buck-baskets!" (3.5.131–3). Owning property and being married – summed up as "this" – makes a husband vulnerable to financial and sexual depletion. This proprietorial burden drives Ford to search his house habitually for signs of sexual pollution long before Falstaff appears on the scene. Dissuading Falstaff from hiding in the chimney, Mrs. Ford explains that her husband knows all household recesses by heart: "He will seek there, on my word. Neither press, coffer, chest, trunk, well, vault, but he hath an abstract for the remembrance of such places and goes to them by his note" (4.2.54–7). Ford takes stock of his luxurious furniture by imagining them as concealing waywardness. In creating an "abstract" of his possessions, he takes the protective duties of the good husband – that of overseeing and ordering resources (Dod and Cleaver 1630) – to such an extreme that he threatens the credit and resources of the family.

While appearing to present a morality lesson in which Ford is cured of his zealous and errant domestic practices, the play reveals skepticism about his declaration of repentance. " 'Tis well, 'tis well; no more. / Be not as extreme in submission / As in offence," Page cautions (4.4.10–12), suggesting that the "cured" Ford still enjoys postures of excess and intemperance. Rather than displaying his newfound good husbandry, Ford histrionically reenacts his self-shaming, here and in the concluding lines of the play. "Sir John," Ford says, turning to Falstaff after the community has festively united, "To Master Brook you yet shall hold your word, / For he to-night shall lie with Mistress Ford" (5.5.241–2). Why would Ford turn attention away from Falstaff's humiliation to remind the community of his role as panderer for his wife? After all, his earlier desire to laugh at Page's unfounded marital security is now granted in a festive register, since Page has been duped by household subordinates. Why, then, does the play end with Ford's rehearsal of an impersonation expressing the paranoid rage he has renounced? *Merry Wives* suggests that Windsor society remains invested in the fantasy of an expansive identity, one which allows Ford to be both cuckold and wittol and to act within and without the proper bounds of marriage. Rather than demonstrating the necessary absorption of civility and control, the play underscores the continuing delights of unreigned selves and immoderate passions. It is at this point that Falstaff turns his own bestial state and the shame back on the town: "When night-dogs run, all sorts of deer are chased," he declares (5.5.235). Opening with charges that Falstaff has stolen deer, *Merry Wives* closes with Falstaff's hint that citizens effect the thefts and improprieties that they themselves condemn.

II

Although arbiters rather than violators of social order, the wives similarly stretch the protocols of domestic management. Upon receiving Falstaff's letter proposing a liaison, Mrs. Page examines her behavior at a party for signs of sexual licentiousness: "I was then frugal of my mirth," she concludes (2.1.27). When impersonating Brook and quantifying female mirth, Mr. Ford comes to an opposite conclusion: his wife, he believes, "enlargeth her mirth so far there is shrewd construction made of her" (2.2.215–16). In thinking about how expansive or unthrifty mirth can be, the characters show that *affect* as well as moral and sexual excesses can be subject to accounting. In doing so, the play links the wives' measurement of merriment to their ethic of self- and property-management. This linkage becomes important when the wives create, in their terms, an "entertainment" that enlarges the bounds of propriety in the name of a greater ethic (2.1.63; Carroll 1977). "I know not which pleases me better," declares Mistress Ford, "that my husband is deceiv'd, or Sir John" (3.3.178–9). The wives' artful and excessive pleasure, emanating out of their domestic work, rights social transgressions, but it also allows them to be less "frugal" of their mirth. As part of their plot to stew, launder, and heal Falstaff, they coach servants John and Robert on their parts, choose a laundry basket and gown to serve as props, and refer to their actions in theatrical terms (Katz 1995). "Mrs. Page, remember your cue," Mrs. Ford commands, to which Mrs. Page replies, "I warrant thee; if I do not act it, hiss me" (3.3.33–4). When Mrs. Page pretends to warn Mrs. Ford of her husband's approach, she acts out a prescribed plot. But unbeknownst to the wives, Ford has in reality organized a search party to descend on the house just as they have scripted. When the wives' imaginary plot materializes, they improvise by folding the wrongly jealous husband into their story; that is, the play foregrounds their eagerness to extend the play of Falstaff in love so as to include the errant Ford in the spectacle. Assuming the roles of dramatically shamed and adulterous woman, morally indignant adviser, wily confidante, and creative abuser, the wives enjoy the flexibility of forged identities: they also position Ford to have Falstaff beaten (but shame Ford for beating a "woman"), and manipulate the decoy basket so that Ford is mocked by the town audience. Though performed discretely (then aired publicly), theatre becomes the wives' means of expending a mirth that they feel social pressure to conserve. In upholding order in Windsor, they, like the disruptive men, test the practices of *oeconomia* by indulging in fantasies of prodigal identity.

In depicting a husband who creates devices to subdue an unruly wife, *A Midsummer Night's Dream* presents a more conventionally gendered version of this plot. Oberon attempts to make Titania respectful of domestic hierarchy through the circuitous route of having her first display even more outrageous and improper behaviors. Turning Bottom into a half-beast, Oberon has Titania erotically substitute an animal lover for the child she has put in her husband's place. The normative family produced by this "joke" remains haunted by the eroticized species- and class-hybridity enabling it. In *Merry Wives* the women similarly produce aberrations as by-products of their moral mission: Mrs. Ford assumes the identity of unfaithful wife; Ford brokers his wife's adultery; Quickly not only impersonates the queen, but also plays the part of supportive messenger to competing suitors; and Anne creates multiple disguises as part of her rebellion against parental control. Is it any wonder that the rectifying arrows in the final scene glance and reverberate through the community? Isn't merriment in Windsor dependent on an ongoing game of pretense and deception?

G. K. Hunter argues that the Folio's final scene uses the queen's authority to "direct fertility away from the bestial and towards its socially approved manifestation in wedlock" (Hunter 1986: 13). Falstaff, branded as lustful, must be taught to husband his desires, and Anne's elopement seals off rivalrous libidos. Yet instead of presenting a well-ordered house, *Merry Wives* moves from the bandy of insults hurled at Falstaff to scrutinize a seemingly sound sexual and domestic unit. Mrs. Page takes the occasion of Sir John's education to taunt her husband: "See you these, husband?" she asks, pointing to Falstaff's horns: "Do not these fair yokes / Become the forest better than the town?" (5.5.108–9). The audience might expect such mockery to be directed to Ford, but the text has Mrs. Page offer this threat masked as an assurance to her decidedly unjealous husband. Described as a "cuckoldy knave" (5.5.111) Falstaff obviously doubles for Ford, as paranoid husband and seducer collapse into one image of flawed masculinity. But Falstaff's "dis-horning" becomes a weapon launched within a marriage guided by good husbandry (4.4.63). Though designed to teach Falstaff to rethink his perverse thrift, the Pages have, after all, used the playlet to deceive each other and redistribute the family wealth. In the Quarto the Pages' glee that they have foiled their partner's plots almost outweighs their grief in having been tricked by a rebellious daughter. Mrs. Page declares: "Altho that I haue missed in my intent, / Yet I am glad my husbands match was crossed" (Shakespeare 1602: G4ᵛ). While the Pages confess their mutual trickery, Ford and Falstaff revel in their shared cozening. Passions that should be tempered circulate fiercely in other registers in the community.[4] Reading *Merry Wives*, Jonathan Hall identifies a type of carnivalesque expulsion that transforms control into pathological symptoms (Hall 1998: 147–8). Falstaff's scapegoating is a primary example, for it extends the combative playing that provides the characters with mirth. Since aggressive and masochistic jests finally help to confirm English culture, the play makes clear that order sometimes rests on the shaky emotional *imbalances* of the domestic economy.

A citizenly ethic based on supervising goods and desires is also undercut by the play's endorsement of a theatricality that makes identities extremely hard to control. In the final act, when the entire community closes ranks against Falstaff by staging a lavish play, Anne Page takes the opportunity afforded by her disguise to multiply herself so that she cannot be husbanded by her parents; that is, she extends her authorized roleplaying beyond the bounds of propriety. While a lower-class woman copies England's Fairy Queen, Anne doubles as transvestite brides carried to the altar by men, with the result that the specter of same-sex marriages challenges the strict gender differentiation and normative sexuality ensured by marriage. "I am cozend: I ha' married un garcon," Dr. Caius cries (5.5.203–4). "If I had not been i' th' church, I would have swinged him," says Slender of the "lubberly boy" he has stolen (5.5.184–5; "swinge" having violent and sexual meanings).

The Quarto returns to the issue of boy-brides in its final presentation of festivity. Calling forth people to a celebration, Ford says to Caius and Slender about Fenton: "He hath got the maiden, each of you a boy / To waite upon you, so God give you ioy" (Shakespeare 1602: G4ᵛ). Since the erotic overtones of "waiting" upon (or "weighting") a master and the allure of boy servants are well documented in early modern discourses (Montrose 1988: 34; Orgel 1996), Ford conjures up a decidedly non-normative wedding party. In doing so he jokingly recalls his earlier sarcastic remark about the wives: "I think, if your husbands were dead, you two would marry," which Mrs. Page corrects: "Be sure of that – two other husbands" (3.2.13–15). Before Mrs. Page directs Ford to another anxious subject – his death and replacement – the text raises the possibility of eroticized female–female ties that rival marital bonds.[5] Though they resist being the duplicates that Falstaff imagines them to be, the wives form the most intimate bonds in the play. "I am sick till I see her," Mrs. Page says of Mrs. Ford, and the two women proceed to conspire to tinker with the protocols of marriage. While Anne's dispersion into boys lands her within a normative marriage, the play ends by unleashing desires not completely husbanded. Instead, the play's ending "is marked by its uneasy relation to 'aberrant' alternatives . . . [I]t becomes clear that the success of the marriages in the play depends on the necessity (at least according to the logic of the normal functioning represented) of some men (Caius and Slender) being paired with boys; one man (Falstaff) dressing up as a woman and another (Ford) fearing that women will marry each other" (Pittenger 1991: 406–7). The play thus draws to a close with Ford again imagining a wayward husbandry. Mr. Brook will indeed seduce Mrs. Ford, he notes, since Ford's multiple identities allow for illicit sexualities. Given that women's parts were played by boys in early modern England, the trick elopements effectively unmask actors to show that *all* theatrical marriages are same-sex unions. Fenton has also stolen away with a boy dressed as girl. Good husbandry runs up against the erotic hybridity of stage business, and citizens and wives are merry when domestic, marital, and social order are not fully guaranteed.

In constructing social order around and through discourses of domesticity, the play endorses a national community based on *oeconomia*. Yet criticism that overestimates the stability of this national community falls prey to what might be called a critical husbandry – an effort to render an overly precise accounting of the "interests" represented by the play. Might *Merry Wives* exemplify instead the "perverse dynamic," defined by Jonathan Dollimore as a "political and sexual ordering . . . always internally disordered by the deviations it produces and displaces and defines itself against" (Dollimore 1991: 160)? Since mirth lies less in hetero-compatibility and more in expressing aggression, manipulating shame, and counterfeiting identity, the citizens' interests appear internally divided. The passions in the play, that is, don't simply underwrite the ideological work outlined by critics. If *Merry Wives* founds English culture on middle-class marriage, it also reveals unmanageable desires that resist the "regime of the normal" (Warner 1993).

In outlining the emotional instabilities within Windsor society, I don't mean to offer an apolitical or ahistorical reading. For in showing resistances within the production of national, social, and political order, the play critically addresses early modern patriarchalism and its relation to domestic ideology. In the seventeenth century the family bore the tremendous burden of inculcating citizenship by structuring the proper dependencies that founded church, state, and body politic. Political treatises, conduct books, and sermons routinely tout the household as the foremost disciplinary site in the period. Minister William Perkins writes that the family is the "Seminary of all other Societies . . . this first Soceitie, is as it were the Schoole, wherein are taught and learned the principles of authoritie and subjection" (Perkins 1609: ¶3).[6] How can this fundamental "Seminary" teach good governance if basic categories (i.e., gender, sexuality, identity) and methods for generating order (i.e., domestic hierarchy, affective bonds) are so radically in flux? So we end where we began: with the unmappable force of desires. Falstaff harnessed to eros? Queen Elizabeth eager to see a fat knight embroiled in romance? Shakespeare in love?

III

For *Merry Wives* the problem of stolen property and counterfeit identities emerges not just as one of its themes, but pervades the language editors use to define the text and its relationship to authorial and national ideologies. Most of Shakespeare's comedies are "disappointingly un-English" to critics because they are set in Padua, Venice, and Illyria, Leah Marcus (1996: 82) wryly notes. As Shakespeare's only English comedy, the Folio *Merry Wives* offers a reassuring national dimension to his canon, one used to "confirm Shakespeare's organic connection and national Genius within a quintessentially English country landscape" (ibid: 88). Arthur Quiller-Couch interjects the autobiography of the writer into the myth of merry old England: "the play is to all intents and purposes an Elizabethan one – almost entire of the time" (Quiller-Couch and Wilson 1921: xix), one in which "Shakespeare gets back from London to the country" (ibid: xxxvii). Insisting on the drama's verisimilitude, Felix Schelling similarly declares: "There is no play of Shakespeare's which draws so unmistakably on his own experience of English life as this, and the dramatist's real source here is indubitably the life of the Elizabethan" (Schelling 1959: II, 324). Presenting our only comedic access to a locale much like the bard's Stratford and inventorying the details of everyday life, this play is unsurprisingly seen as somehow "true" and "truly English"; it forges a crucial identification between Shakespeare and his nation.

The myth of the play's bucolic nationalism, unimpeded by its Italianate and Greek plot structure, assumes an author whose experience founds a story. Yet *Merry Wives'* disorderly textual status makes the notion of a single writer producing an authorized text hard to substantiate. As Elizabeth Pittenger argues, "the story of MWW's textual transmission and reception is already scripted, to some extent, by the play" (Pittenger 1991: 393). The play's verbal slippages, mistranslated texts, and duplicated letters are cases in point. When Mrs. Page compares the love letter she has received from Falstaff to Mrs. Ford's and finds them identical, she calls forth the metaphor of print: "I warrant he hath a thousand of these letters . . . He will print them, out of doubt; for he cares not what he puts into the press, when he would put us two. I had rather be a giantess, and lie under Mount Pelion" (2.1.71–7). Sexualizing print technology as the impressing of women by men, Mrs. Page codes publication as promiscuous; the duplication of letters, in other words, reveals the author and his texts to be counterfeit. A single authentic original might have convinced her that Falstaff was truly in love.

Editors grappling with problems raised by the two versions of *Merry Wives* almost uniformly deem the Quarto to be such a counterfeit: it is labeled as inauthentic, one of the famous "pirated" quartos identified by Pollard and declaimed by the 1623 Folio editors as "stolne . . . maim'd and deformed by the frauds and thefts of injurious imposters" (Pollard 1909; Folio). A suspicion of fiscal mismanagement as well as moral impropriety drives the editorial project: scholars must shun the Quarto, which "robs" speeches of meanings (Oliver 1971: xxxii), correct its "naughtiness" (Quiller-Couch and Wilson 1921: xi), and remedy the "gross corruption" that a "playhouse thief" (Greg 1910: xxvi–xxvii) instilled in this text. The Quarto is "bad" because the product of rogue actors and greedy printers who trafficked in stolen property. Since some of its "errors" (e.g., prose read as verse) don't suggest a reported text, editors then add to the mix compositors' faulty transmissions and actors' spurious additions (Daniel 1881; Oliver 1971: xxviii). The play's editorial machinery, including the legend blaming its faults on a whimsical queen, work to salvage the author by cordoning him off from duplicate, theatrical, or suspect texts. Critics embrace the legend of the queen's commission in part because it ties Shakespeare to a single, handwritten text and to the Elizabethan England he is assumed to represent so faithfully.

Recently, however, critics have suggested that both the Quarto and Folio might have been independent performances which differ in their inscriptions of town life and monarchy (Marcus 1996), of economic conditions (Kinney 1993), and of family relations (Urkowitz 1996). Read as separate plays, these versions differ subtly in their portrayals of class relations, gender, and nationality. Noting that the Quarto is located in a less rural town and contains fewer allusions to the court, Marcus argues that the

Folio creates a court-friendly text amenable to the critical project of validating English nationalism. Because the Quarto Fenton is not associated with the monarch, this earlier text also presents a clearer victory for middle-class housewives whose efforts at thwarting court intruders fully succeed. Yet the text's thematic interest in impersonation unsettles even this reading, for the queen is counterfeited by a laundress whose "womanly" lack of linguistic control is the subject of mockery. Inscribing a shadow Elizabeth in a world of verbal vagaries and forged identities, the citizens hardly pay unqualified compliments to the crown; *their* community revolves around a housekeeper-queen with middle-class credentials and a penchant for garbling the English tongue.[7]

Although editors disparage the Quarto, they include bits from this "filched" text, so that modern readers encounter a composite of two versions. The Quarto is said to offer some passages that correct misprints in the Folio, provide stage directions, and donate the name "Brooke" in lieu of the Folio "Broome" (Oliver 1971: xxxii–xxxiv). As is the usual case for Shakespearean plays, editors are free to create a conflated text because there is no authorized handwritten original; all they have at their disposal are transcribed texts and revised copies. Is the Quarto a first draft of the Folio and if so, is it based on an existing play? Is it an abridgment of the Folio? Or did the actor playing the Host, who is cozened of his horses in the play, then cozen the company by stealing the text? Is either edition authorized by Shakespeare? Were both performed? Just as Windsor order rests on the specter of aberrant copies, *Merry Wives* boasts no untranslated or non-suspect original.

This absence poses a particular problem for the critical project of seeing the bard as *present* in a special way in *Merry Wives*, his experience of Stratford life detectable in its portrayal of an Elizabethan small town. When editors establish a "proper" text that can fulfill this mission, then, they undertake a textual husbandry. Reprimanding piracy, roguery, counterfeiting, and theft, editors seek to protect the possession of goods so important to middle-class national identity and literary history. In their laudable attempts to produce a usable text, editors stylize themselves as righting the acts of cozening that taint a phantasmatic original. Battling with "pirates," they secure the playwright from the vicissitudes that *Shakespeare in Love* advertised in its title. But in their efforts to safeguard a national treasure, might some of their arrows of reprimand "glance," as Falstaff reports, revealing problematic investments in such projects? The property that editors seek to categorize and preserve (namely bad Quartos and good Folios) were never, after all, Shakespeare's possessions. *Shakespeare in Love* combats this problem by introducing us to the playwright in the reassuring position of writing, the hand of Shakespeare yoked to the paper in ways that protect it from the vagaries of textual transmission. But belief in an author producing an unmediated text doesn't accord with what we know about Renaissance theatrical collaboration and printshop practice. The film perhaps acknowledges this problem when the camera zooms in to show that the financially strapped Shakespeare is not scripting a theatrical masterpiece at all, but instead practicing his autograph. Notably he scribbles out variant spellings that render his name into unstable characters and himself into one of those seemingly injurious imposters able to manufacture identities. Is this dilemma perhaps also acknowledged in *Merry Wives* when Anne Page transmutes into counterfeit "pages" (young boys) as part of the production of Windsor society, English culture, and marital fidelity?

NOTES

1   In making this argument I hope to refine some of the assumptions driving historicist and feminist readings of the play. Simply put, I query the ideas postulated in such criticism – that desire is identical to a drive for power and that various social groups' interests are transparently displayed on stage. Do desires for self-shaming or fantasies of indeterminate identity interfere with didactic and political readings?
2   For an assessment of memorial reconstruction, see Maguire (1996); for an excellent overview of the play's textual history, see Roberts (1979: 1–40); and on its topicality, see Freedman (1994). I cite from Oliver's (1971) edition, based on the Folio, unless otherwise noted.
3   But see Kegl (1994: 77–126) on the importance of seeing class designations as a shifting process.
4   On the importance of looking at affect in the production of ideology, see Erickson: "It is in the emotional charge and psychological investment involved in the engagement with a host of issues that we may locate an ideological stance in its full, particularized complexity . . . ideology is thus lived out, not merely thought out" (Erickson 1987: 118).
5   For a reading of male–male normative relations as underwriting Renaissance definitions of husbandry, see Shannon (2002).
6   On patriarchalism and its contradictions, see Orlin (1994: 126–30) and Amussen (1988: 41–7).
7   While building on readings offered by Erickson (1987) and Helgerson (2000) I differ from their assessment of the play as representing domestic, female, and local power as the object of national and aristocratic appropriation.

REFERENCES AND FURTHER READING

Amussen, S. (1988). *An Ordered Society: Gender and Class in Early Modern England.* New York: Columbia University Press.

Cahn, S. (1987). *Industry of Devotion: The Transformation of Women's Work in England, 1500–1650.* New York: Columbia University Press.

Carroll, W. (1977). "A Received Belief": Imagination in *The Merry Wives of Windsor. Studies in Philology,* 74, 186–215.

Clark, S. (1987). "Wives may be merry and yet honest too": Women and Wit in *The Merry Wives of Windsor* and Some Other Plays. In J. W. Mahon and T. A. Pendleton (eds.) *"Fanned and Winnowed Opinions": Shakespearean Essays Presented to Harold Jenkins.* London: Methuen, 249–67.

Cotton, N. (1987). Castrating (W)itches: Impotence and Magic in *The Merry Wives of Windsor. Shakespeare Quarterly,* 38, 3, 320–6.

Daniel, P. A. (ed.) (1881). *The Merry Wives of Windsor.* London: W. Griggs.

Dod, J. and Cleaver, J. (1630). *A Godly Forme of Houshold Government.* London.

Dollimore, J. (1991). *Sexual Dissidence: Augustine to Wilde, Freud to Foucault.* New York: Oxford University Press.

Erickson, P. (1987). The Order of the Garter, the Cult of Elizabeth, and Class–Gender Tension in *The Merry Wives of Windsor.* In J. E. Howard and M. F. O'Connor (eds.) *Shakespeare Reproduced: The Text in History and Ideology.* New York: Methuen, 116–42.

Ezell, M. (1987). *The Patriarch's Wife.* Chapel Hill: University of North Carolina Press.

Freedman, B. (1994). Shakespearean Chronology, Ideological Complicity, and Floating Texts: Something is Rotten in Windsor. *Shakespeare Quarterly*, 45, 190–210.

French, M. (1981). *Shakespeare's Division of Experience*. New York: Summit Books.

Greg, W. W. (ed.) (1910). *The Merry Wives of Windsor: 1602*. Oxford: Clarendon Press.

Hall, J. (1998). The Evacuations of Falstaff (*The Merry Wives of Windsor*). In R. Knowles (ed.) *Shakespeare and Carnival*. New York: St. Martin's Press, 123–51.

Helgerson, R. (2000). *Adulterous Alliances: Home, State and History in Early Modern European Drama and Painting*. Chicago, IL: University of Chicago Press.

Hunter, G. K. (1986). Bourgeois Comedy: Shakespeare and Dekker. In E. A. J. Honigmann (ed.) *Shakespeare and His Contemporaries*. Manchester: Manchester University Press, 1–15.

Hutson, L. (1994). *The Usurer's Daughter: Male Friendship and Fictions of Women in Sixteenth-Century England*. London: Routledge.

Katz, L. (1995). *Merry Wives of Windsor*: Sharing the Queen's Holiday. *Representations*, 51, 77–93.

Kegl, R. (1994). *The Rhetoric of Concealment: Figuring Gender and Class in Renaissance Literature*. Ithaca, NY: Cornell University Press.

Kinney, A. (1993). Textual Signs in The Merry Wives of Windsor. *Yearbook-of-English-Studies*, 23, 206–34.

Korda, N. (2001). "Judicious oeillades": Supervising Marital Property in *The Merry Wives of Windsor*. In J. E. Howard and S. Cutler (eds.) *Marxist Shakespeares*. London: Routledge, 82–103.

Leinwand, T. (1993). Shakespeare and the Middling Sort. *Shakespeare Quarterly*, 44, 284–303.

McRae, A. (1992). Husbandry Manuals and the Language of Agrarian Improvement. In M. Leslie and T. Raylor (eds.) *Culture and Cultivation in Early Modern England: Writing and the Land*. Leicester: Leicester University Press, 35–62.

Maguire, L. (1996). *Shakespearean Suspect Texts: The "Bad" Quartos and Their Contexts*. Cambridge: Cambridge University Press.

Marcus, L. (1996). *Unediting the Renaissance: Shakespeare, Marlowe, Milton*. New York: Routledge.

Markham, G. (1631). *The English House-wife*. London.

Montrose, L. A. (1988). "Shaping Fantasies". Figurations of Gender and Power in Elizabethan Culture. In S. Greenblatt (ed.) *Representing the English Renaissance*. Berkeley: University of California Press, 31–64.

Neely, C. T. (1989). Constructing Female Sexuality in the Renaissance: Stratford, London, Windsor, Vienna. In R. Feldstein and J. Roof (eds.) *Feminism and Psychoanalysis*. Ithaca, NY: Cornell University Press, 208–29.

Oliver, H. J. (ed.) (1971). *The Merry Wives of Windsor*. London: Routledge.

Orgel, S. (1996). *Impersonations: The Performance of Gender in Shakespeare's England*. Cambridge: Cambridge University Press.

Orlin, L. C. (1994). *Private Matters and Public Culture in Post-Reformation England*. Ithaca, NY: Cornell University Press.

Parker, P. (1991). *The Merry Wives of Windsor* and Shakespearean Translation. *Modern Language Quarterly*, 52, 225–61.

Parten, A. (1985). Falstaff's Horns: Masculine Inadequacy and Feminine Mirth in *The Merry Wives of Windsor*. *Studies in Philology*, 82, 184–99.

Perkins, W. (1609) *Christian Oeconomie: Or, A Short Survey of the Right Manner of Erecting and Ordering a Familie*. London.

Pittenger, E. (1991). Dispatch Quickly: The Mechanical Reproduction of Pages. *Shakespeare Quarterly*, 42, 389–408.

Pollard, A. W. (1909). *Shakespeare's Folios and Quartos*. London: Methuen.

Quiller-Couch, A. T. and Wilson, J. D. (eds.) (1921). *The Merry Wives of Windsor*. Cambridge: Cambridge University Press.

Roberts, J. A. (1979). *Shakespeare's English Comedy: The Merry Wives of Windsor in Context*. Lincoln: University of Nebraska Press.

Schelling, F. E. (1959). *Elizabethan Drama, 1558–1642*, 2 vols. New York: Russell and Russell.

Shakespeare in Love (1998). Dir. John Madden. Miramax Films.

Shakespeare, W. (1602). *A Most pleasaunt and excellent conceited Comedie, of Syr John Falstaffe, and the merrie Wives of Windsor.* London.

——(1971). *The Merry Wives of Windsor*, ed. H. J. Oliver. London: Routledge.

Shannon, L. (2002). *Like(en)ings*: Rhetorical Husbandries and Portia's "True Conceit" of Friendship. *Renaissance Drama*, forthcoming.

Thirsk, J. (1967). *Agrarian History of England and Wales, Vol. 4: 1500–1640.* Cambridge: Cambridge University Press.

Tusser, T. (1573). *Five Hundreth Points of Good Husbandry.* London.

Urkowitz, S. (1996). Two Versions of *Romeo and Juliet* 2.6 and *Merry Wives of Windsor* 5.5.215–45: An Invitation to the Pleasures of Textual/Sexual Di(Per)versity. In R. B. Parker and S. P. Zitner (eds.) *Elizabethan Theater: Essays in Honor of S. Schoenbaum.* Newark: University of Delaware Press, 222–38.

Wall, W. (2001). Why Does Puck Sweep?: Fairylore, Merry Wives and Social Struggle. *Shakespeare Quarterly*, 52, 1, 67–106.

Warner, M. (1993). *Fear of a Queer Planet: Queer Politics and Social Theory.* Minneapolis: University of Minnesota Press.

20

Much Ado About Nothing

Alison Findlay

I

Early on the morning of Hero's wedding, Margaret assures her that her wedding dress exceeds that of the duchess of Milan with its "cloth o' gold, and cuts, and laced with silver, set with pearls, down sleeves, side sleeves, and skirts, round underborne with a bluish tinsel" (3.4.14–18).[1] The duchess of Milan's gown evokes memories of Beatrice D'Este, duchess of the glittering court of Milan from 1491–7, and her daughter-in-law Christina of Denmark, who had wittily refused Henry VIII's proposal of marriage on the grounds that, unfortunately, she only had one head, and therefore could not spare one in the king's service (Cartwright, 1926: 378). In 1554 the Catholic English monarch, Mary Tudor, became duchess of Milan on her marriage to Philip II of Spain. This duchess's passionate wish to return England to the Roman faith failed, but by the late sixteenth century Milan was a hotbed of Counter-Reformation zeal. It was the home of Carlo Borromeo, archbishop of Milan from 1566–84 and author of the spiritual testament of which John Shakespeare held a copy (Borromeo 1988; Wilson 2001).

In the light of all these associations, what are we to make of Margaret's lovingly detailed description of the duchess of Milan's gown? Its immediate dramatic effect is to signal the importance of material props, a vital ingredient in the play's creation of meanings. Secondly, it reveals Margaret's character in a highly significant way. Evidence from personal writings and wills shows that women of every class in early modern England had an interest in textiles, but that access to richly decorated silks and satins, lace and cloth of gold or silver was confined to the elite. Nevertheless, "an obsession with the acquisition of beautiful and flattering clothes was a leitmotif of many young women's memoirs at this period, regardless of social rank" (Mendelson and Crawford 1998: 222). Margaret, who admires the duchess of Milan's ornate wedding gown, is a servant who "covets pretty things" in the knowledge that they cannot be hers to wear (Zitner 1983: 44). In Boyd's 1997 RSC production, act 5, scene 2 opened with Margaret wearing Beatrice's dress, parading in front of a large mirror. As I will argue, Margaret's obsession with the clothes of her betters underpins her oddly inconsistent role in the play.

Beyond its material attractions, the gown's cultural associations with Milan endow it with a third dramatic function as an object invested with memories of the Counter-Reformation mission which continued to complicate the position of Catholics in England. Fashioned from many layers and detachable elements, decorated with jewels, and underlaid by a chimeric bluish silk, the duchess of Milan's gown provides a palimpsest for reading *Much Ado About Nothing*. Like the gown, the play is a curiously fashioned comedy. Its witty, patterned dialogue bejewels a plot in which layers of meaning are superimposed through the repeated motif of "noting": overhearing and reportage. The near-tragedies and comic resolutions of the plot depend on a series of pivotal moments demonstrating the detachable nature of signs, whether verbal, or material like the sleeves and skirts of a gown. *Much Ado* presents a kaleidoscopic pattern of meanings. Its superficial brilliance as a comedy of manners set in an elite social world of fashion can deceive us into thinking it lacks the maturity of *As You Like It* or *Twelfth Night*. We need to look differently. Like the bluish tinsel of the gown, whose appearance alters under the shift of light, the play's topos of fashionable clothing is "underborne" by a profound exploration of identity in which gender and religious politics create a mingled yarn of meanings about inwardness.

Fashion, the "deformed thief" (3.3.102), appears in both rhetorical and material guises in *Much Ado About Nothing*. James A. S. McPeek pointed out in 1960 that the events of the play are closely interwoven with its imagery of fashion, a word used more frequently here than in any other Shakespeare text. Costumes are a central feature of the action. Turns in the plot arise from scenes of communal dressing up: a masked ball (2.1), a wedding (4.1), a cloaked ritual of mourning (5.3), and a finale that replays both masked ball and wedding. Clothes function as a material language in the play and much ado is made of their equivocal nature. Benedick hints at the instability of both types of language by telling Don Pedro "the body of your discourse is sometime guarded with fragments, and the guards are but slightly basted on, neither" (1.1.212–14). Clothes, like words, are "nothing" but become something within a signifying system traditionally governed by sumptuary laws. They become something with each wearer, whose use of the costume leaves a trace of meaning (presence) which is appropriated and to a greater or lesser extent transformed by every subsequent wearer.

When Borachio proposes that "the fashion of a doublet, or a hat, or a cloak, is nothing to a man," Conrade objects "Yes, it is apparel" (3.3.96–8). A major question raised by the play is figured here: what power have clothes to shape identity? Coming into the argument on Conrade's side, Jones and Stallybrass (2000) have shown that, far from being nothing to a man, apparel functioned to constitute subjects in early modern England. Livery served to define individuals as possessions of a master or mistress, while aristocratic portraits display a self made up through investiture. At the same time, clothes were detachable from the bodies whose meaning they were designed to signify, and could be exchanged. As valuable commodities, garments were sold, borrowed, bequeathed, and pawned. The rapidly changing fashion market in late Elizabethan England was the most visible element of a vast circulation of apparel. The "phantastical folly of our nation (even from the courtier to the carter) is such that no form of apparel liketh us longer than the first garment is in the wearing," complained William Harrison (1876: 107–8). The transferability of clothes meant they could reform social identity. In *The Anatomie of Abuses* (1583) Philip Stubbes pointed out the dangers of assuming the immanence of selfhood in apparel:

> For if we should accept of men after apparell onely, respecting nothinge els, than shold it come to passe, that we might more esteme of the one, both meane by birth, base without virtue, servyle by calling, & poore in estate, more than of some by birthe, noble, by virtue honorable and by callinge laudable. And the reason is because every one, tagge and ragge, go braver, or at least as brave as those that be both noble, honorable and worshipful. (Ibid: D1)

Because of their semi-detached nature, clothes are a slippery form of signification. Feste in *Twelfth Night* observes that "a sentence is but a cheverel glove to a good wit, how quickly the wrong side may be turned outward" (3.1.10–12). Don John's plots in *Much Ado* rely on the doubleness of garments, detached from their original signifying bodies. The "Much Ado" of the title refers, as much as anything else, to the exchange of apparel through which social status, moral character, and even spiritual identity could change.

Theatre offered the most explicit recycling of clothes and identities, the seductive dream of material self-transformation. The "apparell of the body declareth well the apparell of the minde," Thomas Wright pointed out, arguing that individuals could refashion themselves "not much unlike unto Stage-players, who now adorn themselves gloriously like Gentlemen, then like clownes, after, as women, then like fooles, bicause the fashion of their garments maketh them resemble these persons" (Wright 1601: 219–20). The freedom to author oneself according to one's desires was limited, though. Clothes functioned as an ideological discourse, granting both the illusion of choice, through "fashion," and the power to interpellate subjects into patterns of social convention. Borachio notes: "Seest thou not, I say, what a deformed thief this fashion is, how giddily a turns about all the hot-bloods, between fourteen and five and thirty," manipulating them into the guise of soldiers, priests, or effeminate lovers (3.3.107–13). Bourdieu's (1994: 95) notion of the *habitus* as a "system of durable, transposable dispositions" describes exactly the operations of apparel since, as Joanne Entwhistle remarks, it "recognizes the structuring influences of the social world on the one hand, and the agency of individuals who make choices as to what to wear on the other" (Entwhistle 2000: 37).

The equivocal nature of fashion as choice and prescription is dramatized to comic effect in the Beatrice–Benedick plot. Marriage, into which they are maneuvered, is imaged as a garment. Any distraction to Claudio's wedding night would be "to show a child his new coat and forbid him to wear it" (3.2.5), claims Don Pedro, who spends most of his energy as the master-tailor of the play, trying to stitch everyone into

Messina's social fabric. Beatrice and Benedick's assertive independence threatens to undermine Messina's fashion for wooing, wedding, and marriage. Benedick flatly refuses to exchange the soldier's garb, with its baldrick, for that of the married man, with an invisible strap to hold on cuckold's horns: "the fine is (for which I may go the finer) I will live a bachelor" (1.1.178–82). Through the "force of his will" (1.1.175) he distances himself from romantic love, incredulous that Claudio, who "would have walked ten mile afoot to see a good armour" will now "lie ten nights awake carving the fashion of a new doublet" (2.3.13).

Opposite Benedick stands Beatrice, "the infernall Ate in good apparel" (2.1.193), who turns "every man the wrong side out" (3.1.68) instead of playing her part in romantic courtship. Her assertions of independent self-worth are even more unacceptable to Messina, given her gender. To refuse to be "overmastered with a piece of valiant dust" on the grounds of sexual equality, or to advocate personal choice of marriage partner "as it please me" (2.1.41–4), challenges the patriarchal order outright. Hero points out that "to be so odd, and from all fashions / As Beatrice is, cannot be commendable" (3.1.72–3). Leonato is not the only one who is anxious to see Beatrice "fitted with a husband" (2.1.42). Well aware of the wish to restrain her autonomy with such a marital garment, she is fortified with an answer when Don Pedro makes a surprise proposal. "Your Grace is too costly to wear every day" (2.1.249–50), she jokes, pointing out that she would need another for working days since he is Sunday best. Rather than becoming a *femme covert*, she would prefer to remain "sunburnt" and single (2.1.241–3). Beatrice and Benedick's witty solipsism threatens to pull Messina apart at the seams just as surely as Don John's villainous plots (Taylor 1973: 149–50). Besides constituting eloquent examples of dissent from marriage, their speeches promote masculine fears about women and encourage a barrack-room mentality linked to all-male companionship. The labor of Hercules which Don Pedro undertakes in fashioning a match is not just to reconcile two warring individuals; it is to allay the insecurities that haunt Messina by converting its two most profound heretics into zealous adherents; turning centrifugal energies of dissent into centripetal forces of assent.

Beatrice and Benedick become lovers by shifting apparel, and the swiftness of putting on begs questions about Don Pedro's role. Critics who believe they are "manoeuvred into the union they inwardly desire" (Humphreys 1981: 62) see Don Pedro as a catalyst. His tricks "merely bring into the open what is already implicit in their attention to each other" (Foakes 1968: 13). There are certainly hints about a former relationship in which Beatrice lost her heart to Benedick's "false dice" (2.1.211–13), and the skirmish of wit between the two attests to a mutual fascination. This is not love, however. They also infuriate and tire each other since they have such different value systems: Benedick's flamboyant misogyny angers Beatrice, while her protofeminist statements signal the untrustworthiness that he fears he will find in all women. I agree with Jean E. Howard that "far from discovering Benedick's and Beatrice's pre-existent love, Don Pedro works hard to *create* it" and so fit them into the gendered social order (Howard 1994: 65). They do have emotions, but these involve antagonism and feelings of splendid, but increasingly anxious, isolation. Rather being born to romance, Beatrice and Benedick have it thrust upon them.

In Don Pedro's devised playlet in act 2, scene 3, Beatrice, the "Ate in good apparell," is undressed to a vulnerable love-sick girl who will "sit in her smock" (2.3.115) and modestly tear up the letter with "Benedick and Beatrice between the sheet" (2.3.12). Her fiery "spirit" collapses to a passion of falling down on her knees and weeping. The reduction of Beatrice to a model of female weakness and dependence is a shared male fantasy, enjoyed no less by the creators of the fiction than by the listener. Any final concerns are removed by the testimony "she's an excellent sweet lady, and (out of all suspicion) she is virtuous" (2.3.136–7). Ironically, in her overhearing scene, Beatrice is chastised for being just the opposite but is, very briefly, offered a fantasy Benedick who is consuming away in sighs because he loves her "entirely" (3.1.37). Any delusion that this "entirely" could include her more assertive qualities is swiftly quashed by Hero and Ursula's damning criticisms of Beatrice's behavior: "Disdain and scorn ride sparkling in her eyes / Misprising what they look on" (3.1.51–2). This is a turning point for Beatrice. To hear her assertions of independence and female equality condemned as errors of judgment by two other women shatters her tentative forays into feminism. "Contempt, farewell, and maiden pride, adieu / No glory lives behind the back of such," she reflects, perhaps with a touch of bitterness (3.1.109–10).

Beatrice and Benedick are unaware that they do not choose the lovers' fashions they will adopt. Both describe romance in terms of agency: Benedick declares "I will be horribly in love with her" (2.3.191), while Beatrices vows "I will requite thee / Taming my wild heart to thy loving hand" (3.1.111–12). Their subsequent changes of dress are powerful material signals of their conformity to Messina's ideological fashions. Beatrice appears dressed for the wedding, as if in preparation for her own. She plays the damsel who must die with grieving rather than fighting for her cousin's cause, and appeals to Benedick as her knight errant to "Kill Claudio!" (4.1.279). Traugott (1982) believes she adopts her romantic costume with worldly wisdom, parodying the postures of high romance so as to diffuse the fantastic violence of the genre in which Claudio and Hero are trapped. At the same time, her command is a test of Benedick's primary loyalty. Is his lover's garb merely fancy dress, the kind of false dice on which she is not willing to gamble again?

The soldier Benedick refashions himself with the adoption of "strange disguises" or foreign styles. Don Pedro complains he wears "the shape of two countries at once, as a German from the waist all downward, all slops, and a Spaniard from the hip upward, no doublet" (3.2.26–8). These details draw on contemporary fashions. The Spanish cloak, popular from the mid-sixteenth century, obscured the doublet; bulky German pluderhose was adapted from military fashion. Although seen in England it was not popular, and would have created a ridiculously flamboyant effect (Arnold 1985: 60; Brooke 1950: 56, 66; Linthicum 1936: 209). When Benedick enters in act 3, scene 2 and claims "Gallants, I am not as I have been" (3.2.11), this is perfectly true. The new costume constitutes a successful interpellation into marriage in the belief that "the world must be peopled" whatever the risks of the unknown female

Other (2.3.197). By act 5 Beatrice and Benedick's skirmishing style has returned but they cannot change back. Their costumes safely contain the body of their wit as entertainment, and the finale in which Beatrice is "fitted with a husband" attests to the power of clothes to conscript characters into their proper social roles.

II

The material memories invoked by costume are emphasized in a theatrical context, since the character has no identity except for its costume and the voice and body of the actor who dons it for the performance. Thus, when a character borrows costume from another character she/he also borrows the identity of the owner. In *Much Ado* Shakespeare relies on the witty capacity of clothes to "name, unname and rename" (Jones and Stallybrass 2000: 32). Unless we pay attention to the presence of garments as part of the play's language, we miss the full emphasis of twists and turns in the Hero–Claudio plot. In the ball scene we see likely and telling performance choices which follow upon the logic of the play's fascination with clothing and its role in identity formation. Don Pedro, Benedick, and Claudio and their party are masked, unlike the members of Leonato's household (Jenkins 1987: 102–3). Don Pedro's promise to Claudio that he will "assume thy part in some disguise" (1.1.247) calls for the transfer of a piece of costume, a favor such as a soldier's scarf or a cloak. The ball scene appears to reverse the ladies' favor-changing in *Love's Labour's Lost* (5.1), with the three male companions swapping garments. Don Pedro "assumes Claudio's part" quite literally, since costume constitutes the material presence of the role. Claudio (and the actor playing him) loses the romantic lead and, significantly, has to assume the part of Benedick the confirmed bachelor: "Thus answer I in name of Benedick / But hear these ill news with the ears of Claudio" (2.1.128–9), he remarks, wearing Benedick's favor. This leaves Benedick to temporarily assume Don Pedro's identity during the ball, returning with the good news "the prince hath got your Hero" and Claudio's garment, in order to reclaim his own. The exchange *"Benedicke* Count Claudio. *Claudio* Yes, the same" (Q1: sig. C1r) marks a reaffirmation of identity as they return favors rather than a questioning of it.

The token disguises produce, in each case, a hybrid figure in which costume speaks alongside words. The identity of the disguised and of the garment's owner coexist in a state of partial presence. The ladies with whom the revelers dance play a subtle game of recognizing and not recognizing their partners, "That my lady Beatrice should know me, and not know me" (2.1.155) Benedick exclaims. The exception is Antonio, who, as a member of the household, has not swapped costumes and so can only "counterfeit" himself. Ursula sharply notes that he plays too well to be anything but "the very man" (2.1.85–7). The other dialogues depend on a shared awareness of the gap between counterfeit and original. It is impossible for spectators to rule out the possibility that Don Pedro is wooing for himself, as Borachio and Don John assert (Myhill 1999: 299). He never tells Hero that he is personating Claudio, yet the material presence of Claudio's "suit" (or some part of it) renders Don Pedro's exchange with Hero much easier to read as a proxy wooing. As if alluding to the Claudio he partially represents, Don Pedro invites her to dance "with your friend" rather than with "me." She accepts on condition that Don Pedro plays the part of her shy lover who, as the betrothal shows, is noticeable for "look[ing] sweetly, and say[ing] nothing" (2.1.61–2). Don Pedro's own, higher-status presence is perceived in references to the body beneath the disguise. Jove is behind the lowly visor and Hero teasingly alludes to his counterfeit representation of Claudio by telling him "your visor should be thatched," recognizing that the face beneath has a beard, whereas the complete Claudio, whose "favour" she likes, does not. When he invites her to "speak low if you speak love" this is on the understanding that Claudio is the real, if absent, object of her affections (2.1.67–70).

The dangers of relying upon mediation, "whereby things and words and individuals function not in relation to the world but in a representational capacity" (Lucking 1997: 5), are apparent in the ease with which Don John's plotting succeeds here. Claudio's credulity can be partially explained by the "naturalness" of Don John and Borachio's appeal to the supposed "Benedick," the ideal person to "do the part of an honest man" (2.1.123) and dissuade the Prince from the match. Benedick's own disguise creates a hybrid of himself and Don Pedro, interestingly prophetic in that they have reversed positions in the final scene where Benedick, as "love god," counsels Don Pedro, who is pointedly "sad" outside the betrothal dance, to "get thee a wife" (5.4.114–15). In this first dance, Beatrice's wit relishes the masquerade in which each is partially present, implicitly addressing both the Prince ("Did he never make you laugh?": 2.1.101) and his "jester" ("I am sure you know him well enough": 2.1.99). Verbally and physically she leads Benedick a merry dance,[2] inviting him to "follow the leaders," and thus "egregiously flouts courtly custom" by reversing the usual gender roles in dancing (Howard 1998: 87).

Since, as Skiles Howard argues, the masked ball is "an active metonym of the play's larger actions" (ibid: 85), it would seem highly appropriate for Borachio to partner Margaret. Jenkins persuasively argues that the confusing stage directions in the Quarto arise from an erroneous expansion of the abbreviation for Borachio ("B or") to "Balthasar or" in a scribbled addition, probably added by a playhouse annotator (Jenkins 1987: 104–6). Although the substitution of Borachio for Balthasar here does not rule out the possibility that Balthasar dances with Margaret, Borachio would be by far the more appropriate partner, and would be able to remove his mask after the dance before approaching Don John. To see Hero and Don Pedro "as Claudio" followed by Margaret and Borachio in the dance prepares for their aping of the aristocratic lovers the night before the wedding.

It is of course this borrowing of a costume which leads the play into a tragicomic pattern of naming, unnaming, and renaming. Margaret's willingness to usurp her mistress's attire is the result of her own social ambitions to marry above stairs. Borachio promises to "fashion the matter" so that Don Pedro and Claudio will "see me at her chamber window, hear me call Margaret Hero, hear Margaret term me Claudio" (2.2.32–5). Hearing the supposed Hero call out "Claudio" would make a nonsense of the plot to demonstrate her infidelity. Borachio is thinking about the scenario from the point of view of Margaret and himself rather than the intended onstage audience. Margaret, he assumes, will be unable to resist the temptation of playing her mistress's role opposite his Claudio in a courtship which would appeal to her as a frustrated social climber. Margaret's absence of guilt at this encounter is perhaps explained by her total involvement in the scenario as fantastic play. Muriel Bradbrook points out that the "old worn device" of a maid dressing as her mistress in the hopes of bringing luck to her own romantic affair follows in a long tradition in European fiction (Bradbrook 1951: 180). For Margaret, Borachio's plan offers a safe opportunity to indulge her fancy for elegant fashion and pursue her own quest to secure marriage. Leonato says: "Margaret was in some fault for this / Although against her will" (5.4.4–5). Even though the consequences of her act were not her "will" or aim in dressing up, Margaret is still knowingly guilty of the "fault" of flouting the sumptuary laws: donning Hero's gown and thus imagining herself her aristocratic mistress's equal.

Margaret's interest in wedding dresses, revealed in 3.4, implicitly suggests to spectators that Hero's wedding gown would be Margaret's first choice for the window assignation. Although we are never told which dress Margaret borrowed, it would be a logical and telling choice. She would not have been able to lace it up alone, but the *déshabillé* effect would have increased the erotic charge of the scene, representing to Claudio the very act of marital seduction "even the night before her wedding day" (3.2.83–4). Having watched himself wooing (as Don Pedro) he now watches himself deflowering his bride. The encounter is not staged, for to do so would be to endanger the play's resolution. Myhill points out that "Margaret in Hero's clothes may look enough like Hero to convince an unprepared (or differently prepared) audience of Hero's guilt," so that staging a convincing Margaret-as-Hero would make deception impossible to detect visually, digging a deeper hole to get out of in the play's resolution, which depends on "noting" the lady's innocence (Myhill 1999: 308).

Instead of showing the seduction, Shakespeare presents remnants of it in the details which follow, and probably intended the wedding costume to carry the charge of dishonor. Borachio's report to Conrade begins with his lengthy account of fashion's effects and discussion over whether the apparel doth proclaim the man or not. This, he insists, is not a digression: it leads directly in to his tale of how he wooed "the Lady Hero's gentlewoman, by the name of Hero" (3.3.119). Borachio's confession that he courted Margaret in Hero's garments (5.1.209) merely confirms what the audience has already guessed from verbal and material hints. Particularly pointed is what happens in the following scene in Hero's chamber. Pieces of wedding attire are the main focus of discussion: the "tires" or headdresses are still within, but the rebatos are on stage. In order for their suitability to be assessed, the wedding gown should be on stage too – Margaret and Hero holding up the rebatos against it as they disagree, and then comparing it to the duchess of Milan's dress.

It could be argued that the spectacular appearance of the gown would have been a focus of the wedding scene, but its premature exposure here would materially emphasize the fact that the bride is (supposedly) besmirched goods. To provide a nonverbal parallel to Borachio's confession to Conrade, Margaret should enter carrying the wedding gown she had stolen the night before, noting that the duchess of Milan's is "but a night gown in respect of yours" (3.4.14).[3] McKewin observes that instead of the intimacy which usually characterizes all-female conversations in Shakespeare, this scene is tense with deception, where "waiting women, impatient with keeping below stairs are not allies of their mistresses, but treacherous, if unwitting, imposters at midnight windows" (McKewin 1983: 126). When Hero takes the gown, her comment "God give me joy to wear it, for my heart is exceeding heavy" (3.4.19) signals the danger it holds.

If Hero's identity is shaped by her clothes, when Margaret borrows them for an assignation at the window, Hero's identity is, to some extent, implicated in the crime. Hero becomes "every man's Hero" (3.2.78), because her garments have been "pawned" to another man (Borachio) and tainted with the liaison. Hero's dress is "the sign and semblance of her honour" (4.1.28). She presents herself as a spectacle, according to the fashion, but the dangers of such exposure are staged. In the Bible Solomon defines the woman whose price is above rubies as richly attired in "silk and purple," making textiles for her own household and beyond (Proverbs 31). Barnabe Rich interprets this selectively, in a manner typical of conduct books. His version of the good woman keeps within doors to spin, while she who "is impudent, immodest, shameless, insolent, audacious, a nightwalker, a company keeper, a gadder from place to place" has "the certain signs and marks of a harlot" (Rich 1616: 11). The wedding scene shows how the clothes of the good woman can be misread. When Hero puts on the tainted wedding dress she becomes a fragmented figure, a "contaminated stale" (2.2.20) in the eyes of those who saw the gown at the window, and an innocent maid by those who did not, including the spectators. It is deeply ironic that Claudio's accusations center on a discrepancy between Hero's outward appearance and her "inward impediment":

> Give not this rotten orange to your friend,
> She's but the sign and semblance of her honour:
> Behold how like a maid she blushes here!
> . . .   Would you not swear
> All you that see her, that she were a maid
> By these exterior shows? But she is none. (4.1.27–35)

Since her garments, the material "exterior shows," are tarnished, it is not the inside but the outside of the orange which is rotten. By trying to turn Hero inside out, Claudio demonstrates his own superficial delusions. Having watched her gown, the semblance of Hero, behaving like Solomon's immodest harlot, "a nightwalker, a company-keeper" (Rich 1616: 11), he is unable to perceive the virtuous Hero underneath it:

> Hero itself can blot out Hero's virtue.
> What man was he, talked with you yesternight
> Out at your window betwixt twelve and one? (4.1.74–8)

Claudio's reliance on outward signs likens him to Othello, who seizes on the hand-kerchief, another piece of fabric, as "ocular proof." Maus's astute comparison of Othello to an early modern English jury applies equally well to Claudio. Like the judicial imagination which scrutinized outward symptoms to detect inward crimes, Claudio reads the appearance of Hero's garments at her window as a sign of her inward cor-ruption. Her innocence relies upon an inner, separate sense of self from the clothes, but that is invisible to Claudio. His mistake highlights what Maus refers to as the "double spectatorship" through which inwardness is formulated in early modern England. Claudio's attempt to read the physical and mental interior of his bride is fallibly human, in contrast to the omniscience of God, to whom "all hearts be open, all desires known, and from whom no secrets are hid" (Maus 1995: 167).

Faced with the technical impossibility of plucking out the heart of Hero's mystery (and with no convincing evidence as to her whereabouts), those who judge her must rely on their own intuition, like the jury who looked into their consciences and imag-inations to discover inward corruption in the accused. The dramatic power of the scene lies partly in its curious mirroring of the theatrical context. The judgment of Hero in church and on stage implicitly cautions female spectators of the risks they are taking by entering that public arena, following Gosson's warning "you can forbid no man, that vieweth you, to note you and that noteth you to judge you" (Gosson 1579: F2). Entry to the theatre would signal a "gadder from place to place, a reveller," the sure signs of a harlot in the minds of conduct book writers like Rich. Hero's inabil-ity to defend herself dramatizes the vulnerability of female spectators, subject to the prejudicial inquisitorial gaze of others.

The extent of that prejudice is clear in the judgments on Hero, all of which rely on a process of projection. Beatrice looks inwards in the hopes of imitating divine omniscience and finds Hero innocent "on my soul" (4.1.139). The unworldly Friar carefully observes outward signs to reach the opposite conclusion to Claudio. The corruption which Claudio attributes to Hero is his own, but not just his own; it is a mental pollution shared by the other jurymen of Messina: Don Pedro, Don John, even Leonato. The latter's shocking response to his daughter's distress highlights how quickly the fictional, dishonored Hero is animated by male fear. In a society pol-luted by distrust of women, it is no surprise that a bastard, the embittered product of sex beyond wedlock, promotes the plot. Don John gives voice to a deep insecurity behind masculine identity when he says that the nightmare of female infidelity here articulated is "true" (4.1.61). Loss of faith in woman's chastity means loss of control over one's family, one's offspring, even one's own identity as the child of a particular father. Leonato's selfish reaction, stuffed with 24 personal pronouns in 17 lines, is on one hand a desperate attempt to reclaim ownership, calling Hero "mine so much / That I myself was to myself not mine, / Valuing of her" (4.1.130–2). On the other hand, his wish that Hero was "from unknown loins" (4.1.28) exposes a fear that she might be, an undercurrent which runs through all the jokes about cuckoldry in the play.

The secrets of the female body were nowhere more threatening than in the mystery of conception, where women's work seemed to underlie the production of children, just as it did the production of cloth. *Much Ado* shows that behind the fictional "deformed thief" who deprives men of self-fashioning without their realizing it, is woman. Prior to all the activities of fashion-monging gallants, tailors, clothiers, and weavers lay the female occupation of spinning thread. Jones and Stallybrass (2000: 116–25) demonstrate that early modern images of woman as maker of thread and maker of life are intertwined in the three Fates, with their power to spin, measure, and cut the thread of life, and even in pictures of Eve and the Virgin holding distaffs. Medical textbooks took up the association, and presented the mysteries of the womb emerging from behind swirling cloaks or cloths (Sawday 1995: figs. 26–7). Knowledge that woman was "the materiall cause of the childe" in comparison to the male's insubstantial seed (*Problemes*, 1597: E3v) implicitly led away from the simple virtues of woman as spinster to the more dangerous possibilities of woman weaving children herself. Helkiah Crooke's *Microcosmographia* opens its discussion of reproduction by asserting that life "hath no end, and may be compared unto a clew of yarne, such as the Poets faigned the Destinies to spin, which so long as there is flaxe to supply, may be drawne into an endlesse length" (Crooke 1615: 198). Woman's menses are the "clew of yarne" spun into life by female destinies. Crooke goes on to describe the membrane of the womb as "the wonderful net" which holds the foetus (ibid: 466), and even more remarkably as a "coate": "fleshy or very thick that it might have heat to cherish the seede and Infant" (ibid: 229). Thomas Raynalde's much reprinted *Birth of Mankinde* uses exactly the same imagery, describing three "wrappers," the outer caule "affixed or basted very exactly to the inner face and walles of the matrix" and circling the child "as it were a broad girth or swadling band" (Raynalde 1598: 52–3). Textile imagery is not confined to the womb; Crooke describes the "coats" of the stomach (Crooke 1615: 229), Raynalde the "coates" of fleshy tissue, and the peritoneum as dressing all the entrails in cloth of his "liverie" (Raynalde 1598: 20, 24). These metaphors may be unconscious, but the frequency of their use betrays an awareness that female labor underlies the essence of male identity. In John Banister's *The Historie of Man*, for example, the male genitals are represented as fabrics. The foreskin "is called in Latin *Sutura*, for so it representeth the fashion of a seame"; the right and left testicles are covered by "coates" held together by "fibres" (Banister 1578: 88v, 85v).

Women's power to actively weave as well as spin the thread of life pulled the carpet of command from beneath men's feet. Having heard his daughter accused of wantonness, Leonato veers from selfish anger to passivity: "The smallest twine may lead me" (4.1.243). In *Much Ado* the women recognize their power to cuckold. Beatrice jokes with Margaret that her fondness for dancing to the tune "*Light o' Love*" means that her husband will not lack bastard children. Margaret's exclamation "O illegitimate construction!" (3.4.37) refers to the deconstructive power of female infidelity. Casual allusions to Hercules underline the fragility of masculine prowess. The manly hero is pictured as metaphorically castrated, turning a spit at the command of Beatrice's Omphale (2.1.191–2), his labors reduced to match-making (2.1.275), and to lust in "the smirched worm-eaten tapestry where his cod-piece seems as massy as his club" (3.3.111–12).

Hero's mock death is a means of purifying her clothes and name. The Friar prophesies that "every lovely organ of her life / Shall come apparelled in more precious habit" (4.1.219–20). However, Claudio is not instantly filled with remorse. Instead, he and Don Pedro brush off Leonato's angry challenges, maintain the truth of their accusations, and turn to tease Benedick. Antonio's description of them as "fashion-monging boys" who "Go anticly, and show outward hideousness" (5.1.93–5) highlights the inappropriateness of their festive attire now, and probably gives voice to audience opinion. What does make Claudio change into mourning apparel is Borachio's discovery that the Princes "saw me court Margaret in Hero's garments" (5.1.208–9). He follows this with "how you disgraced her when you should marry her," a detail that has no place in his original confession but makes explicit the connection between the clothes and the shaming (5.1.208–9). Once the bawdy mannequin is exposed, its power to blot out Hero's name fades and Hero's "image doth appear" to Claudio "*in* the rare semblance that I loved it first" (5.1.220–1; my italics).

Claudio's restoration of the original Hero oversimplifies the matter, however. The extraordinary outpouring of grief from Leonato suggests that the fiction of the guilty Hero's death takes on a life of its own (Cook 1986: 197). The specter of bridal infidelity continues to deform the graceful, excellent fashion of the wedding dress even when the truth is known. Hero is not brought straight back on stage to proclaim her innocence, but has to undergo a *petite mort* in the epitaph scene in order to be reborn for her wedding night. Although Cook believes that the funeral ritual paves the way for comic closure by disembodying Hero (ibid: 198), the puns and rhythms of the epitaph and song continue to dwell on the erotic possibilities of sexual transgression by the Hero that here "lies." The guilty Hero "Lives in death with glorious fame" because life comes from sexual "death" (5.3.1–8). The bawdy associations of dying are inescapable (especially following Benedick's "I will die in thy lap and be buried in thy eyes" at the end of the previous scene: 5.2.78) and the song apologizing to Diana climaxes with the words:

> Midnight assist our moan,
> Help us to sigh and groan.
> Heavily, heavily.
> Graves yawn and yield your dead,
> Till death be utterèd,
> Heavily, heavily. (5.3.16–21)

Claudio is spokesman for fears of the female womb/tomb as a swallowing and life-giving place, bound up in the puns on sex, death, and life. In addition to demonstrating his contrition, the funeral ritual expresses in rigidly stylized terms the male population's worst nightmares about female power to construct and deconstruct male identity. Rather than completely exorcizing the threat of Hero's body, the ritual functions like a dark fantasy through which Claudio confronts his own vulnerability, the potential for female infidelity, and the necessity for blind faith as a basis for existence.

Since one function of the ritual is to "achieve the transformation of [Hero's] image in the eyes of the hero" (Neely 1985: 53), it is fitting that she reappears veiled in the final scene. Claudio has to complete the wedding ceremony he interrupted by marrying a dress whose contents are completely unknown to him. Ambiguity surrounds the bride even beyond the discovery. She cannot simply announce herself as "Hero" (and of course even her name is a self-conscious borrowing).[4] She is either "another Hero" (5.4.62) or "the former Hero, Hero that is dead" (5.4.65). The idea of a second marriage, following the sexual experience played out by Margaret and Borachio, is there in Hero's references to being an "other wife" loved by Claudio's "other husband" (5.4.60–1). Even if Margaret stands masked behind Hero in this final scene, she is insignificant since the dual identity of Hero is materialized in the garment. Charged with the weight of its own history, the wedding dress signifies the mystery of the female body, a mystery so threatening that its wearer cannot be granted a unified subject position. "One Hero died defiled, but I do live, / And surely as I live, I am a maid" (5.4.63–4) declares Hero, but her assertion of an independent virginal self, perhaps with an implicit resistance to marriage, is put down by Don Pedro's reconstruction of her as "Hero that is dead" (5.4.65). By redefining her as the "defiled" Hero, he continues to doubt her word. Moreover, he confines her to the realm of the absent, silent, Other whose uncanny return will always threaten the presence of those who assume the authority to fashion themselves and others.

III

Much Ado About Nothing's interrogation of clothing, identity, and inwardness relates as much to spiritual as to sexual politics. The final section of my essay can address the topic only briefly, offering a sketch of the play's densely woven pattern of religious allusion which furthers questions about Shakespeare's relationship to Catholicism. The comic resolution of *Much Ado* relies on a redemptive pattern of sin, death, and resurrection. Janice Hayes believes that Friar Francis functions as an instrument of divine Grace, in which Claudio's redemption is achieved not through his own merit, but through the "passive reception of unmerited favour" (Hayes 1980: 92). This reading acknowledges that Claudio's repentance and reward are beyond human understanding. Omerod and Lewalski both trace Claudio's ascent from reliance on outward appearances to his final recognition of an inner reality. For Lewalski, the play dramatizes a neo-Platonic process which incorporates the Christian model of sacrificial love for the restoration of others enacted in Hero's death and the awakening of Claudio's faith (Lewalski 1968: 250–1). However, to argue that *Much Ado* shows "out of the evil of fashion should be brought the good of a higher faith" (Omerod 1972: 104) fails to engage with the play's own interrogation: the problem of reading faith through fashion.

Clothing is a common trope for hypocrisy in religious propaganda. Catholics complained that Protestants had "assumed a glittering of godlinesse . . . without the substance and trueth thereof" (Walsham 1993: 45), while Puritans like Stubbes scornfully mocked the "Papistes" for placing their religion in "Romish raggs" (Stubbes 1583: C5v). In *The Anatomie of Abuses* his interrogation highlights the problems of displaying religious faith:

> the summe of their religion, doth consiste in apparell. And to speake my conscience I think there is more or as muche holynesse in the apparell, as in them, that is just none at all. But admit that there be holynesse in apparell (as who is so infatuat to beleve it) than it followeth that the holynes pretended is not in them, & so be they plaine Hipocrits to make shew of that, which they have not. And if ye holines by there attire presaged be in them selves, than is it not in the garments, & why do they than attribute that to the garments, whiche is neither adherent to the one nor yet inherent in the other? (Ibid: D1–D1v).

Attempting to proclaim one's faith externally is as pointless as a woman's attempt to proclaim her chastity, since the very act of proclamation is self-defeating. Locating "holiness" in the apparel denies it to the wearer, while to publicly assert one's chastity was to lose the modesty on which it depended.

The problematic relationship between external form and inner conscience was brought to the fore by church papistry, the clerical *bête noire* of early modern England. Following the crippling penalties of anti-recusancy statutes in 1581, 1587, and 1593, more lay Catholics put on the "visard of heresy" by attending church services, even though they were Catholics in mind (H. B. 1587: 32–5). Garnet complained that those with private pews appointed others to impersonate them "that them selves may be deemed present" (Garnet 1593: 62). Their self-division was deeply subversive, since it collapsed the binary oppositions so central to religious controversy. Indeed, disagreements within Catholic ecclesiastical ranks over the extent to which it should be excused flared up when priests were detained in Wisbech in 1595–8 and were a significant factor leading to the Archpriest controversy of 1598–1602 (Walsham 1993: 60). *Much Ado About Nothing's* secular concerns about fashion and identity also address the problem of reading inner faith through outward appearances. Beatrice jokes of Benedick that "he wears his faith but as the fashion of his hat; it ever changes with the next block" (1.1.55–6). Her accusation refers not just to the mold on which felt hats were made, but to the possibility of martyrdom. Even lay Catholics were encouraged to embrace this fate as recusants rather than shifting the outward fashion of their faith to conform. Since Robert Southwell had died for the Catholic cause in 1595, perhaps Lady Disdain's satiric attack is a covert self-mortification on the part of a church papist Shakespeare.

Beneath the romantic shimmer of the duchess of Milan's gown, the play's allusions to spying, betrayal, hanging, and burning at the stake combine with references to heresy, hypocrisy, conversion, and martyrdom, to evoke a bloody religious battleground in 1590s England. The setting of *Much Ado*, which opens just after a great victory, and its bastard villain Don John, seem designed to evoke memories of the Battle of Lepanto (1571). This Catholic crusade against Islamic forces was launched from Messina under the command of Don John of Austria, bastard brother to Philip II of Spain (Paulson 1986). The battle being over, there is no foreign quarrel to busy giddy minds, which turn instead to plotting divisions – in fictional Messina or the ecclesiastical hierarchies of Catholic Europe. The pagan enemy now becomes the antichrist within. An audience living through this religious controversy, violent in its physical as well as rhetorical manifestations, would have been readily attuned to the religious allusions in the play. Viewed through Jesuitically tinted spectacles, the Hero of the church scene, that "pure impiety and impious purity" (4.1.97), is the Roman Bride of Christ, corrupted by Protestants without and church papists within. Claudio's actions aggressively appropriate church ritual when he assumes the authoritative priestly role and rewrites the marriage sacrament according to his will to produce an inverted rite of rejection. The judgment on Hero reflects the schism caused by Margaret's appropriation of her garments. Although the feminized image of the church offered a more positive image of the endlessly divisible female body (Sawday 1995: 218–19), the crisis of schism raised typical prejudices about female pollution. Ralph Buckland complained that the Protestant clergy who had deserted Rome continued to "jet up and downe, cladde in her robes." With a particular nod at those Catholics who attended their services, he asked: "Can the veile of a Virgin, make a strumpet honest, or stolen attire beautifie heresie?" (Buckland 1611: 36). Friar Francis's suggestion that Hero should "die to live" (4.1.246) reiterates the counsel of Jesuits such as Southwell, who advised English Catholics that the responsibility for upholding the faith lay not just with Jesuit martyrs but with them (Walsham 1993: 31). Southwell's own path was confidently expressed in his poem "I dye Alive":

> I live, but such a life as ever dyes;
> I dye, but such a death as never endes (Southwell 1872: 64)

Such memorable lines add another dimension to the ambiguity of the epitaph at Hero's tomb: "So the life that died with shame, / Lives in death with glorious fame" (5.3.7–8).

The comic elements of *Much Ado* also allude wittily to the debates on church papistry, outward conformity, or the recusancy that might lead to martyrdom. Benedick, whose name means "blessed," is associated with exorcist "Benedict" priests (1.1.64) and sees himself as a martyr to the virtues of bachelorhood: "that is the opinion that fire cannot melt out of me: I will die in it at the stake" (1.1.172–3). When he does succumb to romance he turns into the sartorial equivalent of a church papist, appearing "in the shape of two countries at once, as a German from the waist downward, all slops, and a Spaniard from the hip upward, no doublet" (3.3.26–8). Like some English Catholics he can shift spiritual apparel according to the need, appearing in the fashion of a Protestant Dutchman one day and a Catholic Frenchman the next (3.2.25–6). Although this satiric picture of shape-shifting could be read as a critique of the double-dealer Anthony Munday,[5] the sympathetic character of Benedick more fittingly represents the compromise of the church papist. The gift of love from Beatrice ("one who blesses") suggests a sanction for the middling way taken by Shakespeare.

The ridiculous hybrid of Benedick's costume is paralleled in verbal terms by Dogberry, one who reports himself "a fellow that hath had losses, and one that hath two gowns, and everything handsome about him" (4.2.68–70). Dogberry's pride in his clothes is outdone by his meticulous concern with Christian doctrine. He is, as Allen's brilliant essay notes, "the nonpareil of beatific self-appreciation" (Allen 1973: 36). The muddles he makes with language afford wonderfully rich humor and point up the paradoxes that English Catholics, Counter-Reformation zealots, and the English church faced when defining church papists. Dogberry tells Conrade "thou villain, thou art full of piety" (4.2.64). This paradoxical remark is exactly the sort of equivocal judgment made on those who outwardly conformed. If Dogberry is a caricatured picture of English authority, a comic version of inquisitor Topcliffe, then his errors of perception and expression become a mockery of the attempts of Elizabeth's ministers to see the inward heart and conscience of any subject, recusant or apparently conformist. Delighted to have arrested the villains, Dogberry reports that he has "comprehended two aspitious persons" (3.5.35–6), a feat which the play shows is far beyond him. His exclamation against the malefactors, "thou wilt be condemned into everlasting redemption for this" (4.2.47–8), ironically gives voice to a familiar Christian paradox (Allen 1973: 39) and expresses exactly what Catholic martyrs like Southwell set out to achieve. In his endearing warmth, Dogberry is less like a prosecutor than a comic personification of the problems and opportunities offered by church papistry. While the wedding gowns of Hero and the duchess of Milan invoke the tortures of self-division for subject, church, and state, Dogberry's comic inversions suggest how useful it could be to be a person "with two gowns" (4.2.68), shifting between faiths.

Notes

1   References are to *Much Ado About Nothing*, ed. F. H. Mares (Cambridge: Cambridge University Press, 1988). Other references are to *The Norton Shakespeare*.
2   The *Oxford Dictionary of Idioms* dates the figurative use of this phrase to the mid-sixteenth century.
3   Since, by the end of the scene, the men have arrived at the house to escort Hero to church, Hero may be clothed during the scene, her appeal to the other women to "dress me" referring to the finishing touches of headdress and jewelry.
4   Jonathan Bate (1994) suggests it draws on Ovid's *Heroides* as well as the suicidal lover of Leander.
5   On Munday, see Wilson (2001).

References and Further Reading

Allen, J. (1973). Dogberry. *Shakespeare Quarterly*, 24, 35–53.
Arnold, J. (1985). *Patterns of Fashion: The Cut and Construction of Clothes for Men and Women c.1560–1620*. London: Macmillan.
Banister, J. (1578). *The Historie of Man*. London.
Bate, J. (1994). Dying to Live in *Much Ado About Nothing*. In Y. Takada (ed.) *Surprised by Scenes: Essays in Honour of Professor Yasunari Takahashi*. Tokyo: Kenkyusha, 69–85.
Berger, H., Jr. (1982). Against the Sink-a-Pace: Sexual and Family Politics in *Much Ado About Nothing*. *Shakespeare Quarterly*, 33, 302–13.
Borromeo, A. (1988). Archbishop Carlo Borromeo and the Ecclesiastical Policy of Philip II in the State of Milan. In J. M. Headley and J. B. Tomaro (eds.) *San Carlo Borromeo: Catholic Reform and*

Ecclesiastical Politics in the Second Half of the Sixteenth Century. Washington, DC: Folger Shakespeare Library, 85–111.

Bourdieu, P. (1994). Structures, Habitus and Practices. In P. Press (ed.) *The Polity Reader in Social Theory.* Cambridge: Polity Press.

Bradbrook, M. C. (1951). *Shakespeare and Elizabethan Poetry.* Cambridge: Cambridge University Press.

Brooke, I. (1950). *English Costume in the Age of Elizabeth.* London: Adam and Charles Black.

Buckland, R. (1611). *An Embassage From Heaven: Wherein Our Lord and Saviour Christ Jesus giveth to understand, his just indignation against such, as being catholickely minded, dare yeelde their presence to the rites and publicke praier, or the malignant Church.* London.

Cartwright, J. (1926). *Beatrice D'Este: Duchess of Milan 1475–1479.* London: Dent.

Cook, C. (1986). The Sign and Semblance of Her Honour: Reading Gender Difference in *Much Ado. Publications of the Modern Languages Association*, 101, 186–202.

Crooke, H. (1615). *Microcosmographia: A Study of the Body of Man.* London.

Entwhistle, J. (2000). *The Fashioned Body: Fashion, Dress and Modern Social Theory.* Cambridge: Polity Press.

Everett, B. (1994). *Much Ado About Nothing*: The Unsociable Comedy. In M. Cordner, P. Holland, and J. Kerrigan (eds.) *English Comedy.* Cambridge: Cambridge University Press, 186–202.

Foakes, R. A. (ed.) (1968). *Much Ado About Nothing.* Harmondsworth: Penguin Books.

Garnet, H. (1593). *An Apology for the Defence of Schisme.* London.

Gosson, S. (1579). *The Schoole of Abuse.* London.

Greenblatt, S., Cohen, W., Howard, J. E., and Maus, K. E. (eds.) (1997). *The Norton Shakespeare.* New York: W. W. Norton.

H. B. (1587–8). *A Consolatory Letter to all the Afflicted Catholikes in England.* Rouen [London, secret press].

Harrison, W. (1876). *Elizabethan England From "A Description of England" by William Harrison*, ed. L. Withington, introduced by F. J. Furnivall. London: Walter Scott.

Hattaway, M. (1998). "I've processed my guilt": Shakespeare, Branagh and the Movies. In J. Bate, J. L. Levenson, and D. Mehl (eds.) *Shakespeare and the Twentieth Century.* Newark: University of Delaware Press, 194–211.

Hayes, J. (1980). Those "soft and delicate desires": *Much Ado* and the Distrust of Women. In C. Lenz, G. Greene, and C. T. Neely (eds.) *The Woman's Part: Feminist Criticism of Shakespeare.* Urbana: University of Illinois Press, 79–99.

Howard, J. E. (1994). *The Stage and Social Struggle in Early Modern England.* London: Routledge.

Howard, S. (1998). *The Politics of Courtly Dancing in Early Modern England.* Amherst: University of Massachusetts Press.

Humphreys, A. R. (ed.) (1981). *Much Ado About Nothing.* The Arden Shakespeare. London: Methuen.

Jenkins, H. (1987). The Ball Scene in *Much Ado About Nothing.* In B. Fabian and K. T. von Rosador (eds.) *Shakespeare: Text, Language, Criticism.* Hildesheim: Olms-Weidmann, 98–117.

Jones, A. R. and Stallybrass, P. (2000). *Renaissance Clothing and the Materials of Memory.* Cambridge: Cambridge University Press.

Levin, R. (1985). *Love and Society in Shakespearean Comedy: A Study of Dramatic Form and Content.* Newark: University of Delaware Press.

Lewalski, B. (1968). Love, Appearance and Reality: Much Ado About Something. *Studies in English Literature*, 8, 235–51.

Linthicum, M. C. (1936). *Costume in the Drama of Shakespeare and his Contemporaries.* Oxford: Clarendon Press.

Lucking, D. (1997). Bringing Deformed Forth: Engendering Meaning in *Much Ado About Nothing. Renaissance Forum*, 2, 1. http://www.hull.ac.uk/renform/v2no1/lucking.htm

MacIntyre, J. (1982). *Costumes and Scripts in the Elizabethan Theatres.* Edmonton: University of Alberta Press.

McKewin, C. (1983). Counsels of Gall and Grace: Intimate Conversations between Women in Shakespeare's Plays. In C. Ruth, S. Lenz, G. Greene, and C. T. Neely (eds.) *The Woman's Part.* Urbana: University of Illinois Press, 117–32.

Maus, K. E. (1995). Proof and Consequences: Inwardness and Its Exposure in the English Renaissance. In I. Kamps (ed.) *Materialist Shakespeare: A History.* London: Verso, 157–80.

Mendelson, S. and Crawford, P. (1998). *Women in Early Modern England.* Oxford: Clarendon Press.

Myhill, N. (1999). Spectatorship in/of *Much Ado About Nothing. Studies in English Literature 1500–1900,* 39, 2, 291–312.

Neely, C. T. (1985). *Broken Nuptials in Shakespeare's Plays.* New Haven, CT: Yale University Press.

Omerod, D. (1972). Faith and Fashion in *Much Ado About Nothing. Shakespeare Survey,* 25, 93–106.

Paulson, M. G. (1986). *Lepanto: Fact, Fiction and Fantasy.* Lanham, MD: University Press of America.

Problemes of Aristotle, with other philosophers and phisitions, The. (1597). London.

Raynalde, T. (1598). *The Birth of Mankind, otherwise named the womans booke.* London.

Rich B. (1616). *My Lady's Looking Glass.* London.

Sawday, J. (1995). *The Body Emblazoned: Dissection and the Human Body in Renaissance Culture.* London: Routledge.

Southwell, R. (1872). *The Poems of Robert Southwell,* ed. Revd. A. Grosart. London: Fuller Worthies Library.

Stubbes, P. (1583). *The Anatomie of Abuses.* London.

Taylor, M. (1973). *Much Ado About Nothing*: The Individual in Society. *Essays in Criticism,* 23, 146–53.

Traugott, J. (1982). Creating a Rational Rinaldo: A Study in the Mixture of the Genres of Comedy and Romance in *Much Ado About Nothing. Genre,* 15, 157–81.

Walsham, A. (1993). *Church Papists: Catholicism, Conformity and Confessional Polemic in Early Modern England.* Woodbridge: Boydell Press.

Wilson, R. (2001). Every Third Thought: Shakespeare's Milan. Paper presented at "Shakespeare and the Mediterranean": The Seventh World Shakespeare Congress, Valencia, April 18–23.

Wright, T. (1601). *The Passions of the Mind.* London; reprinted Hildesheim: Georg Olms Verlag, 1973.

Zitner, S. P. (ed.) (1983). *Much Ado About Nothing.* Oxford: Oxford University Press.

21

As You Like It

Juliet Dusinberre

Would the first audience of *As You Like It,* probably played both at court and at the
new Globe theatre in 1599, have seen a romantic comedy in which actors and audience
flock to the golden world of the Forest of Arden to escape envy and malice, politics
and perfidy? Or would it have recognized the play's relevance to the two hottest controversies of the time: the anti-theatrical debate, and the crisis developing between
1599 and 1601 around the queen's favorite, Robert Devereux, second earl of Essex?

The critical and theatrical tradition of the fairy-tale *As You Like It* has been challenged by both feminist analysis of gender as performance and new historicist emphasis on social context, particularly the law of the forest and enclosure of common land
at the end of the sixteenth century.[1] I want in this essay to discuss the possible interactions between Shakespeare's comedy and the troubled career of the earl of Essex in
the late 1590s.

The year 1599 marked a key moment in Elizabethan politics as well as in
Shakespeare's theatre. When the court met at Richmond in February 1599 Essex's
fortunes were still precarious, as he awaited the queen's much-delayed decision on his
appointment as Earl Marshall against the Irish rebels. He received his commission
and embarked in March 1599. From early on the expedition seemed doomed, and in
July the queen wrote angrily to him of his failure to quell the rebels. Her discontent
exploded when he knighted a number of his followers, including her godson, Sir John
Harington. Essex compounded his disgrace by bursting in on her unannounced in
September 1599; he was put under house arrest, and eventually staged his unsuccessful rebellion early in 1601.

Essex was a charismatic figure, renowned throughout the 1590s for his military
exploits (Flanders and Rouen) and expeditions on the high seas against the Spanish
(Cadiz and the Azores). Whatever royal displeasure he incurred in the pursuit of these
activities, his popular reputation was for valor and adventure. His dramatic debut as
official court favorite at the 1595 Accession tilt was typical of his propensity for
image-making (Hammer 1999: 199 ff.), and in his downfall he was terrified of the

satire of the players. Although Essex had been in severe disfavor in 1598, his renewed disgrace in Ireland took many people by surprise, including Shakespeare and his fellow dramatists, as can be seen from the final Chorus of *Henry V*, where his glorious return as a conquering Caesar was abruptly cut from the first Quarto.

The extent to which the theatre reflects on Essex's fortunes in this period is under constant debate; it's evident that Jonson, Chapman, and Daniel all referred to him, however covertly. The pastoral setting of *As You Like It*, which has seemed to later ages to ensure its immunity to political intrusion, would have been for the Elizabethans the best reason for its entry into that terrain. Pastoral as a veil for satire and political commentary was familiar from Spenser's *The Shepheardes Calender* (1579) and Sidney's *Arcadia* (1593, reprinted 1598), both of which lie in the hinterland of Shakespeare's play.

Shakespeare in *As You Like It* identifies the alternative court in the Forest of Arden with Elizabeth through the figure of Rosalind, who is associated with the coming of Spring, the season of Flora, to whom Spenser's song to "Elisa, Queene of shepheardes all" in the "April" Eclogue of *The Shepheardes Calender* is addressed (Montrose 1980; Dusinberre 1994: 16–18). The Elizabethans would have recognized in Rosalind-playing-Ganymede the queen's virtuoso exploiting of her gender in the interests of political power, her pastoral metaphors, and her resemblance to Astraea, Virgin of justice, who returns to earth with the restoration of the Golden Age prophesied in Virgil's Fourth Eclogue (Yates 1975: 4). At the end of *As You Like It* the magical power of Rosalind is almost a royal power (Goldberg 1983: 152–3), as she summons the masque of Hymen and unmasks herself from Ganymede the shepherd boy, to herself the banished princess.

If Rosalind would have been recognized by Shakespeare's audiences as a figure akin to the queen, Essex arguably enters the Forest of Arden when a lord reports the melancholy Jaques' lament over a wounded deer

> as he lay along
> Under an oak, whose antique root peeps out
> Upon the brook that brawls along this wood,
> To the which place a poor sequester'd stag,
> That from the hunter's aim had ta'en a hurt,
> Did come to languish. (2.1.30–5)[2]

The deer who stops to drink at the brook while the herd rushes on regardless, abandoned of its "velvet friend," occupies a place of surprising prominence in the first scene played in the Forest of Arden. In the Folio "friend" is not, as one would expect (and as nineteenth-century editors often emended it) plural, "velvet friends," but singular, his "velvet friend": *one* friend (as also in Amiens' song at 2.7.189: "friend remembered not," where Essex again seems to be the focus of the song's emotion). Velvet could only be worn by those of the highest birth, so that the detail seems to point a finger at the queen. The weeping stag, augmenting the brook with his tears, provokes multiple interpretation (Fitter 1999: 193–208; Bath 1986; Strong 1995:

303–24). In the autumn of 1599 the Elizabethans might have seen in the stag abandoned of its velvet friend a pointed reference to Elizabeth's abandoning of Essex. Essex reproached the queen in a passionate letter (written in 1599): "Whatt wordes haue I to offer to such a goddesse?"[3] It was sealed with one of the crests of the Devereux arms: a stag *trippant*. In *Cynthia's Revels* Jonson evokes the Actaeon myth, the youth turned into a stag and destroyed by Diana, in a transparent reference to Essex's untimely intrusion on the queen in her private chambers at Nonsuch in September 1599.

There are other ways in which *As You Like It* might have held a mirror up to the earl of Essex's fortunes in Elizabeth's court. Both the presentation of Orlando and Rosalind's projection of Ganymede can be read in the light of Essex's reputation and behavior as court favorite in the 1590s. Essex never stopped addressing the queen through the conventions of courtly romance, as is evident from the letter quoted above from the Hulton papers. Describing the earl's self-dramatization, Peter Beal (1992: 17) writes:

> Essex (a 'humble vassal') deliberately and histrionically strikes all the various exaggerated attitudes of a lover – now pledging his eternal devotion . . . now faithful . . . now complimenting and adoring, now solicitous and concerned . . . now longing . . . now disappointed, now beseeching, now resolute, now self-sacrificing . . . now jealous, now grateful . . . now abject . . . now protesting, now accusing . . . and so on.

Beal unconsciously echoes Ganymede's impersonation of Rosalind: "Would now like him, now loath him; then entertain him, then forswear him; now weep for him, then spit at him; that I drave my suitor from his mad humour of love, to a living humour of madness" (3.2.396–408). If Elizabeth is conjured up by the figure of Rosalind, Rosalind's impersonation of Ganymede, and fictional creation of herself as wayward mistress, recreates the terms of Essex's courtship of Elizabeth. The effeminizing of the male courtier was a condition of Elizabeth's dominance, and Essex's behavior and writing style make him an exemplar of that situation. He played the great warrior but he was temperamentally as capricious as the courtly lady invented by Ganymede as a means of curing the passion of a lovesick suitor. Essex's letters to Elizabeth suggest a man divided between gender roles, obliged to be a chivalric warrior of the Virgin Queen, and at the same time the rejected mistress of a woman perfectly capable of assuming a "mannish" role, as Essex learnt to his cost on innumerable occasions.

This dualism acknowledges the literary source of Sidney's *Old Arcadia*, a work as important for the genesis of *As You Like It* as Lodge's *Rosalynde*, from which Shakespeare took his main story. Both Sidney's *Arcadia* and Lodge's *Rosalynde* create the subsoil from which Shakespeare's playing with gender grows. Both works are also significant in the antitheatrical impetus which gains velocity in the period up to 1642 and may have been fueled not only by theatregoing, but by the reading of plays made possible by the printing of the First Folio (1623) and its reprint in 1632.

Early in his career Thomas Lodge engaged (probably in 1581) in one of the first defenses of the theatre against Stephen Gosson's *The School of Abuse* (1579). Sidney himself was to enter the debate resoundingly in *An Apology for Poetry*, probably written about 1586, but published posthumously in 1595. His courtly romance *Arcadia*, the most popular of Elizabethan pastorals, made its own intervention in that debate. If there is a shocking text in this period from the Puritan point of view, it isn't a play at all, it's Sidney's *Arcadia*, in which the hero, Pyrocles, disguises himself as a woman. The way in which this disguise is presented taps into one of the chief fears of opponents of the theatre, which was that the fantasy would be taken by the audience for the real thing.

In Francis Rous' *Diseases of the Time*, printed in 1622, there is a chapter called "The Danger of Representation," where the author questions the power of the representation to create feeling in the watchers of it. He asks whether in the case of "the Representation of Women by Men," "the shape of a woman hath not made masculine loues." This goes to the heart of *As You Like It*, in which Orlando embodies the dread of the antitheatricalist because he falls in love with a shadow, the stage-play of a woman, just as in Sidney's *Arcadia* the warlike Pyrocles disguised as an Amazon (Cleophila in the *Old Arcadia*, Zelmane in the revised and amplified *Countess of Pembroke's Arcadia*) presents a counterfeit of a woman. Both Sidney's romance and Shakespeare's play put pressure on the boundaries between homoerotic and heterosexual passion. Sidney's revision of his original pastoral (with the countess of Pembroke's additions, published 1593) was reprinted in 1598 (like Lodge's *Rosalynde*), and no doubt provided a stimulus to Shakespeare's creation of his own pastoral drama (Gibbons 1993: 153–66; Levine 1994: 155 n.9).

However, the *Old Arcadia* is more daring about gender than the revised version. Both contain the song in which Pyrocles declares that "she" is "transformed in show, but more transformed in mind" (Duncan-Jones, in Sidney 1985: 26). In his reworking, Sidney replaces "her" with "his" when describing the disguised Pyrocles, erases Musidorus' erotic admiration for the feminine version of his friend with its suggestive Pygmalion image, and replaces the emblem of eagle-and-dove, with Hercules with his distaff and a Greek motto: "Never more valiant" (Duncan-Jones, in Sidney 1985: 24–6; Sidney 1977: 130–4). The fluidity of gender which the *Old Arcadia* creates at this moment is thus subtly censored in the printed version.

This is true of many other places in the *Old Arcadia* where Sidney highlights the ambiguities surrounding the gender identity of the disguised Pyrocles. The poet often seems uncertain about the nature of the change which takes place in his warlike hero once he dresses himself as the beautiful Amazon lady, Cleophila. It's not clear whether Pyrocles really does undergo some deep process of transformation, and this must have been particularly interesting to Shakespeare as he created his own Rosalind. Does she, or does she not, become Ganymede? In Lodge's *Rosalynde* the heroine, disguised as the page (not shepherd-boy) Ganymede, simply becomes a boy, speaking in an authentic boy's voice. But Shakespeare's Ganymede is a more complex figure.

The dual nature of Pyrocles creates a highly comic interaction in the confrontation in *Old Arcadia* between Dametas, the brutish shepherd, and Pyrocles, disguised as Cleophila: " 'Maid Marian,' demands Dametas, 'am I not a personage to be answered?' " (p. 29). Receiving no response he gives "her" a hefty blow. The title "Maid

Marian" is already double-edged, as in May games and Morris dances Robin Hood's consort, Maid Marian, was always played by a man, so that Sidney's text creates a dramatic irony (Duncan-Jones, in Sidney 1985: 370 n.29). Pyrocles' response to the attack is instantaneous: "Cleophila no sooner felt the blow but that, the fire sparkling out of her eyes, and rising up with a right Pyrocles countenance in a Cleophila face, 'Vile creature,' said she, laying her hand upon her sword, 'force me not to defile this sword in thy base blood!'" (p. 29). At this moment the outer may be the fair Amazon, but the inner is warlike Prince Pyrocles, hand to sword before you can say distaff, just as the Ganymede who swoons at blood is Rosalind within, however much she pretends to be counterfeiting (though of course it is well known that men, not women, swoon at blood). Essex in his relation with Elizabeth encountered many curious dilemmas and dualities created by a role which combined male chivalry with female dependence. Notoriously his hand flew to his sword when she boxed his ear (in 1598), as though he would have challenged her man to "man."

The role of Ganymede, Jove's own page, might have struck the Elizabethan court as particularly applicable to the wayward earl of Essex, in whose character the brash youth played by Rosalind dances a duet with the caricature of feminine caprice which Rosalind invents for Orlando. But what of Orlando himself? He is the love-struck wooer, hanging sonnets on trees (Essex was one of Elizabeth's most prolific sonneteers), and his chivalric descent and ambience is congruent with Essex's image and special inheritance as Elizabeth's favorite. Essex assumed the mantle at court not only of his stepfather, Robert Dudley, earl of Leicester but also of Sir Philip Sidney. Leicester was responsible for introducing his young stepson to court favor, and acted as both guardian and patron to him, launching him on a glamorous career when he took him on his first military engagement in the Low Countries in 1585 to aid the Protestant Dutch against the Spanish Catholics under Philip II. Essex, only 19 when he left for the Low Countries, consciously took over the chivalric and heroic mantle of the dead Sidney, carrying his sword at his funeral, and subsequently marrying his widow, Frances Walsingham.

It has long been a matter of debate whether the Forest of Arden represents Shakespeare's Warwickshire or Ardennes in Flanders, the setting of Lodge's *Rosalynde* (although it is located nearer Bordeaux than Flanders). The first act of the play is at pains to stress the "Frenchness" of the court, perhaps in order to avoid its seeming too near home. The Flanders Ardennes would have evoked Elizabethan memories of Leicester's campaign in the Low Countries in the 1580s which constituted Essex's military debut and made him the natural heir to the chivalric world of Leicester and Sidney.

As You Like It deliberately invokes an age of past chivalry surrounding old Sir Rowland (Orlando's father) and Duke Senior (Rosalind's father), which taps into an area of mingled fiction and past history associated with Leicester, Henry VIII, and the romance world of Ariosto's *Orlando Furioso* (one of the sources of the play, translated into English by the queen's godson, Sir John Harington). The chivalric romance *Chanson de Roland,* a source of stories as well known as the Robin Hood myths, is given an additional gloss by the presence in the Low Countries (alongside Leicester's

Players) of the jester Will Kemp, a man linked, tantalizingly, with his own home brand of Rowland jigs (Baskervill 1965: 181–3, 226 n.3). I have argued elsewhere that Touchstone's teasing of Sir Oliver Mar-text, culminating in the song (also a jig) "O sweet Oliver" in 3.3, makes it certain that the part of Touchstone was conceived not, as usually thought, for Robert Armin, but for Will Kemp, whose role in the stage-baiting of Marprelates is well documented.[4]

When Orlando names his parentage to Duke Senior in 2.7 of *As You Like It* the Duke's response is instantaneous:

> If that you were the good Sir Rowland's son,
> As you have whisper'd faithfully you were,
> And as mine eye doth his effigies witness
> Most truly limn'd and living in your face,
> Be truly welcome hither. I am the Duke
> That lov'd your father. (2.7.194–8)

Leicester and Henry VIII both haunt this passage, but another figure is also drawn into it by the word "limn," usually glossed to mean color painting. Limning was exclusively used for the art of miniature portrait painting.[5] Henry VIII imported illuminators from Flanders, the most renowned being Holbein, from whom the Elizabethan miniaturist Nicholas Hilliard claims in his treatise *The Arte of Limning* (written between 1598 and 1602) to have learnt his art. Hilliard's famous *Young Man among Roses*, once thought to be Southampton, is now generally agreed to represent the young earl of Essex, engarlanded in the queen's flower, the eglantine (Hammer 1999: 68 and n.149).[6] The Duke describes Orlando as the miniature portrait of his father Sir Rowland, as Essex might be said to be the miniature portrait of the earl of Leicester.

Hilliard's connection with Essex's family dates from their shared childhood as Marian exiles in Geneva. The artist named his children after the Knollys children; Essex helped him financially over his house in 1595.[7] But Hilliard not only had close connections with Leicester; in the Elizabethan court in the 1580s he was also considered to have influence with Lord Hunsdon, the Lord Chamberlain (Blakiston 1954). Familiarity with Leicester, Essex, and the Sidney circle blend in Hilliard's career with associations which point to the acting company of the Chamberlain's Men. The reference to "limning" thus carries a complex web of associations with the past which could be read by a court audience and fastened onto the fortunes of Orlando in the present of Shakespeare's play. Orlando's adoration of Rosalind (*rosa linda*, "beautiful rose" in Spanish) recalls not only the heroic past of the earl of Leicester's Flanders campaign, in which his stepson played an important part, but also Essex's present patronage of the arts and his devotion to Elisa, Queene of shepheardes, to whom Hilliard was official court painter.

Essex's career as court favorite after the death of Leicester was marked by a sensational debut in the tilting ceremony and masque of his own making which was presented at the Accession day celebrations in 1595. He deliberately fashioned himself as an aristocrat from an old-world chivalric mode, in contrast to Raleigh, whom he (and others) considered an upstart, and ousted from Elizabeth's favor. Raleigh was nicknamed "Fortune" in the court (May 1980: 87) and the jokes between Rosalind and Celia in the second scene of *As You Like It* about the gifts of Nature and Fortune suggest the terms on which the rivalry between Essex and Raleigh was conducted. Raleigh counter-accused Essex of being successful only because he was Fortune's child (Hammer 1999: 67–8). Raleigh's chequered career lies in the hinterland of the rich composite character of Jaques, as evidenced in Jaques' fondness for travel, his selling of his lands, and his edgy relationship with both Rosalind and the young nobleman who enjoys her favor, the chivalric Orlando.

The sense of conflict between the representatives of an old chivalric order and a race of new upstarts is familiar from Shakespeare's history plays, notably *Richard II*, where the old order of the monarch is superseded by the new efficient order of Bolingbroke. This play was commissioned by the earl of Essex's supporters to be shown on the eve of the rebellion in 1601. However, in that play, Essex was identified by his contemporaries as the rebel Bolingbroke, the champion of the new order which would overthrow the waning monarch (Dutton 1991: 117–27). "Knowst thou not that I am Richard II?" Elizabeth demanded. But in many ways this is a misleading picture of the earl of Essex, whose troubled allegiance to a chivalric past (James 1986) is in stark contrast to the pragmatism and Machiavellian politics of his enemy Robert Cecil. Does *As You Like It* offer an escape into the chivalric golden world in which Essex delighted to wrap himself, or does it cast its own shadow across that Elizabethan fairy-tale?

In the chivalric atmosphere evoked by Orlando's name and parentage, Orlando himself strikes a new note. He uses a telling image to describe his falling in love with Rosalind:

> My better parts
> Are all thrown down, and that which here stands up
> Is but a quintain, a mere lifeless block. (1.2.239–41)

The quintain was a post used in jousting tournaments at court.[8] Orlando is metamorphosed here from a knight riding at tilt at the quintain to a lifeless object, a position the reverse of glorious. He has overcome the wrestler, but his victory is wrested from him:

> O poor Orlando, thou art overthrown!
> Or Charles, or something weaker masters thee. (1.2.249–50)

If he started the play lamenting his deprivations as a nobleman, he continues throughout it to be on the wrong side of the chivalric equation.

This is most noticeable when he bursts, sword drawn, onto the scene of Duke Senior's rustic dinner in the Forest of Arden, seeking food for his old servant, Adam. "Of what kind should this cock come of?" enquires Jaques, as though a real cock from the cock-fighting arena had strayed on to the Globe stage mistaking the night of his performance (cock-fighting being a regular event in that theatre when plays were not on offer). Duke Senior admonishes him:

> What would you have? Your gentleness shall force,
> More than your force move us to gentleness. (2.7.102–3)

Orlando accepts the rebuke:

> Speak you so gently? Pardon me, I pray you.
> I thought that all things had been savage here. (3.3.106–7)

Orlando's situation has led him into the kind of behavior identified by Rosalind when she anticipates mockingly her own impersonation of masculinity in the figure of Ganymede:

> A gallant curtle-axe upon my thigh,
> A boar-spear in my hand, and in my heart,
> Lie there what hidden woman's fear there will,
> We'll have a swashing and a martial outside,
> As many other mannish cowards have
> That do outface it with their semblances. (1.3.114–19)

Orlando is momentarily caught in swash-buckling, although not cowardly, mode, and feels its indecorum in the Forest of Arden. For if in Arden Rosalind can explore new dimensions for being a woman, Orlando also becomes a new man. The touchstone of his difference from traditional masculinity, as defined by Rosalind, is Ganymede, a woman's fiction of a man, just as the capricious Rosalind which Ganymede creates for Orlando is a man's fiction of woman. The play-acting of both roles, the make-believe Rosalind, and the make-believe Ganymede, highlights the different characteristics of the "real" Rosalind and the "real" Orlando.

Orlando is not the chivalric knight of Ariosto's *Orlando Furioso* who goes mad when spurned by his cruel lady. He is a gentle man, as well as a gentleman, a conjunction ironically investigated in the early *Two Gentlemen of Verona*. Essex's conviction that he was automatically superior to Raleigh because he was an aristocrat is exposed to scrutiny in the way in which Shakespeare uses the word "gentle," the adjective which describes birth, and the virtues which should accompany it, but which are lacking in Duke Frederick's court. Oliver is a villain; his brother's wordplay on the word for peasant, "villein," points to Essex's obstinate retort in the autumn of 1598 to Sir Thomas Egerton's plea that he should reconcile himself to the queen: "I haue been contented to doe her the seruice of an Erle, but can neuer serue her as a villaine or slaue."[9] Even as Orlando is identified as well-born, Oliver reluctantly registers his brother's "gentleness" which, while it reinforces gentle birth, is also the medium through which the pretensions of the gently born are, as in many of Shakespeare's plays, undermined: "Yet he's gentle, never schooled and yet learned, full of noble device, of all sorts enchantingly beloved" (1.1.160–1). The word, by moving towards its modern meaning, heralds a new interpretation of masculinity.

The gentle Orlando is much in evidence in his treatment of his old servant, Adam, and although this is identified by Adam himself as old-world virtue, Shakespeare nevertheless gives it a further gloss. Duke Senior, having heard Orlando's apology for his rough behavior, invites him to eat: "And therefore sit you down in gentleness" (2.7.125). But Orlando has to bring Adam to the feast of plenty:

> Then but forbear your food a little while,
> Whiles, like a doe, I go to find my fawn,
> And give it food. (3.3.127–9)

Shakespeare could easily have made Orlando here into a lion fetching its cub, but he chooses instead the feminine image of the doe feeding her fawn. In the autumn of 1599 *As You Like It* could be read as a plea for less concern about who was knighted (Elizabeth's rage at Essex's "Irish" knights) and more discernment about the difference between true and false friends, more recognition of gentle behavior than of gentle birth. Of this the ending of the play is itself witness. Lodge's *Rosalynde* ends in war. Shakespeare's play emphatically does not. Its end is heralded by two key moments which also suggest connections with the earl of Essex, who stood patron to the Italian (Catholic) fencing-master Vincentio Saviolo, who in 1595 dedicated his two works on fencing to Essex (Hammer 1999: 178), and whose two books arguably prompt Touchstone's extravaganza on dueling in 5.4. Even more significantly, Morley's song in 5.3, "It was a lover and his lass," creates connections with Essex which have gone unnoticed.

Morley's relation to the stage is particularly interesting. In the late 1580s he would have been in close contact with the Children of Paul through his position as cathedral organist. This may have fueled his protests against the virulence of the antitheatricalists, from whom he seems to have felt under personal attack. He became Gentleman of the Chapel Royal in 1592, alongside William Byrd, to whom Morley's immensely popular *A Plain and Easy Introduction to Practical Music* (1597) is dedicated (in the hope of protection in "these dayes wherein Enuie raigneth"). But one of the dedicatory poems points out that Morley's fortunes have already changed dramatically because he has acquired a patron among the great:

> But lo, the day star, with his bright beames shining,
> Sent forth his aide to musicks arte refining,
> Which gaue such light for him whose eyes long houered,
> To finde a part where more lay vndiscouered;
> That all his workes, with ayre so sweet perfumed
> Shall liue with fame when foes shall be consumed.

The poet puns on Morley's name ("more lay") and on his "airs": the perfumed air. The "day star" is almost certainly Essex: Elizabeth called him her "evening star." The earl may have become Morley's patron in 1595 after Morley took part in the spectacular masque which Essex mounted for the queen's Accession in 1595 (Chambers 1923: III, 212). Morley's song evoking a Golden Age spring, characterized by descending scales which imitate wedding bells, but which in November would conjure up day-long Accession day ringing, offers a striking reinforcement of the play's Essex associations. Morley had attracted Elizabeth's attention in 1591 at the entertainment given at Elvetham by the earl of Hertford for the queen on her progresses. This elaborate week-long entertainment was marked by spectacular music, and Morley himself was singled out for royal favor when the queen "gave a newe name unto one of their Pavans, made long since by Master Thomas Morley, then organist of Paule's Church." The instrumentalists who played on this occasion provided exactly the same combination of instruments as those in Morley's *Book of Consorts* printed in 1599 (Poulton 1972: 404, 432). Shakespeare and Morley lived in the late 1590s in the same parish of St. Helen's, Bishopsgate, in London and must have known each other. Fellowes noted in 1937 that they had exactly the same tax assessment (Fellowes 1937: v). Like many Elizabethan musicians, Morley was a Catholic, whose religion was tolerated for his musical skill. Essex protected many Catholic musicians who benefited from his reputation for religious tolerance.[10]

That tolerance is in tune with another aspect of Shakespeare's play, which may have been part of its political significance for the troubled times of 1599. Its engagingly throwaway title keys into a debate about the nature of content. In the great central scene of the play, 3.2, Touchstone has a dialogue with the old shepherd, Corin, about the virtues of country life: "How like you this shepherd's life, Master Touchstone?" inquires Corin, and the court jester replies:

> Truly, shepherd, in respect of itself, it is a good life; but in respect that it is a shepherd's life, it is naught. In respect that it is solitary, I like it very well; but in respect that it is private, it is a very vile life. Now in respect it is in the fields, it pleaseth me well, but in respect that it is not in the court, it is tedious. (3.2.11–16)

Corin's response to the jester's prolonged and waspish quizzing is dignified:

> Sir, I am a true labourer: I earn that I eat, get that I wear; owe no man hate, envy no man's happiness; glad of other men's good, content with my harm; and the greatest of my pride is to see my ewes graze and my lambs suck. (3.2.63–6)

There is here a significant change of language. Touchstone speaks the language of "pleasure": "it pleaseth me well, I like it very well." But Corin's credo: "glad of other men's good, content with my harm" is the language of content.

As You Like It opens in discontent; Oliver's envy of Orlando; Frederick's dislike of Orlando's success. But also Orlando's discontent: his opening speech complains that he is debarred from his patrimony (his gold and lands) and deprived of education: the nurturing of good soil. The Elizabethans understood perfectly that the golden world might be equally Raleigh's *El Dorado* or Ovid's *Metamorphoses*: real travel, or reading: the travel of the mind. Orlando resents being excluded from the education enjoyed by his brother Jaques: "Report speaks goldenly of his profit" (1.1.5). Oliver's envy of Orlando is mirrored in Duke Frederick's fear of Rosalind's overshadowing Celia: "Thou wilt show more bright . . . / When she is gone" (1.3.77–8). The absence of envy becomes the touchstone of Arden: "Are not these woods / More free from peril than the envious court?" asks the Duke at the opening of act 2. The only enemy is winter and rough weather; there are none of the false friends and flatterers whose ingratitude and betrayal enter the forest only in Amiens' songs: "benefits forgot," "friend remembered not" (2.7.186, 189).

In 1599 James Roberts reprinted three sermons originally published in 1590 and 1591 by Henry Smith, Chaplain of Lincoln's Inn, a compilation which went into a surprising number of editions. In the sermon called "The Benefit of Contentation" Smith declares: "Contentation wanteth nothing . . . Therefore if you see a man contented with that he hath, it is a great signe that godlines is entred into him" (sigs. B4–B4v). It's difficult not to see Roberts's new edition of Smith's immensely popular sermon as politically grounded in a year when the discontent of the earl of Essex (his apologia printed in 1601 was entitled "The passion of a discontented mind") caused so much alarm.

In *As You Like It* the cornerstone of court life is ambition:

> Who doth ambition shun,
> And loves to live i' th' sun (2.5.35–6)

sings Amiens, and if the play carries an admonition for the Elizabethan court and for Essex in particular, it lies in the shunning of ambition. "Living i' th' sun" translates easily into "living in the queen's favor." Sir John Harington reports an occasion when Sir Christopher Hatton emerged from the queen's presence "with ill countenance, and pulled me aside by the girdle, and saide in secrete waie, If you have any suite to daie, I praye you put it aside. The sunne dothe not shine" (Harington 1779: II: 220–1). Ambition undermines content.

The difference between pleasure and content in the play is articulated by Rosalind, when she turns to Silvius, promising to grant him his heart's desire: "If what pleases you, contents you" (5.2.116). When Hymen blesses the four couples in the marriage masque, he says:

> Here's eight that must take hands,
> To join in Hymen's bands.
> If truth holds true contents. (5.4.115)

Hymen's "if" is one of many conditionals in the play (Traub 1992: 128; Sedinger 1997: 72–3), but it also partakes in the triumphant affirmation of Sonnet 116: "If this be error and upon me proved / I never writ, and no man ever loved." On one important level truth and content do join hands in the Forest of Arden: "Now go we in content / To liberty and not banishment," cries Rosalind. The play celebrates reconciliation.

If *As You Like It*'s intervention in politics is couched in such conciliatory terms it is hard to see why it could have caused offense. Nevertheless, a silence surrounds it at the turn of the century, and the suggestion that it was played at Wilton in November 1603 for James I (the first play of his reign), though attractive in view of the Sidney connections, is not a certainty. It was in the repertoire of the old Blackfriars theatre, according to the 1669 list of plays assigned to Thomas Killigrew for the new Theatre Royal (PRO LC 5/12). What may have happened was that it was deemed prudent to keep it off the stage after 1600 because of the possibility of its seeming to animadvert on Essex's fortunes, as Samuel Daniel's *Philotas* was later accused of having done (Pitcher 1998). Daniel claimed (disingenuously) that any resemblance was purely coincidental, and if *As You Like It* was written before July 1599 Shakespeare might have said the same with perfect good faith. But the reading of works with hindsight was a well-known Elizabethan pastime, and Elizabeth herself was a canny discerner of unwelcome references in apparently innocent works.

In 1599 it would have touched two raw nerves. In the first place it defies with extraordinary audacity the vociferous critics of the theatre to whom the crossdressed boy actor was anathema. Secondly, it presents not only a hostile picture of an actual court, but dares to complement it with an alternative court peopled by courtiers who have taken to the highway as though they were vagabonds (gypsies like the players, in antitheatrical parlance), and are cavorting in the Forest of Arden with a banished Duke who is openly compared to the outlawed Robin Hood.

To take the second objection first. The ruling figure in the Forest is Rosalind, whom Shakespeare is at pains to associate with the queen. However, if, as Bullough suggests, the play offered a sophisticated version of the 1598 Robin Hood plays to entertain the Essex circle (Bullough 1968: II, 143), it's hard to believe that the earl's supporters would not have seen in the banished greenwood Duke and the figure of Robin Hood a prototype for their own hero. Essex, like Leicester, was Elizabeth's "Robin." Moreover the famous speech: "They say many young gentlemen flock to him every day and fleet the time carelessly as they did in the golden world" (1.1.91–4) uses the same word – "flock" – which Elizabeth used in her renewed proclamation against vagabonds on 15 February 1601, just ten days before Essex's execution:

> There is at this time dispersed within our Citie of London, and *the Suburbs thereof*, a great multitude of base and loose people, such as neither haue any certeine place of abode, nor any good or lawful cause of businesse to attend hereabouts, but lie priuily in corners and bad houses, listning after newes and stirres, and spreading rumours and tales . . . And likewise that further numbers of such sort of vagabond people do continually *flocke* and gather to our City, and the places confining about the same. (*Book of Proclamations*, 1600, p. 420; my emphasis).

Citizens are not to flock to new leaders. The word "flock" connects automatically with subversion, and is used by Gosson in his attack on playgoing: "To celebrate the Sabboth, [men] flock to Theaters" (Gosson 1579: sig. C2). Players, vagabonds, rebels, and Robin Hood. Put them all together, stick them in a forest, and call their way of life *As You Like It*, and put it on the public stage. The recipe, at least by 1600, sounds too hot for happiness. The withdrawal of *As You Like It* from performance by the early summer of 1600 would help to explain the "staying" order of August 4 of the same year in the *Stationers' Register* (alongside *Henry V*, *Much Ado About Nothing*, and Jonson's *Every Man In His Humour*), and its not being subsequently printed, as the three other plays were, perhaps reflecting the well-known caution of the printer James Roberts, who made the staying order.

To understand more about the ways in which the play gave offense to antitheatricalists it's instructive to look ahead to the Caroline period. Charles I wrote "Rosalind" in his copy of the First Folio opposite its title, so presumably had seen the play. But whether or not most of his subjects saw it, they would for the first time have been able to read it, for 1623 marks its first appearance in print. The First Folio is a book aimed not at theatregoers but at private readers.

Prynne's onslaught on the theatre, *Histrio-Mastix* (1633), while primarily concerned with theatregoing, takes time to consider the difference between seeing and reading a play. The latter is less vicious, in his view, because it involves no outlay of money. It is done privately rather than in "ill company," and without the seducing effects of lewd gestures, "kisses, dalliances, or embracements; any whorish, immodest, fantastique, womanish apparell, Vizards, disguises." Furthermore, a reader can be his own Bowdler:

> He that reades a Stage-play may passe by all obscene or amorous passages, all prophane or scurrill Iests, all heathenish oathes and execrations even with detestation; but he who makes, who acts, who heares, or viewes a Stage-play acted, hath no such liberty left him, but hee must act, recite, behold and heare them all. (Prynne 1633: 930)

The play exerts less power over the mind if it is not witnessed in company with others. "The eyes, the eares of Play-readers want all those lust-enraging objects, which Actors and Spectators meet with in the Play-house" (ibid: 931). Reading is not representation. The eye of the mind is much less powerful than the eye. But other aspects of the written word rile the Puritan.

Prynne's tract contains interesting evidence of the popularity of the First Folio, reprinted in 1632, the year Prynne's work was written. He declares in his third dedication "To the Christian Reader":[11] "*Some Play-books since I first undertooke this subject, are growne from* Quarto *into* Folio"; in the margin he notes: "*Ben-Iohnsons, Shackspeers, and others*." He's desperately disappointed that the books are so well-produced and sell so well: "*which yet beare so good a price and sale, that I cannot but with griefe relate it, they are now (e) new-printed in farre better paper than most Octavo or Quarto* Bibles, *which hardly finde such vent as they*." The marginal note (e) adds: "Shackspeers Plaies are printed in the best Crowne paper, far better than most Bibles." Just as the theatre in Shakespeare's time drew crowds whom the antitheatricalists thought should be attending sermons in church, so here the private reader is spending money to buy a book of plays when he should be reading the Bible, and the printer is pandering to this preference.

It is not only Folios which have caused the trouble: "Besides, our Quarto-Play-bookes since the first sheetes of this my Treatise came unto the Presse, have come forth in such *abundance, and found so many customers, that they almost exceed all number, one studie being scarce able to holde them, and two yeares time too little to peruse them all." The asterisk refers the reader again to "Ben-Iohnsons, Shackspeers, and others," but it may be a printer's mistake for the note (f) which declares: "Above forty thousand Play-bookes have beene printed and vented within these two yeares." This opens a window on the world in which theatres were about to be closed. People seem to have been stocking up on texts to read even if they couldn't go to the play.

Lodge's *Rosalynde* is a reading text, not a play, although it's possible that James Roberts, its printer, thought of it as in some ways a text for Shakespeare's play, which he then printed so that performances of the play might boost its sales. *Rosalynde* was printed in 1623, again in 1634 (both times hard on the First Folio), and cannily in 1642, so that audiences banished from the theatre might keep on reading the book (if they couldn't afford Shakespeare's Folio, then available in its second printing of 1632). Sidney's *Old Arcadia*, written to be read aloud to his sister, Mary Sidney, countess of Pembroke, and her ladies at Wilton, is presented as though it were a play. Sidney cajoles, solicits sympathy from, and flirts with his female audience in a way that Lodge, writing for a reading public (and "Gentlemen readers" at that) does not. The ladies' pleasure is part of Sidney's performance, just as it is for Rosalind: "I charge you, O women, for the love you bear to men, to like as much of this play as please you" (5.4.205–7). Shakespeare's *As You Like It*, while seeming to be a preeminently theatrical work, has had great success as a reading text. The nineteenth-century actress Frances Kemble never played Rosalind, but her readings of the play were renowned. It may be true that the subversive aspects of the play's treatment of gender, its evocation of political and social events which rocked Elizabethan political and court life, emerge fully not from dramatic representation but from reading. Theatre in our time cannot recreate the complex interaction which *As You Like It* presents between the fictions of the stage and the vanished masquerades and realities of Elizabeth's reign at the end of the sixteenth century, although to try to represent the hidden tensions in the play is a long overdue mission for theatre directors.

For the play's relation to the crises of its time — the onslaught on theatre and the earl of Essex's tragic downfall — color its mood and preconceptions, creating the sort of reverberation that might be made by the tolling of bells, an image invoked in the play by Orlando. However, the end of the play is at pains to underline its fictive nature.

The last scene of *As You Like It* resembles Elizabethan masques put on for the queen's entertainment at her numerous progresses. In Marston's *Histrio-Mastix* (1610), a play probably written for the Children of Paul's in 1599, Astraea at the end "mounts vnto the Throne" (annotated in ink "Qu. Eliza" (sig. H2v) in the only extant quarto in the British Library). But Shakespeare's play ends not with the casting aside of disguise and the princess restored to her rightful position, but with a startlingly original Epilogue: "If I were a woman, I would kiss as many of you as had beards that pleased me, complexions that liked me, and breaths that I defied not" (5.4.212–15). Shakespeare's Epilogue places at the center of the stage not the queen, but the primacy of theatrical illusion: "All the world's a stage," or as the Globe's motto declared: *"Totus mundus agit histrionem."* Rosalind, playing the boy who has played her, defies the audience to root the play in either the fictions it has created, or in the sensitive political and social reality of its own world, racked in 1599 by the factions created by the unstable fortunes of the earl of Essex.

Shakespeare's play captures the spirit which made the earl of Essex a lodestar for his own culture: insouciant, vital, exuberant, audacious. Essex was, as any reading of his letters to Elizabeth demonstrates, a tremendous role-player, himself a Rosalind/ Ganymede, now a woman to be wooed, now a brash young man. In July 1599 Elizabeth wrote sternly to Essex about her dissatisfaction with his conduct in Ireland, adding: "These things we would pass over but that we see your pen flatters you with phrases" (Elizabeth I 2000: 392). Like Touchstone, the queen knew the difference between a fiction and a lie, and like Rosalind, she knew when the revels were ended.

There was to be no marriage of minds between Essex and the queen who would not brook a master, no Golden world of Robin Hood fleeting the time carelessly (without care). The court was too envious and the young nobleman too ambitious. *As You Like It* captures a moment in 1599 when the young earl, poised between triumph and disaster, could still be shadowed by Orlando, Hilliard's *Young Man among Roses*, and by Ganymede, a shepherd-boy, in a play whose mood of genial reconciliation seems to plead for a leniency which never happened. Egerton warned Essex in 1598: "My verie good L. It is often seene, that a stands by seeth more then he that plaieth."[12] Some at least of that first audience of *As You Like It* must have known that it saw more than Essex did, and that for the earl, Orlando's "I can live no longer by thinking" would be a tragic, not a comic line.

NOTES

1 Summarized by Michael Hattaway in the New Cambridge edition of the play (2000).

2 All quotations are from *The Arden Shakespeare, The Complete Works* (1998).

3 By permission of the British Library, Additional MS 74268, Letter 43, folio 119.

4 See Dusinberre (2002). Dutton (2000: 34–5) believes that Kemp was still with the Chamberlain's Men to play the Poet – "jigging fools" (4.3.137) – in *Julius Caesar* in the autumn of 1599 and that he may still have been with the company after his dance to Norwich in Lent 1600.

5 In the Induction (132–3) to Marston's *Antonio and Mellida* a character remarks: "I fear it is not possible to limn so many persons in so small a tablet as the compass of our plays afford" (Marston 1965: 9).

6 The identification was first suggested by Piper (1957: II, 300–3), developed by Strong (1977), and by Fumerton in a fascinating discussion of Hilliard's unique place in the rise of the Elizabethan "miniature craze" (Fumerton 1986: 65, 68–71).

7 Strong (1995: 181–6); Edmond (1983: 28, 126). Hilliard's fortunes had declined by the end of the century, possibly reflecting Essex's disfavor at court (Strong). He pleaded to Cecil for help, which he received in March 1599. Shakespeare's reference may have brought Hilliard's plight to court notice.

8 Yates (1975) reproduces Antoine Caron's drawing "The Quintain" (Witt Collection, Courtauld Institute) from the Duc de Joyeuse's *Magnificences* (1581), which demonstrates the courtliness of jousting with the quintain.

9 By permission of the British Library, Additional MS 48126, folio 100.

10 Fellowes (1937) refers to the Roll of Assessments for subsidies in St. Helen's parish in 1598 (PRO E.179.146/369). If Shakespeare was a covert Catholic, the connection with Morley becomes even more interesting.

11 The first is to the "Masters of the Bench" of Lincoln's Inn, the second "To the Right Christian, Generovs Yovng Gentlemen-Students of the famous Innes of Court and especially that *of* Lincolnes Inne." Prynne's title-page advertises him as a member of Lincoln's Inn, as were Donne, Lodge, Harington, and the dedicatee of Morley's *First Book of Ayres* (1600), Sir Ralph Bosvile. *As You Like It* may have been one of many plays performed at the Inns of Court, and therefore in Prynne's view in need of reform, but by the 1630s Lincoln's Inn harbored a number of Puritans.

12 By permission of the British Library, Additional MS 48126, folio 99.

References and Further Reading

Baskervill, C. R. (1965) [1929]. *The Elizabethan Jig.* New York: Columbia University Press.

Bath, M. (1986). Weeping Stags and Melancholy Lovers: The Iconography of *As You Like It. Emblematica,* 1, 13–52.

Beal, P. (1992). *Elizabeth and Essex: The Hulton Papers.* London: Sotheby's Catalogue.

Belsey, C. (2001). *Shakespeare and the Loss of Eden.* Basingstoke: Palgrave.

Berry, P. (1989). *Of Chastity and Power: Elizabethan Literature and the Unmarried Queen.* London: Routledge.

Bevington, D. (1968). Heywood's Comic Pleading for Reconciliation. In *Tudor Drama and Politics: A Critical Approach to Topical Meaning.* Cambridge, MA: Harvard University Press.

Blakiston, N. (1954). Nicholas Hilliard at Court. *Burlington Magazine,* 96, 17–18.

Bono, B. (1986). Mixed Gender, Mixed Genre in Shakespeare's *As You Like It.* In B. K. Lewalski (ed.) *Renaissance Genres.* Cambridge, MA: Harvard University Press, 189–212.

Book of Proclamations (1600). London: Robert Barker.

Brissenden, A. (1994). *As You Like It.* Oxford: Oxford University Press.

Bullough, G. (1968). '*As You Like It*', 143–266. In *Narrative and Dramatic Sources of Shakespeare, Vol. 2, The Comedies,* 1597–1603. London: Eyre and Spottiswoode.

Callaghan, D., Helms, L., and Jyotsna S. (eds.) (1994). *The Weyward Sisters: Shakespeare and Feminist Politics.* Oxford: Blackwell.

Calvo, C. (1992). Pronouns of Address and Social Negotiation in *As You Like It. Language and Literature,* 1, 5–27.

Chambers, E. K. (1923). *The Elizabethan Stage,* 4 vols. Oxford: Oxford University Press.

Chapman, G. (1607). *Bussy D'Ambois.* London: William Aspley.

Daley, A. S. (1985). The Dispraise of the Country in *As You Like It. Shakespeare Quarterly,* 36, 300–14.

Devereux, Robert, 2nd earl of Essex, and Egerton, Thomas, Lord Kepper [1599]. Two Letters. British Library Additional MS 48126.

——[1599]. ORIGINAL LETTERS from Robert Dudley, Earl of Leicester and Robert Devereux, Earl of Essex to QUEEN ELIZABETH. The Hulton Papers. British Library Additional MS 74286.

Dusinberre, J. (1994). As *Who* Liked It? *Shakespeare Survey,* 46, 9–21.

——(1996). *Shakespeare and the Nature of Women,* 2nd edn. London: Macmillan.

——(2002). Topical Forest: Kemp and Mar-text in Arden. In A. Thompson and G. McMullan (eds.) *In Arden: Editing Shakespeare, Essays in Honor of G. R. Proudfoot.* London: The Arden Shakespeare, Thomson Learning.

Dutton, R. (1991). *Mastering the Revels.* London: Macmillan.

——(2000). *Licensing, Censorship and Authorship in Early Modern England.* Basingstoke: Palgrave.

Edmond, M. (1983). *Hilliard and Oliver*. London: Robert Hale.

Elizabeth I (2000). *Collected Works*, ed. L. S. Marcus, J. Mueller, and M. B. Rose. Chicago, IL: University of Chicago Press.

Fellowes, E. H. (1937). Introduction. In *A Plaine and Easie Introduction to Practicall Musicke*, by Thomas Morley. London: Shakespeare Association, Oxford University Press.

Fitter, C. (1999). The Slain Deer and Political *Imperium*: *As You Like It* and Andrew Marvell's "Nymph Complaining for the Death of her Fawn." *Journal of English and Germanic Philology*, 98, 193–218.

Fumerton, P. (1986). "Secret" Arts: Elizabethan Miniatures and Sonnets. *Representations*, 15, 57–97.

Gibbons, B. (1993). Amorous Fictions in *As You Like It*. In *Shakespeare and Multiplicity*. Cambridge: Cambridge University Press, 153–81.

Goldberg, J. (1983). *James I and the Politics of Literature*. Baltimore, MD: Johns Hopkins University Press.

Gosson, S. (1579). *The School of Abuse*. London: Thomas Woodstocke.

Hammer, P. E. J. (1999). *The Polarisation of Elizabethan Politics: The Political Career of Robert Devereux, 2nd Earl of Essex, 1585–1597*. Cambridge: Cambridge University Press.

Harington, Sir John (1779). *Nugae Antiquae. Being a Miscellaneous Collection of Original Papers in Prose and Verse*, selected by Henry Harington, 3 vols. London: J. Dodsley.

Hattaway, M. (2000). *As You Like It*. Cambridge: Cambridge University Press.

Heffner, R. (1934). Essex the Ideal Courtier. *English Literary History*, 1, 7–36.

Herford, C. H. and Simpson, P. (1925–52). *Ben Jonson*. Oxford: Oxford University Press.

Hilliard, N. (1981). *A Treatise concerning the Arte of Limning*, ed. R. K. R. Thornton and T. G. S. Cain. Advington, Northumberland: Carcanet Press.

Howard, J. E. (1994). *The Stage and Social Struggle in Early Modern England*. London: Routledge.

James, M. (1986). At a Crossroads of the Political Culture: The Essex Revolt, 1601. In *Society, Politics and Culture*. Cambridge: Cambridge University Press, 416–65.

Jonson, B. (1920) [1600]. *Every Man Out of His Humour*. Oxford: Oxford University Press, Malone Society Reprints.

Killigrew, T. (1669). A Catalogue of part of his Ma[te] Servants Playes as they were formerly acted at the Blackfryers and now allowed to his Ma[te] Servants at y[e] New Theatre. [Margin: Playes Acted at the Theatre Royall]. PRO LC 5/12.

Levine, L. (1994). *Men in Women's Clothing: Anti-Theatricality and Effeminization 1572–1642*. Cambridge: Cambridge University Press.

McCoy, R. (1983). "A Dangerous Image": The Earl of Essex and Elizabethan Chivalry. *Journal of Medieval and Renaissance Studies*, 13, 313–29.

McDonald, M. A. (1995). The Elizabethan Poor Laws and the Stage in the Late 1590s. *Medieval and Renaissance Drama in England*, 7, 121–44.

Marston, J. (1610). *Histrio-mastix. Or, the player whipt*. London: G. Eld for T. Thorp.

——(1965) [1599]. *Antonio and Mellida, The First Part*, ed. G. K. Hunter. London: Edward Arnold.

May, S. W. (1980). The Poems of Edward de Vere, Seventeenth Earl of Oxford and of Robert Devereux, Second Earl of Essex. *Studies in Philology*, 77.

Montrose, L. A. (1980). "Elisa, queen of shepheardes", and the Pastoral of Power. *English Literary Renaissance*, 10, 153–82.

Morley, T. (1608) [1597]. *A Plain and Easy Introduction to Practical Music*. London: Humfrey Lownes.

——(1937). *A Plaine and Easie Introduction to Practiall Musicke*, ed. E. Fellowes. Oxford: Humphrey Milford, Oxford University Press. Shakespeare Association Facsimiles, No. 14.

Neely, C. T. (2000). Lovesickness, Gender, and Subjectivity: *Twelfth Night* and *As You Like It*. In D. Callaghan (ed.) *A Feminist Companion to Shakespeare*. Oxford: Blackwell.

Neill, M. (1998). "This gentle gentleman": Social Change and the Language of Status in *Arden of Feversham*. *Medieval and Renaissance Drama in England*, 10, 73–97.

Orgel, S. (1996). *Impersonations: The Performance of Gender in Shakespeare's England*. Cambridge: Cambridge University Press.

Ostovich, H. M. (1992). 'So sudden and strange a cure': A Rudimentary Masque in *Every Man Out of His Humour*. *English Literary Renaissance*, 22, 315–32.

Parrott, T. M. (1908). The Date of Chapman's *Bussy D'Ambois*. *Modern Language Review*, 3, 126–40.

Piper, D. (1957). The 1590 Lumley Inventory: Hilliard, Segar and the Earl of Essex. *Burlington Magazine*, 99 (2 parts), 224–31, 299–303.

Pitcher, J. (1998). Samuel Daniel and the Authorities. *Medieval and Renaissance Drama in England*, 10, 113–48.

Platter, T. (1937) [1599]. *Thomas Platter's Travels in England 1599*, trans. C. Williams. London: Jonathan Cape.

Poulton, D. (1972). *John Dowland*. London: Faber and Faber.

Proudfoot, R., Thompson, A., and Kastan, D. S. (eds.) (1998). *The Arden Shakespeare Complete Works*. London: Thomas Nelson.

Prynne, W. (1633). *Histrio-Mastix*. London: E. Allde et al.

Rackin, P. (1987). Androgyny, Mimesis and the Marriage of the Boy Actor on the English Renaissance Stage. *Publications of the Modern Languages Association*, 102, 113–33.

Ronk, M. (2001). Locating the Visual in *As You Like It*. *Shakespeare Quarterly*, 52, 255–76.

Rous, F. (1622). *Diseases of the Time*. London.

Ruff, L. M. and Wilson, D. A. (1969). The Madrigal, the Lute Song and Elizabethan Politics. *Past and Present*, 44, 3–51.

Sedinger, T. (1997). "If sight and shape be true": The Epistemology of Crossdressing on the London Stage. *Shakespeare Quarterly*, 48, 63–79.

Sidney, Sir Philip (1977) [1590]. *The Countess of Pembroke's Arcadia*, ed. M. Evans. Harmondsworth: Penguin Books.

——(1985). *The Old Arcadia*, ed. K. Duncan-Jones. Oxford: Oxford University Press.

Singh, J. (1989). Renaissance Antitheatricality, Antifeminism, and Shakespeare's *Antony and Cleopatra*. *Renaissance Drama*, n.s., 20, 99–121.

Smith, H. (1599). The Benefit of Contentation. In *Three Sermons*. London: James Roberts for Nicholas Ling.

Strong, R. (1977). Hilliard's *Young Man amongst [sic] Roses*. In *The Cult of Elizabeth*. London: Thames and Hudson, 56–83.

——(1995). Queen Elizabeth, the Earl of Essex and Nicholas Hilliard, 181–6. "My weeping stagge I crowne": The Persian Lady Reconsidered, 303–24. In *The Tudor and Stuart Monarchy: Pageantry, Painting, Iconography, Vol. 2: Elizabethan*. Woodbridge: Boydell Press.

Tiffany, G. (1994). "That reason wonder may diminish": *As You Like It*, Androgyny, and the Theater Wars. *Huntington Library Quarterly*, 57, 213–39.

Traub, V. (1992). *Desire and Anxiety: Circulations of Sexuality in Shakespearean Drama*. London: Routledge.

Wilson, J. (1980). *Entertainments for Elizabeth*. Woodbridge: D. S. Brewer.

Wilson, R. (1993). Like the Old Robin Hood: *As You Like It* and the Enclosure Riots. In *Will Power*. London: Macmillan, 66–87.

Yates, F. A. (1975). *Astraea: The Imperial Theme in the Sixteenth Century*. London: Routlege and Kegan Paul.

22

Twelfth Night: "The Babbling Gossip of the Air"

Penny Gay

> *Malvolio.* . . . Is there no respect of place, persons, or time in you?
> *Sir Toby.* We did keep time, sir, in our catches.
>
> (2.6.79–80)[1]

Punning on the multiple connotations of one word, "time," Sir Toby puts down Malvolio ("Sneck up!"), asserts his position as the worthy representative of the good life (cakes, ale, and song), and utters a "chime" with one of the play's key phrases – Viola's rhyming tag to the previous scene, "O time, thou must untangle this, not I; / It is too hard a knot for me t' untie." This is one of *Twelfth Night*'s most characteristic habits: words echo, chime, jingle, rhyme; they pun, tie themselves in knots, riddles, and anagrams. At the end of the play Orsino claims that Viola, when seen "in other habits," will be his "fancy's queen." But I doubt whether any audience member ever really cares about the married life of Viola and Orsino, for she won't then be in the "habit" (situational, verbal, costumed) of the play; she won't be the Viola we've come to know, who is essentially a linguistic being, a speaker of blank verse and rhyme, a quick-witted wordsmith. Her last speech in the play is (significantly) bald and prosaic, with just the faintest echo of the punning habit (garments/suit) as she prepares to doff her doublet's doubleness:

> The captain that did bring me first on shore
> Hath my maid's garments; he upon some action
> Is now in durance, at Malvolio's suit,
> A gentleman and follower of my lady's. (5.1.258–61)

Who remembers this, when asked to quote Viola? Rather, they will launch into "I left no ring with her . . ." or "Make me a willow cabin at your gate . . ." or "She never told her love . . ." (though she does, with this speech, which is partly what makes it so memorable). And in fact almost all the play's characters talk poetry, or at least a punning prose. Even poor Sir Andrew can on occasion – when he's lucky – manage a feeble pun: "And your horse now would make him an ass." (2.3.142)

The play's uniqueness, I will argue, is as much to do with the aural experience it imposes – whether in the two hours' traffic of the stage or in the mind's ear as we read it – as with the romantic fable it tells. We cannot resist its seductive musicality, its wit, its linguistic games: they seem, ultimately, to be part of the *meaning* of the play, if the meaningful is that which we remember. We will always have the story of separation and rediscovery; always the story of disguise and frustrated loves finally resolved (these first two are in Shakespeare's sources); always the story of the bringing-down of the pompous Puritan, clearly a perpetually relevant theme in the theatre. But there's also always more: "babble" (used at least three times in *Twelfth Night*); nonsense, rhyme, and word-play; echoes, all the time. A modern audience may not have as sophisticated an aural capacity as an Elizabethan one, and may be distracted by technical marvels of the modern stage, but we can still hear a pun, a jingle, a chime. I want to propose something I call temp/aurality: in the context of the *action*, *temporality*, and *narrative drive* of theatre, what happens to the audience – the listeners – in *Twelfth Night*? Significantly, exactly midway through the play an aural symbol – a literal chime – is provided, in the stage direction "*Clock strikes*" at 3.1.126. "The clock upbraids me with the waste of time," Olivia reflects; does not the audience at this point subconsciously register that the play delightfully wastes time, and that the return to the "every day" of work is inevitably approaching?

Jean Howard argued in 1984 (though few critics seem since to have heeded her observations) that

> in experiencing [this] play in the theatre, the audience does not start . . . with a summation of the play's overriding symbolic or psychological concerns . . . In the theatre we begin, not with abstract reflections on the sterility of egocentricity, but with the sound of a particular kind of music and a particular man's reaction to that music. What we subsequently experience is not a psychological treatise, but a particular succession of sights, sounds, and events that create a unique theatrical experience with its own tempo, rhythm, and pauses, its own moments of engagement and detachment, and its own natural points of emphasis.
>
> What is remarkable about this and other Shakespeare plays is the extent to which the temporal experience of them – what the play *does* in its progressive mode – constitutes and controls what the play *means*. (Howard 1984: 178–9)

In this essay I will focus particularly on the aural aspect of the "progressive mode," assisted by theorizations of language and the theatre experience that have become available in the last three decades. There is undoubtedly the danger, in a reading which emphasizes linguistic play, of reducing everything to what Malcolm Evans calls "a delirium of dissent which is also a babble of compliance, an equalizing of all voices in the irreducibility of *écriture*" (Evans 1985: 89). My intention, however, is to uncover the political potential of the aesthetic and affective experience of *attending to* the play.[2]

"More than any of his contemporaries, Shakespeare discovered how to use the erotic power that the theatre could appropriate" (Greenblatt 1988: 88). Actors will admit that seducing the audience – through embodying the script – is what the process is all about; perhaps I might be allowed the first of several anagrammatic observations when I point out that *rhetoric*, this play's habit of verbal troping, contains *erotic*. Consider the function of questions in the theatre: speech acts they undoubtedly are, and their principal function is to elicit (either immediately or within the play's playing time) information that clarifies plot and situation. But they are also utterances heard by an audience that, by convention, cannot respond, and so feels itself deliciously at the mercy of the players: if they don't tell us, no one will. I will return to this issue of the player's power in my discussion of the riddling with which *Twelfth Night* is stuffed. Here, meanwhile, are some of the play's opening questions:

> *Viola.* What country, friends, is this?
> . . . And what should I do in Illyria?
> Who governs here? . . . What is his name?
> . . . What's she? (1.2)

Naming will be a major issue in this play, both as regards plot and as one of the signs of its thematizing of identity, and although the names of the other two members of Viola's erotic triad are here supplied (Orsino, Olivia), Viola herself is not named in the spoken script until the last scene of the play. Here's a puzzle, then, for the audience: what is the heroine's name? How can we know who she is, this sea-born(e) sibling who will only tell us that she can "sing, and speak . . . in many sorts of music" (1.2.57–8)?

Down at the other end of the affective spectrum, Sir Andrew's questions in the next scene (1.3) all revolve around his perplexity with the meaning of words and phrases: "Is that the meaning of 'accost'?" "What's your metaphor?" "But what's your jest?" etc. In 1.5 Feste and Maria match wits in classic vaudeville banter ("I am resolved on two points –" "That if one break, the other will hold, or if both break, your gaskins fall"), the prelude to Feste's "catechizing" Olivia. This is in turn the prelude to the play's first climactic sequence, the arrival of Viola in Olivia's garden, turning Olivia into a questioner: "What is he at the gate?" "What kind o' man is he?" "What manner of man?" – to which Malvolio replies with his own snide word-play, "Of very ill manner: he'll speak with you, will you or no." Finally there begins the first encounter between Olivia and the disguised Viola, an extraordinary litany of questions, for the first time making explicit the play's interest in identity:[3]

> *Viola.* The honourable lady of the house, which is she?
> . . . *Olivia.* Whence came you, sir?
> . . . Are you a comedian?
> . . . What are you? What would you?
> . . . Where lies your text?
> . . . In what chapter of his bosom?
> . . . Have you no more to say?
> . . . How does he love me?
> . . . Why, what would you?

– the climactic question of this scene, to which the astonishing answer is:

> *Viola.* Make me a willow cabin at your gate,
> And call upon my soul within the house;
> Write loyal cantons of contemned love,
> And sing them loud even in the dead of night;
> Hallow your name to the reverberate hills,
> And make the babbling gossip of the air
> Cry out, "Olivia!" . . .

Demonstrably, the play is not yet a fifth of the way through, and the "air" in the theatre is indeed "babbling" with questions, word-play, echoes. Viola's "ring" solilo-quy at the end of 2.2 is the first moment at which the audience, directly addressed, can pause to appreciate this Alice-in-Wonderland, identity-questioning quality of Illyria (Lewis Carroll might have heard *Illyria* as a portmanteau word in the seman-tic universe of nonsense: *Ill*usion–de*liri*um, Oliv*ia*; the name is emphatically used – ten occurrences – in the first act of the play, as though to impress its resonances on our auditory memory):

> I left no ring with her: what means this lady?
> . . . How will this fadge? My master loves her dearly,
> And I, poor monster, fond as much on him:
> And she, mistaken, seems to dote on me.[4]
> What will become of this? As I am man,
> My state is desperate for my master's love;
> As I am woman – now alas the day! –
> What thriftless sighs shall poor Olivia breathe!
> O time, thou must entangle this, not I;
> It is too hard a knot for me t' untie.

"Knot" echoes "not." Knots are the physical figure of riddles; riddles are particular types of questions ("What is . . . ?" "Why is . . . ?" "What means . . . ?"), with answers usually based on puns, i.e., the nonsensical echoes caused by the semantic clash of homophones. Puns are the aural equivalent of (near-)identical twins (just as Sebastian and Viola can't actually be identical; it's a biological impossibility – they are "frater-nal" twins). They are sometimes deliberate, always playful confusions of semantic identity, which may, of course, arise unbidden. As Jonathan Culler argues:

> Puns, like portmanteaux, limn for us a model of language where the word is derived rather than primary and combinations of letters suggest meanings while at the same time illustrating the instability of meanings, their as yet ungrasped or undefined rela-tions to one another, relations which further discourse (further play of similarity and difference) can produce. When one thinks of how puns characteristically demonstrate the applicability of a single signifying sequence to two different contexts with quite dif-

ferent meanings, one can see how puns both evoke prior formulations, with the meanings they have deployed, and demonstrate their instability, the mutability of meaning,
the production of meaning by linguistic motivation. (Culler 1988: 14)

Culler's acknowledgment of the importance of temporality in punning is important. If we agree that the experience of drama is that of privileged voyeuristic entry
into a temporary fantasy world (a Globe, for example), we might further argue that
such worlds have their own little language, which we "learn" in the course of the play
(and always retain traces of, as my opening comments suggest). *Music, food, love, sea,
fancy, time, Illyria* are words from the play's first two scenes which will chime phon-
emically throughout the play, insisting on being remembered and creating strange
subliminal connections which we try to order by sorting them into "themes." Citing
Freudian theory (especially as revisited by the punster Lacan), Culler points out that
"Puns are a mechanism of the psyche and in numerous cases the connections of puns
flagrantly structure a subject's experience" (ibid: 11). In the theatre we are indeed
subject to the actors' speech, to language embodied; and every performance will create
subtly different connections for each of us, as the play's language sensually intertwines
with what we bring to it, creating in us a linguistic incubus.

But we can also see in Culler's formulation why Feste and Viola should joust for
punning superiority, why Feste is Olivia's "corrupter of words" (3.1.30), and why Viola
should be proud of her ability to "sing and speak . . . in *many sorts of music*," i.e., poetry.
It's a kind of power – a temporary or occasional demonstration of control over the
instability of language. And, at pun's perhaps most elementary level, it delivers the
power of the riddle.

Riddles

Riddling is a challenge to both onstage and auditorium auditors, a variety of
question that assumes the auditor is willing to play games with words, rather than
use them for the sober purpose of gaining information. A riddle implies "Solve this
one and join me (the riddle-setter) as a member of the intellectual elite." The very
title *Twelfth Night, or What You Will*, is a riddle set by the elusive author, and never
yet satisfactorily solved. (Literally, the answer to the question implied by the title –
"What am I?" – is "A play." But that only raises more questions.) And riddling
is the focus of the play's two central scenes, 2.5 (the box-tree scene) and 3.1
(Feste/Viola/Olivia).

The forged and enigmatic letter that Maria throws in Malvolio's way centers on a
riddle, of the classic rhymed variety:

> I may command where I adore,
> But silence, like a Lucrece knife,
> With bloodless stroke my heart doth gore;
> M.O.A.I. doth sway my life.

"A fustian riddle,"[5] as Fabian comments; it is less fine than it looks (sounds); thus it is deliberately misleading, or insoluble. But Malvolio cannot conceive of that, of a meaningless riddle addressed to *him*:

> 'M' – but then there is no consonancy in the sequel that suffers under probation. 'A' should follow, but 'O' does.

Malvolio thinks that if he tries hard enough, he can *make* the "alphabetical position portend" ("to crush this a little; it would bow to me, for every one of these letters are in my name!"), as Puritans probed the Bible to make it yield meanings which justified their views (we already know Malvolio is "a kind of Puritan," 2.3.119). But instead of this high intellectual and spiritual endeavor, the commentary of the three observers in the box-tree emphasizes the farcical ("I'll cudgel him and make him cry 'O!'") and the indecent potential of riddling ("thus makes she her great P's").[6] The scene becomes, on stage, an object-lesson in the proverb "Pride goeth before a fall." Malvolio's deliberate perversion ("crushing") of the riddle leads to an incorrect solution – or rather to the self-deceiving solution that the pranksters want (they know his vain character well enough to know that he will misread "M.O.A.I."). "It did come to his hands, and commands shall be executed," he says smugly, thinking he has cracked the code, as he arrives a couple of scenes later before Olivia, ludicrously yellow-stockinged and cross-gartered, smiling fatuously, and humming an indecent song. Malvolio's reading of the riddle is, as Feste/Sir Topas says, "*vain* bibble babble" (4.2.82: both senses of *vain* resonate here, outside the dark house where "mad" Malvolio is confined), and it leads to the humiliating transformation of the Puritan into the clown, complete with yellow and black motley. The misinterpretation of the riddle produces a coarse, visual comedy with farce's typical undercurrent of violence.

The play, however, has other stories to tell, other knots to untie. It is interested in a more complex form of babble or riddle, embodied in Viola's shifting gender, and in the "corrupter of words" Feste's aslant observations on the world (of the play, and of "every day"). Viola is, on any count, Shakespeare's most riddling heroine; riddling is her particular "habit," her conscious, teasing (and thus flirtatious) signaling of disguise:

> *Olivia.* What is your parentage?
> *Viola.* Above my fortunes, yet my state is well:
>   I am a gentleman. (1.5.233–4)

> *Viola.* I am all the daughters of my father's house
>   And all the brothers too. (2.4.116–17)

> *Feste.* . . . Now Jove, in his next commodity of hair, send thee a beard!
> *Viola.* By my troth, I'll tell thee, I am almost sick for one – though I would not have it grow on my chin. (3.1.39–40)

Act 3, scene 1, which begins with Viola and Feste's quibbling and deep-riddling dialogue, is the temporal center of the play: it often begins a performance's second half. And just as "M.O.A.I." does not quite yield "Malvolio," Malvolio's performance in his bravura scene of self-mirroring soliloquy ("practising behaviour to his own shadow") is *not quite* the center of the play: it and its comic consequence flank this extraordinary scene. It begins with vaudeville banter, but quickly shifts (as the comparable early scene with Maria does not) to witty philosophizing about wit itself:

> *Feste.* ... A sentence is but a cheveril glove to a good wit – how quickly the wrong side may be turned outward.
> *Viola.* Nay, that's certain: they that dally nicely with words may quickly make them wanton.
> *Feste.* ... words are grown so false, I am loath to prove reason with them.
> ... Who you are, and what you would are out of my welkin – I might say 'element', but the word is overworn. [*Exit.*]

"This fellow is wise enough to play the fool," Viola concludes, in a soliloquy in which she underlines – i.e., asks the audience to notice, just as she did in the "ring" scene – the thematic importance of this dramatically unnecessary exchange. It has forced the audience to contemplate the idea that nothing can be tied down to a single meaning, that the world is, in an important sense, always "mad" – one of the play's peculiar phonemes (*mad*onna, *mad*am, *mad*ness) – because always uncontrollable and unpredictable (as acknowledged by the dialogue on "chance" in Viola's opening scene). Language's unpredictability of connotation, or infinite deferral of meaning, is a specific instance of this generalization: word as world.

As we should then expect, Viola continues to riddle in her second encounter with Olivia, as 3.1 ends:

> *Olivia.* I prithee tell me what thou think'st of me,
> *Viola.* That you do think you are not what you are.
> *Olivia.* If I think so, I think the same of you.
> *Viola.* Then think you right: I am not what I am.
> ... By innocence I swear, and by my youth,
> I have one heart, one bosom, and one truth,
> And that no woman has, nor never none
> Shall mistress be of it, save I alone.

"What am I?" she might conclude, but she prefers not to stay Olivia's guessing.

The play has other riddles besides Viola's identity and Malvolio's letter; perhaps most notably the near-anagrams of the names Olivia, Viola, Malvolio. This is deliberate: the names aren't thus in Shakespeare's sources. They are an orthographic and aural reinforcement of the riddle of identity. If Viola and Sebastian are "identical" (though not in behavior), so, in a different sense, are Olivia and Viola (except in the autocratic behavior represented by the extra "I" in Olivia's name): they are both young women suffering unrequited love. And Malvolio ("Ill-I-will"), the same again, except with a masculine ending and a prefix that signifies the wrongness of *his* "will" read as both sexual desire and will-to-power. Alternatively, one might solve this ana-grammatic riddle by observing with Malvolio "... O, A and I" – all these letters are in *all three names*; and so are L and V. You can make LOV with all three names. Only Malvolio's M marks him as different: male, or male-volent. Finally (for the time being), M is the middle letter of the alphabet, and as a capital it is a perfect reflec-tion of itself: so Malvolio prides and preens himself as he imagines his centrality in the letter scene: "To be *Count* Malvolio." But a minute or two later Sir Andrew's incomprehension of the vulgar textual joke – "Her C's, her U's and her T's – why that?" – will underline and reflect Malvolio's fantasies in a very unflattering light: "To be *cunt* Malvolio": to be for ever the feminized, effeminate, despised steward of the house (even the fantasized "in my branched velvet gown . . ." is as effete an image as the play's opening one of the *Count* Orsino).[7]

Even while I sit in the theatre, I am encouraged – or compelled – to join in this verbal game-playing; puns and anagrammatism are as much an aural as an ortho-graphic experience (more so for the play's first audience, considering the fluidity of Elizabethan spelling and the primacy of the idea of "hearing" a play when attending it). This play shows it knows about the power of aurality: not only is "music . . . the food of love" in its opening line, as early as 1.5 Viola's "willow-cabin" speech exemplifies the (uncontrollable) resonances set up by echoes. As well as invoking the idealized unity of Petrarchan lovers – "call upon my soul within the house" – the speech also demonstrates the near-identity of Viola and Olivia in aural terms. In "hallow[ing] your name to the reverberate hills" Viola invokes the Chinese-whispers effect of "the babbling gossip of the air": "OLIVIA! . . . O'VIA . . . vi[o]la". This is truly a performative speech, eliciting from Olivia the overwhelmed response: "You might do [have done just now] much!"

Children riddle in order to gain the power of adult language; riddles are the first sort of questions children ask of which *they* know the (punning) answer. Further, the modern child's understanding of the metaphorical nature of riddles seems to coincide with the development of literacy,[8] the equivalent of the Elizabethan's delighted atten-dance at "the great feast of languages" (*Love's Labour's Lost*, 5.1).[9] Our players – his-torically powerless and dependent on aristocratic patrons for their legitimacy (as much now as in 1601) – through Feste, their spokesman and corrupter of words, acknowl-edge their childlike subordinacy even while they flaunt their power to keep us in our seats, in the theatre, until such time as *they* "will":

> . . . our play is done,
> And we'll strive to please you every day.

Here is another of the play's echoing words: Orsino's opening instruction is "*play on.*" Hearing this, as the text's eighth word, the audience might well feel itself, as well as the actors, called into play. Finally, the audience is told "Our play is done": the actors separate themselves from any fantasy-identity we may have con-structed with them, and we return to our separate identities as "you," the theatre's adult patrons.

Rhyme

Rhyme supplies memory with a comforting mnemonic, though too much can be exhausting. But a little positively enriches the experience of temp/aurality. In her essay "Rhyming as comedy: body, ghost, and banquet", Gillian Beer argues that

> Rhyme suggests pun: dislodged likenesses, delayed differences . . . rhyme gets under the guard of reason and teases words out of their autonomy, doubling, dissolving, and playing across the rim of meaning.
> . . . Rhyme is de-formation; a first, apparently rationally sanctioned word, is tripped and changed (both semantically and aurally) by the rhyme-word . . . endoubling, estrangement, twinning and disconnecting: the first word in the sound pair is tricked, transfigured, ghosted, sometimes grotesque-ed. (Beer 1994: 180–1)

Beer's formulations (though she is talking about lyric, not dramatic poetry) are wonderfully pertinent to my case:[10] here is a Shakespearean play about twins, tricks, transformations, and mistakes – a play which in fact contains more rhyme than any of the other middle comedies. All scenes that end with verse end with a single or double couplet. Olivia's declaration of love at the end of 3.1 is entirely in couplets, as is Viola's response and Olivia's closing speech. Sebastian and Antonio at 3.3 collapse into prose – as though consonance were not possible – a striking contrast with Sebastian and Olivia in 4.2's first encounter, which concludes with *four* couplets as they go off together. Climactically, in 5.1, there is the sixteen-line sequence which begins with Orsino's admission that he loves Cesario, then Viola's reciprocation, Olivia's accusation – the couplets being broken up more and more as the speakers get more frantic. Beer speaks of a "theatre of division and condensation" caused by the "sounds in contention . . . the helpless excess of possibility that poises it always on the brink of comedy" (Beer 1994: 190), which well suggests the farcicality of this moment of the play; at the same tune, I suggest, the pleasing nonsense yet consonance of rhyme reassures us that the situation will be resolved:

> *Orsino.* . . . I'll sacrifice the lamb that I do *love*,
>   To spite a raven's heart within a *dove*.
> *Viola.* And I most jocund, apt, and willing*ly*,
>   To do you rest, a thousand deaths would *die*.
> *Olivia.* Where goes Cesario?
> *Viola.*   After him I *love*
>   More than I love these eyes, more than my *life*,
>   More, by all mores, than e'er I shall love *wife*.
>   If I do feign, you witnesses *above*
>   Punish my life for tainting of my *love*!

Here are five lines rhyming with *love*, as well as the internal repetitions of the echoing word.

> *Olivia.* Ay me, detested! How am I beguiled!
> *Viola.* Who does beguile you? Who does do you *wrong*?
> *Olivia.* Hast thou forgot thyself? Is it so *long*?

Questions, mirroring those at their first encounter, about identity and agency, are here reinforced by the rhyme. The non-rhyming line (". . . beguiled") has an internal echo in the following line, which might be heard as reinforcing the "wiliness" of this verb.

> *Olivia.* Call forth the holy father.
> *Orsino.*   Come, *away*!
> *Olivia.* Whither, my lord? Cesario, husband, *stay*!
> *Orsino.* Husband?
> *Olivia.*   Ay, husband. Can he that *deny*?
> *Orsino.* Her husband, sirrah?
> *Viola.*   No, my lord, not *I*.

"Not I," the climax of this frenetic exchange about identity. "Not I," then who? Who is this person who claims she is not "feigning" now, though at the same moment, subliminally, aurally, she is admitting her doubleness: "More than I love these *eyes*," punning on *I*'s, selves? The riddle is answered by Sebastian's manly and courteous entrance, claiming agency and confident in his identity, in measured and rhyme-free blank verse:

> I am sorry, madam, I have hurt your kinsman.
> But had it been the brother of my blood,
> I must have done no less with wit and safety. (5.1.193–5)

Namings follow emphatically: "Sebastian" three times, "Viola" also (symmetrically) three times – though she has not previously been named in the spoken playtext. These two, though so similar physically, are *essentially* different, in that they are *named* differently (so Sebastian is *more* different than Illyrian residents Viola/Olivia/Malvolio are from each other, and thus more *like* the outsider Antonio who "adores" him). Names provide clarity and closure at the representational or ideational level of the fable/romance. But the games go on: is not the ear, in fact, gratified by the grave antiphony of Sebastian and Viola's exchange of the speech-acts of identification? Anything else might seem aurally and emotionally parsimonious.

The word-play itself ("One face, one voice, one habit, and two persons"), while providing a satisfying thematic conclusion, as ever turns and twists upon itself, continuing to puzzle ("A natural perspective, that *is and is not*"). We are not to be let off into a perfect, poetry-less, Platonic world. Although there are several more substantial speeches in verse in the play (including Malvolio's great self-justifying complaint), there are just two more couplets after the outbreak of rhyme at the scene's climax: one shared, fittingly – at last – by Orsino and Olivia as they both embrace Viola (a trio in a couplet; the *master–mistress* of Olivia's passion translated into the assonant *sister*):

Orsino. Here is my hand; you shall from this time be
　　　Your master's mistress.
Olivia. 　　　　　　　　　　A sister, you are she.

And one by Orsino to close the play and lead into Feste's song, but it hardly provides the closure that the speech of this figure of authority should. Viola is *renamed* "Cesario" by her master/lover:

> Cesario, come –
> For so you shall be while you are a man,
> But when in other habits you are seen,
> Orsino's mistress, and his fancy's queen.

Orsino's resonant phrase disconcertingly echoes the play's opening speech, with its signaling of the self-reflectiveness of both art and romantic love, "So full of shapes is fancy, / That it alone is high fantastical" (1.1.14–15). Our ears tell us that Orsino's world remains narcissistic, hermetically enclosed; ripe, it would seem, for deconstruction.

And so to the "food of love" which feeds this narcissism (and perhaps our own). Songs are rhymes doubly reinforced by music. The play has plenty: "O Mistress mine," "Come away, Death," "When that I was and a little tiny boy," as well as the snatches of popular song sung by Sir Toby, Feste, and even Malvolio. The three named songs are philosophical despite their catchiness: their themes (in all three) love, death, and time. Here then is a "theme" or meaning to take away from the play, a choice of three tunes that memorably (hummably) embody the melancholy that seems to haunt it, however funny the comic moments might be. But then, isn't there *too much* rhyme in Feste's last song, the play's epilogue? Lines 2 and 4 of each verse (except the last) are identical: is this just a catchy iteration of everyday reality, or are we being sent back to some sort of existential treadmill? Perhaps Feste, as musician, is the agent of "the whirligig of time" – and rhyme – which brings in its revenges on us, house-stewards all.

Seeing What We Hear

If word-games, riddles, puns, and rhymes constitute the chief element of the aural texture of the play, this richness of doubled and redoubled sounds reinforces, subliminally, what we see: the narrative of hidden identity, gender confusion, and concealed love. The play is full of disconcerting *visual* echoes, in the non-identical but recognizable doublings of character types: two clowns (Feste and Malvolio), two romantic/Petrarchan lovers (Orsino and Sir Andrew), two boys (Cesario and Sebastian), two sea captains, two "ladies of the house" in 1.5, two priests (Olivia's "real" chaplain and Feste's Sir Topas), even Sir Toby and Fabian as a pair of controlling puppeteers flanking the gormless Sir Andrew in the box-tree scene.

Robert Weimann has recently returned to his influential reading of early modern stage space as comprising the symbolic (representational) *locus* and the unlocalized (presentational) *platea*, inflecting it now with an awareness of the "new poetics of cultural response." The *locus* is "a fairly specific imaginary locale or self-contained space in the world of the play," the *platea* "an opening in *mise-en-scène* through which the place and time of the stage-as-stage and the cultural occasion itself are made either to assist or resist the socially and verbally elevated, spatially and temporally remote representation" (Weimann 2000: 181). I am interested in developing the notion of *resistance* through performance in the *platea*: its tendency to be inhabited by outsiders, "players doing porters, vendors, grave diggers, but also crossdressed women and other figures in disguise and madness" (ibid: 196). Surprisingly, he does not mention *Twelfth Night*, but Weimann's subtle political analysis of the plays he does discuss constantly returns to the idea of doubleness, and thus, to my mind, inescapably brings up *Twelfth Night*. For example, he argues,

> Shakespearean word-play in miniature exemplifies how the quibbling, juggling and corporeal uses of play jarred with a dramatic mode of representation which sought to render an imaginary picture, possibly a world-picture, informed by notions, doctrines, and abstractions quite remote from the traditional world of common players and nonverbal performers . . . The quibble, the jingle, the riddle, much like other types of playful practice . . . marr[ed] the mirror of the world. (Ibid: 178–9)

This theory is not dependent on an architectural wooden O for resonance: it is based on a reading of linguistic styles and registers in the playtexts: performance directives to the actors. In terms of *Twelfth Night* what this means is a habit of crossing the stage/audience barrier, a foregrounding of the consciously performative actor, whose work in the *platea* deconstructs the aesthetic high ground of the *locus* and its romantic fable. For example, the social power represented in the figures of Orsino and Olivia, which has been the subject of some new historicist analyses (Malcolmson 1996; Suzuki 1992). Orsino, opening the play – presumably upstage, seated perhaps, surrounded by musicians and attendants – speaks something close to high-sounding nonsense, as close analysis will show (Booth 1998: 121–42) and (more importantly) as Feste underlines in his speech and song in 2.4. "Come away, death," *as well as* thematizing the play's melancholy, is also capable of undermining that mood's self-importance; it will be the choice of the actor playing the clown whether to underline this satire. The song's linguistic excess ("sad cypress . . . Not a flower . . . not a friend . . . A thousand thousand sighs," etc.) recalls the self-indulgence of Orsino's opening scene. And by this stage in the play the audience can easily recognize that we need not take Orsino's posturing very seriously – which is exactly what Feste's post-song quibbling suggests, without actually openly insulting his social superior:

> Now the melancholy god protect thee, and the tailor make thy doublet of changeable taffeta, for thy mind is a very opal. I would have men of such constancy put to sea, that their business might be everything and their intent everywhere, for that's it that always makes a good voyage of nothing. Farewell. (2.4.70–4)

A quick exit is clearly in order, just in case Orsino has understood the verbally disguised insults here. Almost impossible to construe, Feste's speech has the quality of what Halliday calls an "antilanguage," "a *counter*-reality, set up *in opposition to* some established norm" (Halliday 1979: 171), on which it depends for its social identity. Criminals' cant is the best-known example; Halliday makes reference to the vigorous language of the Elizabethan "counterculture of vagabonds" (ibid: 165). And *Twelfth Night's* clown is a vagabond, a wanderer; he is encountered by the characters of the fable when *he* chooses. He is equally at home in Olivia's or Orsino's household, yet lives in neither: "tell me where thou hast been, or . . ." is Maria's greeting and threat as he makes his first appearance. Feste is thus not "placed" in the *locus*, and this fact paradoxically gives him a subversive power which he signals through his characteristic word-play ("Let her hang me: he that is well hanged in this world need fear no colours"). As with the song for Orsino, his nonsensical "simple syllogism" (1.5.40) for Olivia positions him safely to commit *lèse-majesté*: "Good madonna, give me leave to prove you a fool" (1.5.47). Malvolio protests on behalf of the hierarchical order: "I marvel your ladyship takes delight in such a barren *rascal*," putting Feste in his social place as a quasi-criminal (the actor, "rogue and vagabond" in Elizabethan law); but Olivia is charmed enough already to begin her move away from the social high ground: "There is no slander in an allowed fool." Feste concludes by offering her the ultimate compliment of his trade – but as with Orsino, it is defensively disguised in the antilanguage of clowns' cant: "Now Mercury endue thee with leasing, for thou speak'st well of fools!" (1.5.79–80; *leasing*, an obscure word used only once elsewhere in the Shakespeare canon, is "lying"). Scenes such as these depend on the clown's complicity with the audience, based on the latter's appreciation of witty "babble" or antilanguage, a wink, a nod, a self-consciously performative energy which is the characteristic of the *platea*.

With wonderful subversiveness, the authority of Malvolio is turned into unwitting clownship by his inhabiting the *platea* in the letter scene's long prose soliloquy, as he parades around Olivia's garden, asking himself – or the audience – questions that are more genuinely puzzled than rhetorically self-serving.[11] If the onstage watchers – Sir Toby, Sir Andrew, and Fabian – consciously inhabit the *platea* in their clown-like behavior in the box-tree and their derisive or indignant commentary ("And does not Toby take you a blow o' the lips then?"), Malvolio is inadvertently betrayed into exemplifying Weimann's formulation of the linguistic aspects of this stage space: "the *platea* was used to foreground . . . drink and desire, sexuality and the body in its regenerative and decaying dimensions . . . using monosyllabic, Anglo-Saxon language" (Weimann 2000: 195). Malvolio's "C.U.'n'.T." is the first guarantee of his downfall – or humanization.

The most extraordinary inhabitant of the *platea*, however, is Viola. In discussing 3.1, I have already commented on the play's emphasis on the intellectual likeness between Feste and Viola. That scene is not something we expect of the romantic heroine of 1.2 or 2.4 – though perhaps we are not as surprised as we might be, since she has already shown herself also to be a wit and a riddler – in, for example, 1.5. But it is in her soliloquizing addresses to the audience that she most fully inhabits the *platea*. Viola in fact is the only comic heroine up to this point in the Shakespearean canon who soliloquizes and exhibits a consciousness of the audience as *amused* listeners. This is demonstrated by the register of her questions in the "ring" soliloquy (2.2.14–38) – "What means this lady?" "How will this fadge?" – and her explanations – "She loves me sure; the cunning of her passion / Invites me in this churlish messenger"; "I am the man!" followed by a comic spelling-out of the situation for the audience's benefit:

> My master loves her dearly,
> And I, poor monster, fond as much on him:
> And she (mistaken) seems to dote on me.
> What will become of this?

This amused, confiding note is adopted again in "This fellow is wise enough to play the fool," complete with a tag that rhymes *fit* and *wit* (3.1.50–8) as she explains to the audience the ambivalent role of clowns. Her final soliloquy comes in 3.4, Viola's last scene before the play's denouement; it combines an excitement that must be shared – "He named Sebastian" – with an (almost pedantic) explanation that reminds the audience of the play's thematic interest in doubleness. The rhymes aurally redouble this theme:

> I my brother know
> Yet living in my glass; even such and so
> In favour was my brother, and he went
> Still in this fashion, colour, ornament,
> For him I imitate. (3.4.330–4)

The character Viola, being by virtue of her crossdressing a liminal figure like the clown, nevertheless *exceeds* Weimann's linguistic formula for clowns ("invariably using monosyllabic, Anglo-Saxon language" (Weimann 2000: 195); he might have added "and prose"). She literally transgresses it by taking her blank verse from the *locus* of her romance to present it consciously and wittily to the audience, thus deconstructing its "poetical" authority (1.5.185; here Olivia represents the audience). In her doubleness – which is embodied as much in her wit and riddling as in her gender ambiguity – Viola crosses between Weimann's two stage aspects, constantly shifting between the representative figure of the pathos-producing romantic heroine in a fable, who "never told her love," and the self-aware, self-delighting performer (boy/girl/boy) chatting wittily to the audience about "her" situation.

Twentieth-century productions of the play – always under the sign of "romantic comedy", i.e., a love story with comic relief – have usually insisted on creating a self-consistent society (Orsino's court, Olivia's house, the town, with church, shops, a pub, constables). Actors, in thrall to Stanislavskian ideology (however modified by fashionable techniques), have aimed for "realism" in their performances: "continuous characterization, an organic connection between scenes, the need to develop an inner life for the role, a consistent through-line of action" (Worthen 1997: 212). Yet Shakespeare's plays keep contradicting this classic realist model. *Twelfth Night* inhabits an Illyria of linguistic play, poetry, and improbable fictions. Its characters are continually caught up in language-games, often games which language itself seems to be playing with them. Gregory Ulmer argues that "in the new [postmodernist] paradigm one thinks less with or about the *idea* – *eidos*, form, clear and distinct outline or shape, dependent on the sense of sight – and more by means of the *moira*, having to do with the way the aleatory cuts across a necessity in the event of a pun" (Ulmer 1988: 187). This suggests that postmodernist or twenty-first-century Shakespearean production would be more at home foregrounding the playful chanciness of aurality than sticking with the "design concepts" of the strongly visual and technological twentieth-century stage. There is nothing, of course, to stop a postmodernist director or designer *visualizing* a pun. A set which is entirely covered with the play's echo-words; mirrors in which characters meet (or ignore) themselves; cross-gender casting; doubling of roles so that the actor "is" Viola or Sebastian[12] just for the duration of a speech – neither performers' nor audiences' imaginations need be limited by the repressive demands of realism or consistency. The audience can be challenged to work with the actors' embodiment of the text, not by simply suspending disbelief in a romantic fiction but by skeptically and gleefully assisting in the "play" implicit in the idea of performance, foregrounded by verbal and aural games.

Play is separate from the adult workaday (realist) world. Overlaying those cultural narratives or fantasies that are easily identifiable – to do with love, desire, gender, class, and identity – there is this text's "babble" of rhyme, riddle, and quibble. Mapping Weimann's conceptualizing of the stage onto the auditory aspect, and specifically its *process*, its temp/aurality, we see how that process itself can create a political intervention; its riddling and echoes can deconstruct the metaphysical certainties of the heterosexual romance, the casting-off of disguise, the assertion of gender and class identity, the play's conservative ending. Malvolio, that unwitting embodiment of a pun, crying "I'll be revenged on the whole pack of you!" might stand for the very denial of closure. Like a pun – like Feste, in fact – he threatens to turn up inopportunely, indecorously, subversively – not "when golden time convents" (5.1.359), but when *he* chooses.

NOTES

1 All quotations from *Twelfth Night* are from the Cambridge University Press edition, ed. Elizabeth Story Donno (1985).

2 Howard herself commented in a later book that her account of *Twelfth Night* here ignored "the political implications of the text's insistence on the return to an 'undisguised' state . . . In short, I accepted the play's dominant ideologies as a mimesis of the true and natural order of things" (Howard 1994: 161, n.14). Patricia Parker's observation that "in the larger discourse and

structures of rhetoric, is embedded . . . [a language] that would enable us to pose, in different ways from those so far pursued, questions of politics and gender, of social biography and ideology," is helpful in my effort here to reread the play (Parker 1987: 94). See also Lloyd Davis's subtle discussion of the nexus between rhetoric and personation in this volume. Using these historical observations as a basis, my focus is on the postmodern rather than early modern audience.

3   Following on the primary puzzle of Viola's name in 1.2, in 1.3 Sir Andrew thinks that "Accost" is Maria's surname, committing a significant category error on perfectly good, but ambiguous, syntactic grounds, in the way that a child learning language does. (See below for further discussion of children and language.)

4   I have altered Donno's editorial "As" back to the Folio's "And," and retained F's punctuation in the previous line.

5   "Fustian . . . was a 'velure' cloth made either from cotton or from a mixture of flax and wool, so silky in appearance it could be used in place of velvet . . . So the natural metaphorical use of the term was for the pretentious and the bogus – things which appeared more valuable or exotic than they really were" (Malcolm 1997: 36–7).

6   Peter J. Smith's (1998) "solution" to Malvolio's riddle is to my mind the most convincing of the many attempts, because it develops the theme of Malvolio's humiliation through the grotesquing of the body. Smith reads it as a contemporary reference to Sir John Harington's (notorious and much reprinted) *Metamorphosis Of A Iakes*, i.e., the treatise on the water-closet (1596). In several recent productions of *Twelfth Night* Malvolio in the dark house has had the contents of a chamber-pot emptied over him.

   Acrostics such as this are probably easier to "hear" and decode than anagrams; however, the emphasis and repetition of the letters would encourage those of an anagrammatic turn in the audience. Smith offers a comprehensive survey of the attempts to solve Malvolio's riddle, as well as an illuminating discussion of Renaissance (especially Puritan) interest in anagrams.

7   For the pun Count/cunt, see the Folio's spelling in *Henry V*, 3.4: "*Le Foot, & le Count: O Seignieur Dieu, il sont le mots de son mauvais corruptible grosse & impudique.*" Dympna Callaghan argues regarding Malvolio's unwitting indecency: "*Twelfth Night*, then, treats the corporeal representation of sexuality, which is equated with femininity . . . the very thing that justified women's exclusion from the stage is *graphically* [my emphasis] foregrounded in this play. But the play does not therefore subversively evade the strictures against female bodies on stage; rather it adds weight to them by presenting the female body in its most biologically essential form – the cunt" (Callaghan 1996: 145). Modern actors and audiences are fortunate in not being obliged to contemplate this female abjection in the figure of a boy playing the romantic heroine.

8   I am indebted for these observations on children and language to the unpublished research of my colleague Geoff Williams (Williams 2000: 5, 7; and conversations).

9   Given that *Twelfth Night* was performed at Middle Temple Hall in 1601/2, Noel Malcolm's comment is pertinent: "During the second half of the sixteenth century . . . verbal humour and rhetorical parody gradually took on a more and more important role in the Christmas festivities of the Inns of Court. Increasingly, these occasions were used as opportunities to practice, in a comically self-conscious manner, courtly and rhetorical skills; in this the lawyers were no doubt also influenced by the literary exercises and plays performed at Christmas in several of the Cambridge colleges" (Malcolm 1997: 123).

10   Beer points out that the first English rhyming dictionary, *Manipulus Vocabulorum*, by Peter Levins, was published in 1570 (Beer 1994: 181).

11   Donald Sinden, Royal Shakespeare Company, 1970 and Desmond Barrit, RSC 1995, are two notably funny Malvolios in this scene who have deliberately taken the audience into their confidence, that is, played Malvolio as clown. For Sinden's conscious reflection on his performance, see Brockbank (1985: 41–66).

12   As was done to exciting effect by the Cambridge group Dramatic Stuff on a bare stage, in unchanging neutral costume, in an Edinburgh Fringe production in 2000: particularly telling was the doubling of Feste and Malvolio, the two "clowns."

REFERENCES AND FURTHER READING

Appler, K. (1995). Deconstructing the Regional Theater with "Performance Art" Shakespeare. *Theatre Topics*, March, 35–49.

Bartels, E. C. (1994). Breaking the Illusion of Being: Shakespeare and the Performance of Self. *Theatre Journal*, 46, 171–85.

Beer, G. (1994). Rhyming as Comedy: Body, Ghost, and Banquet. In M. Cordner, P. Holland, and J. Kerrigan (eds.) *English Comedy*. Cambridge: Cambridge University Press, 180–96.

Belsey, C. (1985). Disrupting Sexual Difference: Meaning and Gender in the Comedies. In J. Drakakis (ed.) *Alternative Shakespeares*. London: Methuen, 166–90.

Berry, R. (1985). *Shakespeare and the Awareness of the Audience*. London: Macmillan.

Booth, S. (1998). *Precious Nonsense: The Gettysburg Address, Ben Jonson's Epitaphs on his Children, and Twelfth Night*. Berkeley: University of California Press.

Brockbank, P. (ed.) (1985). *Players of Shakespeare*. Cambridge: Cambridge University Press.

Callaghan, D. (1996). 'And all is semblative a woman's part': Body Politics and *Twelfth Night*. In R. S. White (ed.) *New Casebooks: Twelfth Night*. London: Macmillan, 129–59.

Charles, C. (1997). Gender trouble in *Twelfth Night*. *Theatre Journal*, 49, 121–41.

Crane, M. T. (2001). *Shakespeare's Brain: Reading with Cognitive Theory*. Princeton, NJ: Princeton University Press.

Culler, J. (ed.) (1988). *On Puns: The Foundation of Letters*. Oxford: Blackwell.

Elam, K. (1996). 'In what chapter of his bosom?' Reading Shakespeare's Bodies. In T. Hawkes (ed.) *Alternative Shakespeares 2*. London: Routledge, 140–63.

——(2000). Language and the Body. In A. Thompson, L. Hunter, and L. Magnusson (eds.) *Shakespeare's Dramatic Language*. London: Routledge, 173–87.

Evans, M. (1985). Deconstructing Shakespeare's Comedies. In J. Drakakis (ed.) *Alternative Shakespeares*. London: Methuen, 67–94.

Gay, P. (1994). *As She Likes It: Shakespeare's Unruly Women*. London: Routledge.

Greenblatt, S. (1988). *Shakespearean Negotiations*. Oxford: Clarendon Press.

Halliday, M. A. K. (1979). *Language as Social Semiotic*. London: Edward Arnold.

Hamburger, M. (1988). A Spate of *Twelfth Nights*: Illyria Rediscovered? In W. Habicht, D. J. Palmer, and R. Pringle (eds.) *Images of Shakespeare: Proceedings of the Third Congress of the International Shakespeare Association*. Newark: University of Delaware Press, 236–44.

Hartman, G. H. (1996). Shakespeare's Poetical Character. In R. S. White (ed.) *New Casebooks: Twelfth Night*. London: Macmillan, 16–36.

Howard, J. E. (1984). *Shakespeare's Art of Orchestration*. Urbana: University of Illinois Press.

——(1994). *The Stage and Social Struggle in Early Modern England*. London: Routledge.

Malcolm, N. (1997). *The Origins of English Nonsense*. London: HarperCollins.

Malcolmson, C. (1996). 'What You Will': Social Mobility and Gender in *Twelfth Night*. In R. S. White (ed.) *New Casebooks: Twelfth Night*. London: Macmillan, 160–93.

Neely, C. T. (2000). Lovesickness, Gender, and Subjectivity: *Twelfth Night* and *As You Like It*. In D. Callaghan (ed.) *A Feminist Companion to Shakespeare*. Oxford: Blackwell.

Osborne, L. E. (1996). *The Trick of Singularity: Twelfth Night and the Performance Editions*. Iowa City: University of Iowa Press.

Parker, P. (1987). *Literary Fat Ladies: Rhetoric, Gender, Property*. London: Methuen.

Redfern, W. (1984). *Puns*. Oxford: Blackwell.

Shapiro, M. (1996). *Gender in Play on the Shakespearean Stage: Boy Heroines and Female Pages*. Ann Arbor: University of Michigan Press.

Smith, B. J. (1999). *The Acoustic World of Early Modern England: Attending to the O-Factor*. Chicago, IL: University of Chicago Press.

Smith, P. J. (1998). M.O.A.I. 'What should that alphabetical position portend?' An Answer to the Metamorphic Malvolio. *Renaissance Quarterly*, 51, 1199–224.

Suzuki, M. (1992). Gender, Class, and the Social Order in Late Elizabethan Drama. *Theatre Journal*, 44, 31–45.

Traub, V. (1992). *Desire and Anxiety: Circulations of Sexuality in Shakespearean Drama*. London: Routledge.

Ulmer, G. (1988). The Puncept in Grammatology. In J. Culler (ed.) *On Puns: The Foundation of Letters*. Oxford: Blackwell, 164–89.

Weimann, R. (2000). *Author's Pen and Actor's Voice: Playing and Writing in Shakespeare's Theatre*. Cambridge: Cambridge University Press.

Williams, G. (2000). Young Children Learning to Talk About Seriously Playful Texts. Report to the Spencer Foundation. Sydney: Department of English.

Worthen, W. (1997). *Shakespeare and the Authority of Performance*. Cambridge: Cambridge University Press.

Index